Colleen Doran

A Distant Soil™

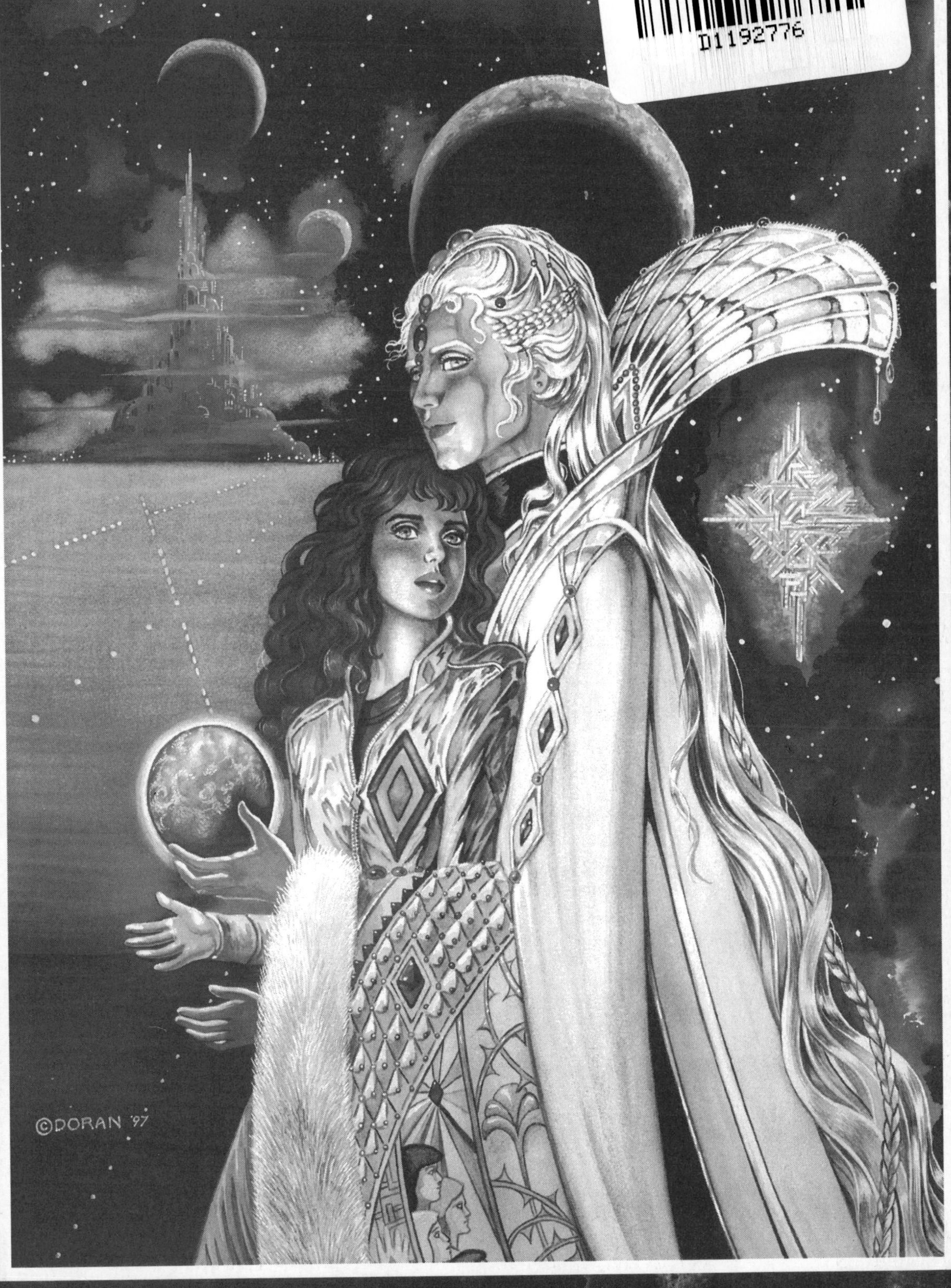
©DORAN '97

Colleen Doran
A Distant Soil
The Gathering

THIRD PRINTING

MAY 2001

Image Comics
1071 North Batavia Street, Ste. A
Orange, CA 92867

Printed in Canada
ISBN # 1-887279-51-2

IMAGE COMICS

PUBLISHER
Jim Valentino

DIRECTOR OF PRODUCTION
Brent Braun

DIRECTOR OF MARKETING
Anthony Bozzi

ART DIRECTOR
Doug Griffith

GRAPHIC DESIGNER
Kenny Felix

ACCOUNTING MANAGER
Traci Hale

ACCOUNTING ASSISTANT
Cindie Espinoza

INVENTORY CONTROLLER
Sean O'Brien

A Distant Soil™

The Gathering

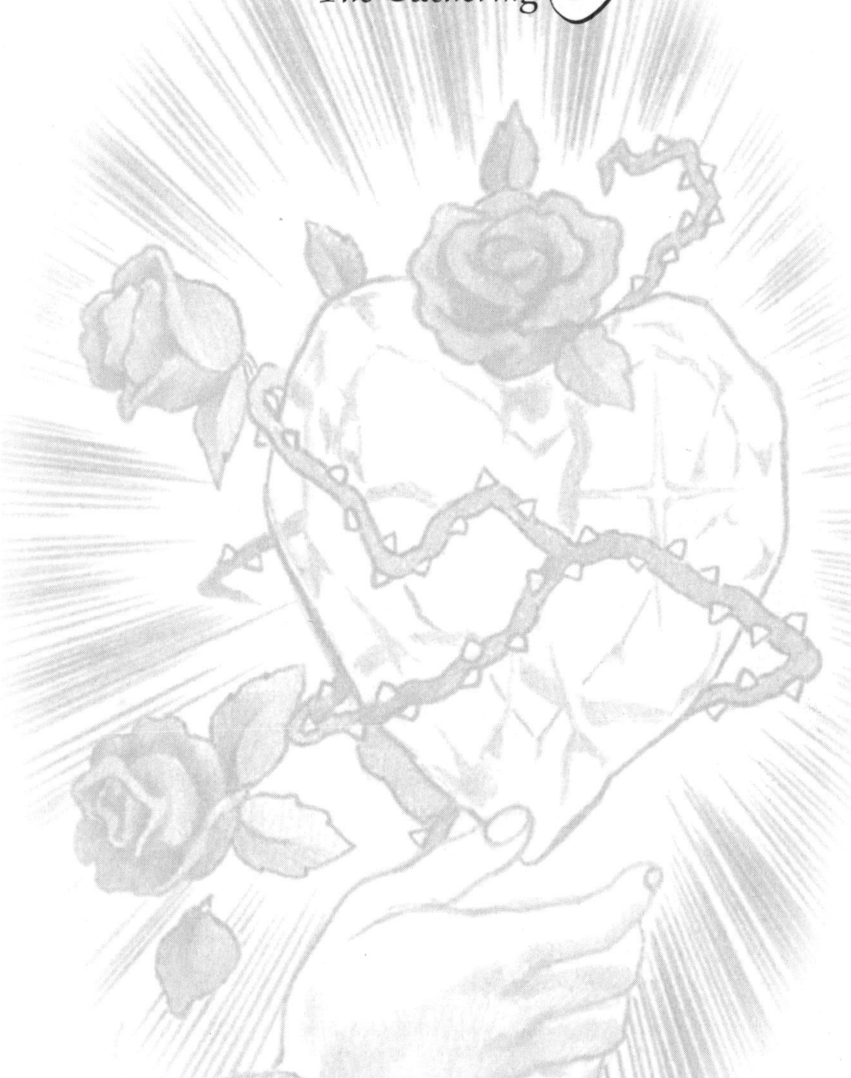

for

Mom and Dad

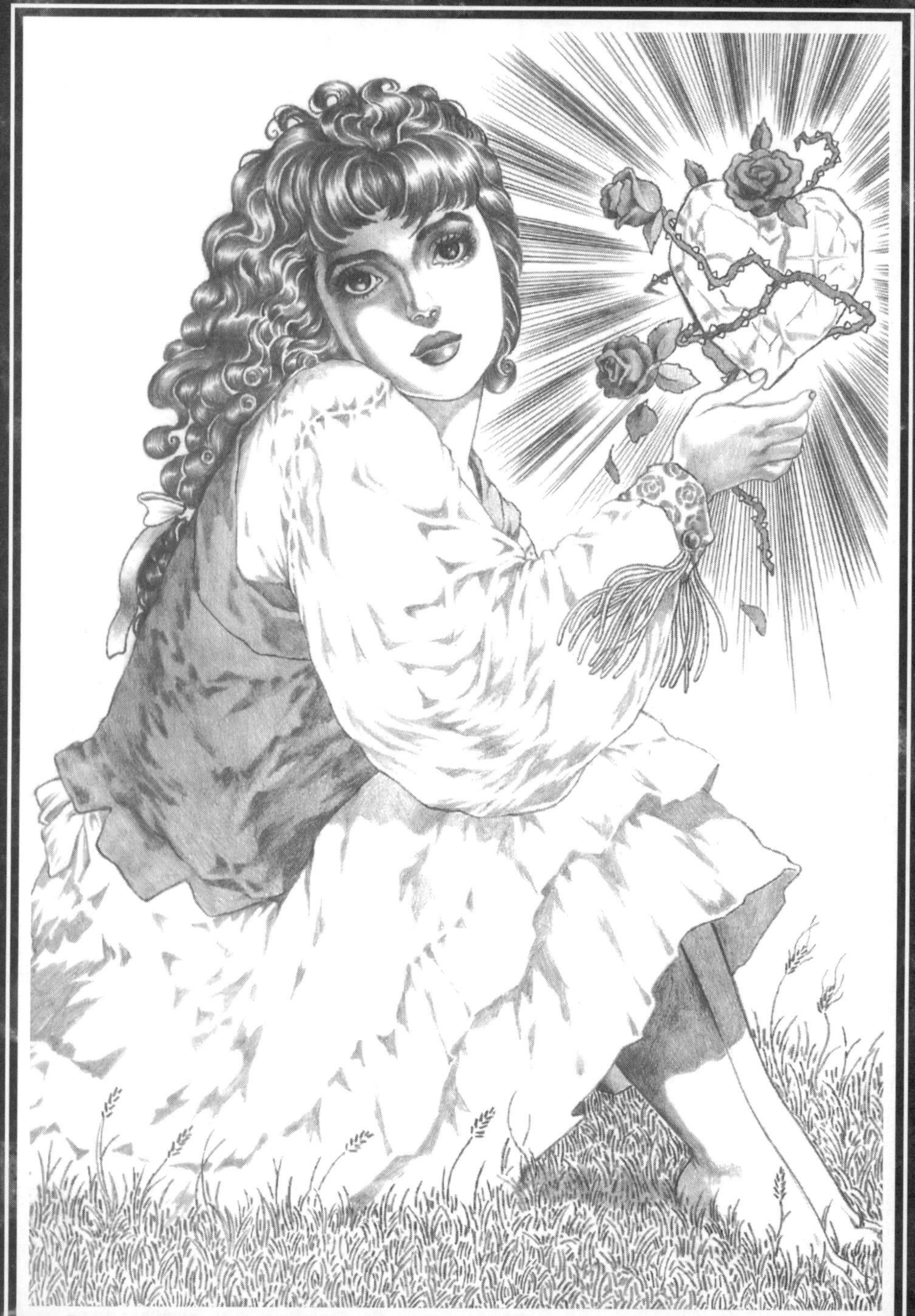

A Distant Soil™
The Gathering

Colleen Doran
CREATOR

Anita Doran
ASSISTANT

Bob Pinaha with Colleen Doran
LETTERING

Mary Gray
COPY EDITOR

AN INTRODUCTION

When I was young I used to make up stories. The one I made up when I was twelve was an enormous epic involving an interdimensional empire that placed all its power into twelve stones, which were scattered across time and space and had to be recovered by the various sons and daughters of the ruling faction. Each stone was a different gem: a ruby, an emerald, an amethyst, a sapphire, and so on. The recovery of each stone would take a whole novel, which would be named after the stone in question. The stories would have ranged from space opera to sword and sorcery to fairy tale to jungle adventure and on from there. It takes a certain sort of twelve year old madness to decide that the first thing you'll write will be a twelve volume epic of linked novels, and, of course, it goes without saying that I did not put pen to paper to ever write a word of it, but I made it up whenever I could. Mostly in geography lessons. Which means, while even today I remember the imaginary political set-up of the multiverse I created, I'm still a little foggy on the exact whereabouts of the Caspian Sea.

(I was about to say something about never using any of that story, but I realized as I typed that last paragraph that, of course, I had taken a sliver of that story [because writers never forget stories, even the ones they don't write—especially the ones they don't write] and slipped it into SANDMAN.)

Every writer out there has a story that he or she has known since he or she was twelve. Mostly we don't ever write them. (But then, I knew Hob Gadling's story when I was about sixteen, although I began it in ancient Egypt, and it took Mr. Croup and Mr. Vandemar eighteen years between their first turning up in my head and the publication of NEVERWHERE.) Sometimes we don't write them for a while.

Colleen Doran began working on A DISTANT SOIL when she was twelve. It was a superhero adventure story back then, as we can see from her reprinted sketch book sketches. The story continued to evolve for the next decade, gaining SF roots, a galactic empire, faerie, magic, shape-shifters, an heroic resistance, government conspiracies, hard-boiled cops, knights in armour—everything that Colleen loved or was interested in, every genre and archetype, went in there, indiscriminately. The young are magpies, and, sensibly, see no reason why any story cannot contain everything.

And then, when she was barely twenty she began to tell the story you will read in this collection. The publishing history of A

DISTANT SOIL is tangled and unlikely, and is, besides, Colleen's story to tell, not mine: suffice it to say that there's about ten years, creatively, between the beginning of this book and the end. The artist's and writer's craft improves as it goes, but it still grabs you from the first and keeps going. You know that the tale-teller knows who these people are, what they are doing, knows more than she will ever tell you about them; knowing this, you know that you are in safe hands, and relax while the tale begins to unfold.

This is what kind of person Colleen Doran is:

She's nice and she's funny and she's bright. She has a very dirty laugh, but is, otherwise a perfect lady in every respect. She is not what most people would describe, on oath, as astonishingly tall. I see her once every couple of years, whenever we're both at the same convention, and mostly I don't immediately recognize her because her hair changes colour so if I'm looking for an albino ice-queen a perky redhead comes over, or if I'm looking for a blonde lady with a fluffy sort of mane a brunette lady with straight hair turns up. She tends to be outspoken, and says exactly what is on her mind; thus she is both beloved and feared in the comics community. Also, she makes killer fudge.

While Colleen has drawn many other things, for many publishers, in many different styles, this is her dream and her story, and I suspect it always will be, and is closest to her heart.

The strangest and the best thing about reading this, the collected initial story-arc of Colleen Doran's life's work, is watching a talent evolve. It's like watching a flower bud and open in stop-motion, as we watch a maturing sensibility craft a story using characters and ideas that started when she was a schoolgirl, and which began as a set of schoolgirl fantasies, a mingling of paranoid esper fantasy, with galactic empire fiction with Arthurian fantasy with proto superheroics, while at the same time learning and refining her craft. And she does it with aplomb, with soul, and with a sense of joy that makes me wish I'd written some of the stories I'd dreamed up when I was twelve.

Neil Gaiman
August 1997

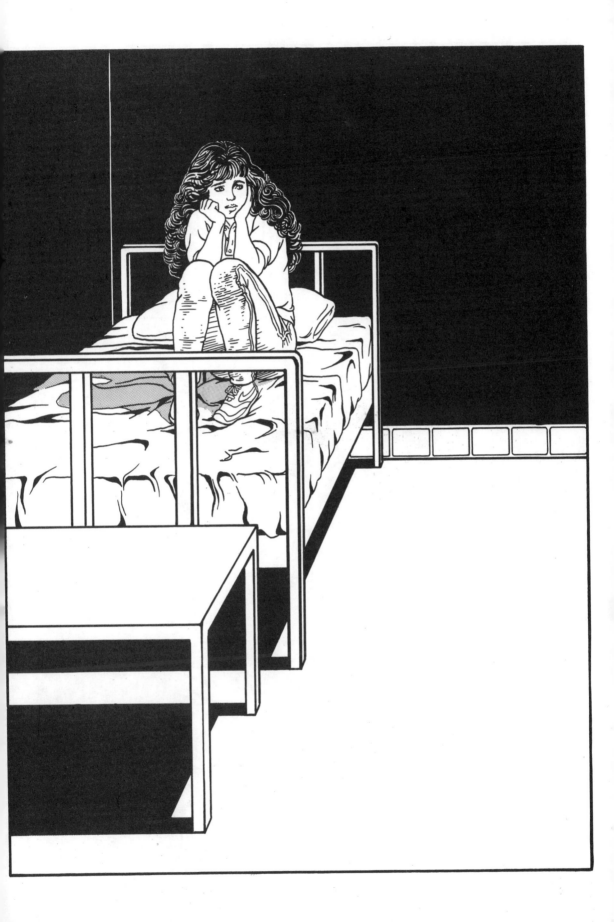

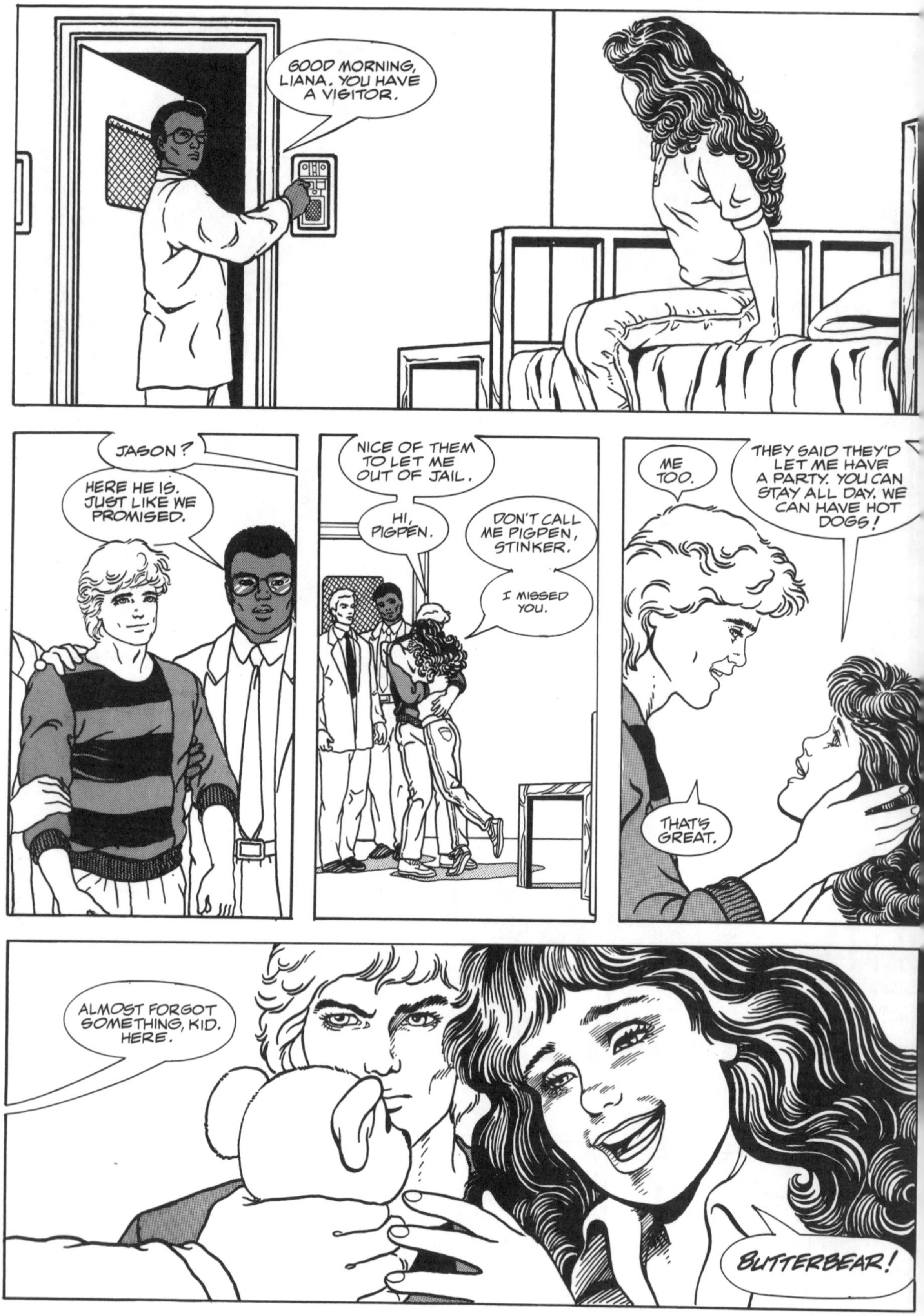
GOOD MORNING, LIANA. YOU HAVE A VISITOR.
JASON?
HERE HE IS. JUST LIKE WE PROMISED.
NICE OF THEM TO LET ME OUT OF JAIL.
HI, PIGPEN.
DON'T CALL ME PIGPEN, STINKER.
I MISSED YOU.
ME TOO.
THEY SAID THEY'D LET ME HAVE A PARTY. YOU CAN STAY ALL DAY. WE CAN HAVE HOT DOGS!
THAT'S GREAT.
ALMOST FORGOT SOMETHING, KID. HERE.
BUTTERBEAR!

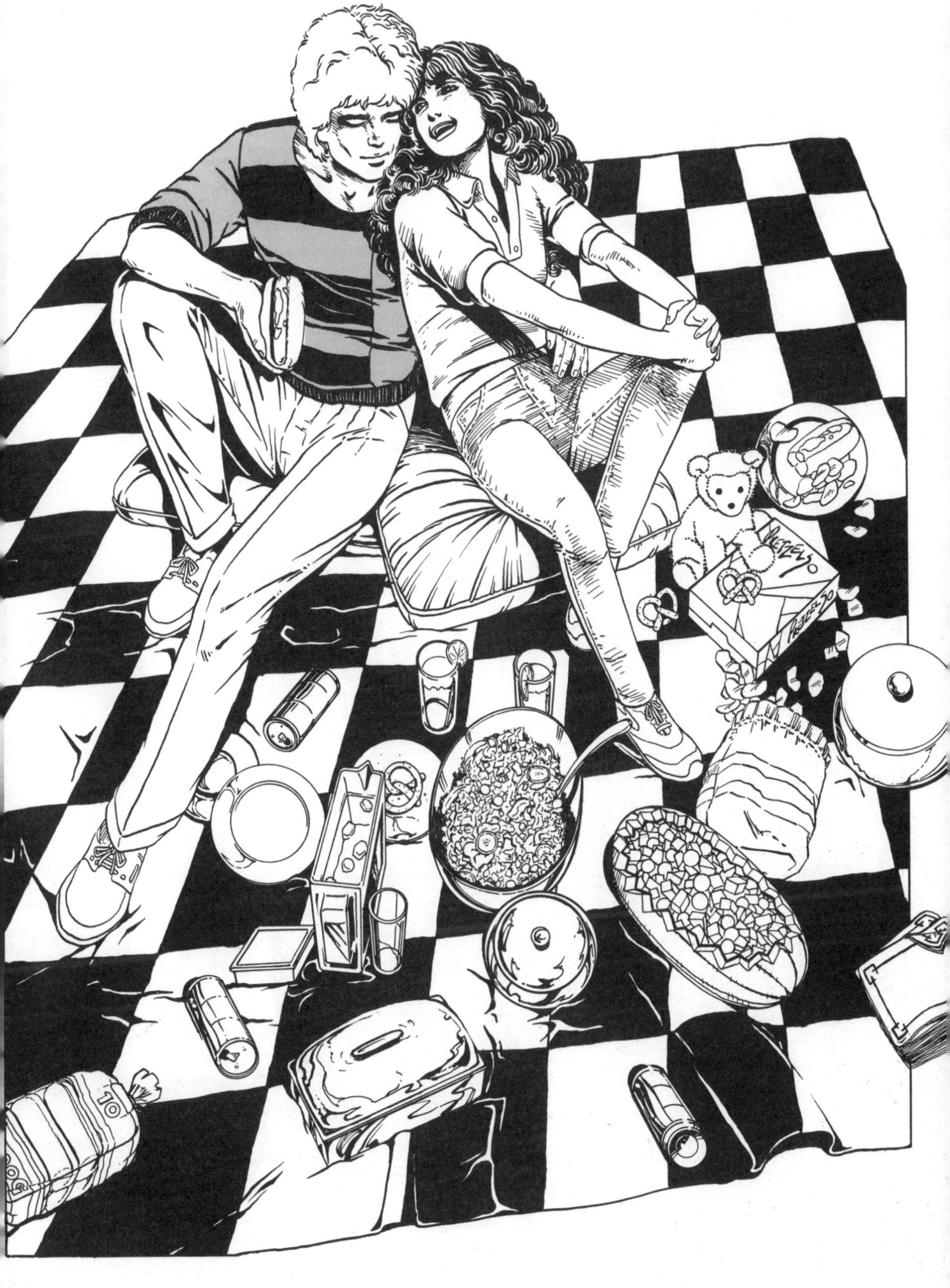

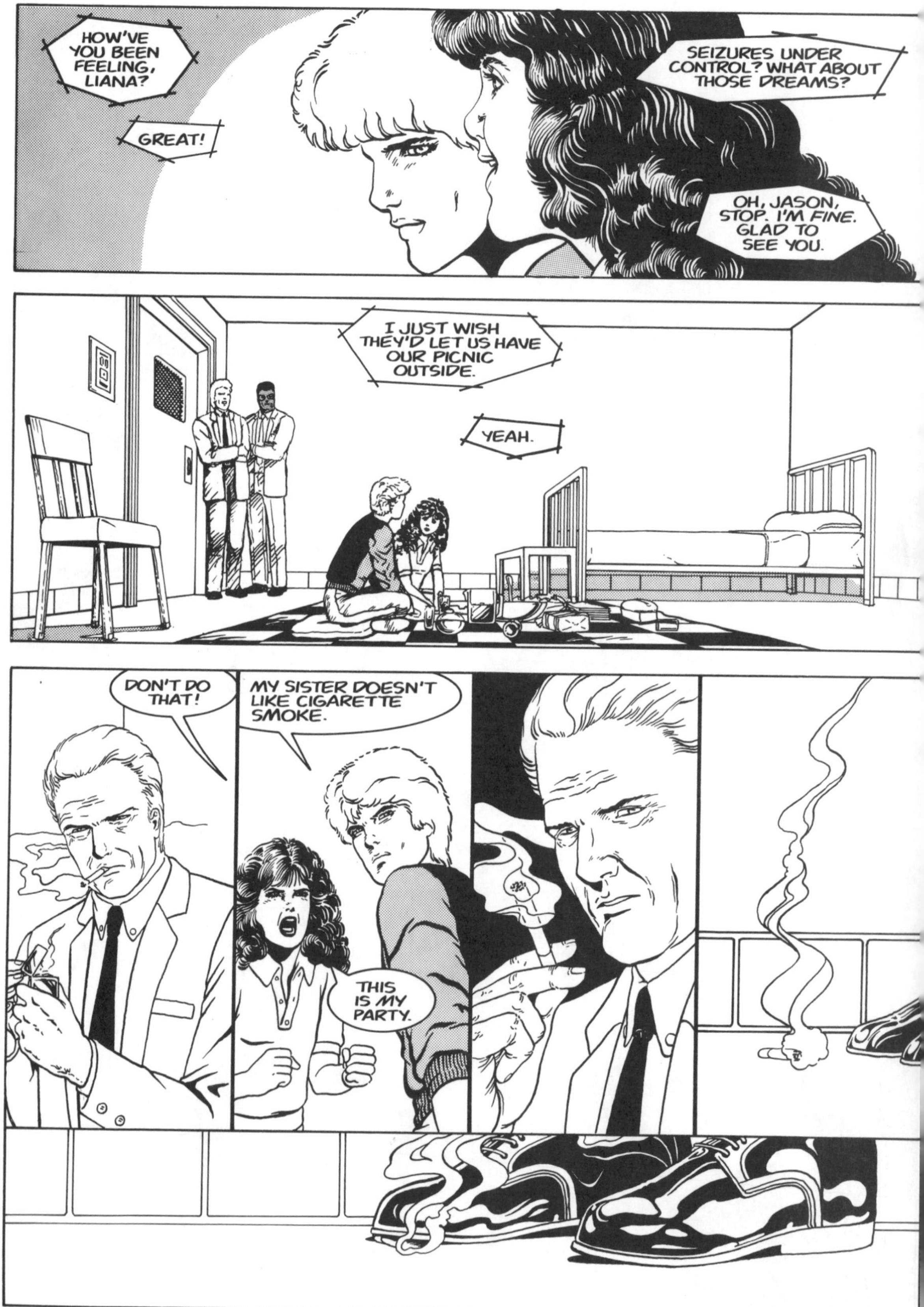
HOW'VE YOU BEEN FEELING, LIANA?
GREAT!
SEIZURES UNDER CONTROL? WHAT ABOUT THOSE DREAMS?
OH, JASON, STOP. I'M FINE. GLAD TO SEE YOU.
I JUST WISH THEY'D LET US HAVE OUR PICNIC OUTSIDE.
YEAH.
DON'T DO THAT!
MY SISTER DOESN'T LIKE CIGARETTE SMOKE.
THIS IS MY PARTY.

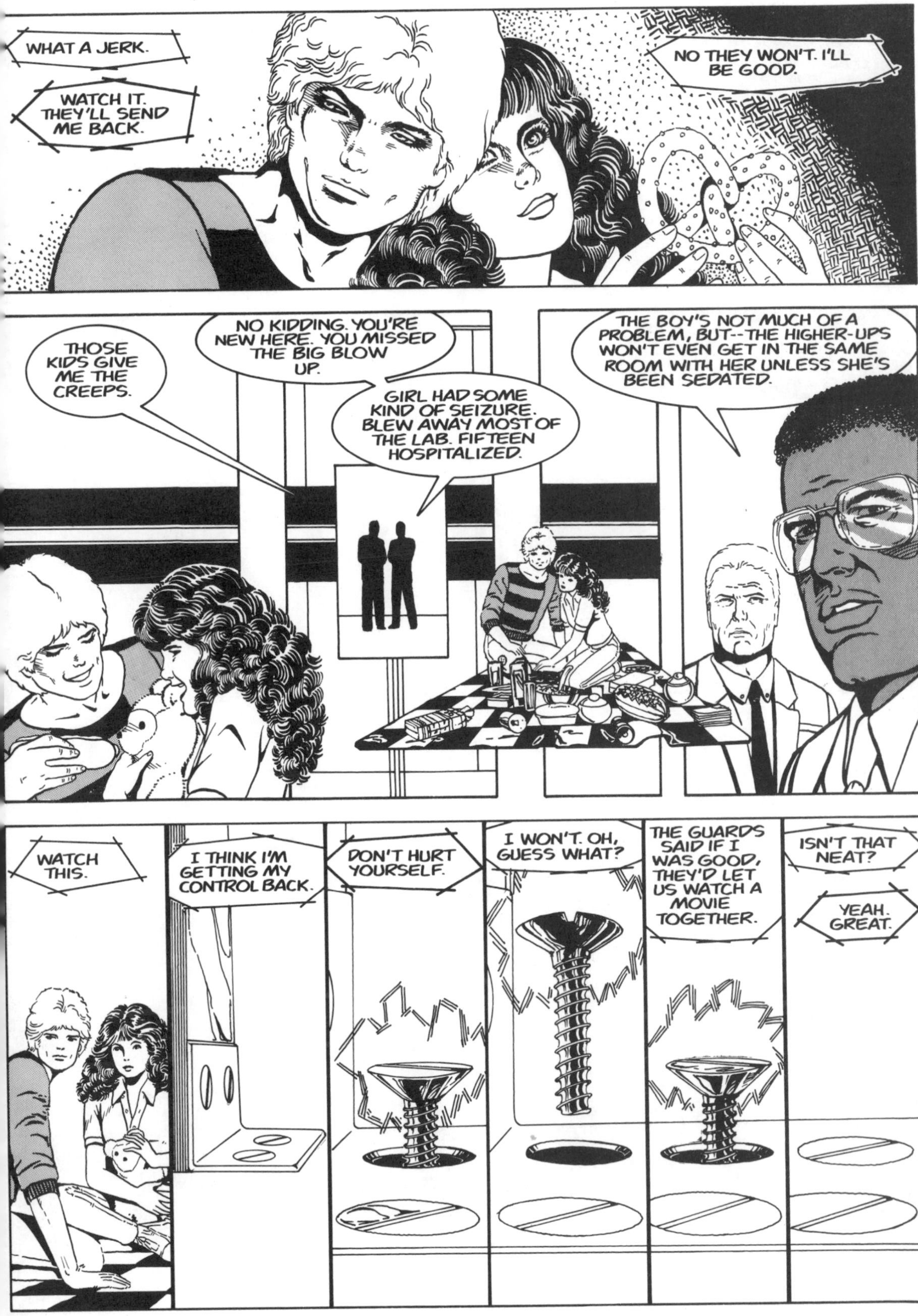
WHAT A JERK.
WATCH IT. THEY'LL SEND ME BACK.
NO THEY WON'T. I'LL BE GOOD.
THOSE KIDS GIVE ME THE CREEPS.
NO KIDDING. YOU'RE NEW HERE. YOU MISSED THE BIG BLOW UP.
GIRL HAD SOME KIND OF SEIZURE. BLEW AWAY MOST OF THE LAB. FIFTEEN HOSPITALIZED.
THE BOY'S NOT MUCH OF A PROBLEM, BUT--THE HIGHER-UPS WON'T EVEN GET IN THE SAME ROOM WITH HER UNLESS SHE'S BEEN SEDATED.
WATCH THIS.
I THINK I'M GETTING MY CONTROL BACK.
DON'T HURT YOURSELF.
I WON'T. OH, GUESS WHAT?
THE GUARDS SAID IF I WAS GOOD, THEY'D LET US WATCH A MOVIE TOGETHER.
ISN'T THAT NEAT?
YEAH. GREAT.

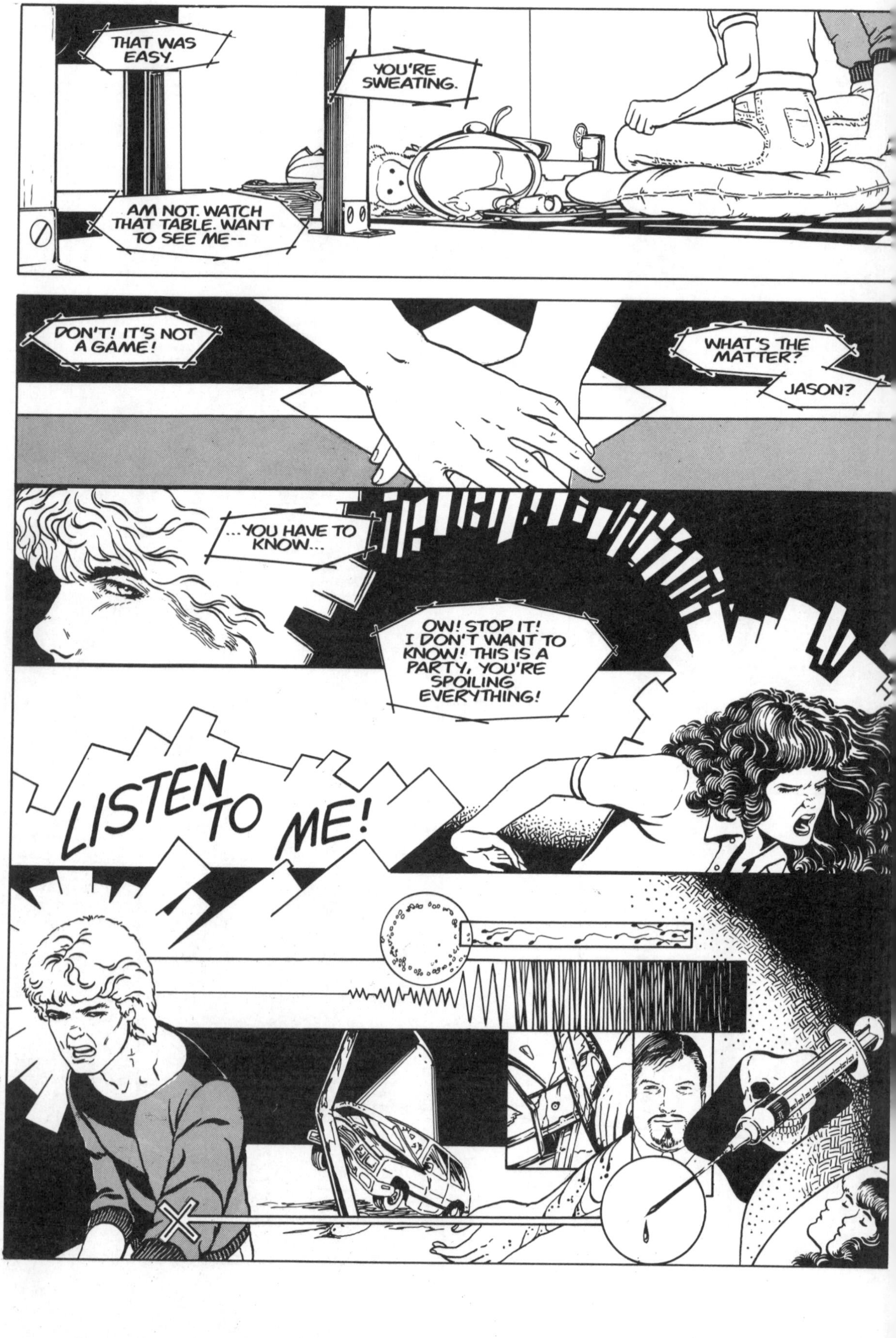
THAT WAS EASY.
YOU'RE SWEATING.
AM NOT. WATCH THAT TABLE. WANT TO SEE ME--
DON'T! IT'S NOT A GAME!
WHAT'S THE MATTER?
JASON?
...YOU HAVE TO KNOW...
OW! STOP IT! I DON'T WANT TO KNOW! THIS IS A PARTY, YOU'RE SPOILING EVERYTHING!
LISTEN TO ME!

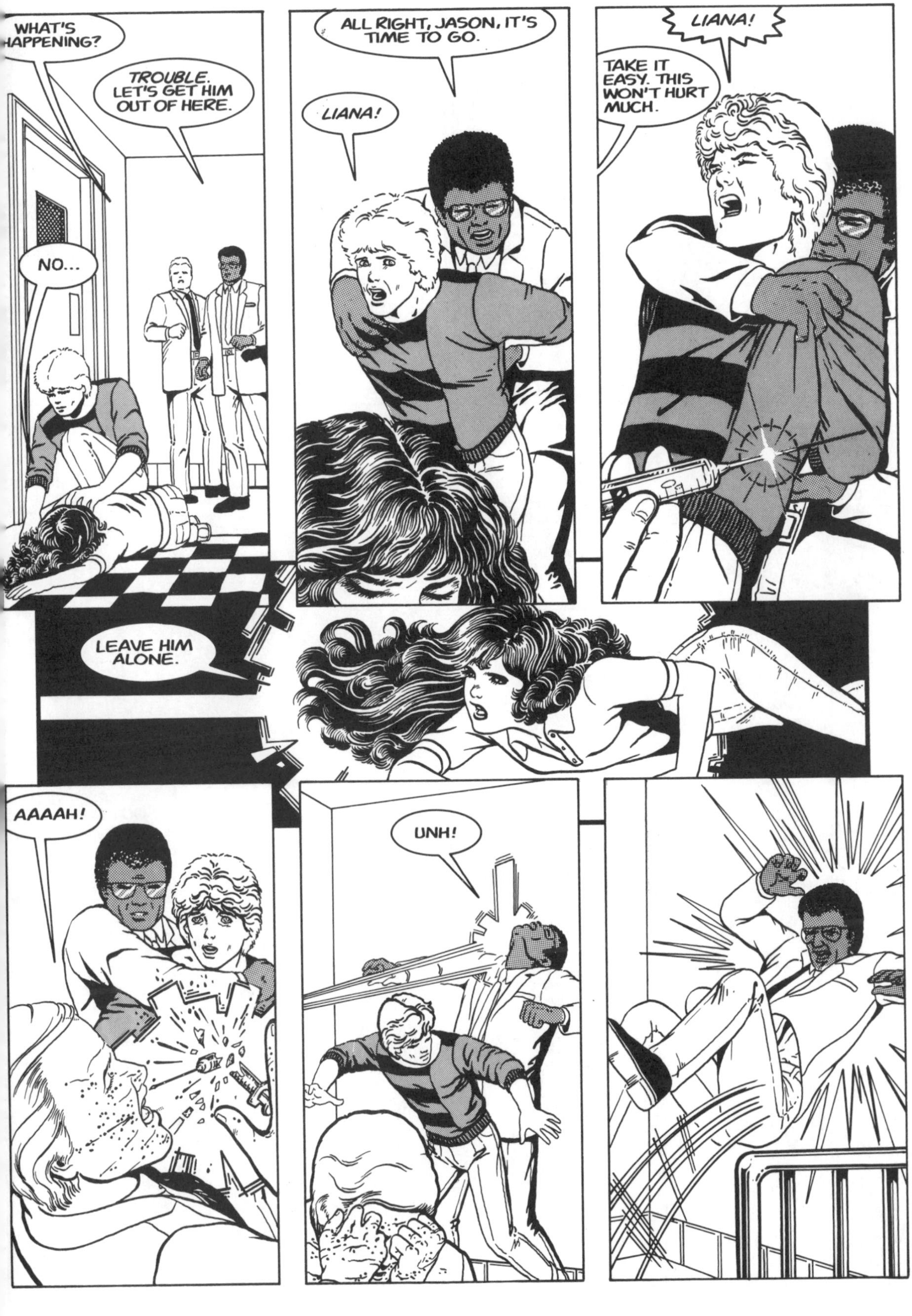
WHAT'S HAPPENING?
TROUBLE. LET'S GET HIM OUT OF HERE.
NO...
ALL RIGHT, JASON, IT'S TIME TO GO.
LIANA!
LIANA!
TAKE IT EASY. THIS WON'T HURT MUCH.
LEAVE HIM ALONE.
AAAAH!
UNH!

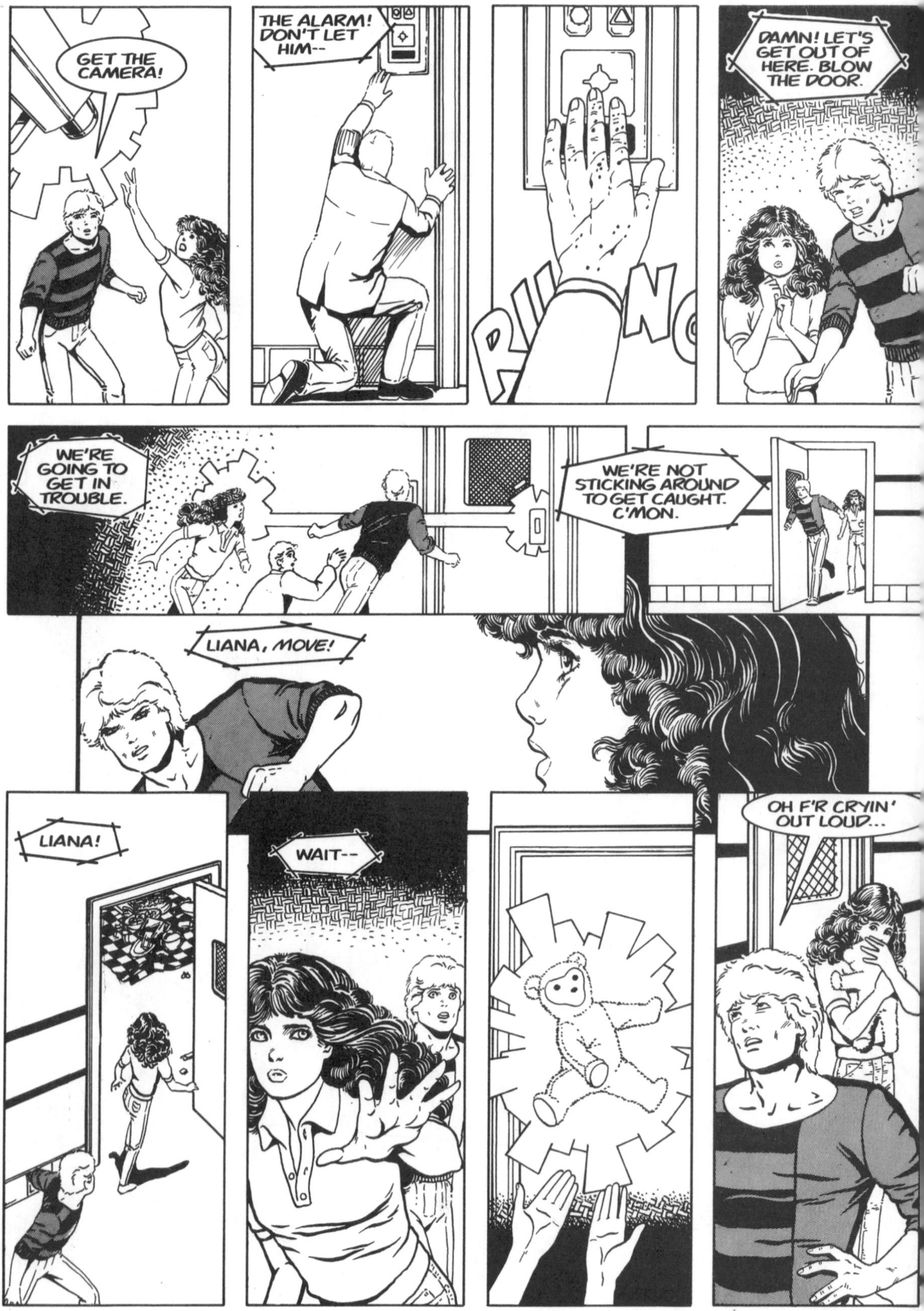
GET THE CAMERA!
THE ALARM! DON'T LET HIM--
RING
DAMN! LET'S GET OUT OF HERE. BLOW THE DOOR.
WE'RE GOING TO GET IN TROUBLE.
WE'RE NOT STICKING AROUND TO GET CAUGHT. C'MON.
LIANA, MOVE!
LIANA!
WAIT--
OH F'R CRYIN' OUT LOUD...

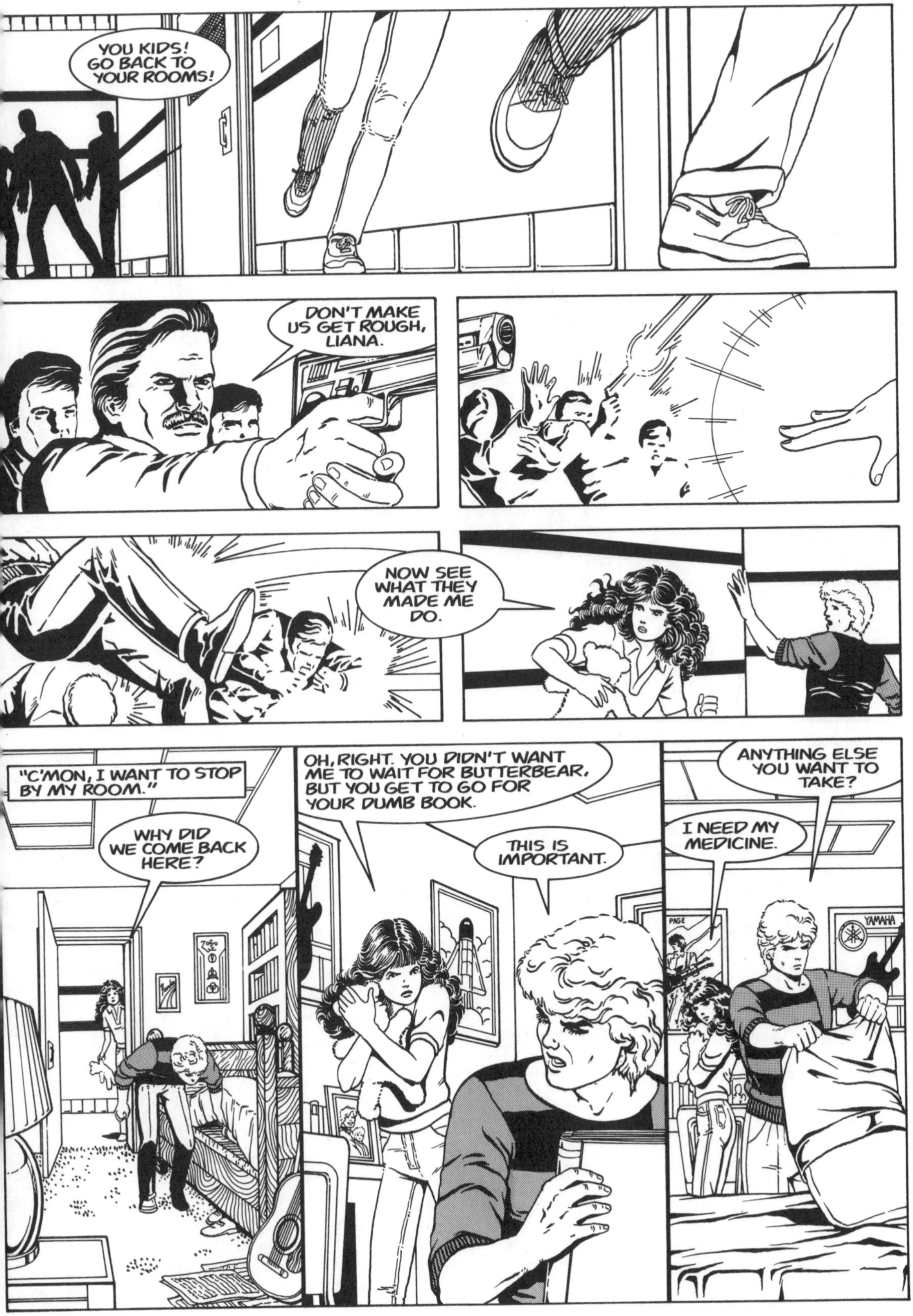
YOU KIDS! GO BACK TO YOUR ROOMS!
DON'T MAKE US GET ROUGH, LIANA.
NOW SEE WHAT THEY MADE ME DO.
"C'MON, I WANT TO STOP BY MY ROOM."
WHY DID WE COME BACK HERE?
OH, RIGHT. YOU DIDN'T WANT ME TO WAIT FOR BUTTERBEAR, BUT YOU GET TO GO FOR YOUR DUMB BOOK.
THIS IS IMPORTANT.
ANYTHING ELSE YOU WANT TO TAKE?
I NEED MY MEDICINE.

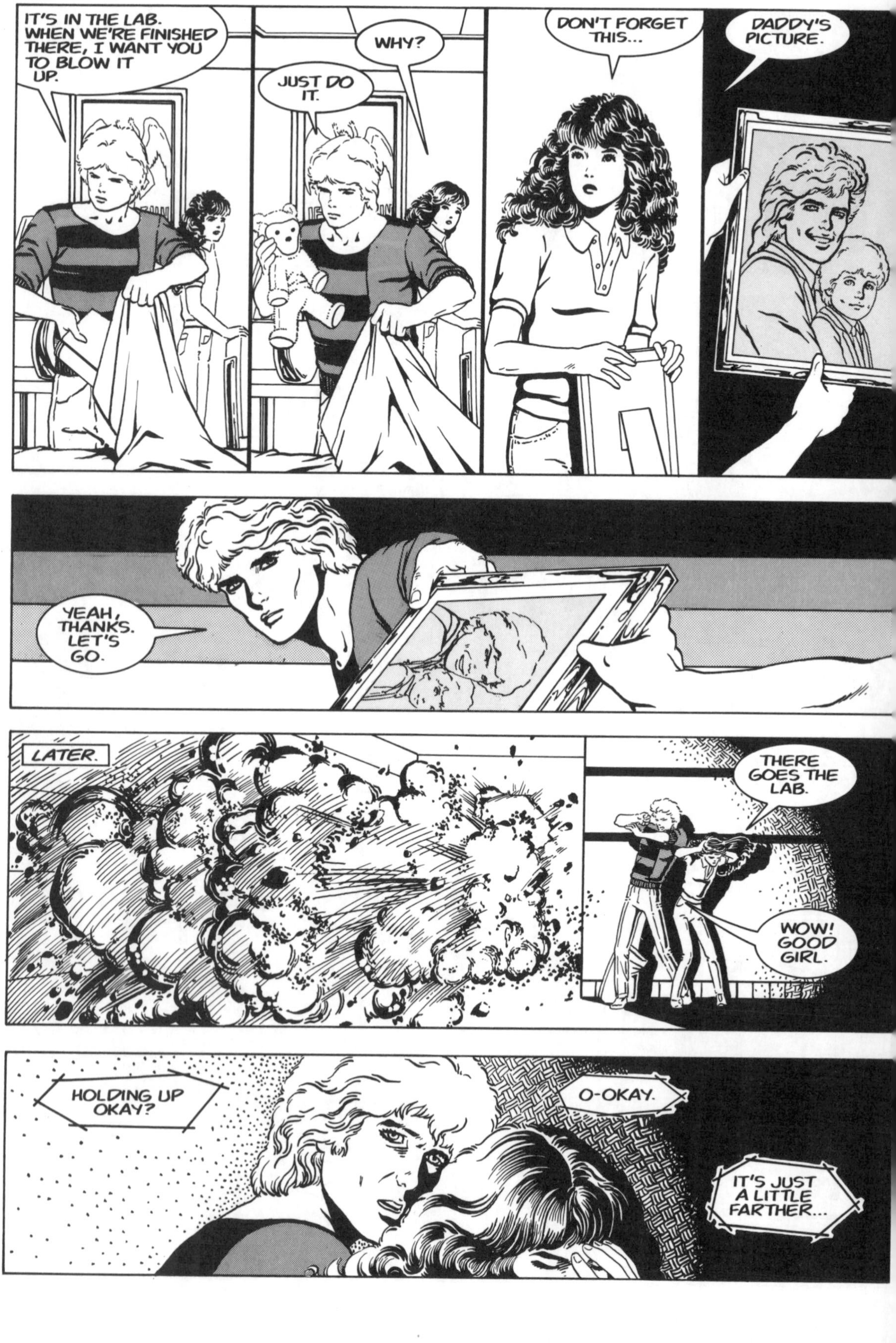
IT'S IN THE LAB. WHEN WE'RE FINISHED THERE, I WANT YOU TO BLOW IT UP.
WHY?
JUST DO IT.
DON'T FORGET THIS...
DADDY'S PICTURE.
YEAH, THANKS. LET'S GO.
LATER.
THERE GOES THE LAB.
WOW! GOOD GIRL.
HOLDING UP OKAY?
O-OKAY.
IT'S JUST A LITTLE FARTHER...

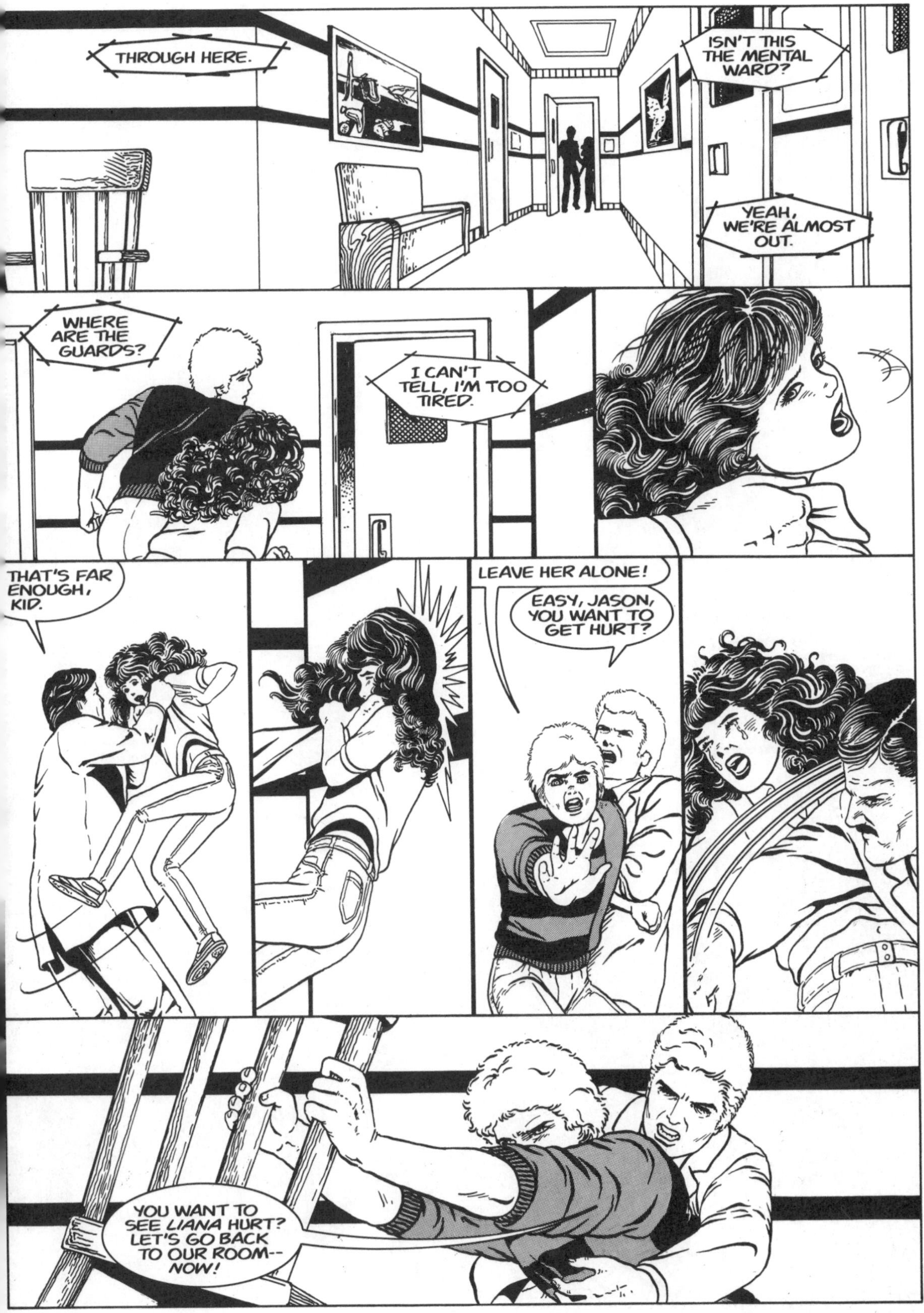
THROUGH HERE.
ISN'T THIS THE MENTAL WARD?
YEAH, WE'RE ALMOST OUT.
WHERE ARE THE GUARDS?
I CAN'T TELL, I'M TOO TIRED.
THAT'S FAR ENOUGH, KID.
LEAVE HER ALONE!
EASY, JASON, YOU WANT TO GET HURT?
YOU WANT TO SEE *LIANA* HURT? LET'S GO BACK TO OUR ROOM-- NOW!

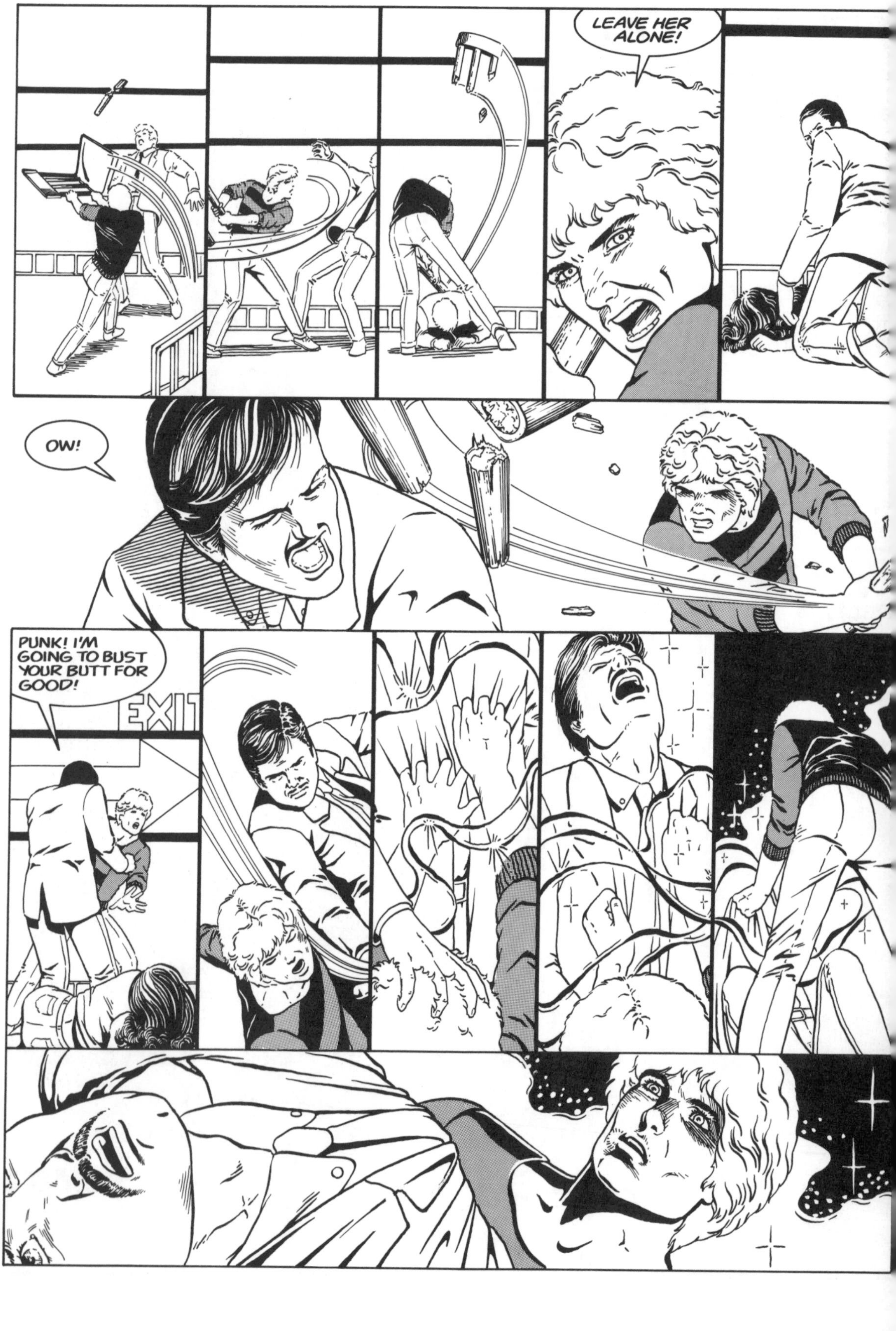
LEAVE HER ALONE!
OW!
PUNK! I'M GOING TO BUST YOUR BUTT FOR GOOD!
EXIT

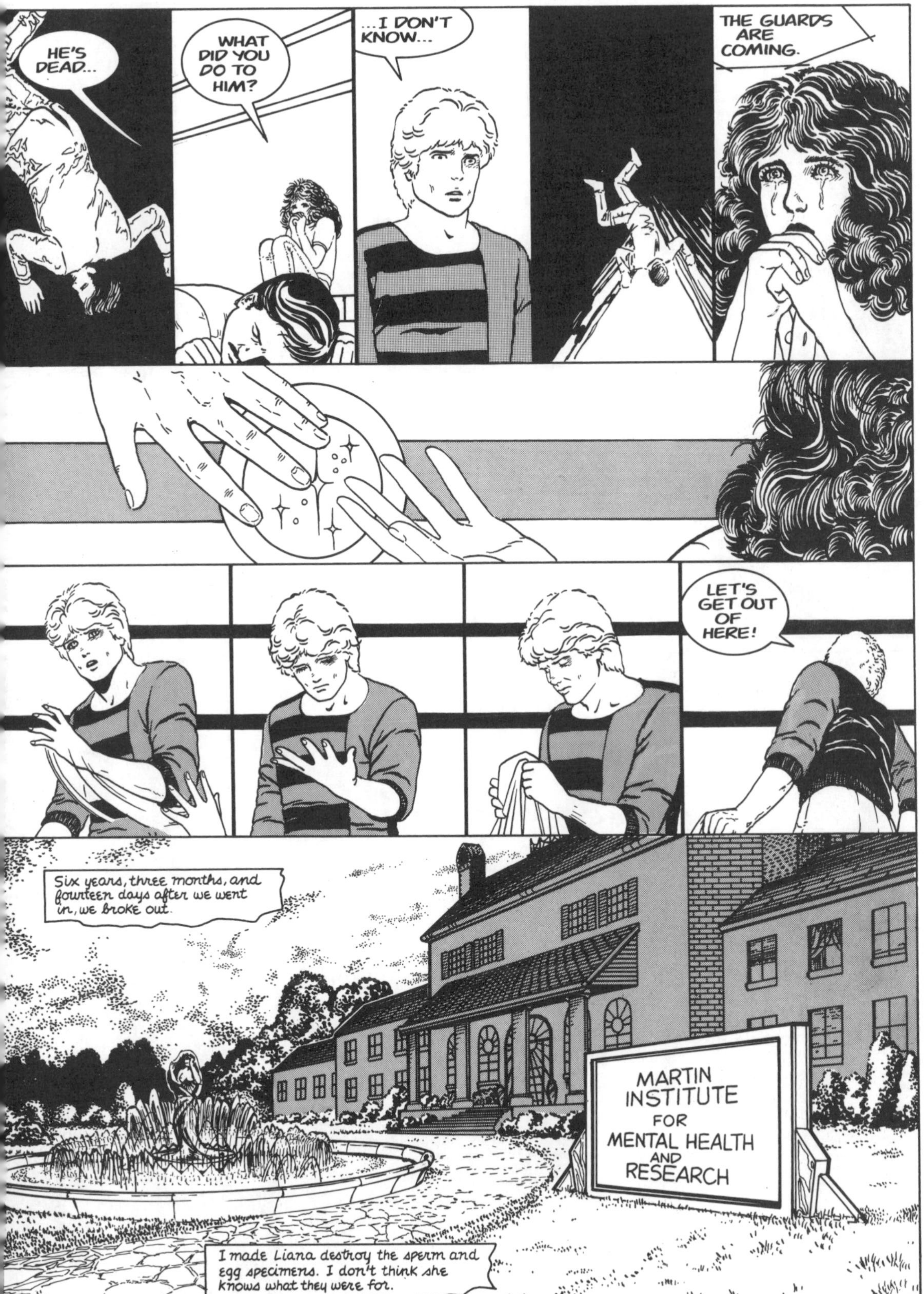
HE'S DEAD...
WHAT DID YOU DO TO HIM?
...I DON'T KNOW...
THE GUARDS ARE COMING.
LET'S GET OUT OF HERE!
Six years, three months, and fourteen days after we went in, we broke out.
MARTIN INSTITUTE FOR MENTAL HEALTH AND RESEARCH
I made Liana destroy the sperm and egg specimens. I don't think she knows what they were for.

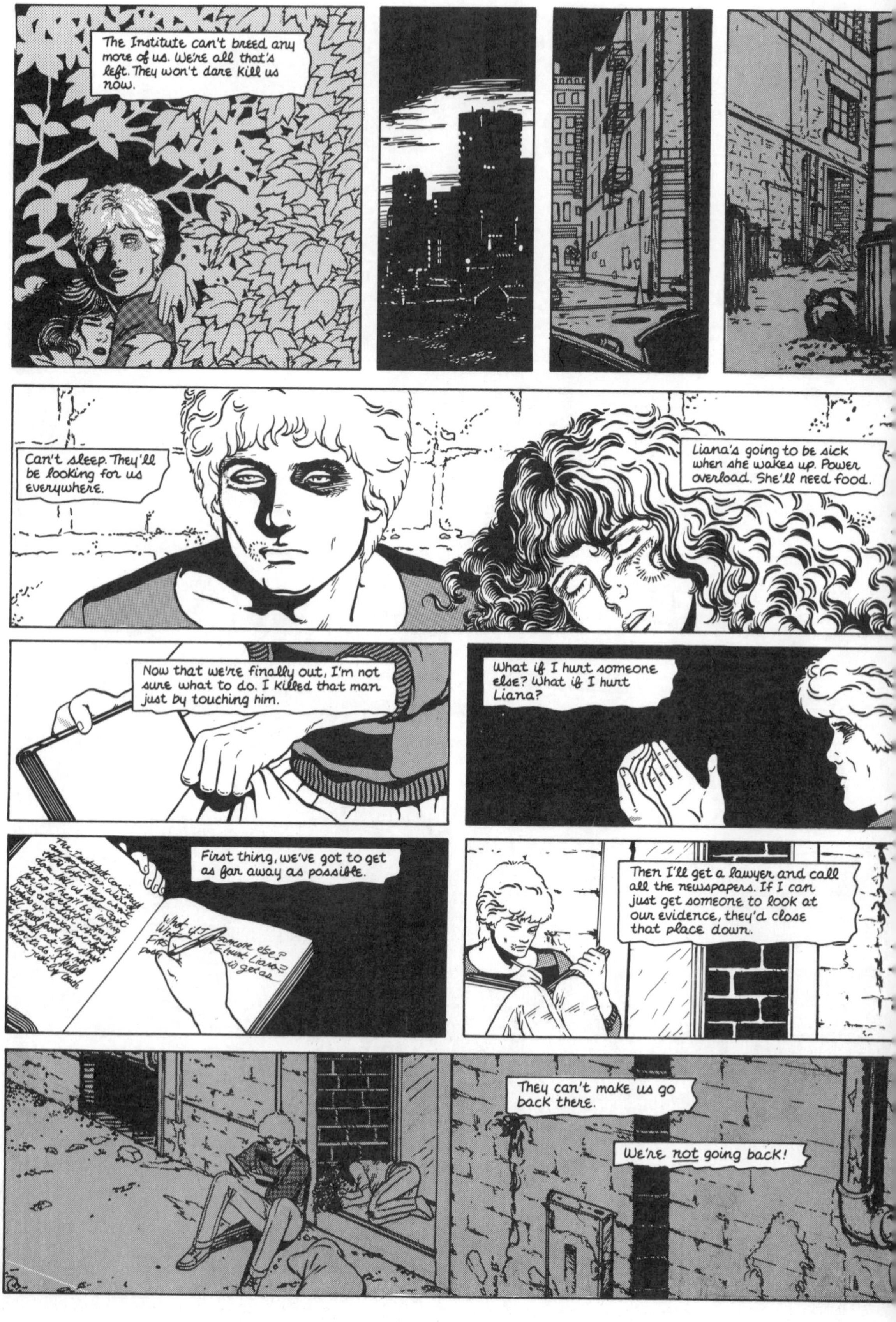
The Institute can't breed any more of us. We're all that's left. They won't dare Kill us now.
Can't sleep. They'll be looking for us everywhere.
Liana's going to be sick when she wakes up. Power overload. She'll need food.
Now that we're finally out, I'm not sure what to do. I Killed that man just by touching him.
What if I hurt someone else? What if I hurt Liana?
First thing, we've got to get as far away as possible.
Then I'll get a lawyer and call all the newspapers. If I can just get someone to look at our evidence, they'd close that place down.
They can't make us go back there.
We're not going back!

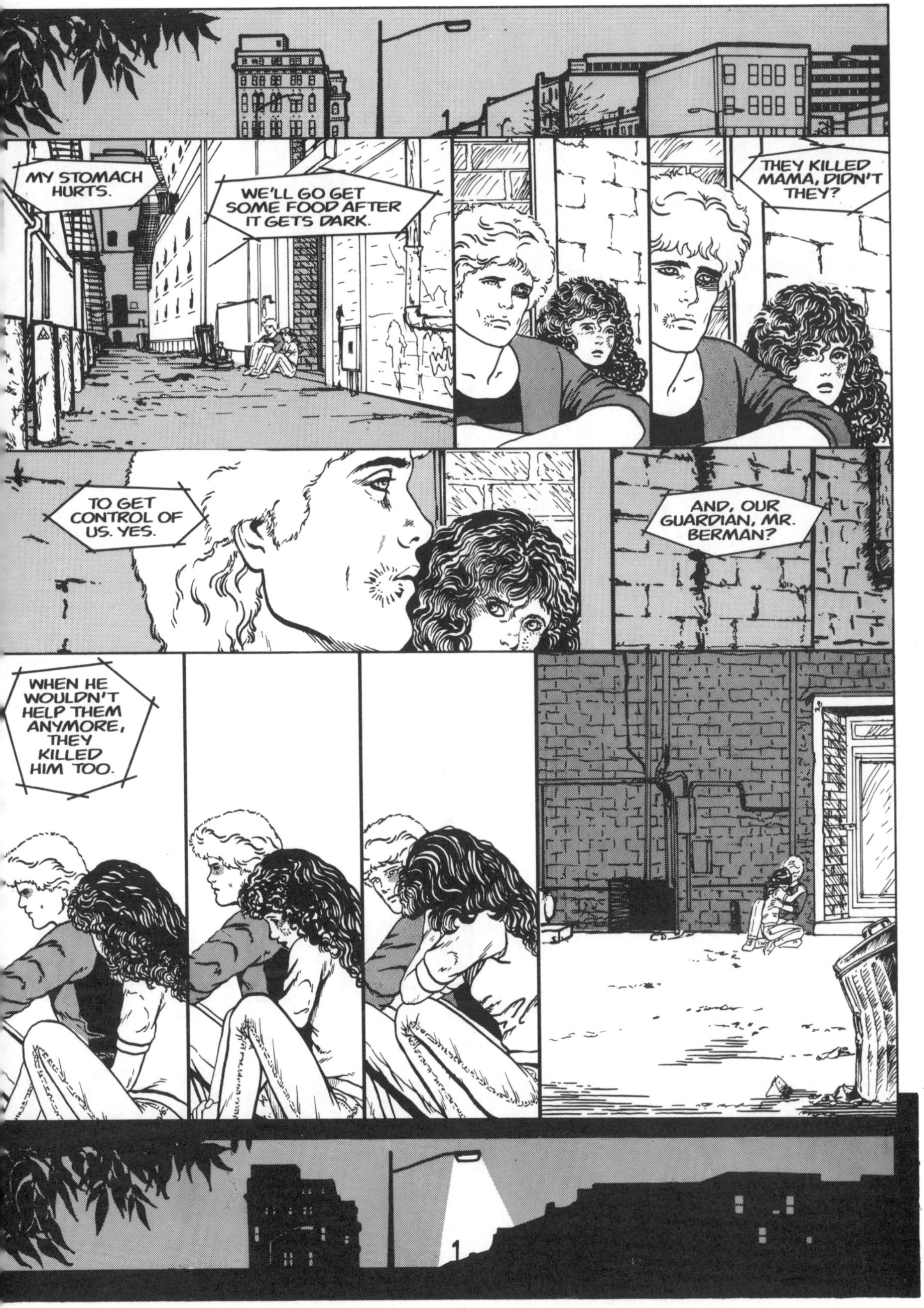
MY STOMACH HURTS.
WE'LL GO GET SOME FOOD AFTER IT GETS DARK.
THEY KILLED MAMA, DIDN'T THEY?
TO GET CONTROL OF US. YES.
AND, OUR GUARDIAN, MR. BERMAN?
WHEN HE WOULDN'T HELP THEM ANYMORE, THEY KILLED HIM TOO.

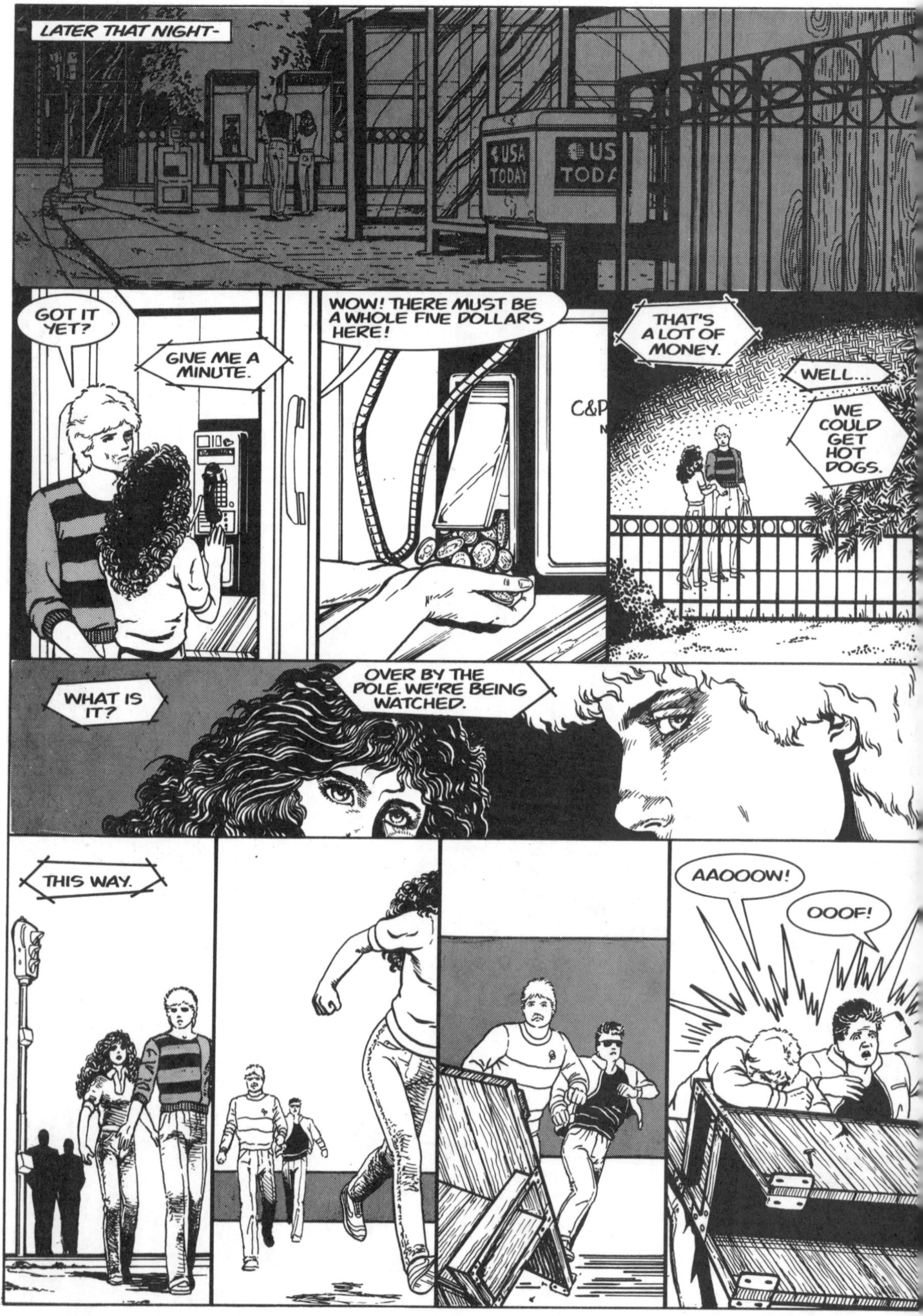
LATER THAT NIGHT-
USA TODAY
GOT IT YET?
GIVE ME A MINUTE.
WOW! THERE MUST BE A WHOLE FIVE DOLLARS HERE!
THAT'S A LOT OF MONEY.
WELL...
WE COULD GET HOT DOGS.
WHAT IS IT?
OVER BY THE POLE. WE'RE BEING WATCHED.
THIS WAY.
AAOOOW!
OOOF!

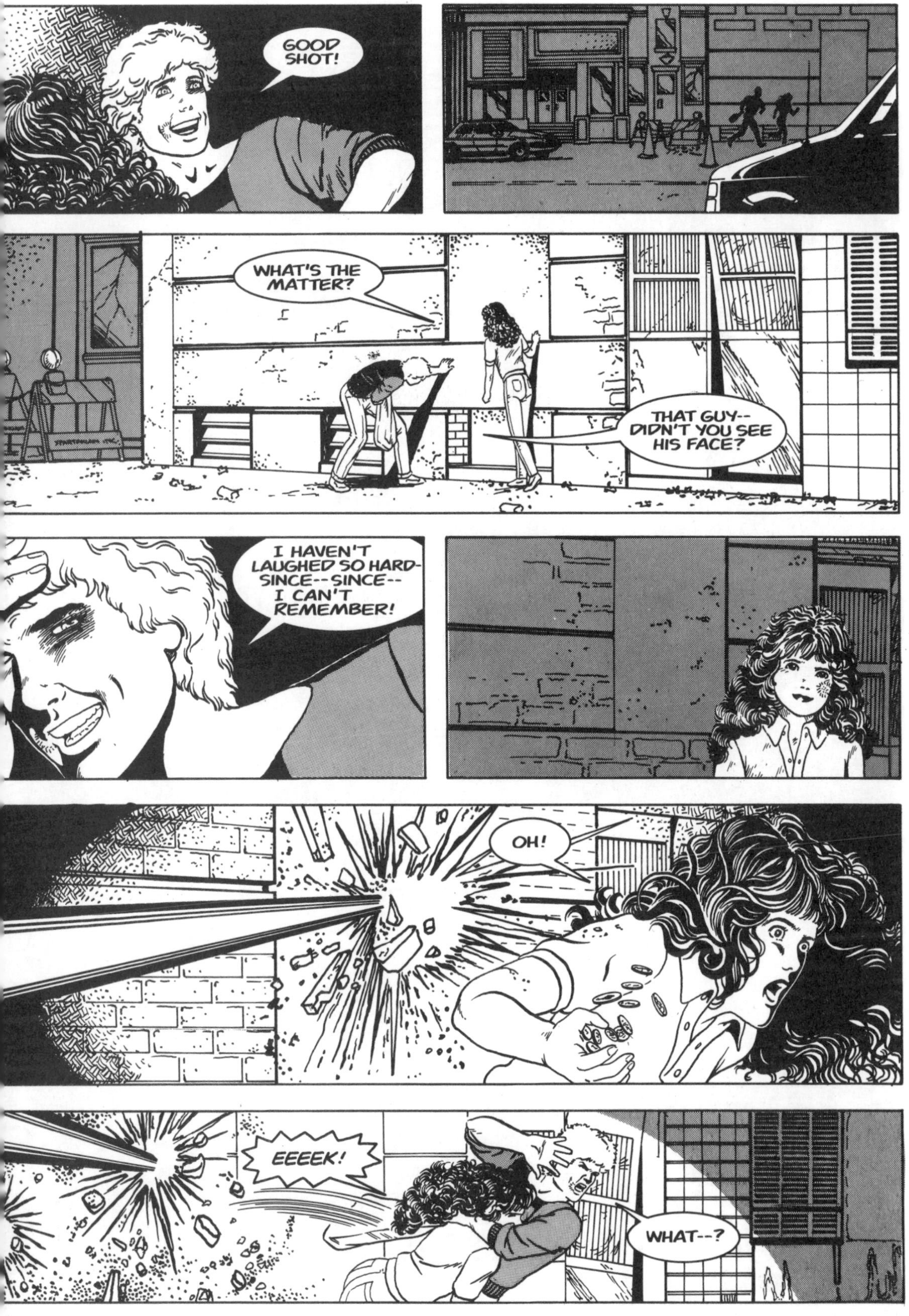
GOOD SHOT!
WHAT'S THE MATTER?
THAT GUY-- DIDN'T YOU SEE HIS FACE?
I HAVEN'T LAUGHED SO HARD-SINCE--SINCE-- I CAN'T REMEMBER!
OH!
EEEEK!
WHAT--?

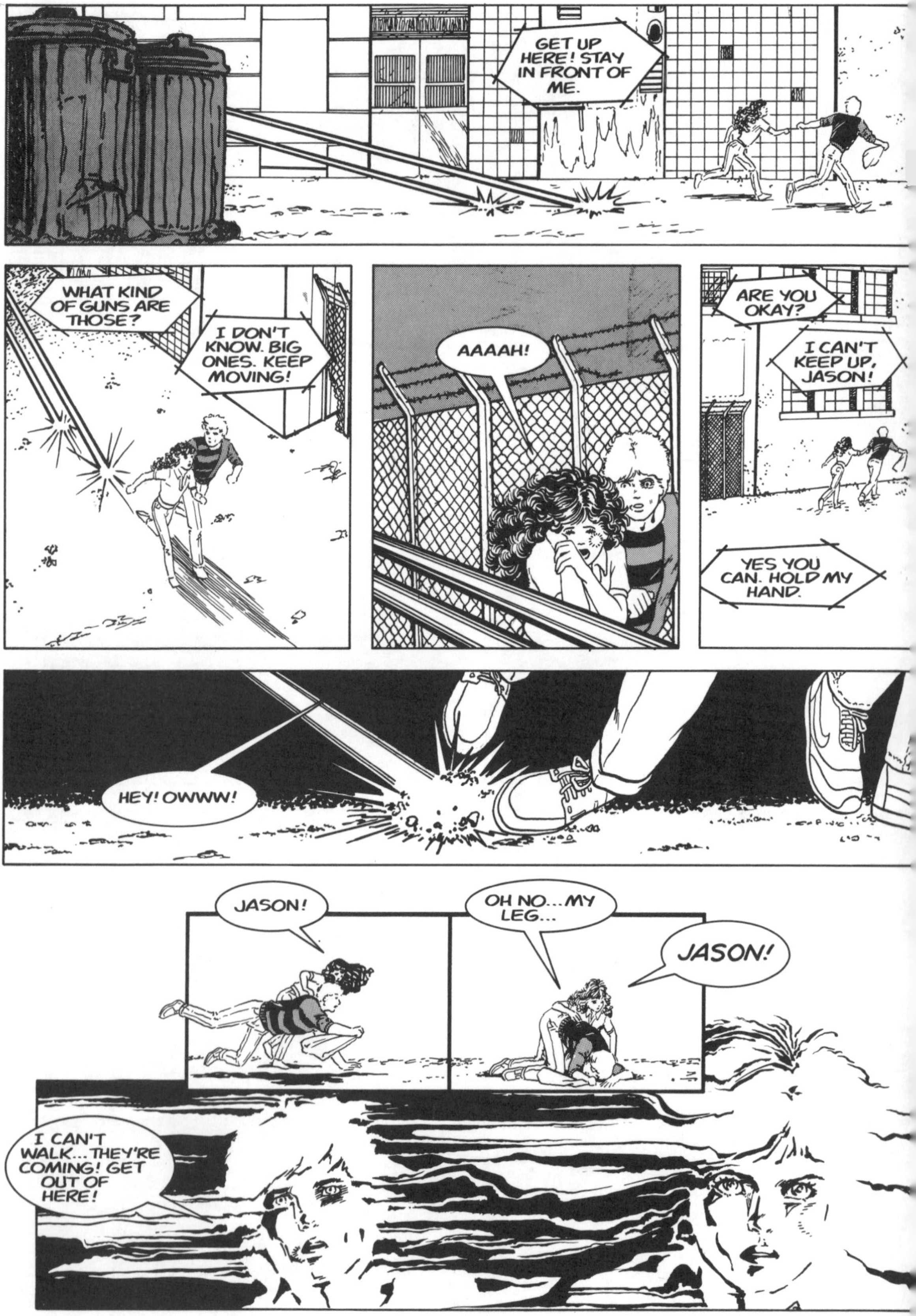
GET UP HERE! STAY IN FRONT OF ME.
WHAT KIND OF GUNS ARE THOSE?
I DON'T KNOW. BIG ONES. KEEP MOVING!
AAAAH!
ARE YOU OKAY?
I CAN'T KEEP UP, JASON!
YES YOU CAN. HOLD MY HAND.
HEY! OWWW!
JASON!
OH NO... MY LEG...
JASON!
I CAN'T WALK... THEY'RE COMING! GET OUT OF HERE!

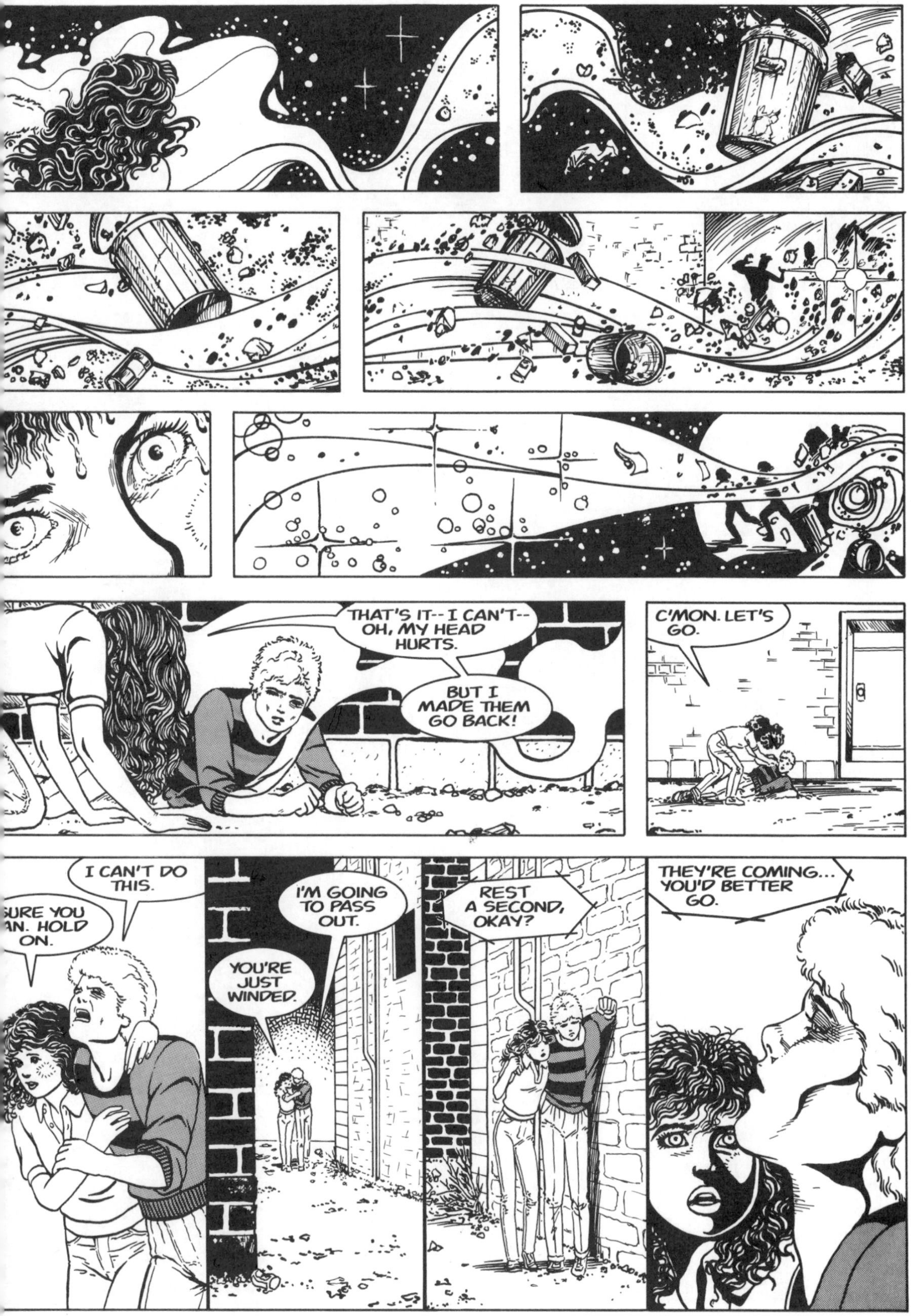
THAT'S IT-- I CAN'T-- OH, MY HEAD HURTS.
BUT I MADE THEM GO BACK!
C'MON. LET'S GO.
I CAN'T DO THIS.
SURE YOU CAN. HOLD ON.
I'M GOING TO PASS OUT.
YOU'RE JUST WINDED.
REST A SECOND, OKAY?
THEY'RE COMING... YOU'D BETTER GO.

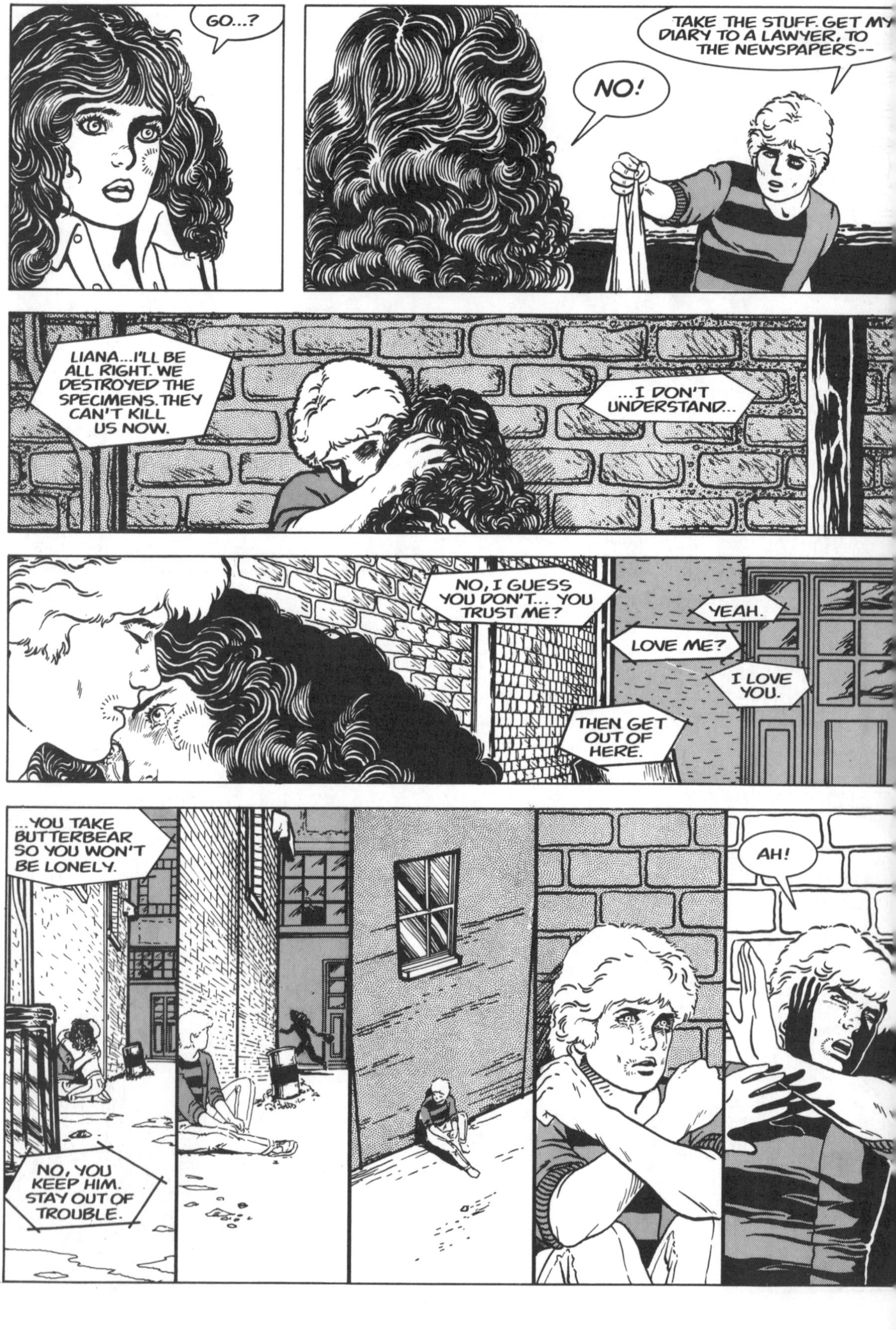
GO...?
TAKE THE STUFF. GET MY DIARY TO A LAWYER, TO THE NEWSPAPERS--
NO!
LIANA...I'LL BE ALL RIGHT. WE DESTROYED THE SPECIMENS. THEY CAN'T KILL US NOW.
...I DON'T UNDERSTAND...
NO, I GUESS YOU DON'T... YOU TRUST ME?
YEAH.
LOVE ME?
I LOVE YOU.
THEN GET OUT OF HERE.
...YOU TAKE BUTTERBEAR SO YOU WON'T BE LONELY.
NO, YOU KEEP HIM. STAY OUT OF TROUBLE.
AH!

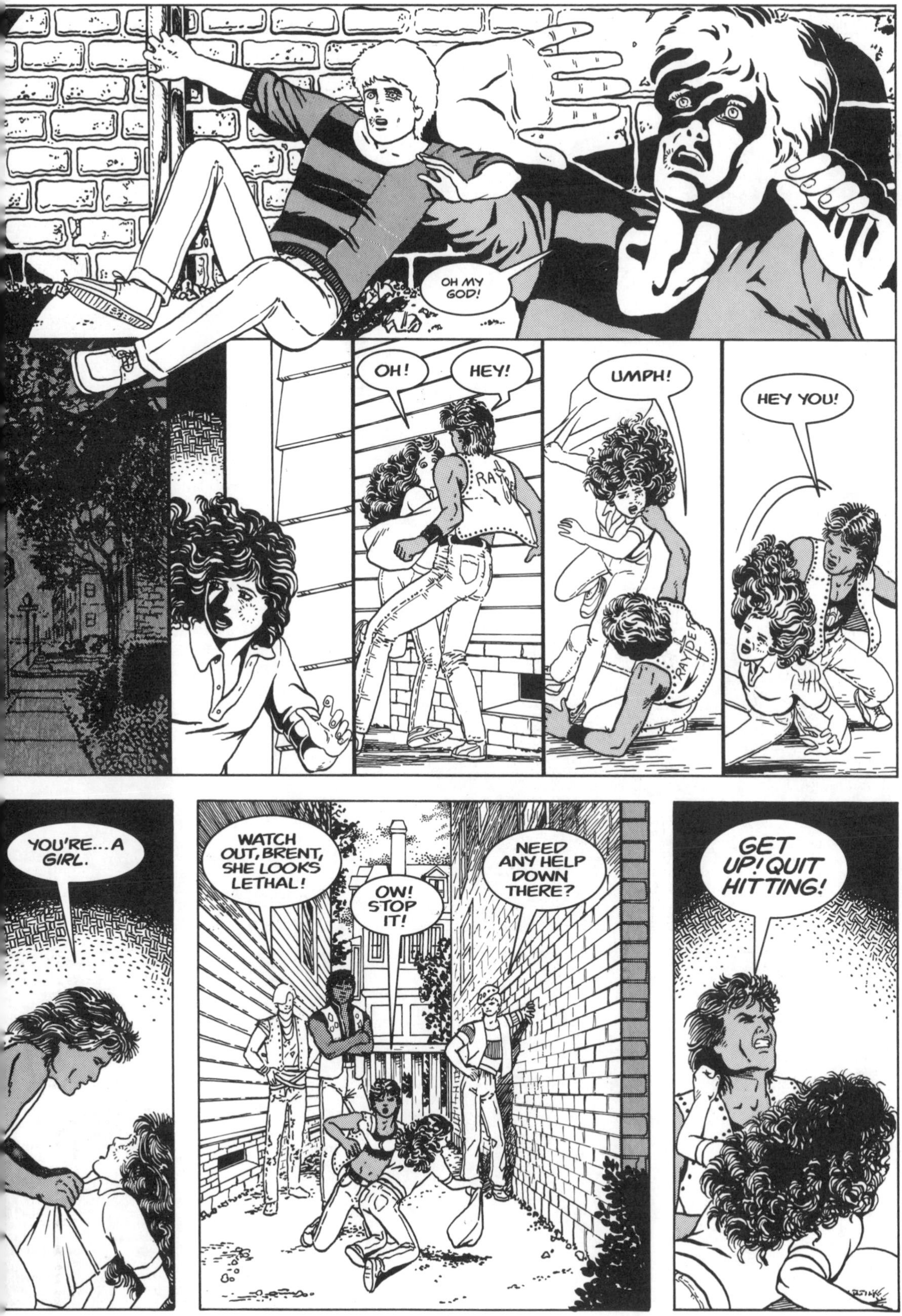
OH MY GOD!
OH!
HEY!
UMPH!
HEY YOU!
YOU'RE... A GIRL.
WATCH OUT, BRENT, SHE LOOKS LETHAL!
OW! STOP IT!
NEED ANY HELP DOWN THERE?
GET UP! QUIT HITTING!

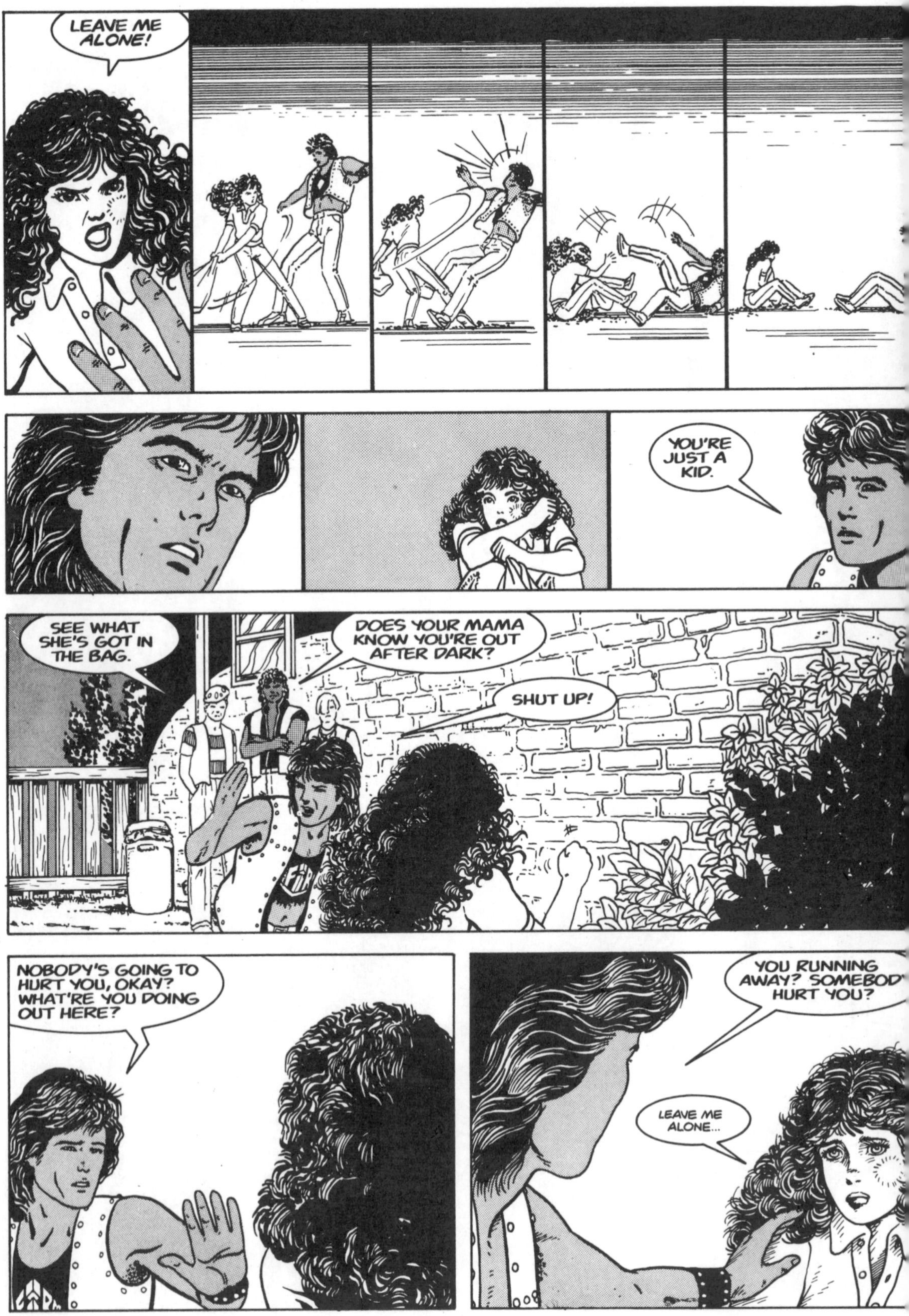
LEAVE ME ALONE!
YOU'RE JUST A KID.
SEE WHAT SHE'S GOT IN THE BAG.
DOES YOUR MAMA KNOW YOU'RE OUT AFTER DARK?
SHUT UP!
NOBODY'S GOING TO HURT YOU, OKAY? WHAT'RE YOU DOING OUT HERE?
YOU RUNNING AWAY? SOMEBOD HURT YOU?
LEAVE ME ALONE...

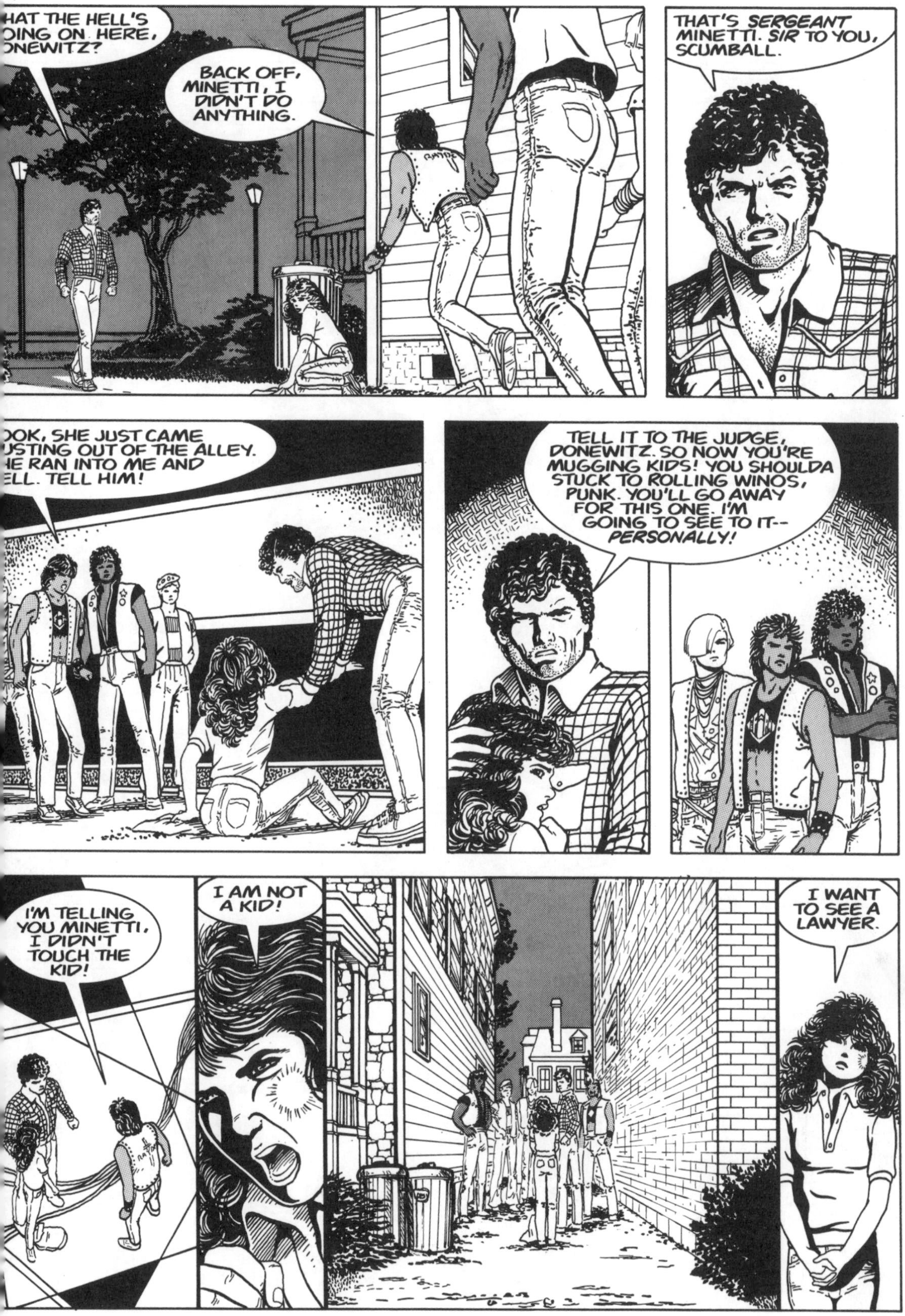
HAT THE HELL'S
OING ON HERE,
ONEWITZ?
BACK OFF, MINETTI, I DIDN'T DO ANYTHING.
THAT'S SERGEANT MINETTI. SIR TO YOU, SCUMBALL.
OOK, SHE JUST CAME
USTING OUT OF THE ALLEY.
HE RAN INTO ME AND
ELL. TELL HIM!
TELL IT TO THE JUDGE, DONEWITZ. SO NOW YOU'RE MUGGING KIDS! YOU SHOULDA STUCK TO ROLLING WINOS, PUNK. YOU'LL GO AWAY FOR THIS ONE. I'M GOING TO SEE TO IT-- PERSONALLY!
I'M TELLING YOU MINETTI, I DIDN'T TOUCH THE KID!
I AM NOT A KID!
I WANT TO SEE A LAWYER.

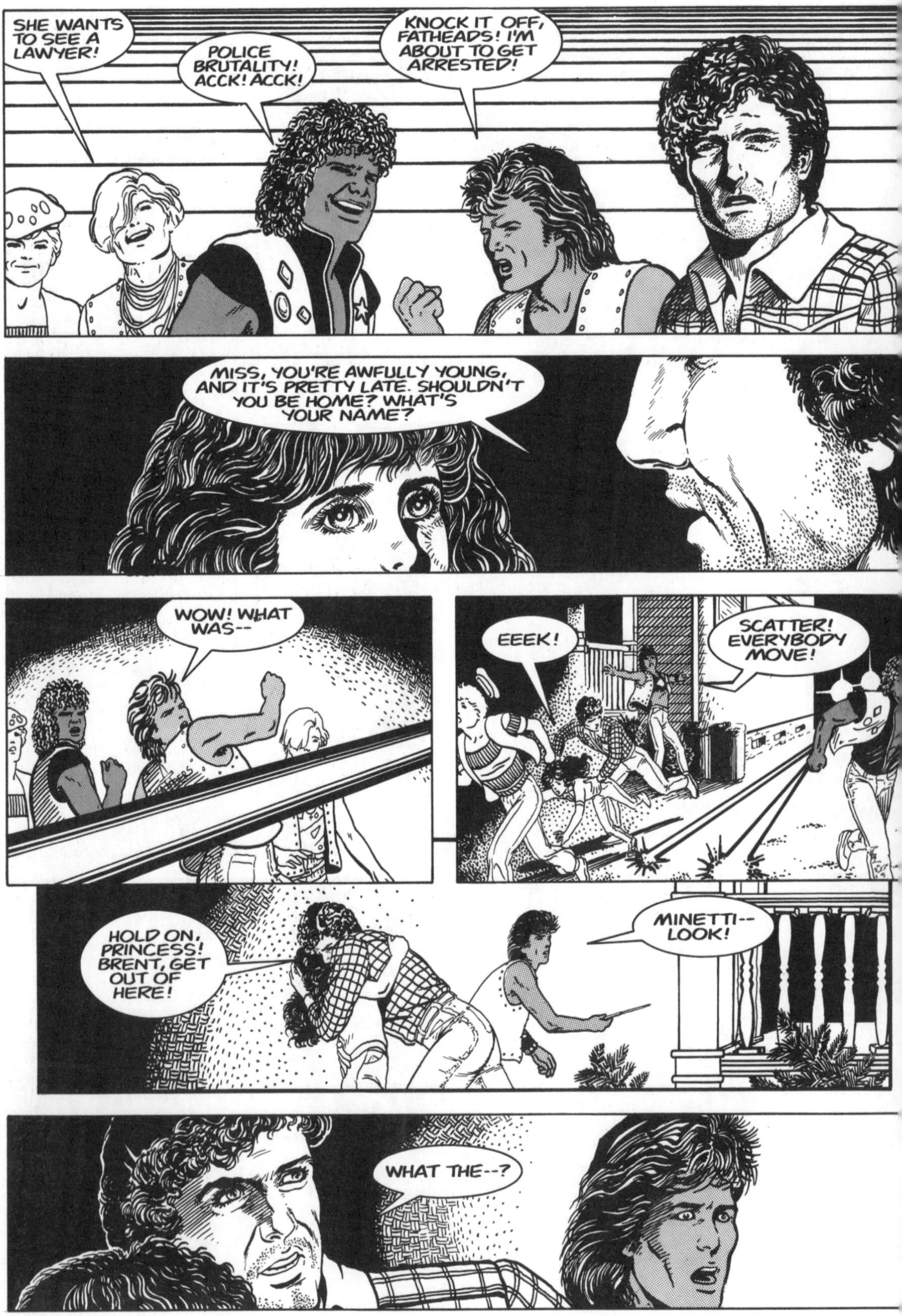
SHE WANTS TO SEE A LAWYER!
POLICE BRUTALITY! ACCK! ACCK!
KNOCK IT OFF, FATHEADS! I'M ABOUT TO GET ARRESTED!
MISS, YOU'RE AWFULLY YOUNG, AND IT'S PRETTY LATE. SHOULDN'T YOU BE HOME? WHAT'S YOUR NAME?
WOW! WHAT WAS--
EEEK!
SCATTER! EVERYBODY MOVE!
HOLD ON, PRINCESS! BRENT, GET OUT OF HERE!
MINETTI-- LOOK!
WHAT THE--?

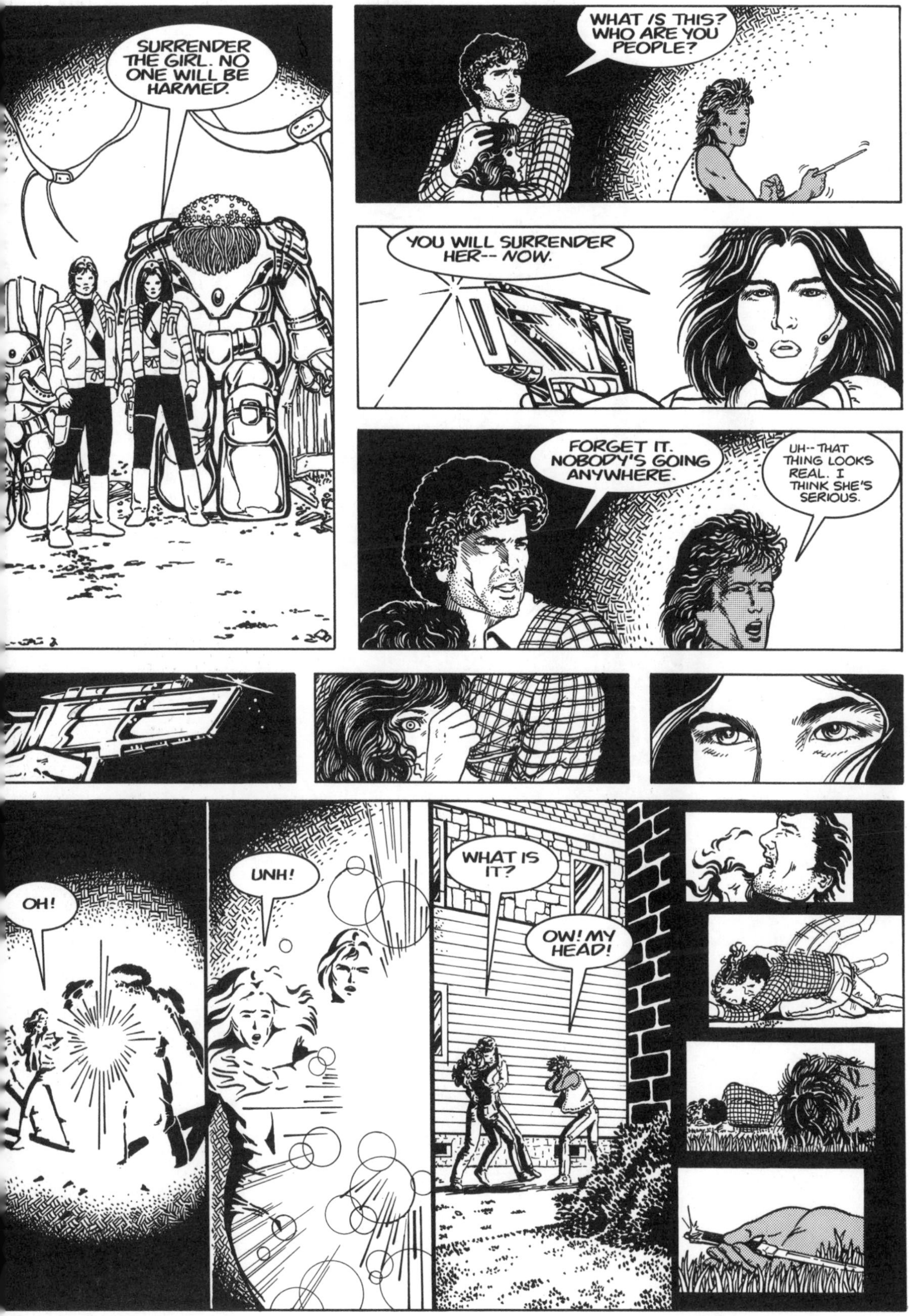
SURRENDER THE GIRL. NO ONE WILL BE HARMED.
WHAT IS THIS? WHO ARE YOU PEOPLE?
YOU WILL SURRENDER HER-- NOW.
FORGET IT. NOBODY'S GOING ANYWHERE.
UH--THAT THING LOOKS REAL. I THINK SHE'S SERIOUS.
OH!
UNH!
WHAT IS IT?
OW! MY HEAD!

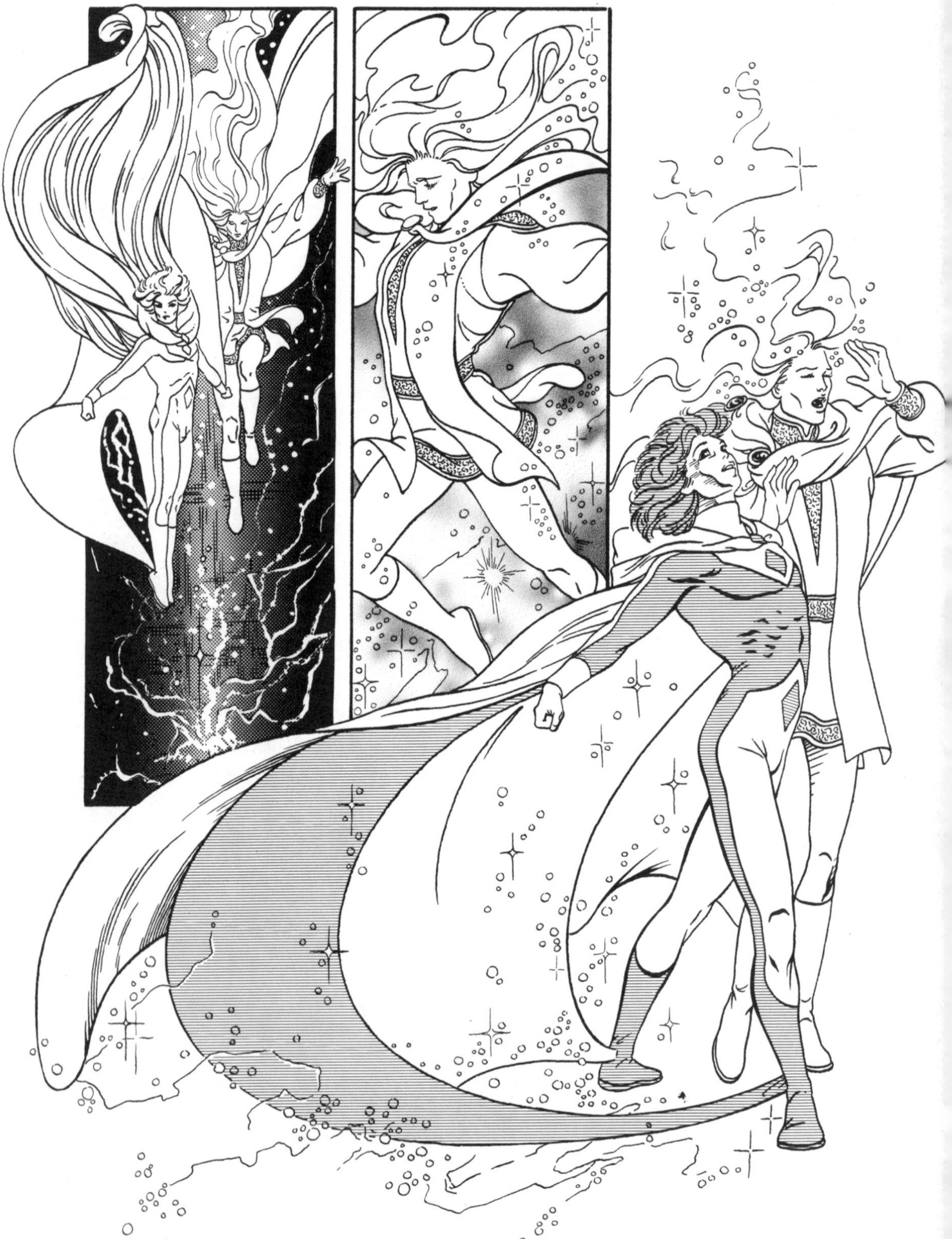

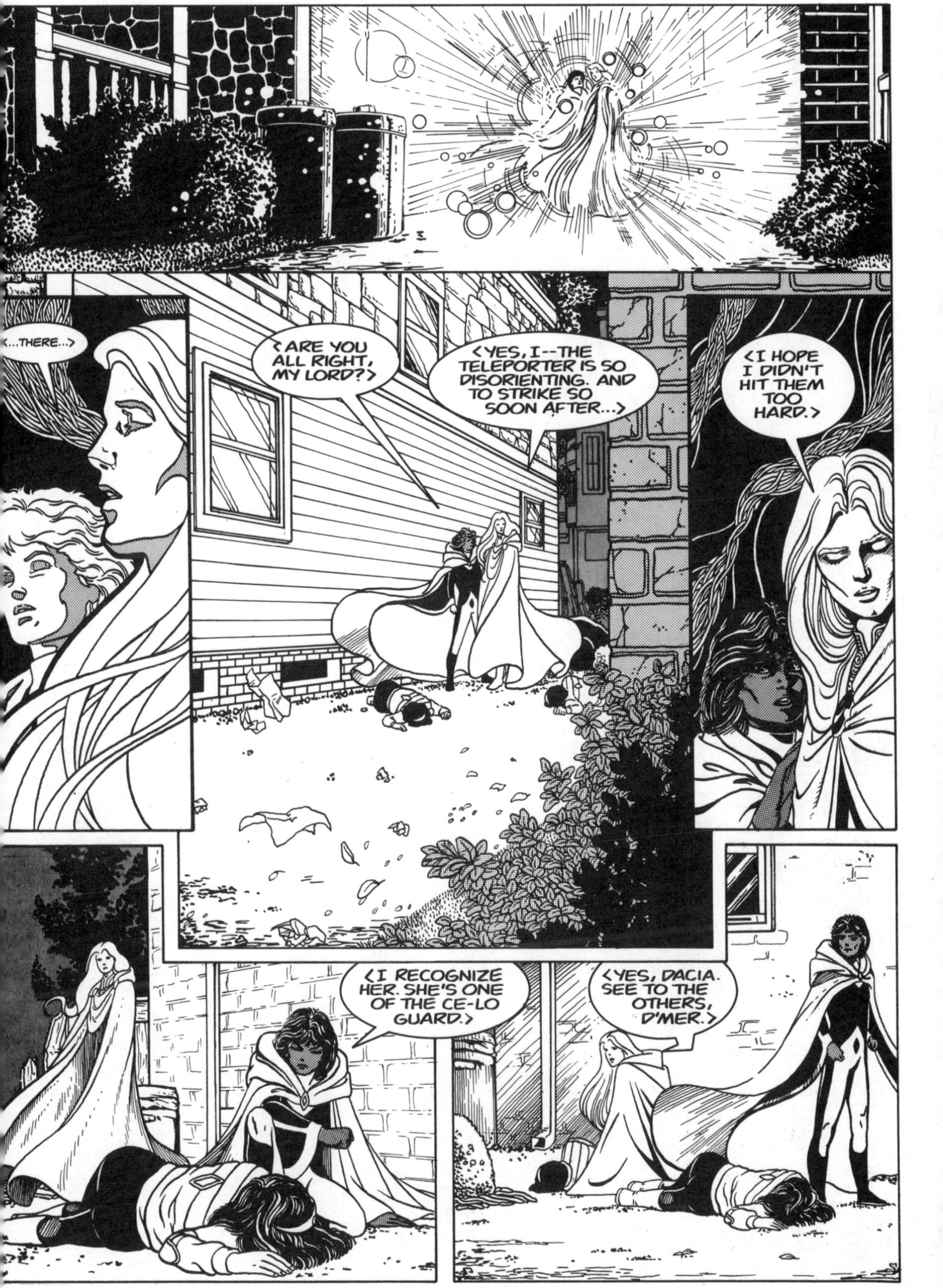
<...THERE...>
<ARE YOU ALL RIGHT, MY LORD?>
<YES, I--THE TELEPORTER IS SO DISORIENTING. AND TO STRIKE SO SOON AFTER...>
<I HOPE I DIDN'T HIT THEM TOO HARD.>
<I RECOGNIZE HER. SHE'S ONE OF THE CE-LO GUARD.>
<YES, DACIA. SEE TO THE OTHERS, D'MER.>

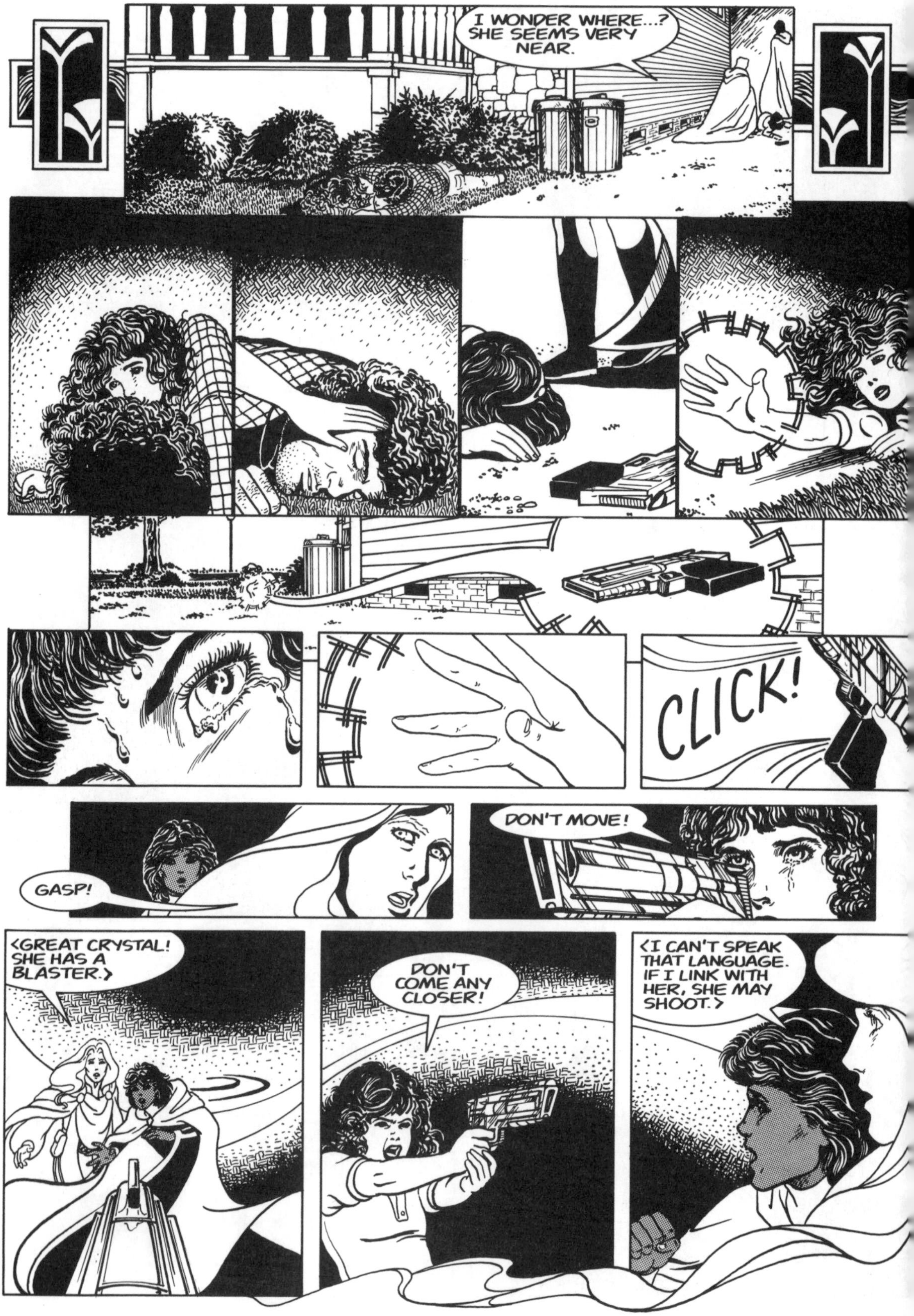
I WONDER WHERE...? SHE SEEMS VERY NEAR.
CLICK!
GASP!
DON'T MOVE!
<GREAT CRYSTAL! SHE HAS A BLASTER.>
DON'T COME ANY CLOSER!
<I CAN'T SPEAK THAT LANGUAGE. IF I LINK WITH HER, SHE MAY SHOOT.>

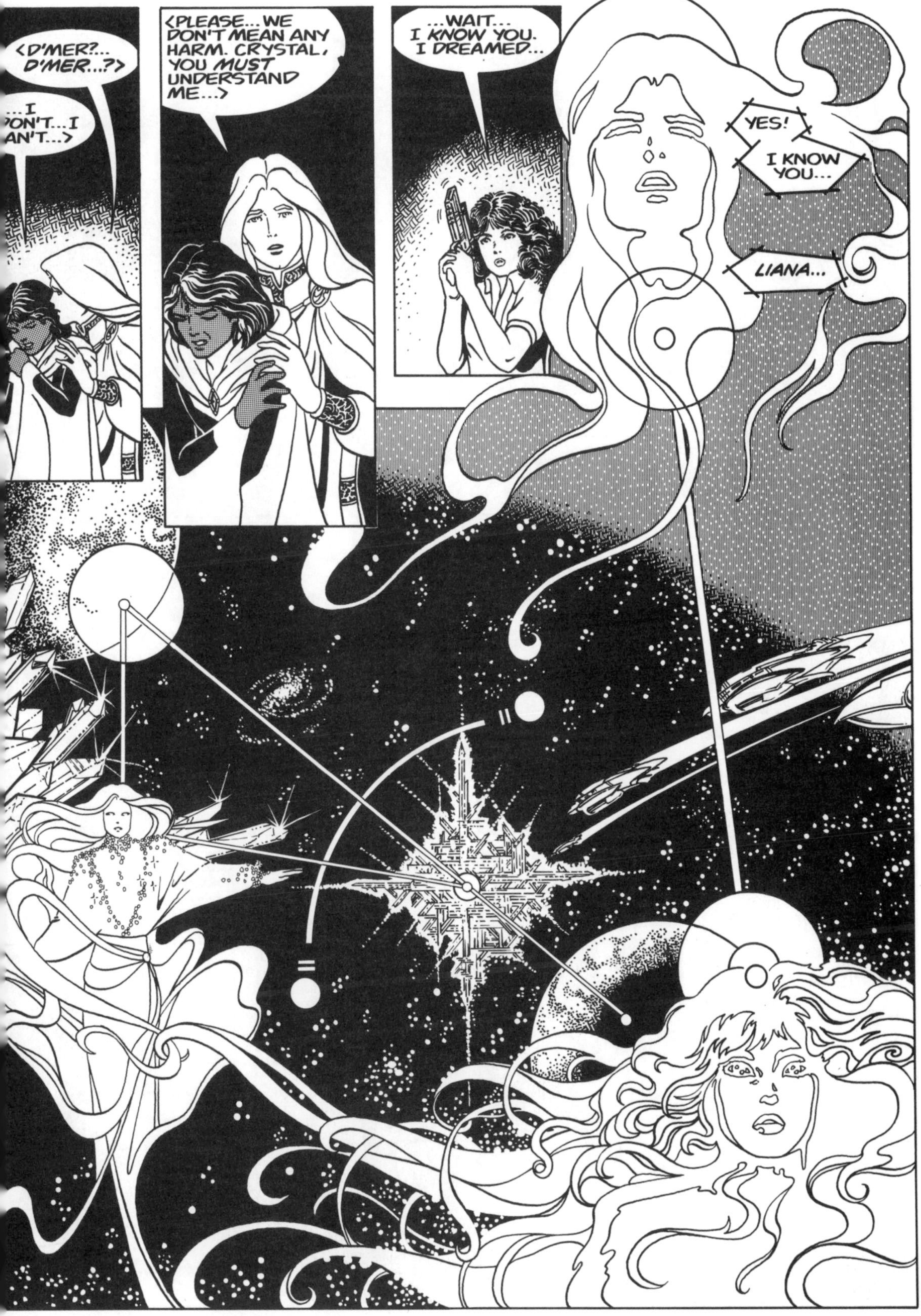

<D'MER?... D'MER...?>
...I DON'T...I CAN'T...>
<PLEASE... WE DON'T MEAN ANY HARM. CRYSTAL, YOU MUST UNDERSTAND ME...>
...WAIT... I KNOW YOU. I DREAMED...
YES!
I KNOW YOU...
LIANA...

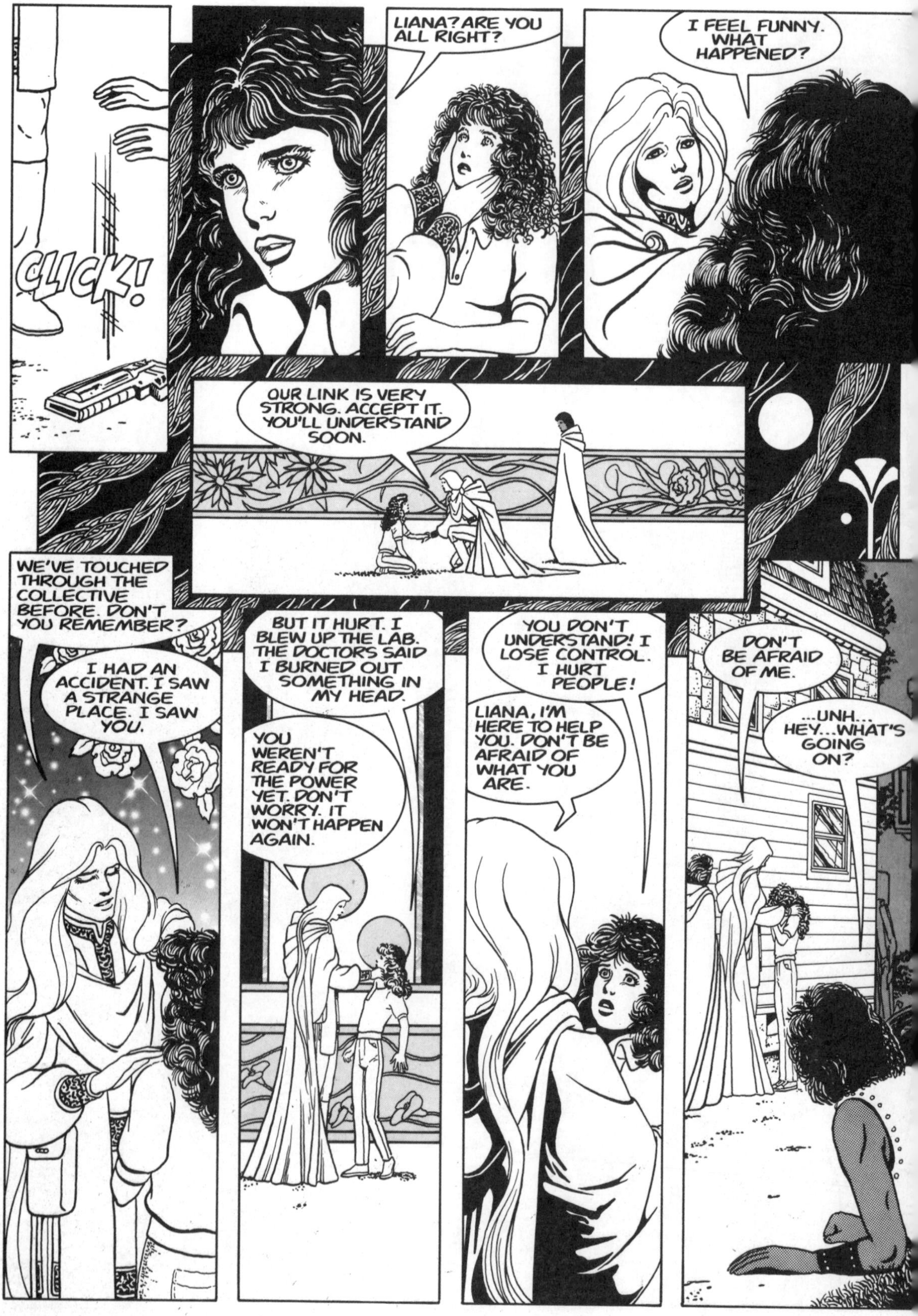
CLICK!
LIANA? ARE YOU ALL RIGHT?
I FEEL FUNNY. WHAT HAPPENED?
OUR LINK IS VERY STRONG. ACCEPT IT. YOU'LL UNDERSTAND SOON.
WE'VE TOUCHED THROUGH THE COLLECTIVE BEFORE. DON'T YOU REMEMBER?
I HAD AN ACCIDENT. I SAW A STRANGE PLACE. I SAW YOU.
BUT IT HURT. I BLEW UP THE LAB. THE DOCTORS SAID I BURNED OUT SOMETHING IN MY HEAD.
YOU WEREN'T READY FOR THE POWER YET. DON'T WORRY. IT WON'T HAPPEN AGAIN.
YOU DON'T UNDERSTAND! I LOSE CONTROL. I HURT PEOPLE!
LIANA, I'M HERE TO HELP YOU. DON'T BE AFRAID OF WHAT YOU ARE.
DON'T BE AFRAID OF ME.
...UNH... HEY...WHAT'S GOING ON?

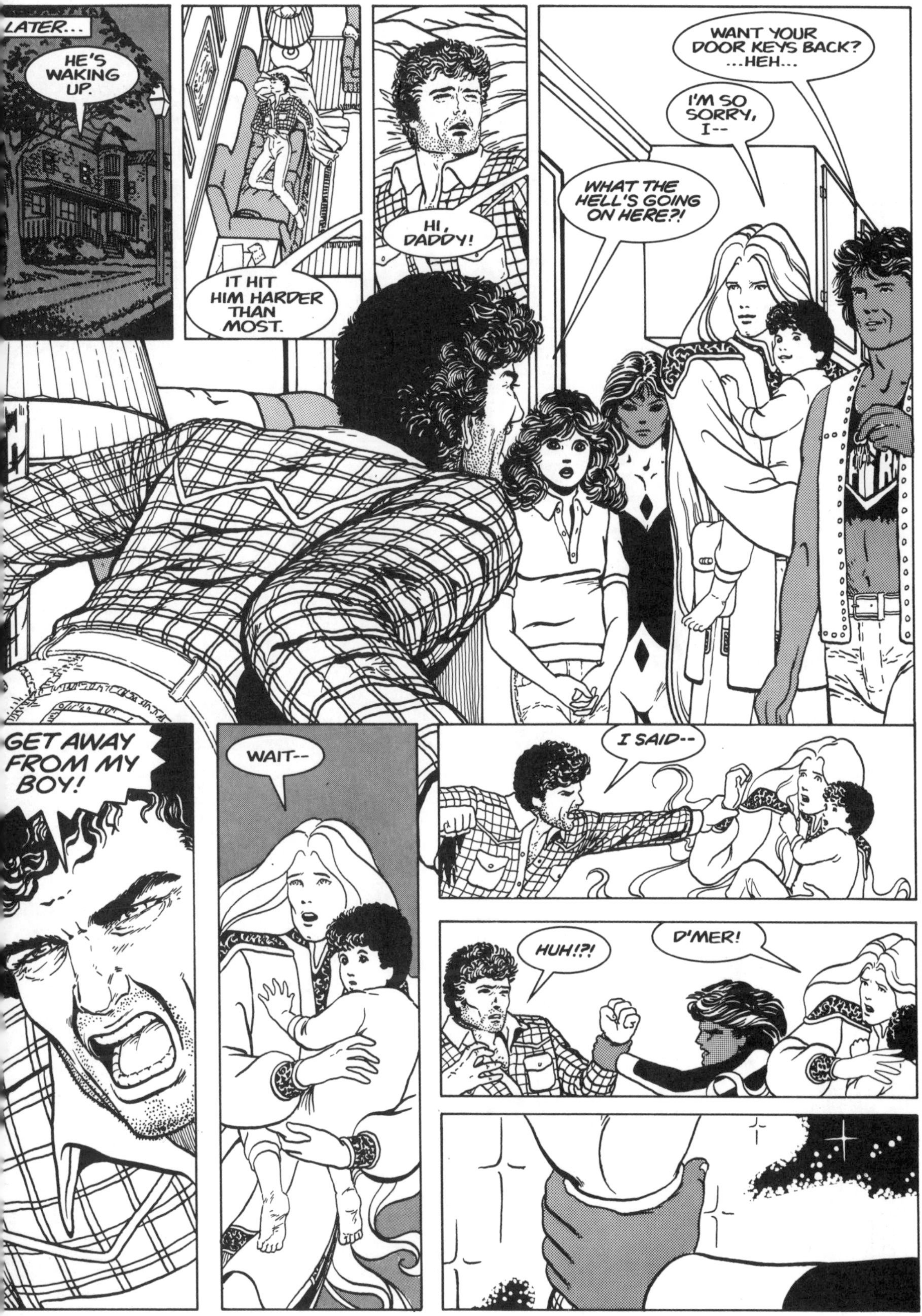
LATER...
HE'S WAKING UP.
IT HIT HIM HARDER THAN MOST.
HI, DADDY!
WHAT THE HELL'S GOING ON HERE?!
I'M SO SORRY, I--
WANT YOUR DOOR KEYS BACK? ...HEH...
GET AWAY FROM MY BOY!
WAIT--
I SAID--
HUH!?!
D'MER!

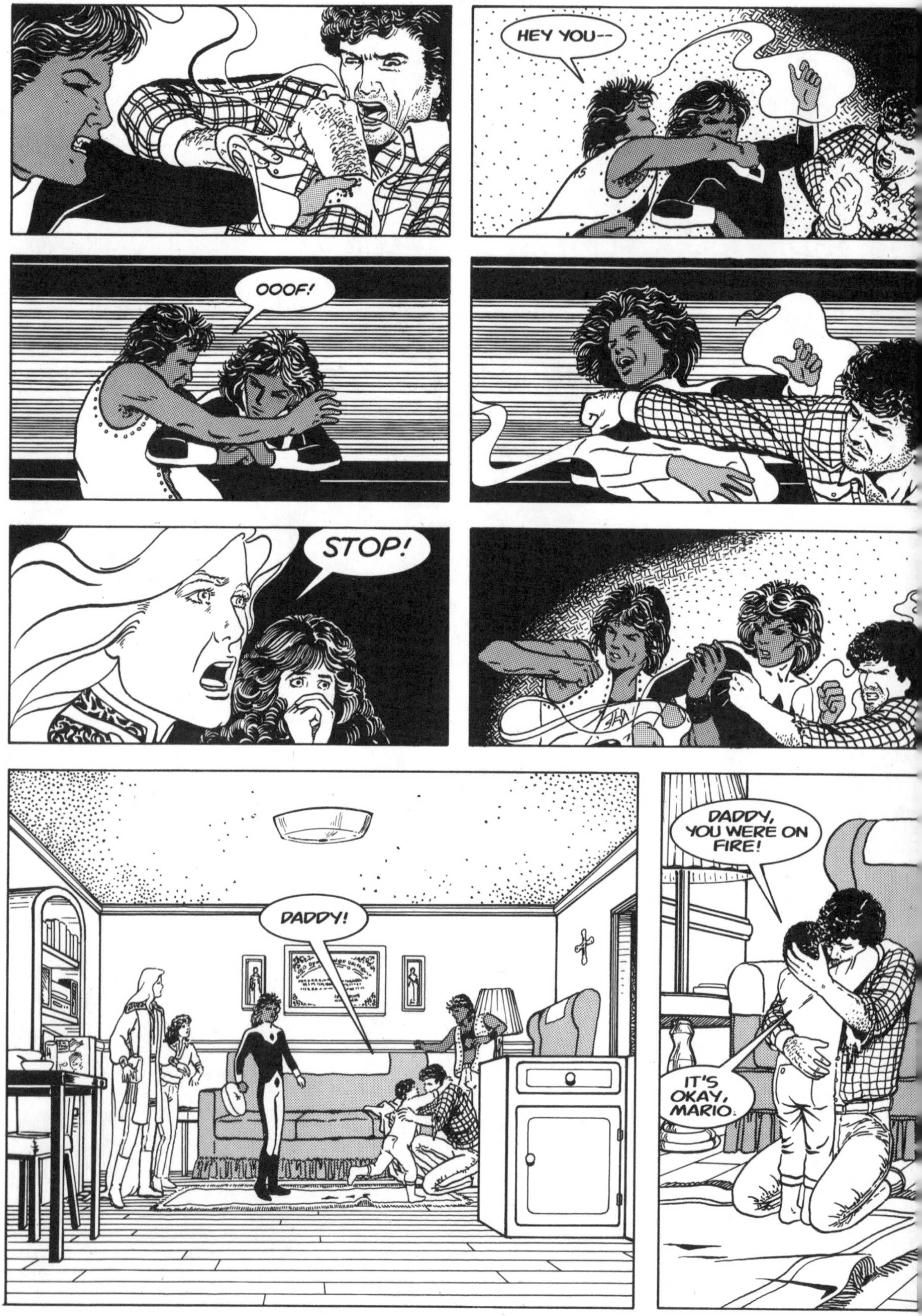
HEY YOU--
OOOF!
STOP!
DADDY!
DADDY, YOU WERE ON FIRE!
IT'S OKAY, MARIO.

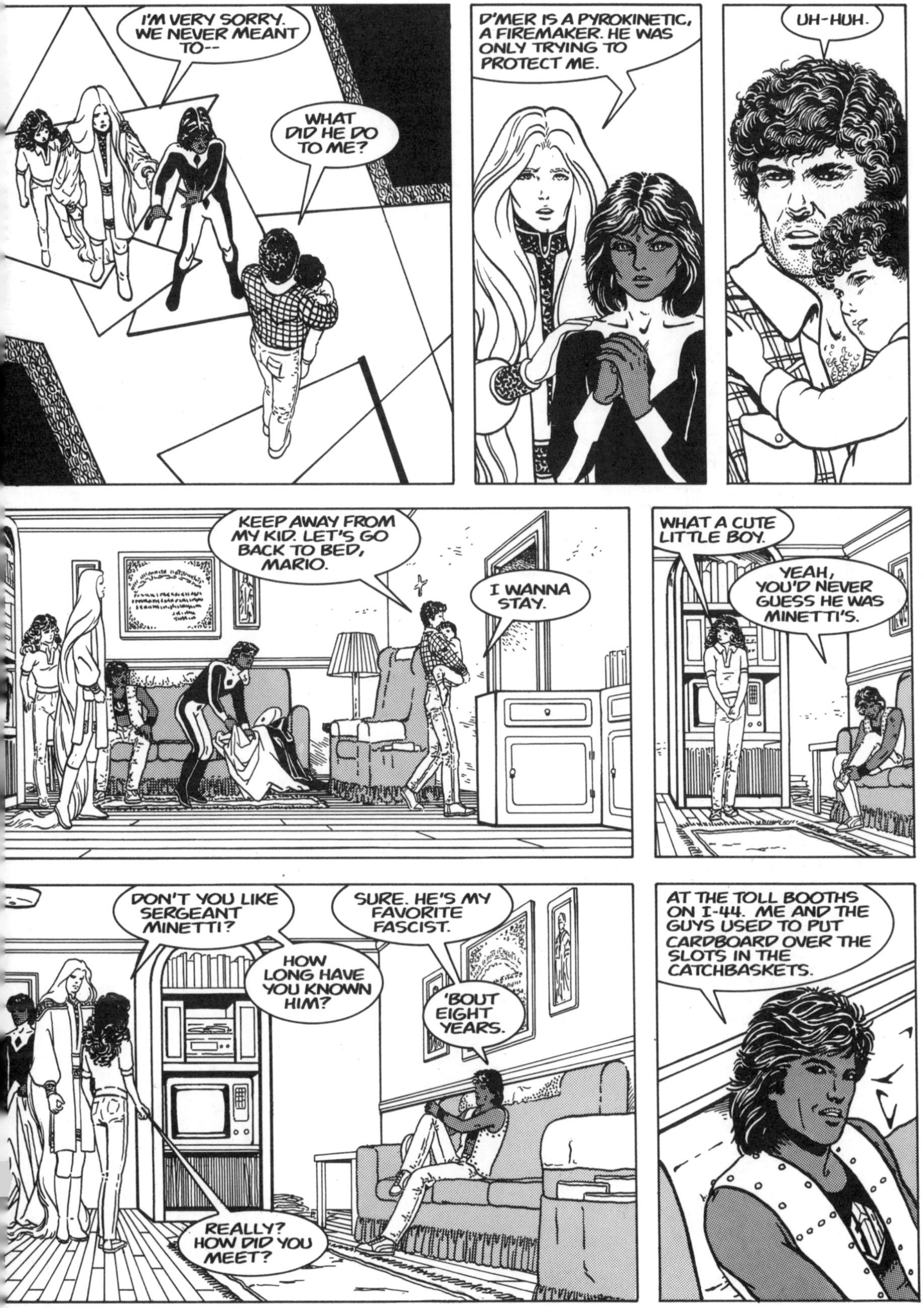
I'M VERY SORRY. WE NEVER MEANT TO--
WHAT DID HE DO TO ME?
D'MER IS A PYROKINETIC, A FIREMAKER. HE WAS ONLY TRYING TO PROTECT ME.
UH-HUH.
KEEP AWAY FROM MY KID. LET'S GO BACK TO BED, MARIO.
I WANNA STAY.
WHAT A CUTE LITTLE BOY.
YEAH, YOU'D NEVER GUESS HE WAS MINETTI'S.
DON'T YOU LIKE SERGEANT MINETTI?
SURE. HE'S MY FAVORITE FASCIST.
HOW LONG HAVE YOU KNOWN HIM?
'BOUT EIGHT YEARS.
REALLY? HOW DID YOU MEET?
AT THE TOLL BOOTHS ON I-44. ME AND THE GUYS USED TO PUT CARDBOARD OVER THE SLOTS IN THE CATCHBASKETS.

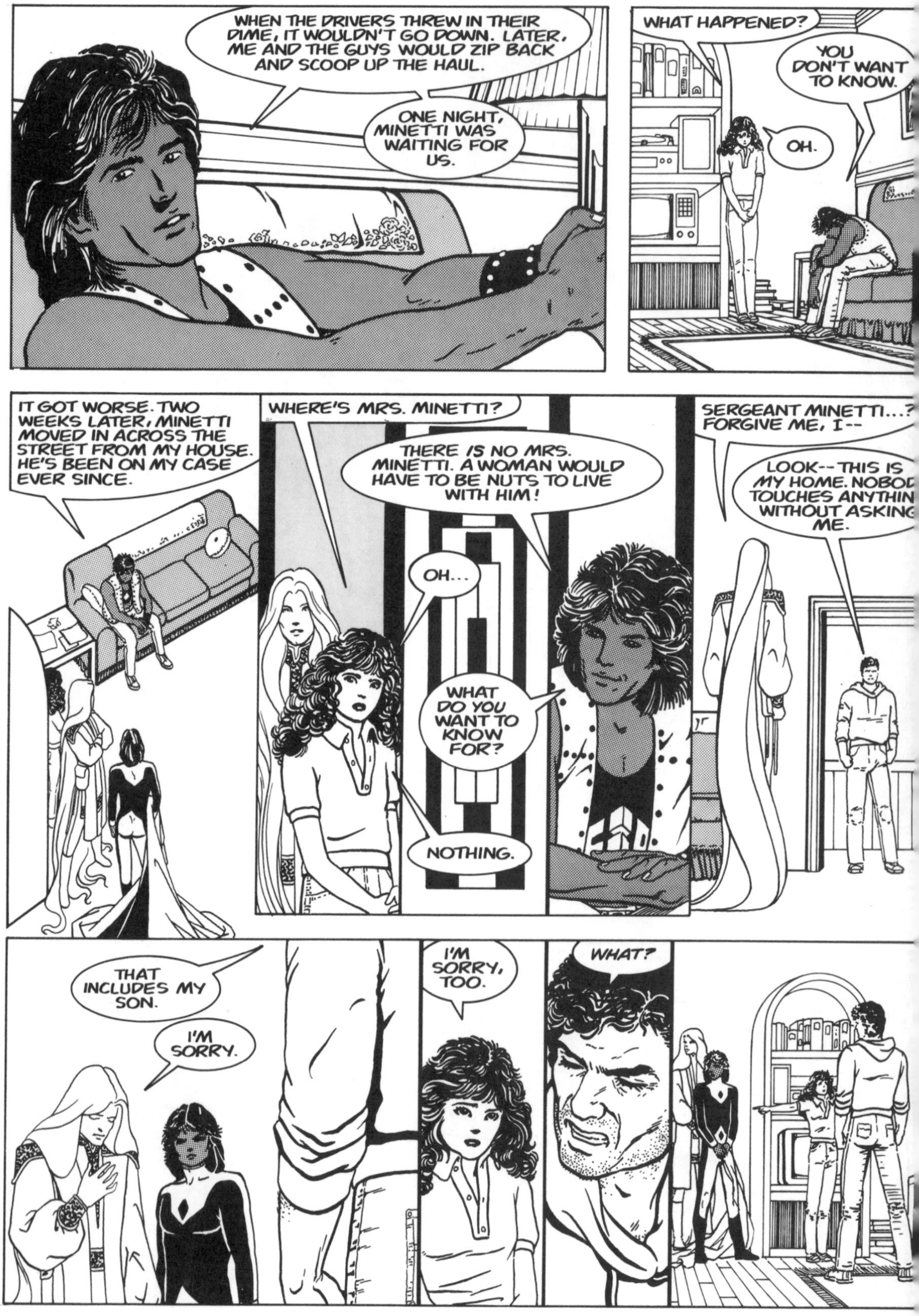
WHEN THE DRIVERS THREW IN THEIR DIME, IT WOULDN'T GO DOWN. LATER, ME AND THE GUYS WOULD ZIP BACK AND SCOOP UP THE HAUL.
ONE NIGHT, MINETTI WAS WAITING FOR US.
WHAT HAPPENED?
YOU DON'T WANT TO KNOW.
OH.
IT GOT WORSE. TWO WEEKS LATER, MINETTI MOVED IN ACROSS THE STREET FROM MY HOUSE. HE'S BEEN ON MY CASE EVER SINCE.
WHERE'S MRS. MINETTI?
THERE IS NO MRS. MINETTI. A WOMAN WOULD HAVE TO BE NUTS TO LIVE WITH HIM!
OH...
WHAT DO YOU WANT TO KNOW FOR?
NOTHING.
SERGEANT MINETTI...? FORGIVE ME, I--
LOOK-- THIS IS MY HOME. NOBOD TOUCHES ANYTHIN WITHOUT ASKING ME.
THAT INCLUDES MY SON.
I'M SORRY.
I'M SORRY, TOO.
WHAT?

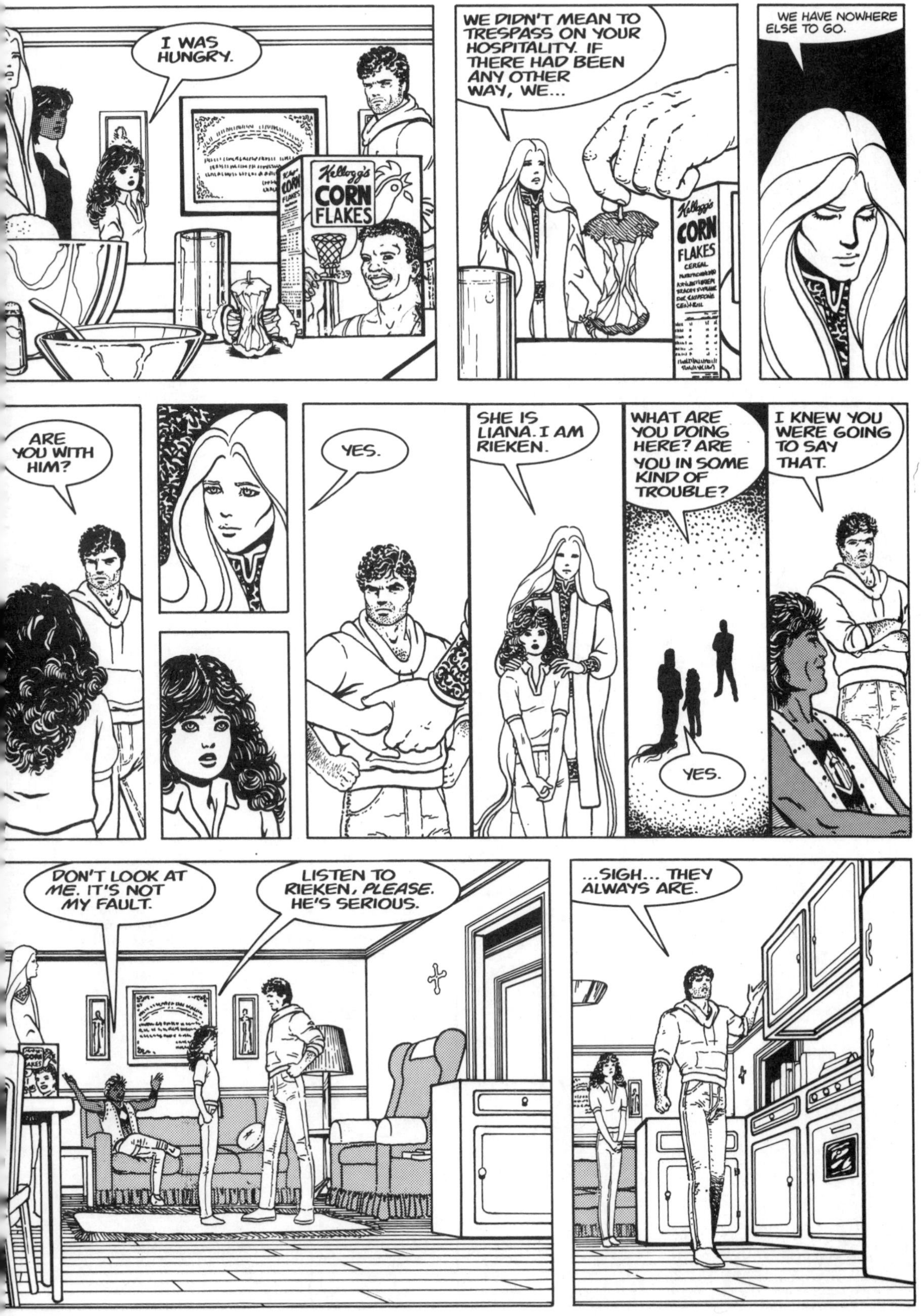
I WAS HUNGRY.
WE DIDN'T MEAN TO TRESPASS ON YOUR HOSPITALITY. IF THERE HAD BEEN ANY OTHER WAY, WE...
WE HAVE NOWHERE ELSE TO GO.
ARE YOU WITH HIM?
YES.
SHE IS LIANA. I AM RIEKEN.
WHAT ARE YOU DOING HERE? ARE YOU IN SOME KIND OF TROUBLE?
YES.
I KNEW YOU WERE GOING TO SAY THAT.
DON'T LOOK AT ME. IT'S NOT MY FAULT.
LISTEN TO RIEKEN, PLEASE. HE'S SERIOUS.
...SIGH... THEY ALWAYS ARE.

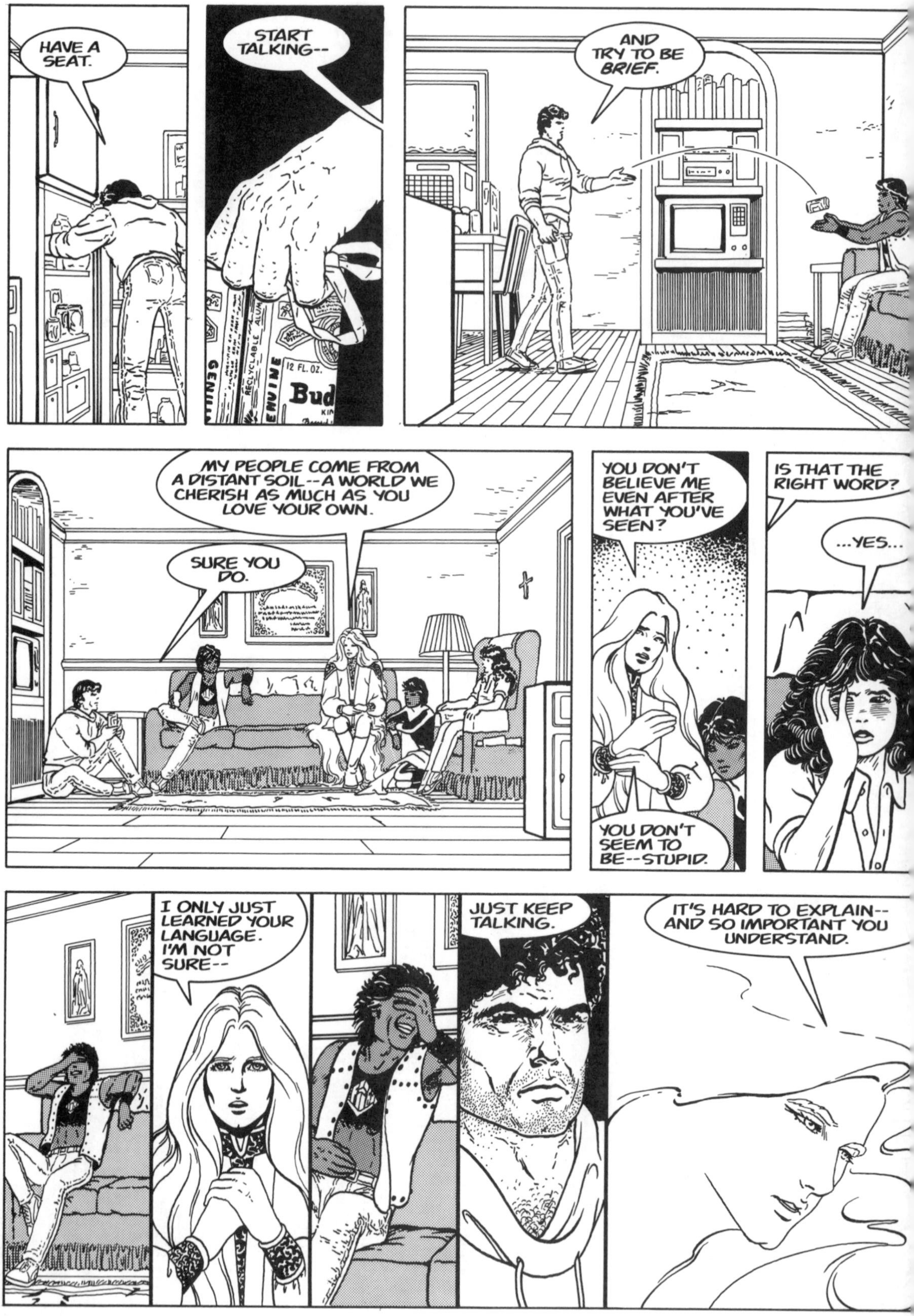
HAVE A SEAT.
START TALKING--
12 FL. OZ.
Bud
AND TRY TO BE BRIEF.
MY PEOPLE COME FROM A DISTANT SOIL--A WORLD WE CHERISH AS MUCH AS YOU LOVE YOUR OWN.
SURE YOU DO.
YOU DON'T BELIEVE ME EVEN AFTER WHAT YOU'VE SEEN?
YOU DON'T SEEM TO BE--STUPID.
IS THAT THE RIGHT WORD?
...YES...
I ONLY JUST LEARNED YOUR LANGUAGE. I'M NOT SURE--
JUST KEEP TALKING.
IT'S HARD TO EXPLAIN--AND SO IMPORTANT YOU UNDERSTAND.

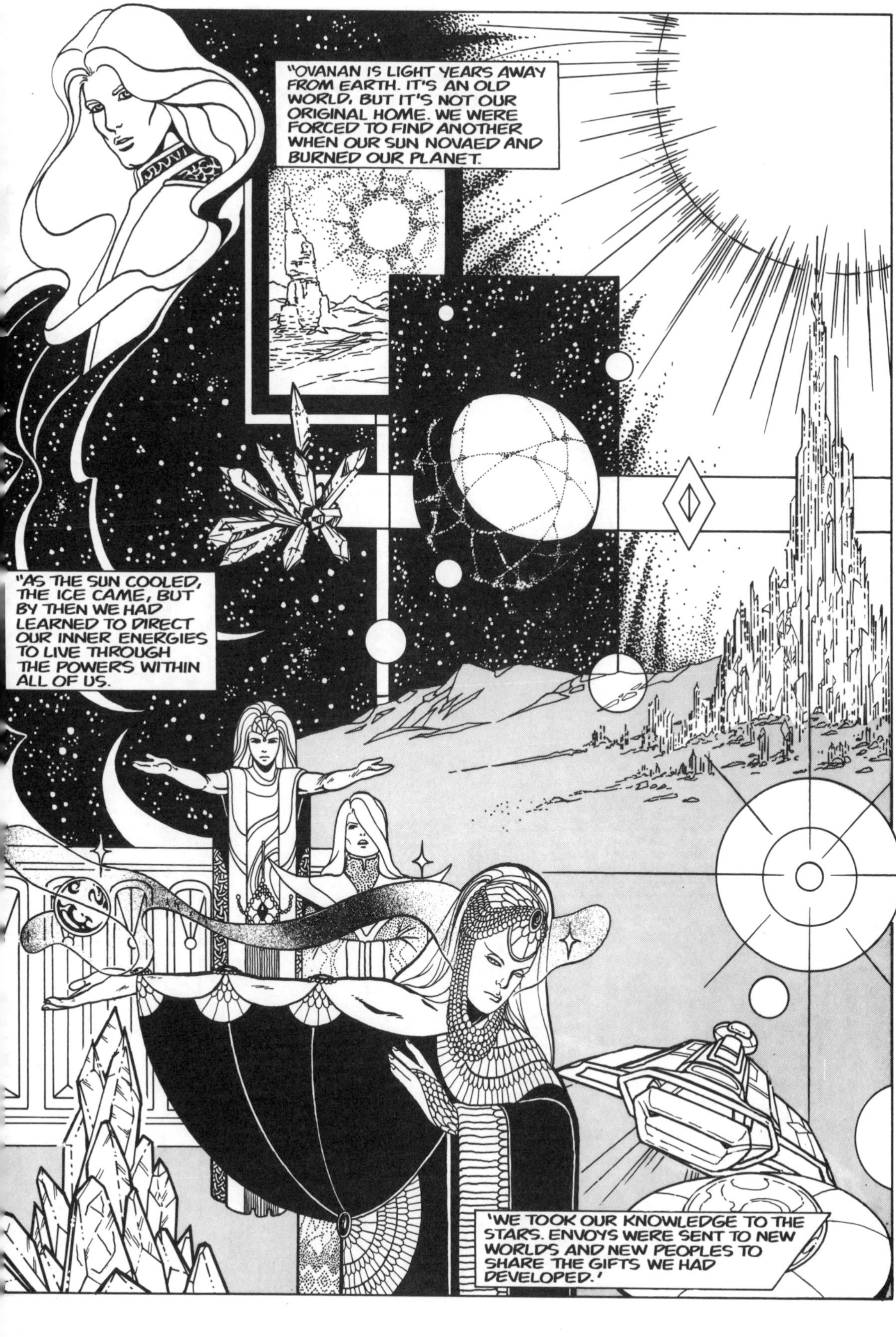
"OVANAN IS LIGHT YEARS AWAY FROM EARTH. IT'S AN OLD WORLD, BUT IT'S NOT OUR ORIGINAL HOME. WE WERE FORCED TO FIND ANOTHER WHEN OUR SUN NOVAED AND BURNED OUR PLANET.
"AS THE SUN COOLED, THE ICE CAME, BUT BY THEN WE HAD LEARNED TO DIRECT OUR INNER ENERGIES TO LIVE THROUGH THE POWERS WITHIN ALL OF US.
'WE TOOK OUR KNOWLEDGE TO THE STARS. ENVOYS WERE SENT TO NEW WORLDS AND NEW PEOPLES TO SHARE THE GIFTS WE HAD DEVELOPED.'

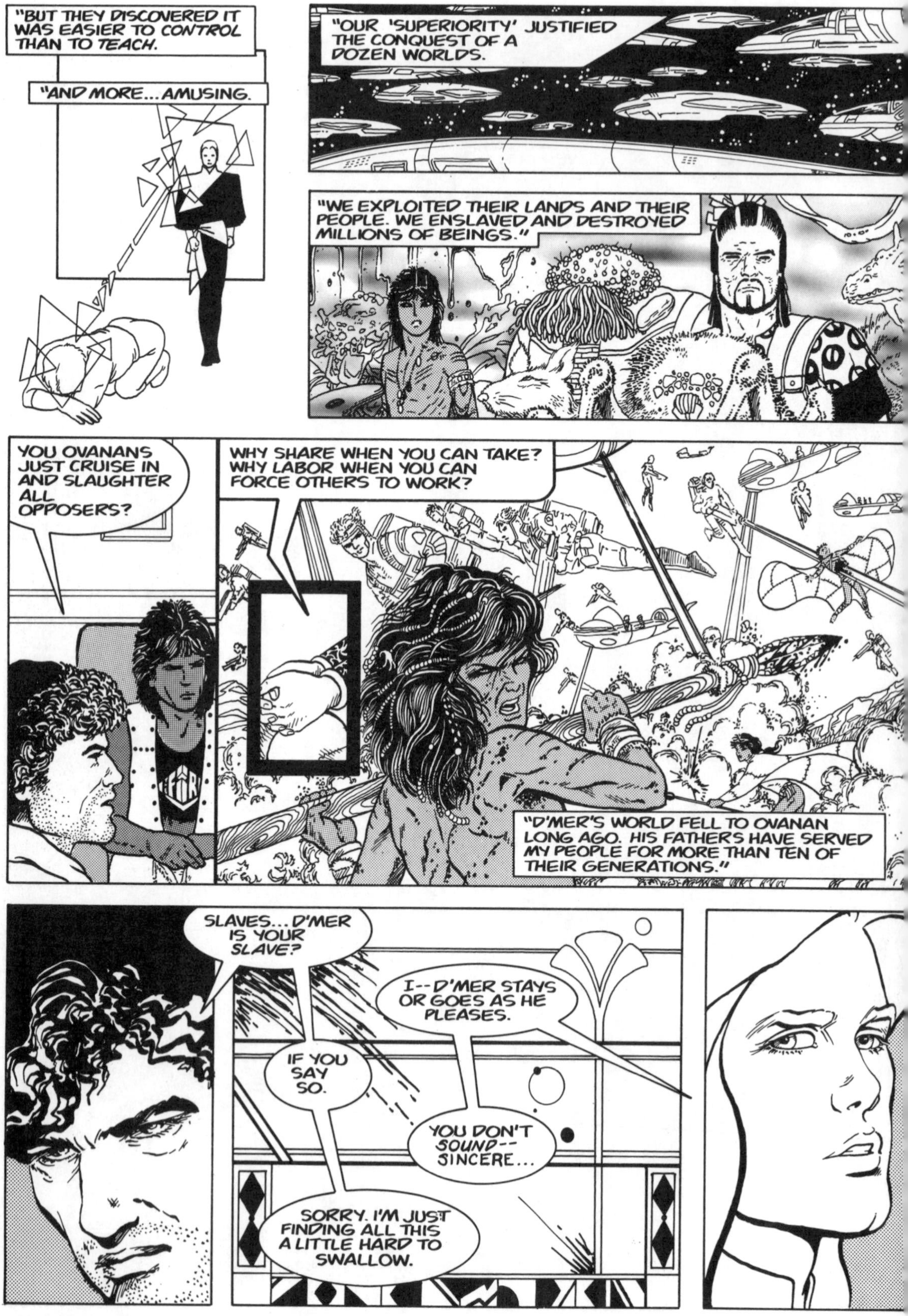
"BUT THEY DISCOVERED IT WAS EASIER TO CONTROL THAN TO TEACH.
"AND MORE... AMUSING.
"OUR 'SUPERIORITY' JUSTIFIED THE CONQUEST OF A DOZEN WORLDS.
"WE EXPLOITED THEIR LANDS AND THEIR PEOPLE. WE ENSLAVED AND DESTROYED MILLIONS OF BEINGS."
YOU OVANANS JUST CRUISE IN AND SLAUGHTER ALL OPPOSERS?
WHY SHARE WHEN YOU CAN TAKE? WHY LABOR WHEN YOU CAN FORCE OTHERS TO WORK?
"D'MER'S WORLD FELL TO OVANAN LONG AGO. HIS FATHERS HAVE SERVED MY PEOPLE FOR MORE THAN TEN OF THEIR GENERATIONS."
SLAVES... D'MER IS YOUR SLAVE?
I--D'MER STAYS OR GOES AS HE PLEASES.
IF YOU SAY SO.
YOU DON'T SOUND-- SINCERE...
SORRY. I'M JUST FINDING ALL THIS A LITTLE HARD TO SWALLOW.

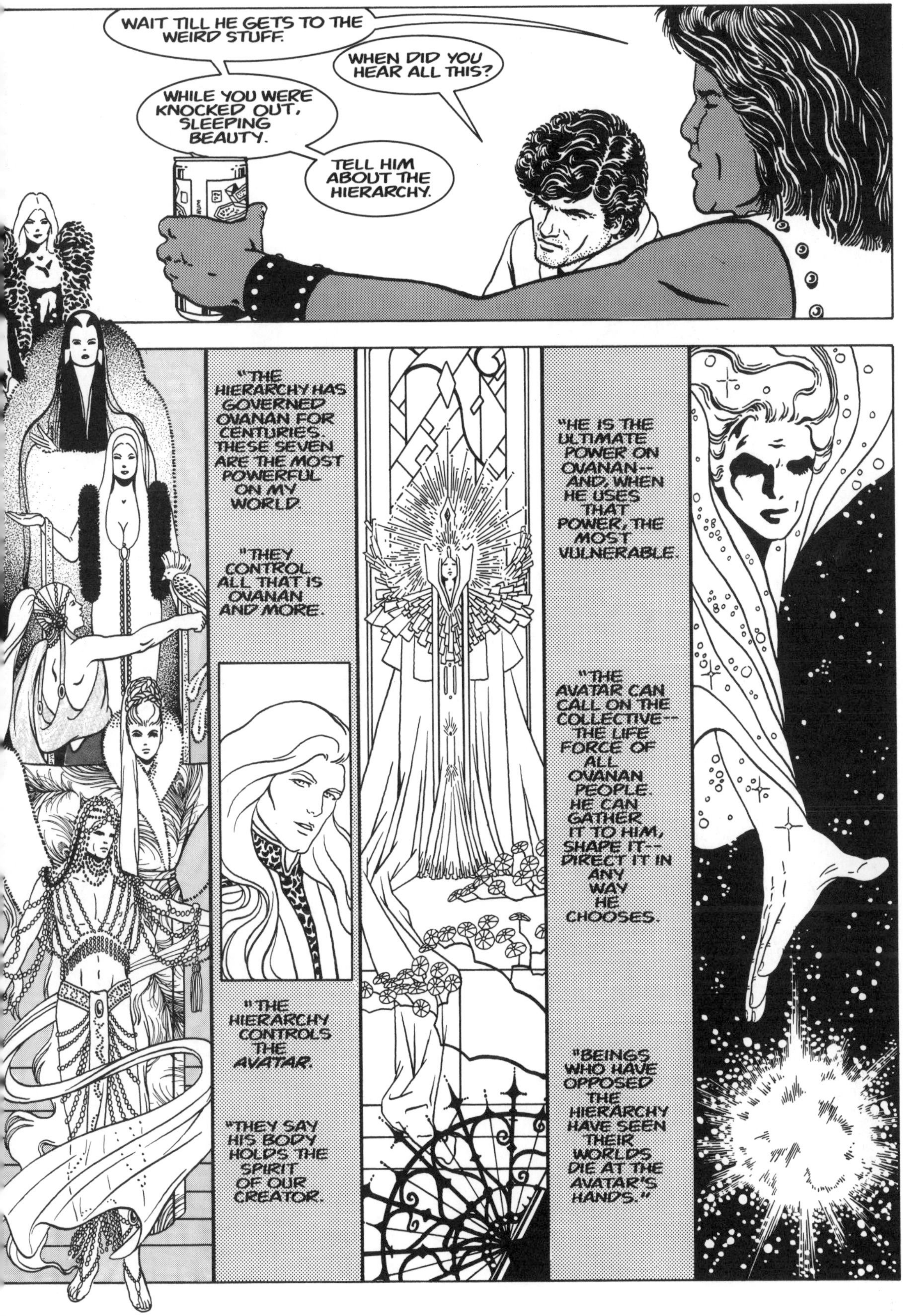

WAIT TILL HE GETS TO THE WEIRD STUFF.
WHEN DID YOU HEAR ALL THIS?
WHILE YOU WERE KNOCKED OUT, SLEEPING BEAUTY.
TELL HIM ABOUT THE HIERARCHY.
"THE HIERARCHY HAS GOVERNED OVANAN FOR CENTURIES. THESE SEVEN ARE THE MOST POWERFUL ON MY WORLD.
"THEY CONTROL ALL THAT IS OVANAN AND MORE.
"THE HIERARCHY CONTROLS THE AVATAR.
"THEY SAY HIS BODY HOLDS THE SPIRIT OF OUR CREATOR.
"HE IS THE ULTIMATE POWER ON OVANAN-- AND, WHEN HE USES THAT POWER, THE MOST VULNERABLE.
"THE AVATAR CAN CALL ON THE COLLECTIVE-- THE LIFE FORCE OF ALL OVANAN PEOPLE. HE CAN GATHER IT TO HIM, SHAPE IT-- DIRECT IT IN ANY WAY HE CHOOSES.
"BEINGS WHO HAVE OPPOSED THE HIERARCHY HAVE SEEN THEIR WORLDS DIE AT THE AVATAR'S HANDS."

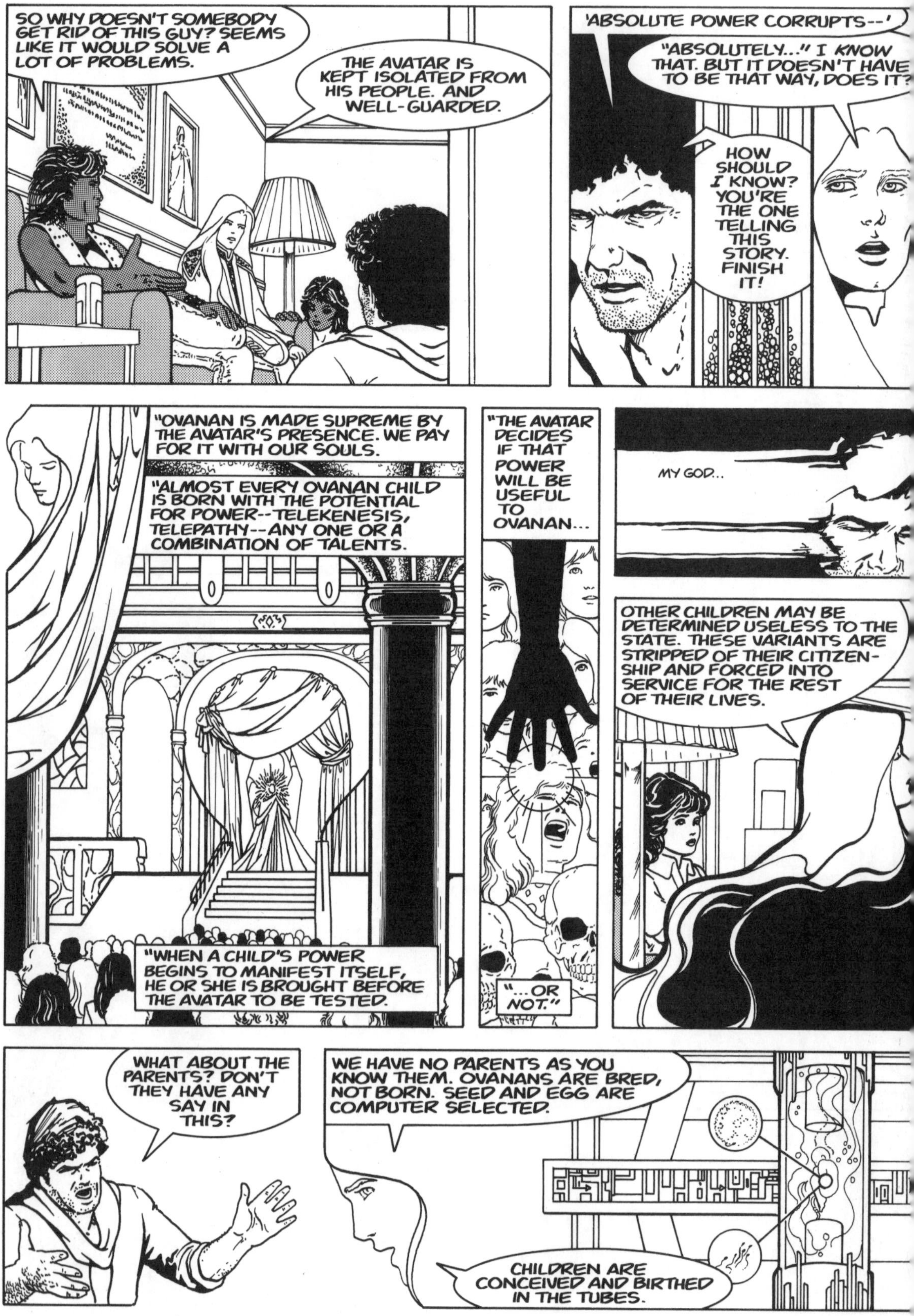

SO WHY DOESN'T SOMEBODY GET RID OF THIS GUY? SEEMS LIKE IT WOULD SOLVE A LOT OF PROBLEMS.
THE AVATAR IS KEPT ISOLATED FROM HIS PEOPLE. AND WELL-GUARDED.
'ABSOLUTE POWER CORRUPTS--'
"ABSOLUTELY..." I KNOW THAT. BUT IT DOESN'T HAVE TO BE THAT WAY, DOES IT?
HOW SHOULD I KNOW? YOU'RE THE ONE TELLING THIS STORY. FINISH IT!
"OVANAN IS MADE SUPREME BY THE AVATAR'S PRESENCE. WE PAY FOR IT WITH OUR SOULS.
"ALMOST EVERY OVANAN CHILD IS BORN WITH THE POTENTIAL FOR POWER--TELEKENESIS, TELEPATHY--ANY ONE OR A COMBINATION OF TALENTS.
"WHEN A CHILD'S POWER BEGINS TO MANIFEST ITSELF, HE OR SHE IS BROUGHT BEFORE THE AVATAR TO BE TESTED.
"THE AVATAR DECIDES IF THAT POWER WILL BE USEFUL TO OVANAN...
"...OR NOT."
MY GOD...
OTHER CHILDREN MAY BE DETERMINED USELESS TO THE STATE. THESE VARIANTS ARE STRIPPED OF THEIR CITIZENSHIP AND FORCED INTO SERVICE FOR THE REST OF THEIR LIVES.
WHAT ABOUT THE PARENTS? DON'T THEY HAVE ANY SAY IN THIS?
WE HAVE NO PARENTS AS YOU KNOW THEM. OVANANS ARE BRED, NOT BORN. SEED AND EGG ARE COMPUTER SELECTED.
CHILDREN ARE CONCEIVED AND BIRTHED IN THE TUBES.

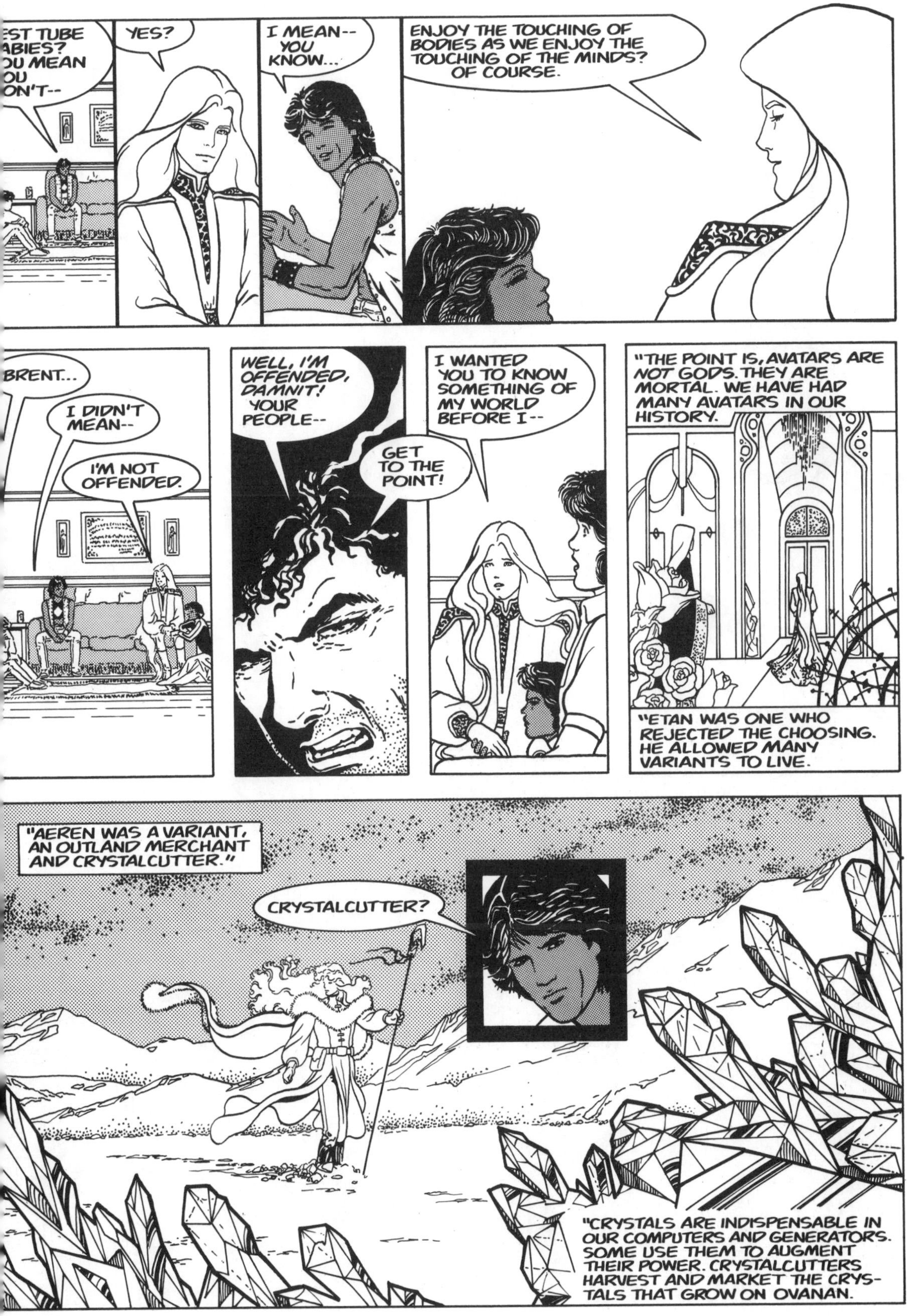

EST TUBE ABIES? OU MEAN OU ON'T--
YES?
I MEAN-- YOU KNOW...
ENJOY THE TOUCHING OF BODIES AS WE ENJOY THE TOUCHING OF THE MINDS? OF COURSE.
BRENT...
I DIDN'T MEAN--
I'M NOT OFFENDED.
WELL, I'M OFFENDED, DAMNIT! YOUR PEOPLE--
GET TO THE POINT!
I WANTED YOU TO KNOW SOMETHING OF MY WORLD BEFORE I--
"THE POINT IS, AVATARS ARE NOT GODS. THEY ARE MORTAL. WE HAVE HAD MANY AVATARS IN OUR HISTORY.
"ETAN WAS ONE WHO REJECTED THE CHOOSING. HE ALLOWED MANY VARIANTS TO LIVE.
"AEREN WAS A VARIANT, AN OUTLAND MERCHANT AND CRYSTALCUTTER."
CRYSTALCUTTER?
"CRYSTALS ARE INDISPENSABLE IN OUR COMPUTERS AND GENERATORS. SOME USE THEM TO AUGMENT THEIR POWER. CRYSTALCUTTERS HARVEST AND MARKET THE CRYSTALS THAT GROW ON OVANAN.

"AEREN WAS A SIMPLE MAN, I THINK. HE LIVED ALONE IN OVANAN'S OUTLANDS.

"HE WAS A MASTER OF HIS TRADE AND ONLY CAME INTO THE CITIES TO SELL AND SHOW HIS WORK.

"ON ONE OF THESE TRIPS, HE SAW AN OVANAN WOMAN PUNISHING HER SLAVE. THERE WAS NOTHING UNUSUAL ABOUT IT. IT'S THE OVANAN WAY.

"BUT AEREN THOUGHT IT WAS WRONG. AND HE SAID SO.

"HE TRIED TO BUY THE SLAVE. IT WAS A TERRIBLE INSULT IMPLYING THE OWNER WAS UNFIT, WORTH LESS THAN HER PROPERTY.

"SHE STRUCK AEREN. WHEN AEREN REACHED TO STOP HER...

"SHE DIED.

"AEREN LEARNED HE WAS A DISRUPTOR. WHEN THE HIERARCHY DISCOVERED THIS, THEY ORDERED THOUSANDS TO BE RESCREENED.

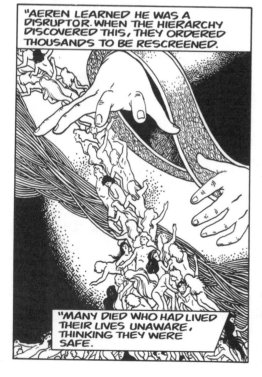

"MANY DIED WHO HAD LIVED THEIR LIVES UNAWARE, THINKING THEY WERE SAFE.

"AEREN BECAME AN OUTLAW. HE ESCAPED, STEALING A SMALL SHUTTLE.

"A MALFUNCTION SENT HIM TOWARDS EARTH.

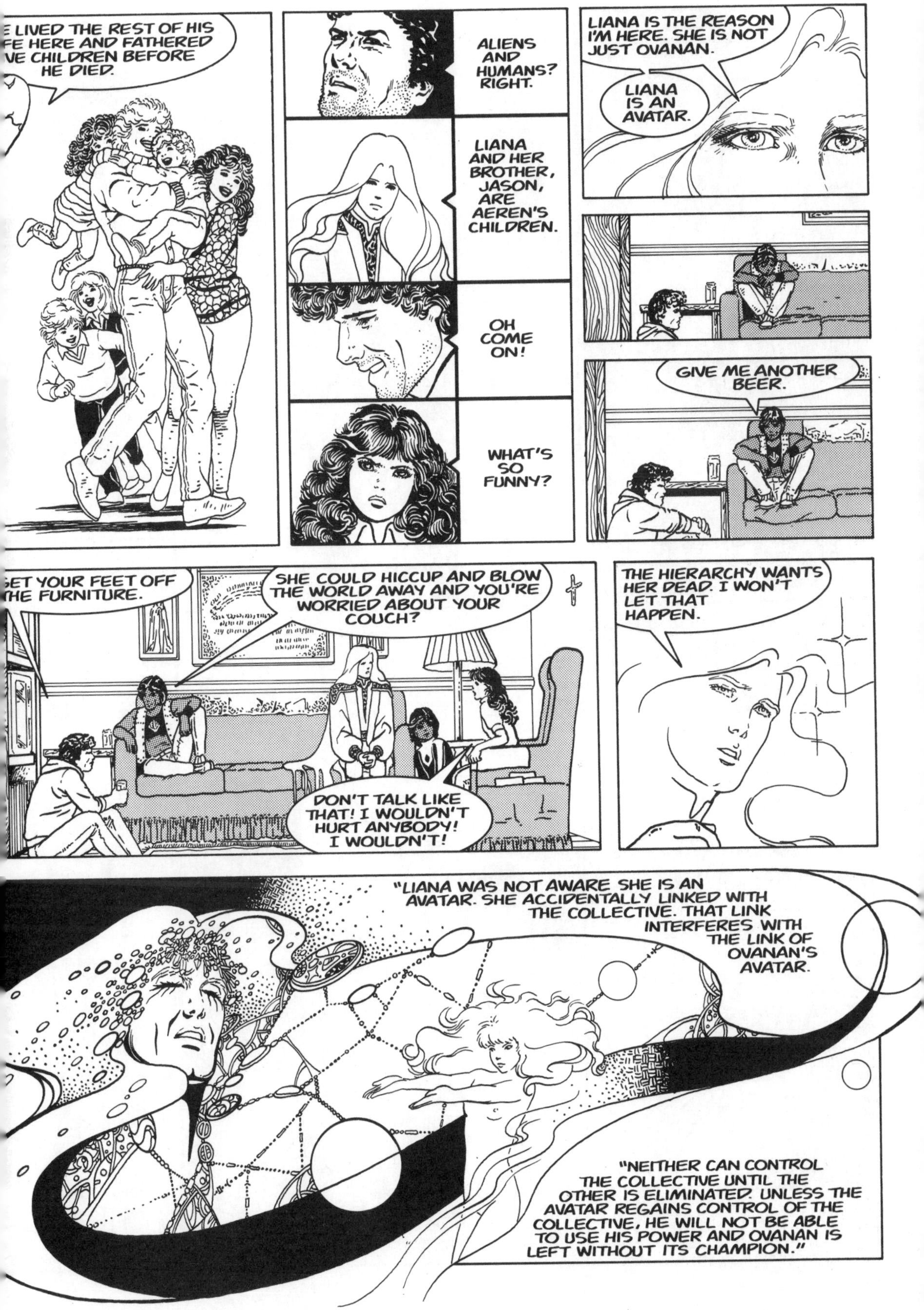

E LIVED THE REST OF HIS FE HERE AND FATHERED VE CHILDREN BEFORE HE DIED.
ALIENS AND HUMANS? RIGHT.
LIANA AND HER BROTHER, JASON, ARE AEREN'S CHILDREN.
OH COME ON!
WHAT'S SO FUNNY?
LIANA IS THE REASON I'M HERE. SHE IS NOT JUST OVANAN.
LIANA IS AN AVATAR.
GIVE ME ANOTHER BEER.
GET YOUR FEET OFF THE FURNITURE.
SHE COULD HICCUP AND BLOW THE WORLD AWAY AND YOU'RE WORRIED ABOUT YOUR COUCH?
DON'T TALK LIKE THAT! I WOULDN'T HURT ANYBODY! I WOULDN'T!
THE HIERARCHY WANTS HER DEAD. I WON'T LET THAT HAPPEN.
"LIANA WAS NOT AWARE SHE IS AN AVATAR. SHE ACCIDENTALLY LINKED WITH THE COLLECTIVE. THAT LINK INTERFERES WITH THE LINK OF OVANAN'S AVATAR.
"NEITHER CAN CONTROL THE COLLECTIVE UNTIL THE OTHER IS ELIMINATED. UNLESS THE AVATAR REGAINS CONTROL OF THE COLLECTIVE, HE WILL NOT BE ABLE TO USE HIS POWER AND OVANAN IS LEFT WITHOUT ITS CHAMPION."

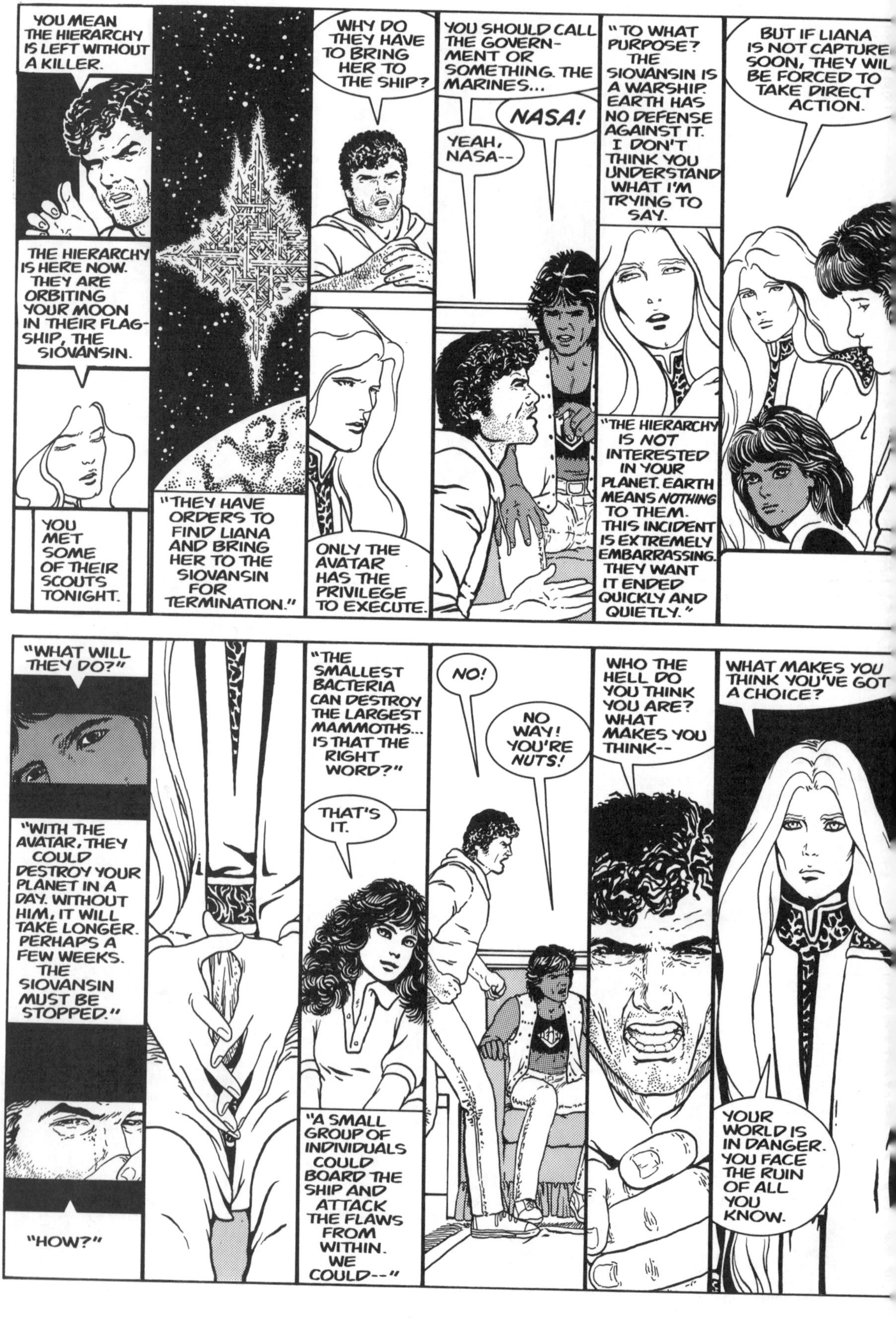

YOU MEAN THE HIERARCHY IS LEFT WITHOUT A KILLER.
THE HIERARCHY IS HERE NOW. THEY ARE ORBITING YOUR MOON IN THEIR FLAG-SHIP, THE SIOVANSIN.
YOU MET SOME OF THEIR SCOUTS TONIGHT.
"THEY HAVE ORDERS TO FIND LIANA AND BRING HER TO THE SIOVANSIN FOR TERMINATION."
WHY DO THEY HAVE TO BRING HER TO THE SHIP?
ONLY THE AVATAR HAS THE PRIVILEGE TO EXECUTE.
YOU SHOULD CALL THE GOVERN-MENT OR SOMETHING. THE MARINES...
YEAH, NASA--
NASA!
"TO WHAT PURPOSE? THE SIOVANSIN IS A WARSHIP. EARTH HAS NO DEFENSE AGAINST IT. I DON'T THINK YOU UNDERSTAND WHAT I'M TRYING TO SAY.
"THE HIERARCHY IS NOT INTERESTED IN YOUR PLANET. EARTH MEANS NOTHING TO THEM. THIS INCIDENT IS EXTREMELY EMBARRASSING. THEY WANT IT ENDED QUICKLY AND QUIETLY."
BUT IF LIANA IS NOT CAPTURE SOON, THEY WIL BE FORCED TO TAKE DIRECT ACTION.
"WHAT WILL THEY DO?"
"WITH THE AVATAR, THEY COULD DESTROY YOUR PLANET IN A DAY. WITHOUT HIM, IT WILL TAKE LONGER. PERHAPS A FEW WEEKS. THE SIOVANSIN MUST BE STOPPED."
"HOW?"
"THE SMALLEST BACTERIA CAN DESTROY THE LARGEST MAMMOTHS... IS THAT THE RIGHT WORD?"
THAT'S IT.
"A SMALL GROUP OF INDIVIDUALS COULD BOARD THE SHIP AND ATTACK THE FLAWS FROM WITHIN. WE COULD--"
NO!
NO WAY! YOU'RE NUTS!
WHO THE HELL DO YOU THINK YOU ARE? WHAT MAKES YOU THINK--
WHAT MAKES YOU THINK YOU'VE GOT A CHOICE?
YOUR WORLD IS IN DANGER. YOU FACE THE RUIN OF ALL YOU KNOW.

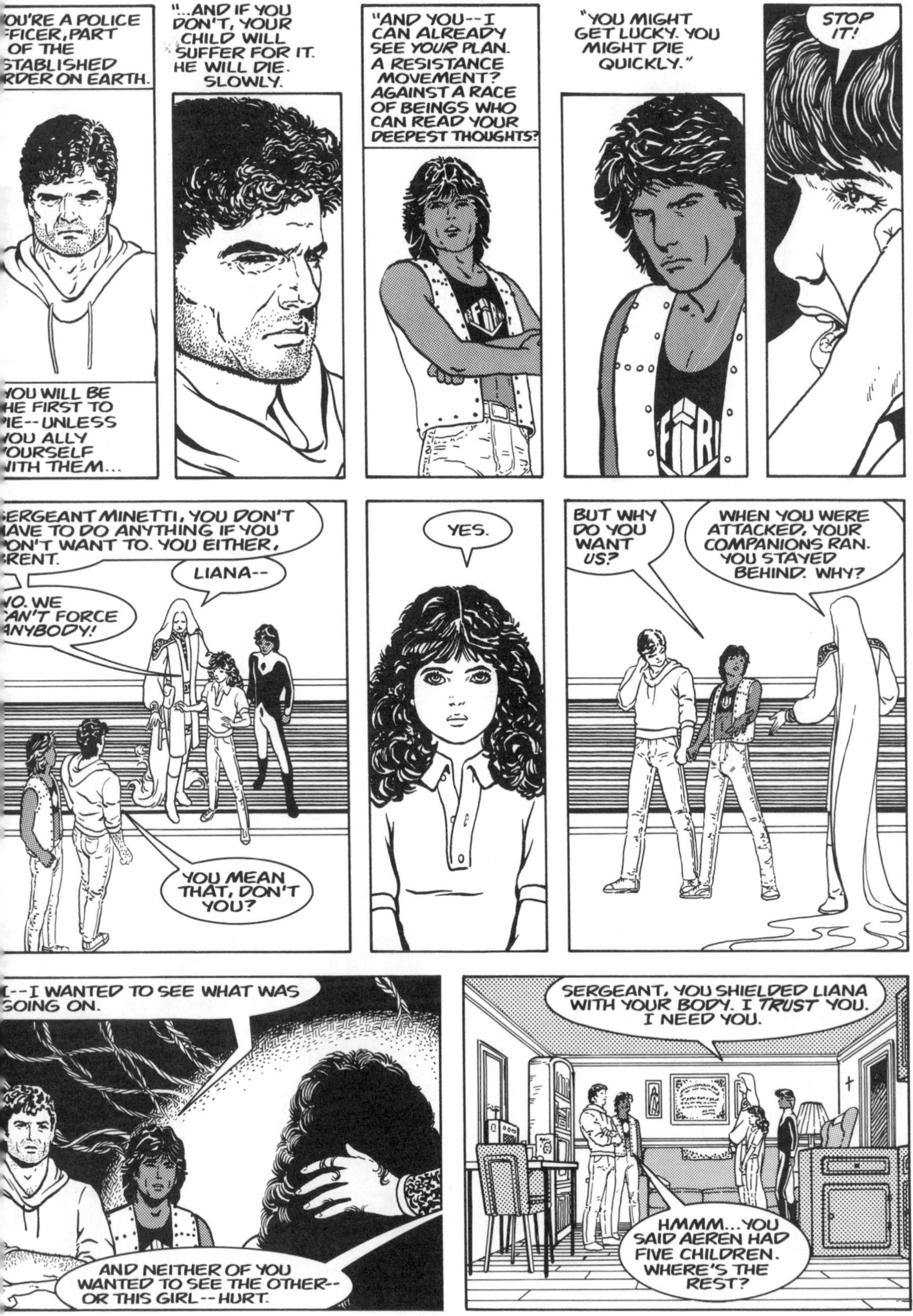
OU'RE A POLICE FFICER, PART OF THE STABLISHED RDER ON EARTH.
YOU WILL BE HE FIRST TO DIE--UNLESS YOU ALLY YOURSELF WITH THEM...
"...AND IF YOU DON'T, YOUR CHILD WILL SUFFER FOR IT. HE WILL DIE. SLOWLY.
"AND YOU--I CAN ALREADY SEE YOUR PLAN. A RESISTANCE MOVEMENT? AGAINST A RACE OF BEINGS WHO CAN READ YOUR DEEPEST THOUGHTS?
"YOU MIGHT GET LUCKY. YOU MIGHT DIE QUICKLY."
STOP IT!
SERGEANT MINETTI, YOU DON'T HAVE TO DO ANYTHING IF YOU DON'T WANT TO. YOU EITHER, BRENT.
LIANA--
NO. WE CAN'T FORCE ANYBODY!
YOU MEAN THAT, DON'T YOU?
YES.
BUT WHY DO YOU WANT US?
WHEN YOU WERE ATTACKED, YOUR COMPANIONS RAN. YOU STAYED BEHIND. WHY?
I--I WANTED TO SEE WHAT WAS GOING ON.
AND NEITHER OF YOU WANTED TO SEE THE OTHER--OR THIS GIRL--HURT.
SERGEANT, YOU SHIELDED LIANA WITH YOUR BODY. I TRUST YOU. I NEED YOU.
HMMM...YOU SAID AEREN HAD FIVE CHILDREN. WHERE'S THE REST?

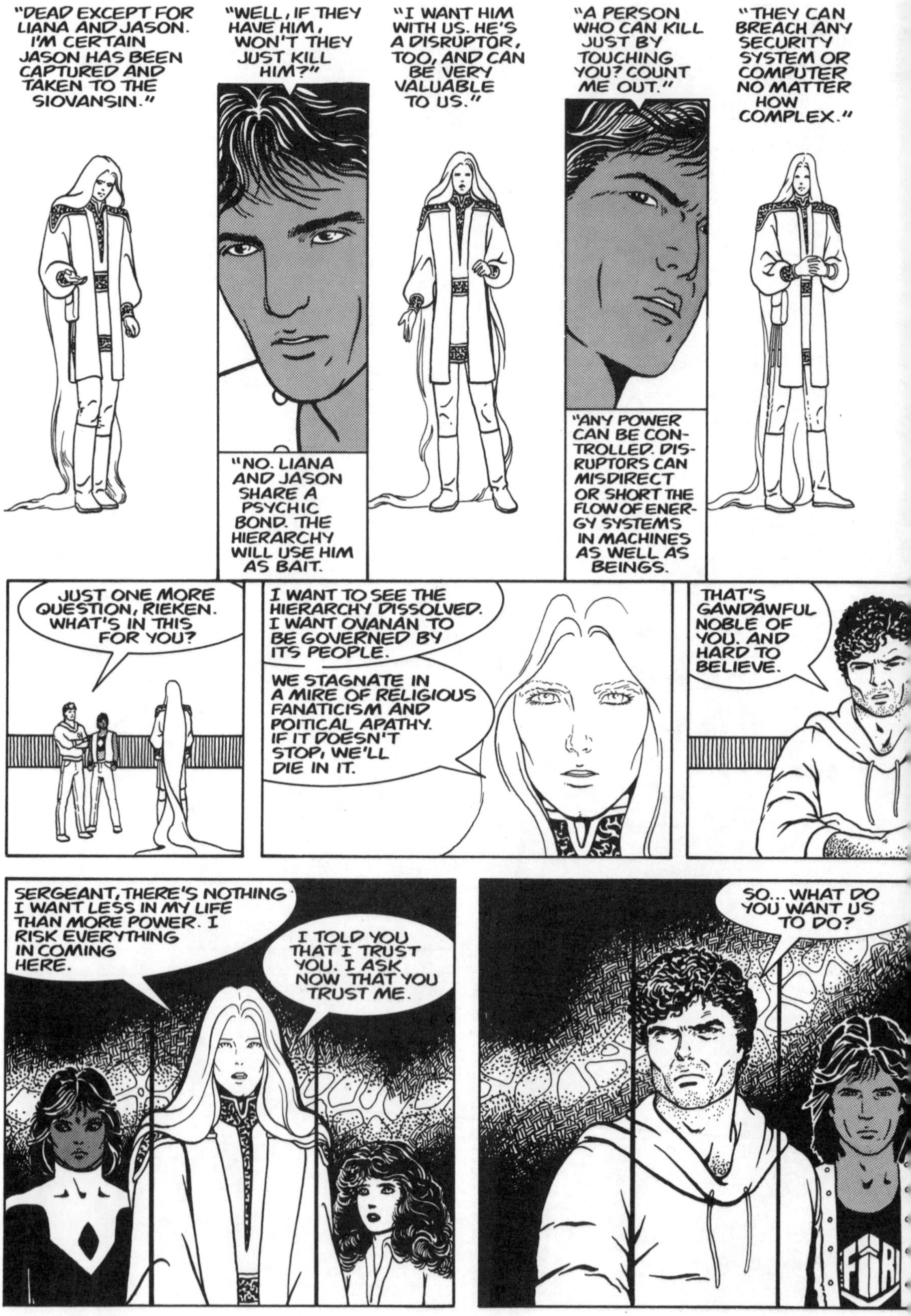
"DEAD EXCEPT FOR LIANA AND JASON. I'M CERTAIN JASON HAS BEEN CAPTURED AND TAKEN TO THE SIOVANSIN."
"WELL, IF THEY HAVE HIM, WON'T THEY JUST KILL HIM?"
"NO. LIANA AND JASON SHARE A PSYCHIC BOND. THE HIERARCHY WILL USE HIM AS BAIT.
"I WANT HIM WITH US. HE'S A DISRUPTOR, TOO, AND CAN BE VERY VALUABLE TO US."
"A PERSON WHO CAN KILL JUST BY TOUCHING YOU? COUNT ME OUT."
"ANY POWER CAN BE CONTROLLED. DISRUPTORS CAN MISDIRECT OR SHORT THE FLOW OF ENERGY SYSTEMS IN MACHINES AS WELL AS BEINGS.
"THEY CAN BREACH ANY SECURITY SYSTEM OR COMPUTER NO MATTER HOW COMPLEX."
JUST ONE MORE QUESTION, RIEKEN. WHAT'S IN THIS FOR YOU?
I WANT TO SEE THE HIERARCHY DISSOLVED. I WANT OVANAN TO BE GOVERNED BY ITS PEOPLE.
WE STAGNATE IN A MIRE OF RELIGIOUS FANATICISM AND POITICAL APATHY. IF IT DOESN'T STOP, WE'LL DIE IN IT.
THAT'S GAWDAWFUL NOBLE OF YOU. AND HARD TO BELIEVE.
SERGEANT, THERE'S NOTHING I WANT LESS IN MY LIFE THAN MORE POWER. I RISK EVERYTHING IN COMING HERE.
I TOLD YOU THAT I TRUST YOU. I ASK NOW THAT YOU TRUST ME.
SO... WHAT DO YOU WANT US TO DO?

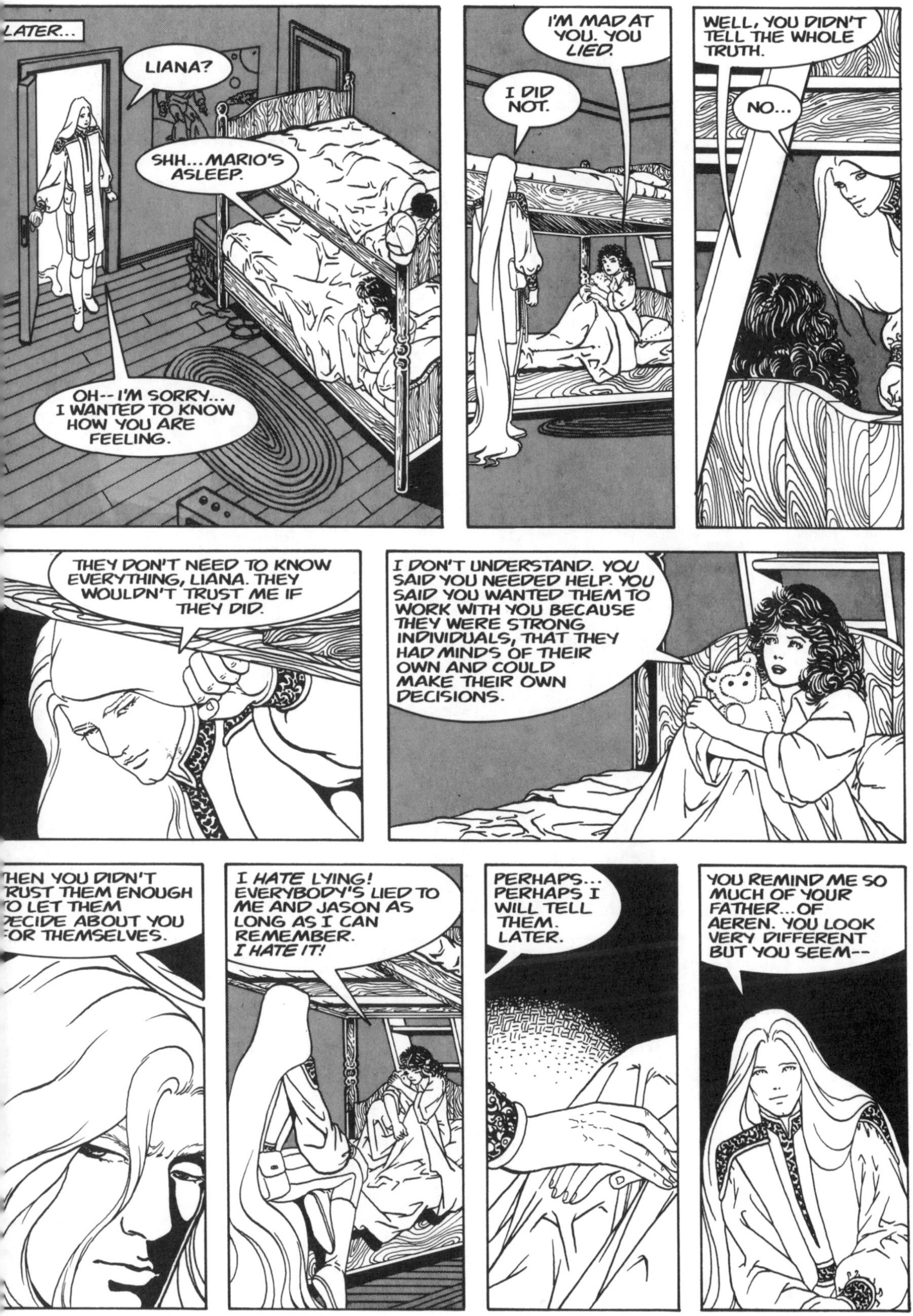
LATER...
LIANA?
SHH... MARIO'S ASLEEP.
OH-- I'M SORRY... I WANTED TO KNOW HOW YOU ARE FEELING.
I'M MAD AT YOU. YOU LIED.
I DID NOT.
WELL, YOU DIDN'T TELL THE WHOLE TRUTH.
NO...
THEY DON'T NEED TO KNOW EVERYTHING, LIANA. THEY WOULDN'T TRUST ME IF THEY DID.
I DON'T UNDERSTAND. YOU SAID YOU NEEDED HELP. YOU SAID YOU WANTED THEM TO WORK WITH YOU BECAUSE THEY WERE STRONG INDIVIDUALS, THAT THEY HAD MINDS OF THEIR OWN AND COULD MAKE THEIR OWN DECISIONS.
THEN YOU DIDN'T TRUST THEM ENOUGH TO LET THEM DECIDE ABOUT YOU FOR THEMSELVES.
I HATE LYING! EVERYBODY'S LIED TO ME AND JASON AS LONG AS I CAN REMEMBER. I HATE IT!
PERHAPS... PERHAPS I WILL TELL THEM. LATER.
YOU REMIND ME SO MUCH OF YOUR FATHER... OF AEREN. YOU LOOK VERY DIFFERENT BUT YOU SEEM--

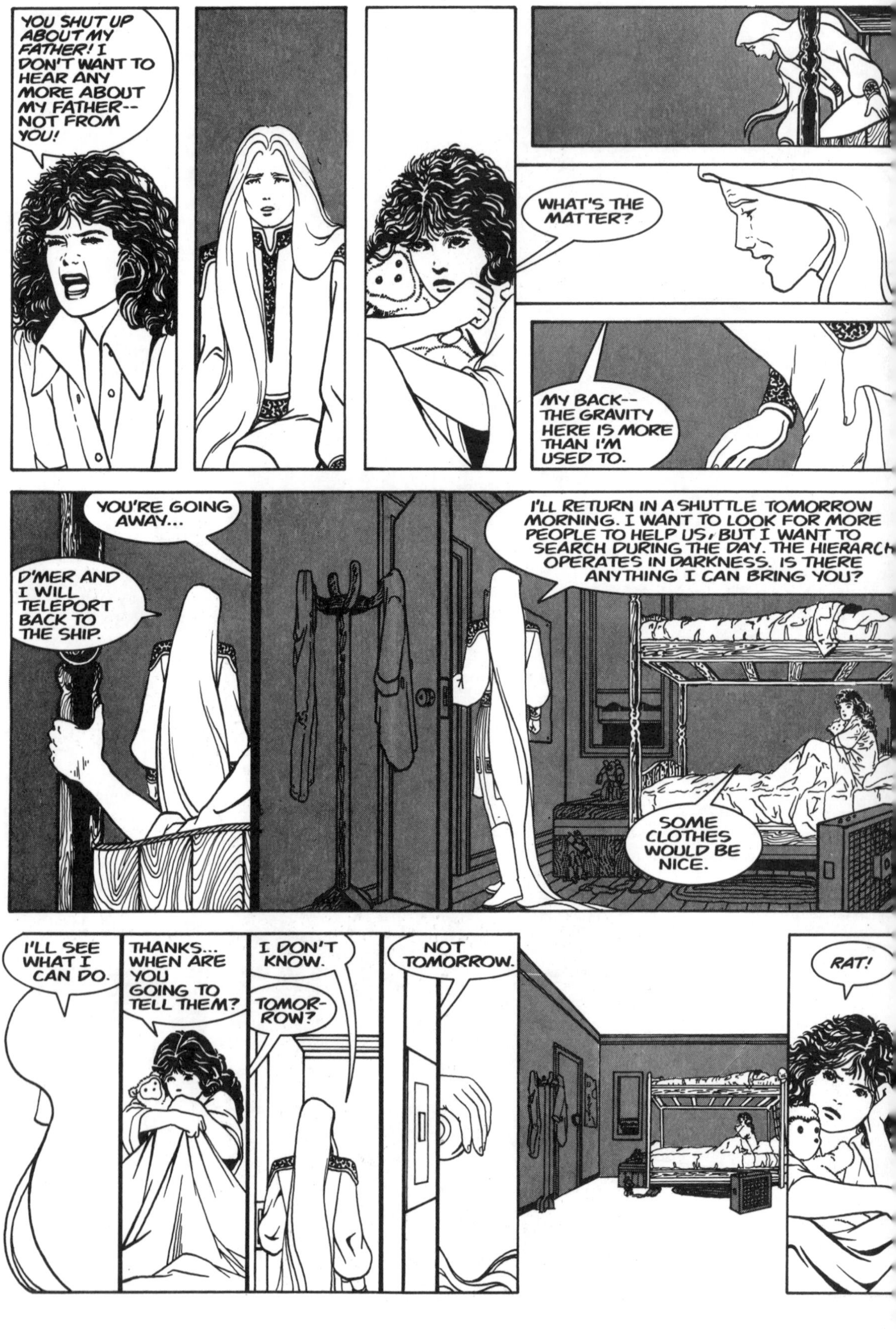
YOU SHUT UP ABOUT MY FATHER! I DON'T WANT TO HEAR ANY MORE ABOUT MY FATHER-- NOT FROM YOU!
WHAT'S THE MATTER?
MY BACK-- THE GRAVITY HERE IS MORE THAN I'M USED TO.
YOU'RE GOING AWAY...
D'MER AND I WILL TELEPORT BACK TO THE SHIP.
I'LL RETURN IN A SHUTTLE TOMORROW MORNING. I WANT TO LOOK FOR MORE PEOPLE TO HELP US, BUT I WANT TO SEARCH DURING THE DAY. THE HIERARCH OPERATES IN DARKNESS. IS THERE ANYTHING I CAN BRING YOU?
SOME CLOTHES WOULD BE NICE.
I'LL SEE WHAT I CAN DO.
THANKS... WHEN ARE YOU GOING TO TELL THEM?
I DON'T KNOW.
TOMORROW?
NOT TOMORROW.
RAT!

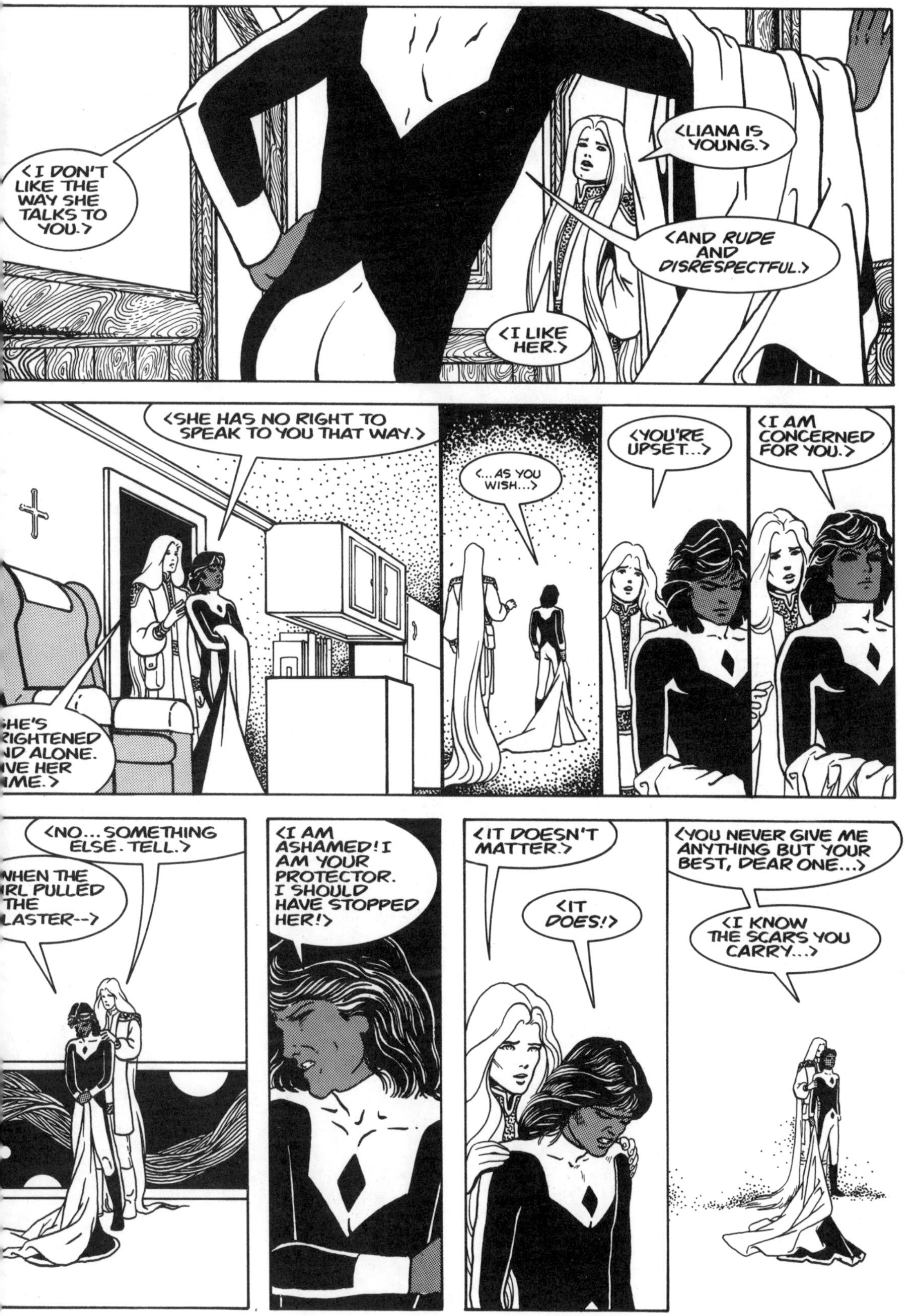

<I DON'T LIKE THE WAY SHE TALKS TO YOU.>
<LIANA IS YOUNG.>
<AND RUDE AND DISRESPECTFUL.>
<I LIKE HER.>
<SHE HAS NO RIGHT TO SPEAK TO YOU THAT WAY.>
HE'S RIGHTENED ND ALONE. VE HER IME.>
<...AS YOU WISH...>
<YOU'RE UPSET...>
<I AM CONCERNED FOR YOU.>
<NO... SOMETHING ELSE. TELL.>
HEN THE IRL PULLED THE LASTER-->
<I AM ASHAMED! I AM YOUR PROTECTOR. I SHOULD HAVE STOPPED HER!>
<IT DOESN'T MATTER.>
<IT DOES!>
<YOU NEVER GIVE ME ANYTHING BUT YOUR BEST, DEAR ONE...>
<I KNOW THE SCARS YOU CARRY...>

<SEREN...MY AVATAR...>

<PLEASE, I'M NOT A HOLY RELIC. AND YOU MUST REMEMBER TO CALL ME RIEKEN-- NOT SEREN.>

<I SHOULD CALL YOU ANGEL.>

<IT ONLY NOW BEGINS AND I AM TIRED ALREADY. IF I SHOULD FAIL...>

<...PLEASE...>

<YOU WON'T FAIL.>

<THEY'RE SIGNALLING US.>

<SO THEY ARE.>

<STOP. WE HAVE TO GO.>

<OUCH! NOW WHO'S BEING DISRESPECT-FUL?>

<YOU'RE IMPOSSIBLE.>

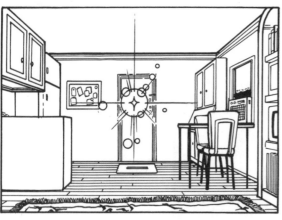

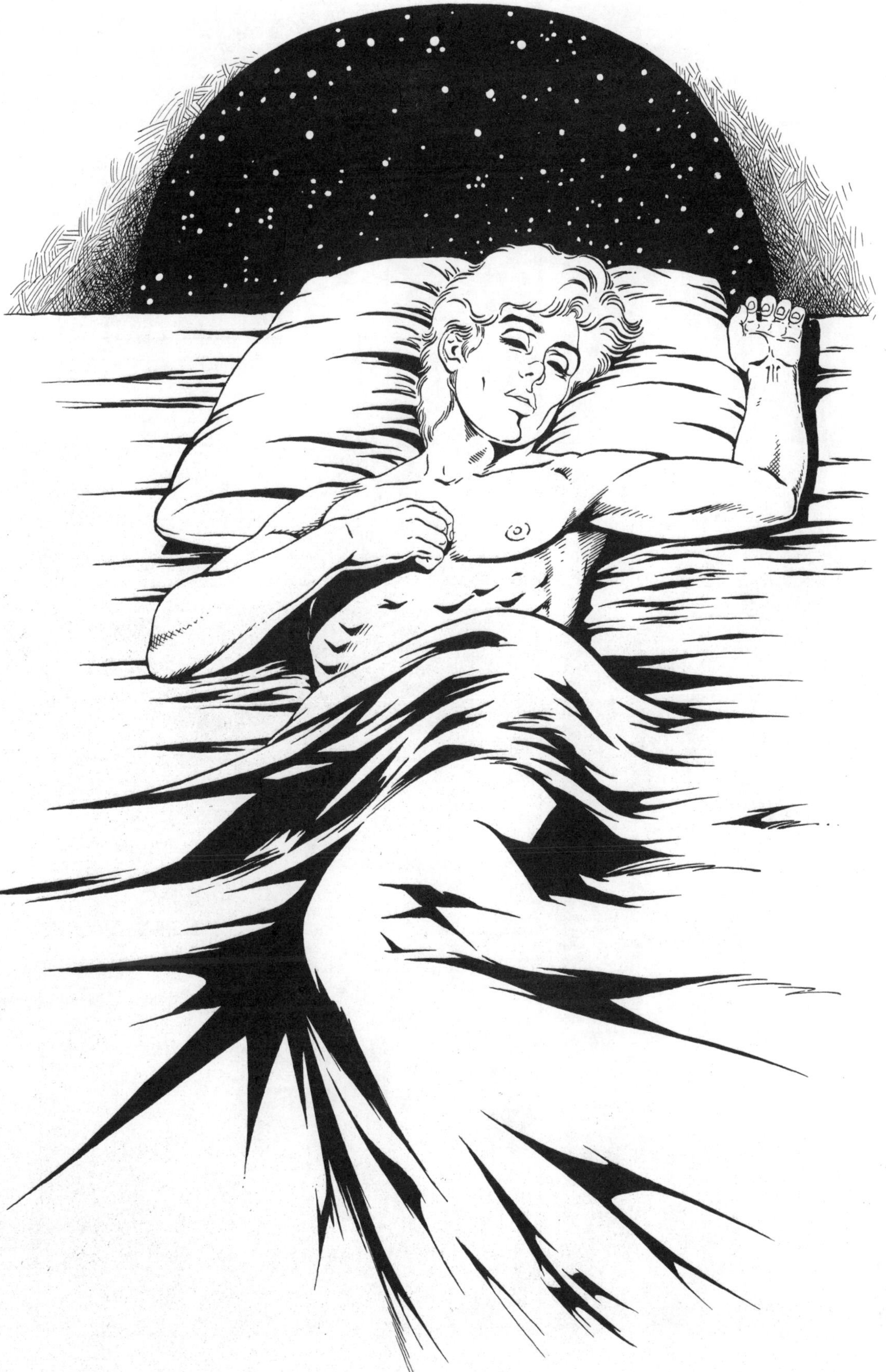

ON THE DARK SIDE OF EARTH'S MOON...

THE SIOVANSIN...

YOU USED TOO MUCH RIESVEMIN.

NONSENSE. I GAVE HIM THE STANDARD DOSE. LOOK, HE'S COMING AROUND NOW.

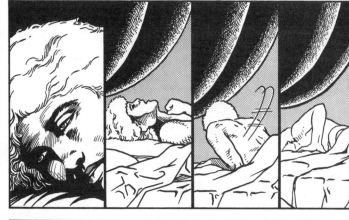

I TOLD YOU SO

ME?

CLEAN IT UP, FRI.

I'M IN CHARGE HERE. IF I SAY CLEAN, YOU CLEAN!

HOW ARE YOU FEELING?

UHHH...NOT SO GOOD...OH...NOT YOU AGAIN. WHERE AM I?

I TOLD YOU BEFORE, YOU'RE IN A SAFE PLACE. CAN I GET YOU ANYTHING?

WHAT KIND OF "SAFE" PLACE?

WOULDN'T YOU LIKE SOMETHING TO CALM YOUR STOMACH?

I'D LIKE TO KNOW WHAT'S GOING ON HERE!

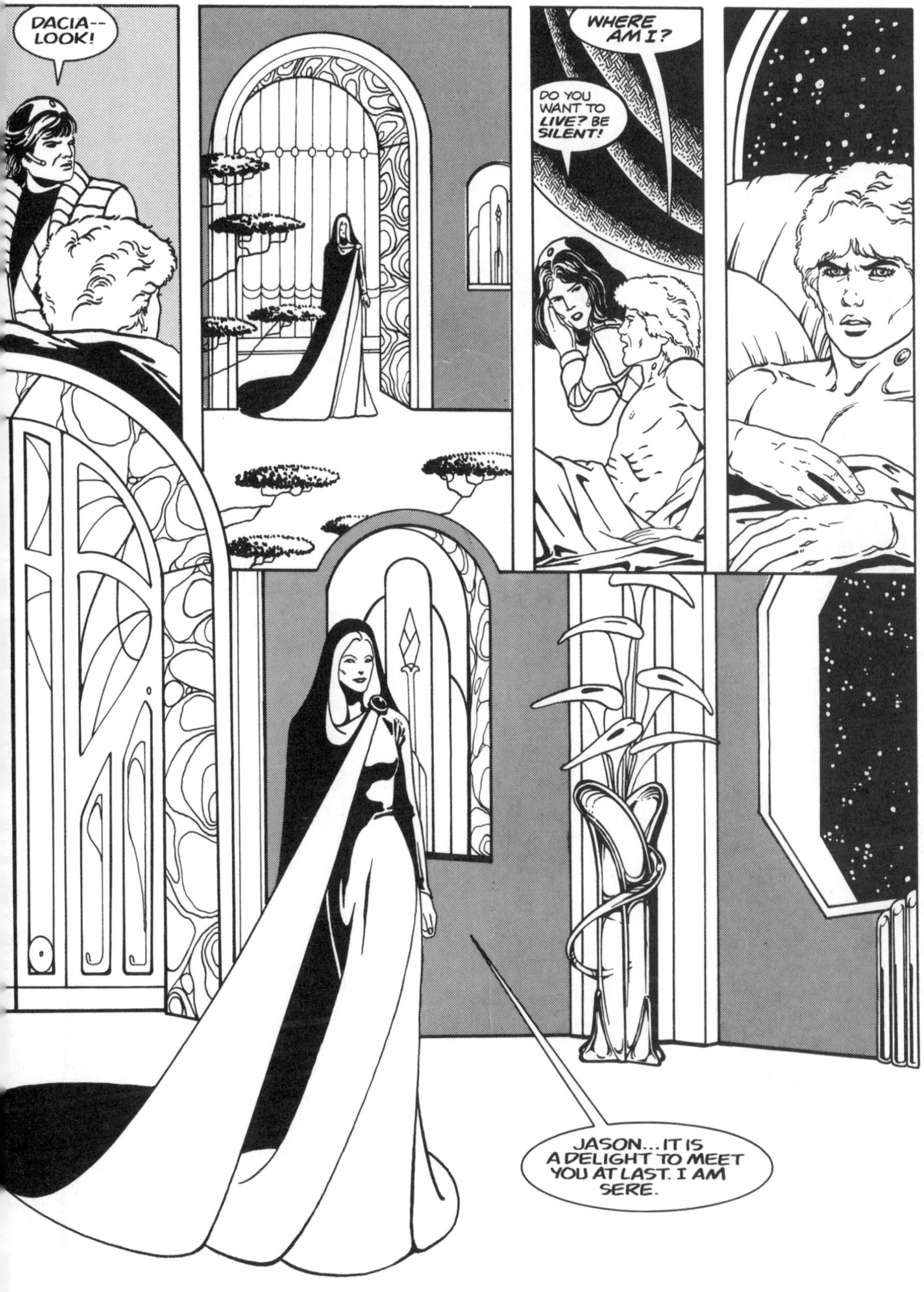
DACIA-- LOOK!
WHERE AM I?
DO YOU WANT TO LIVE? BE SILENT!
JASON... IT IS A DELIGHT TO MEET YOU AT LAST. I AM SERE.

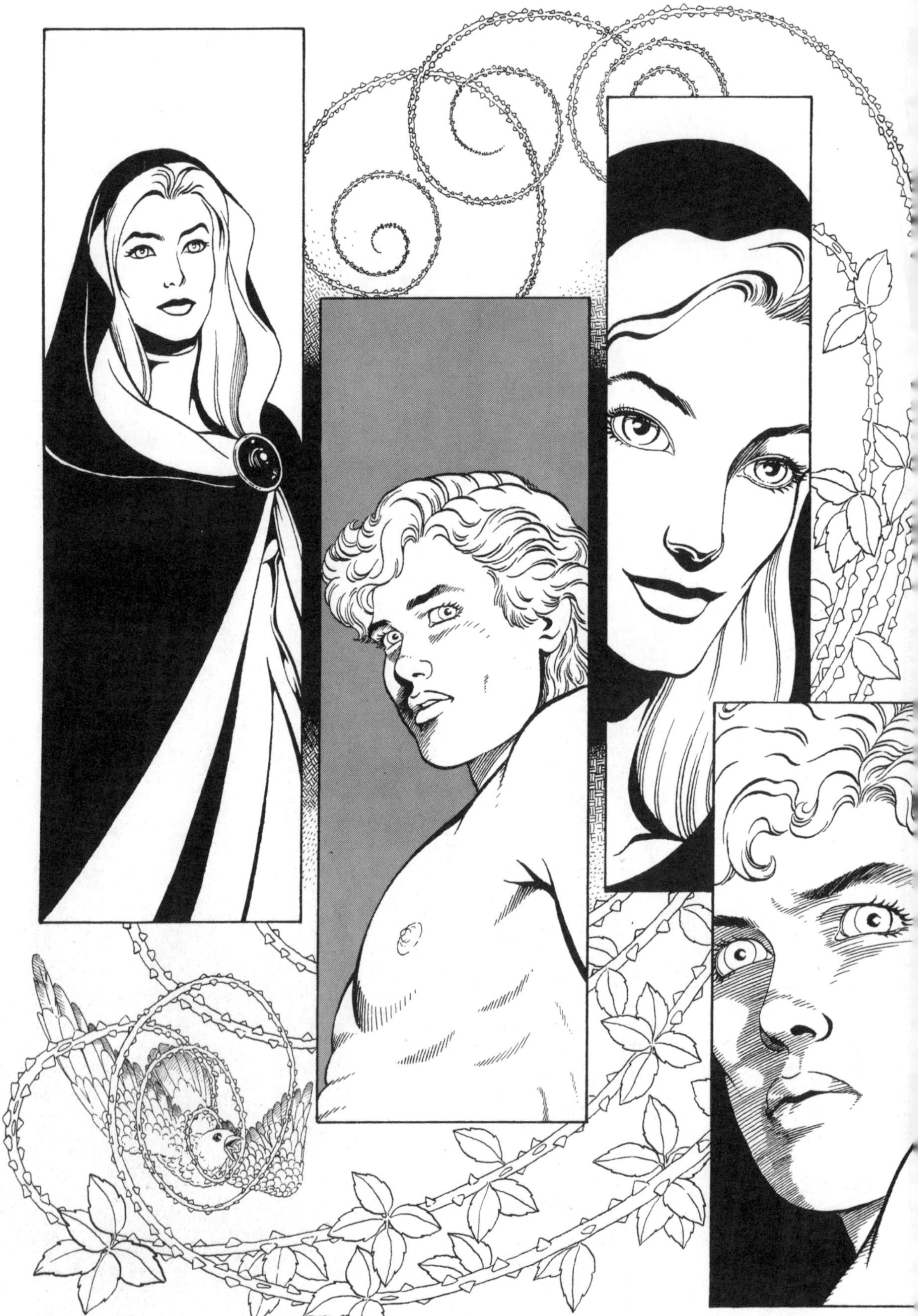

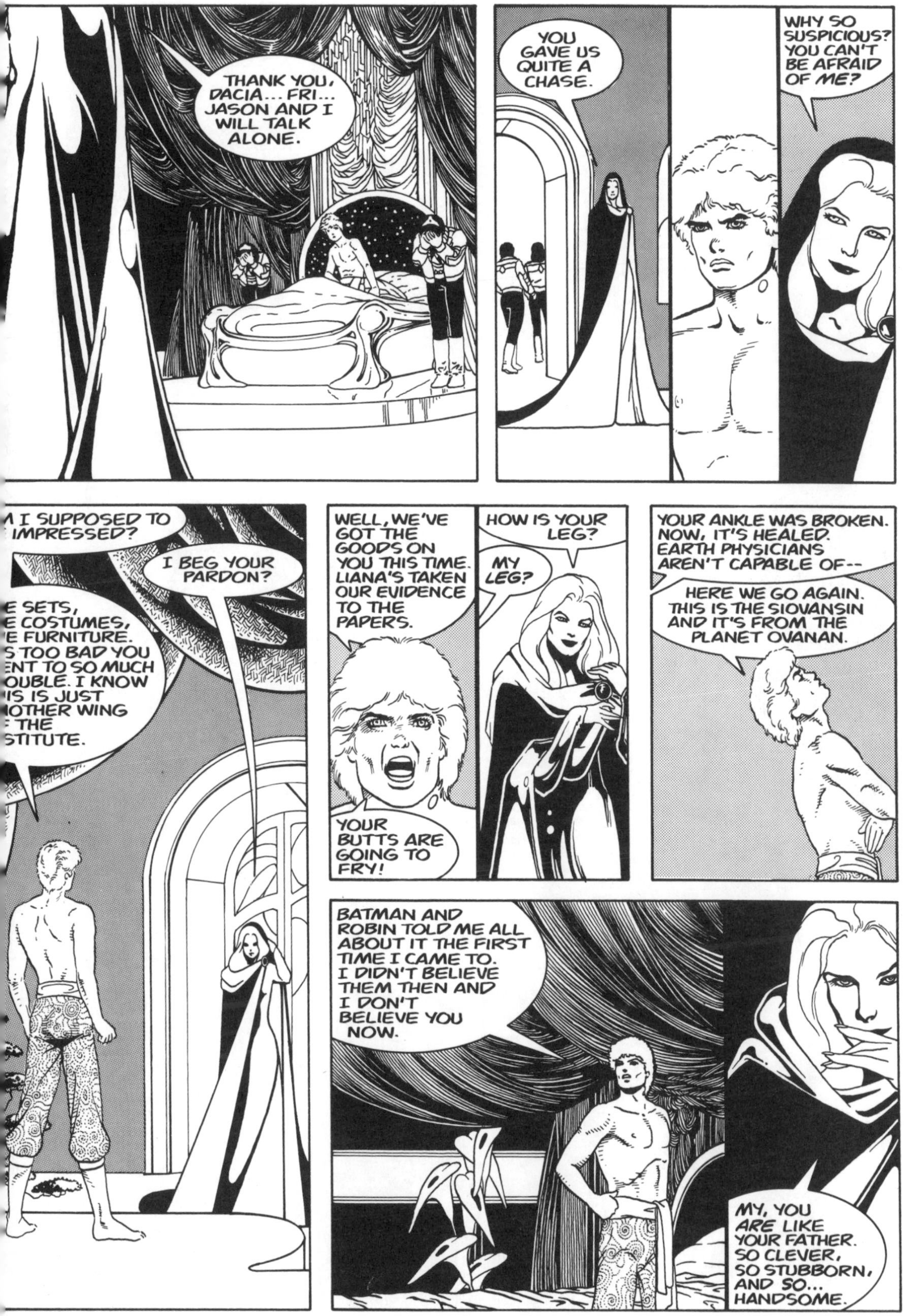

THANK YOU, DACIA... FRI... JASON AND I WILL TALK ALONE.
YOU GAVE US QUITE A CHASE.
WHY SO SUSPICIOUS? YOU CAN'T BE AFRAID OF *ME*?
M I SUPPOSED TO IMPRESSED?
I BEG YOUR PARDON?
E SETS, E COSTUMES, E FURNITURE. S TOO BAD YOU ENT TO SO MUCH OUBLE. I KNOW IS IS JUST NOTHER WING F THE STITUTE.
WELL, WE'VE GOT THE GOODS ON YOU THIS TIME. LIANA'S TAKEN OUR EVIDENCE TO THE PAPERS.
YOUR BUTTS ARE GOING TO FRY!
HOW IS YOUR LEG?
MY LEG?
YOUR ANKLE WAS BROKEN. NOW, IT'S HEALED. EARTH PHYSICIANS AREN'T CAPABLE OF--
HERE WE GO AGAIN. THIS IS THE SIOVANSIN AND IT'S FROM THE PLANET OVANAN.
BATMAN AND ROBIN TOLD ME ALL ABOUT IT THE FIRST TIME I CAME TO. I DIDN'T BELIEVE THEM THEN AND I DON'T BELIEVE YOU NOW.
MY, YOU *ARE* LIKE YOUR FATHER. SO CLEVER, SO STUBBORN, AND SO... HANDSOME.

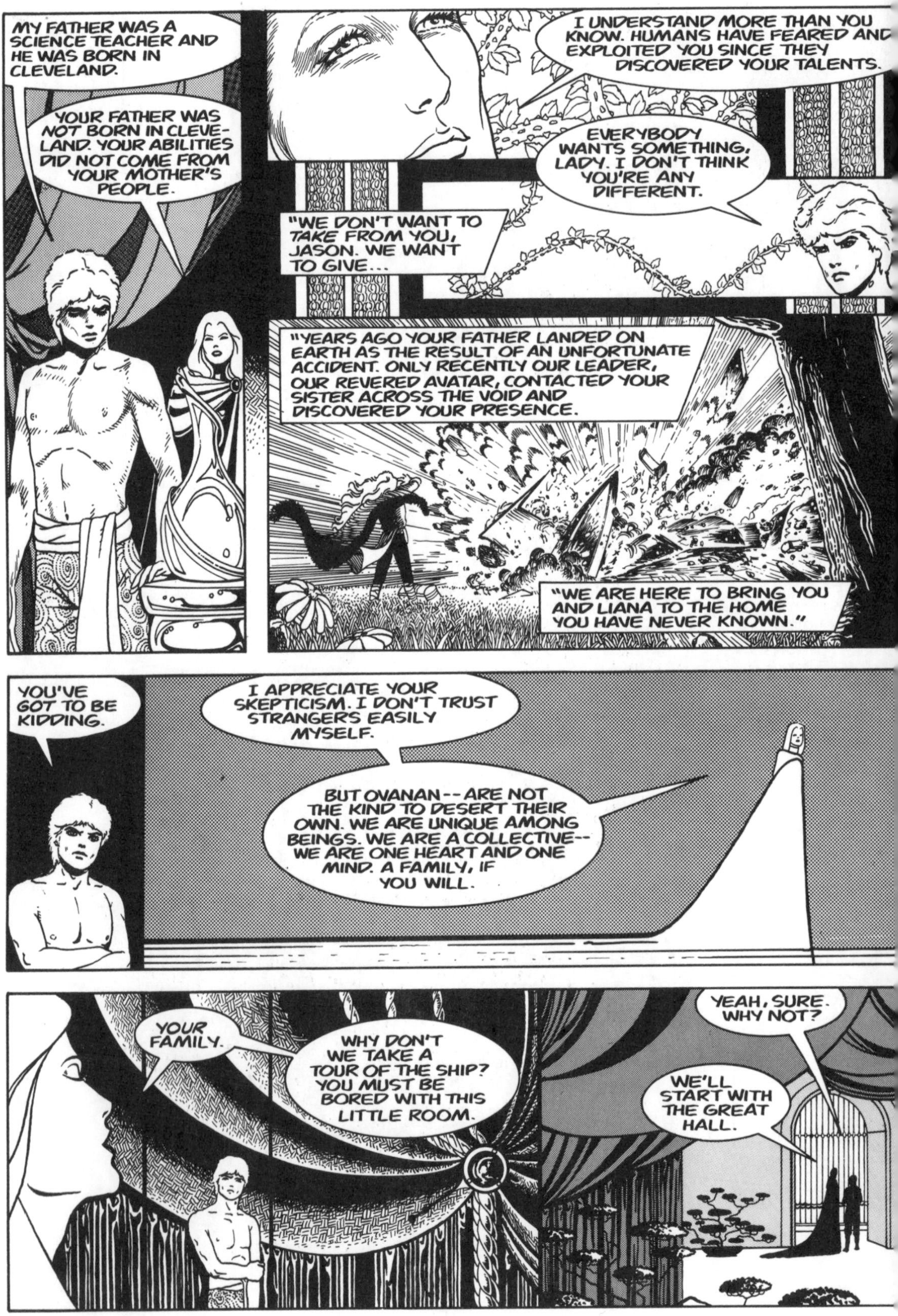
MY FATHER WAS A SCIENCE TEACHER AND HE WAS BORN IN CLEVELAND.
YOUR FATHER WAS NOT BORN IN CLEVELAND. YOUR ABILITIES DID NOT COME FROM YOUR MOTHER'S PEOPLE.
I UNDERSTAND MORE THAN YOU KNOW. HUMANS HAVE FEARED AND EXPLOITED YOU SINCE THEY DISCOVERED YOUR TALENTS.
EVERYBODY WANTS SOMETHING, LADY. I DON'T THINK YOU'RE ANY DIFFERENT.
"WE DON'T WANT TO TAKE FROM YOU, JASON. WE WANT TO GIVE...
"YEARS AGO YOUR FATHER LANDED ON EARTH AS THE RESULT OF AN UNFORTUNATE ACCIDENT. ONLY RECENTLY OUR LEADER, OUR REVERED AVATAR, CONTACTED YOUR SISTER ACROSS THE VOID AND DISCOVERED YOUR PRESENCE.
"WE ARE HERE TO BRING YOU AND LIANA TO THE HOME YOU HAVE NEVER KNOWN."
YOU'VE GOT TO BE KIDDING.
I APPRECIATE YOUR SKEPTICISM. I DON'T TRUST STRANGERS EASILY MYSELF.
BUT OVANAN--ARE NOT THE KIND TO DESERT THEIR OWN. WE ARE UNIQUE AMONG BEINGS. WE ARE A COLLECTIVE--WE ARE ONE HEART AND ONE MIND. A FAMILY, IF YOU WILL.
YOUR FAMILY.
WHY DON'T WE TAKE A TOUR OF THE SHIP? YOU MUST BE BORED WITH THIS LITTLE ROOM.
YEAH, SURE. WHY NOT?
WE'LL START WITH THE GREAT HALL.

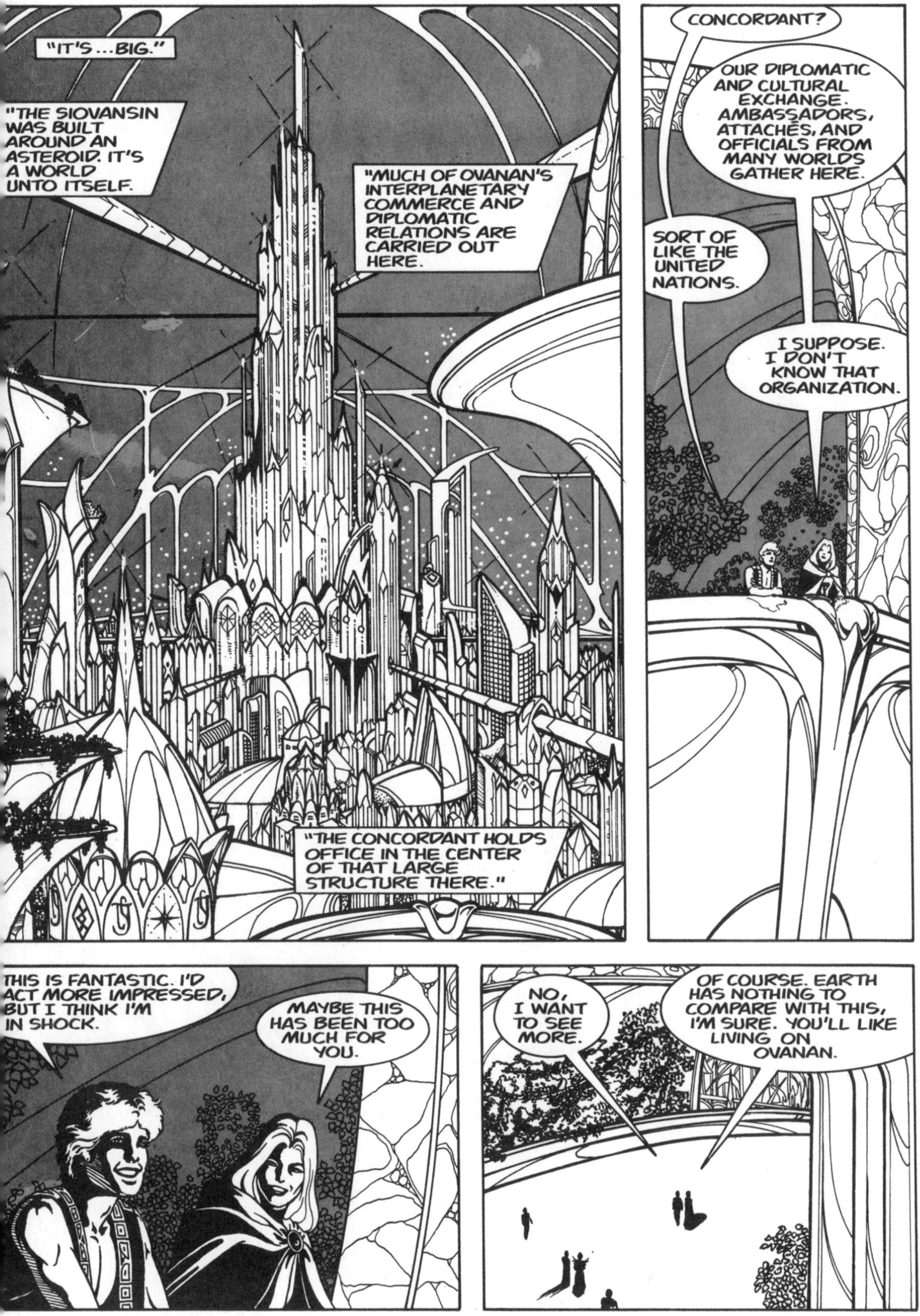
"IT'S...BIG."
"THE SIOVANSIN WAS BUILT AROUND AN ASTEROID. IT'S A WORLD UNTO ITSELF.
"MUCH OF OVANAN'S INTERPLANETARY COMMERCE AND DIPLOMATIC RELATIONS ARE CARRIED OUT HERE.
"THE CONCORDANT HOLDS OFFICE IN THE CENTER OF THAT LARGE STRUCTURE THERE."
CONCORDANT?
OUR DIPLOMATIC AND CULTURAL EXCHANGE. AMBASSADORS, ATTACHÉS, AND OFFICIALS FROM MANY WORLDS GATHER HERE.
SORT OF LIKE THE UNITED NATIONS.
I SUPPOSE. I DON'T KNOW THAT ORGANIZATION.
THIS IS FANTASTIC. I'D ACT MORE IMPRESSED, BUT I THINK I'M IN SHOCK.
MAYBE THIS HAS BEEN TOO MUCH FOR YOU.
NO, I WANT TO SEE MORE.
OF COURSE. EARTH HAS NOTHING TO COMPARE WITH THIS, I'M SURE. YOU'LL LIKE LIVING ON OVANAN.

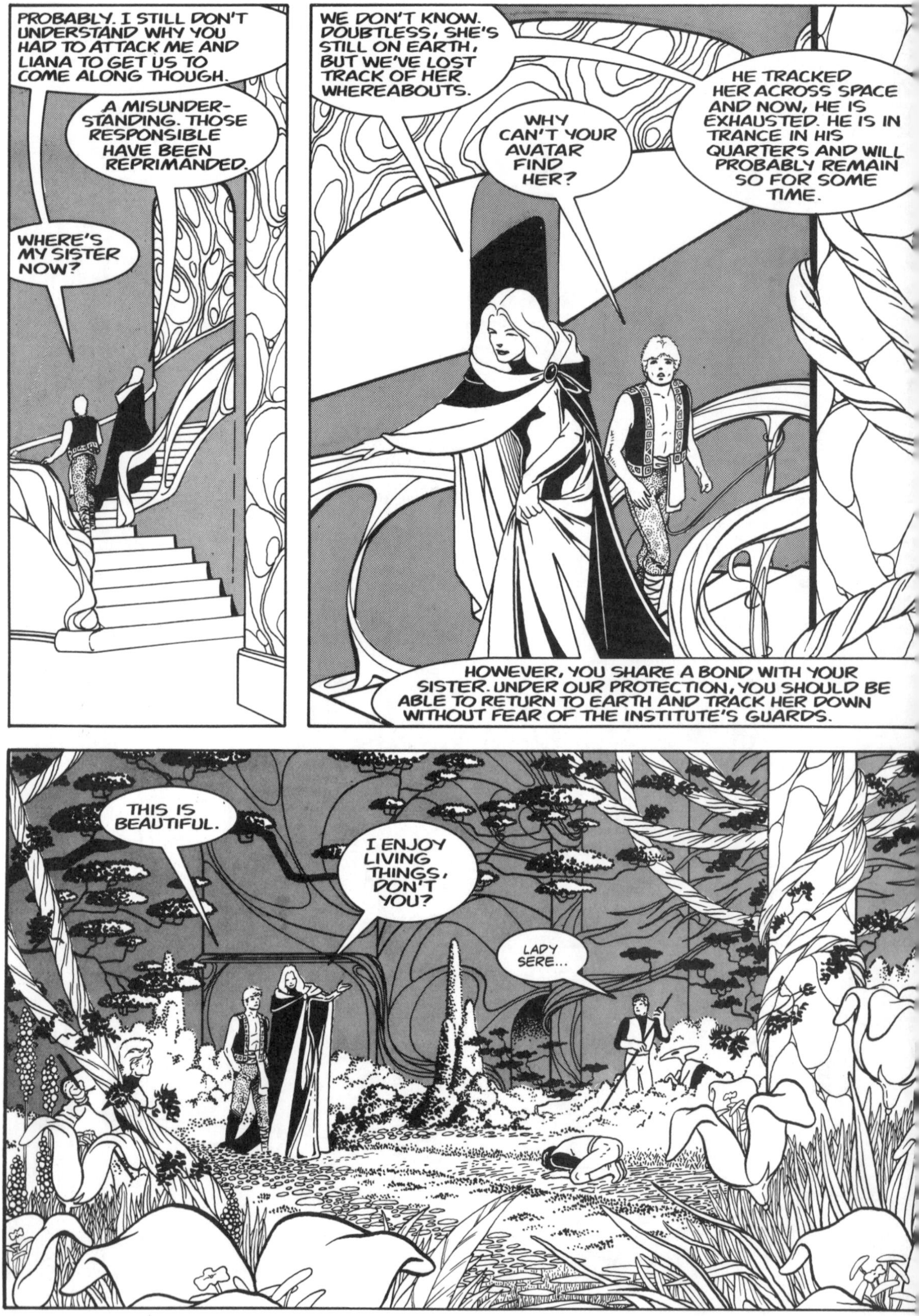
PROBABLY. I STILL DON'T UNDERSTAND WHY YOU HAD TO ATTACK ME AND LIANA TO GET US TO COME ALONG THOUGH.
A MISUNDERSTANDING. THOSE RESPONSIBLE HAVE BEEN REPRIMANDED.
WHERE'S MY SISTER NOW?
WE DON'T KNOW. DOUBTLESS, SHE'S STILL ON EARTH, BUT WE'VE LOST TRACK OF HER WHEREABOUTS.
WHY CAN'T YOUR AVATAR FIND HER?
HE TRACKED HER ACROSS SPACE AND NOW, HE IS EXHAUSTED. HE IS IN TRANCE IN HIS QUARTERS AND WILL PROBABLY REMAIN SO FOR SOME TIME.
HOWEVER, YOU SHARE A BOND WITH YOUR SISTER. UNDER OUR PROTECTION, YOU SHOULD BE ABLE TO RETURN TO EARTH AND TRACK HER DOWN WITHOUT FEAR OF THE INSTITUTE'S GUARDS.
THIS IS BEAUTIFUL.
I ENJOY LIVING THINGS, DON'T YOU?
LADY SERE...

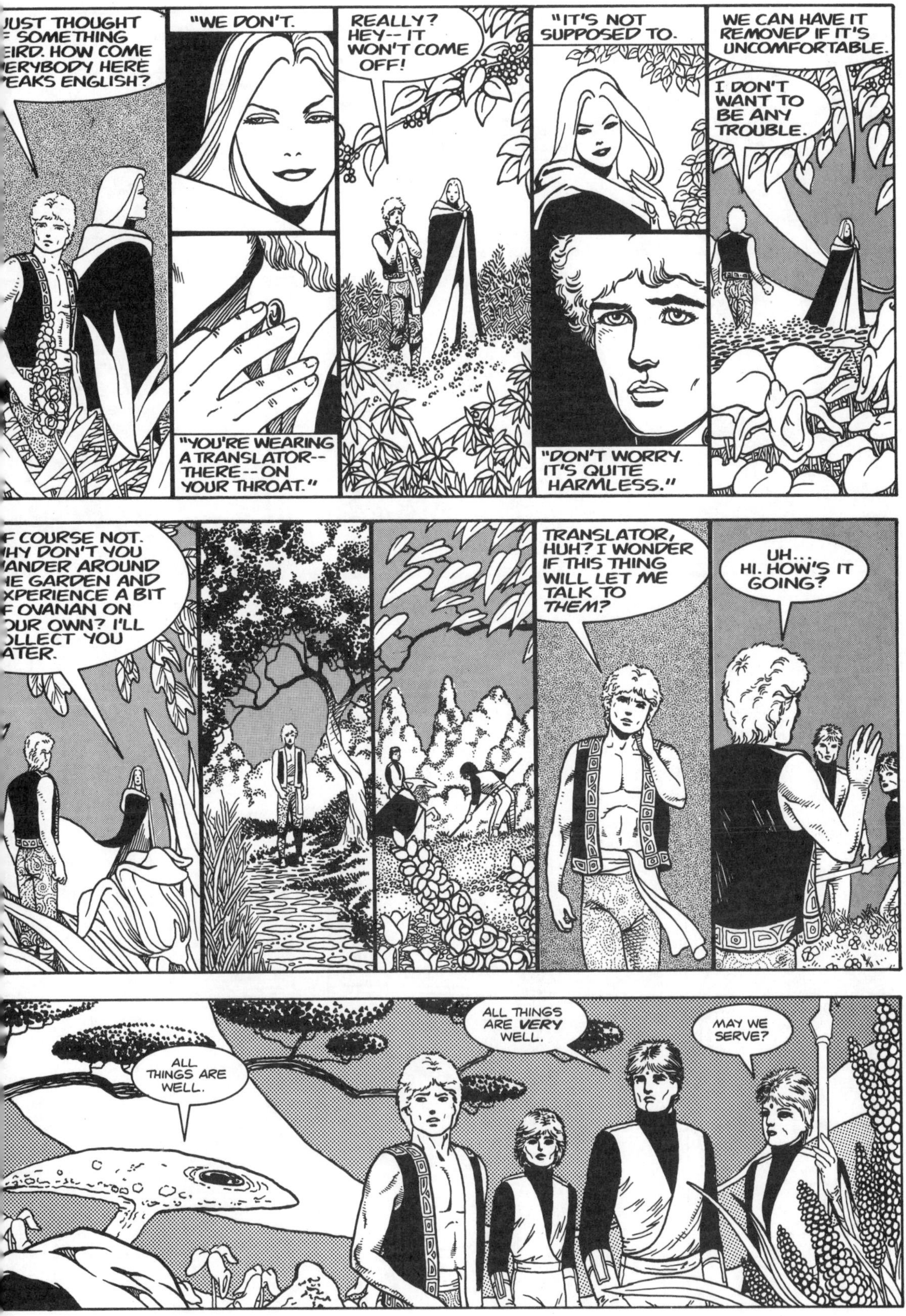
JUST THOUGHT
F SOMETHING
EIRD. HOW COME
ERYBODY HERE
PEAKS ENGLISH?
"WE DON'T.
"YOU'RE WEARING A TRANSLATOR-- THERE--ON YOUR THROAT."
REALLY? HEY-- IT WON'T COME OFF!
"IT'S NOT SUPPOSED TO.
"DON'T WORRY. IT'S QUITE HARMLESS."
WE CAN HAVE IT REMOVED IF IT'S UNCOMFORTABLE.
I DON'T WANT TO BE ANY TROUBLE.
F COURSE NOT.
HY DON'T YOU
ANDER AROUND
HE GARDEN AND
XPERIENCE A BIT
F OVANAN ON
OUR OWN? I'LL
OLLECT YOU
ATER.
TRANSLATOR, HUH? I WONDER IF THIS THING WILL LET ME TALK TO *THEM*?
UH... HI. HOW'S IT GOING?
ALL THINGS ARE WELL.
ALL THINGS ARE *VERY* WELL.
MAY WE SERVE?

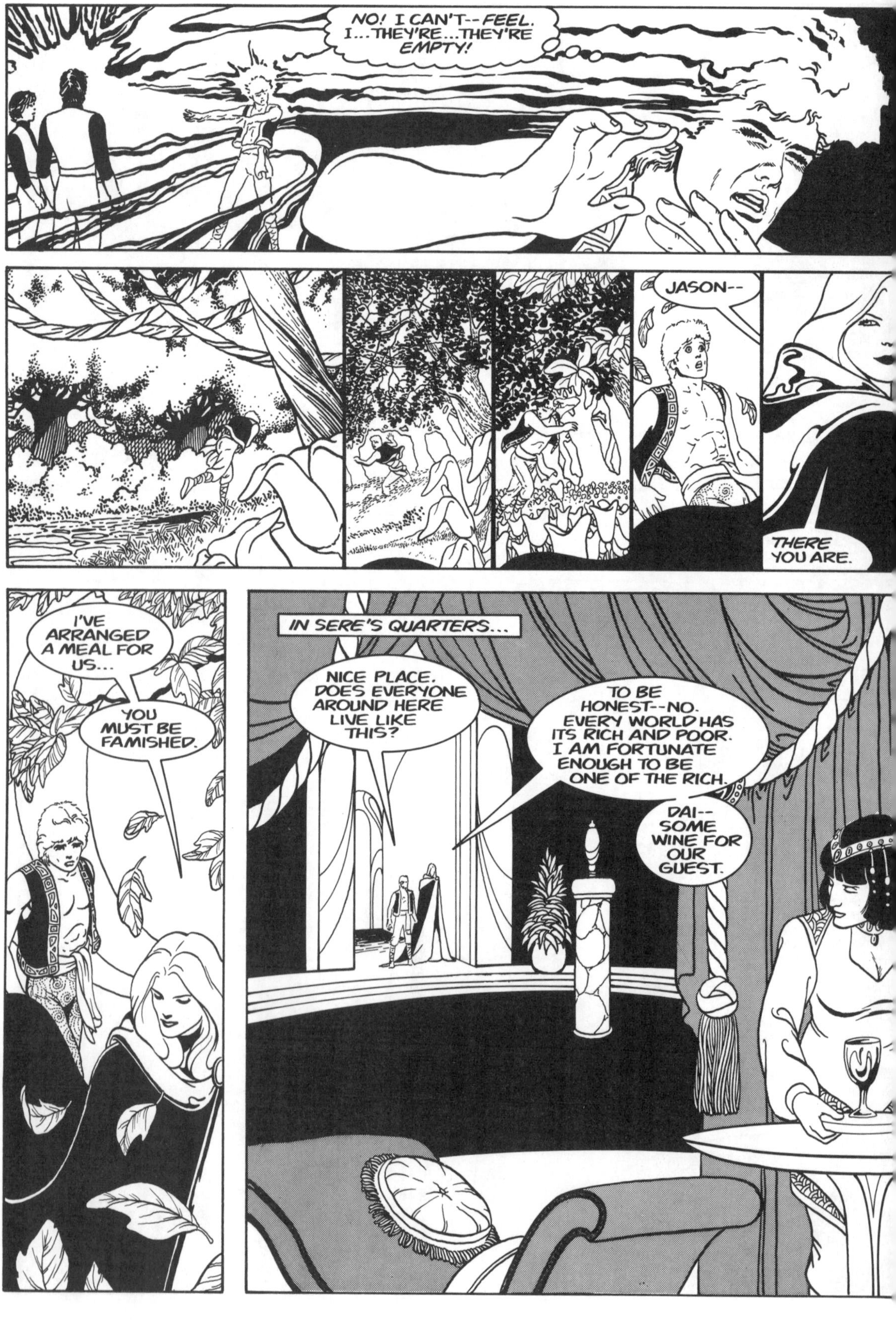
NO! I CAN'T--FEEL. I...THEY'RE...THEY'RE EMPTY!
JASON--
THERE YOU ARE.
I'VE ARRANGED A MEAL FOR US...
YOU MUST BE FAMISHED.
IN SERE'S QUARTERS...
NICE PLACE. DOES EVERYONE AROUND HERE LIVE LIKE THIS?
TO BE HONEST--NO. EVERY WORLD HAS ITS RICH AND POOR. I AM FORTUNATE ENOUGH TO BE ONE OF THE RICH.
DAI--SOME WINE FOR OUR GUEST.

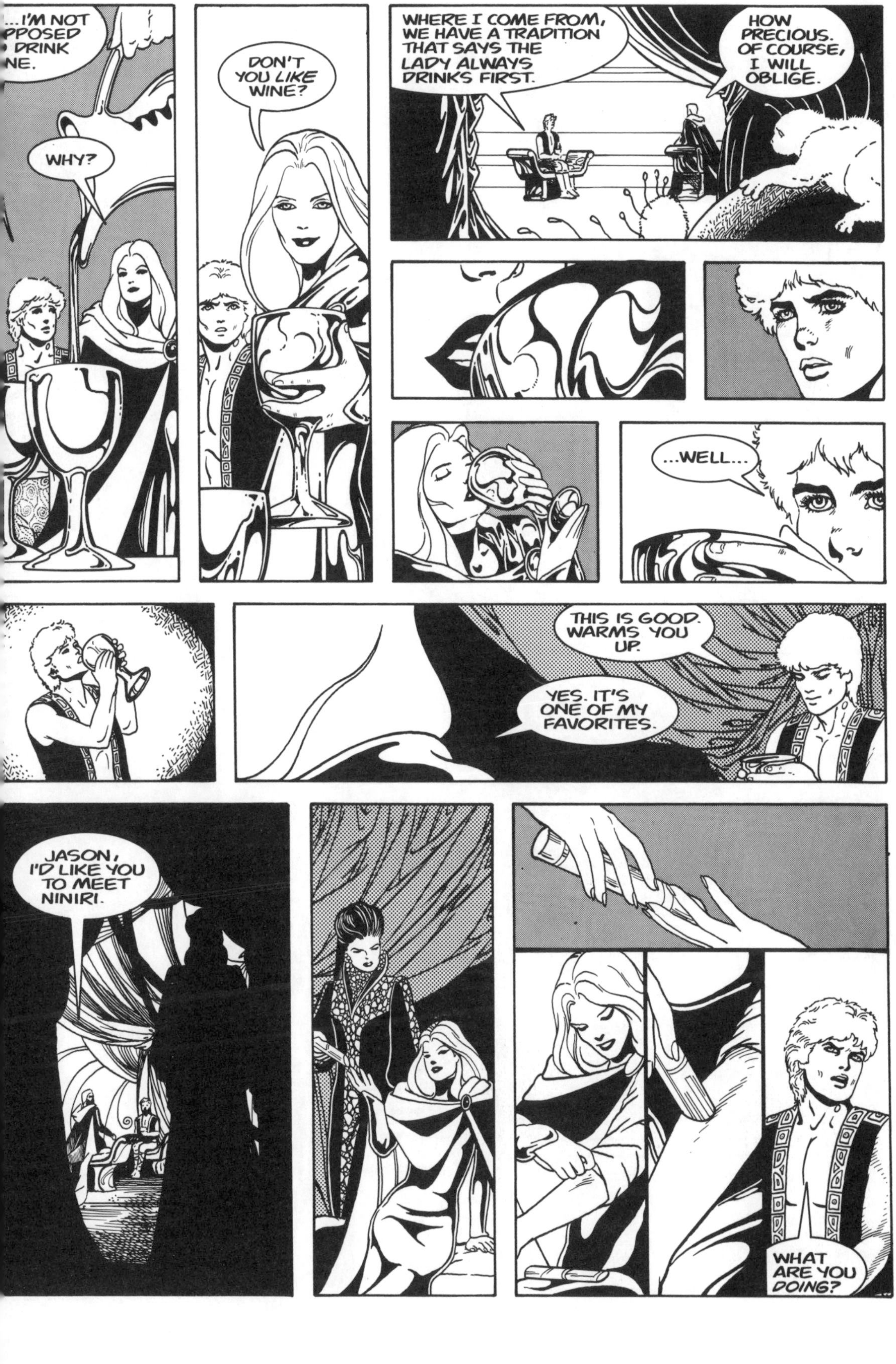
...I'M NOT PPOSED DRINK NE.
WHY?
DON'T YOU LIKE WINE?
WHERE I COME FROM, WE HAVE A TRADITION THAT SAYS THE LADY ALWAYS DRINKS FIRST.
HOW PRECIOUS. OF COURSE, I WILL OBLIGE.
...WELL...
THIS IS GOOD. WARMS YOU UP.
YES. IT'S ONE OF MY FAVORITES.
JASON, I'D LIKE YOU TO MEET NINIRI.
WHAT ARE YOU DOING?

I THOUGHT YOU SAID THIS WOULDN'T BE NECESSARY.

HE'S A SENSITIVE, TOO. HE KNEW I WAS LYING. DIDN'T YOU, JASON?

...OH GOD...

I'M VERY CONTROLLED, BUT YOU SAW RIGHT THROUGH ME. YOU'RE QUITE TALENTED.

I CAN'T WAIT TO MEET YOUR SISTER.

...LIANA...!

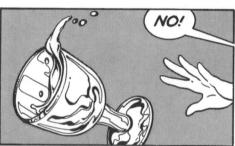

NO!

YOU LET HIM SEE THROUGH YOU. I KNOW YOU TOO WELL, SERE.

HE REALLY DOES LOOK LIKE AEREN, DON'T YOU THINK?

CALL ME WHEN YOU'RE FINISHED WITH YOUR NEW TOY. REMEMBER-- WE NEED HIM.

OH NO...

NOTHING PERMANENT...

DON'T INFLICT ANY DEBILITATING DAMAGE.

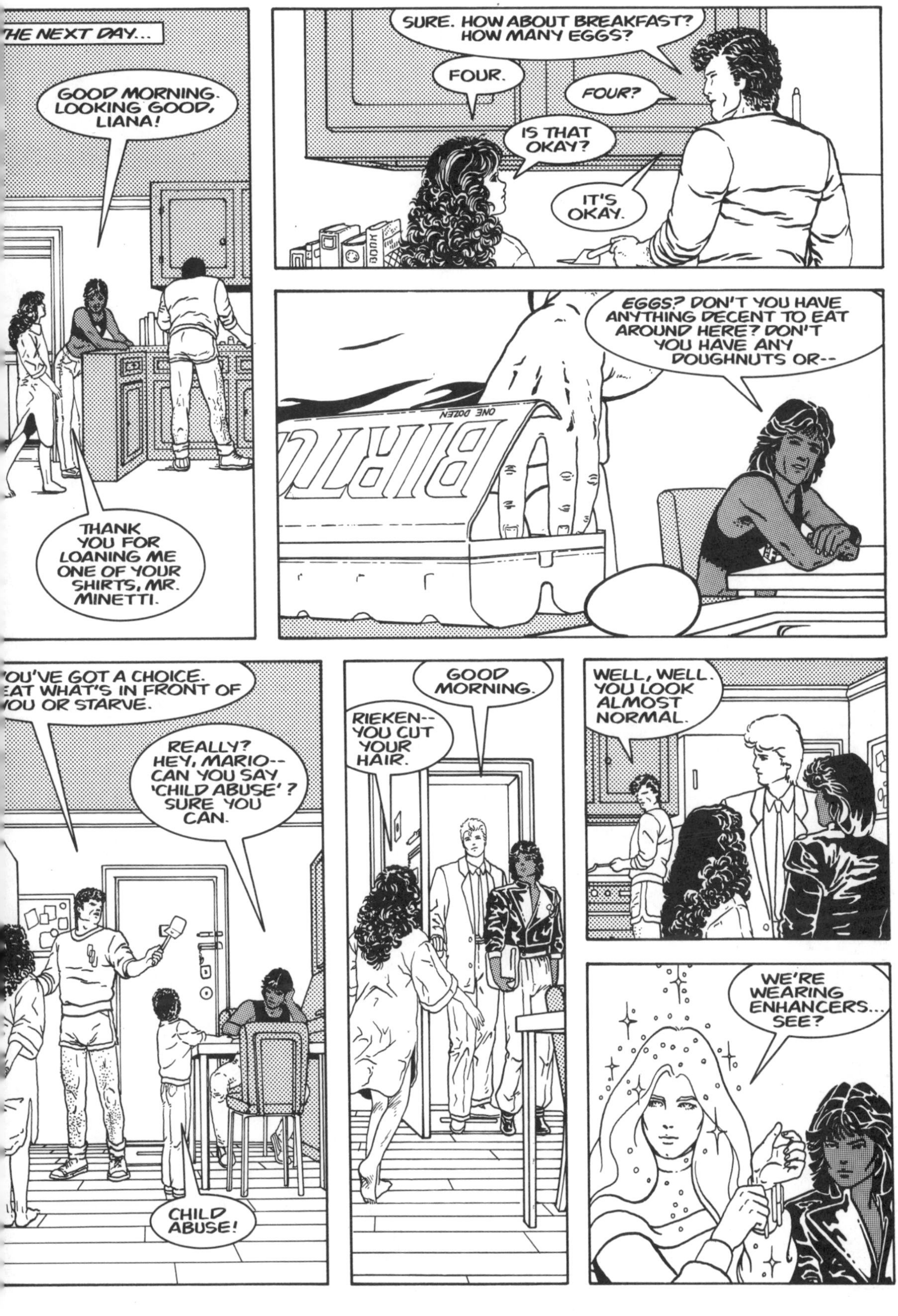
THE NEXT DAY...
GOOD MORNING. LOOKING GOOD, LIANA!
THANK YOU FOR LOANING ME ONE OF YOUR SHIRTS, MR. MINETTI.
SURE. HOW ABOUT BREAKFAST? HOW MANY EGGS?
FOUR.
FOUR?
IS THAT OKAY?
IT'S OKAY.
EGGS? DON'T YOU HAVE ANYTHING DECENT TO EAT AROUND HERE? DON'T YOU HAVE ANY DOUGHNUTS OR--
ONE DOZEN
YOU'VE GOT A CHOICE. EAT WHAT'S IN FRONT OF YOU OR STARVE.
REALLY? HEY, MARIO-- CAN YOU SAY 'CHILD ABUSE'? SURE YOU CAN.
CHILD ABUSE!
RIEKEN-- YOU CUT YOUR HAIR.
GOOD MORNING.
WELL, WELL. YOU LOOK ALMOST NORMAL.
WE'RE WEARING ENHANCERS... SEE?

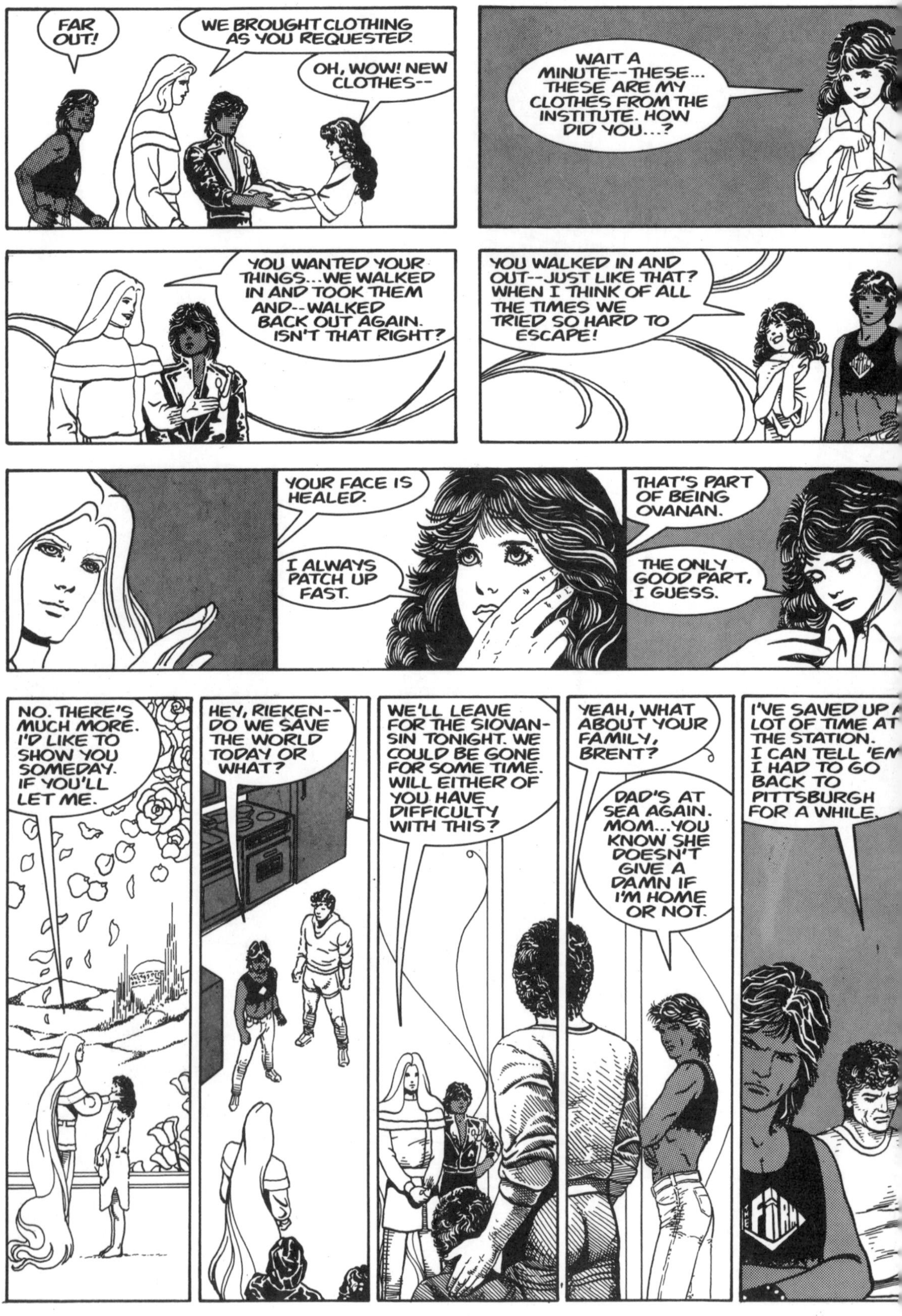
FAR OUT!
WE BROUGHT CLOTHING AS YOU REQUESTED.
OH, WOW! NEW CLOTHES--
WAIT A MINUTE--THESE... THESE ARE MY CLOTHES FROM THE INSTITUTE. HOW DID YOU...?
YOU WANTED YOUR THINGS...WE WALKED IN AND TOOK THEM AND--WALKED BACK OUT AGAIN. ISN'T THAT RIGHT?
YOU WALKED IN AND OUT--JUST LIKE THAT? WHEN I THINK OF ALL THE TIMES WE TRIED SO HARD TO ESCAPE!
YOUR FACE IS HEALED.
I ALWAYS PATCH UP FAST.
THAT'S PART OF BEING OVANAN.
THE ONLY GOOD PART, I GUESS.
NO. THERE'S MUCH MORE. I'D LIKE TO SHOW YOU SOMEDAY. IF YOU'LL LET ME.
HEY, RIEKEN-- DO WE SAVE THE WORLD TODAY OR WHAT?
WE'LL LEAVE FOR THE SIOVAN-SIN TONIGHT. WE COULD BE GONE FOR SOME TIME. WILL EITHER OF YOU HAVE DIFFICULTY WITH THIS?
YEAH, WHAT ABOUT YOUR FAMILY, BRENT?
DAD'S AT SEA AGAIN. MOM...YOU KNOW SHE DOESN'T GIVE A DAMN IF I'M HOME OR NOT.
I'VE SAVED UP A LOT OF TIME AT THE STATION. I CAN TELL 'EM I HAD TO GO BACK TO PITTSBURGH FOR A WHILE.

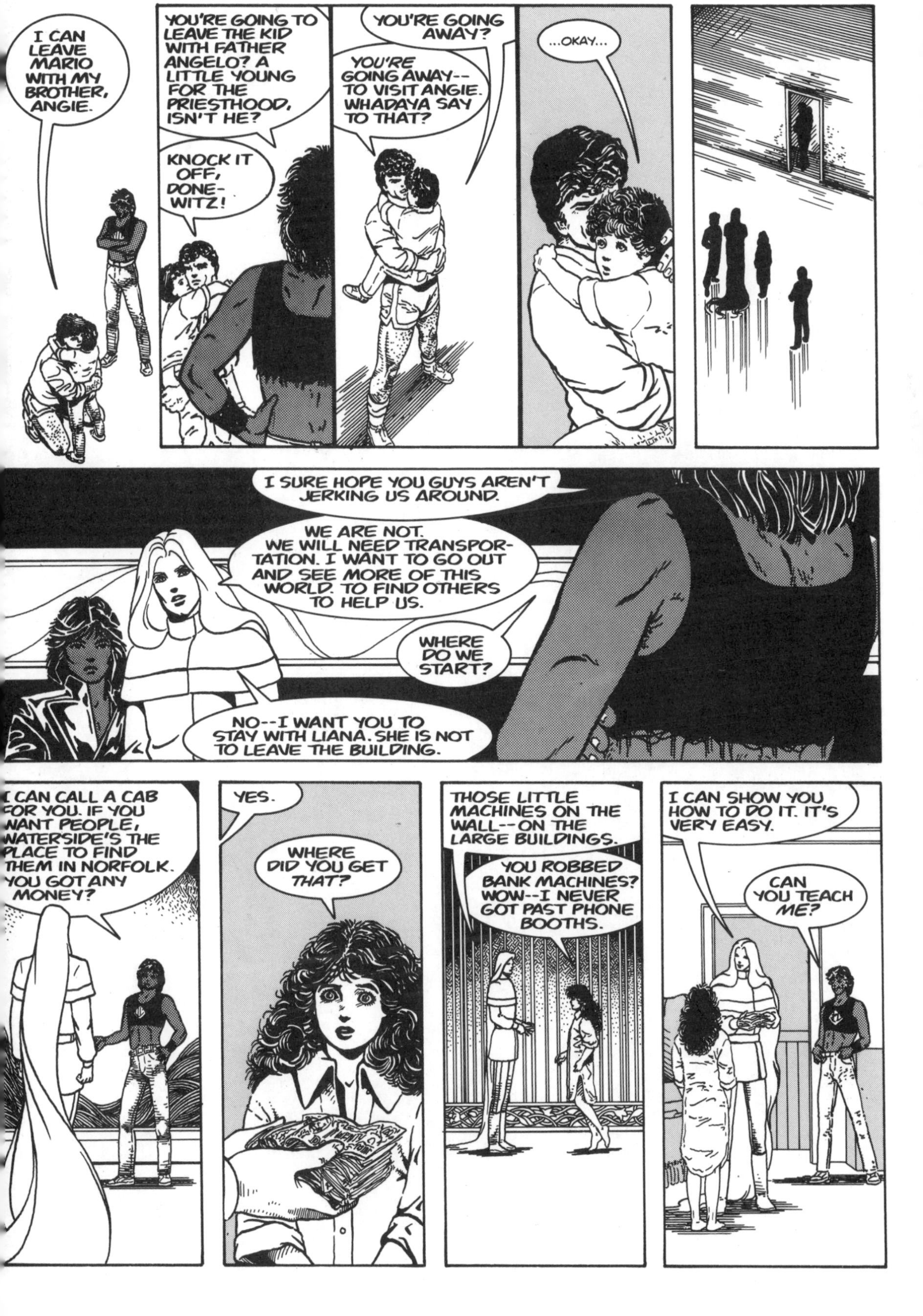
I CAN LEAVE MARIO WITH MY BROTHER, ANGIE.
YOU'RE GOING TO LEAVE THE KID WITH FATHER ANGELO? A LITTLE YOUNG FOR THE PRIESTHOOD, ISN'T HE?
KNOCK IT OFF, DONE-WITZ!
YOU'RE GOING AWAY?
YOU'RE GOING AWAY-- TO VISIT ANGIE. WHADAYA SAY TO THAT?
...OKAY...
I SURE HOPE YOU GUYS AREN'T JERKING US AROUND.
WE ARE NOT. WE WILL NEED TRANSPORTATION. I WANT TO GO OUT AND SEE MORE OF THIS WORLD. TO FIND OTHERS TO HELP US.
WHERE DO WE START?
NO--I WANT YOU TO STAY WITH LIANA. SHE IS NOT TO LEAVE THE BUILDING.
I CAN CALL A CAB FOR YOU. IF YOU WANT PEOPLE, WATERSIDE'S THE PLACE TO FIND THEM IN NORFOLK. YOU GOT ANY MONEY?
YES.
WHERE DID YOU GET THAT?
THOSE LITTLE MACHINES ON THE WALL--ON THE LARGE BUILDINGS.
YOU ROBBED BANK MACHINES? WOW--I NEVER GOT PAST PHONE BOOTHS.
I CAN SHOW YOU HOW TO DO IT. IT'S VERY EASY.
CAN YOU TEACH ME?

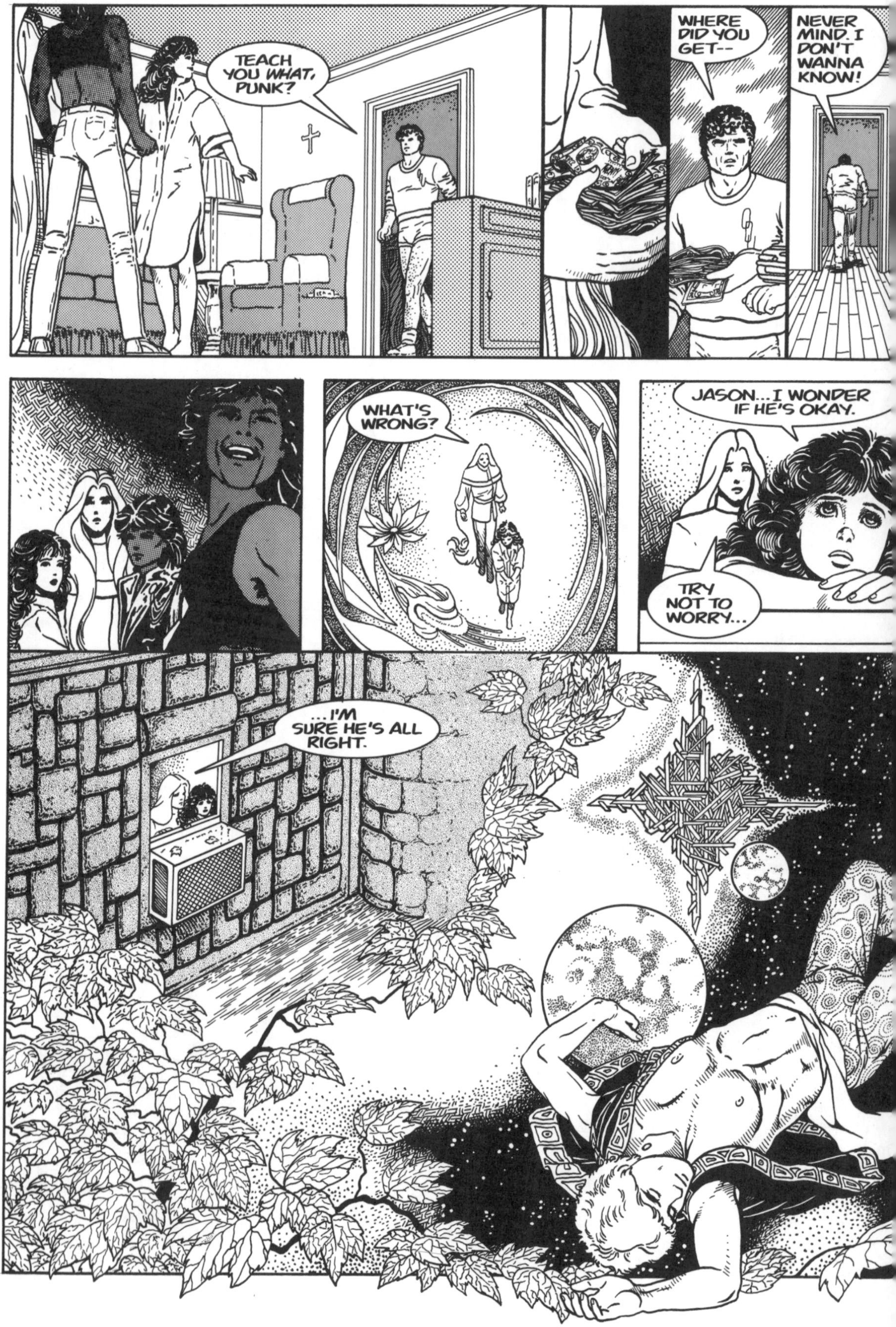
TEACH YOU WHAT, PUNK?
WHERE DID YOU GET--
NEVER MIND, I DON'T WANNA KNOW!
WHAT'S WRONG?
JASON... I WONDER IF HE'S OKAY.
TRY NOT TO WORRY...
...I'M SURE HE'S ALL RIGHT.

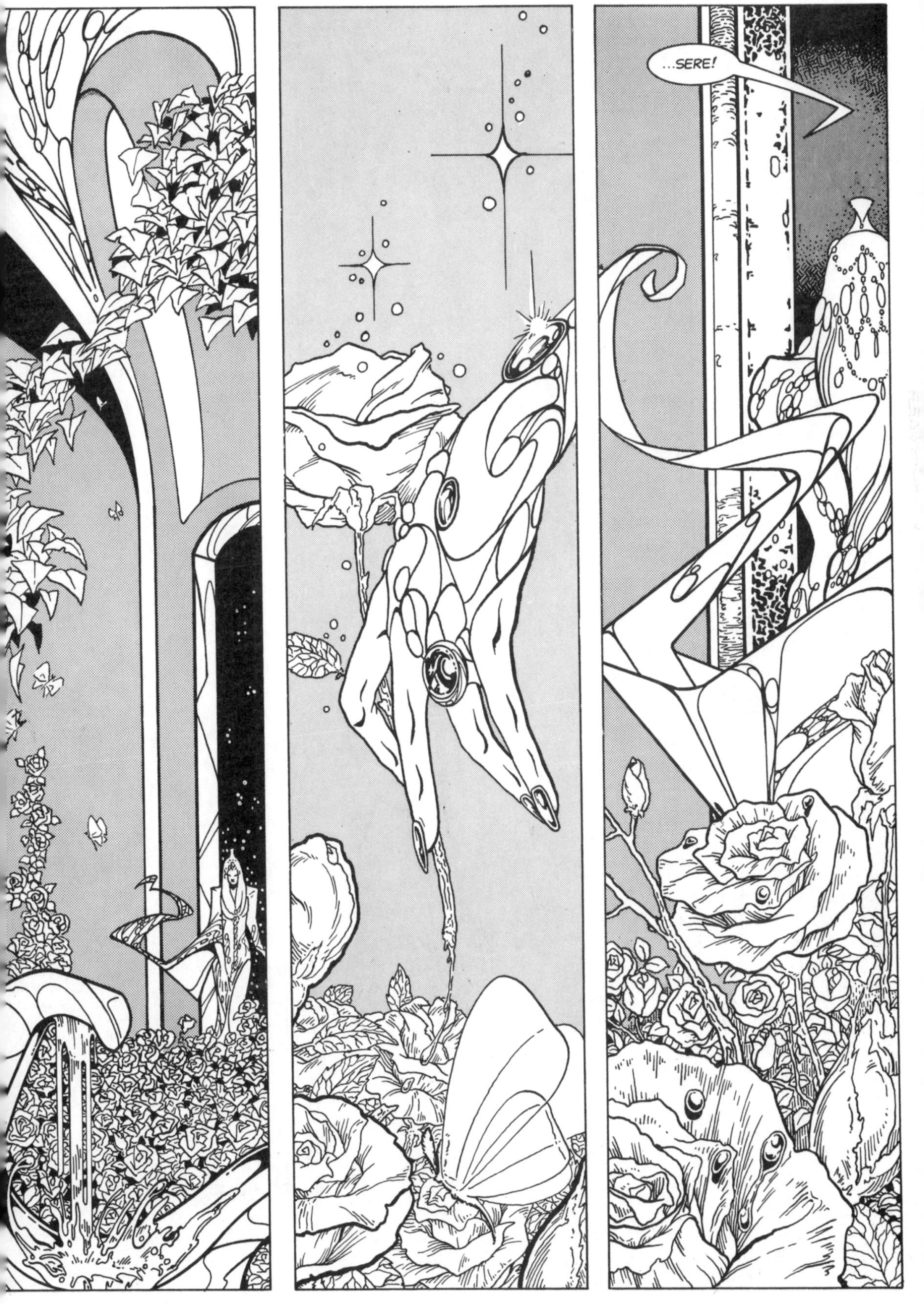
...SERE!

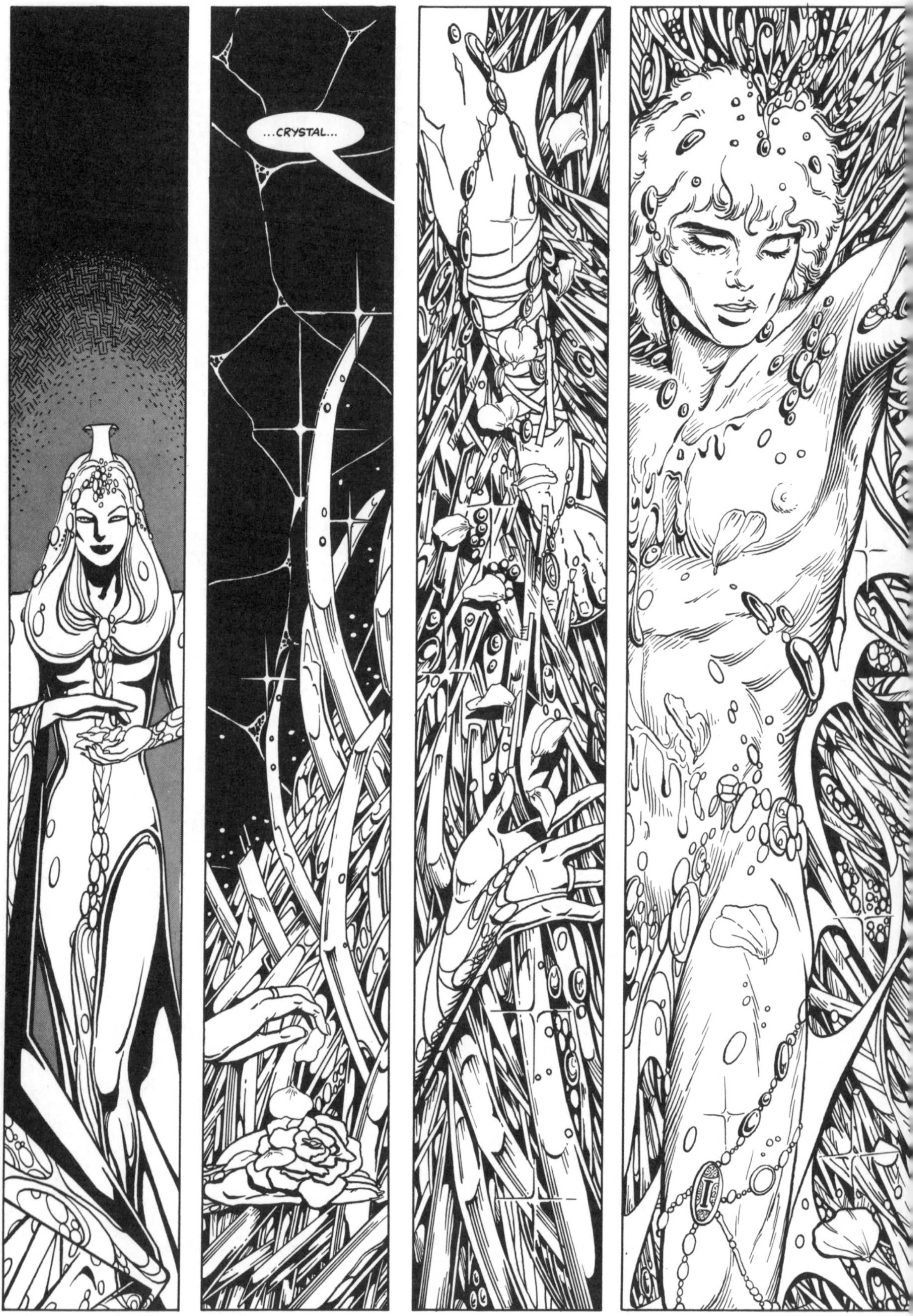
...CRYSTAL...

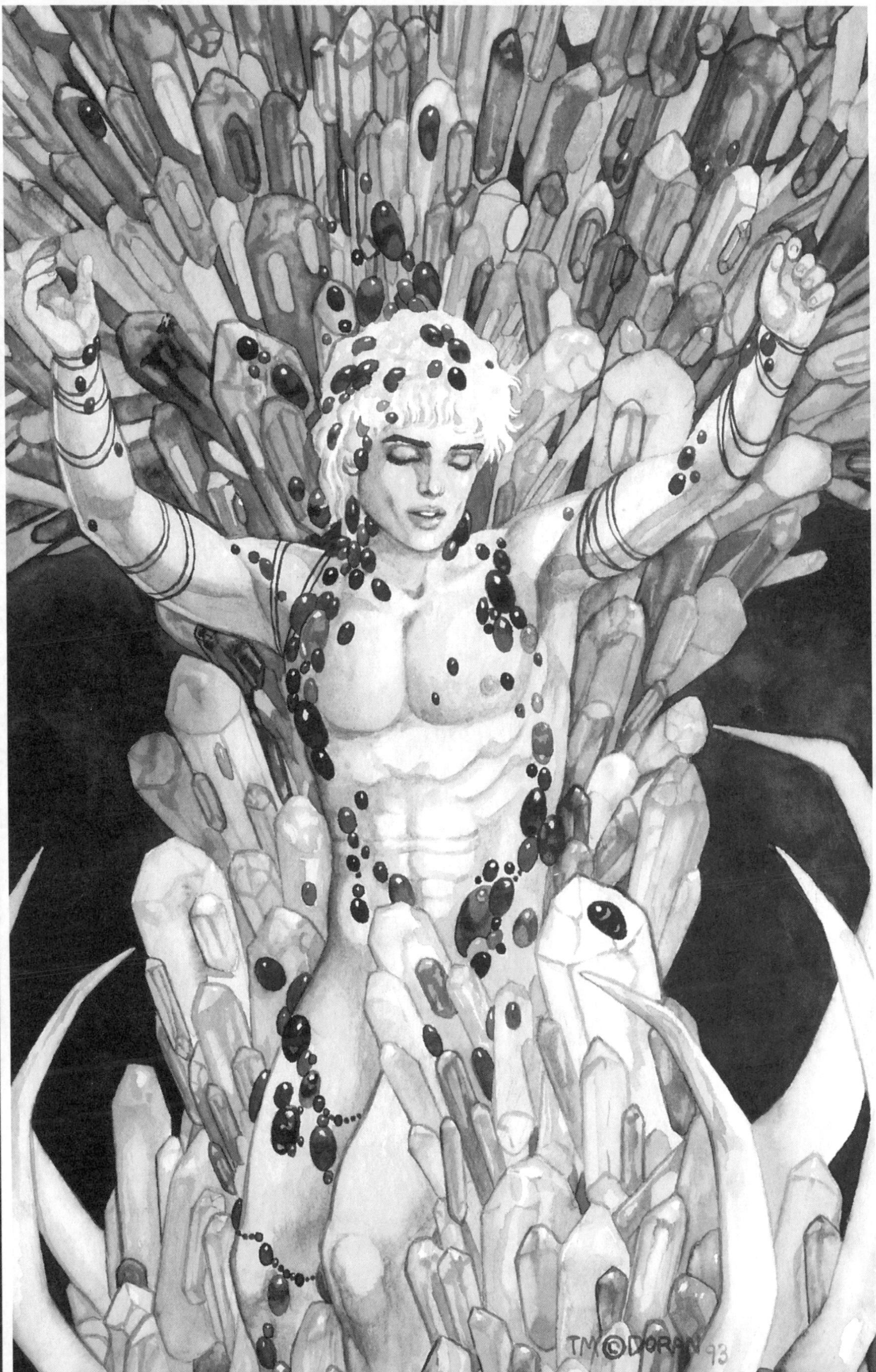
TM©DORAN 93

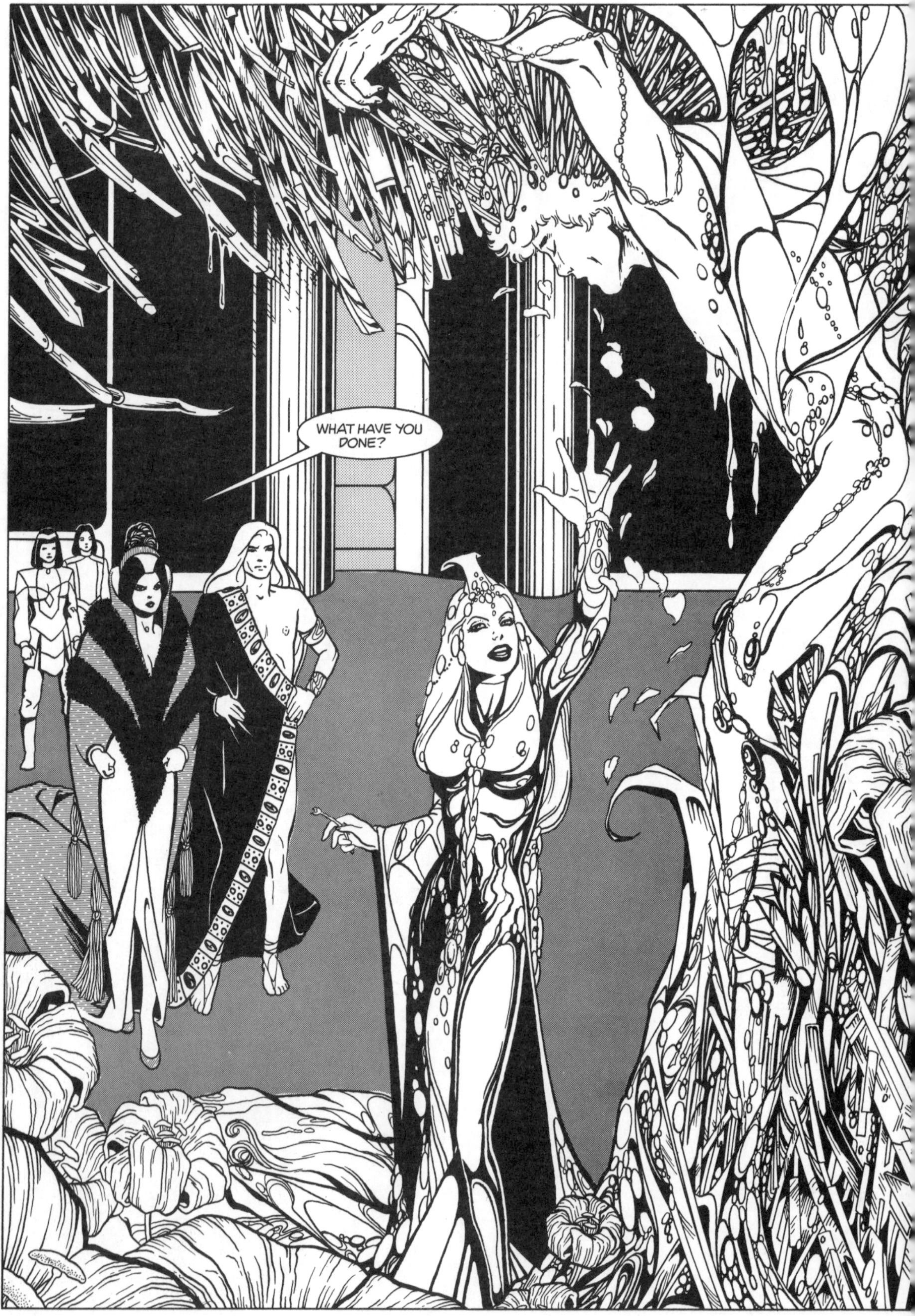
WHAT HAVE YOU DONE?

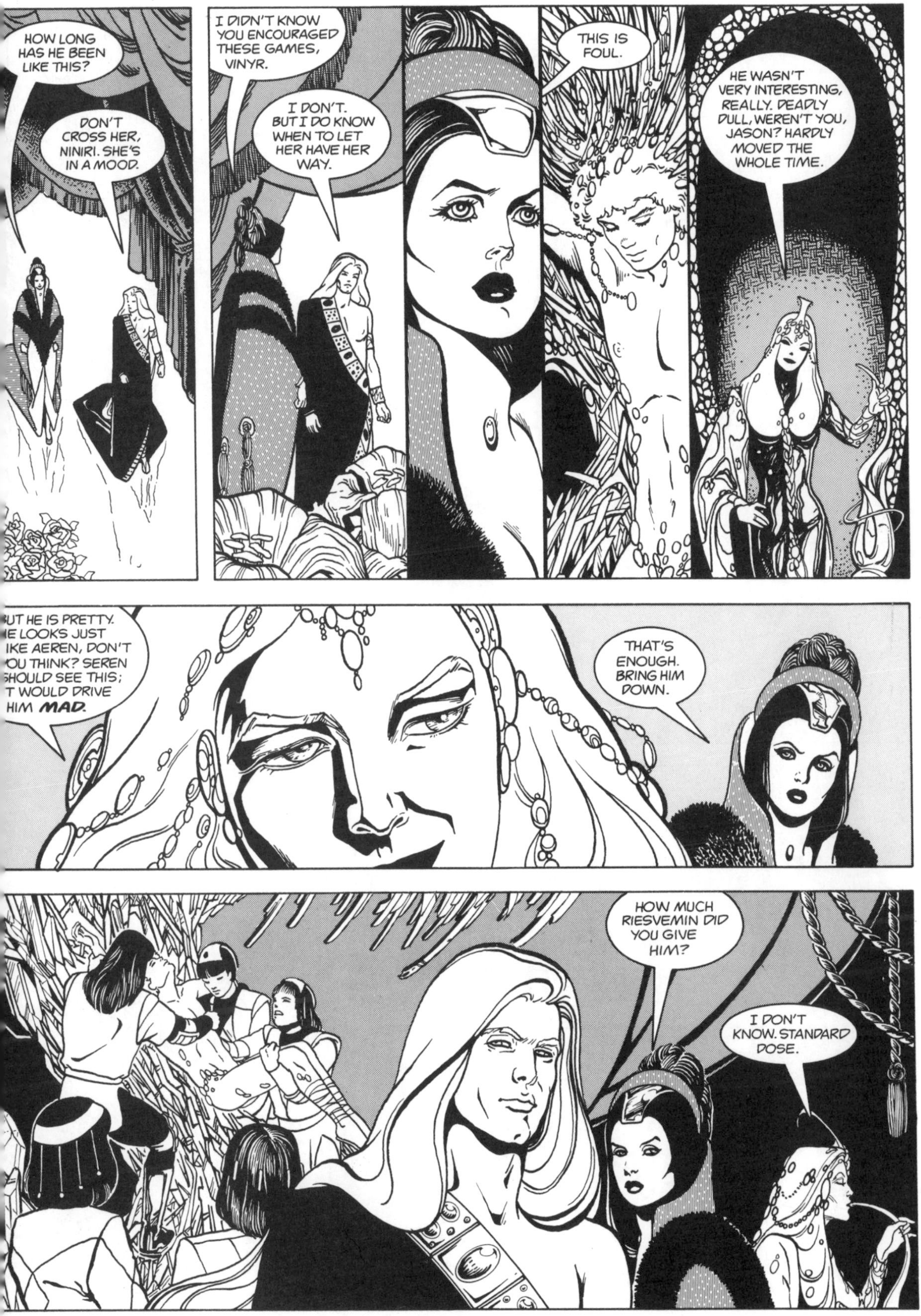
HOW LONG HAS HE BEEN LIKE THIS?
DON'T CROSS HER, NINIRI. SHE'S IN A MOOD.
I DIDN'T KNOW YOU ENCOURAGED THESE GAMES, VINYR.
I DON'T. BUT I DO KNOW WHEN TO LET HER HAVE HER WAY.
THIS IS FOUL.
HE WASN'T VERY INTERESTING, REALLY. DEADLY DULL, WEREN'T YOU, JASON? HARDLY MOVED THE WHOLE TIME.
UT HE IS PRETTY. E LOOKS JUST IKE AEREN, DON'T OU THINK? SEREN SHOULD SEE THIS; T WOULD DRIVE HIM MAD.
THAT'S ENOUGH. BRING HIM DOWN.
HOW MUCH RIESVEMIN DID YOU GIVE HIM?
I DON'T KNOW. STANDARD DOSE.

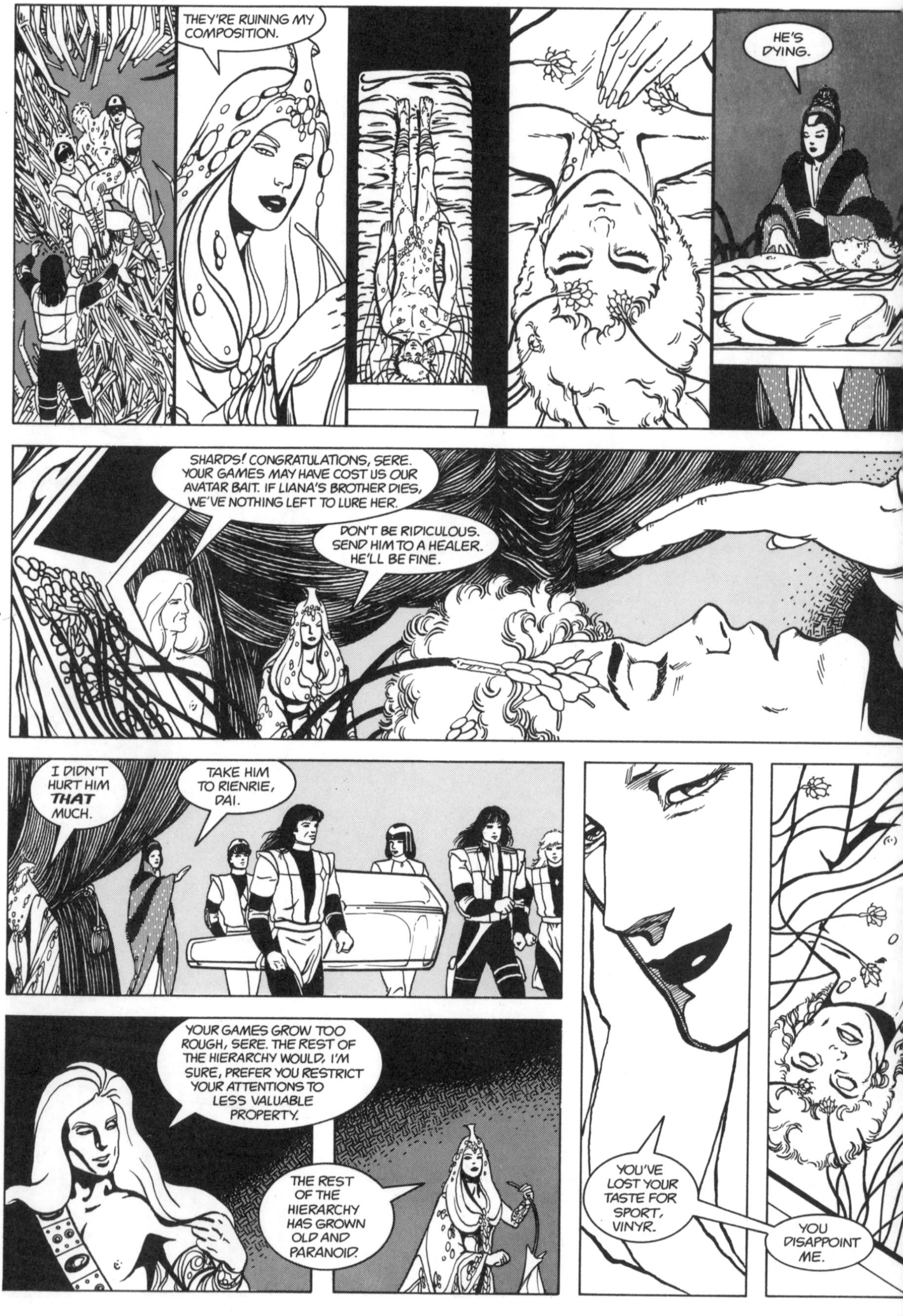
THEY'RE RUINING MY COMPOSITION.
HE'S DYING.
SHARDS! CONGRATULATIONS, SERE. YOUR GAMES MAY HAVE COST US OUR AVATAR BAIT. IF LIANA'S BROTHER DIES, WE'VE NOTHING LEFT TO LURE HER.
DON'T BE RIDICULOUS. SEND HIM TO A HEALER. HE'LL BE FINE.
I DIDN'T HURT HIM THAT MUCH.
TAKE HIM TO RIENRIE, DAI.
YOUR GAMES GROW TOO ROUGH, SERE. THE REST OF THE HIERARCHY WOULD, I'M SURE, PREFER YOU RESTRICT YOUR ATTENTIONS TO LESS VALUABLE PROPERTY.
THE REST OF THE HIERARCHY HAS GROWN OLD AND PARANOID.
YOU'VE LOST YOUR TASTE FOR SPORT, VINYR.
YOU DISAPPOINT ME.

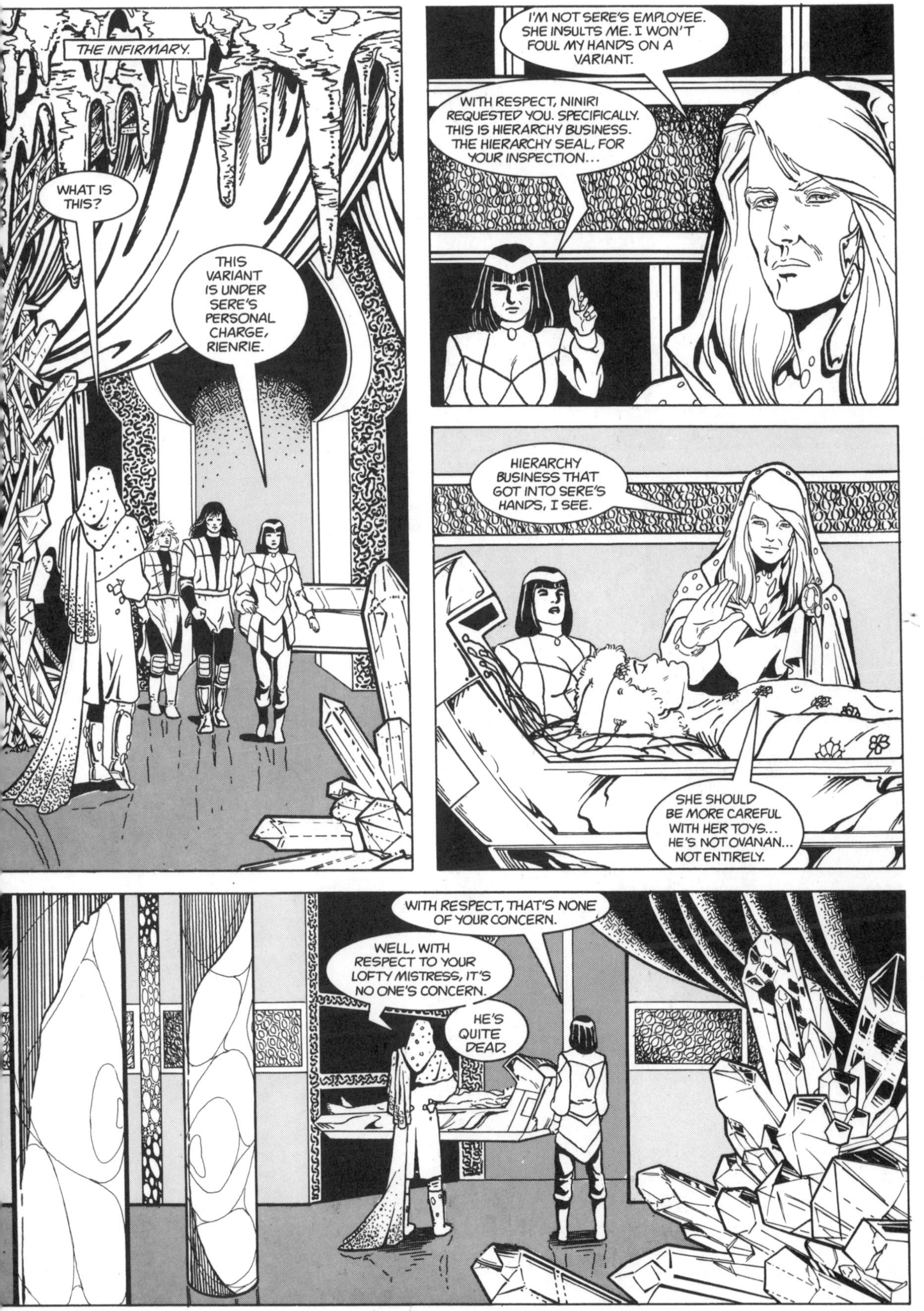
THE INFIRMARY.
WHAT IS THIS?
THIS VARIANT IS UNDER SERE'S PERSONAL CHARGE, RIENRIE.
I'M NOT SERE'S EMPLOYEE. SHE INSULTS ME. I WON'T FOUL MY HANDS ON A VARIANT.
WITH RESPECT, NINIRI REQUESTED YOU. SPECIFICALLY. THIS IS HIERARCHY BUSINESS. THE HIERARCHY SEAL, FOR YOUR INSPECTION...
HIERARCHY BUSINESS THAT GOT INTO SERE'S HANDS, I SEE.
SHE SHOULD BE MORE CAREFUL WITH HER TOYS... HE'S NOT OVANAN... NOT ENTIRELY.
WITH RESPECT, THAT'S NONE OF YOUR CONCERN.
WELL, WITH RESPECT TO YOUR LOFTY MISTRESS, IT'S NO ONE'S CONCERN.
HE'S QUITE DEAD.

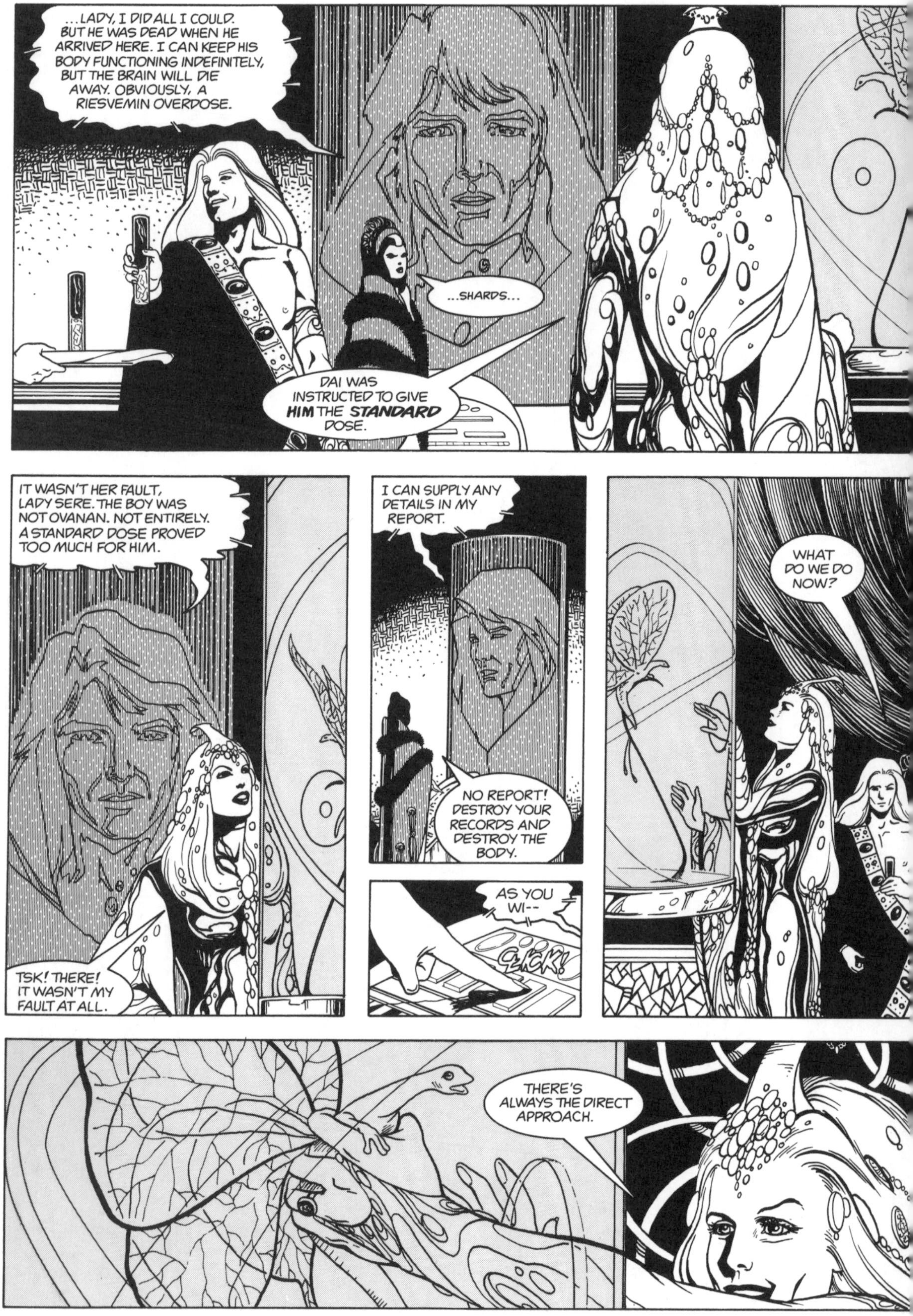
...LADY, I DID ALL I COULD. BUT HE WAS DEAD WHEN HE ARRIVED HERE. I CAN KEEP HIS BODY FUNCTIONING INDEFINITELY, BUT THE BRAIN WILL DIE AWAY. OBVIOUSLY, A RIESVEMIN OVERDOSE.
...SHARDS...
DAI WAS INSTRUCTED TO GIVE HIM THE STANDARD DOSE.
IT WASN'T HER FAULT, LADY SERE. THE BOY WAS NOT OVANAN. NOT ENTIRELY. A STANDARD DOSE PROVED TOO MUCH FOR HIM.
TSK! THERE! IT WASN'T MY FAULT AT ALL.
I CAN SUPPLY ANY DETAILS IN MY REPORT.
NO REPORT! DESTROY YOUR RECORDS AND DESTROY THE BODY.
AS YOU WI--
CLICK!
WHAT DO WE DO NOW?
THERE'S ALWAYS THE DIRECT APPROACH.

NO! I WON'T AUTHORIZE THAT.

NINIRI, OUR SENTRIES HAVEN'T MET WITH MUCH SUCCESS. AND NOW WE'VE LOST OUR LURE. FULL SCALE INVASION MAY BE EXTREME, BUT HOW LONG CAN WE WAIT? AS LONG AS THE GIRL REMAINS ALIVE, OVANAN IS VULNERABLE.

NO. WE WAIT. IT'S ONLY ONE YOUNG GIRL. SHE CAN'T ELUDE OUR SENTRIES FOREVER.

YOU'RE RIGHT. I ENJOY A GOOD CHASE. LET'S WAIT AND SEE WHAT HAPPENS, VINYR. GOOD SPORT!

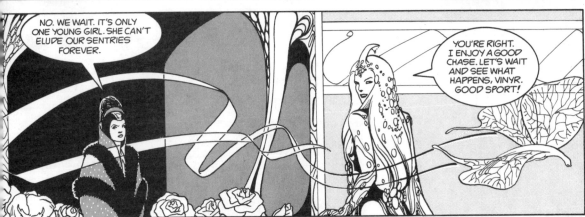

THIS SHOULD LIVEN THINGS.

ANOTHER GAME, SERE? THIS ONE IS, PERHAPS, TOO DANGEROUS. EVEN FOR YOU.

THEN PERHAPS THIS GAME WILL BE THE MOST FUN OF ALL.

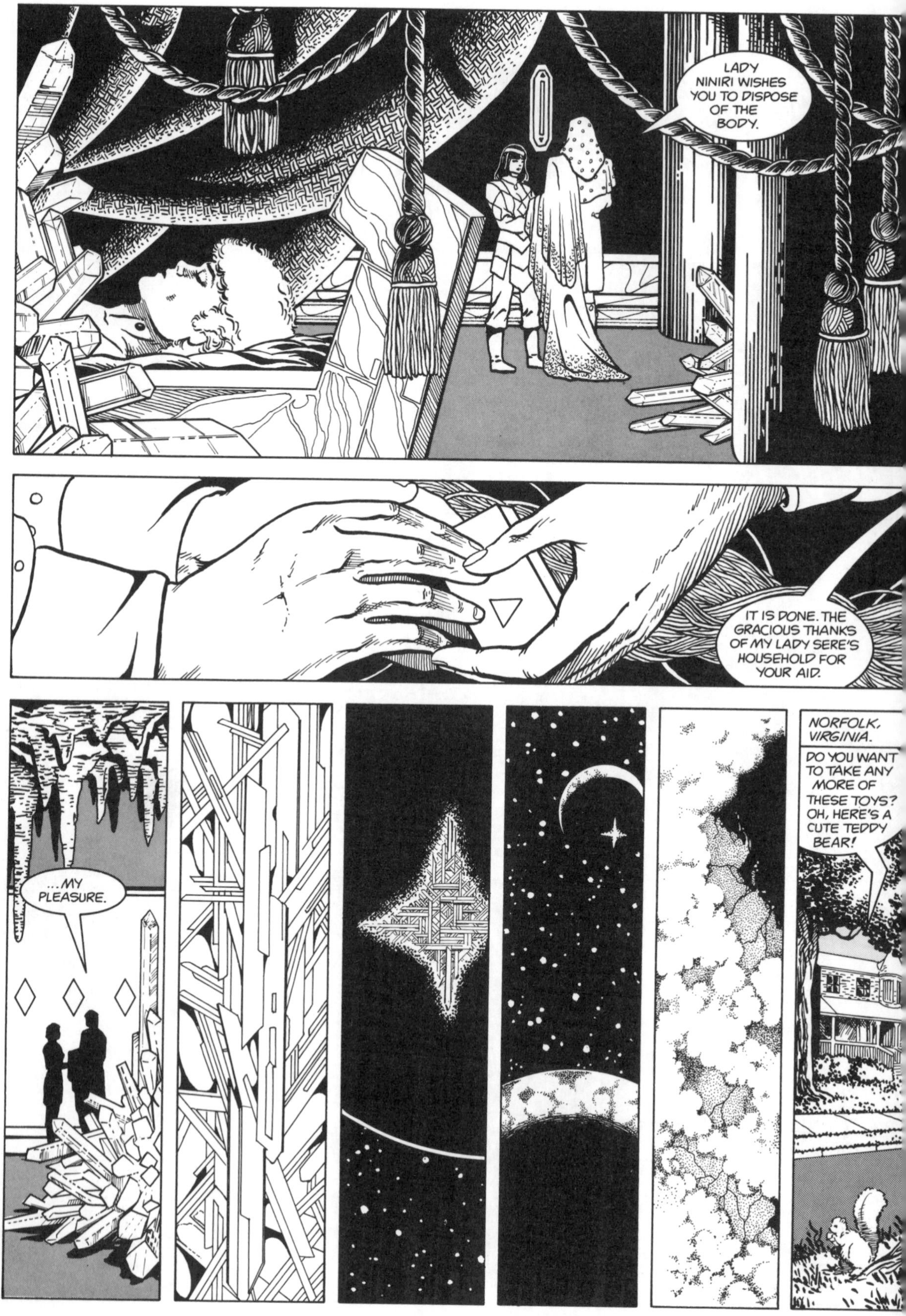
LADY NINIRI WISHES YOU TO DISPOSE OF THE BODY.
IT IS DONE. THE GRACIOUS THANKS OF MY LADY SERE'S HOUSEHOLD FOR YOUR AID.
...MY PLEASURE.
NORFOLK, VIRGINIA.
DO YOU WANT TO TAKE ANY MORE OF THESE TOYS? OH, HERE'S A CUTE TEDDY BEAR!

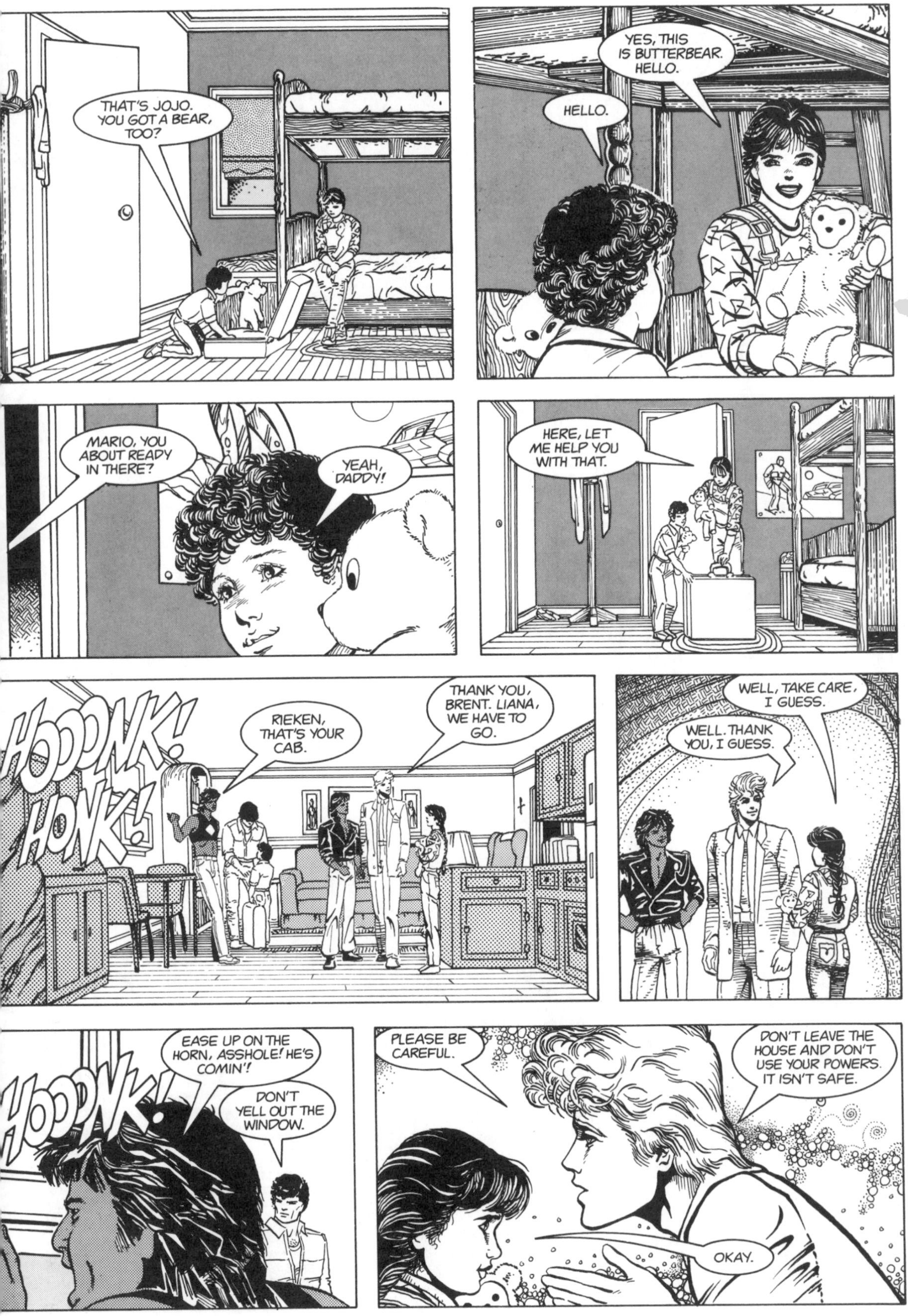
THAT'S JOJO. YOU GOT A BEAR, TOO?
YES, THIS IS BUTTERBEAR. HELLO.
HELLO.
MARIO, YOU ABOUT READY IN THERE?
YEAH, DADDY!
HERE, LET ME HELP YOU WITH THAT.
HOOONK! HONK!
RIEKEN, THAT'S YOUR CAB.
THANK YOU, BRENT. LIANA, WE HAVE TO GO.
WELL, TAKE CARE, I GUESS.
WELL. THANK YOU, I GUESS.
HOOONK!
EASE UP ON THE HORN, ASSHOLE! HE'S COMIN'!
DON'T YELL OUT THE WINDOW.
PLEASE BE CAREFUL.
DON'T LEAVE THE HOUSE AND DON'T USE YOUR POWERS. IT ISN'T SAFE.
OKAY.

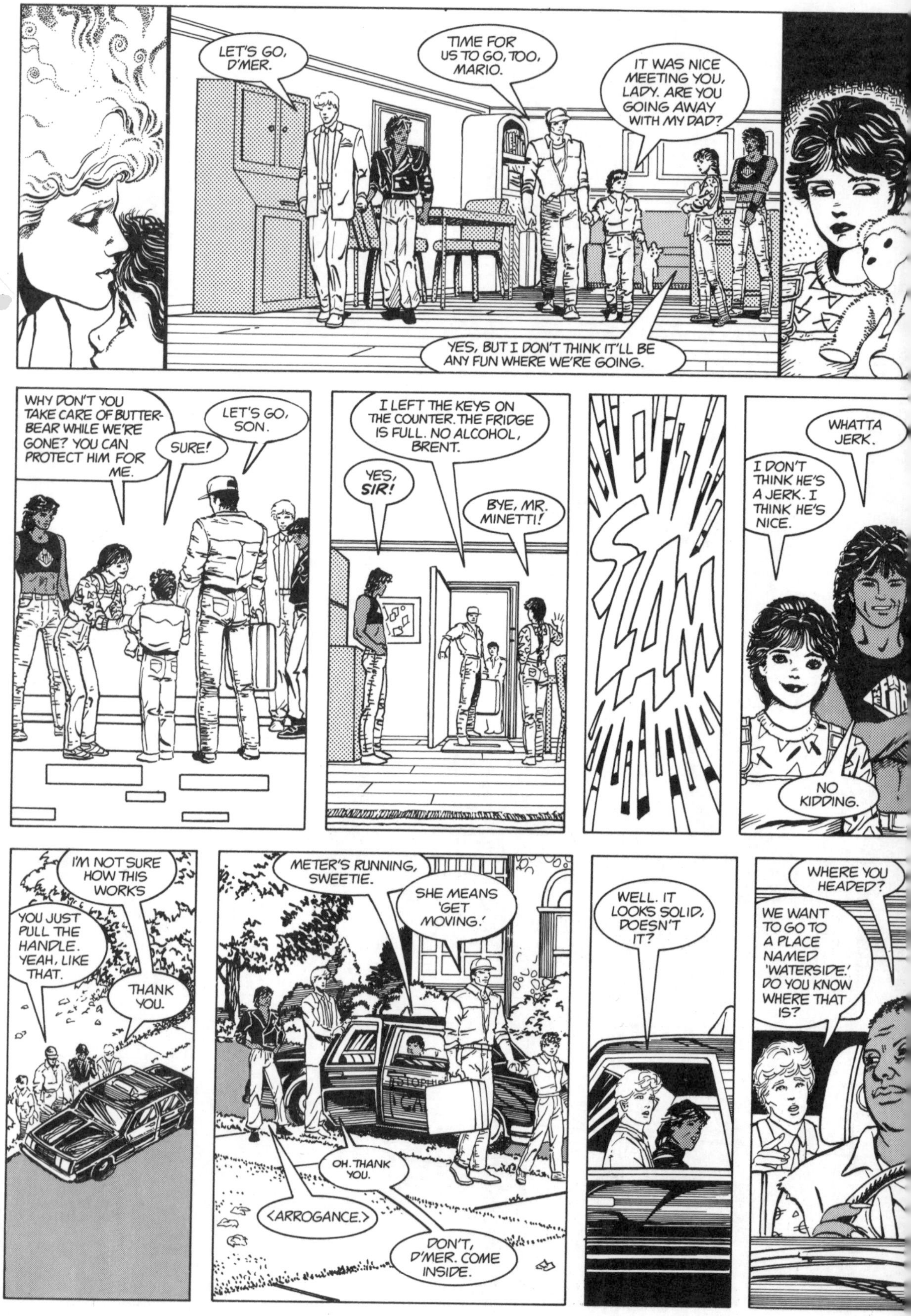
LET'S GO, D'MER.
TIME FOR US TO GO, TOO, MARIO.
IT WAS NICE MEETING YOU, LADY. ARE YOU GOING AWAY WITH MY DAD?
YES, BUT I DON'T THINK IT'LL BE ANY FUN WHERE WE'RE GOING.
WHY DON'T YOU TAKE CARE OF BUTTER-BEAR WHILE WE'RE GONE? YOU CAN PROTECT HIM FOR ME.
SURE!
LET'S GO, SON.
I LEFT THE KEYS ON THE COUNTER. THE FRIDGE IS FULL. NO ALCOHOL, BRENT.
YES, SIR!
BYE, MR. MINETTI!
SLAM
WHATTA JERK.
I DON'T THINK HE'S A JERK. I THINK HE'S NICE.
NO KIDDING.
I'M NOT SURE HOW THIS WORKS
YOU JUST PULL THE HANDLE. YEAH, LIKE THAT.
THANK YOU.
METER'S RUNNING, SWEETIE.
SHE MEANS 'GET MOVING.'
OH. THANK YOU.
<ARROGANCE.>
DON'T, D'MER. COME INSIDE.
WELL. IT LOOKS SOLID, DOESN'T IT?
WHERE YOU HEADED?
WE WANT TO GO TO A PLACE NAMED 'WATERSIDE.' DO YOU KNOW WHERE THAT IS?

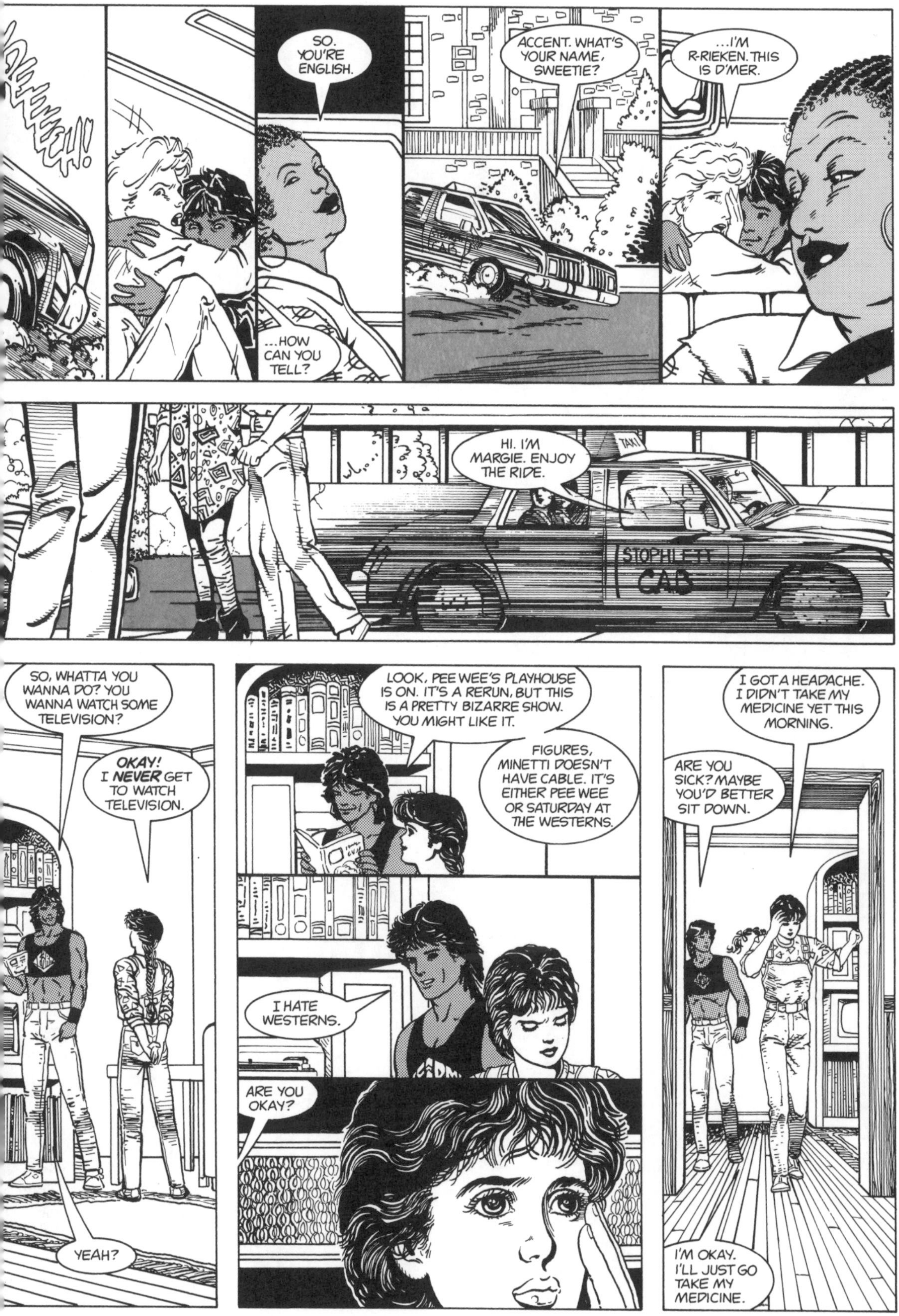
SKREEEECH!
SO. YOU'RE ENGLISH.
...HOW CAN YOU TELL?
ACCENT. WHAT'S YOUR NAME, SWEETIE?
...I'M R-RIEKEN. THIS IS D'MER.
TAXI
HI. I'M MARGIE. ENJOY THE RIDE.
STOPHLETT CAB
SO, WHATTA YOU WANNA DO? YOU WANNA WATCH SOME TELEVISION?
OKAY! I NEVER GET TO WATCH TELEVISION.
YEAH?
LOOK, PEE WEE'S PLAYHOUSE IS ON. IT'S A RERUN, BUT THIS IS A PRETTY BIZARRE SHOW. YOU MIGHT LIKE IT.
FIGURES, MINETTI DOESN'T HAVE CABLE. IT'S EITHER PEE WEE OR SATURDAY AT THE WESTERNS.
I HATE WESTERNS.
ARE YOU OKAY?
I GOT A HEADACHE. I DIDN'T TAKE MY MEDICINE YET THIS MORNING.
ARE YOU SICK? MAYBE YOU'D BETTER SIT DOWN.
I'M OKAY. I'LL JUST GO TAKE MY MEDICINE.

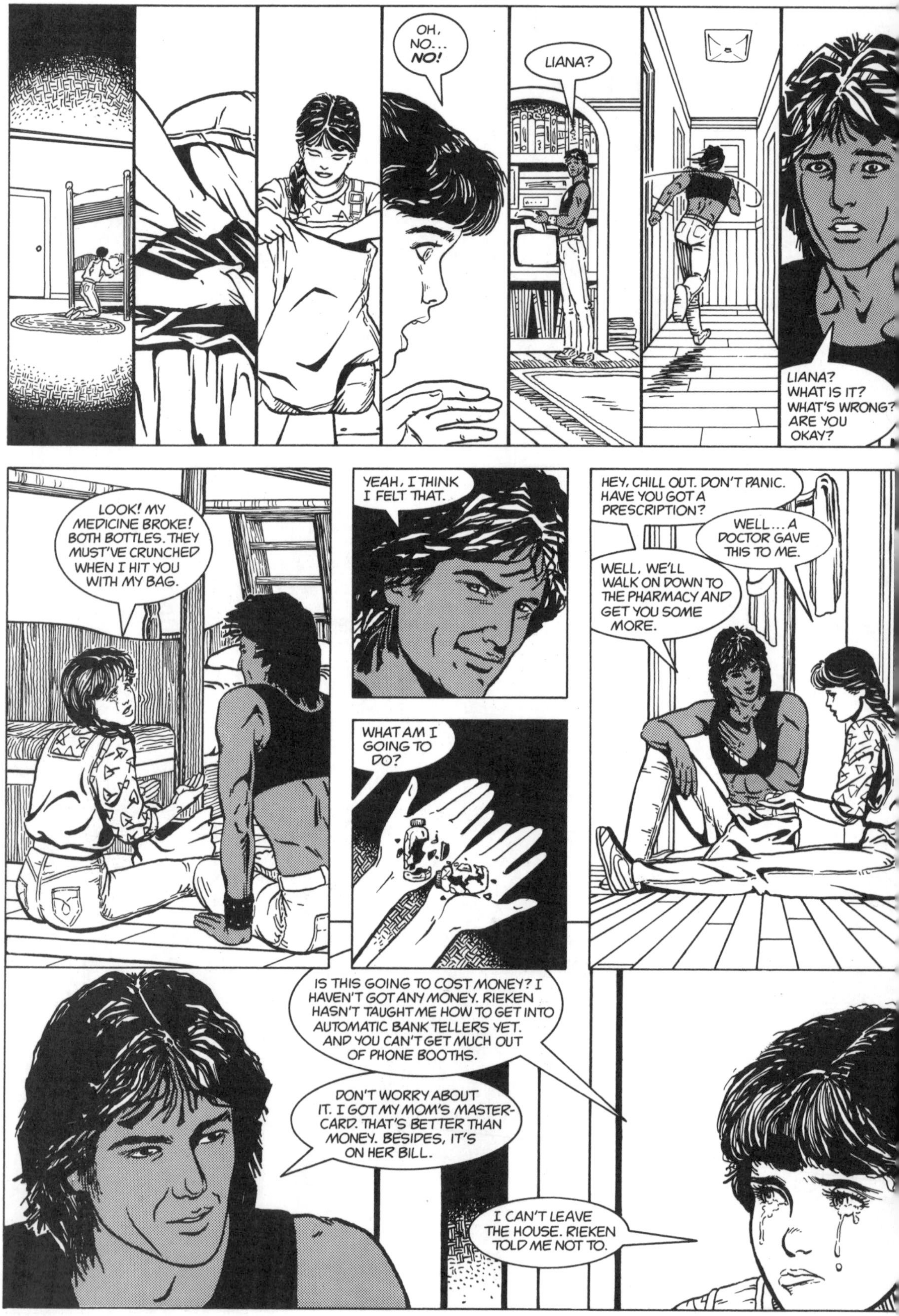
OH, NO... **NO!**
LIANA?
LIANA? WHAT IS IT? WHAT'S WRONG? ARE YOU OKAY?
LOOK! MY MEDICINE BROKE! BOTH BOTTLES. THEY MUST'VE CRUNCHED WHEN I HIT YOU WITH MY BAG.
YEAH, I THINK I FELT THAT.
WHAT AM I GOING TO DO?
HEY, CHILL OUT. DON'T PANIC. HAVE YOU GOT A PRESCRIPTION?
WELL... A DOCTOR GAVE THIS TO ME.
WELL, WE'LL WALK ON DOWN TO THE PHARMACY AND GET YOU SOME MORE.
IS THIS GOING TO COST MONEY? I HAVEN'T GOT ANY MONEY. RIEKEN HASN'T TAUGHT ME HOW TO GET INTO AUTOMATIC BANK TELLERS YET. AND YOU CAN'T GET MUCH OUT OF PHONE BOOTHS.
DON'T WORRY ABOUT IT. I GOT MY MOM'S MASTER-CARD. THAT'S BETTER THAN MONEY. BESIDES, IT'S ON HER BILL.
I CAN'T LEAVE THE HOUSE. RIEKEN TOLD ME NOT TO.

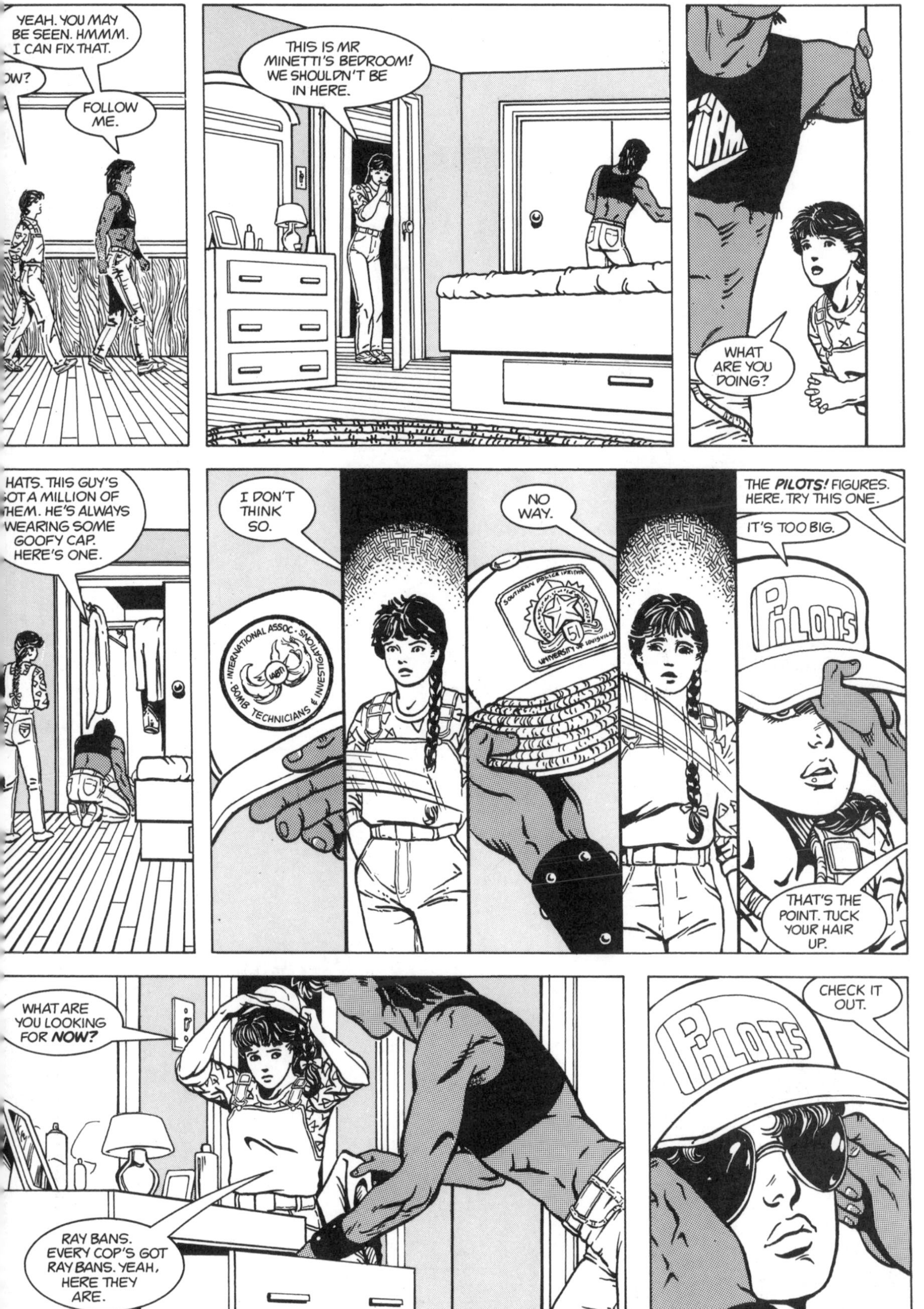
YEAH. YOU MAY BE SEEN. HMMM. I CAN FIX THAT.
OW?
FOLLOW ME.
THIS IS MR MINETTI'S BEDROOM! WE SHOULDN'T BE IN HERE.
WHAT ARE YOU DOING?
HATS. THIS GUY'S OT A MILLION OF HEM. HE'S ALWAYS WEARING SOME GOOFY CAP. HERE'S ONE.
I DON'T THINK SO.
INTERNATIONAL ASSOC. BOMB TECHNICIANS & INVESTIGATIONS
NO WAY.
THE PILOTS! FIGURES. HERE, TRY THIS ONE.
IT'S TOO BIG.
PILOTS
THAT'S THE POINT. TUCK YOUR HAIR UP.
WHAT ARE YOU LOOKING FOR NOW?
RAY BANS. EVERY COP'S GOT RAY BANS. YEAH, HERE THEY ARE.
CHECK IT OUT.
PILOTS

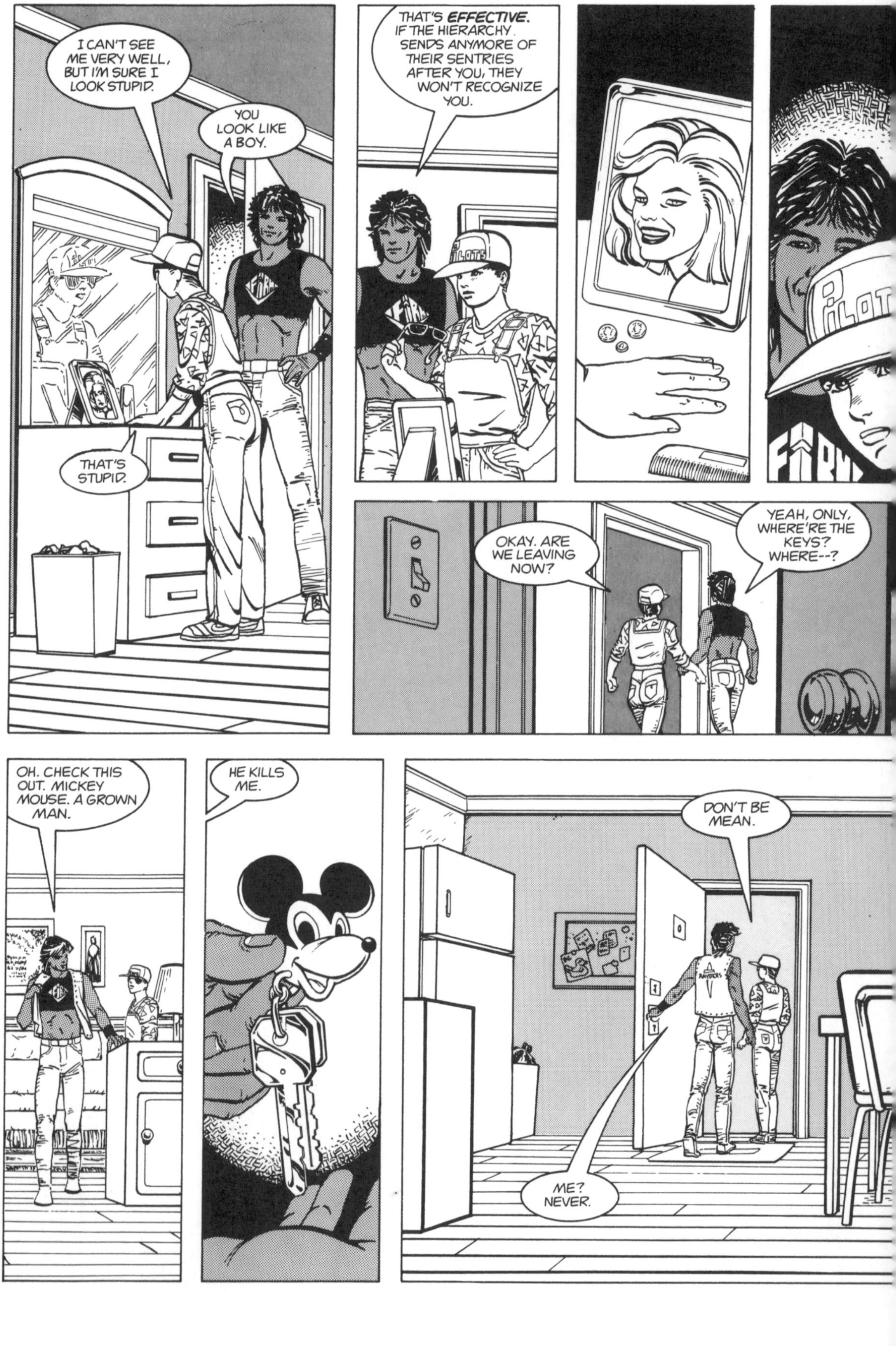
I CAN'T SEE ME VERY WELL, BUT I'M SURE I LOOK STUPID.
YOU LOOK LIKE A BOY.
THAT'S STUPID.
THAT'S *EFFECTIVE.* IF THE HIERARCHY SENDS ANYMORE OF THEIR SENTRIES AFTER YOU, THEY WON'T RECOGNIZE YOU.
OKAY. ARE WE LEAVING NOW?
YEAH, ONLY, WHERE'RE THE KEYS? WHERE--?
OH. CHECK THIS OUT. MICKEY MOUSE. A GROWN MAN.
HE KILLS ME.
DON'T BE MEAN.
ME? NEVER.

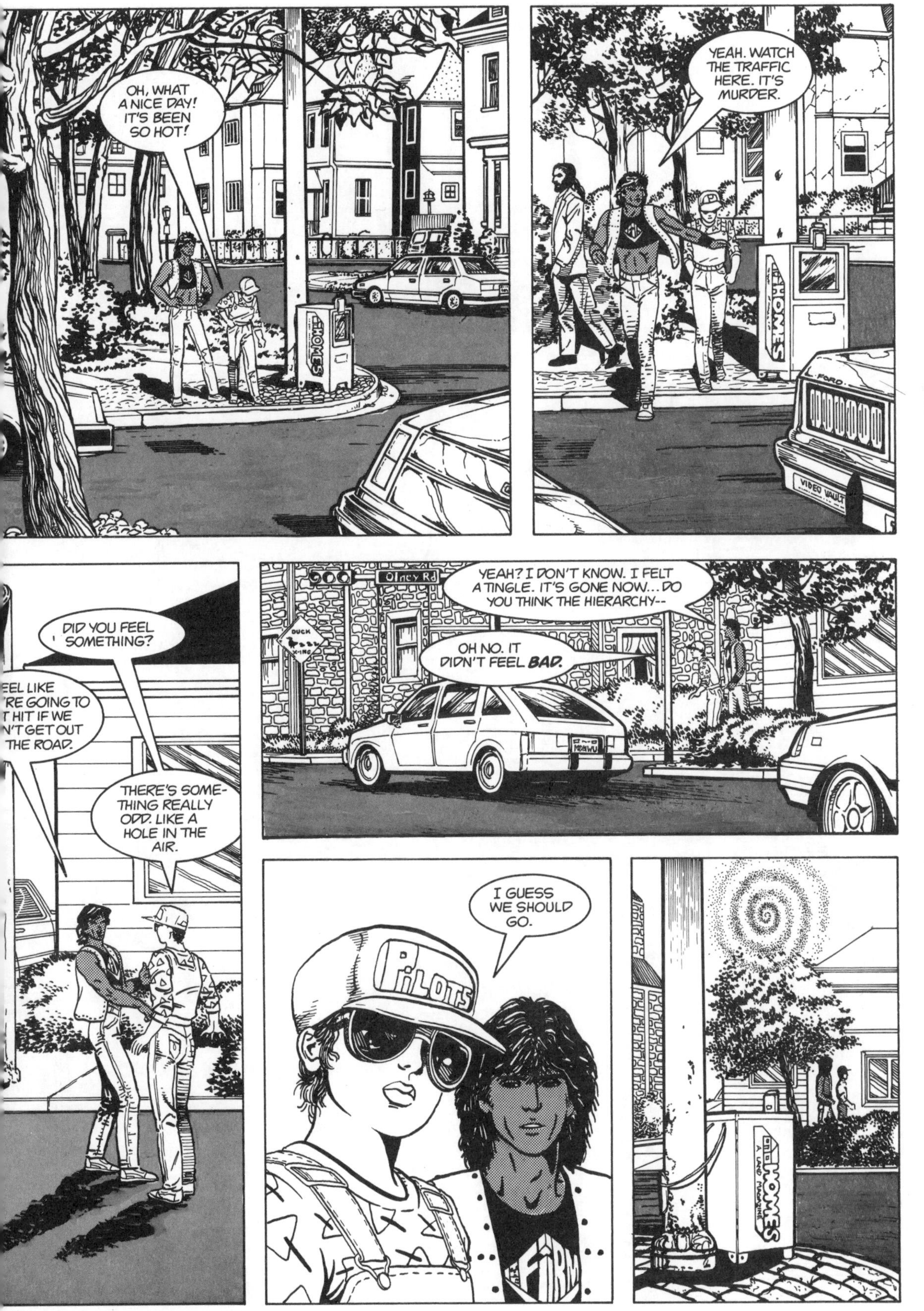
OH, WHAT A NICE DAY! IT'S BEEN SO HOT!
YEAH. WATCH THE TRAFFIC HERE. IT'S MURDER.
DID YOU FEEL SOMETHING?
EEL LIKE 'RE GOING TO T HIT IF WE N'T GET OUT THE ROAD.
THERE'S SOMETHING REALLY ODD. LIKE A HOLE IN THE AIR.
YEAH? I DON'T KNOW. I FELT A TINGLE. IT'S GONE NOW... DO YOU THINK THE HIERARCHY--
OH NO. IT DIDN'T FEEL **BAD.**
I GUESS WE SHOULD GO.

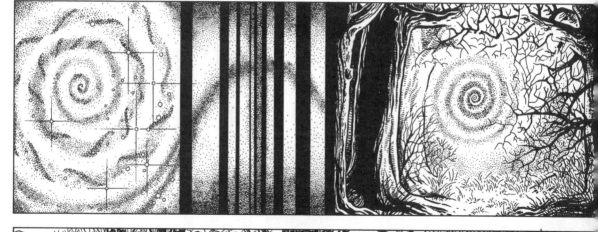

AVALON.

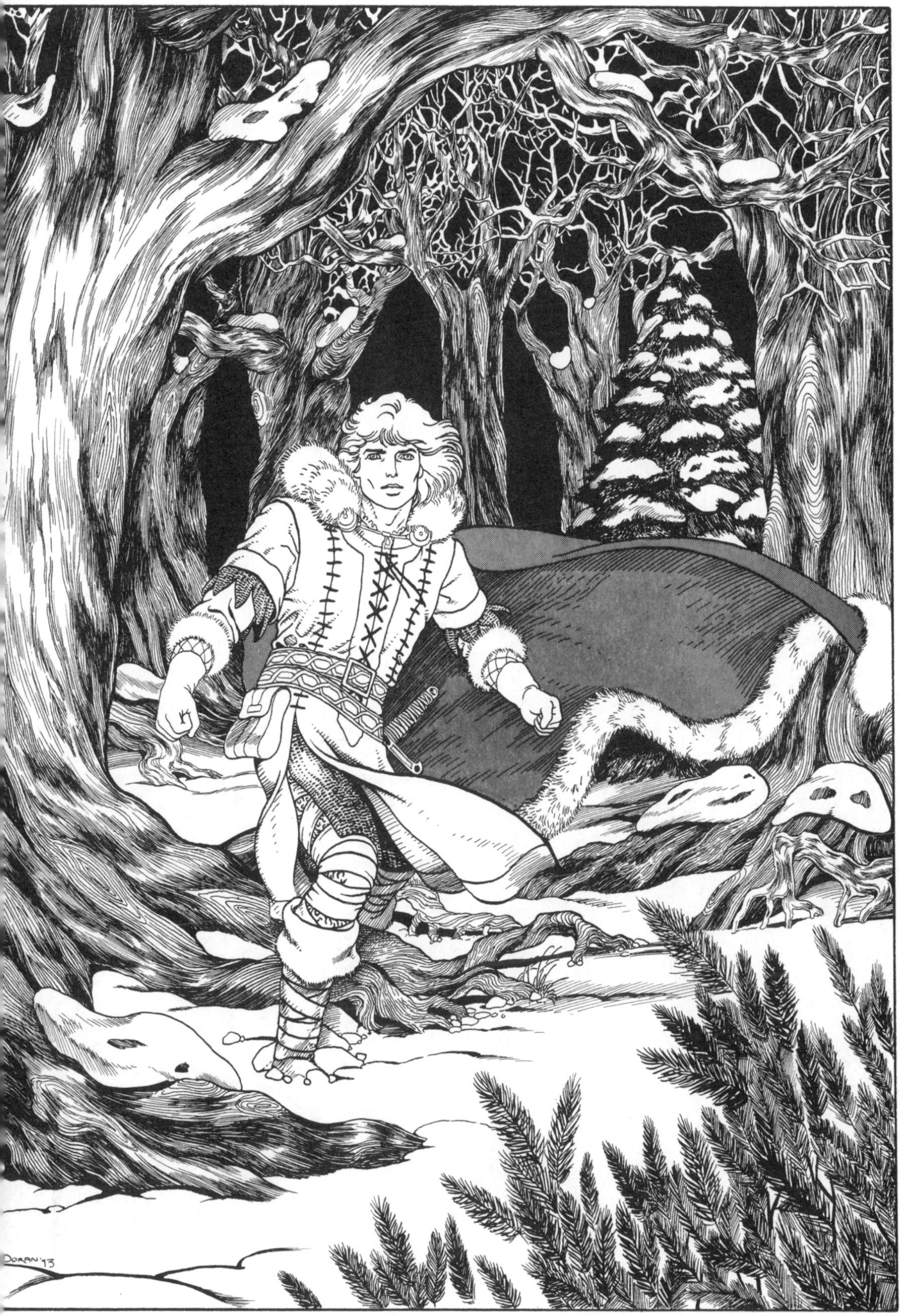
DORAN '93

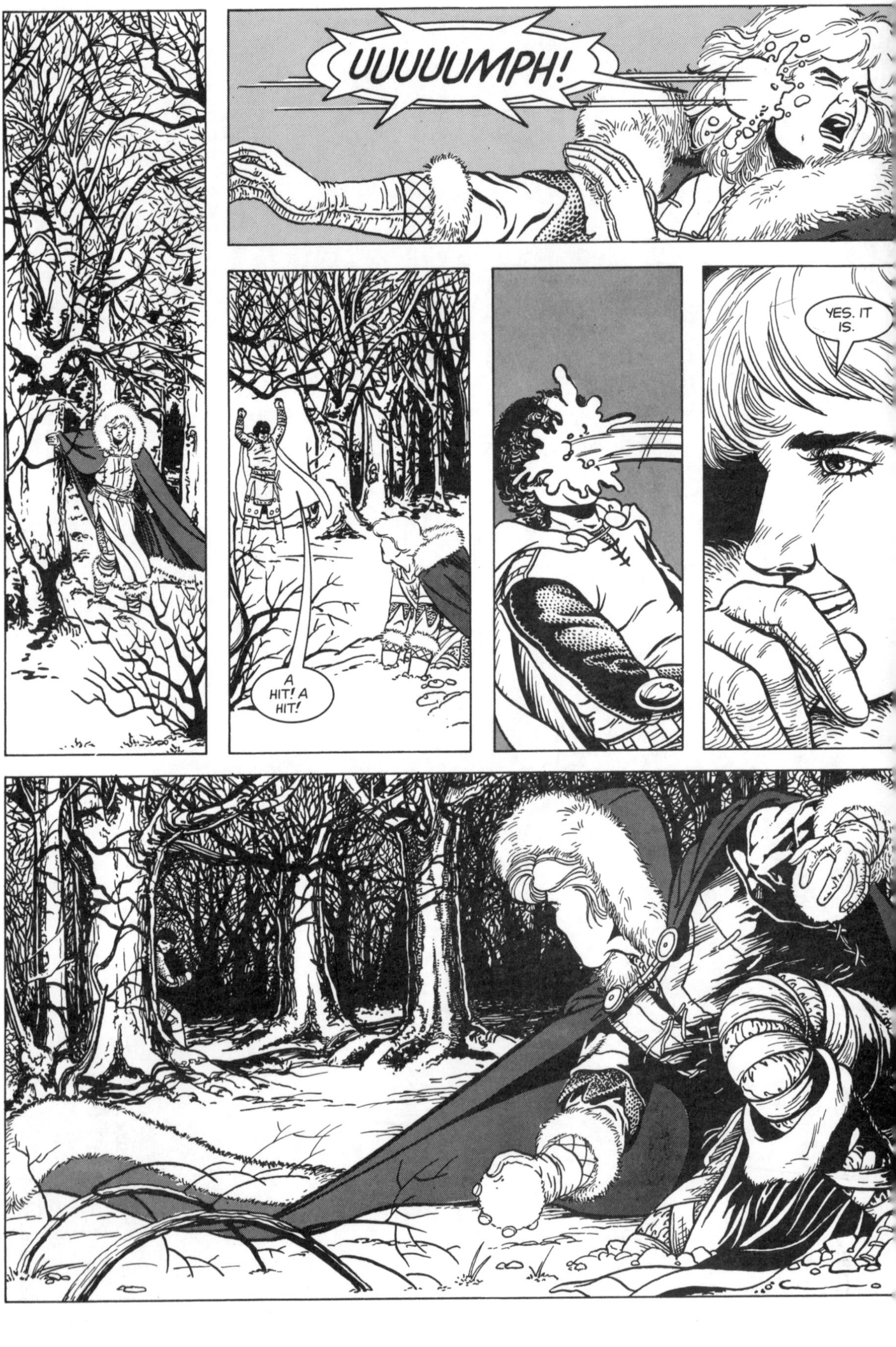
UUUUUMPH!
A HIT! A HIT!
YES. IT IS.

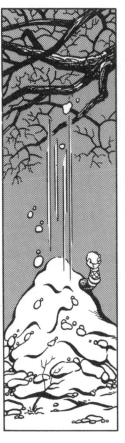

READY TO GIVE UP, PERCIVAL?

NO, YOU TOAD!

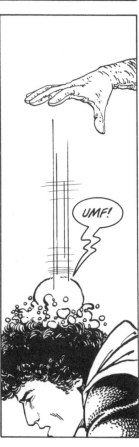

UMF!

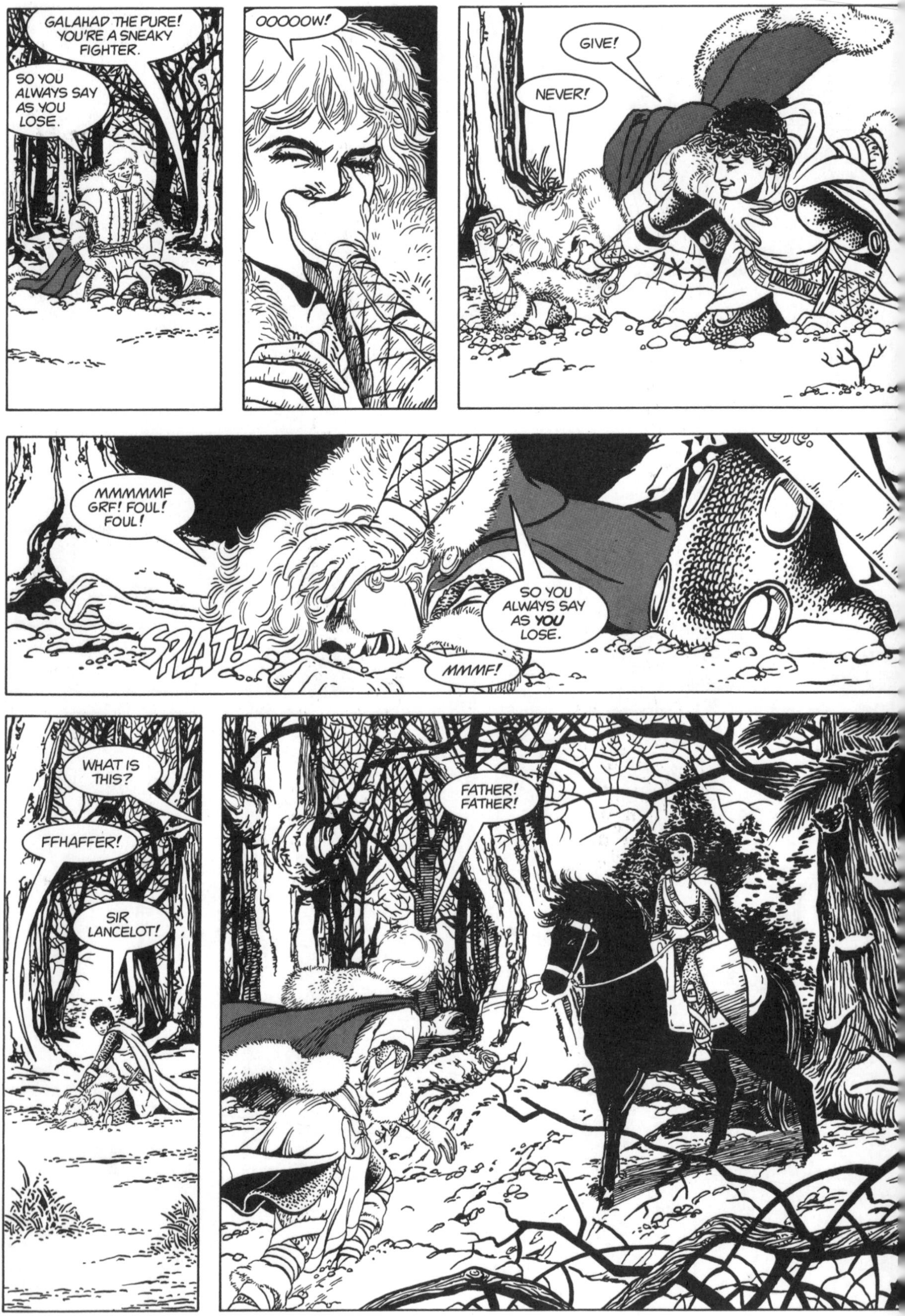

GALAHAD THE PURE! YOU'RE A SNEAKY FIGHTER.
SO YOU ALWAYS SAY AS YOU LOSE.
OOOOOW!
GIVE!
NEVER!
MMMMMF GRF! FOUL! FOUL!
SPLAT!
SO YOU ALWAYS SAY AS **YOU** LOSE.
MMMF!
WHAT IS THIS?
FFHAFFER!
SIR LANCELOT!
FATHER! FATHER!

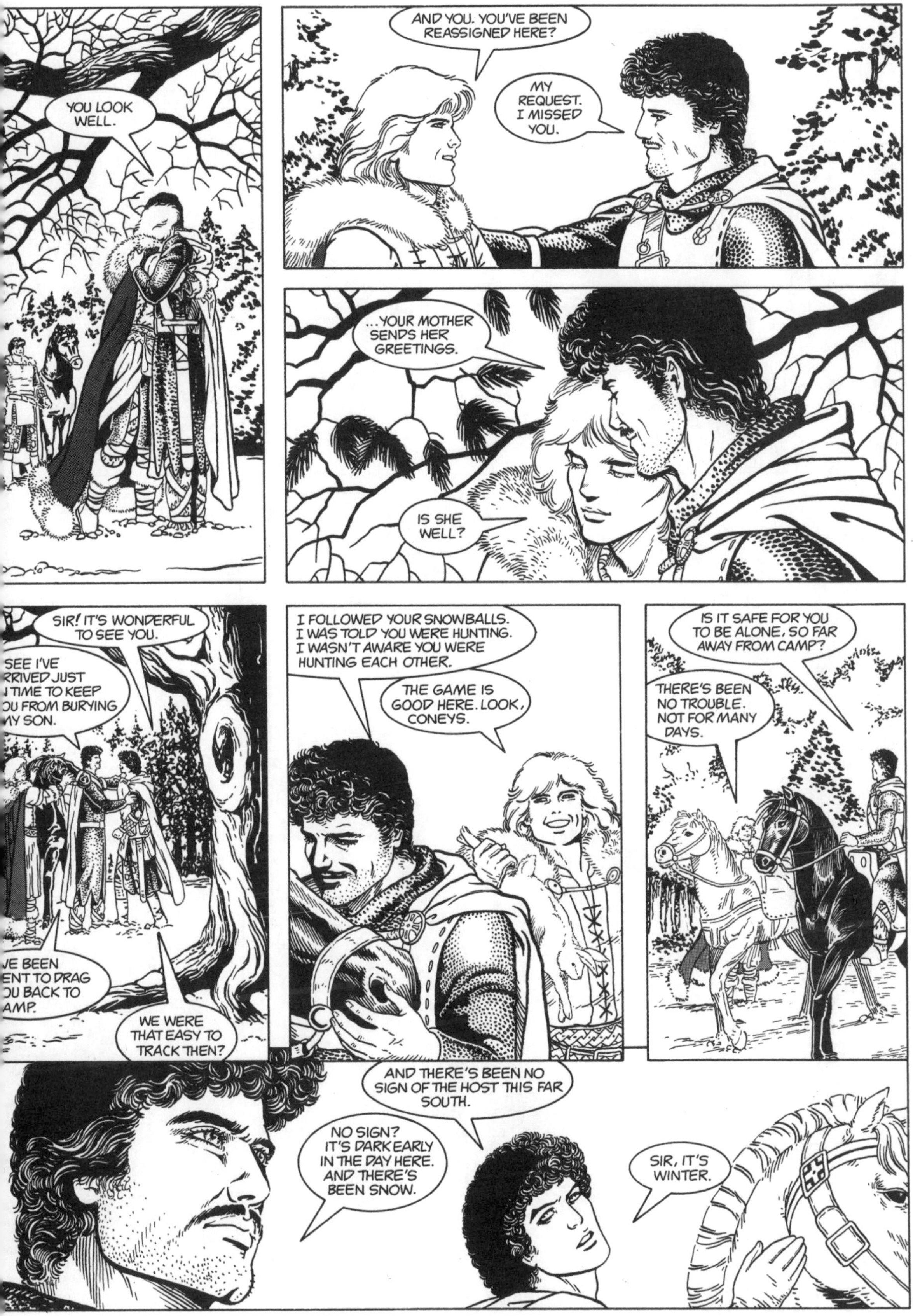
YOU LOOK WELL.
AND YOU. YOU'VE BEEN REASSIGNED HERE?
MY REQUEST. I MISSED YOU.
...YOUR MOTHER SENDS HER GREETINGS.
IS SHE WELL?
SIR! IT'S WONDERFUL TO SEE YOU.
SEE I'VE RRIVED JUST N TIME TO KEEP OU FROM BURYING MY SON.
VE BEEN ENT TO DRAG OU BACK TO AMP.
WE WERE THAT EASY TO TRACK THEN?
I FOLLOWED YOUR SNOWBALLS. I WAS TOLD YOU WERE HUNTING. I WASN'T AWARE YOU WERE HUNTING EACH OTHER.
THE GAME IS GOOD HERE. LOOK, CONEYS.
IS IT SAFE FOR YOU TO BE ALONE, SO FAR AWAY FROM CAMP?
THERE'S BEEN NO TROUBLE. NOT FOR MANY DAYS.
AND THERE'S BEEN NO SIGN OF THE HOST THIS FAR SOUTH.
NO SIGN? IT'S DARK EARLY IN THE DAY HERE. AND THERE'S BEEN SNOW.
SIR, IT'S WINTER.

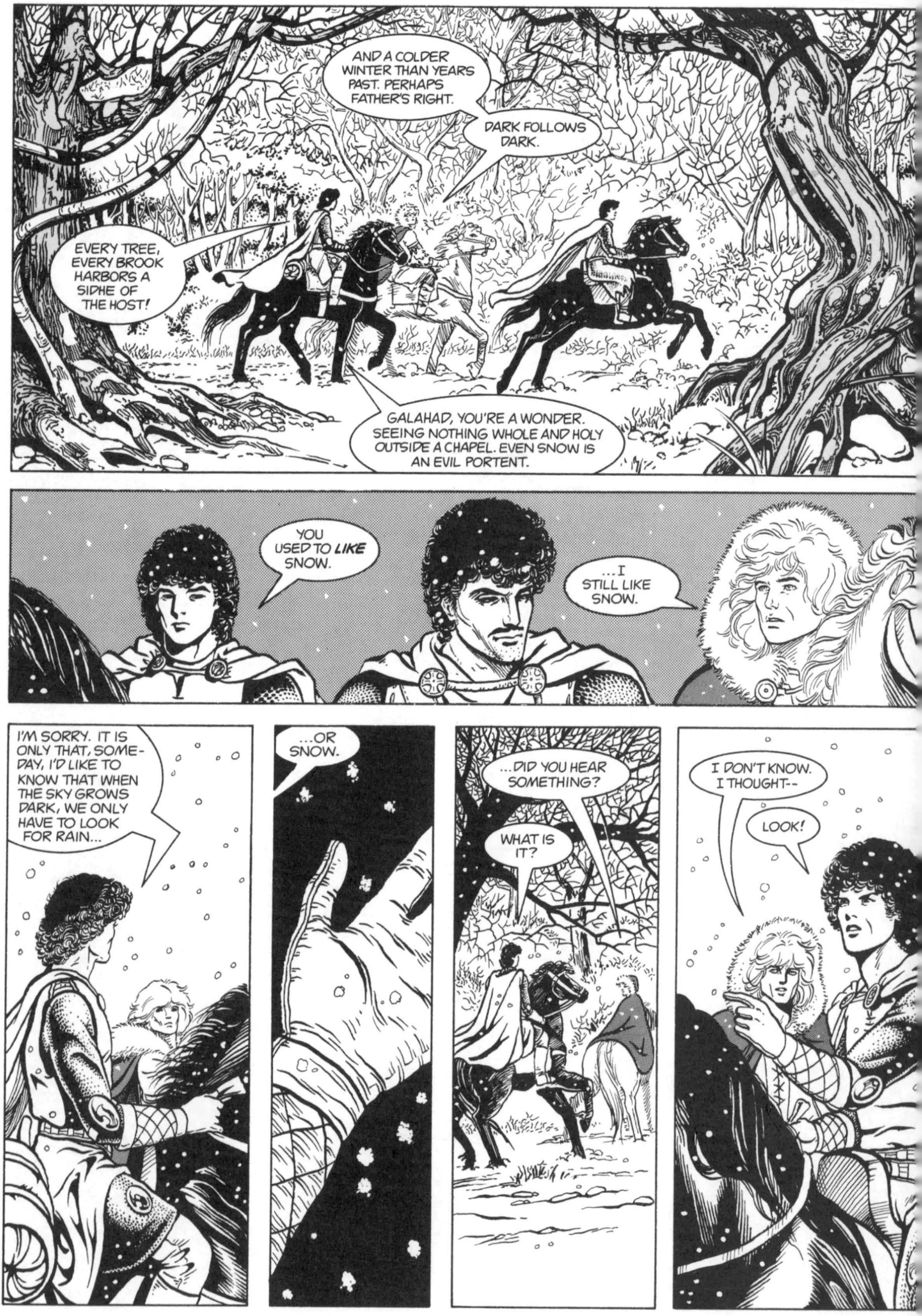
AND A COLDER WINTER THAN YEARS PAST. PERHAPS FATHER'S RIGHT.
DARK FOLLOWS DARK.
EVERY TREE, EVERY BROOK HARBORS A SIDHE OF THE HOST!
GALAHAD, YOU'RE A WONDER. SEEING NOTHING WHOLE AND HOLY OUTSIDE A CHAPEL. EVEN SNOW IS AN EVIL PORTENT.
YOU USED TO LIKE SNOW.
...I STILL LIKE SNOW.
I'M SORRY. IT IS ONLY THAT, SOME-DAY, I'D LIKE TO KNOW THAT WHEN THE SKY GROWS DARK, WE ONLY HAVE TO LOOK FOR RAIN...
...OR SNOW.
...DID YOU HEAR SOMETHING?
WHAT IS IT?
I DON'T KNOW. I THOUGHT--
LOOK!

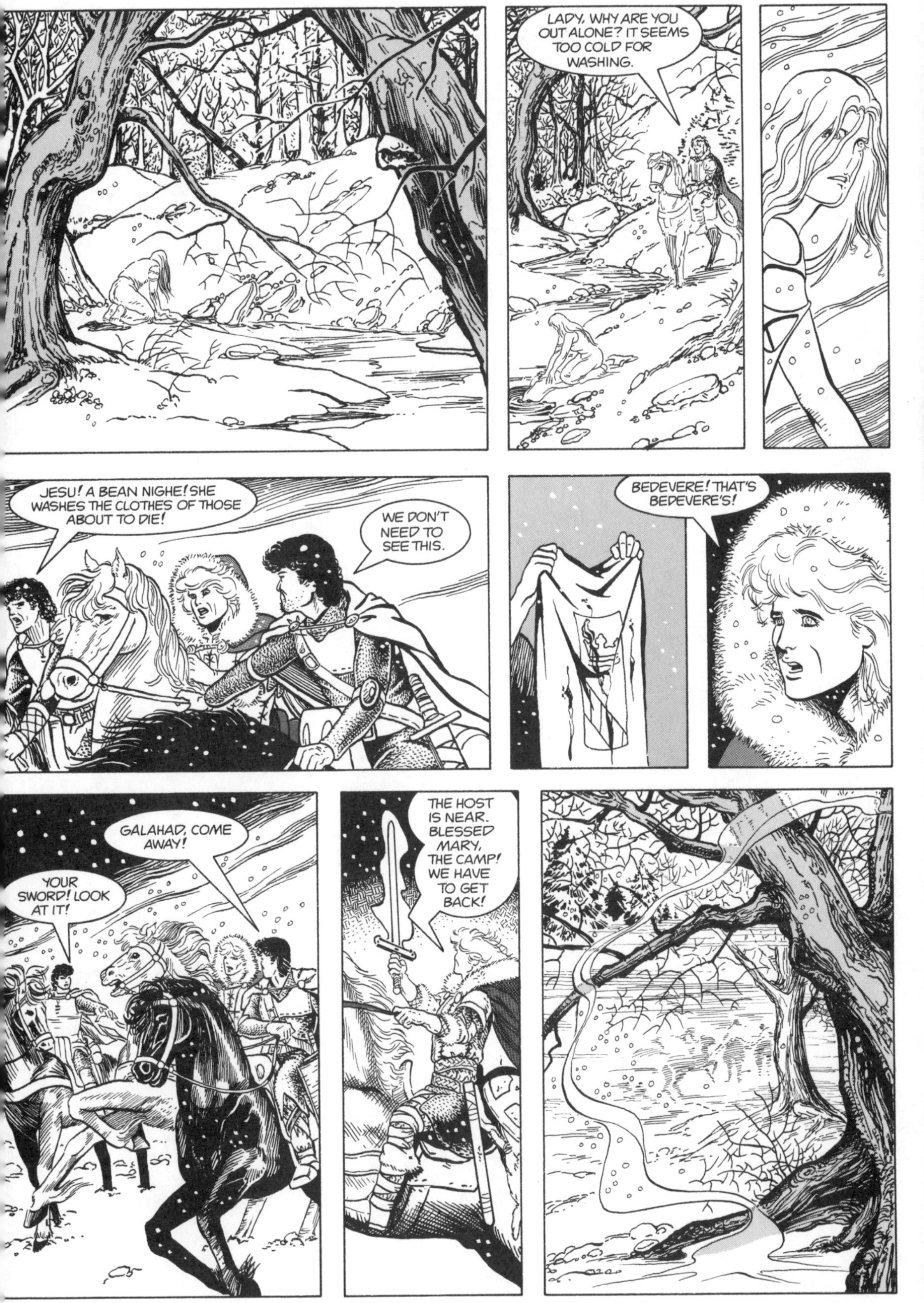
LADY, WHY ARE YOU OUT ALONE? IT SEEMS TOO COLD FOR WASHING.
JESU! A BEAN NIGHE! SHE WASHES THE CLOTHES OF THOSE ABOUT TO DIE!
WE DON'T NEED TO SEE THIS.
BEDEVERE! THAT'S BEDEVERE'S!
GALAHAD, COME AWAY!
YOUR SWORD! LOOK AT IT!
THE HOST IS NEAR. BLESSED MARY, THE CAMP! WE HAVE TO GET BACK!

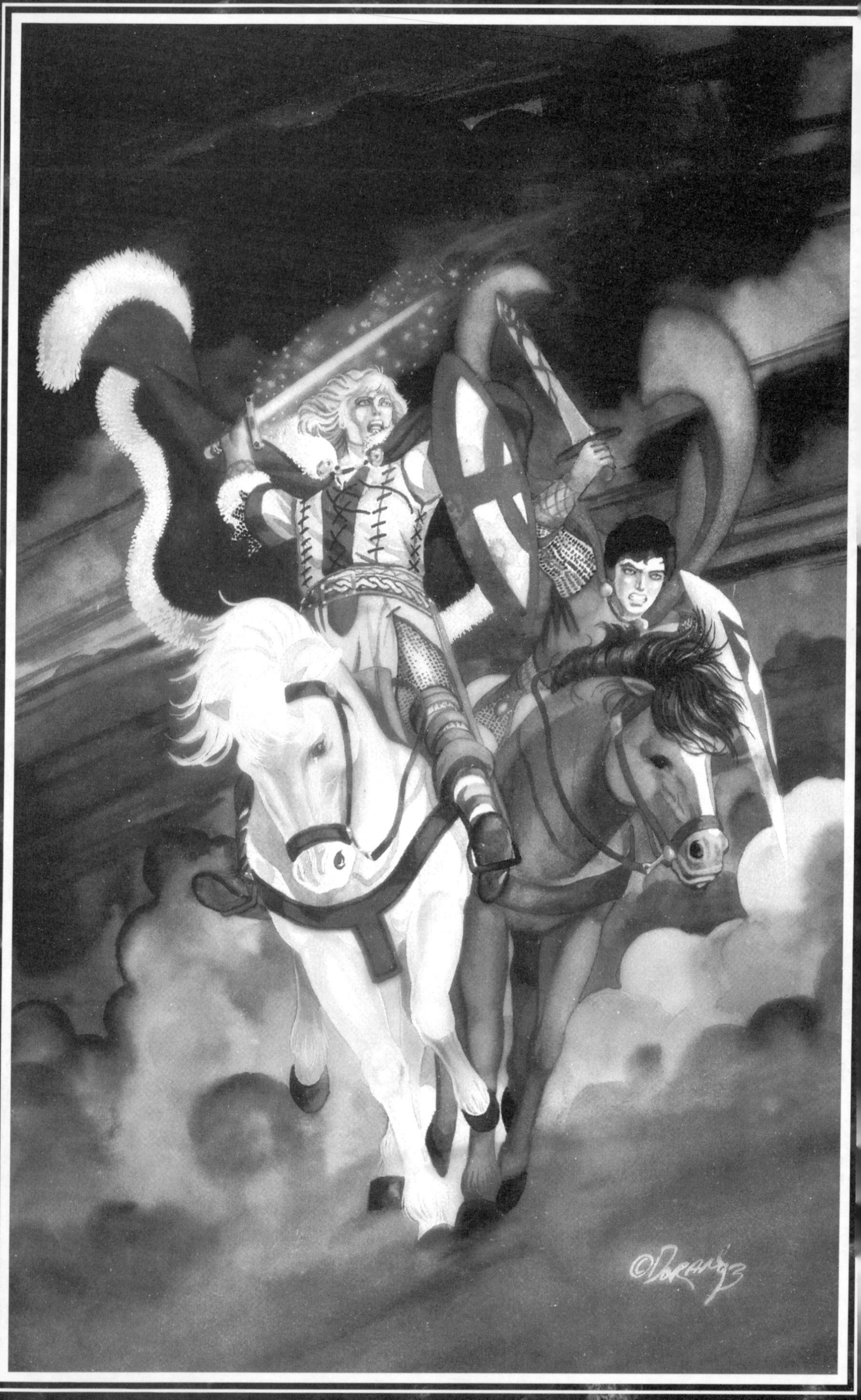
©Doran'93

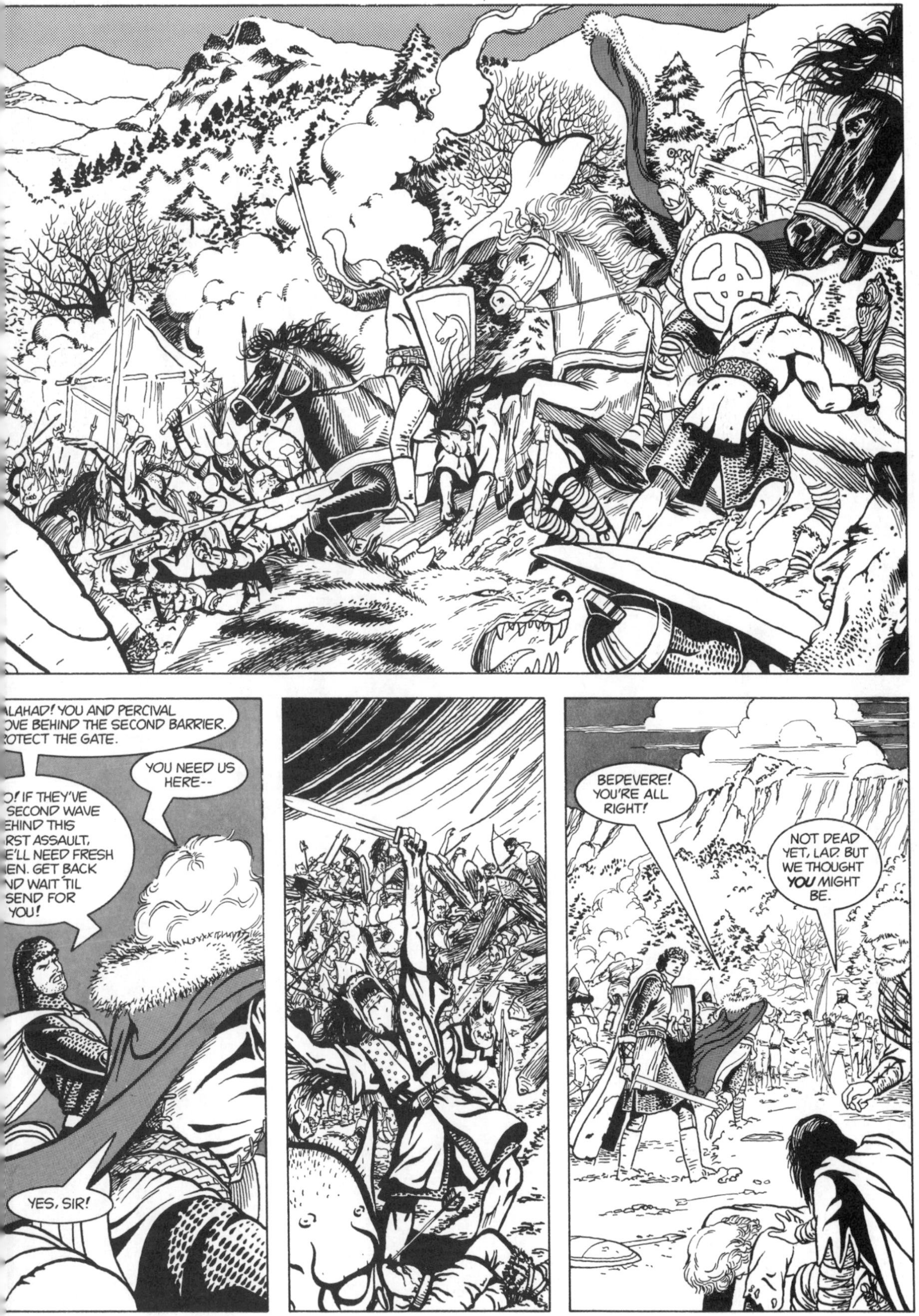
ALAHAD! YOU AND PERCIVAL
OVE BEHIND THE SECOND BARRIER.
ROTECT THE GATE.
YOU NEED US HERE--
O! IF THEY'VE SECOND WAVE EHIND THIS ARST ASSAULT, E'LL NEED FRESH IEN. GET BACK ND WAIT 'TIL SEND FOR YOU!
YES, SIR!
BEDEVERE! YOU'RE ALL RIGHT!
NOT DEAD YET, LAD. BUT WE THOUGHT YOU MIGHT BE.

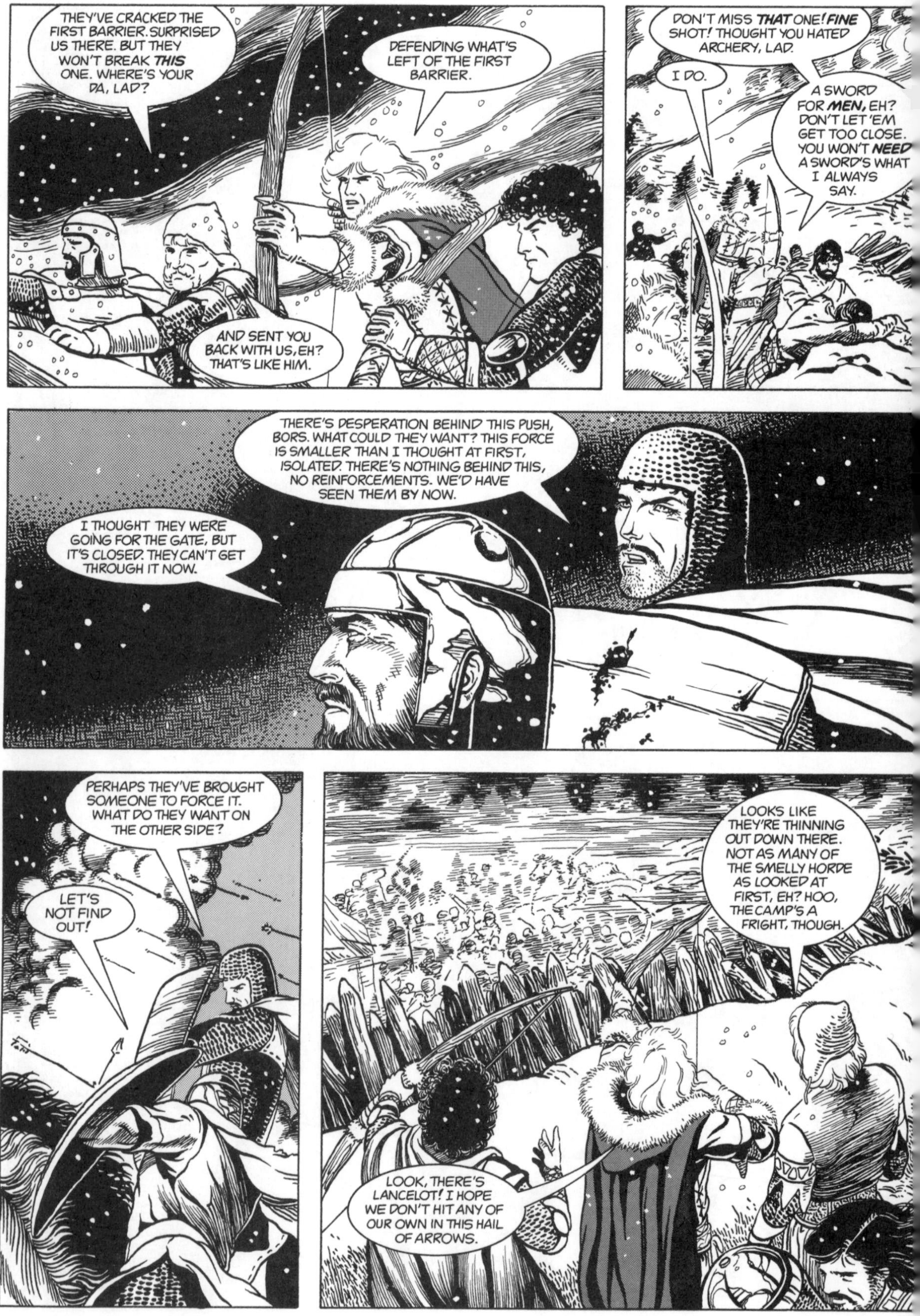
THEY'VE CRACKED THE FIRST BARRIER. SURPRISED US THERE. BUT THEY WON'T BREAK **THIS** ONE. WHERE'S YOUR DA, LAD?
DEFENDING WHAT'S LEFT OF THE FIRST BARRIER.
AND SENT YOU BACK WITH US, EH? THAT'S LIKE HIM.
DON'T MISS **THAT** ONE! **FINE** SHOT! THOUGHT YOU HATED ARCHERY, LAD.
I DO.
A SWORD FOR **MEN,** EH? DON'T LET 'EM GET TOO CLOSE. YOU WON'T **NEED** A SWORD'S WHAT I ALWAYS SAY.
THERE'S DESPERATION BEHIND THIS PUSH, BORS. WHAT COULD THEY WANT? THIS FORCE IS SMALLER THAN I THOUGHT AT FIRST, ISOLATED. THERE'S NOTHING BEHIND THIS, NO REINFORCEMENTS. WE'D HAVE SEEN THEM BY NOW.
I THOUGHT THEY WERE GOING FOR THE GATE, BUT IT'S CLOSED. THEY CAN'T GET THROUGH IT NOW.
PERHAPS THEY'VE BROUGHT SOMEONE TO FORCE IT. WHAT DO THEY WANT ON THE OTHER SIDE?
LET'S NOT FIND OUT!
LOOKS LIKE THEY'RE THINNING OUT DOWN THERE. NOT AS MANY OF THE SMELLY HORDE AS LOOKED AT FIRST, EH? HOO, THE CAMP'S A FRIGHT, THOUGH.
LOOK, THERE'S LANCELOT! I HOPE WE DON'T HIT ANY OF OUR OWN IN THIS HAIL OF ARROWS.

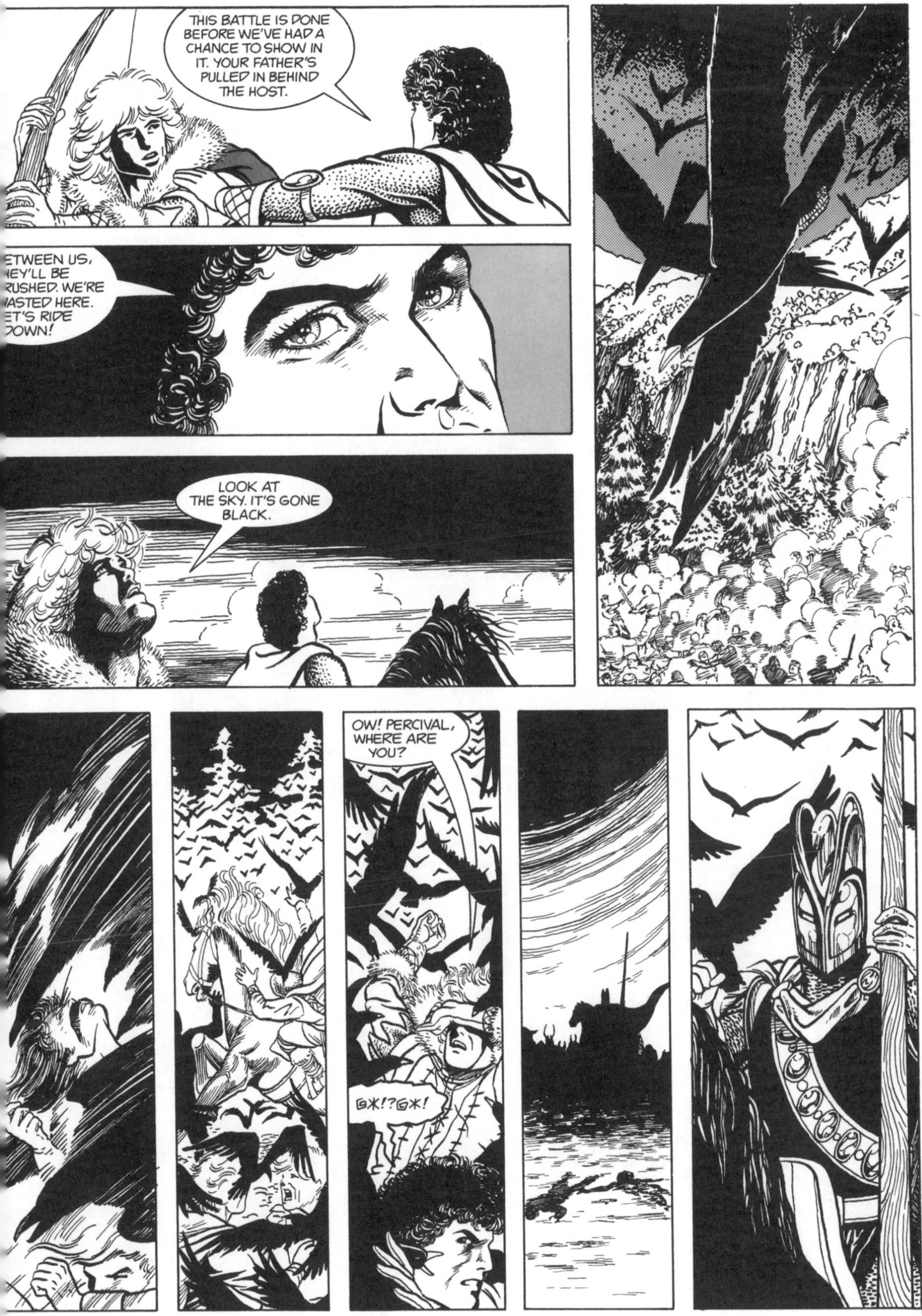
THIS BATTLE IS DONE BEFORE WE'VE HAD A CHANCE TO SHOW IN IT. YOUR FATHER'S PULLED IN BEHIND THE HOST.
ETWEEN US, HEY'LL BE RUSHED. WE'RE WASTED HERE. ET'S RIDE DOWN!
LOOK AT THE SKY. IT'S GONE BLACK.
OW! PERCIVAL, WHERE ARE YOU?
GЖ!?GЖ!

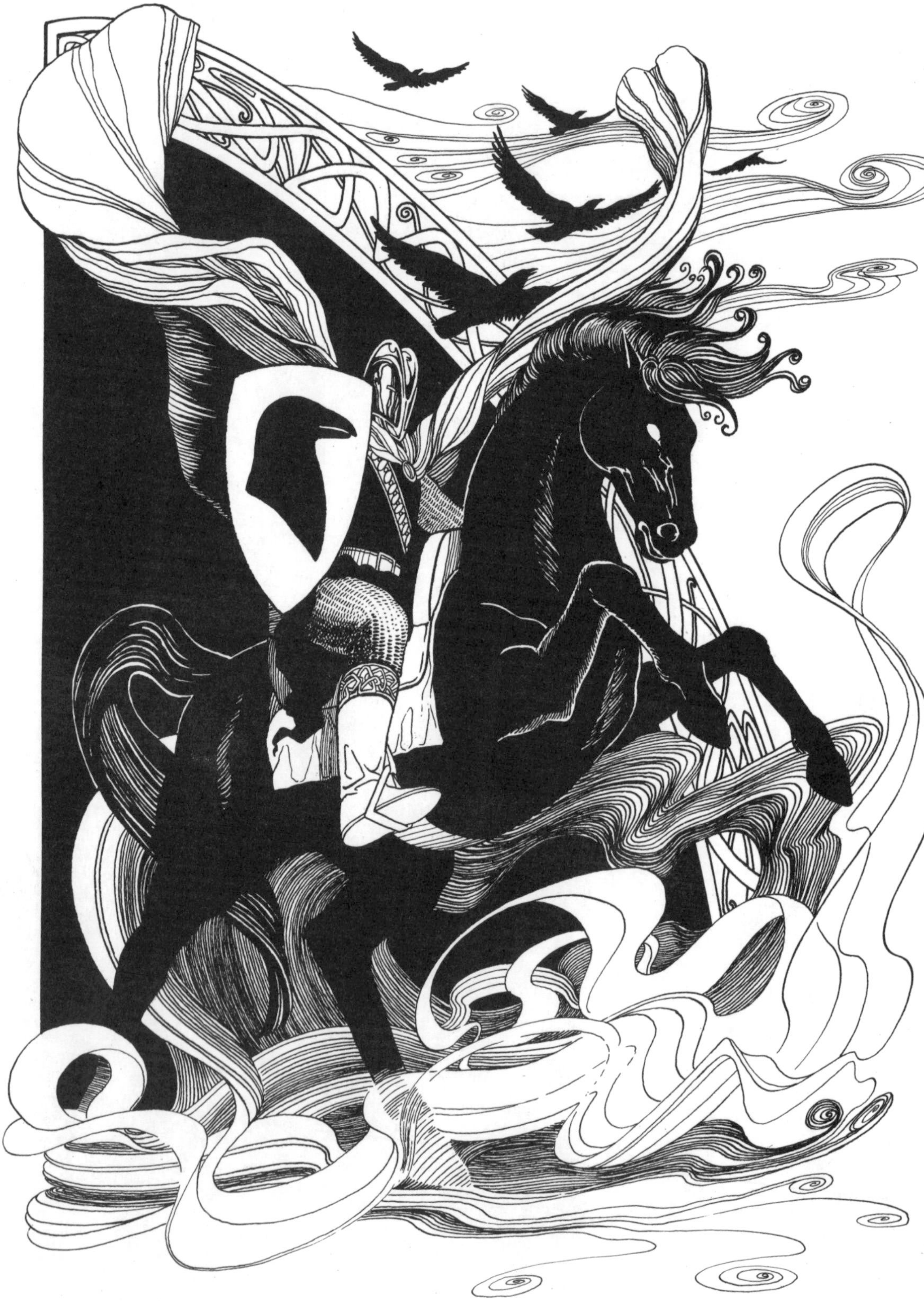

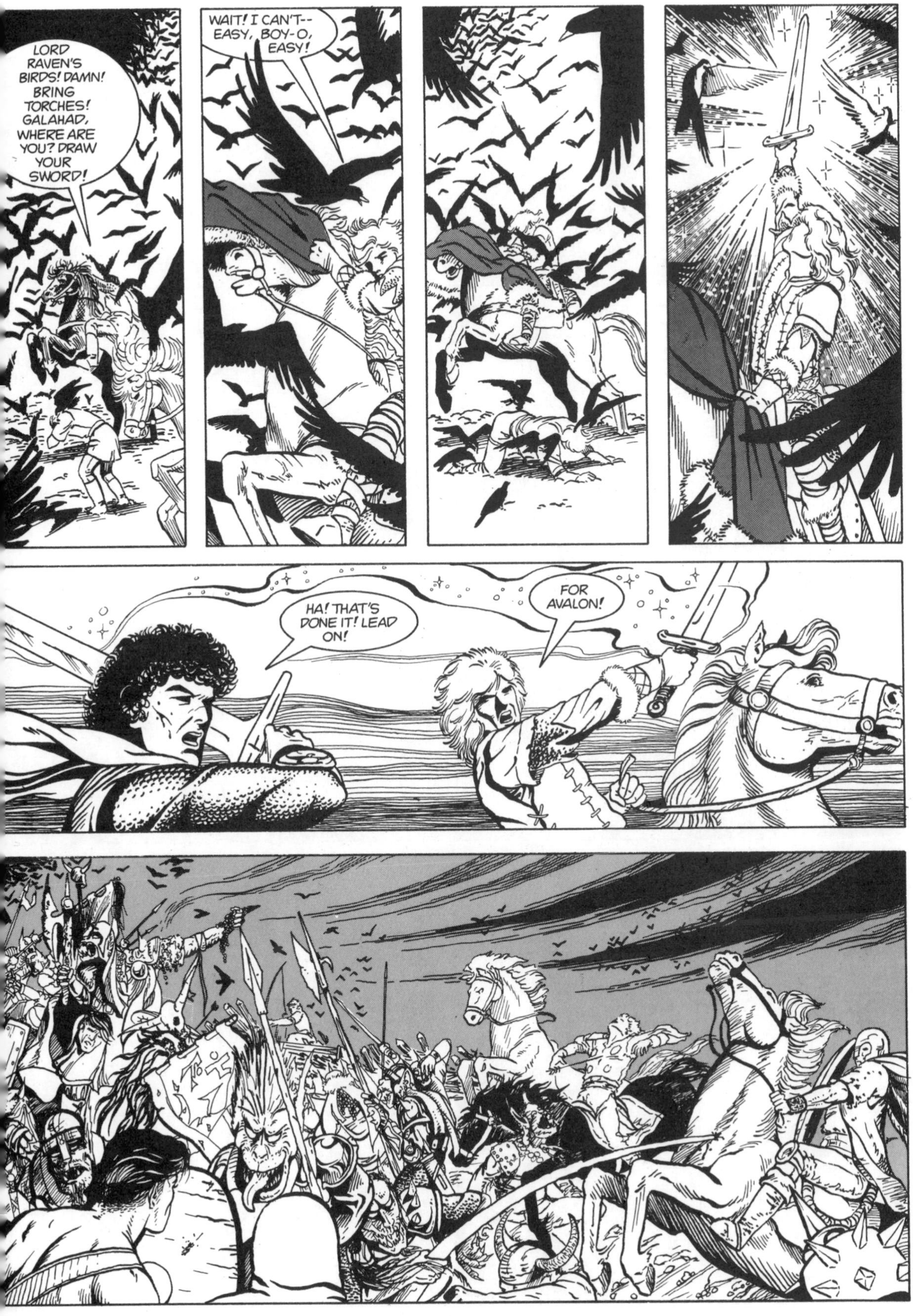
LORD RAVEN'S BIRDS! DAMN! BRING TORCHES! GALAHAD, WHERE ARE YOU? DRAW YOUR SWORD!
WAIT! I CAN'T--
EASY, BOY-O, EASY!
HA! THAT'S DONE IT! LEAD ON!
FOR AVALON!

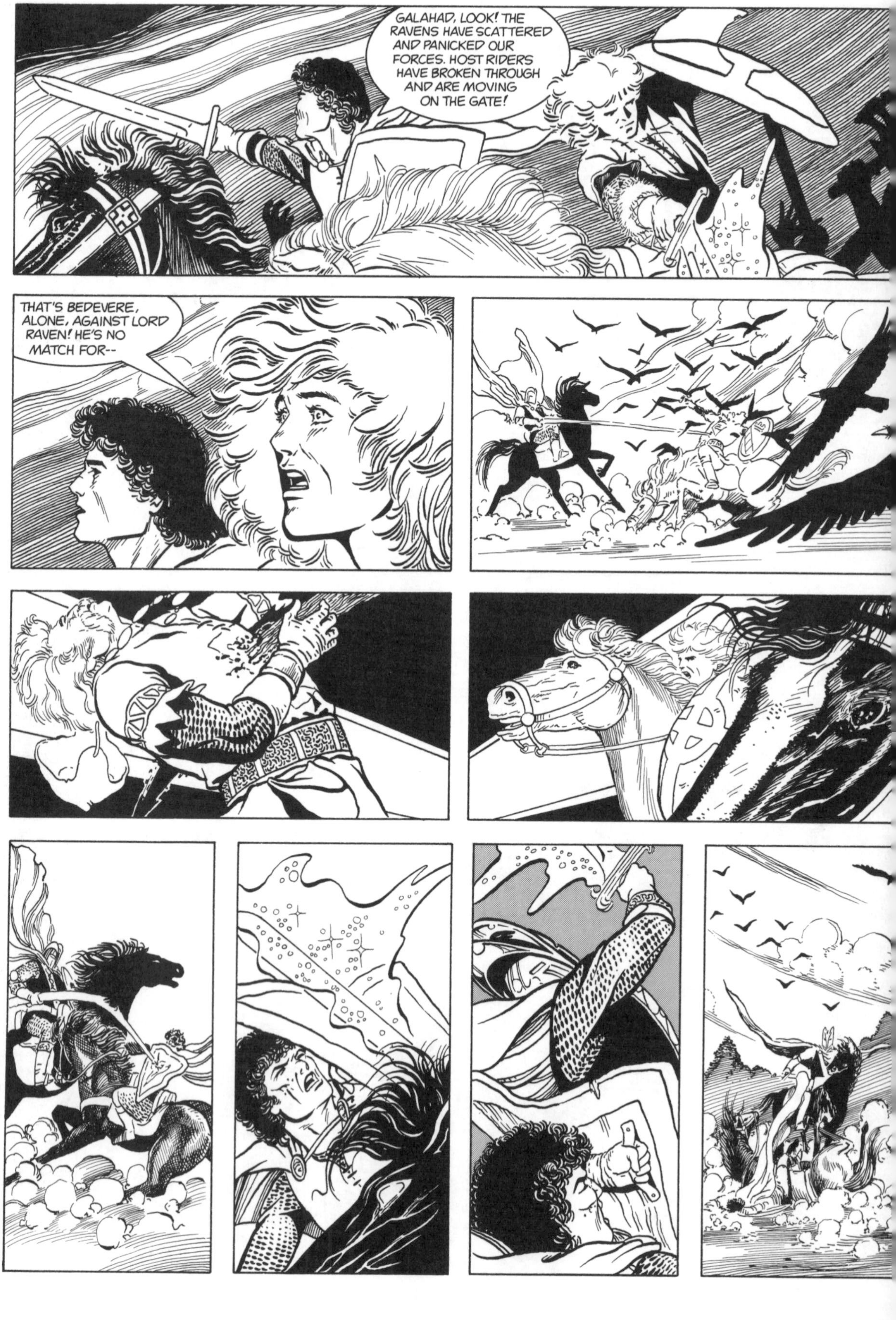
GALAHAD, LOOK! THE RAVENS HAVE SCATTERED AND PANICKED OUR FORCES. HOST RIDERS HAVE BROKEN THROUGH AND ARE MOVING ON THE GATE!
THAT'S BEDEVERE, ALONE, AGAINST LORD RAVEN! HE'S NO MATCH FOR--

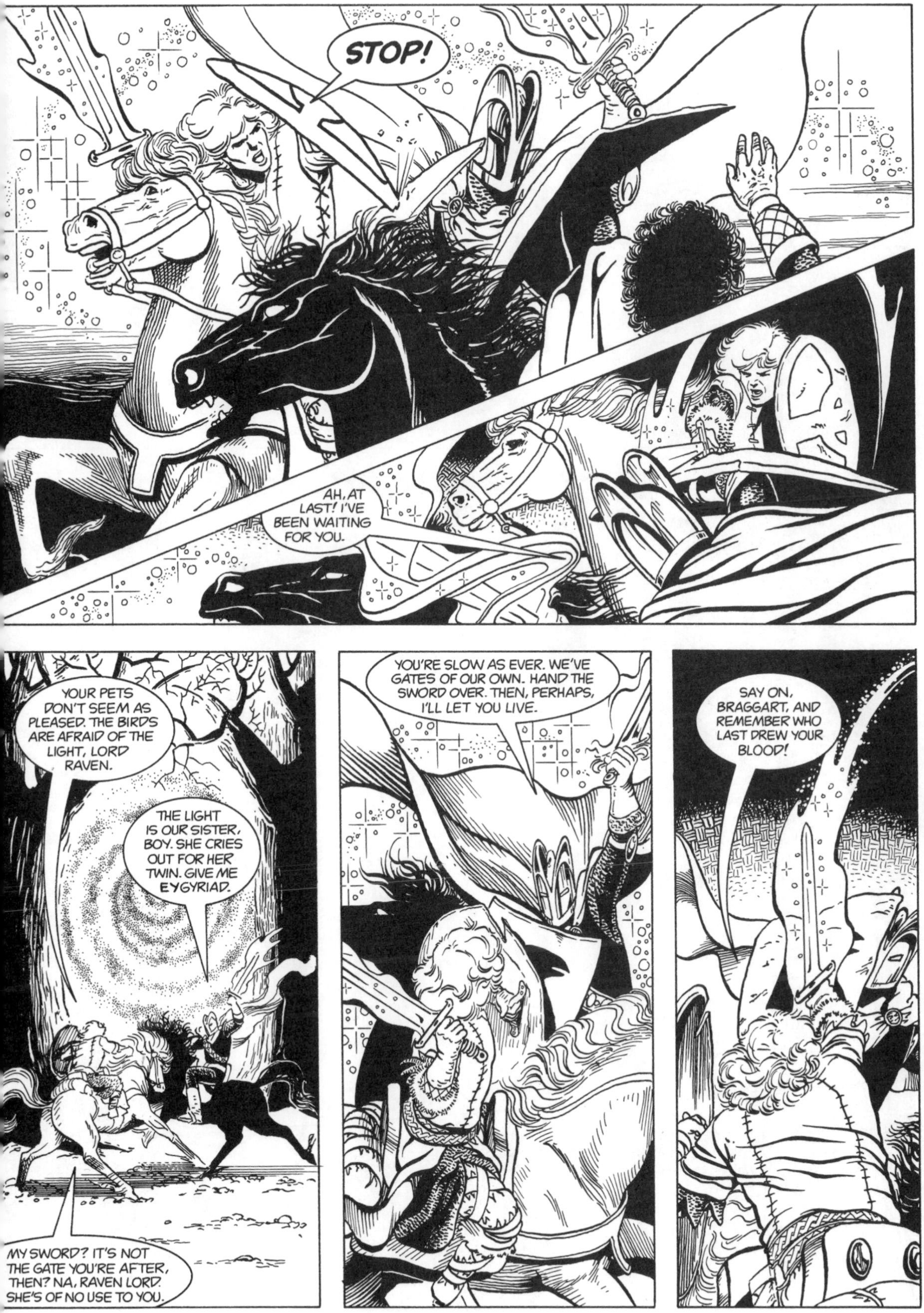
STOP!
AH, AT LAST! I'VE BEEN WAITING FOR YOU.
YOUR PETS DON'T SEEM AS PLEASED. THE BIRDS ARE AFRAID OF THE LIGHT, LORD RAVEN.
THE LIGHT IS OUR SISTER, BOY. SHE CRIES OUT FOR HER TWIN. GIVE ME EYGYRIAD.
MY SWORD? IT'S NOT THE GATE YOU'RE AFTER, THEN? NA, RAVEN LORD. SHE'S OF NO USE TO YOU.
YOU'RE SLOW AS EVER. WE'VE GATES OF OUR OWN. HAND THE SWORD OVER. THEN, PERHAPS, I'LL LET YOU LIVE.
SAY ON, BRAGGART, AND REMEMBER WHO LAST DREW YOUR BLOOD!

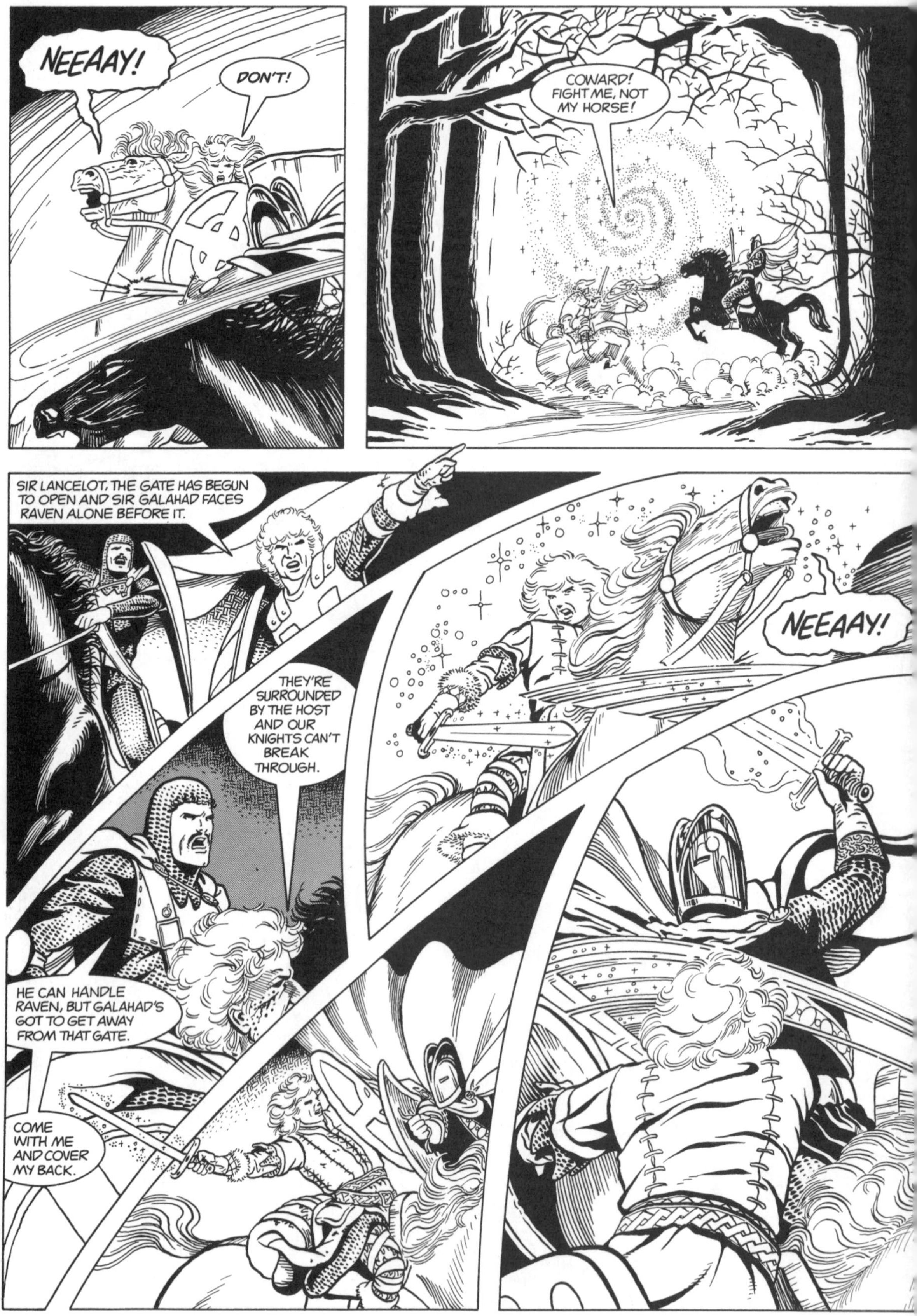
NEEAAY!
DON'T!
COWARD! FIGHT ME, NOT MY HORSE!
SIR LANCELOT, THE GATE HAS BEGUN TO OPEN AND SIR GALAHAD FACES RAVEN ALONE BEFORE IT.
NEEAAY!
THEY'RE SURROUNDED BY THE HOST AND OUR KNIGHTS CAN'T BREAK THROUGH.
HE CAN HANDLE RAVEN, BUT GALAHAD'S GOT TO GET AWAY FROM THAT GATE.
COME WITH ME AND COVER MY BACK.

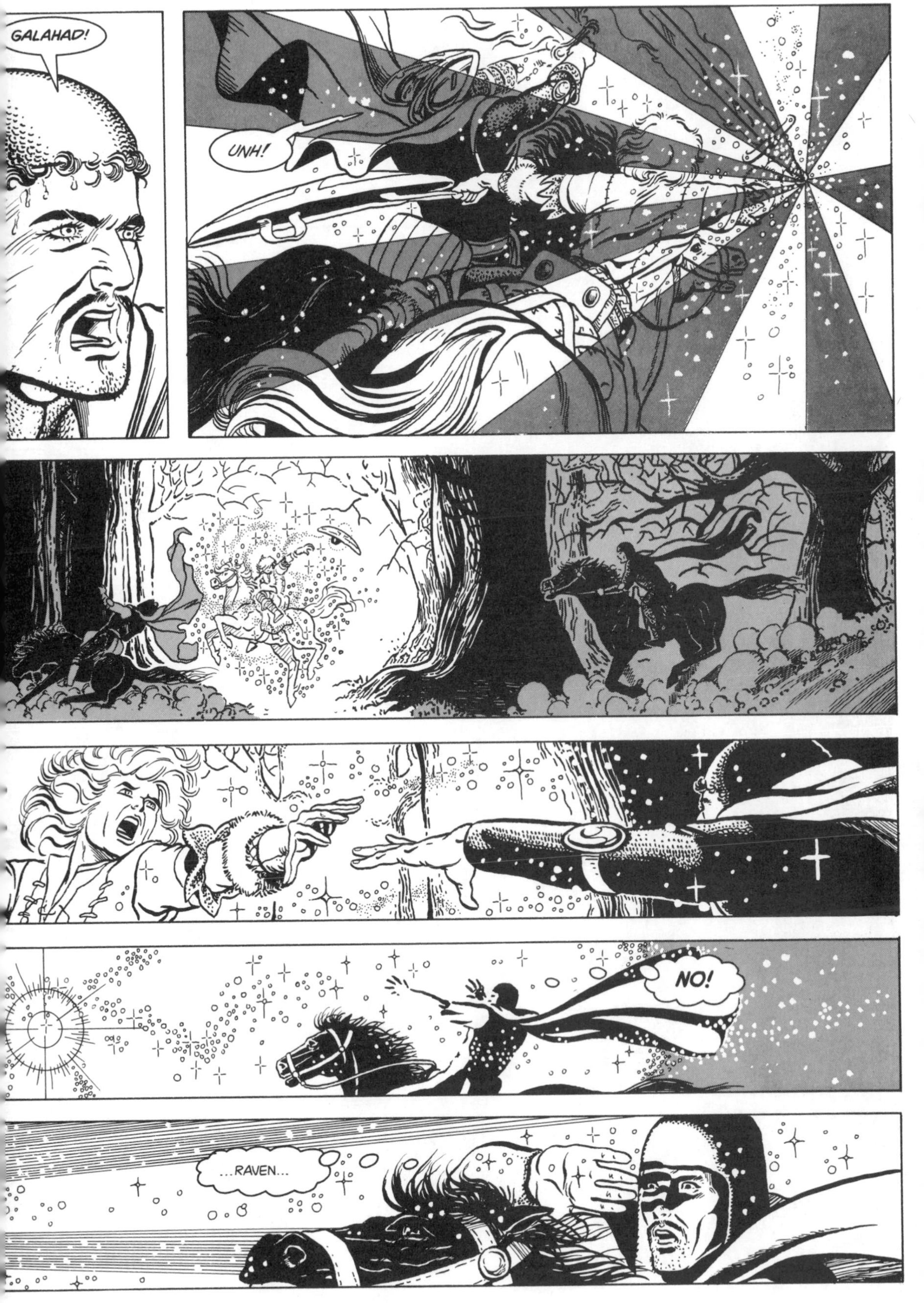
GALAHAD!
UNH!
NO!
...RAVEN...

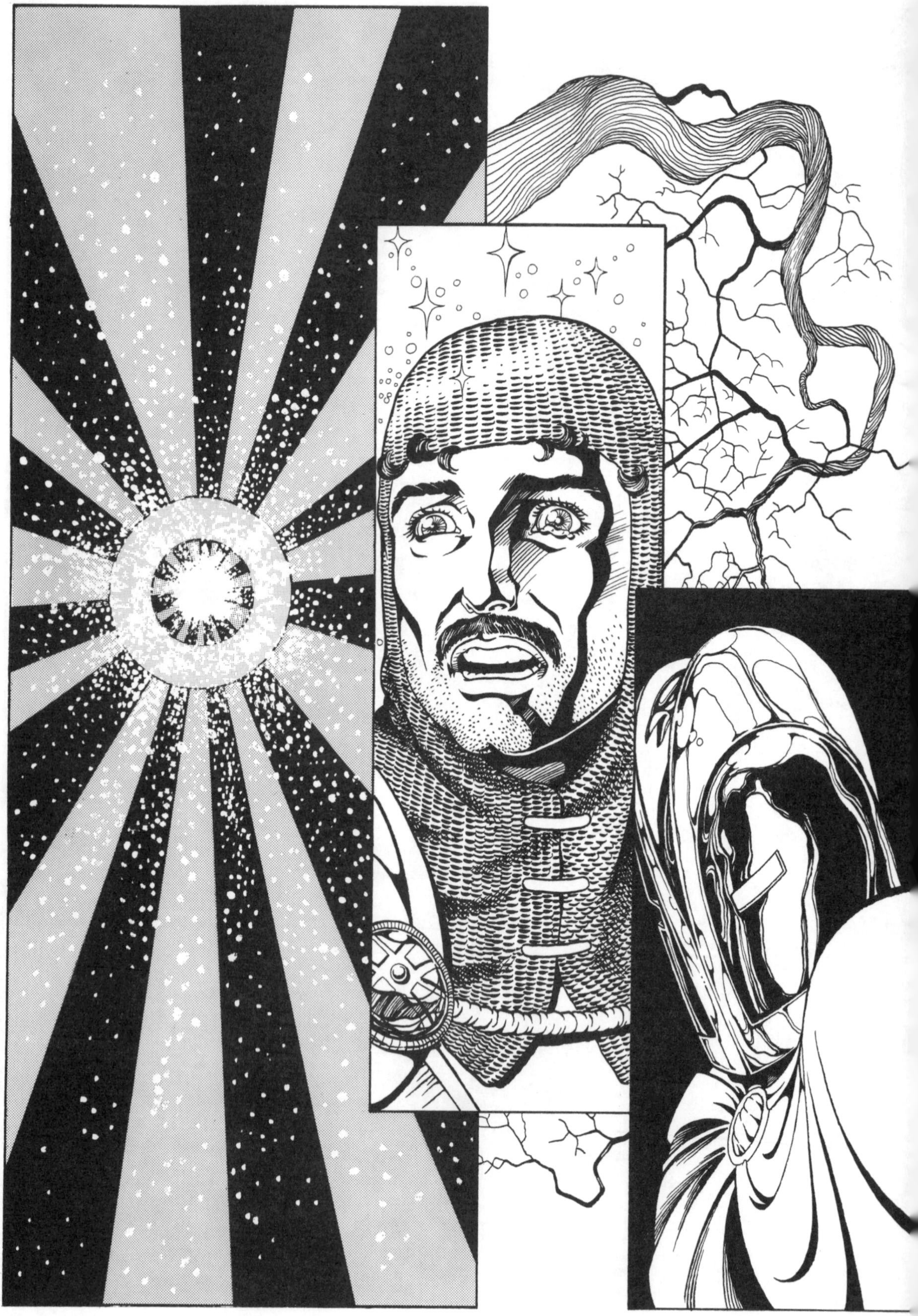

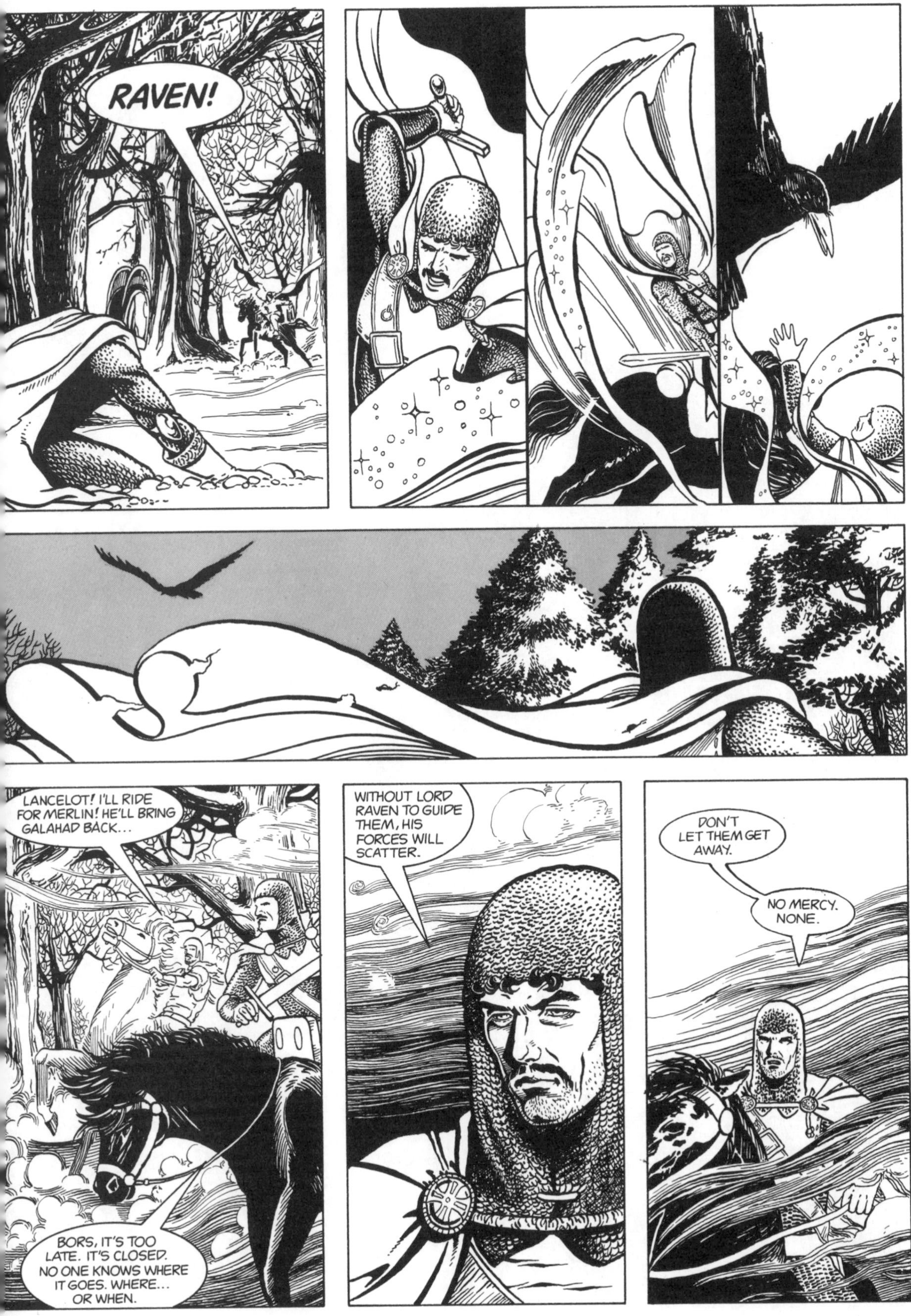
RAVEN!
LANCELOT! I'LL RIDE FOR MERLIN! HE'LL BRING GALAHAD BACK...
BORS, IT'S TOO LATE. IT'S CLOSED. NO ONE KNOWS WHERE IT GOES. WHERE... OR WHEN.
WITHOUT LORD RAVEN TO GUIDE THEM, HIS FORCES WILL SCATTER.
DON'T LET THEM GET AWAY.
NO MERCY. NONE.

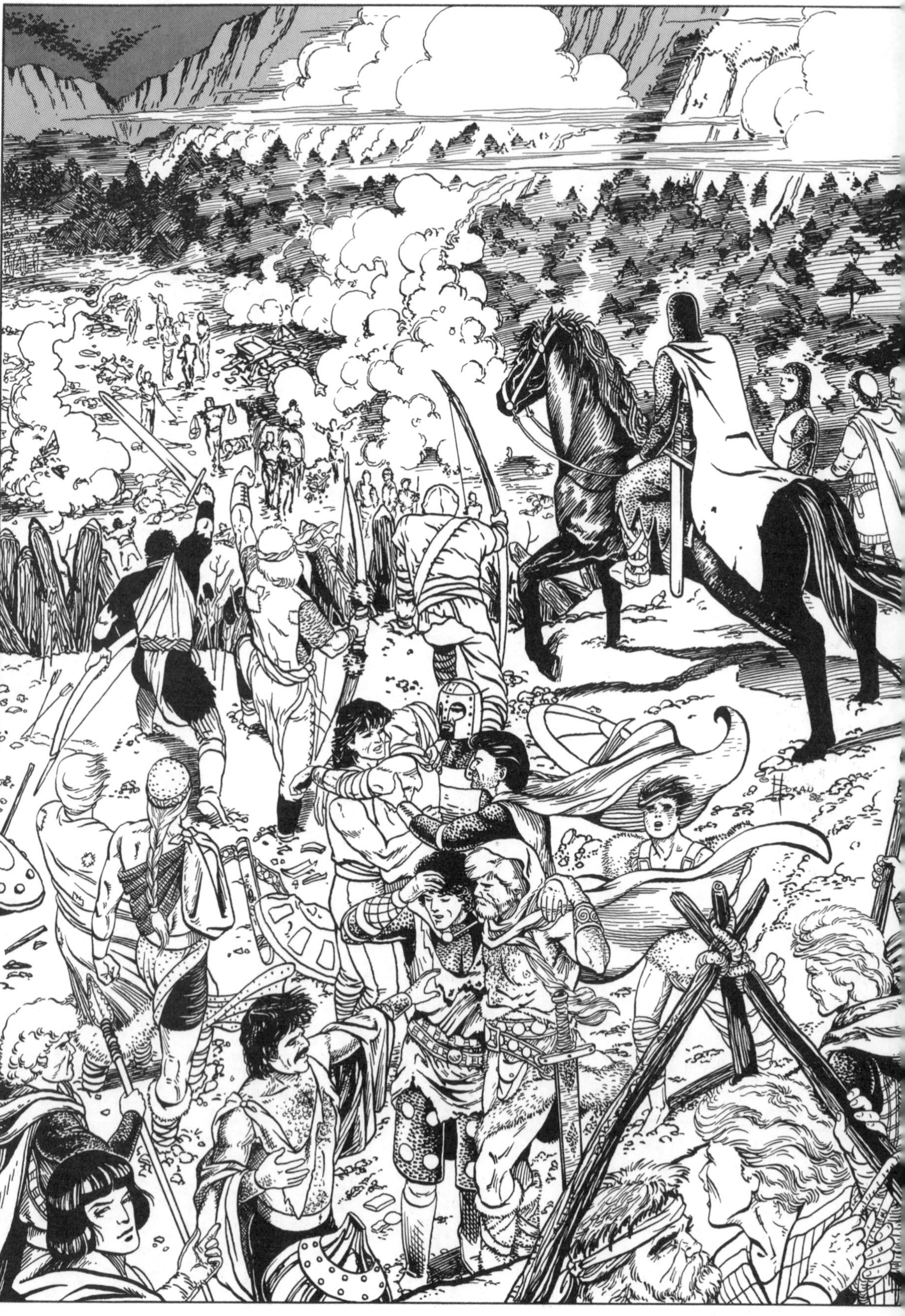

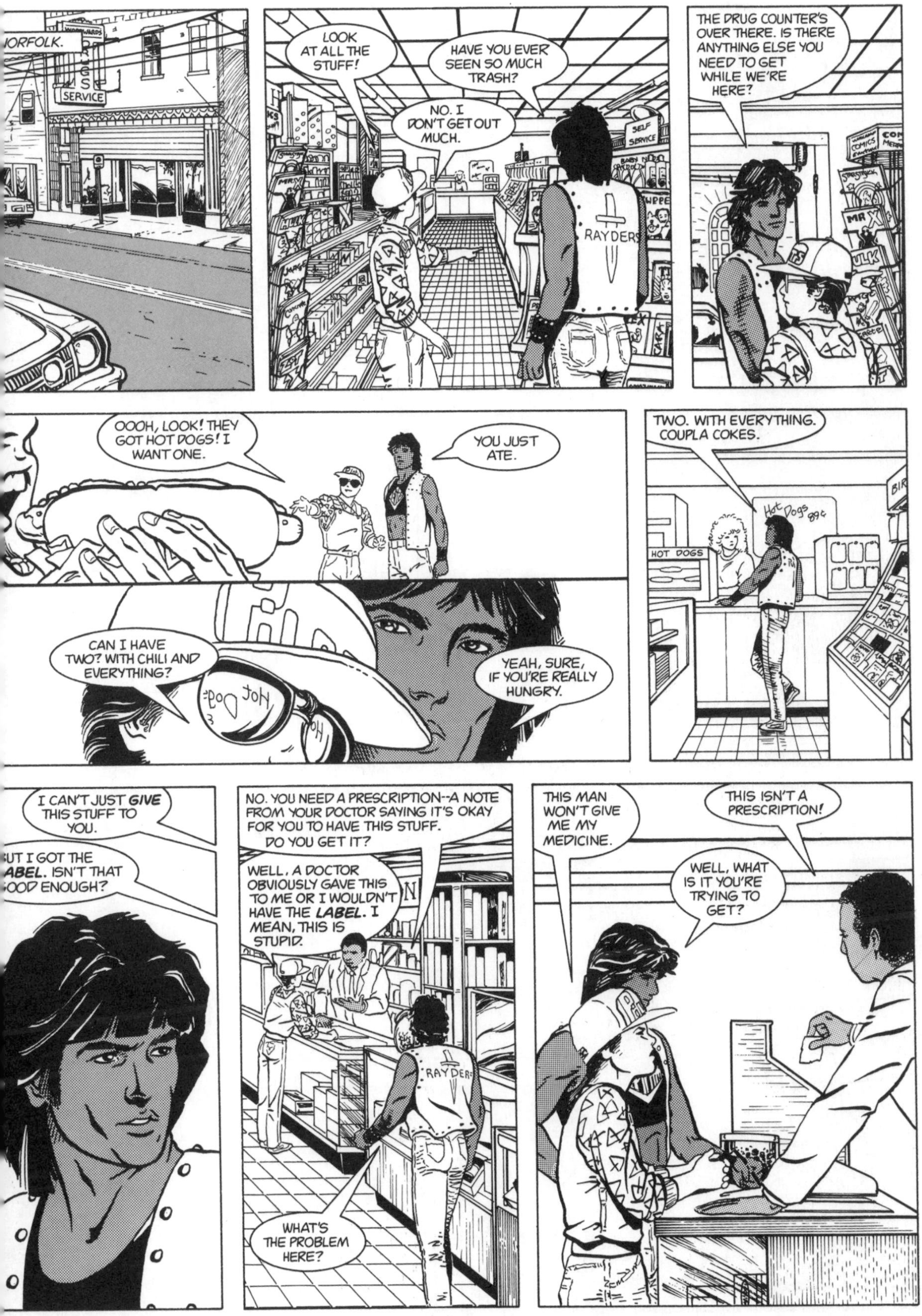
NORFOLK.
LOOK AT ALL THE STUFF!
HAVE YOU EVER SEEN SO MUCH TRASH?
NO. I DON'T GET OUT MUCH.
SELF SERVICE
RAYDERS
THE DRUG COUNTER'S OVER THERE. IS THERE ANYTHING ELSE YOU NEED TO GET WHILE WE'RE HERE?
OOOH, LOOK! THEY GOT HOT DOGS! I WANT ONE.
YOU JUST ATE.
CAN I HAVE TWO? WITH CHILI AND EVERYTHING?
YEAH, SURE, IF YOU'RE REALLY HUNGRY.
TWO. WITH EVERYTHING. COUPLA COKES.
Hot Dogs 89¢
HOT DOGS
I CAN'T JUST GIVE THIS STUFF TO YOU.
BUT I GOT THE LABEL. ISN'T THAT GOOD ENOUGH?
NO. YOU NEED A PRESCRIPTION--A NOTE FROM YOUR DOCTOR SAYING IT'S OKAY FOR YOU TO HAVE THIS STUFF. DO YOU GET IT?
WELL, A DOCTOR OBVIOUSLY GAVE THIS TO ME OR I WOULDN'T HAVE THE LABEL. I MEAN, THIS IS STUPID.
RAYDERS
WHAT'S THE PROBLEM HERE?
THIS MAN WON'T GIVE ME MY MEDICINE.
THIS ISN'T A PRESCRIPTION!
WELL, WHAT IS IT YOU'RE TRYING TO GET?

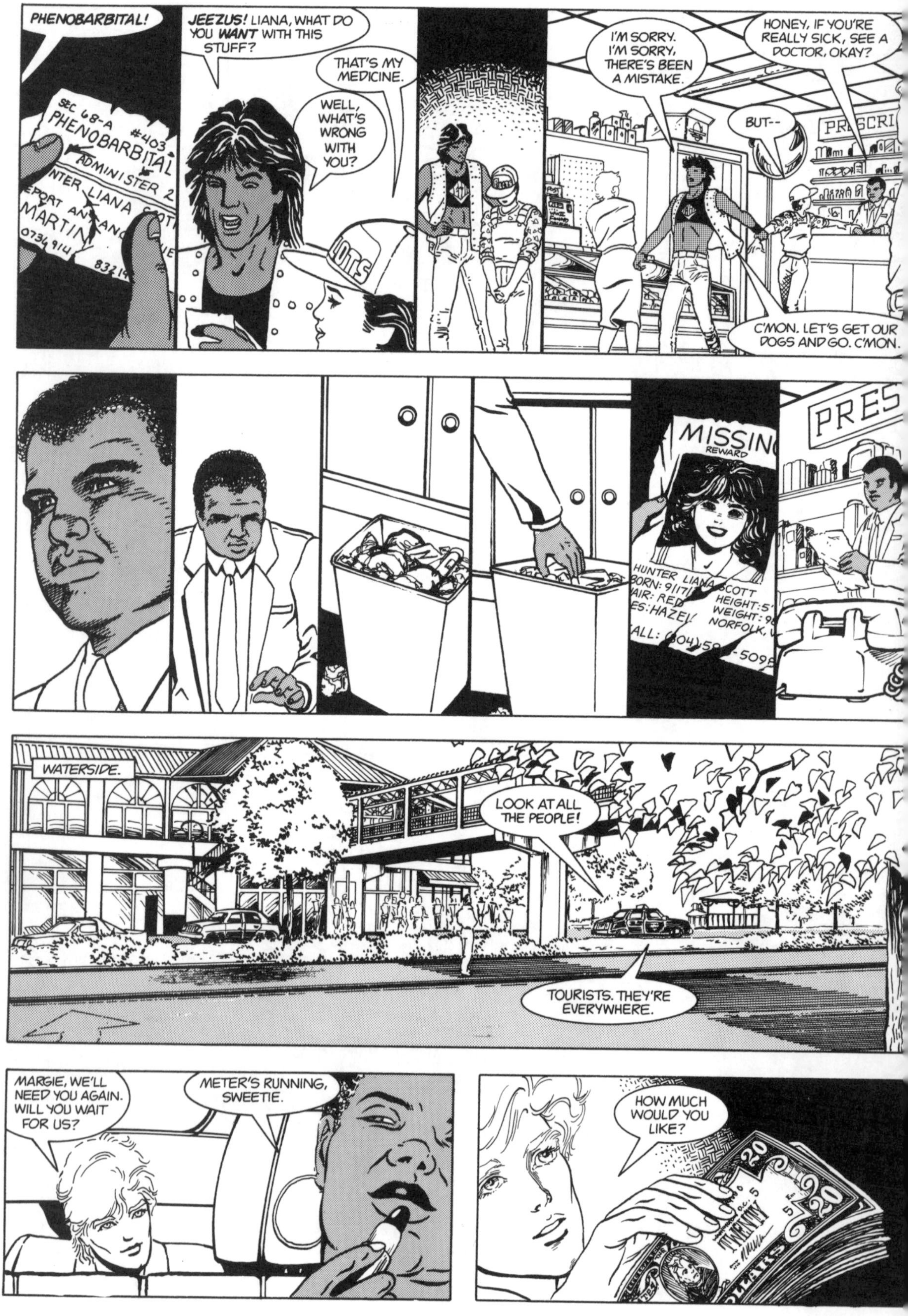
PHENOBARBITAL!
SEC 68-A #403 PHENOBARBITAL ADMINISTER 2 NTER LIANA SCOTT EPORT AN ANCE MARTIN 0734914 8321
JEEZUS! LIANA, WHAT DO YOU WANT WITH THIS STUFF?
THAT'S MY MEDICINE.
WELL, WHAT'S WRONG WITH YOU?
I'M SORRY. I'M SORRY, THERE'S BEEN A MISTAKE.
HONEY, IF YOU'RE REALLY SICK, SEE A DOCTOR, OKAY?
BUT--
PRESCRI
C'MON. LET'S GET OUR DOGS AND GO. C'MON.
PRES
MISSING REWARD
HUNTER LIANA SCOTT BORN: 9/17/ HEIGHT: 5' HAIR: RED WEIGHT: 9 EYES: HAZEL NORFOLK, CALL: (804) 5 -5098
WATERSIDE.
LOOK AT ALL THE PEOPLE!
TOURISTS. THEY'RE EVERYWHERE.
MARGIE, WE'LL NEED YOU AGAIN. WILL YOU WAIT FOR US?
METER'S RUNNING, SWEETIE.
HOW MUCH WOULD YOU LIKE?

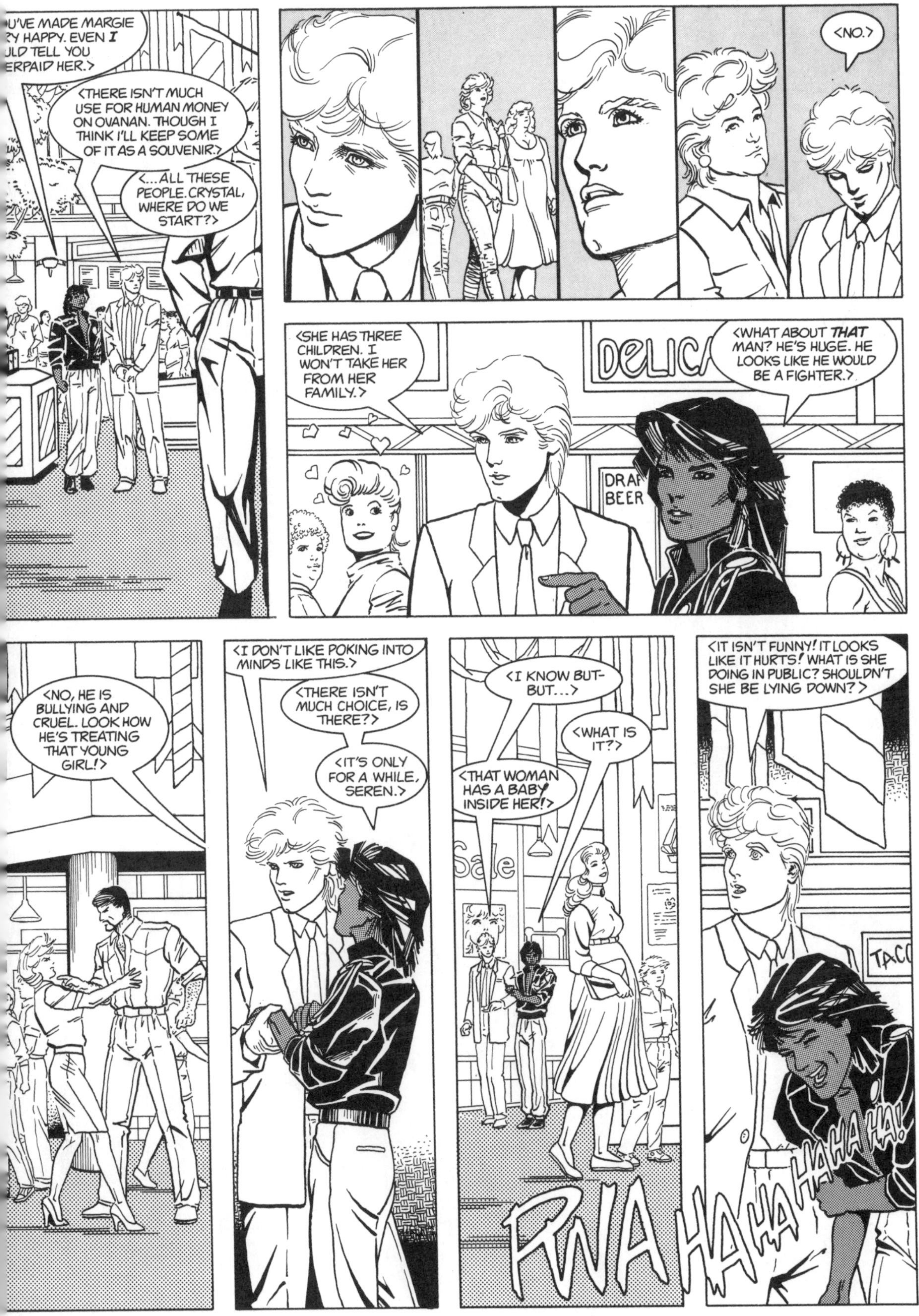

U'VE MADE MARGIE
RY HAPPY. EVEN I
ULD TELL YOU
ERPAID HER.>
<THERE ISN'T MUCH USE FOR HUMAN MONEY ON OVANAN. THOUGH I THINK I'LL KEEP SOME OF IT AS A SOUVENIR.>
<...ALL THESE PEOPLE. CRYSTAL, WHERE DO WE START?>
<NO.>
<SHE HAS THREE CHILDREN. I WON'T TAKE HER FROM HER FAMILY.>
DELICA
<WHAT ABOUT THAT MAN? HE'S HUGE. HE LOOKS LIKE HE WOULD BE A FIGHTER.>
DRAF BEER
<NO, HE IS BULLYING AND CRUEL. LOOK HOW HE'S TREATING THAT YOUNG GIRL!>
<I DON'T LIKE POKING INTO MINDS LIKE THIS.>
<THERE ISN'T MUCH CHOICE, IS THERE?>
<IT'S ONLY FOR A WHILE, SEREN.>
<I KNOW BUT- BUT...>
<WHAT IS IT?>
<THAT WOMAN HAS A BABY INSIDE HER!>
Sale
<IT ISN'T FUNNY! IT LOOKS LIKE IT HURTS! WHAT IS SHE DOING IN PUBLIC? SHOULDN'T SHE BE LYING DOWN?>
TACO
RWA HA HA HA HA HA HA!

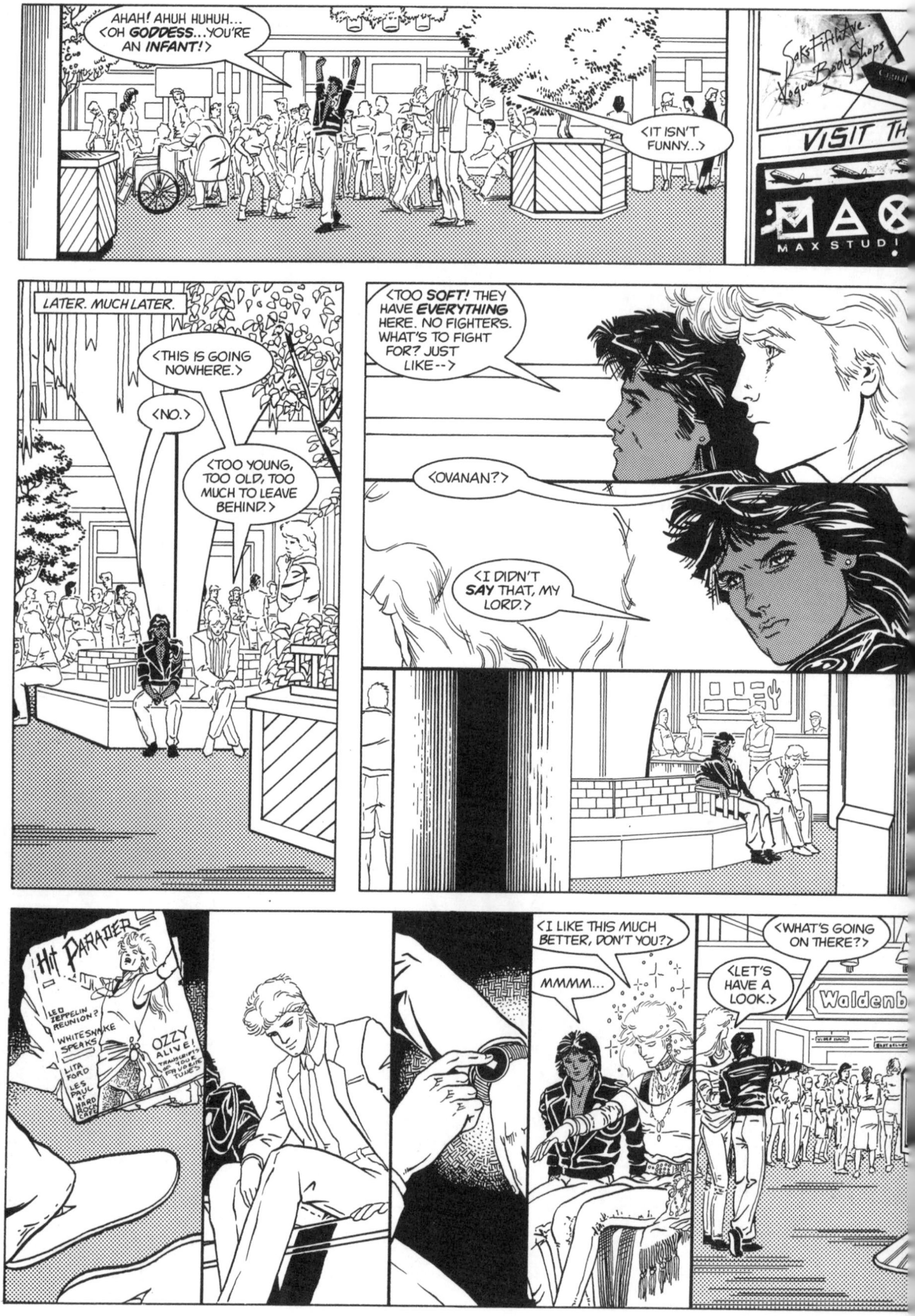

AHAH! AHUH HUHUH... <OH GODDESS... YOU'RE AN INFANT!>
<IT ISN'T FUNNY...>
Saks Fifth Ave.
Vogue Body Shops
VISIT TH
MAX STUDI
LATER. MUCH LATER.
<THIS IS GOING NOWHERE.>
<NO.>
<TOO YOUNG, TOO OLD, TOO MUCH TO LEAVE BEHIND.>
<TOO SOFT! THEY HAVE EVERYTHING HERE. NO FIGHTERS. WHAT'S TO FIGHT FOR? JUST LIKE-->
<OVANAN?>
<I DIDN'T SAY THAT, MY LORD.>
Hit Parader
LED ZEPPELIN REUNION?
WHITESNAKE SPEAKS
OZZY ALIVE!
LITA FORD
LES PAUL AT HARD ROCK CAFE
<I LIKE THIS MUCH BETTER, DON'T YOU?>
MMMM...
<WHAT'S GOING ON THERE?>
<LET'S HAVE A LOOK.>
Waldenb

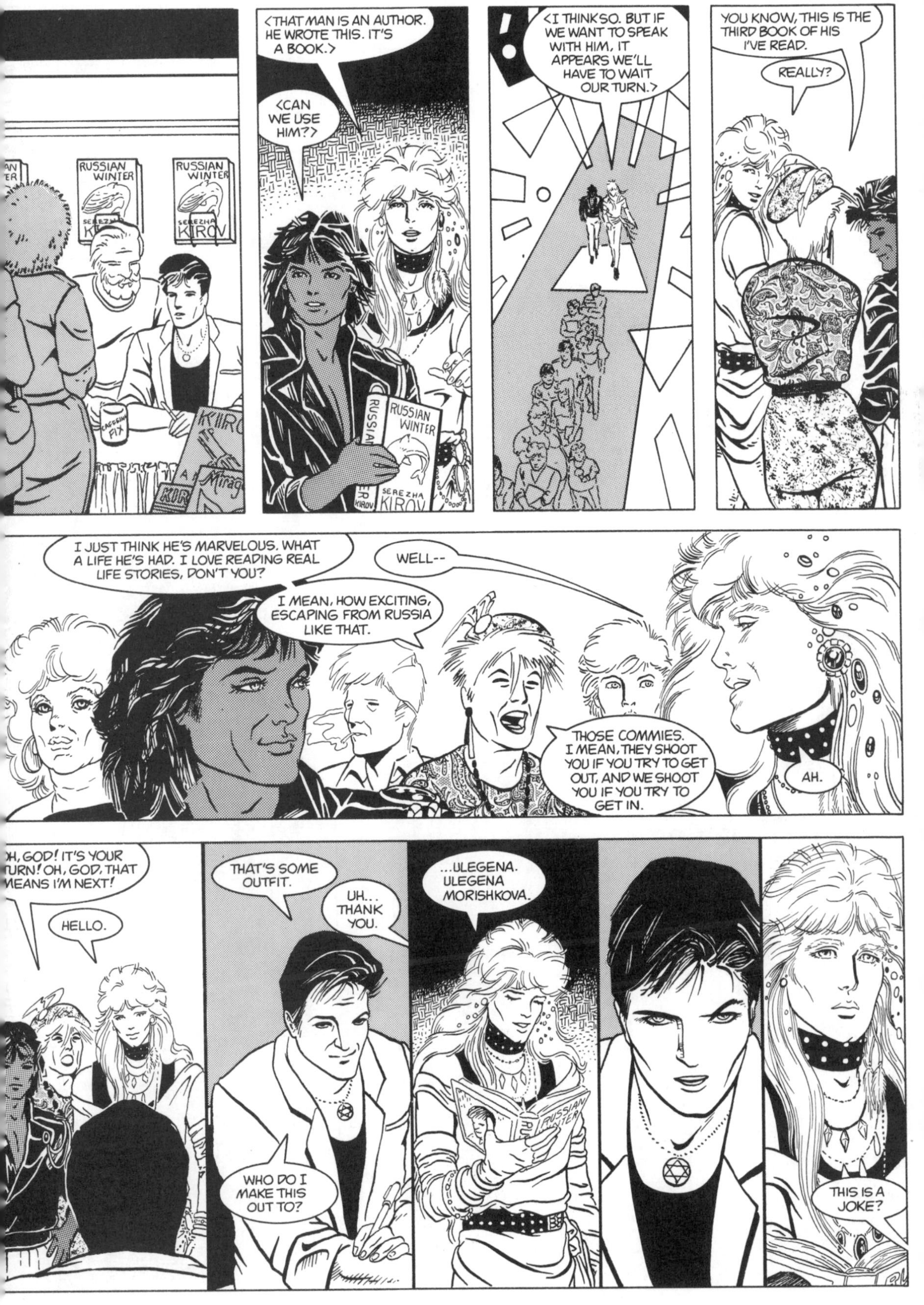
RUSSIAN WINTER
SEREZHA KIROV
RUSSIAN WINTER
SEREZHA KIROV
<THAT MAN IS AN AUTHOR. HE WROTE THIS. IT'S A BOOK.>
<CAN WE USE HIM?>
RUSSIAN WINTER
SEREZHA KIROV
<I THINK SO. BUT IF WE WANT TO SPEAK WITH HIM, IT APPEARS WE'LL HAVE TO WAIT OUR TURN.>
YOU KNOW, THIS IS THE THIRD BOOK OF HIS I'VE READ.
REALLY?
I JUST THINK HE'S MARVELOUS. WHAT A LIFE HE'S HAD. I LOVE READING REAL LIFE STORIES, DON'T YOU?
WELL--
I MEAN, HOW EXCITING, ESCAPING FROM RUSSIA LIKE THAT.
THOSE COMMIES. I MEAN, THEY SHOOT YOU IF YOU TRY TO GET OUT, AND WE SHOOT YOU IF YOU TRY TO GET IN.
AH.
H, GOD! IT'S YOUR URN! OH, GOD, THAT MEANS I'M NEXT!
HELLO.
THAT'S SOME OUTFIT.
UH... THANK YOU.
WHO DO I MAKE THIS OUT TO?
...ULEGENA. ULEGENA MORISHKOVA.
THIS IS A JOKE?

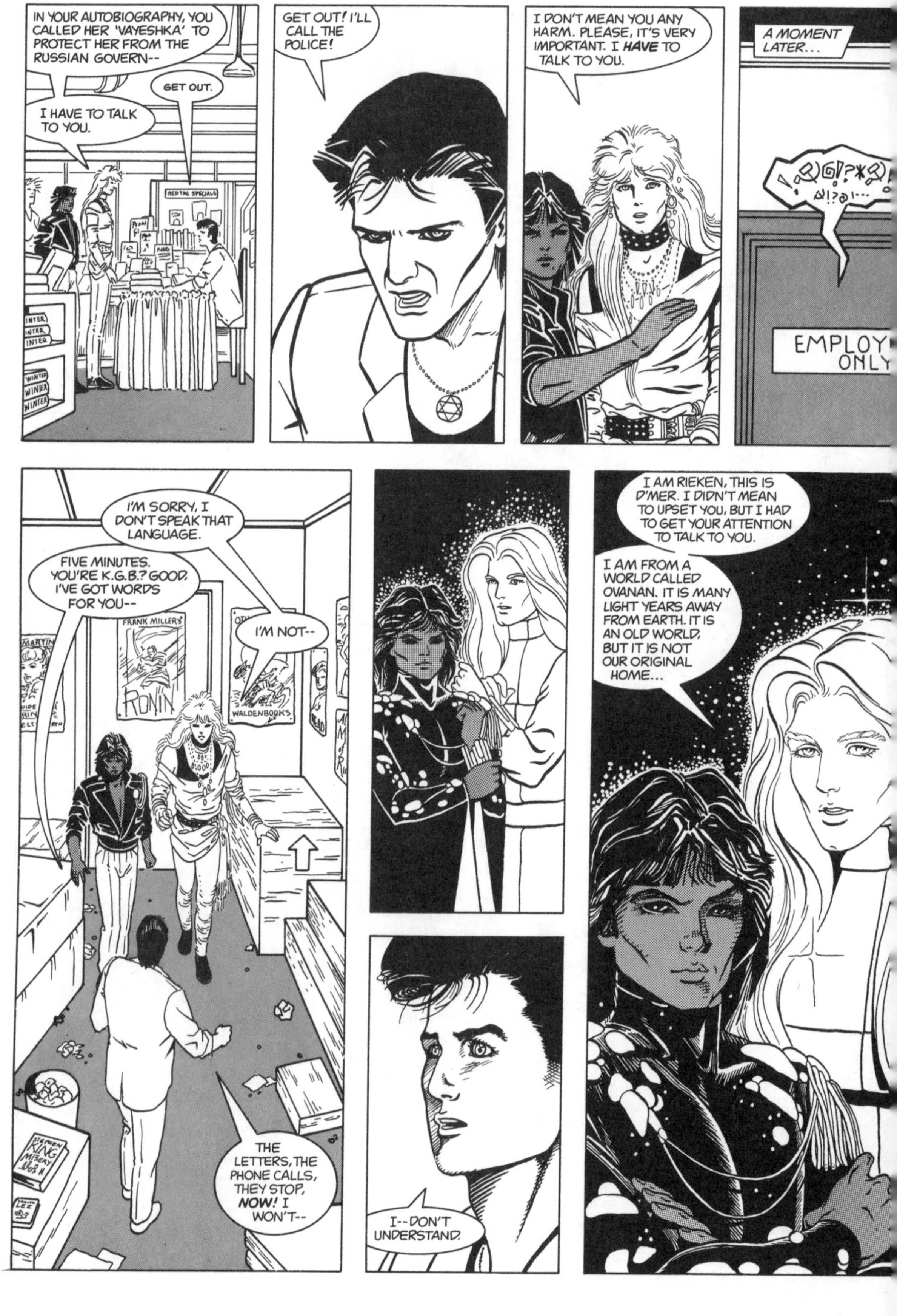
IN YOUR AUTOBIOGRAPHY, YOU CALLED HER 'VAYESHKA' TO PROTECT HER FROM THE RUSSIAN GOVERN--
GET OUT.
I HAVE TO TALK TO YOU.
RED TAG SPECIALS
GET OUT! I'LL CALL THE POLICE!
I DON'T MEAN YOU ANY HARM. PLEASE, IT'S VERY IMPORTANT. I HAVE TO TALK TO YOU.
A MOMENT LATER...
EMPLOY ONLY
I'M SORRY, I DON'T SPEAK THAT LANGUAGE.
FIVE MINUTES. YOU'RE K.G.B.? GOOD. I'VE GOT WORDS FOR YOU--
I'M NOT--
FRANK MILLER'S RONIN
WALDENBOOKS
THE LETTERS, THE PHONE CALLS, THEY STOP, NOW! I WON'T--
STEPHEN KING MISERY
I AM RIEKEN, THIS IS D'MER. I DIDN'T MEAN TO UPSET YOU, BUT I HAD TO GET YOUR ATTENTION TO TALK TO YOU.
I AM FROM A WORLD CALLED OVANAN. IT IS MANY LIGHT YEARS AWAY FROM EARTH. IT IS AN OLD WORLD, BUT IT IS NOT OUR ORIGINAL HOME...
I--DON'T UNDERSTAND.

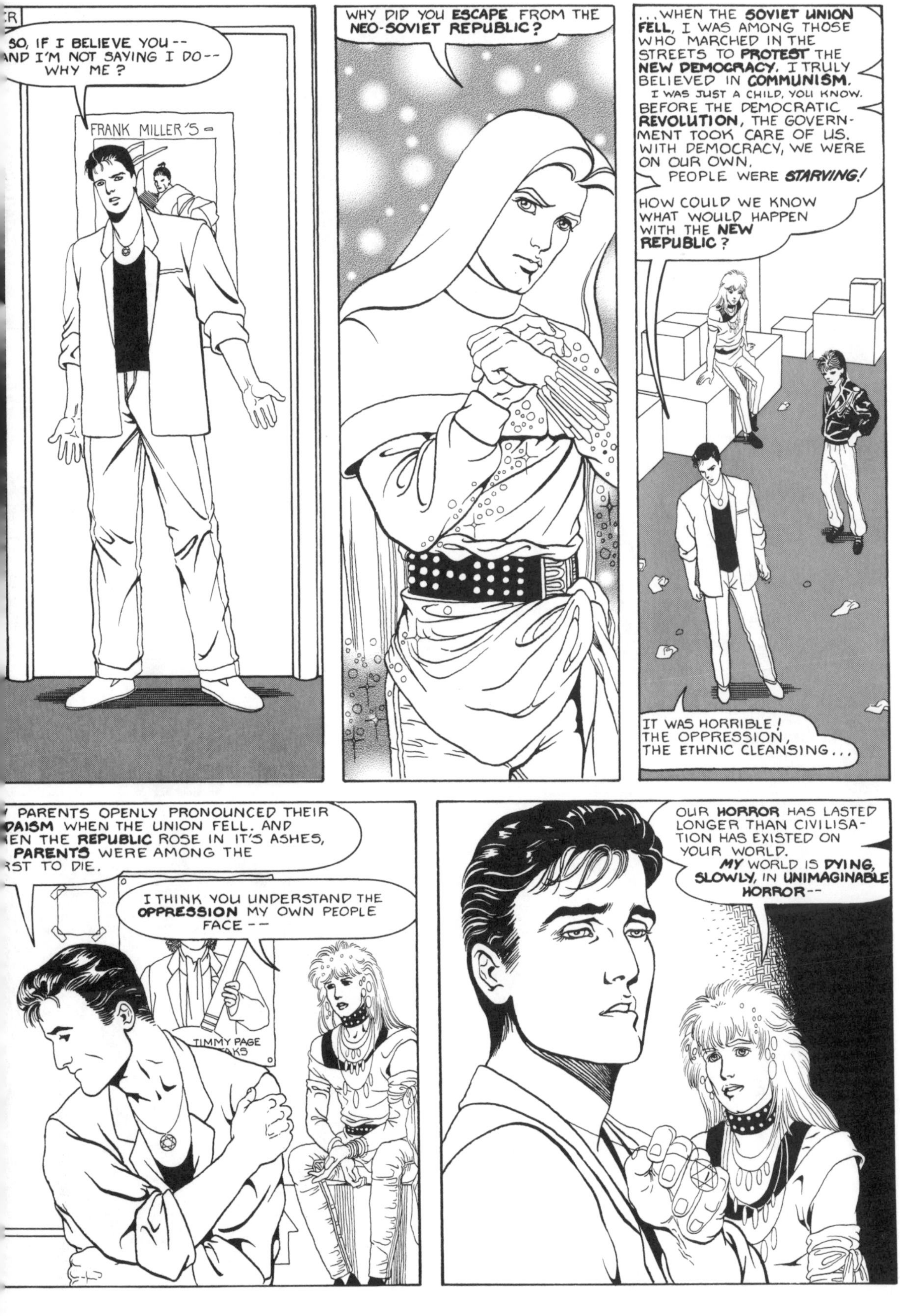

FRANK MILLER'S
SO, IF I BELIEVE YOU -- AND I'M NOT SAYING I DO -- WHY ME?
WHY DID YOU ESCAPE FROM THE NEO-SOVIET REPUBLIC?
...WHEN THE SOVIET UNION FELL, I WAS AMONG THOSE WHO MARCHED IN THE STREETS TO PROTEST THE NEW DEMOCRACY. I TRULY BELIEVED IN COMMUNISM. I WAS JUST A CHILD, YOU KNOW. BEFORE THE DEMOCRATIC REVOLUTION, THE GOVERNMENT TOOK CARE OF US. WITH DEMOCRACY, WE WERE ON OUR OWN. PEOPLE WERE STARVING!
HOW COULD WE KNOW WHAT WOULD HAPPEN WITH THE NEW REPUBLIC?
IT WAS HORRIBLE! THE OPPRESSION, THE ETHNIC CLEANSING...
PARENTS OPENLY PRONOUNCED THEIR DAISM WHEN THE UNION FELL. AND EN THE REPUBLIC ROSE IN IT'S ASHES, PARENTS WERE AMONG THE RST TO DIE.
I THINK YOU UNDERSTAND THE OPPRESSION MY OWN PEOPLE FACE --
TIMMY PAGE
OUR HORROR HAS LASTED LONGER THAN CIVILISATION HAS EXISTED ON YOUR WORLD. MY WORLD IS DYING, SLOWLY, IN UNIMAGINABLE HORROR--

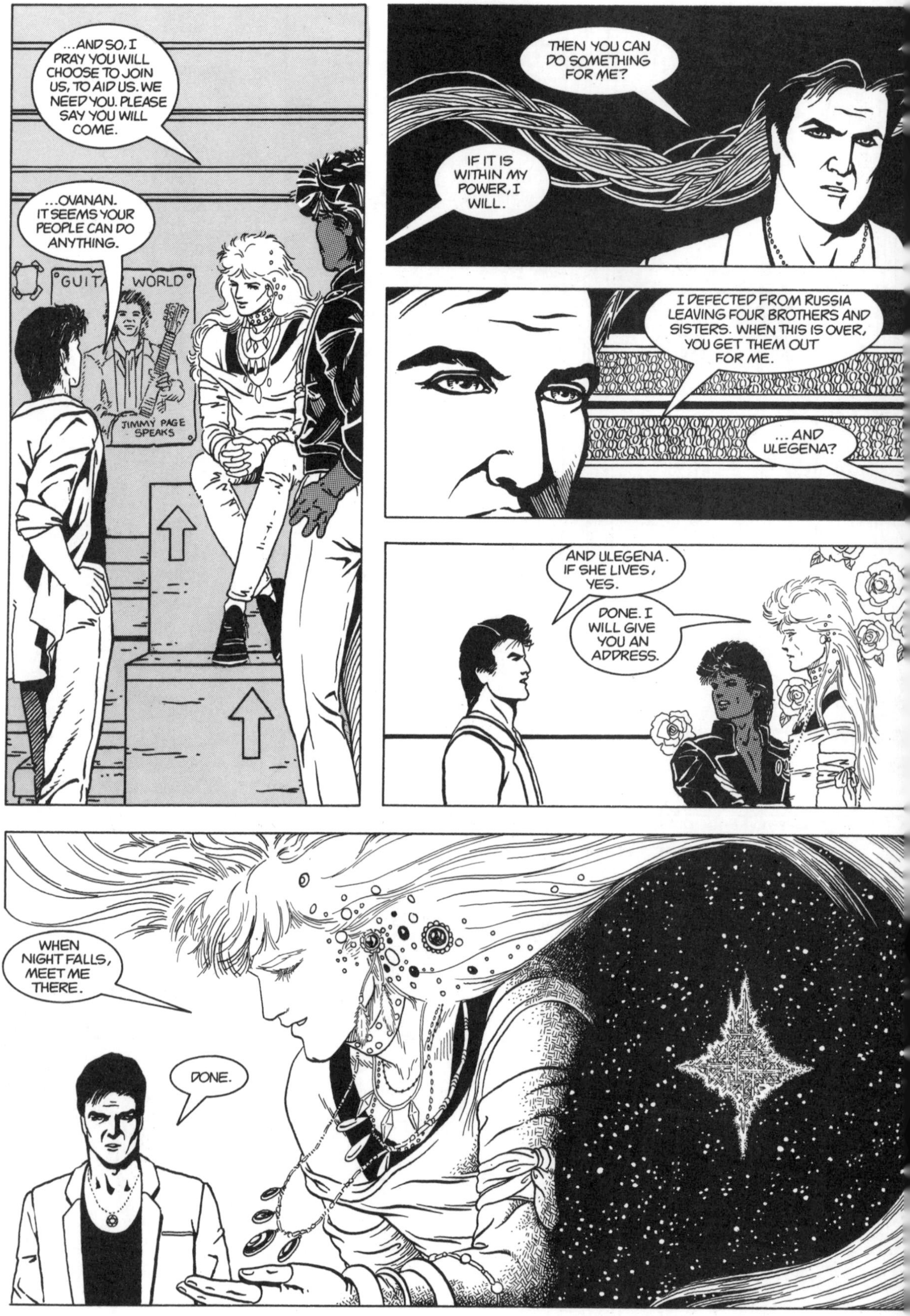
...AND SO, I PRAY YOU WILL CHOOSE TO JOIN US, TO AID US. WE NEED YOU. PLEASE SAY YOU WILL COME.
...OVANAN. IT SEEMS YOUR PEOPLE CAN DO ANYTHING.
GUITA WORLD
JIMMY PAGE SPEAKS
THEN YOU CAN DO SOMETHING FOR ME?
IF IT IS WITHIN MY POWER, I WILL.
I DEFECTED FROM RUSSIA LEAVING FOUR BROTHERS AND SISTERS. WHEN THIS IS OVER, YOU GET THEM OUT FOR ME.
...AND ULEGENA?
AND ULEGENA. IF SHE LIVES, YES.
DONE. I WILL GIVE YOU AN ADDRESS.
WHEN NIGHT FALLS, MEET ME THERE.
DONE.

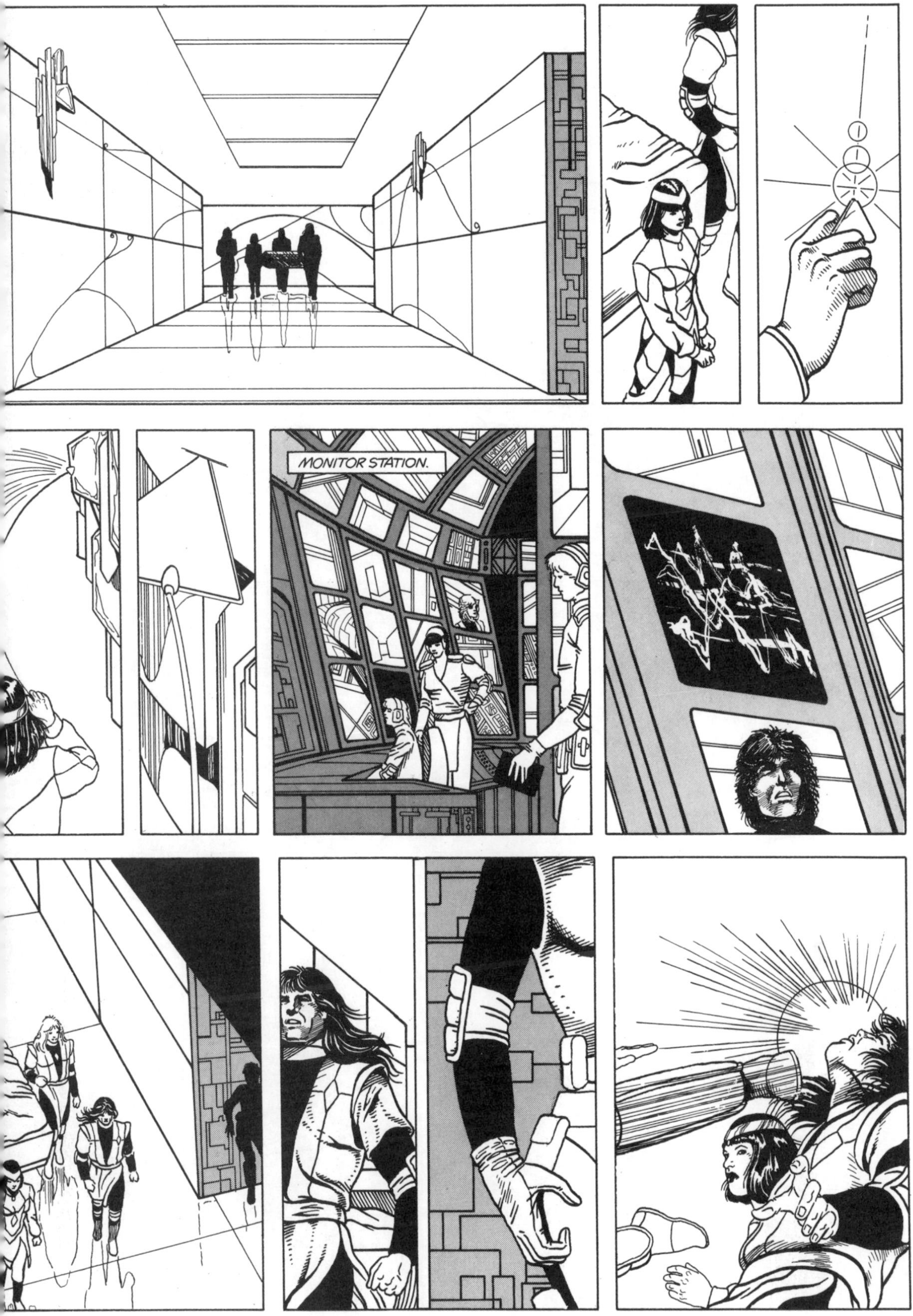
MONITOR STATION.

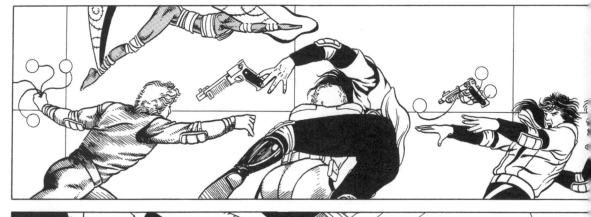

CRACK

LET'S GET RID OF THESE BODIES. D'RENI, DUMP THEM ON THE PLATFORM.

RIGHT.

I'VE GOT THE ANTIDOTE, BEYS.

WELL DONE, DAI. NINIVIR, HOW'S THE BOY?

HE LOOKS DEAD. THIS HAD BETTER WORK.

IT WILL.

THE ANTIDOTE, DAI.

HERE. FREEDOM.

FREEDOM. D'RENI, NINIVIR, LET'S GO.

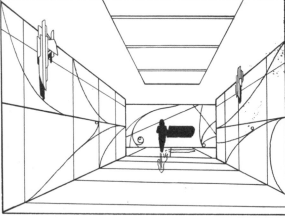

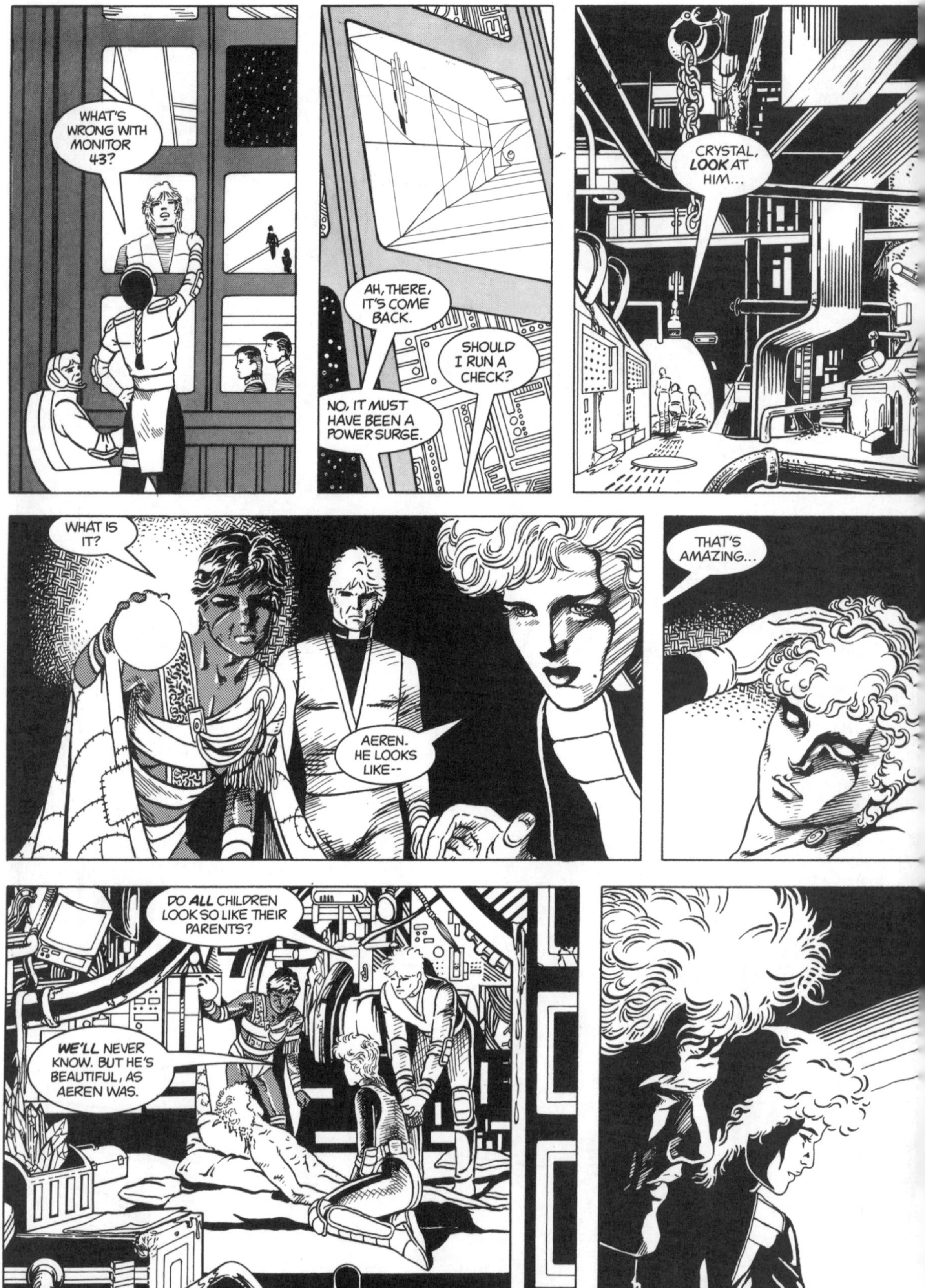
WHAT'S WRONG WITH MONITOR 43?
AH, THERE, IT'S COME BACK.
SHOULD I RUN A CHECK?
NO, IT MUST HAVE BEEN A POWER SURGE.
CRYSTAL, LOOK AT HIM...
WHAT IS IT?
AEREN. HE LOOKS LIKE--
THAT'S AMAZING...
DO ALL CHILDREN LOOK SO LIKE THEIR PARENTS?
WE'LL NEVER KNOW. BUT HE'S BEAUTIFUL, AS AEREN WAS.

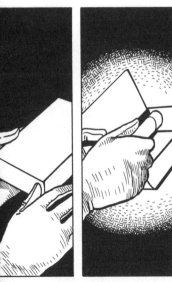

JASON...

NOTHING. NO READING.

THIS ISN'T GOING TO WORK.

GIVE IT A MOMENT.

...YES, I'M GETTING SOMETHING. VERY STRONG NOW. RIENRIE DID IT!

YES...

OUR DISRUPTOR. OUR VICTORY. THE AVATAR IS AS GOOD AS DEAD.

WELL, I **DON'T** SEE WHAT THE PROBLEM IS.

LIANA, YOU CAN'T GET THIS STUFF WITHOUT A DOCTOR'S PRESCRIPTION. IT'S REALLY STRONG.

OOH! WHAT A PRETTY DRESS.

YEAH, NICE.

MISSING

LIANA, WHAT'S THIS?

HUNTER L
BORN: 9/
HAIR: RE
S: HA
ALL (8

THAT LOOKS LIKE ME.

IT **IS** YOU.

Uh-Oh.

DO ALIENS SEND OUT MISSING CHILDREN POSTERS?

PROBABLY NOT.

C'MON, LET'S GET OUT OF HERE.

WHO **ELSE** IS LOOKING FOR YOU?

WELL...

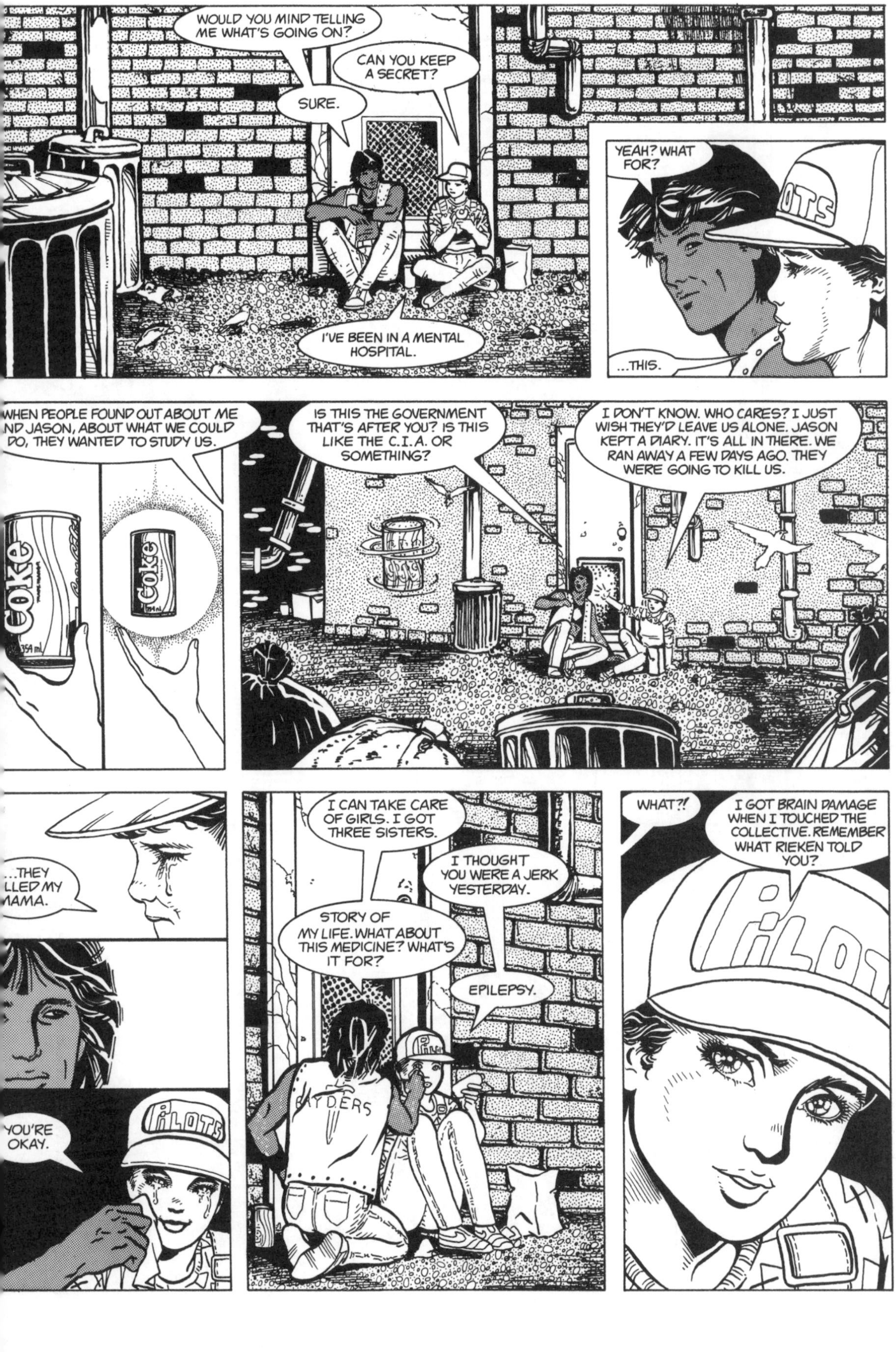
WOULD YOU MIND TELLING ME WHAT'S GOING ON?
CAN YOU KEEP A SECRET?
SURE.
I'VE BEEN IN A MENTAL HOSPITAL.
YEAH? WHAT FOR?
...THIS.
WHEN PEOPLE FOUND OUT ABOUT ME AND JASON, ABOUT WHAT WE COULD DO, THEY WANTED TO STUDY US.
IS THIS THE GOVERNMENT THAT'S AFTER YOU? IS THIS LIKE THE C.I.A. OR SOMETHING?
I DON'T KNOW. WHO CARES? I JUST WISH THEY'D LEAVE US ALONE. JASON KEPT A DIARY. IT'S ALL IN THERE. WE RAN AWAY A FEW DAYS AGO. THEY WERE GOING TO KILL US.
...THEY KILLED MY MAMA.
YOU'RE OKAY.
I CAN TAKE CARE OF GIRLS. I GOT THREE SISTERS.
I THOUGHT YOU WERE A JERK YESTERDAY.
STORY OF MY LIFE. WHAT ABOUT THIS MEDICINE? WHAT'S IT FOR?
EPILEPSY.
WHAT?!
I GOT BRAIN DAMAGE WHEN I TOUCHED THE COLLECTIVE. REMEMBER WHAT RIEKEN TOLD YOU?

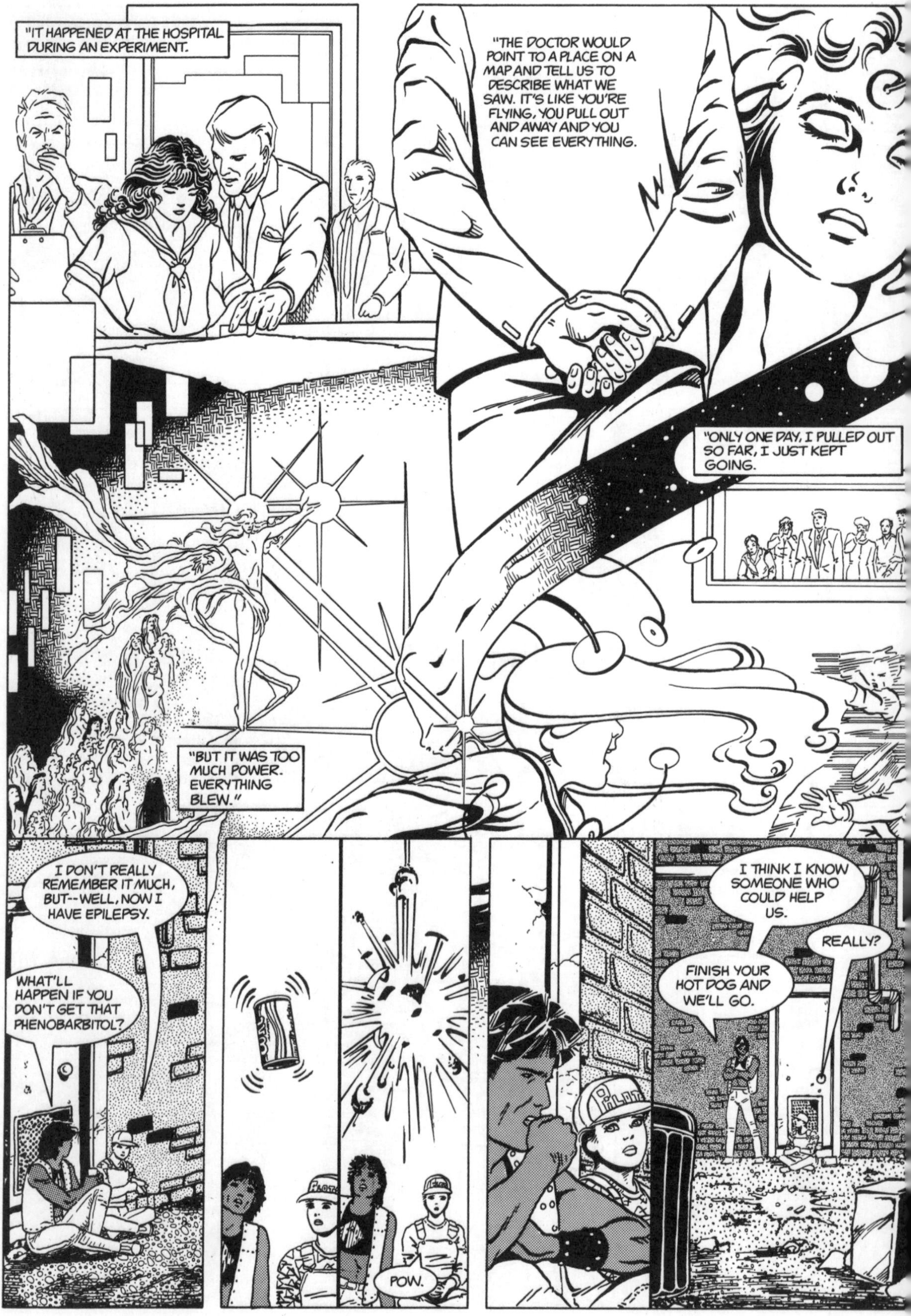
"IT HAPPENED AT THE HOSPITAL DURING AN EXPERIMENT.
"THE DOCTOR WOULD POINT TO A PLACE ON A MAP AND TELL US TO DESCRIBE WHAT WE SAW. IT'S LIKE YOU'RE FLYING, YOU PULL OUT AND AWAY AND YOU CAN SEE EVERYTHING.
"ONLY ONE DAY, I PULLED OUT SO FAR, I JUST KEPT GOING.
"BUT IT WAS TOO MUCH POWER. EVERYTHING BLEW."
I DON'T REALLY REMEMBER IT MUCH, BUT--WELL, NOW I HAVE EPILEPSY.
WHAT'LL HAPPEN IF YOU DON'T GET THAT PHENOBARBITOL?
POW.
I THINK I KNOW SOMEONE WHO COULD HELP US.
REALLY?
FINISH YOUR HOT DOG AND WE'LL GO.

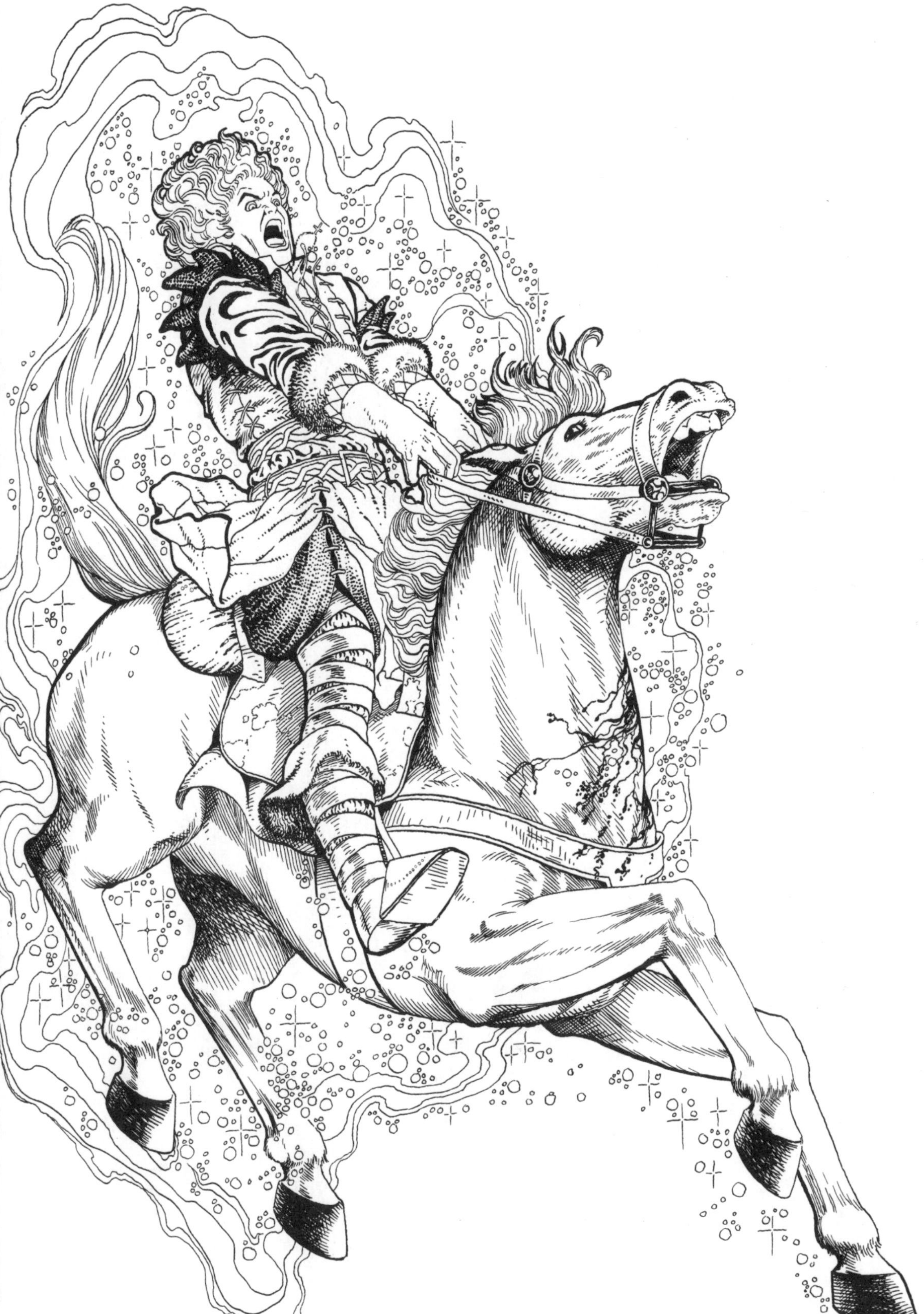

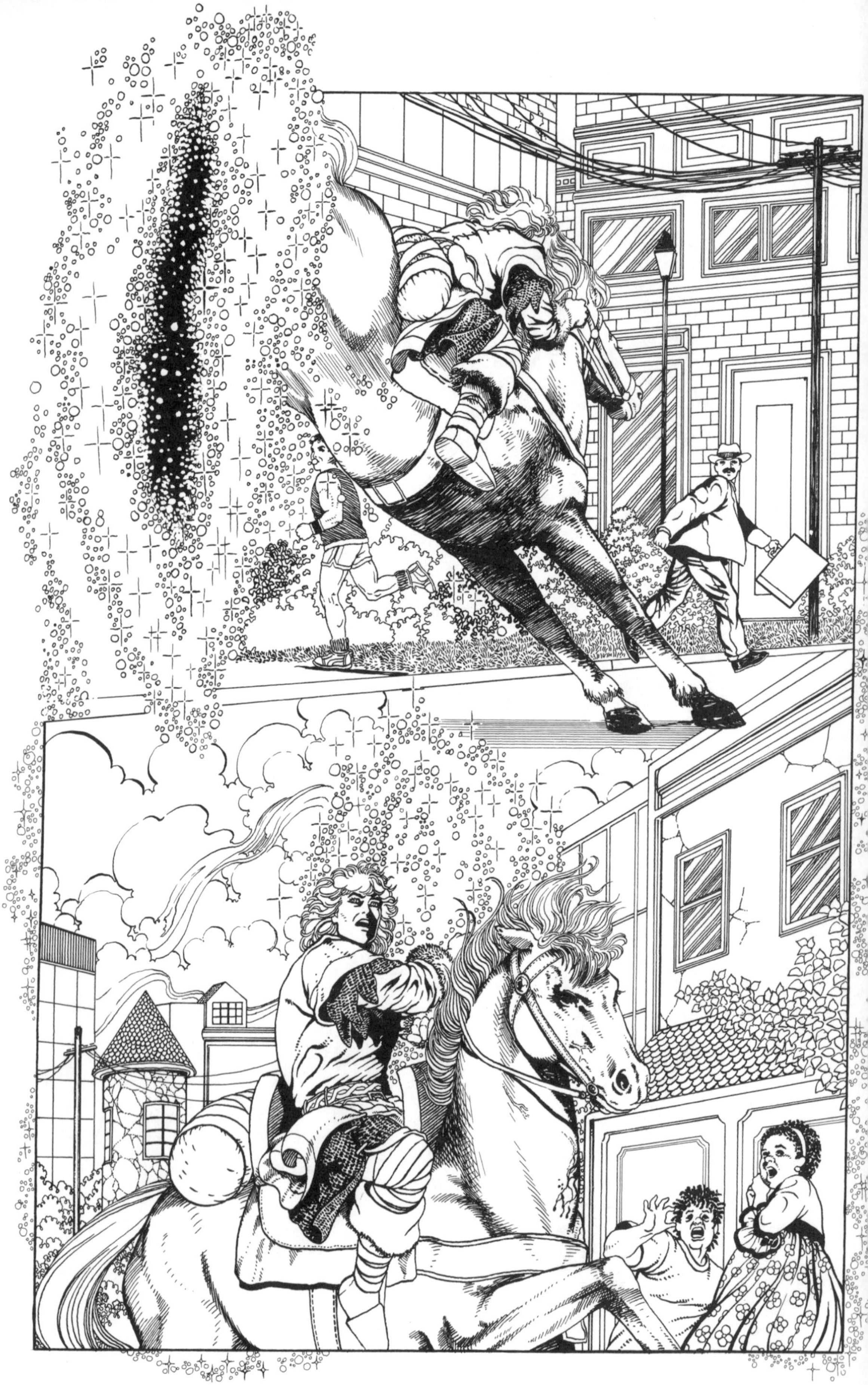

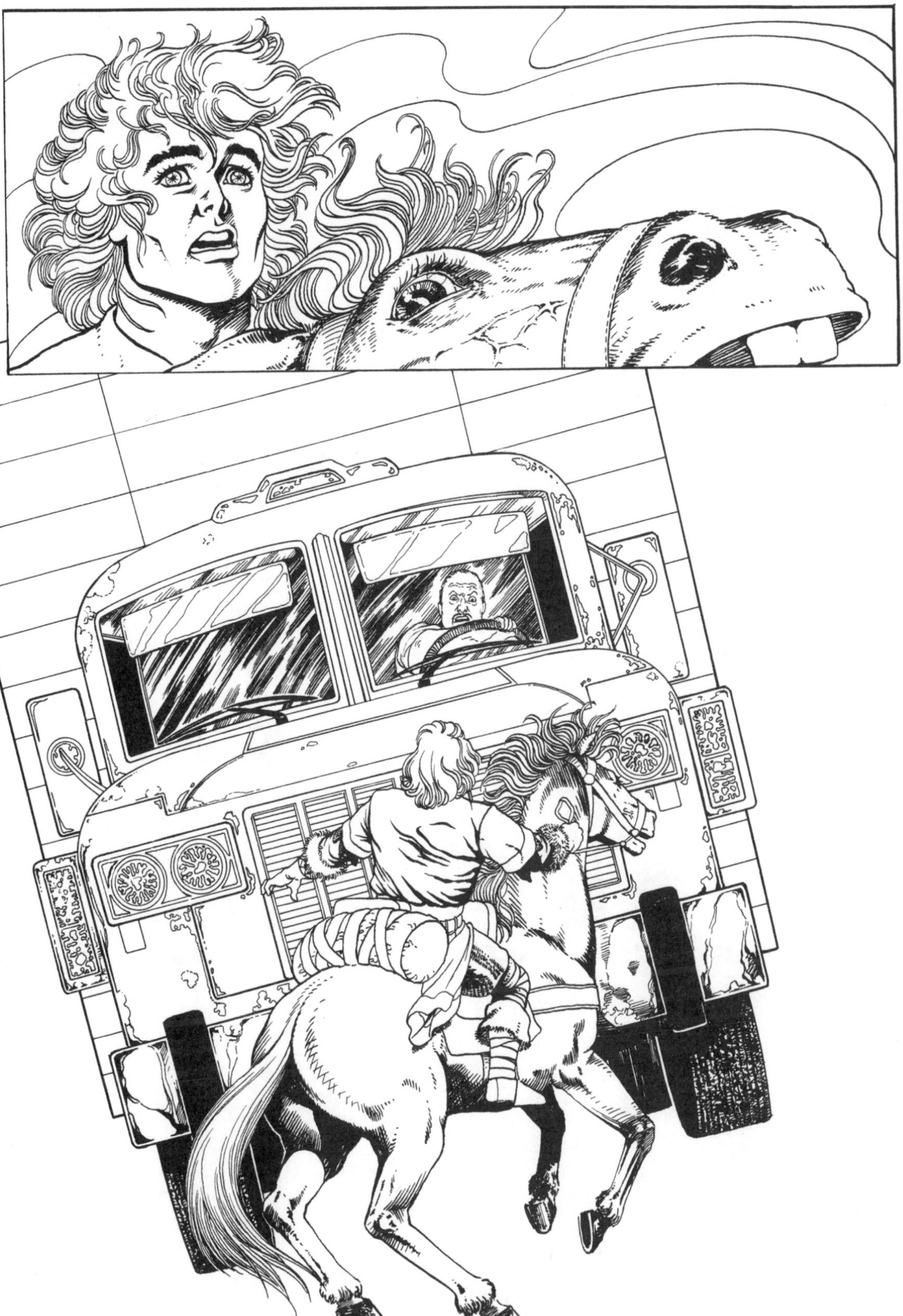

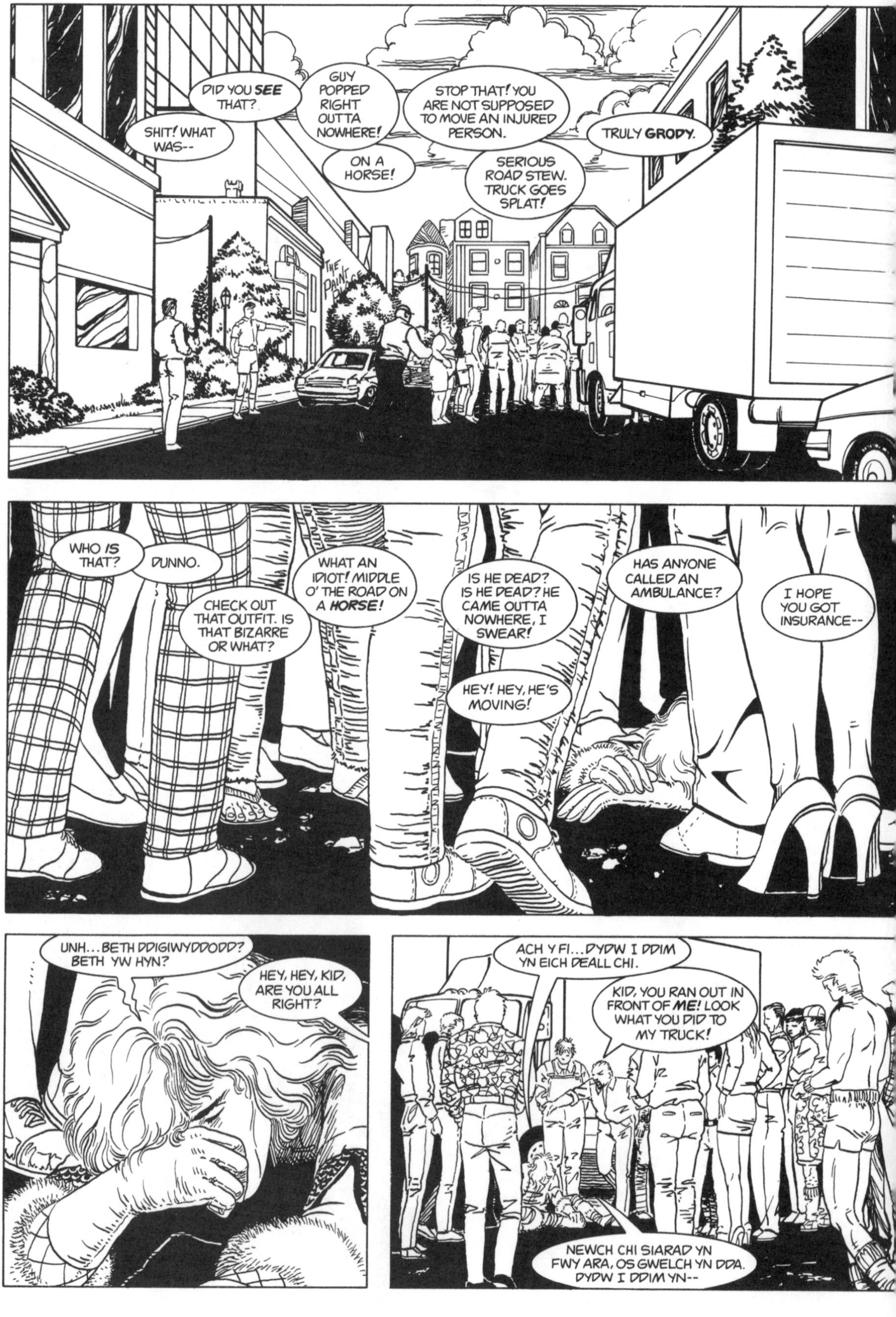

SHIT! WHAT WAS--
DID YOU SEE THAT?
GUY POPPED RIGHT OUTTA NOWHERE!
ON A HORSE!
STOP THAT! YOU ARE NOT SUPPOSED TO MOVE AN INJURED PERSON.
SERIOUS ROAD STEW. TRUCK GOES SPLAT!
TRULY GRODY.
THE PAINT PLACE
WHO IS THAT?
DUNNO.
CHECK OUT THAT OUTFIT. IS THAT BIZARRE OR WHAT?
WHAT AN IDIOT! MIDDLE O' THE ROAD ON A HORSE!
IS HE DEAD? IS HE DEAD? HE CAME OUTTA NOWHERE, I SWEAR!
HEY! HEY, HE'S MOVING!
HAS ANYONE CALLED AN AMBULANCE?
I HOPE YOU GOT INSURANCE--
UNH... BETH DDIGIWYDDODD? BETH YW HYN?
HEY, HEY, KID, ARE YOU ALL RIGHT?
ACH Y FI... DYDW I DDIM YN EICH DEALL CHI.
KID, YOU RAN OUT IN FRONT OF ME! LOOK WHAT YOU DID TO MY TRUCK!
NEWCH CHI SIARAD YN FWY ARA, OS GWELCH YN DDA. DYDW I DDIM YN--

BACHGEN!

BETH SY WEDI DIDWYDD! NA! NA...

I'LL SUE, I SWEAR!

KNOCK IT OFF MISTER, THE KID'S HURT.

IT'S NOT MY FAULT! YOU SAW!

YOU'LL HEAR FROM MY LAWYER, PUNK!

PIEDIWCH!

OH, MY GOD!

LOOK OUT!

DRUAN O BACHGEN... FE HELPA CHI.

PAID A SYMUDI.

CHUK

AH, NO...

GROSS!

WHERE'RE THE COPS? COPS EVERY-WHERE 'CEPT WHEN YOU NEED 'EM.

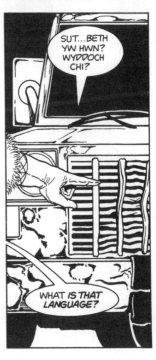

SUT...BETH YW HWN? WYDDOCH CHI?

WHAT IS THAT LANGUAGE?

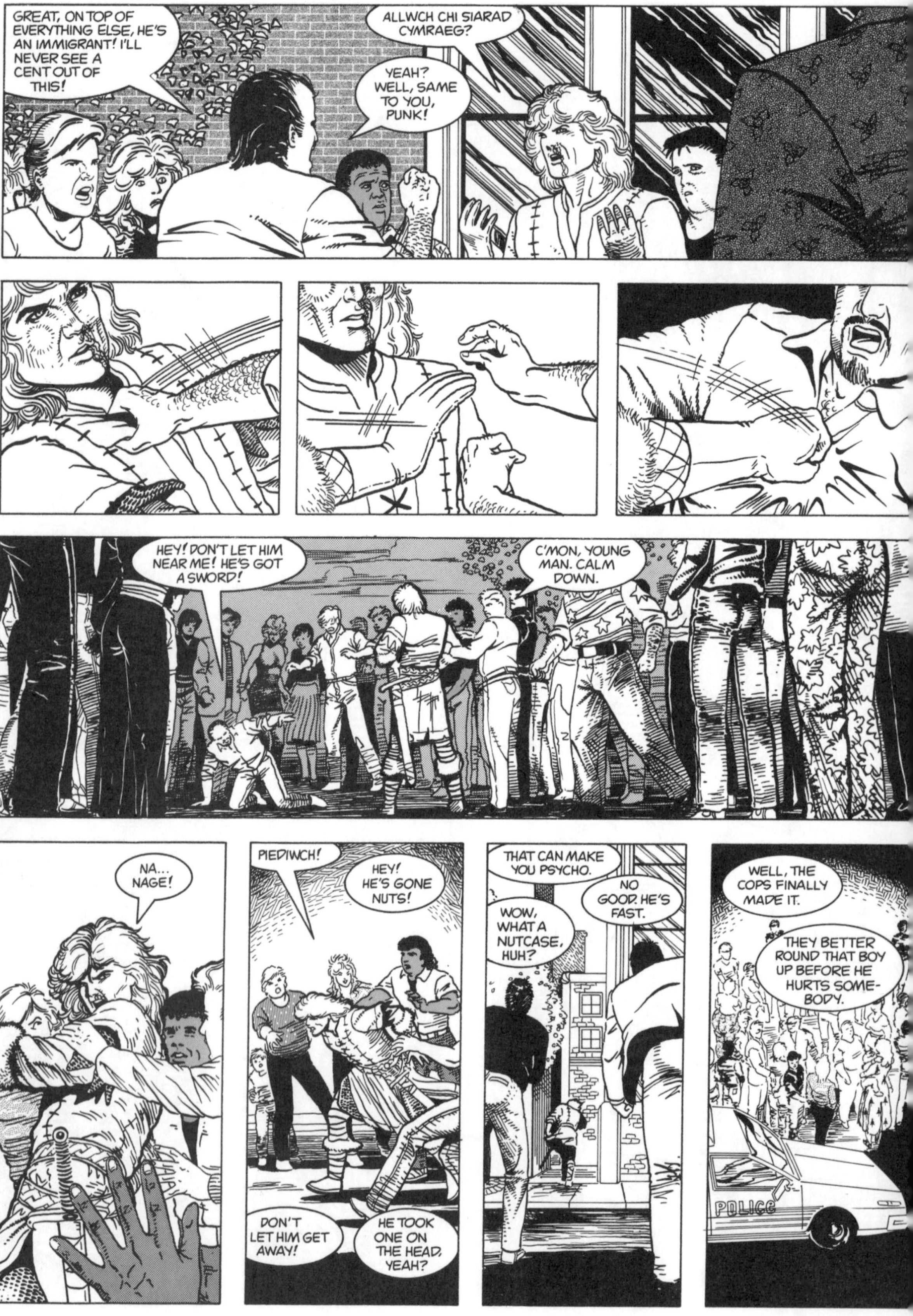
GREAT, ON TOP OF EVERYTHING ELSE, HE'S AN IMMIGRANT! I'LL NEVER SEE A CENT OUT OF THIS!
ALLWCH CHI SIARAD CYMRAEG?
YEAH? WELL, SAME TO YOU, PUNK!
HEY! DON'T LET HIM NEAR ME! HE'S GOT A SWORD!
C'MON, YOUNG MAN. CALM DOWN.
NA... NAGE!
PIEDIWCH!
HEY! HE'S GONE NUTS!
DON'T LET HIM GET AWAY!
HE TOOK ONE ON THE HEAD, YEAH?
THAT CAN MAKE YOU PSYCHO.
WOW, WHAT A NUTCASE, HUH?
NO GOOD. HE'S FAST.
WELL, THE COPS FINALLY MADE IT.
THEY BETTER ROUND THAT BOY UP BEFORE HE HURTS SOME-BODY.
POLICE

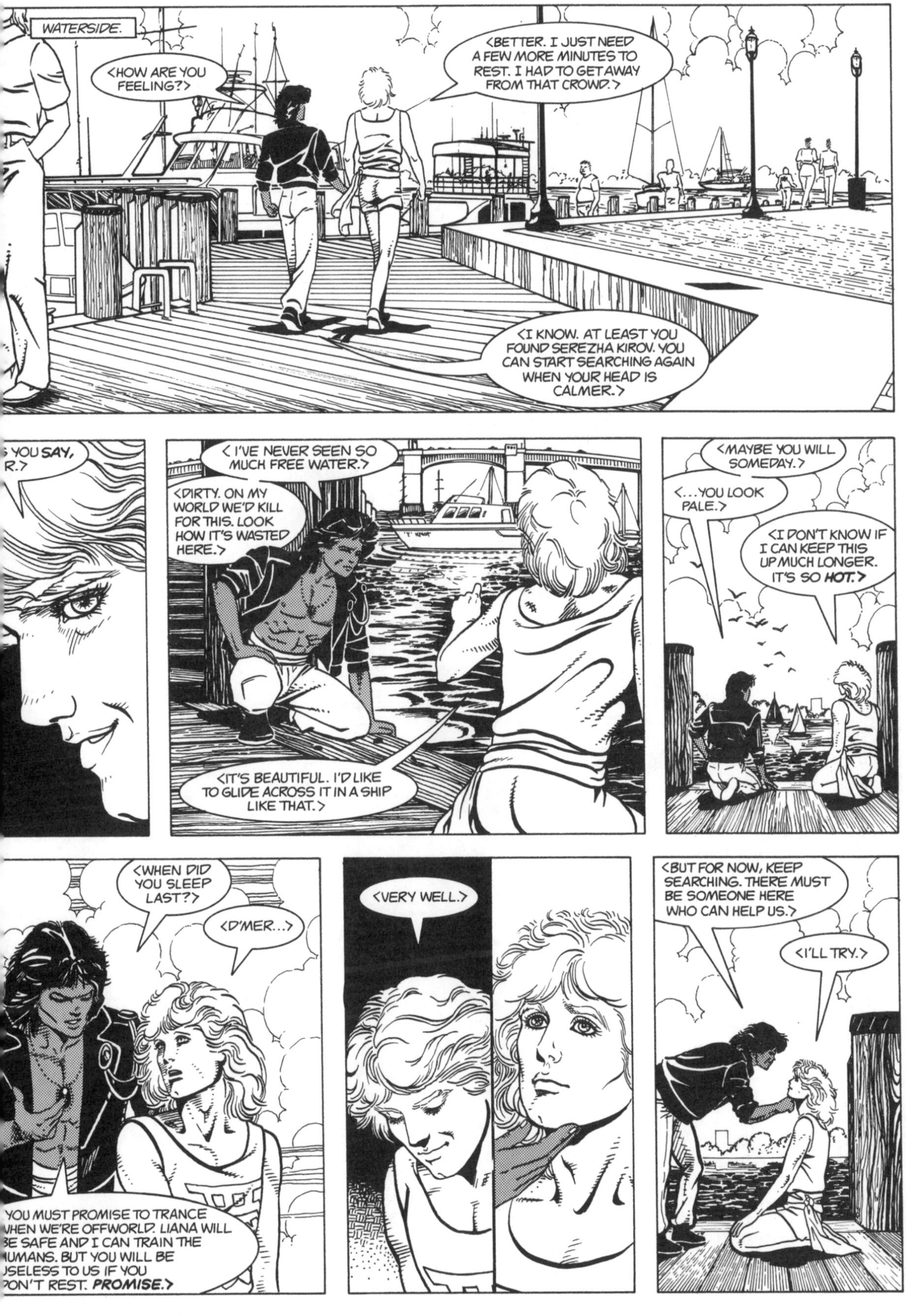
WATERSIDE.
<HOW ARE YOU FEELING?>
<BETTER. I JUST NEED A FEW MORE MINUTES TO REST. I HAD TO GET AWAY FROM THAT CROWD.>
<I KNOW. AT LEAST YOU FOUND SEREZHA KIROV. YOU CAN START SEARCHING AGAIN WHEN YOUR HEAD IS CALMER.>
YOU SAY,
R.>
< I'VE NEVER SEEN SO MUCH FREE WATER.>
<DIRTY. ON MY WORLD WE'D KILL FOR THIS. LOOK HOW IT'S WASTED HERE.>
<IT'S BEAUTIFUL. I'D LIKE TO GLIDE ACROSS IT IN A SHIP LIKE THAT.>
<MAYBE YOU WILL SOMEDAY.>
<...YOU LOOK PALE.>
<I DON'T KNOW IF I CAN KEEP THIS UP MUCH LONGER. IT'S SO HOT.>
<WHEN DID YOU SLEEP LAST?>
<D'MER...>
YOU MUST PROMISE TO TRANCE WHEN WE'RE OFFWORLD. LIANA WILL BE SAFE AND I CAN TRAIN THE HUMANS. BUT YOU WILL BE USELESS TO US IF YOU DON'T REST. PROMISE.>
<VERY WELL.>
<BUT FOR NOW, KEEP SEARCHING. THERE MUST BE SOMEONE HERE WHO CAN HELP US.>
<I'LL TRY.>

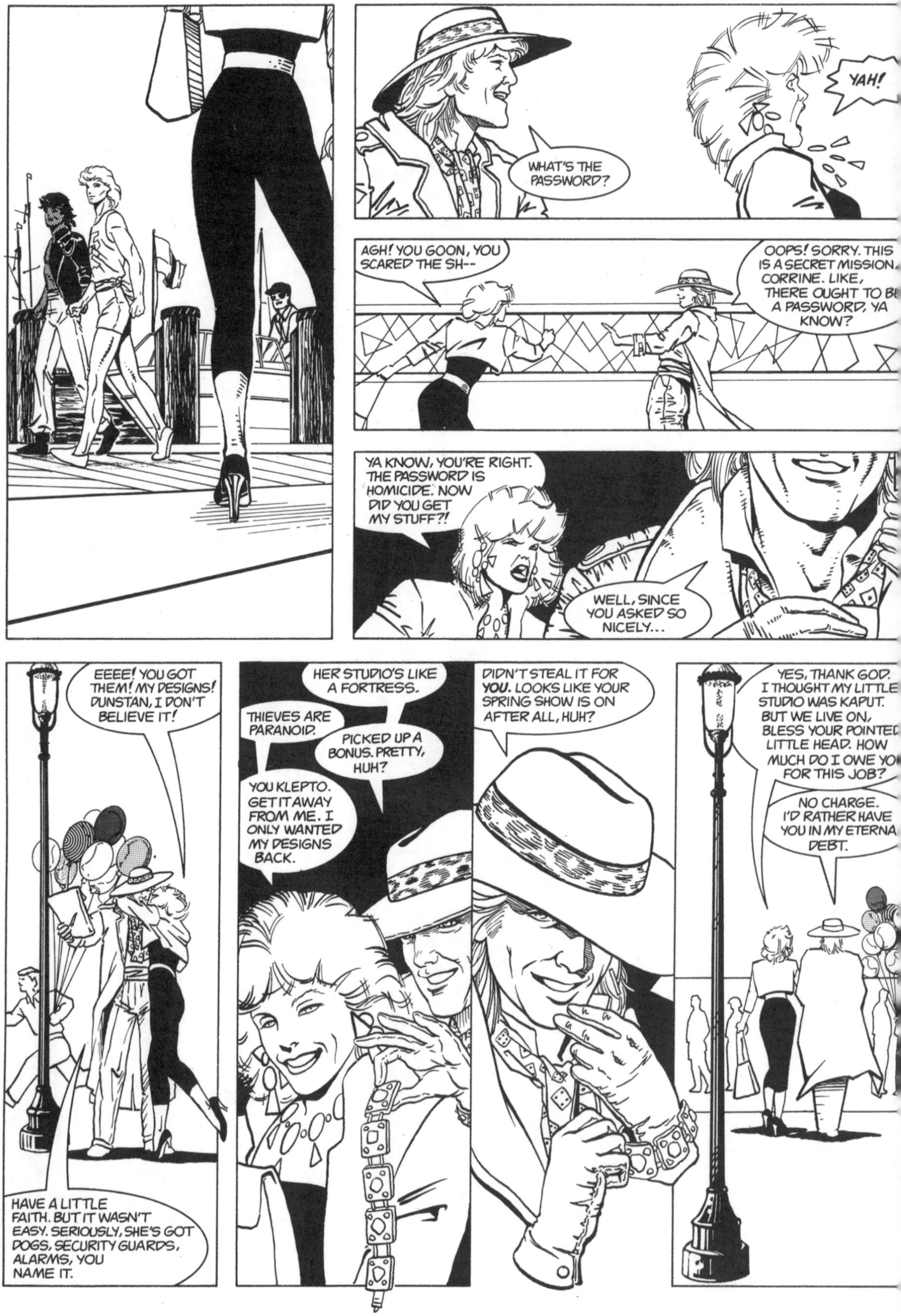

WHAT'S THE PASSWORD?
YAH!
AGH! YOU GOON, YOU SCARED THE SH--
OOPS! SORRY. THIS IS A SECRET MISSION, CORRINE. LIKE, THERE OUGHT TO BE A PASSWORD, YA KNOW?
YA KNOW, YOU'RE RIGHT. THE PASSWORD IS "HOMICIDE." NOW DID YOU GET MY STUFF?!
WELL, SINCE YOU ASKED SO NICELY...
EEEE! YOU GOT THEM! MY DESIGNS! DUNSTAN, I DON'T BELIEVE IT!
HAVE A LITTLE FAITH. BUT IT WASN'T EASY. SERIOUSLY, SHE'S GOT DOGS, SECURITY GUARDS, ALARMS, YOU NAME IT.
HER STUDIO'S LIKE A FORTRESS.
THIEVES ARE PARANOID.
PICKED UP A BONUS. PRETTY, HUH?
YOU KLEPTO. GET IT AWAY FROM ME. I ONLY WANTED MY DESIGNS BACK.
DIDN'T STEAL IT FOR YOU. LOOKS LIKE YOUR SPRING SHOW IS ON AFTER ALL, HUH?
YES, THANK GOD. I THOUGHT MY LITTLE STUDIO WAS KAPUT. BUT WE LIVE ON, BLESS YOUR POINTED LITTLE HEAD. HOW MUCH DO I OWE YOU FOR THIS JOB?
NO CHARGE. I'D RATHER HAVE YOU IN MY ETERNAL DEBT.

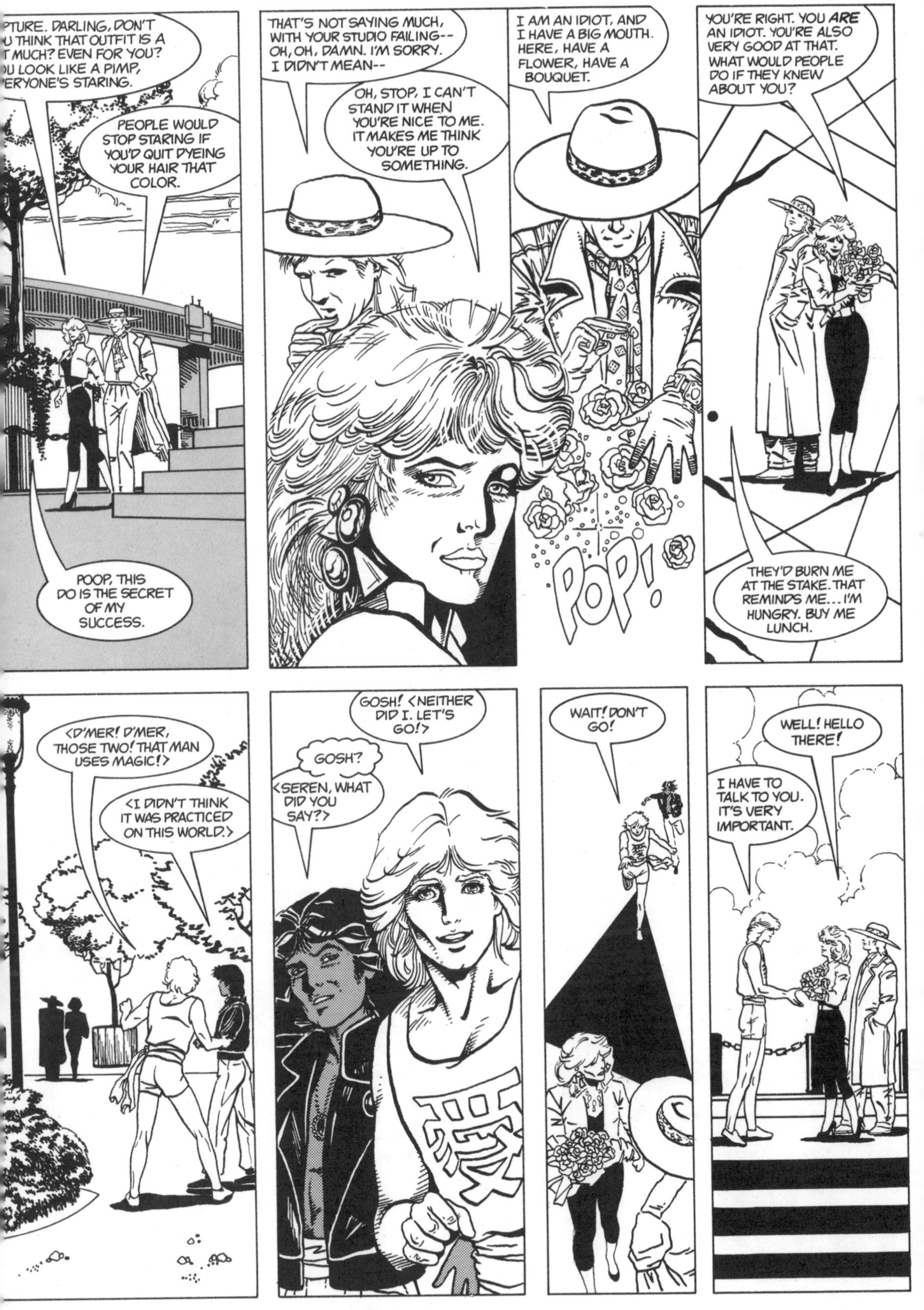
PTURE. DARLING, DON'T U THINK THAT OUTFIT IS A T MUCH? EVEN FOR YOU? U LOOK LIKE A PIMP. ERYONE'S STARING.
PEOPLE WOULD STOP STARING IF YOU'D QUIT DYEING YOUR HAIR THAT COLOR.
POOP, THIS DO IS THE SECRET OF MY SUCCESS.
THAT'S NOT SAYING MUCH, WITH YOUR STUDIO FAILING-- OH, OH, DAMN. I'M SORRY. I DIDN'T MEAN--
OH, STOP, I CAN'T STAND IT WHEN YOU'RE NICE TO ME. IT MAKES ME THINK YOU'RE UP TO SOMETHING.
I AM AN IDIOT, AND I HAVE A BIG MOUTH. HERE, HAVE A FLOWER, HAVE A BOUQUET.
POP!
YOU'RE RIGHT. YOU **ARE** AN IDIOT. YOU'RE ALSO VERY GOOD AT THAT. WHAT WOULD PEOPLE DO IF THEY KNEW ABOUT YOU?
THEY'D BURN ME AT THE STAKE. THAT REMINDS ME... I'M HUNGRY. BUY ME LUNCH.
<D'MER! D'MER, THOSE TWO! THAT MAN USES MAGIC!>
<I DIDN'T THINK IT WAS PRACTICED ON THIS WORLD.>
GOSH! <NEITHER DID I. LET'S GO!>
GOSH?
<SEREN, WHAT DID YOU SAY?>
WAIT! DON'T GO!
WELL! HELLO THERE!
I HAVE TO TALK TO YOU. IT'S VERY IMPORTANT.

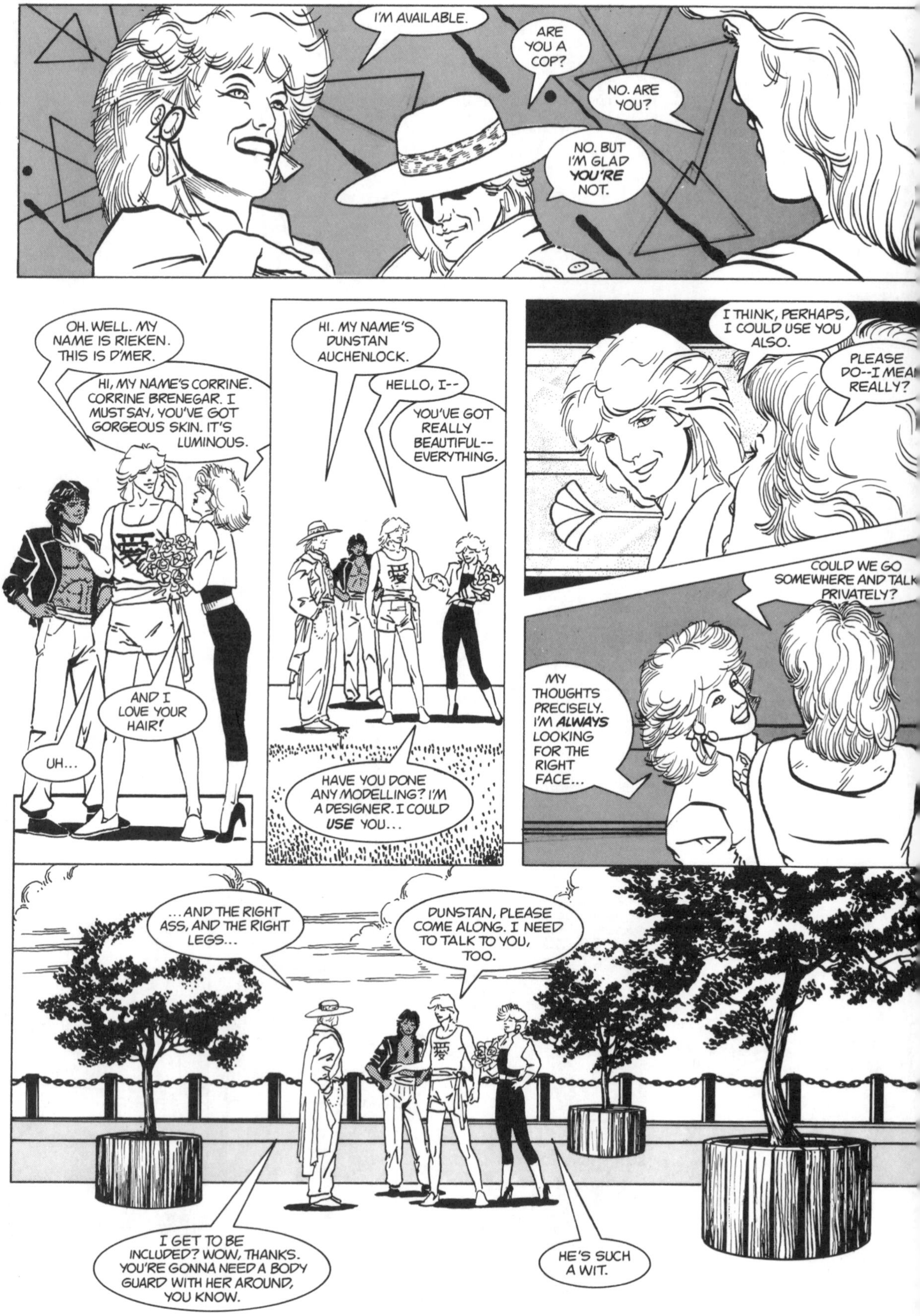

I'M AVAILABLE.
ARE YOU A COP?
NO. ARE YOU?
NO. BUT I'M GLAD ***YOU'RE*** NOT.
OH. WELL. MY NAME IS RIEKEN. THIS IS D'MER.
HI, MY NAME'S CORRINE. CORRINE BRENEGAR. I MUST SAY, YOU'VE GOT GORGEOUS SKIN. IT'S LUMINOUS.
AND I LOVE YOUR HAIR!
UH...
HI. MY NAME'S DUNSTAN AUCHENLOCK.
HELLO, I--
YOU'VE GOT REALLY BEAUTIFUL-- EVERYTHING.
HAVE YOU DONE ANY MODELLING? I'M A DESIGNER. I COULD ***USE*** YOU...
I THINK, PERHAPS, I COULD USE YOU ALSO.
PLEASE DO--I MEA REALLY?
COULD WE GO SOMEWHERE AND TALK PRIVATELY?
MY THOUGHTS PRECISELY. I'M ***ALWAYS*** LOOKING FOR THE RIGHT FACE...
...AND THE RIGHT ASS, AND THE RIGHT LEGS...
DUNSTAN, PLEASE COME ALONG. I NEED TO TALK TO YOU, TOO.
I GET TO BE INCLUDED? WOW, THANKS. YOU'RE GONNA NEED A BODY GUARD WITH HER AROUND, YOU KNOW.
HE'S SUCH A WIT.

THIS IS REALLY HEAVY.

WILL YOU JOIN US, DUNSTAN? AND YOU, CORRINE?

I THINK THIS IS FABULOUS, BUT I DON'T KNOW WHAT YOU EXPECT ME TO DO. IT'S BEEN A WHILE SINCE I WAS A PUNKY KID ON THE STREETS. I'M NOT MUCH OF A FIGHTER ANYMORE.

WE'LL TRAIN YOU. AND I THINK YOU COULD TAKE CARE OF YOURSELF IN ANY SITUATION, MS. BRENEGAR.

HE'S RIGHT. LIKE, I SAW YOU PUNCH OUT THAT GUY AT THE CHRISTMAS PARTY LAST YEAR. OUTRAGEOUS.

OH GOD, I REMEMBER THAT CREEP. HE HAD SWEATY HANDS. HOW EMBARRASSING.

I'M GOING...RIEKEN? IS THAT HOW YOU PRONOUNCE IT?

THAT'S FINE.

I CAN'T LEAVE HIM TO HIMSELF. HE CAN'T REMEMBER TO KEEP HIS FLY UP. I'D BETTER GO TOO.

I'M GLAD. THANK YOU. THIS MEANS EVERYTHING TO ME.

WELL, I GUESS THIS MEANS YOU WON'T BE MODELLING FOR MY SPRING LINE.

NO, I DON'T THINK SO.

YOU ARE SO DEEP.

I KNOW THIS GUY NAMED CHRIS D'ERRICO. HE'S A MEDICAL STUDENT.

FALLEN ANGELS

STOP GENTRIFICATION IN LOWELL

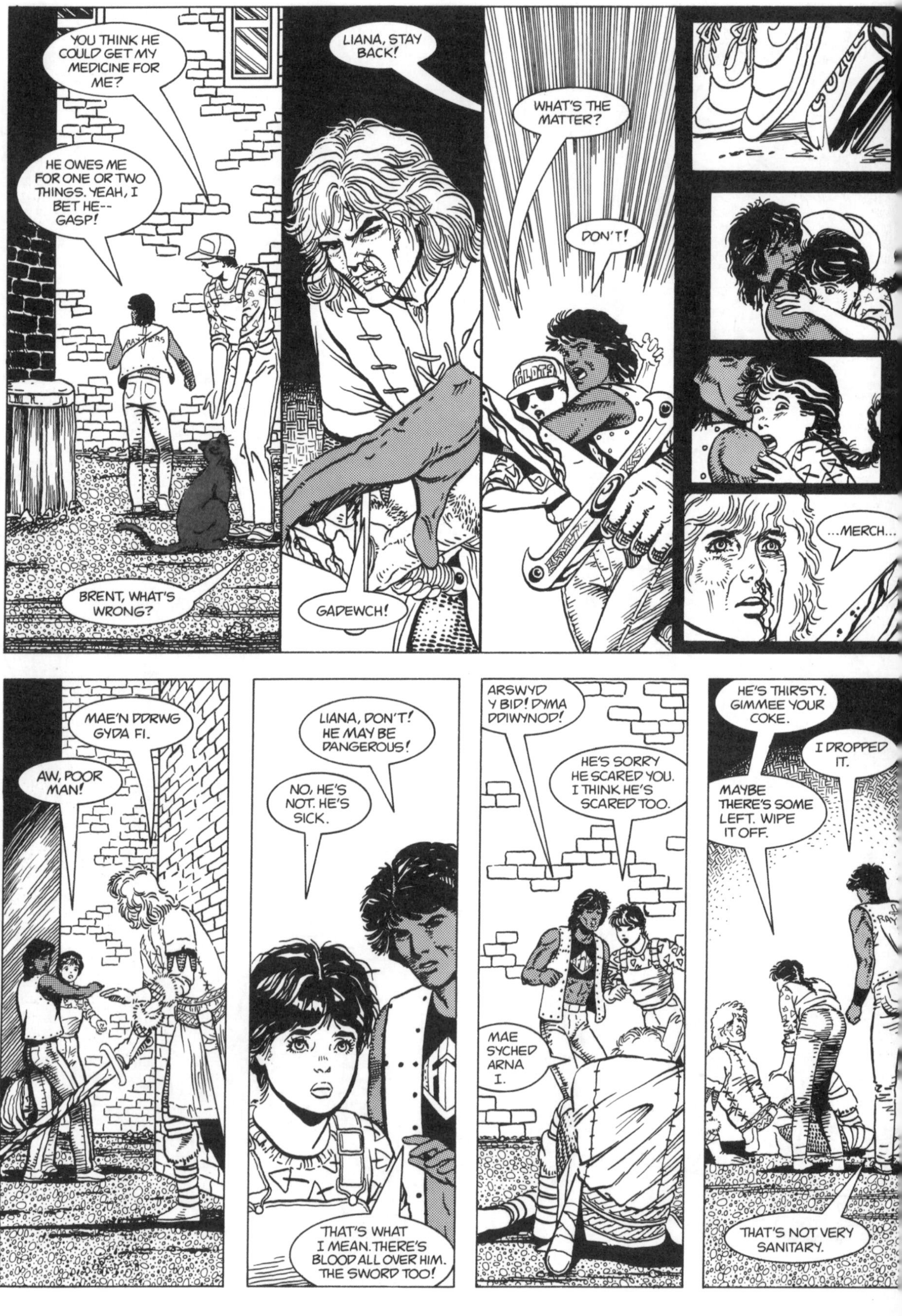

YOU THINK HE COULD GET MY MEDICINE FOR ME?
HE OWES ME FOR ONE OR TWO THINGS. YEAH, I BET HE-- GASP!
BRENT, WHAT'S WRONG?
LIANA, STAY BACK!
GADEWCH!
WHAT'S THE MATTER?
DON'T!
...MERCH...
MAE'N DDRWG GYDA FI.
AW, POOR MAN!
LIANA, DON'T! HE MAY BE DANGEROUS!
NO, HE'S NOT. HE'S SICK.
THAT'S WHAT I MEAN. THERE'S BLOOD ALL OVER HIM. THE SWORD TOO!
ARSWYD Y BID! DYMA DDIWYNOD!
HE'S SORRY HE SCARED YOU. I THINK HE'S SCARED TOO.
MAE SYCHED ARNA I.
HE'S THIRSTY. GIMMEE YOUR COKE.
I DROPPED IT.
MAYBE THERE'S SOME LEFT. WIPE IT OFF.
THAT'S NOT VERY SANITARY.

DIOLCH I CHI.

GO DDA!

HE LIKES IT!

YOU *SPEAK* THAT LANGUAGE?

NO, BUT I CAN TELL SOME OF WHAT HE'S THINKING, WHAT'S ON THE SURFACE. BUT I DON'T WANT TO GO POKING AROUND WHERE I'M NOT INVITED.

PSYCHIC ETHICS? RIGHT. THAT'S NICE TO KNOW, THOUGH. AS LONG AS HE'S NOT AN AXE MURDERER OR-- WOW, THIS ARMOUR'S REAL!

WE CAN'T LEAVE HIM HERE. HE'S ALL BANGED UP.

I'M BRENT. BRENT! BRRRENT!

I FEEL LIKE TARZAN, MAYBE I SHOULD GRUNT. BRENT! UGH!

AH! BRENT! RYDYCH CHI BRENT!

AH, OKAY...UM...I'D BE [MO]RE COMFORTABLE IF HE'D [PU]T THE SWORD AWAY. [WO]ULD YOU...UM...YOU [KN]OW, PUT THAT BACK?

HE DOESN'T UNDERSTAND A WORD YOU'RE SAYING.

AH. HYLO. RYDYCH CHI LIANA. RYDYCH CHI BRENT. O'R GOR.

HEY! HE GOT IT!

NOSWAITH DDA! RYDWI GALAHAD. GALAHAD!

HIS NAME'S GALAHAD? I WOULDN'T BRAG ABOUT A NAME LIKE THAT.

I THINK IT'S NICE, LIKE IN KING ARTHUR. I'M LIANA. LIANA!

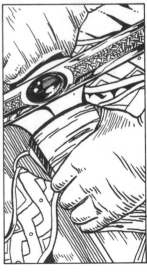

OKAY, HELP ME GET HIM UP HERE. YEAH, THAT'S--PHEW! HE REALLY STINKS!

HE SMELLS LIKE HORSES. I USED TO RIDE THEM WHEN I WAS LITTLE.

IS THAT WHAT THEY SMELL LIKE? GREAT. C'MON, LET'S GO.

DIOLCH I CHI... FFRIND?

YEAH, GREAT.

CHRIS! HEY, CHRIS! OPEN THE DOOR!

BAM!
BAM
5B
BAM!

HOLD ON A SEC-- BRENT, IS THAT YOU

BRENT...? GOOD GOD!

5B

SORRY ABOUT THIS, BUT IT'S SORT OF AN EMERGENCY.

THERE, SET HIM DOWN ON THE COUCH. WHAT HAPPENED?

CHRIS, THIS'LL RUIN YOUR--

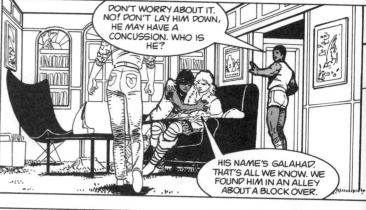

DON'T WORRY ABOUT IT. NO! DON'T LAY HIM DOWN, HE MAY HAVE A CONCUSSION. WHO IS HE?

HIS NAME'S GALAHAD. THAT'S ALL WE KNOW. WE FOUND HIM IN AN ALLEY ABOUT A BLOCK OVER.

LET'S HAVE A LOOK.

SHOULD WE CALL AN AMBULANCE? I KNOW YOU'RE NOT SUPPOSED TO MOVE AN INJURED PERSON, BUT--

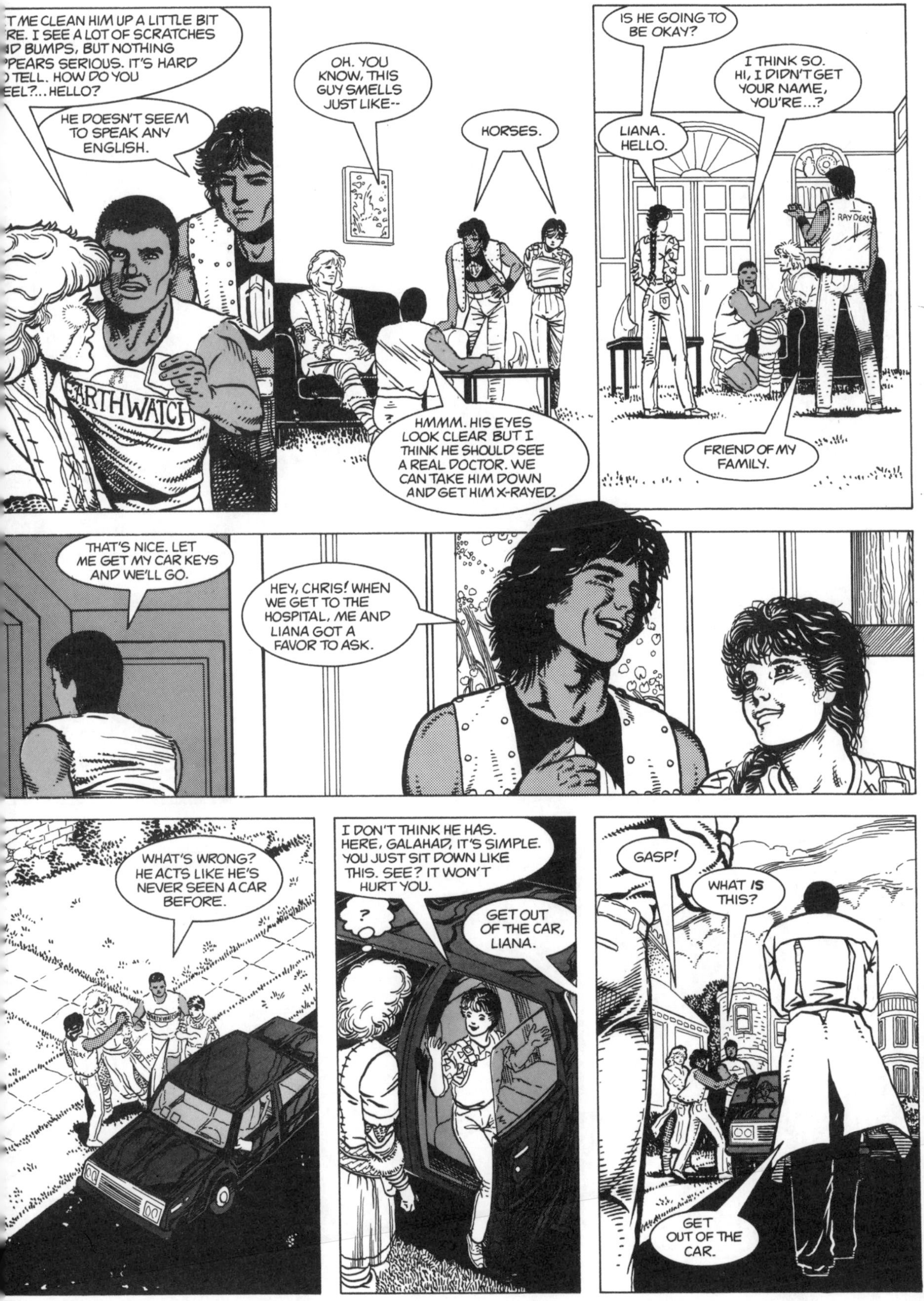

T ME CLEAN HIM UP A LITTLE BIT RE. I SEE A LOT OF SCRATCHES D BUMPS, BUT NOTHING PEARS SERIOUS. IT'S HARD TELL. HOW DO YOU EEL?... HELLO?
HE DOESN'T SEEM TO SPEAK ANY ENGLISH.
EARTHWATCH
OH. YOU KNOW, THIS GUY SMELLS JUST LIKE--
HORSES.
HMMM. HIS EYES LOOK CLEAR BUT I THINK HE SHOULD SEE A REAL DOCTOR. WE CAN TAKE HIM DOWN AND GET HIM X-RAYED.
IS HE GOING TO BE OKAY?
I THINK SO. HI, I DIDN'T GET YOUR NAME, YOU'RE...?
LIANA. HELLO.
RAYDERS
FRIEND OF MY FAMILY.
THAT'S NICE. LET ME GET MY CAR KEYS AND WE'LL GO.
HEY, CHRIS! WHEN WE GET TO THE HOSPITAL, ME AND LIANA GOT A FAVOR TO ASK.
WHAT'S WRONG? HE ACTS LIKE HE'S NEVER SEEN A CAR BEFORE.
I DON'T THINK HE HAS. HERE, GALAHAD, IT'S SIMPLE. YOU JUST SIT DOWN LIKE THIS. SEE? IT WON'T HURT YOU.
?
GET OUT OF THE CAR, LIANA.
GASP!
WHAT IS THIS?
GET OUT OF THE CAR.

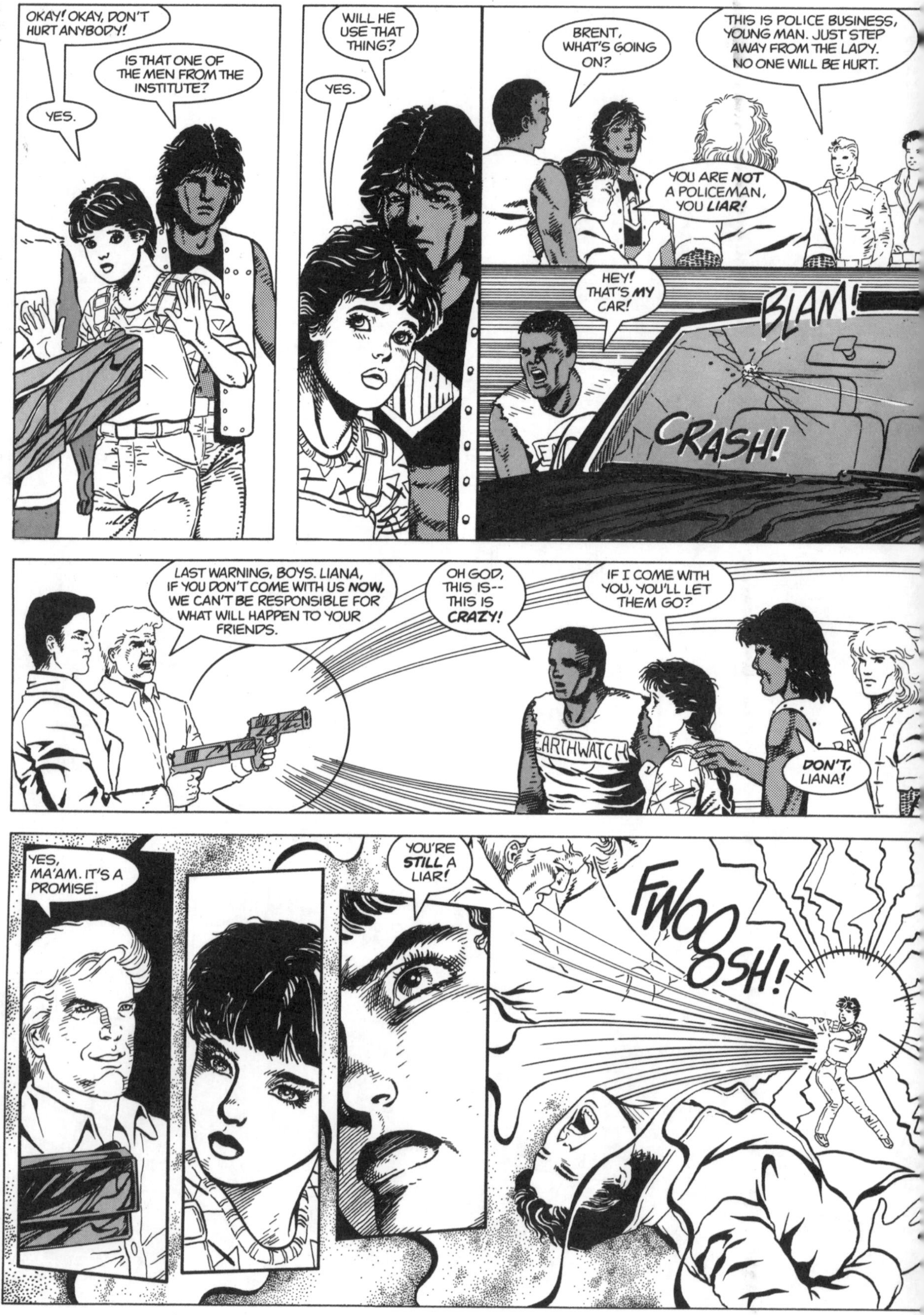
OKAY! OKAY, DON'T HURT ANYBODY!
IS THAT ONE OF THE MEN FROM THE INSTITUTE?
YES.
WILL HE USE THAT THING?
YES.
BRENT, WHAT'S GOING ON?
THIS IS POLICE BUSINESS, YOUNG MAN. JUST STEP AWAY FROM THE LADY. NO ONE WILL BE HURT.
YOU ARE NOT A POLICEMAN, YOU LIAR!
HEY! THAT'S MY CAR!
BLAM!
CRASH!
LAST WARNING, BOYS. LIANA, IF YOU DON'T COME WITH US NOW, WE CAN'T BE RESPONSIBLE FOR WHAT WILL HAPPEN TO YOUR FRIENDS.
OH GOD, THIS IS-- THIS IS CRAZY!
IF I COME WITH YOU, YOU'LL LET THEM GO?
EARTHWATCH
DON'T, LIANA!
YES, MA'AM. IT'S A PROMISE.
YOU'RE STILL A LIAR!
FWOOOSH!

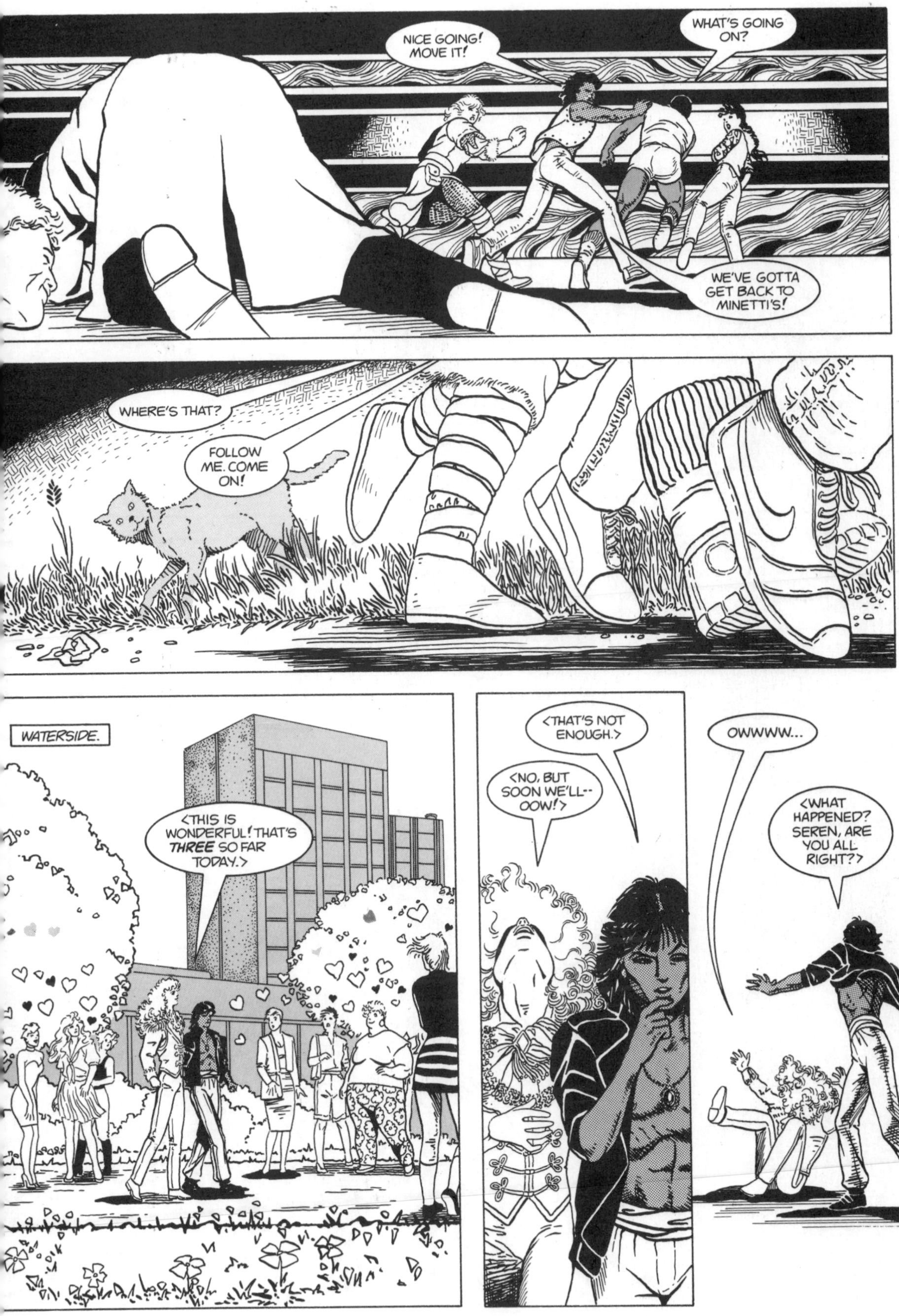
NICE GOING! MOVE IT!
WHAT'S GOING ON?
WE'VE GOTTA GET BACK TO MINETTI'S!
WHERE'S THAT?
FOLLOW ME. COME ON!
WATERSIDE.
<THIS IS WONDERFUL! THAT'S THREE SO FAR TODAY.>
<THAT'S NOT ENOUGH.>
<NO, BUT SOON WE'LL-- OOW!>
OWWWW...
<WHAT HAPPENED? SEREN, ARE YOU ALL RIGHT?>

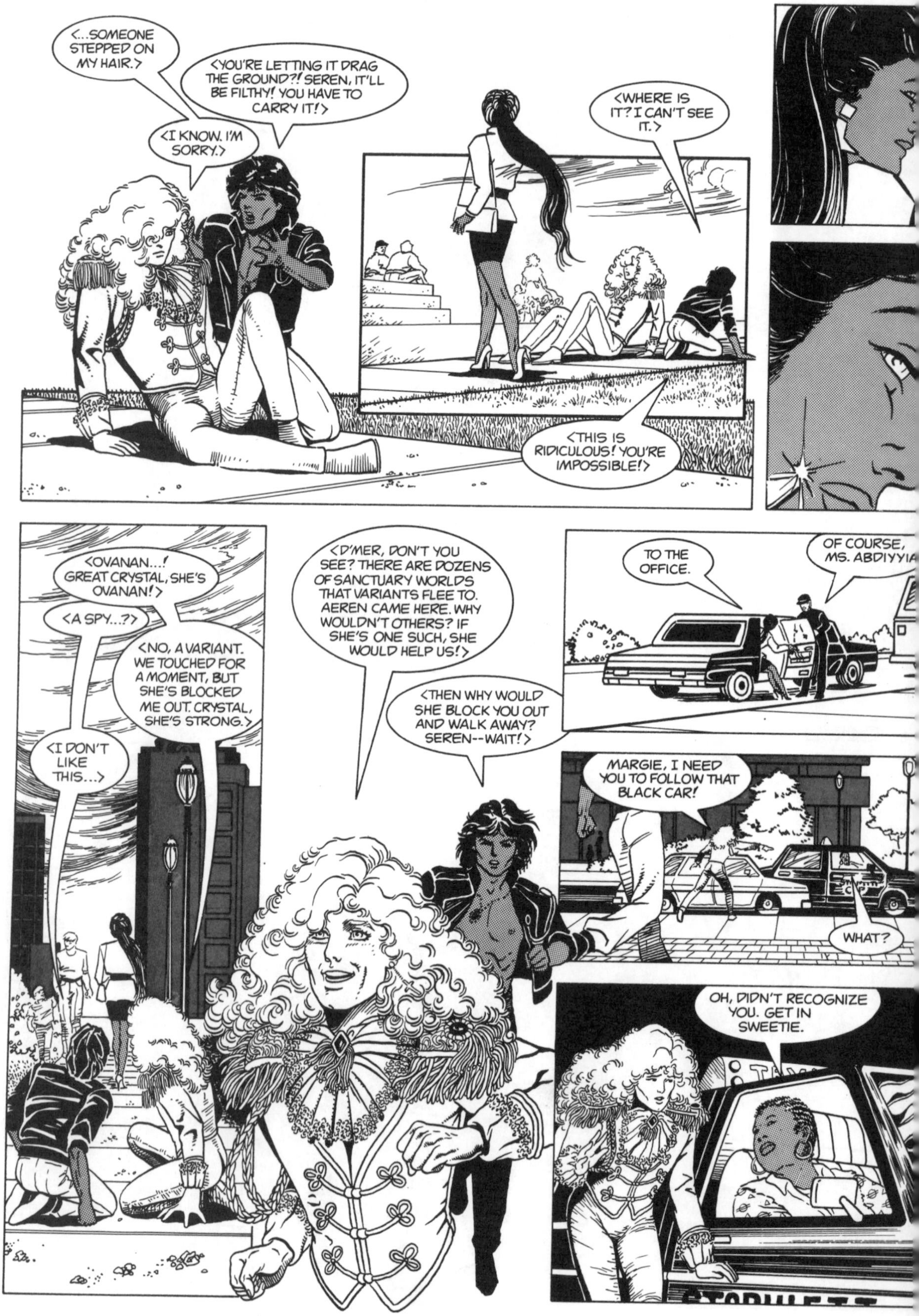
<...SOMEONE STEPPED ON MY HAIR.>
<YOU'RE LETTING IT DRAG THE GROUND?! SEREN, IT'LL BE FILTHY! YOU HAVE TO CARRY IT!>
<I KNOW. I'M SORRY.>
<WHERE IS IT? I CAN'T SEE IT.>
<THIS IS RIDICULOUS! YOU'RE IMPOSSIBLE!>
<OVANAN...! GREAT CRYSTAL, SHE'S OVANAN!>
<A SPY...?>
<NO, A VARIANT. WE TOUCHED FOR A MOMENT, BUT SHE'S BLOCKED ME OUT. CRYSTAL, SHE'S STRONG.>
<I DON'T LIKE THIS...>
<D'MER, DON'T YOU SEE? THERE ARE DOZENS OF SANCTUARY WORLDS THAT VARIANTS FLEE TO. AEREN CAME HERE. WHY WOULDN'T OTHERS? IF SHE'S ONE SUCH, SHE WOULD HELP US!>
<THEN WHY WOULD SHE BLOCK YOU OUT AND WALK AWAY? SEREN--WAIT!>
TO THE OFFICE.
OF COURSE, MS. ABDIYYIA
MARGIE, I NEED YOU TO FOLLOW THAT BLACK CAR!
WHAT?
OH, DIDN'T RECOGNIZE YOU. GET IN SWEETIE.

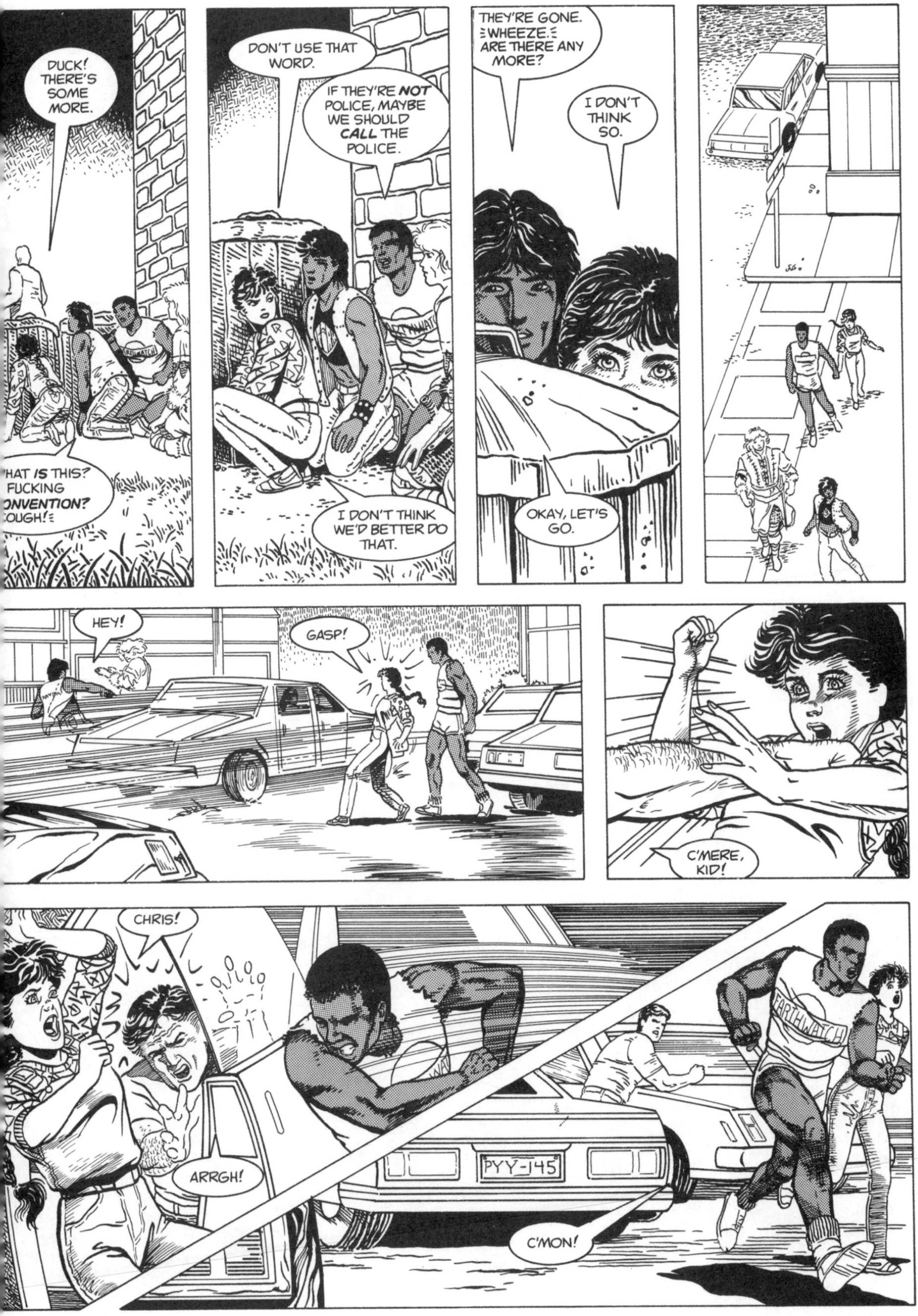
DUCK! THERE'S SOME MORE.
HAT IS THIS? FUCKING ONVENTION? OUGH!
DON'T USE THAT WORD.
IF THEY'RE NOT POLICE, MAYBE WE SHOULD CALL THE POLICE.
I DON'T THINK WE'D BETTER DO THAT.
THEY'RE GONE. WHEEZE. ARE THERE ANY MORE?
I DON'T THINK SO.
OKAY, LET'S GO.
HEY!
GASP!
C'MERE, KID!
CHRIS!
ARRGH!
PYY-145
C'MON!

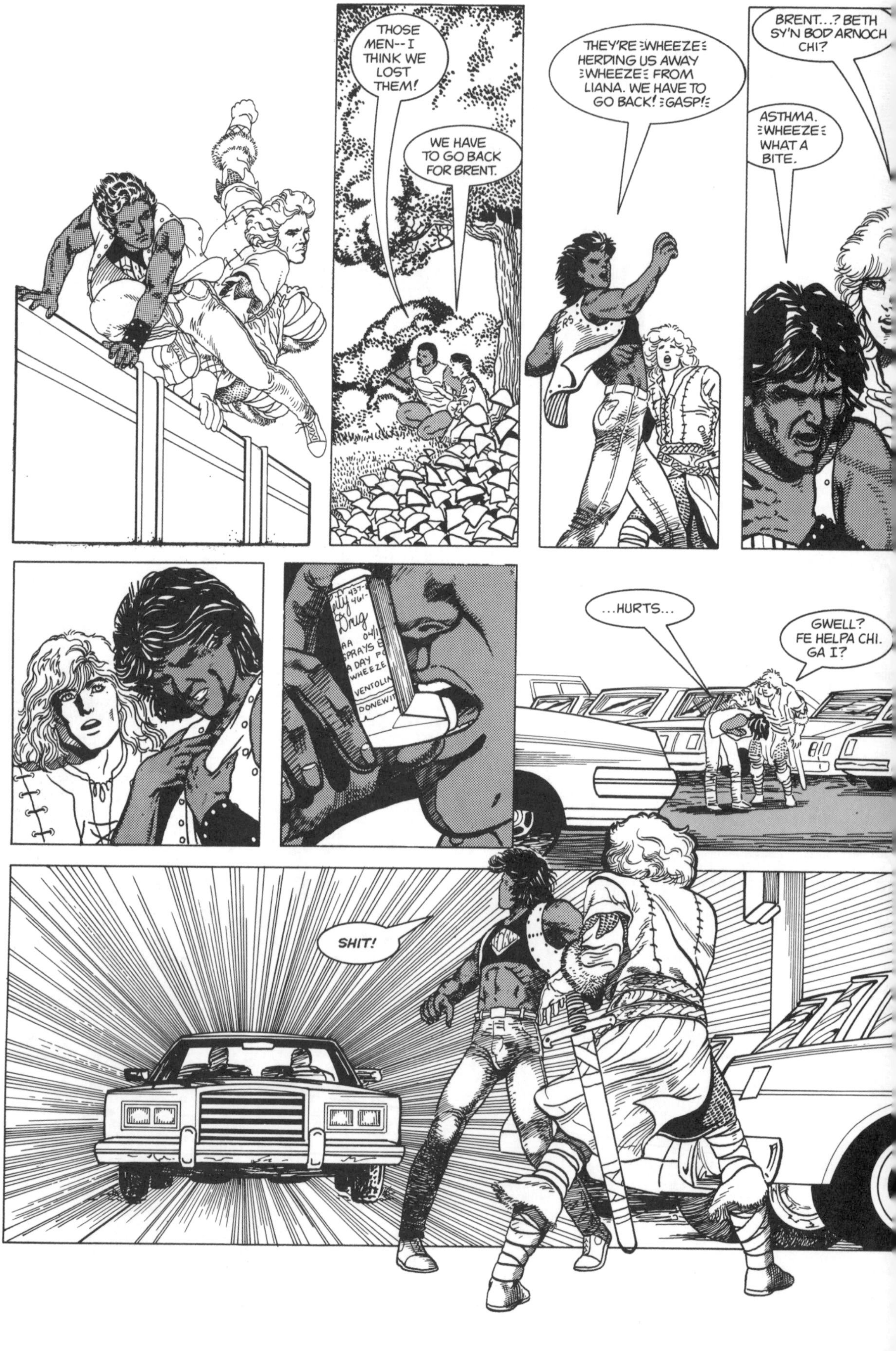
THOSE MEN--I THINK WE LOST THEM!
WE HAVE TO GO BACK FOR BRENT.
THEY'RE ≡WHEEZE≡ HERDING US AWAY ≡WHEEZE≡ FROM LIANA. WE HAVE TO GO BACK! ≡GASP!≡
BRENT...? BETH SY'N BOD ARNOCH CHI?
ASTHMA. ≡WHEEZE≡ WHAT A BITE.
...HURTS...
GWELL? FE HELPA CHI. GA I?
SHIT!

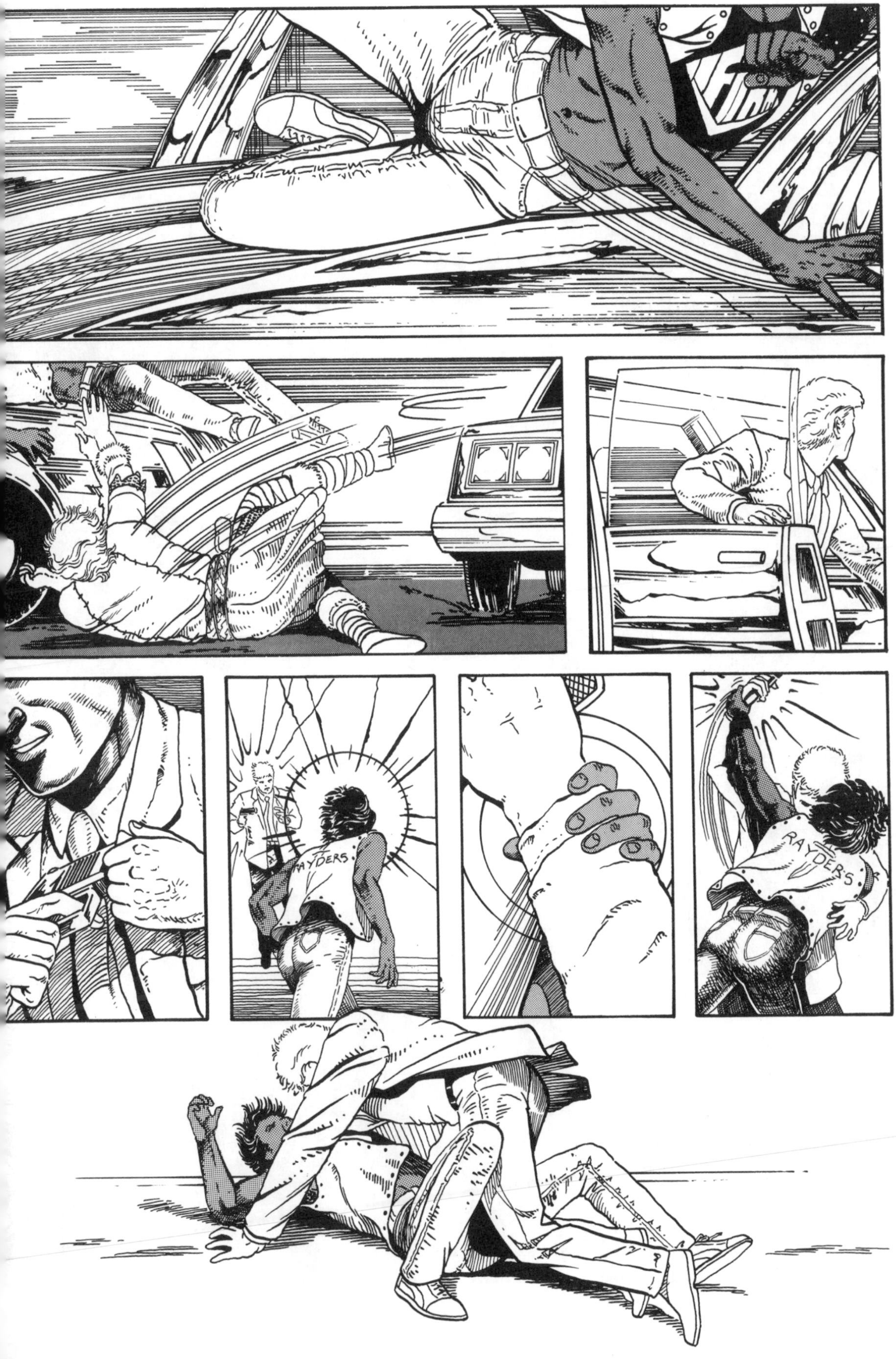
RAYDERS
RAYDERS

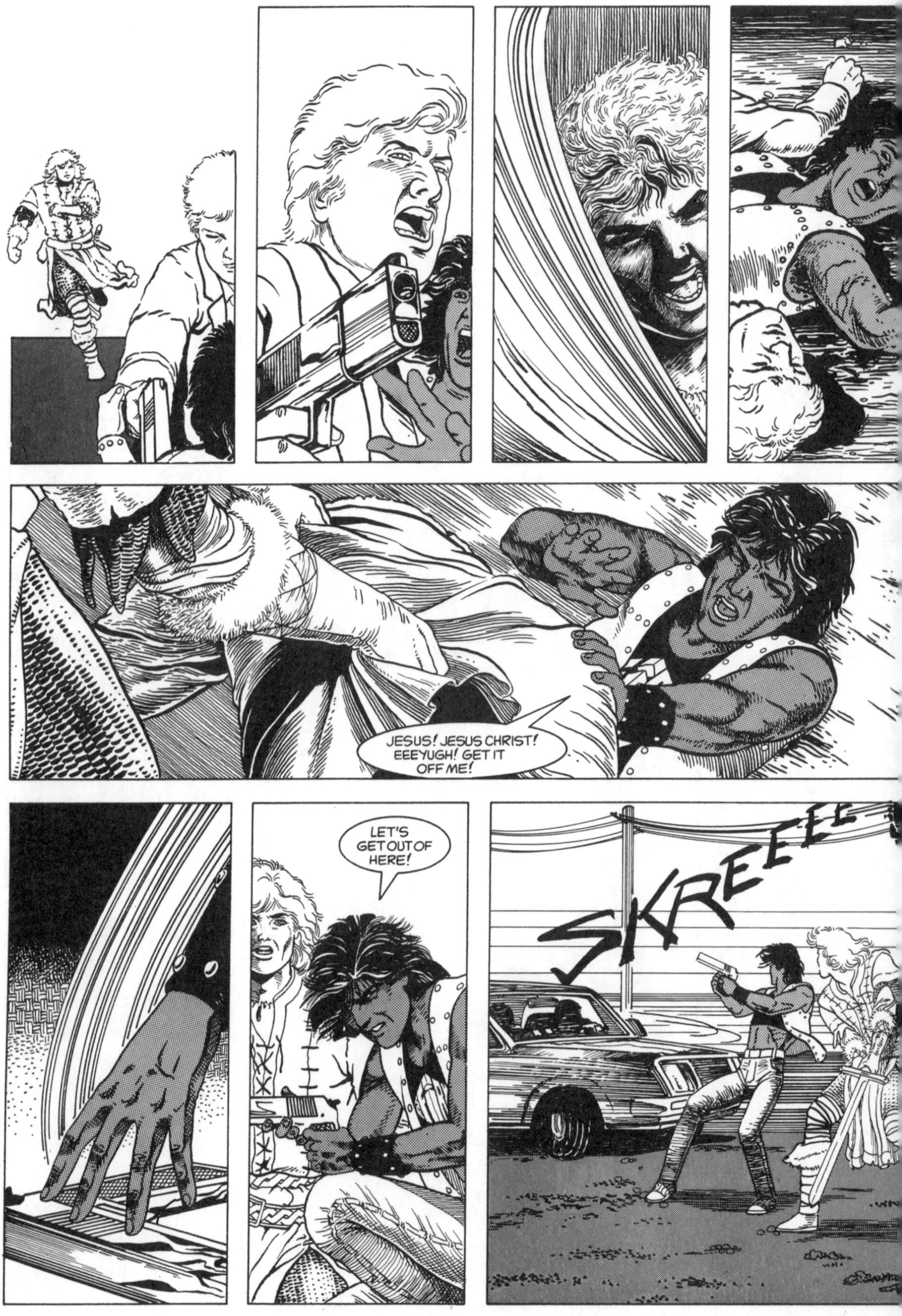
JESUS! JESUS CHRIST! EEEYUGH! GET IT OFF ME!
LET'S GET OUT OF HERE!
SKREEEE

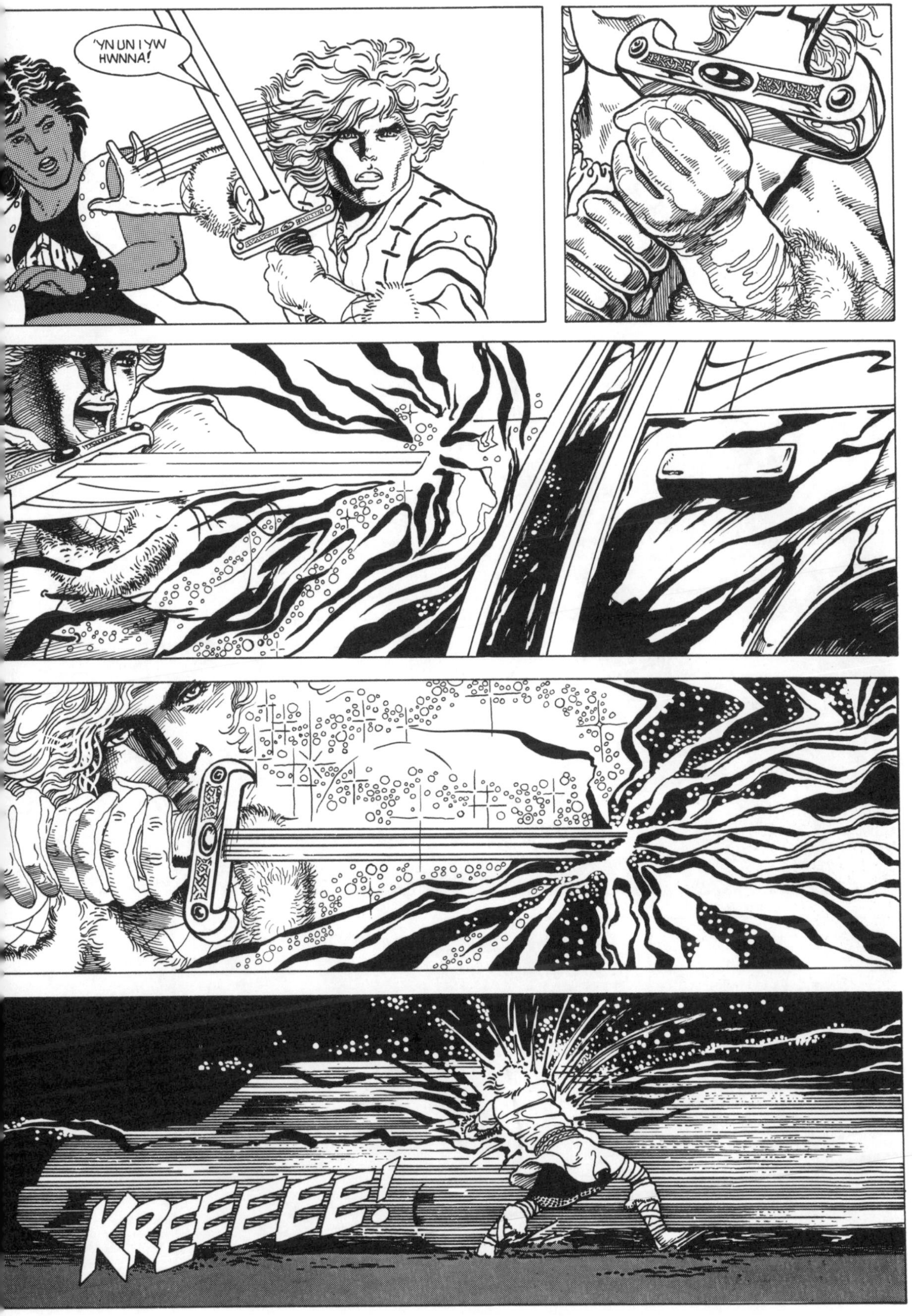
'YN UN I YW HWNNA!
KREEEEEE!

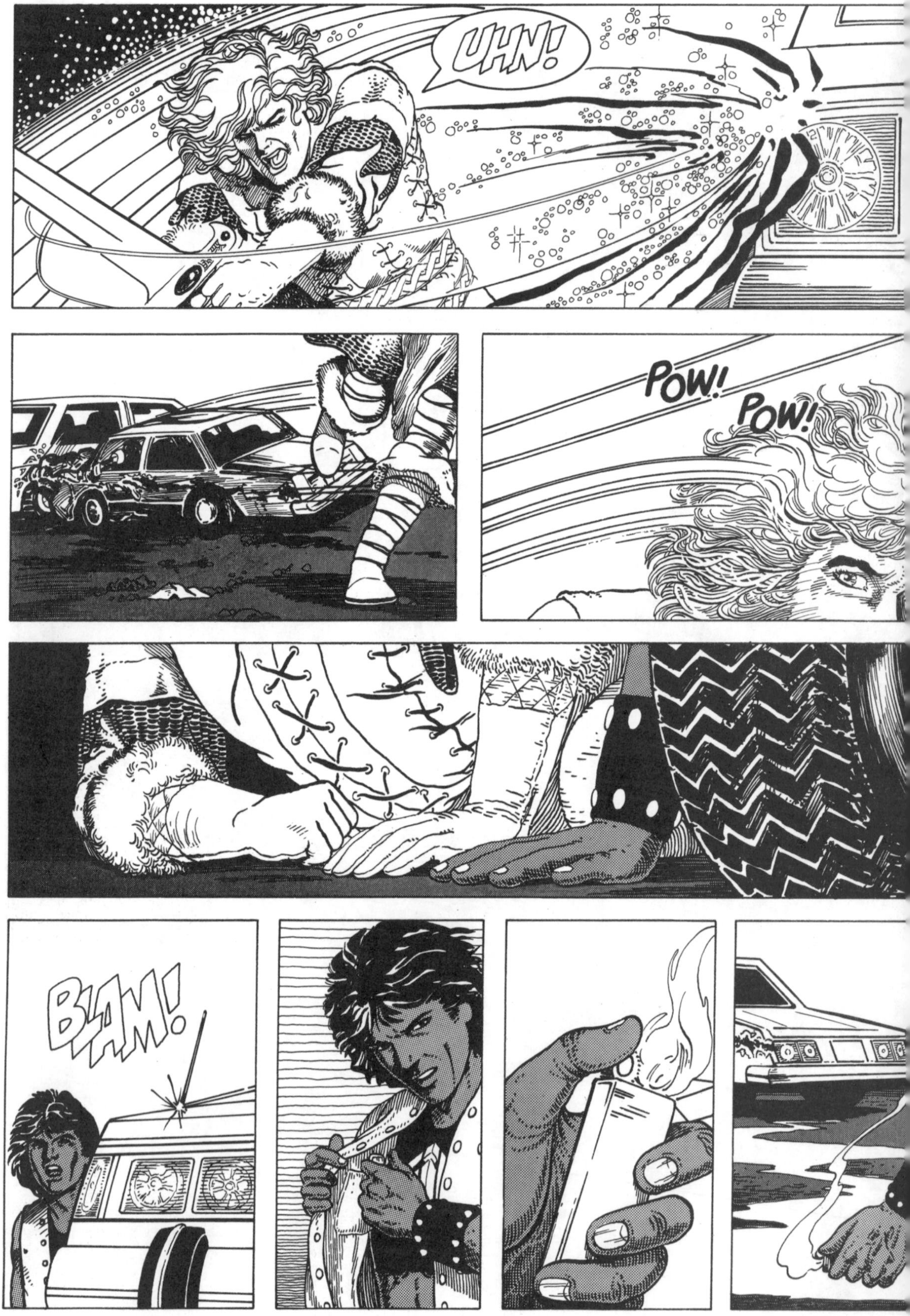
UHN!
POW!
POW!
BLAM!

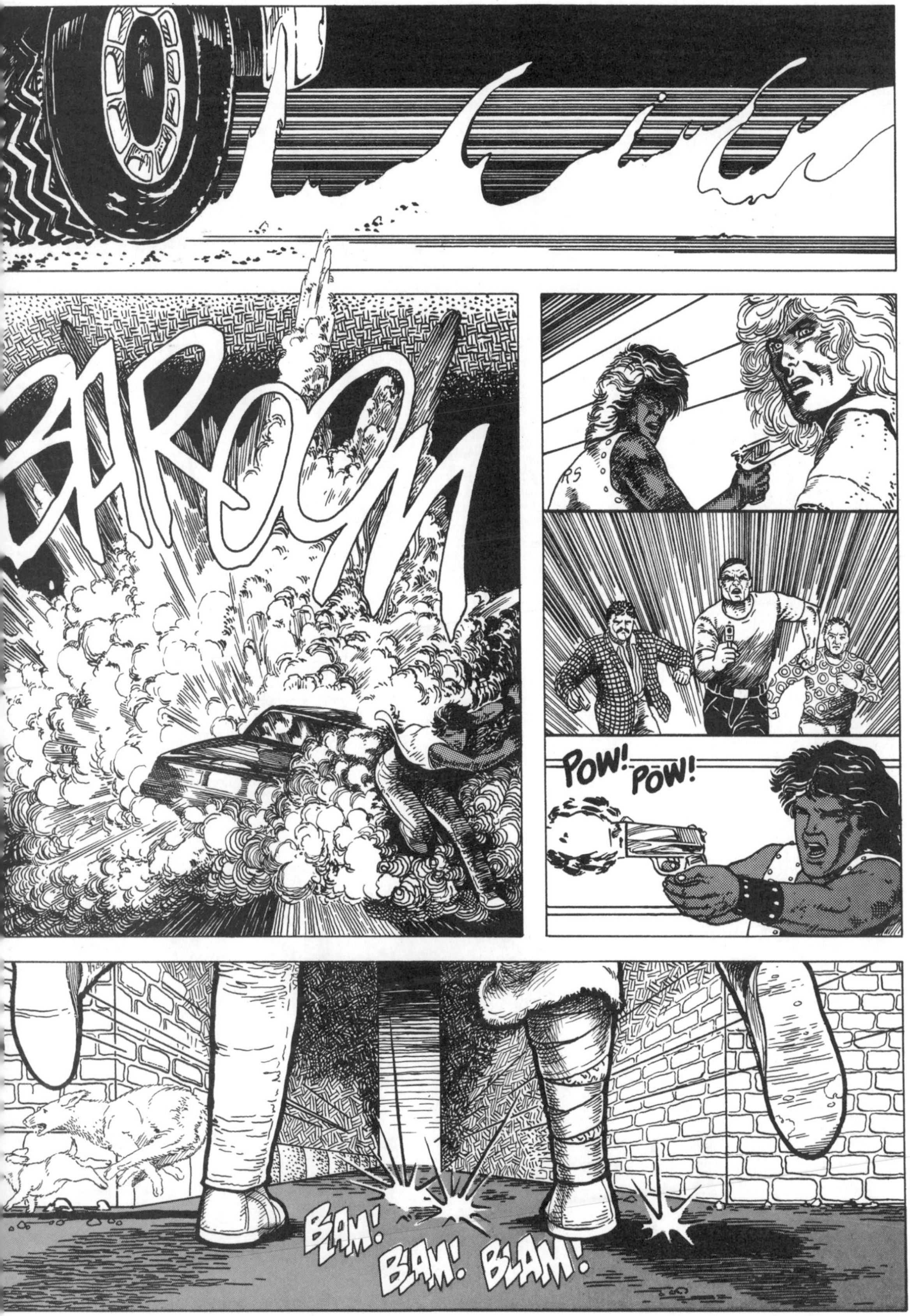
BAROOM
POW! POW!
BLAM!
BLAM! BLAM!

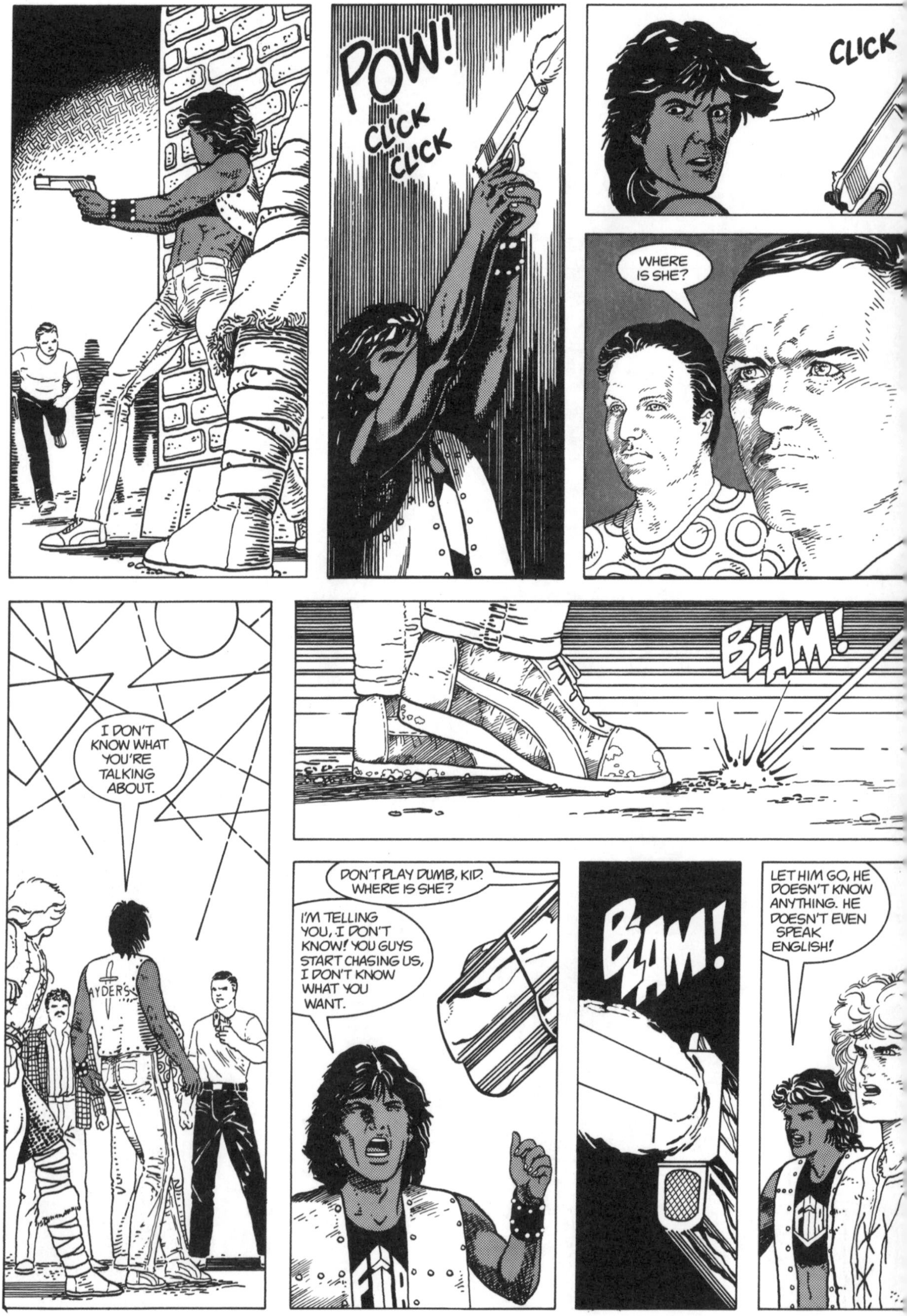
POW!
CLICK
CLICK
CLICK
WHERE IS SHE?
I DON'T KNOW WHAT YOU'RE TALKING ABOUT.
AYDERS
BLAM!
DON'T PLAY DUMB, KID. WHERE IS SHE?
I'M TELLING YOU, I DON'T KNOW! YOU GUYS START CHASING US, I DON'T KNOW WHAT YOU WANT.
BLAM!
LET HIM GO, HE DOESN'T KNOW ANYTHING. HE DOESN'T EVEN SPEAK ENGLISH!

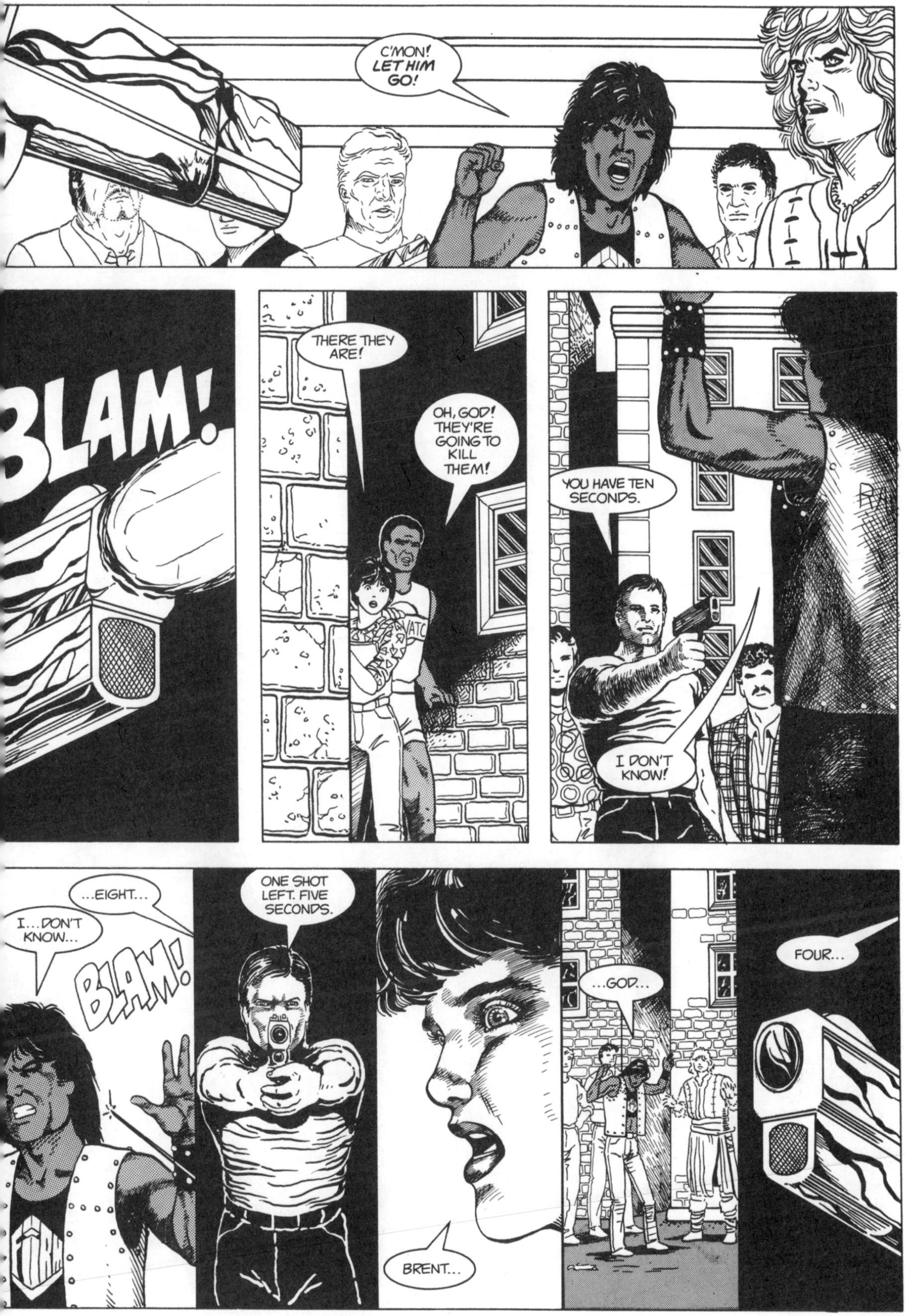
C'MON! LET HIM GO!
BLAM!
THERE THEY ARE!
OH, GOD! THEY'RE GOING TO KILL THEM!
YOU HAVE TEN SECONDS.
I DON'T KNOW!
...EIGHT...
I...DON'T KNOW...
BLAM!
ONE SHOT LEFT. FIVE SECONDS.
BRENT...
...GOD...
FOUR...

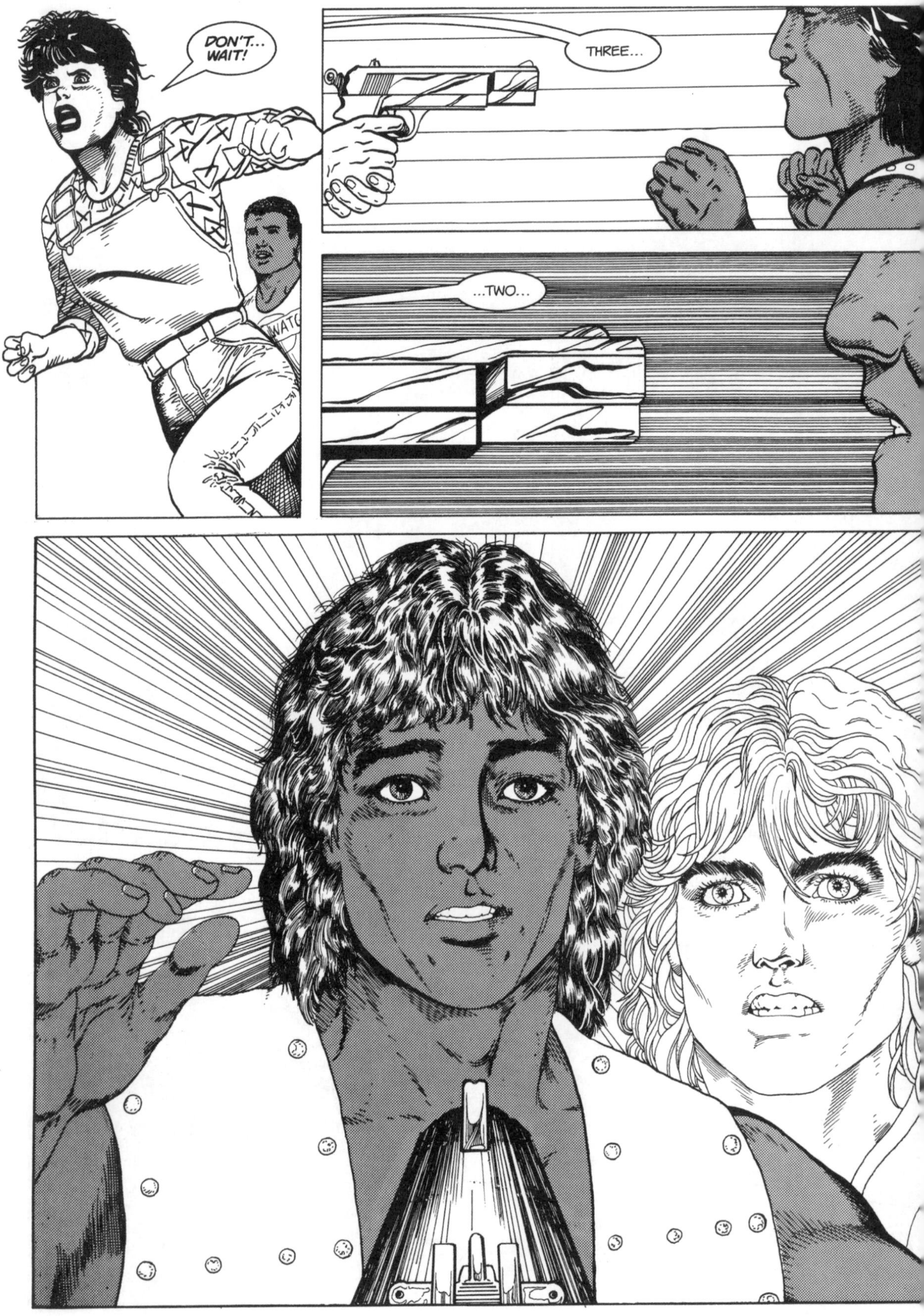
DON'T... WAIT!
THREE...
...TWO...

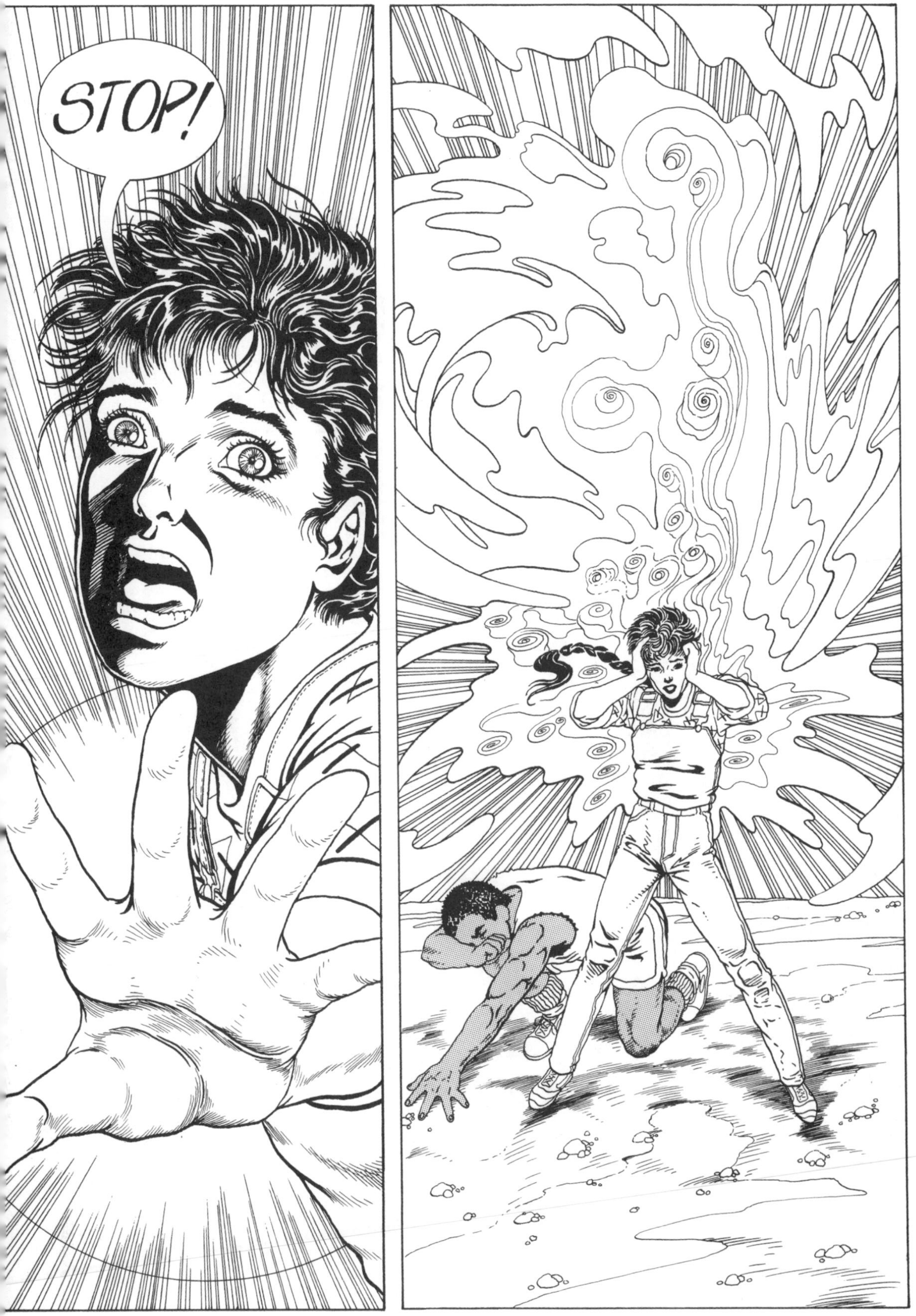
STOP!

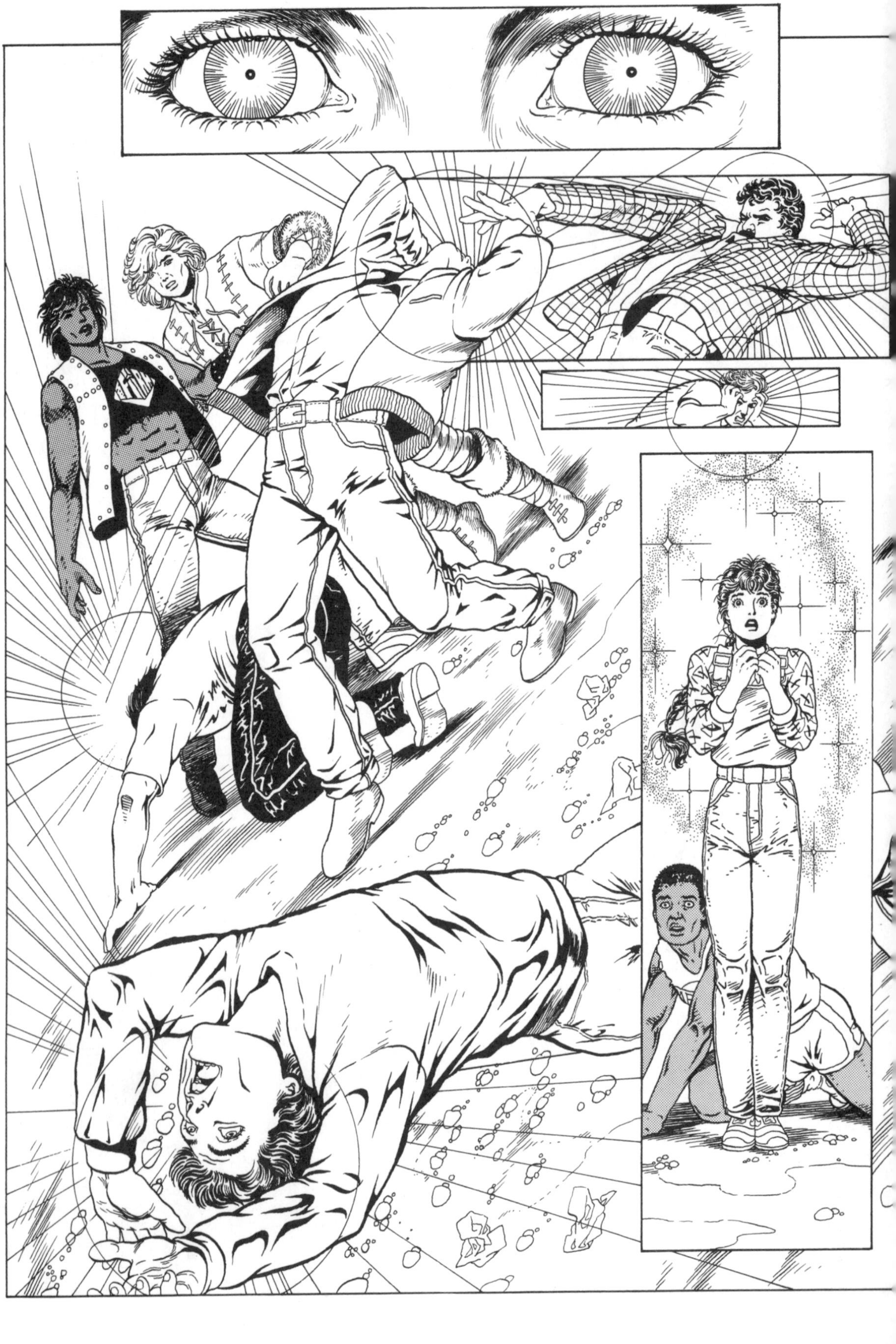

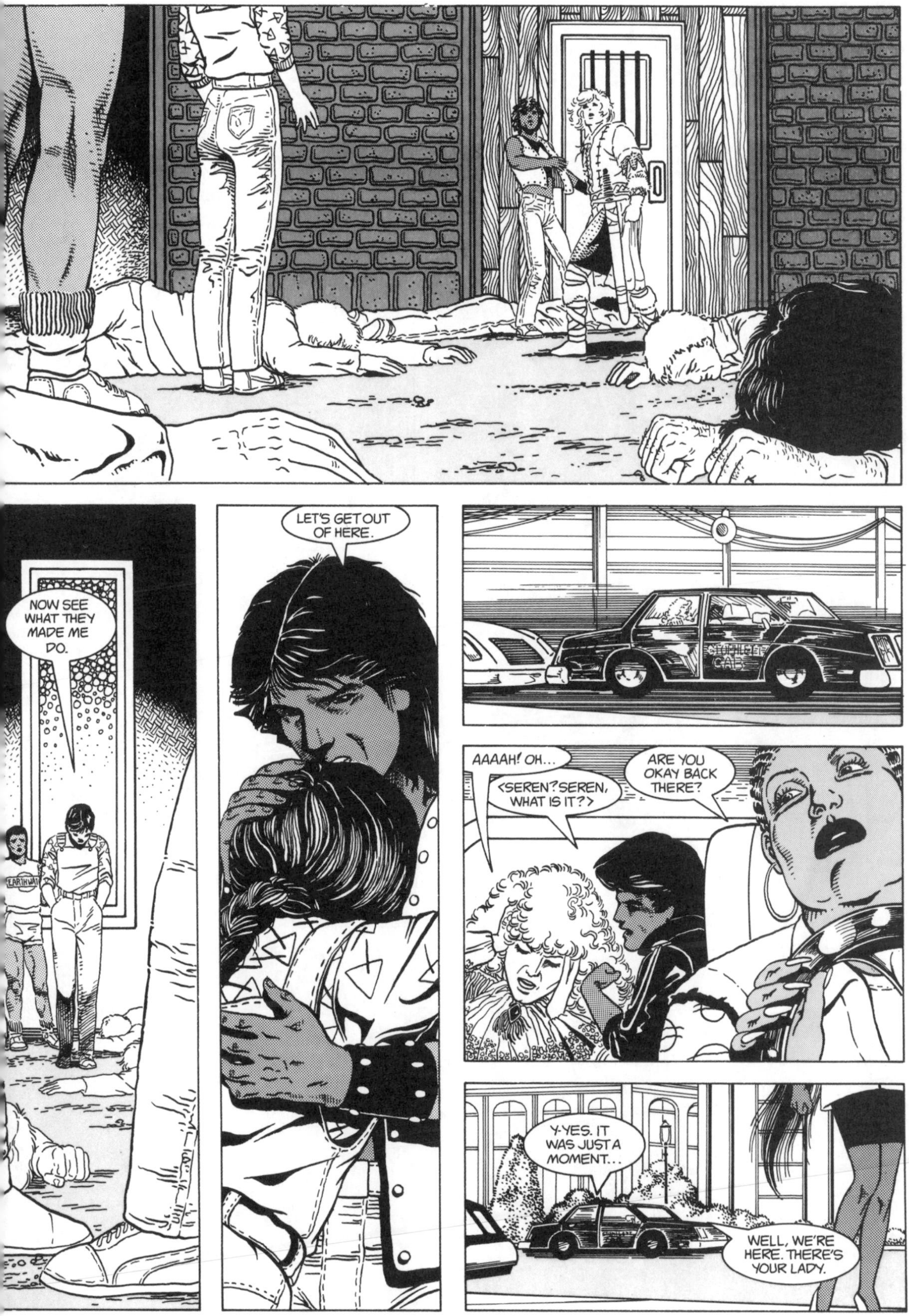
NOW SEE WHAT THEY MADE ME DO.
LET'S GET OUT OF HERE.
CITYLIGHT CAB
AAAAH! OH...
<SEREN? SEREN, WHAT IS IT?>
ARE YOU OKAY BACK THERE?
Y-YES. IT WAS JUST A MOMENT...
WELL, WE'RE HERE. THERE'S YOUR LADY.

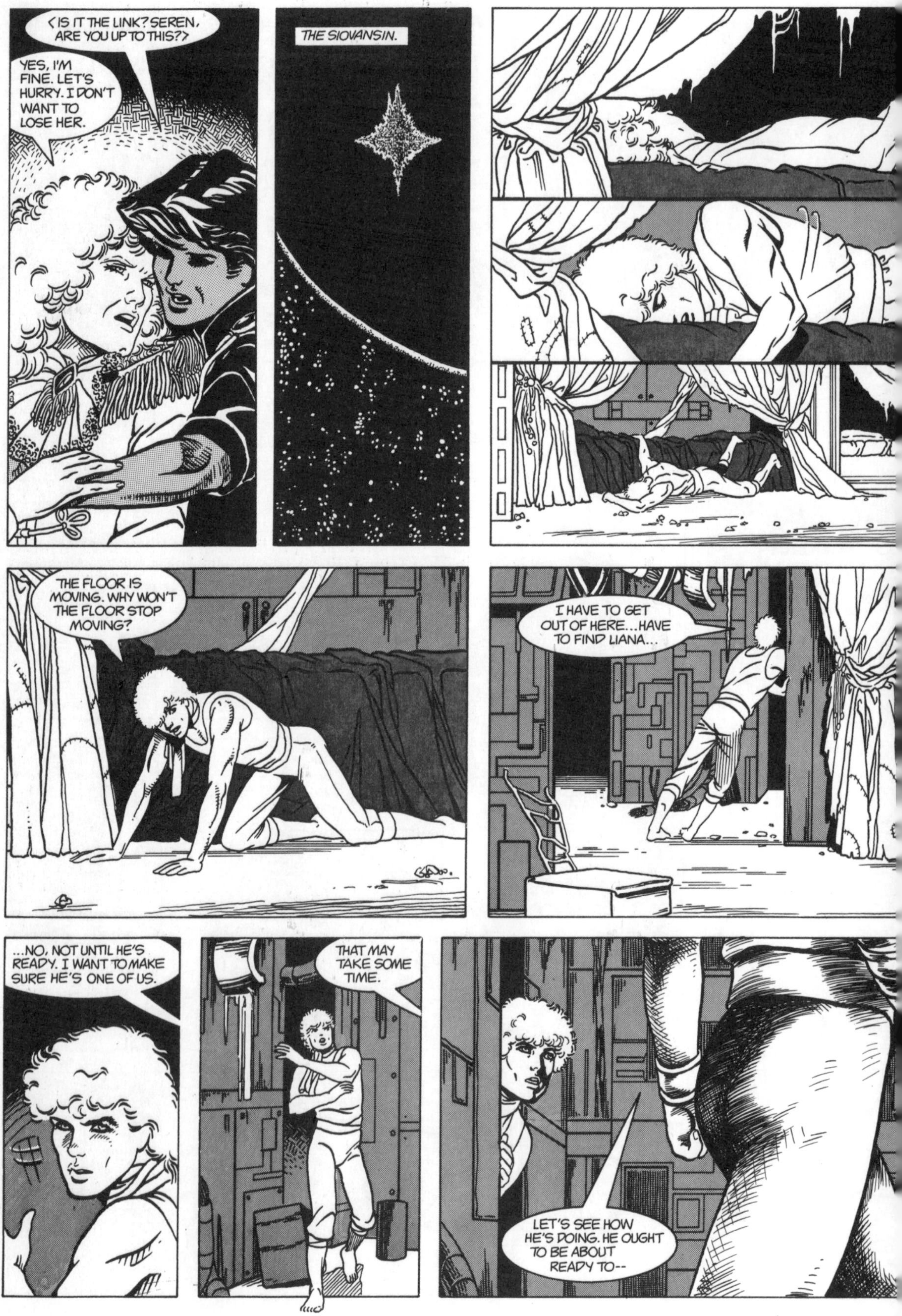
<IS IT THE LINK? SEREN, ARE YOU UP TO THIS?>
YES, I'M FINE. LET'S HURRY. I DON'T WANT TO LOSE HER.
THE SIOVANSIN.
THE FLOOR IS MOVING. WHY WON'T THE FLOOR STOP MOVING?
I HAVE TO GET OUT OF HERE...HAVE TO FIND LIANA...
...NO, NOT UNTIL HE'S READY. I WANT TO MAKE SURE HE'S ONE OF US.
THAT MAY TAKE SOME TIME.
LET'S SEE HOW HE'S DOING. HE OUGHT TO BE ABOUT READY TO--

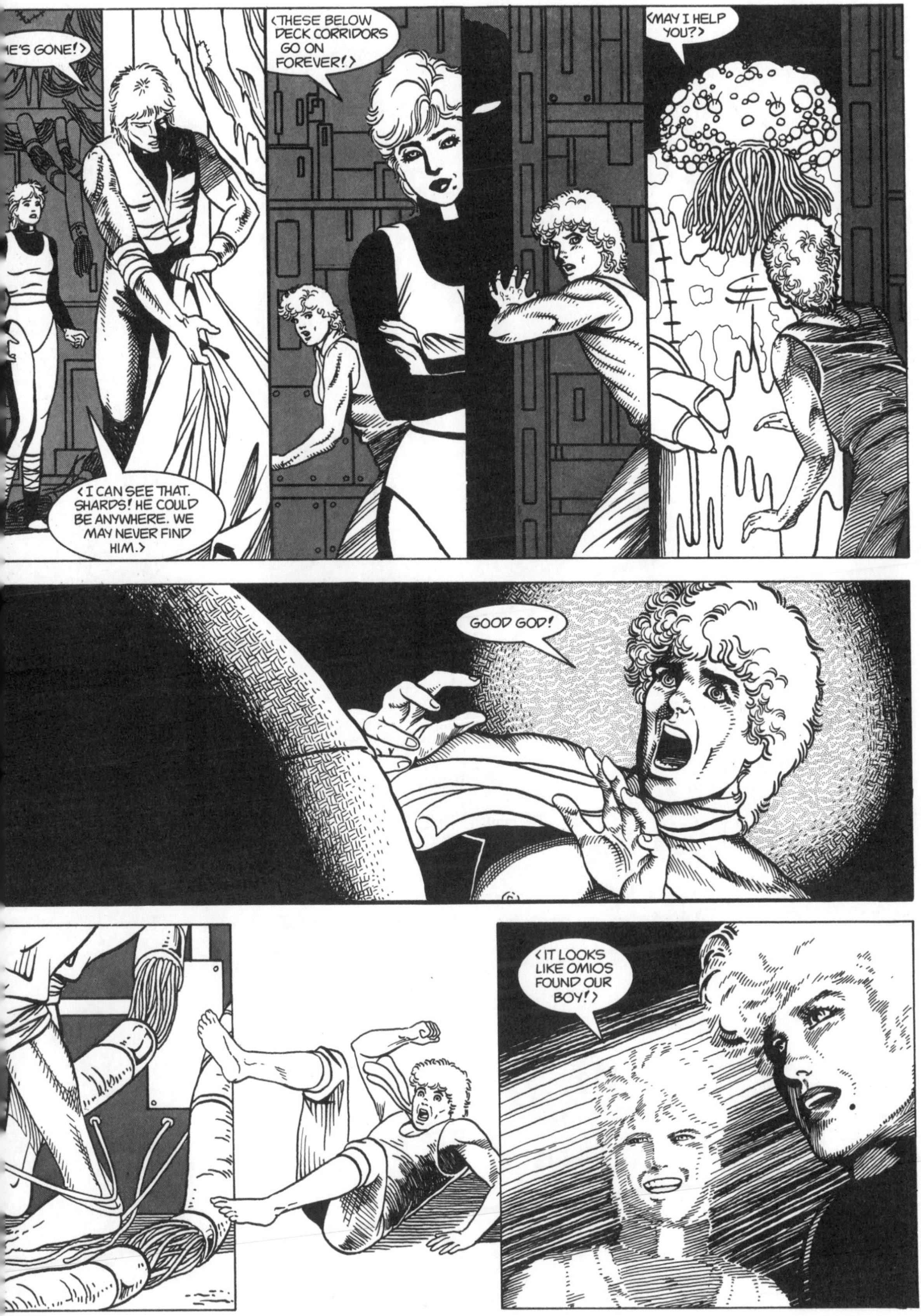

HE'S GONE!>
<I CAN SEE THAT. SHARDS! HE COULD BE ANYWHERE. WE MAY NEVER FIND HIM.>
<THESE BELOW DECK CORRIDORS GO ON FOREVER!>
<MAY I HELP YOU?>
GOOD GOD!
<IT LOOKS LIKE OMIOS FOUND OUR BOY!>

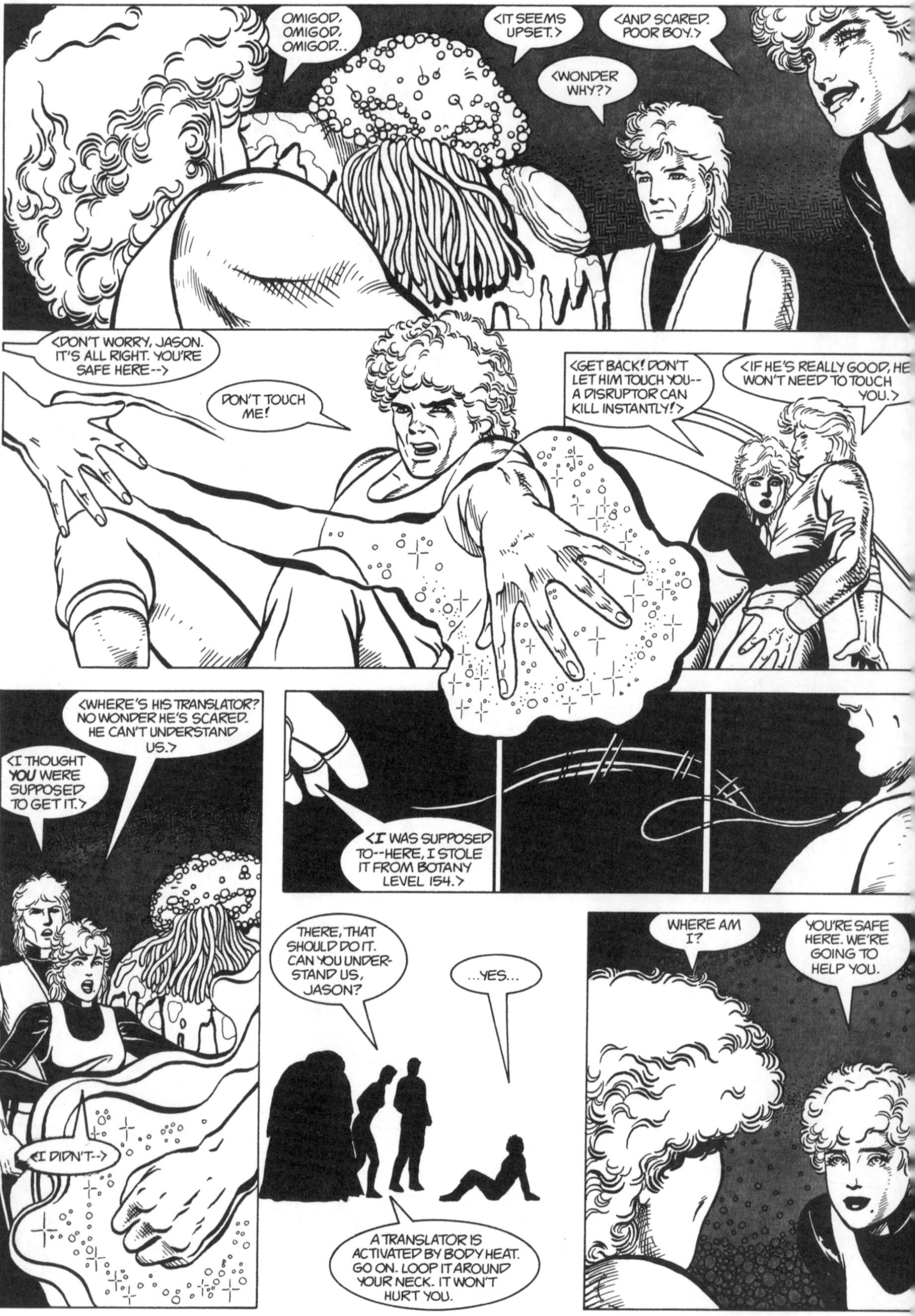
OMIGOD, OMIGOD, OMIGOD...
<IT SEEMS UPSET.>
<AND SCARED. POOR BOY.>
<WONDER WHY?>
<DON'T WORRY, JASON. IT'S ALL RIGHT. YOU'RE SAFE HERE-->
DON'T TOUCH ME!
<GET BACK! DON'T LET HIM TOUCH YOU--A DISRUPTOR CAN KILL INSTANTLY!>
<IF HE'S REALLY GOOD, HE WON'T NEED TO TOUCH YOU.>
<WHERE'S HIS TRANSLATOR? NO WONDER HE'S SCARED. HE CAN'T UNDERSTAND US.>
<I THOUGHT YOU WERE SUPPOSED TO GET IT.>
<I DIDN'T-->
<I WAS SUPPOSED TO--HERE, I STOLE IT FROM BOTANY LEVEL 154.>
THERE, THAT SHOULD DO IT. CAN YOU UNDERSTAND US, JASON?
...YES...
A TRANSLATOR IS ACTIVATED BY BODY HEAT. GO ON. LOOP IT AROUND YOUR NECK. IT WON'T HURT YOU.
WHERE AM I?
YOU'RE SAFE HERE. WE'RE GOING TO HELP YOU.

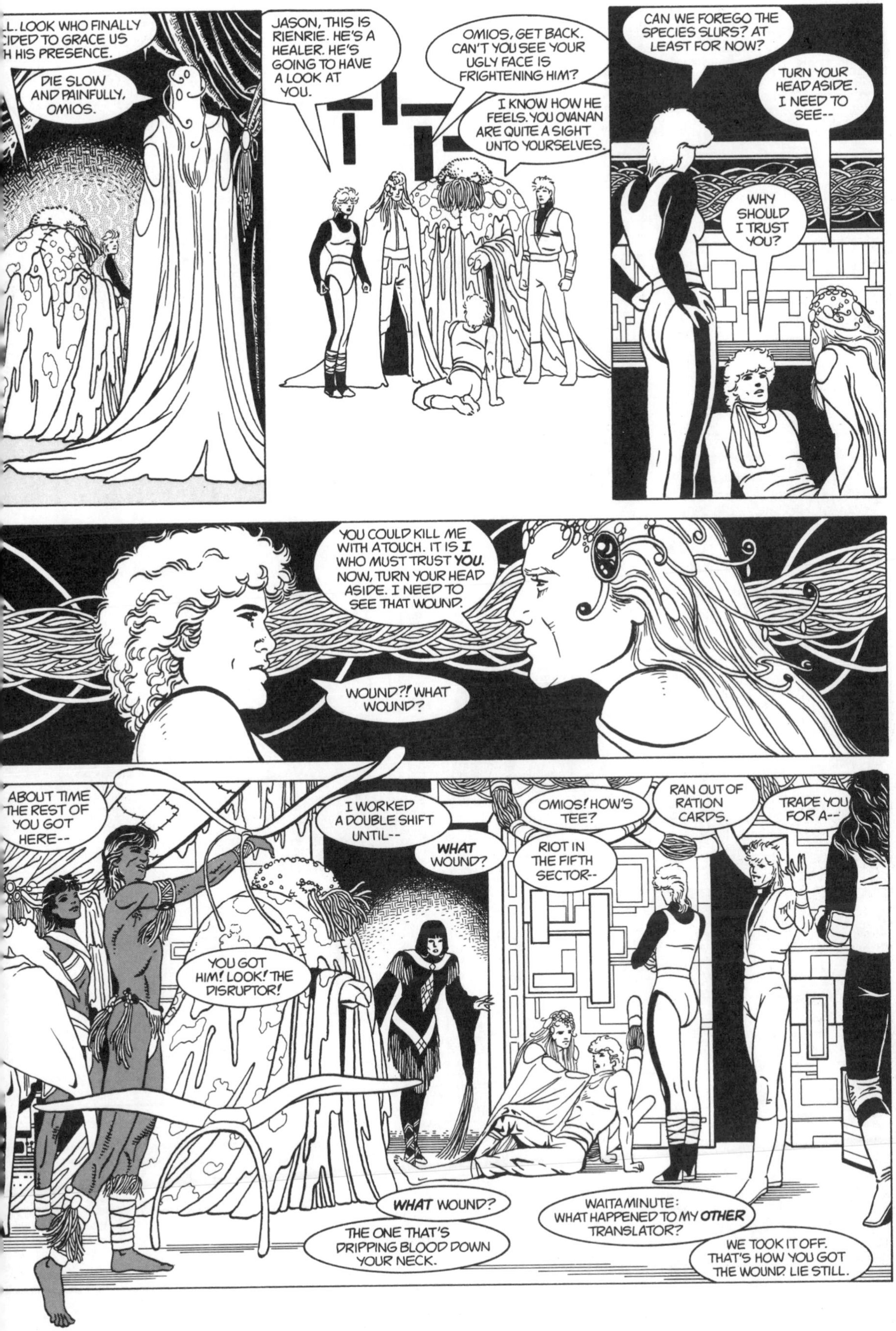
L. LOOK WHO FINALLY CIDED TO GRACE US H HIS PRESENCE.
DIE SLOW AND PAINFULLY, OMIOS.
JASON, THIS IS RIENRIE. HE'S A HEALER. HE'S GOING TO HAVE A LOOK AT YOU.
OMIOS, GET BACK. CAN'T YOU SEE YOUR UGLY FACE IS FRIGHTENING HIM?
I KNOW HOW HE FEELS. YOU OVANAN ARE QUITE A SIGHT UNTO YOURSELVES.
CAN WE FOREGO THE SPECIES SLURS? AT LEAST FOR NOW?
TURN YOUR HEAD ASIDE. I NEED TO SEE--
WHY SHOULD I TRUST YOU?
YOU COULD KILL ME WITH A TOUCH. IT IS I WHO MUST TRUST YOU. NOW, TURN YOUR HEAD ASIDE. I NEED TO SEE THAT WOUND.
WOUND?! WHAT WOUND?
ABOUT TIME THE REST OF YOU GOT HERE--
I WORKED A DOUBLE SHIFT UNTIL--
WHAT WOUND?
OMIOS! HOW'S TEE?
RIOT IN THE FIFTH SECTOR--
RAN OUT OF RATION CARDS.
TRADE YOU FOR A--
YOU GOT HIM! LOOK! THE DISRUPTOR!
WHAT WOUND?
THE ONE THAT'S DRIPPING BLOOD DOWN YOUR NECK.
WAIT A MINUTE: WHAT HAPPENED TO MY OTHER TRANSLATOR?
WE TOOK IT OFF. THAT'S HOW YOU GOT THE WOUND. LIE STILL.

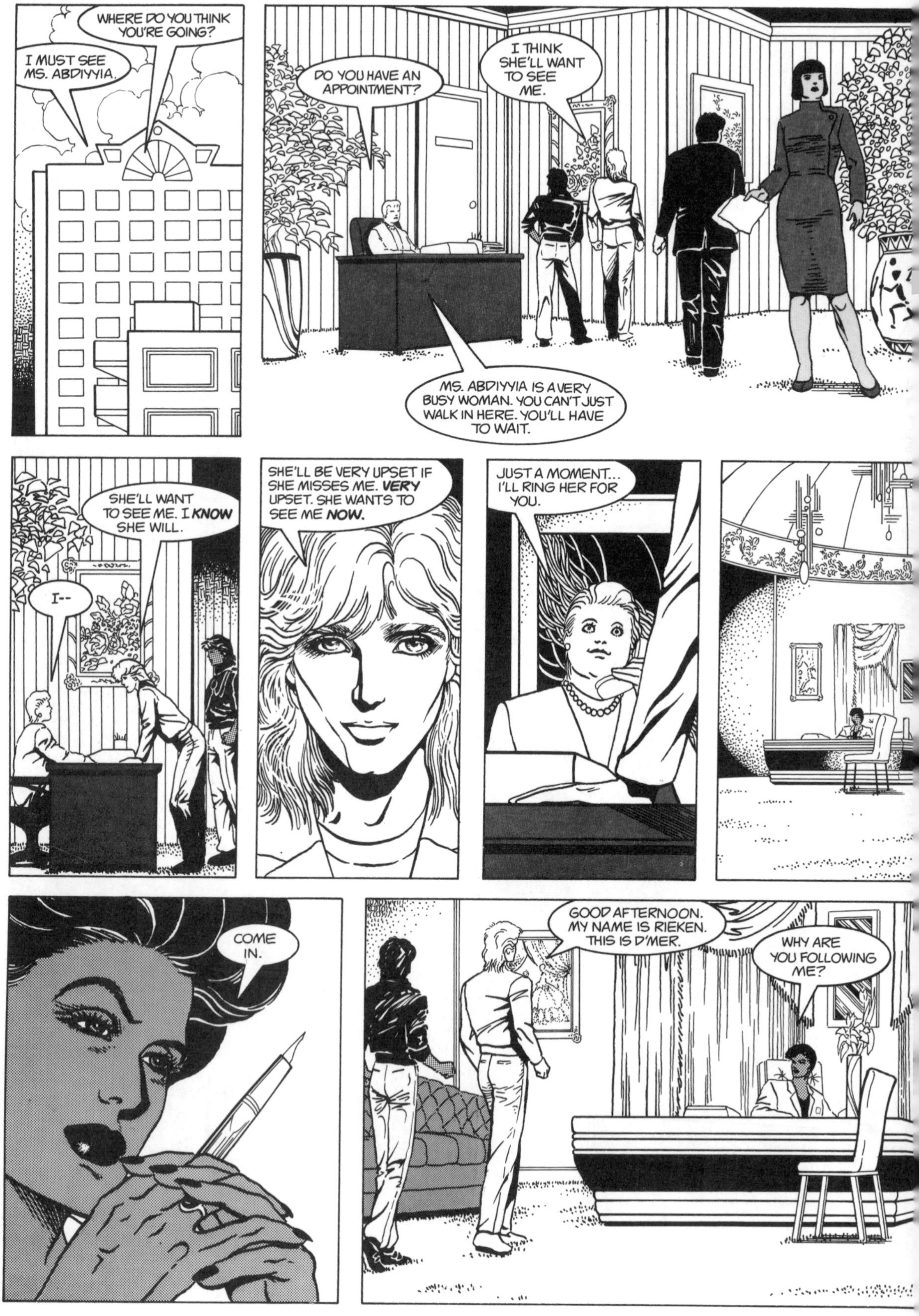

I MUST SEE MS. ABDIYYIA.
WHERE DO YOU THINK YOU'RE GOING?
DO YOU HAVE AN APPOINTMENT?
I THINK SHE'LL WANT TO SEE ME.
MS. ABDIYYIA IS A VERY BUSY WOMAN. YOU CAN'T JUST WALK IN HERE. YOU'LL HAVE TO WAIT.
SHE'LL WANT TO SEE ME. I **KNOW** SHE WILL.
I--
SHE'LL BE VERY UPSET IF SHE MISSES ME. **VERY** UPSET. SHE WANTS TO SEE ME **NOW.**
JUST A MOMENT... I'LL RING HER FOR YOU.
COME IN.
GOOD AFTERNOON. MY NAME IS RIEKEN. THIS IS D'MER.
WHY ARE YOU FOLLOWING ME?

T'S BEEN
TRING
Y. MAY
SIT
WN?

. IF SETH
ENT YOU, I AM
O LONGER AFFILIATED
TH THE NETWORK.
LL HIM I'M NOT
TERESTED IN ANYTHING
HAS TO OFFER.
U MAY GO.

I DON'T KNOW WHAT YOU MEAN. I'VE COME FROM THE HOMEWORLD. I'M FROM OVANAN.

CRYSTAL!

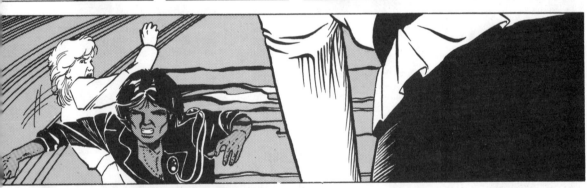

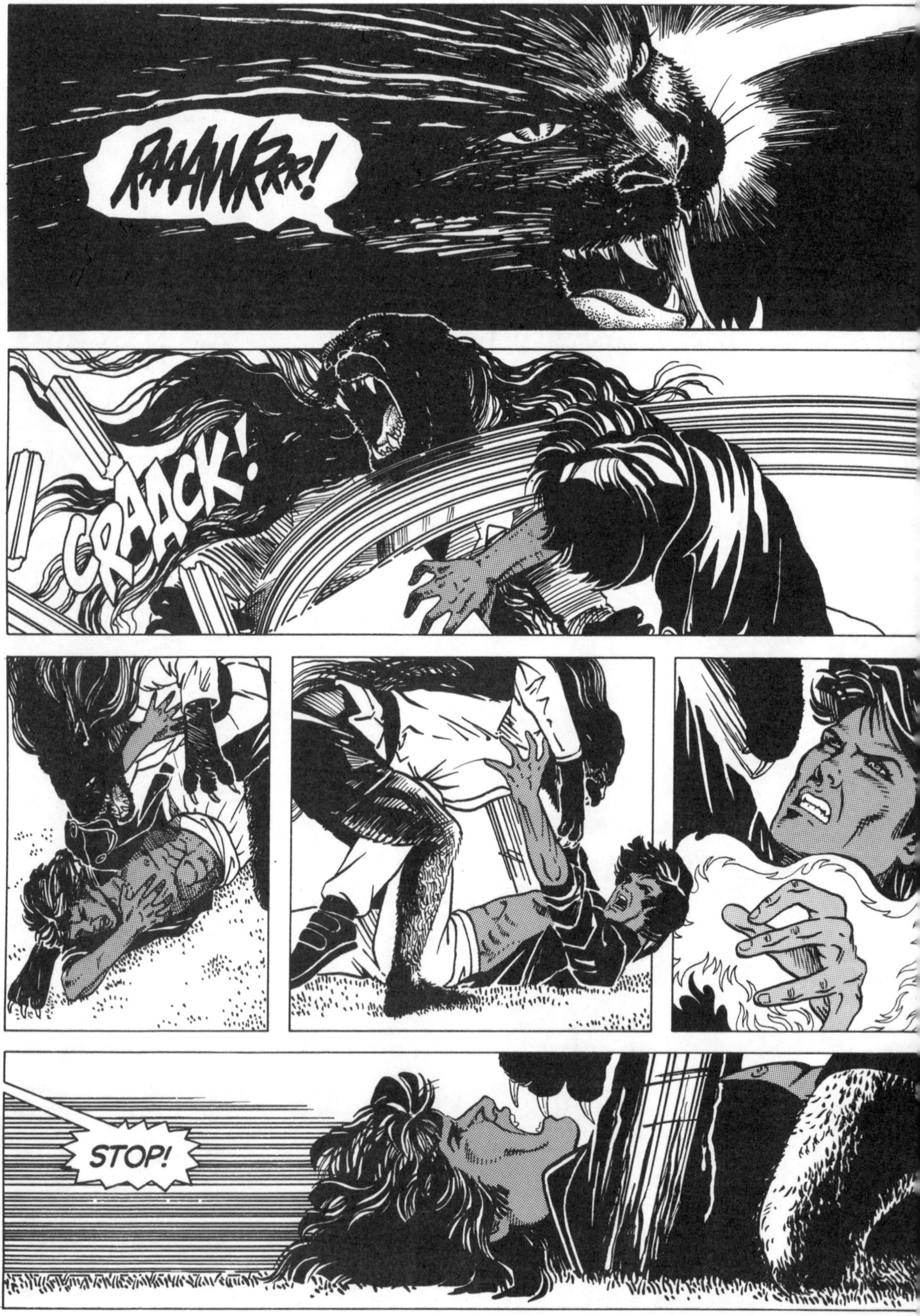
RAAAWRrrr!
CRAACK!
STOP!

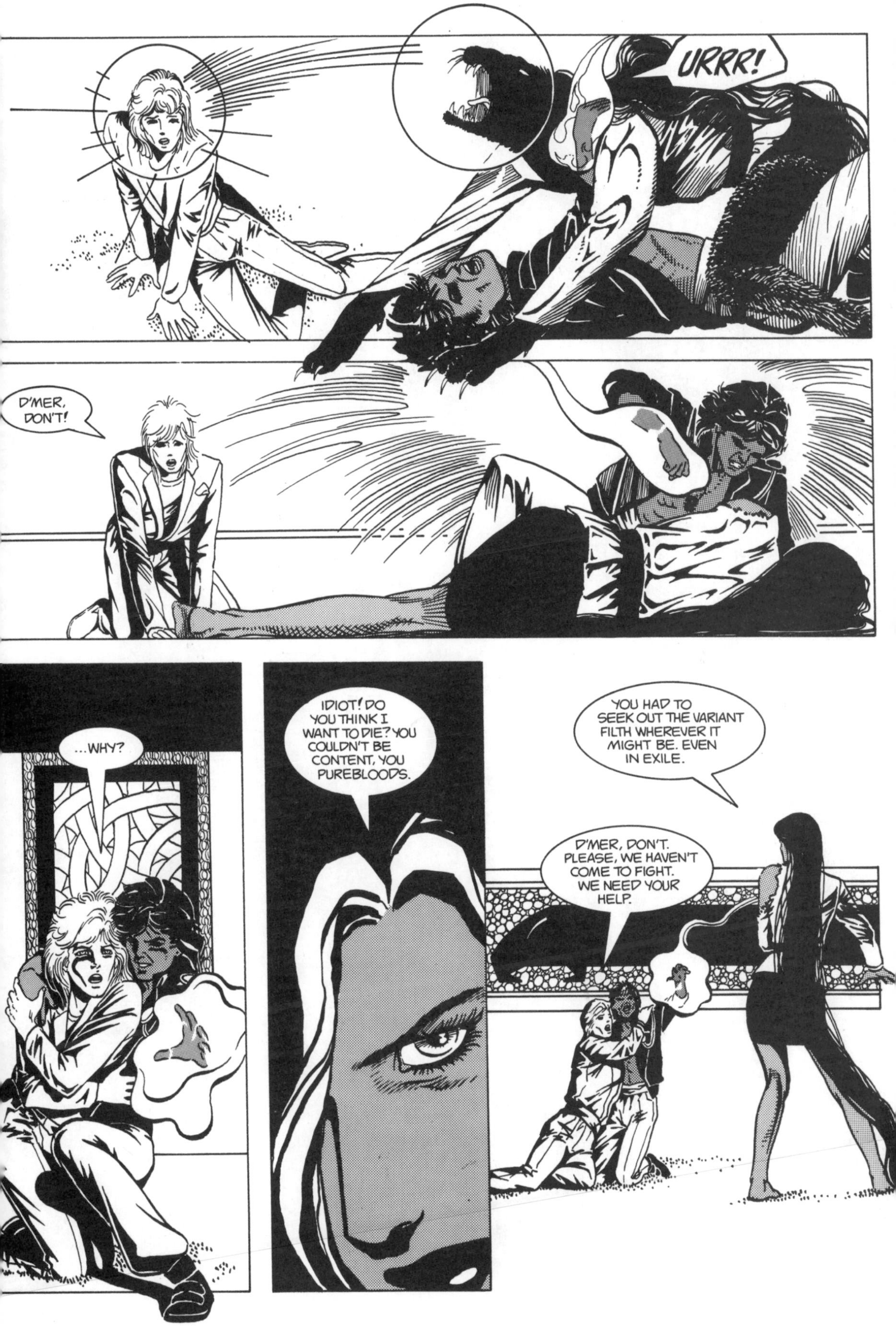
URRR!
D'MER, DON'T!
...WHY?
IDIOT! DO YOU THINK I WANT TO DIE? YOU COULDN'T BE CONTENT, YOU PUREBLOODS.
YOU HAD TO SEEK OUT THE VARIANT FILTH WHEREVER IT MIGHT BE. EVEN IN EXILE.
D'MER, DON'T. PLEASE, WE HAVEN'T COME TO FIGHT. WE NEED YOUR HELP.

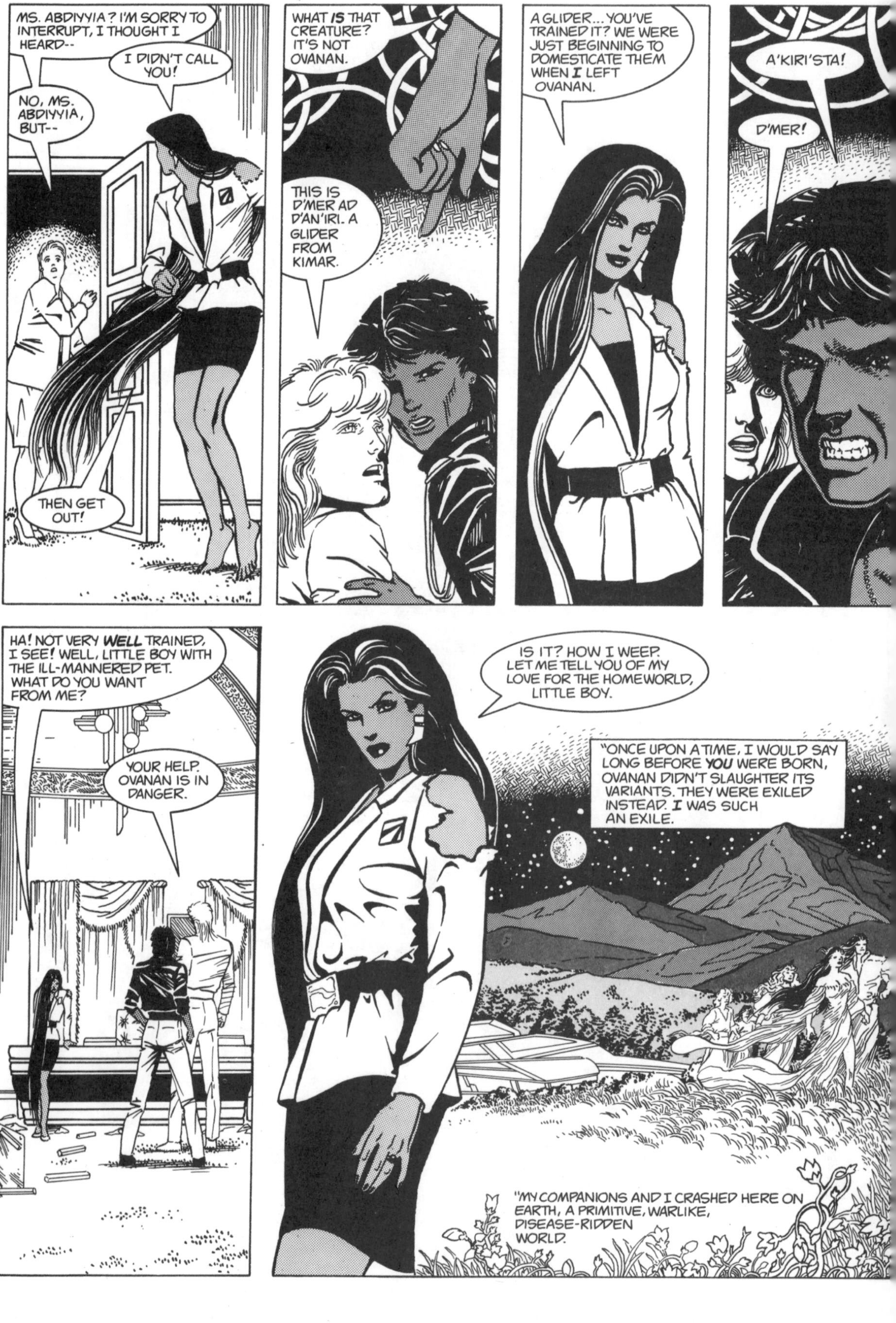
MS. ABDIYYIA? I'M SORRY TO INTERRUPT, I THOUGHT I HEARD--
I DIDN'T CALL YOU!
NO, MS. ABDIYYIA, BUT--
THEN GET OUT!
WHAT IS THAT CREATURE? IT'S NOT OVANAN.
THIS IS D'MER AD D'AN'IRI. A GLIDER FROM KIMAR.
A GLIDER... YOU'VE TRAINED IT? WE WERE JUST BEGINNING TO DOMESTICATE THEM WHEN I LEFT OVANAN.
A'KIRI'STA!
D'MER!
HA! NOT VERY WELL TRAINED, I SEE! WELL, LITTLE BOY WITH THE ILL-MANNERED PET. WHAT DO YOU WANT FROM ME?
YOUR HELP. OVANAN IS IN DANGER.
IS IT? HOW I WEEP. LET ME TELL YOU OF MY LOVE FOR THE HOMEWORLD, LITTLE BOY.
"ONCE UPON A TIME, I WOULD SAY LONG BEFORE YOU WERE BORN, OVANAN DIDN'T SLAUGHTER ITS VARIANTS. THEY WERE EXILED INSTEAD. I WAS SUCH AN EXILE.
"MY COMPANIONS AND I CRASHED HERE ON EARTH, A PRIMITIVE, WARLIKE, DISEASE-RIDDEN WORLD.

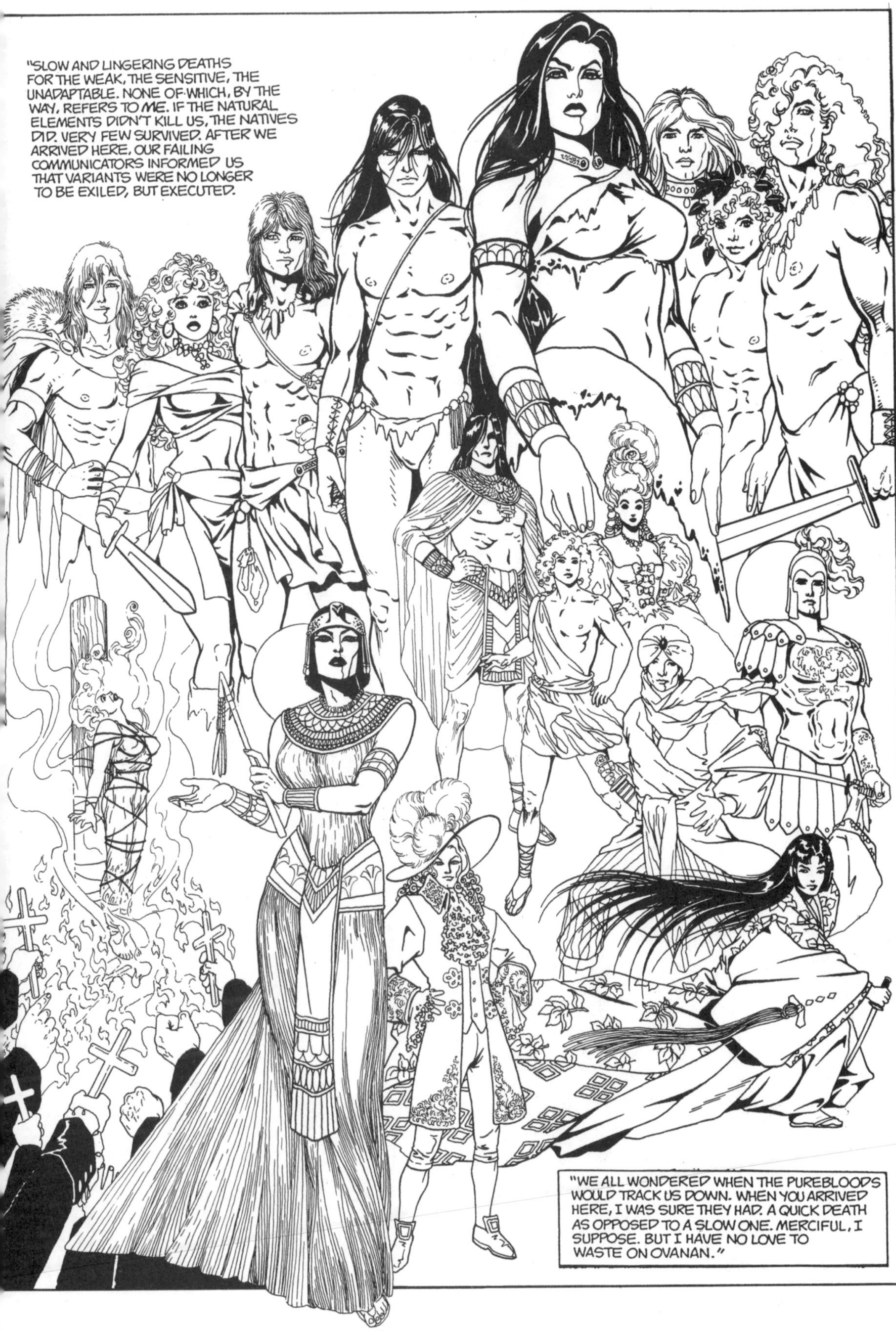
"SLOW AND LINGERING DEATHS FOR THE WEAK, THE SENSITIVE, THE UNADAPTABLE. NONE OF WHICH, BY THE WAY, REFERS TO ME. IF THE NATURAL ELEMENTS DIDN'T KILL US, THE NATIVES DID. VERY FEW SURVIVED. AFTER WE ARRIVED HERE, OUR FAILING COMMUNICATORS INFORMED US THAT VARIANTS WERE NO LONGER TO BE EXILED, BUT EXECUTED.
"WE ALL WONDERED WHEN THE PUREBLOODS WOULD TRACK US DOWN. WHEN YOU ARRIVED HERE, I WAS SURE THEY HAD. A QUICK DEATH AS OPPOSED TO A SLOW ONE. MERCIFUL, I SUPPOSE. BUT I HAVE NO LOVE TO WASTE ON OVANAN."

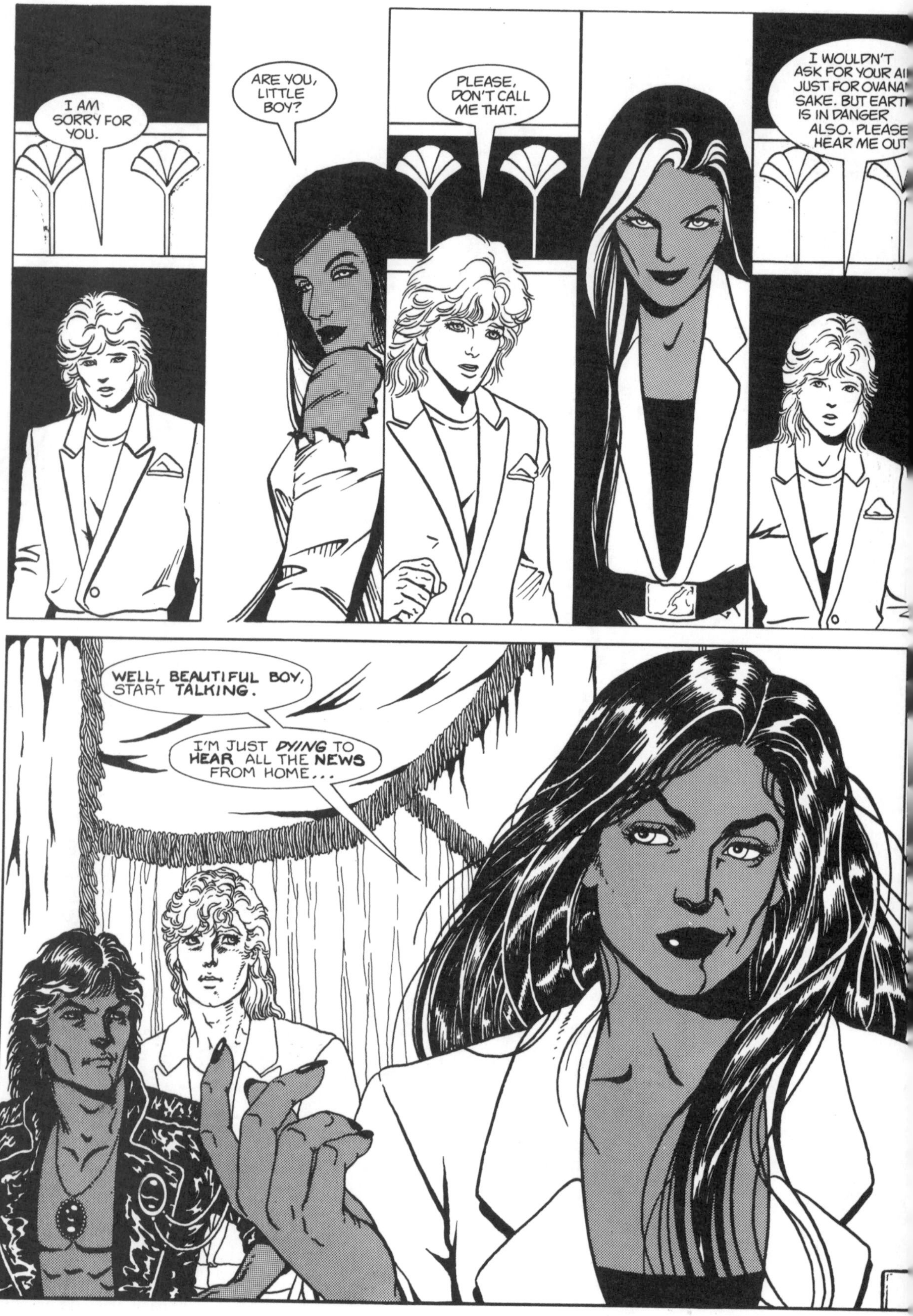

I AM SORRY FOR YOU.
ARE YOU, LITTLE BOY?
PLEASE, DON'T CALL ME THAT.
I WOULDN'T ASK FOR YOUR AI JUST FOR OVANA SAKE. BUT EART IS IN DANGER ALSO. PLEASE HEAR ME OUT
WELL, BEAUTIFUL BOY, START TALKING.
I'M JUST DYING TO HEAR ALL THE NEWS FROM HOME...

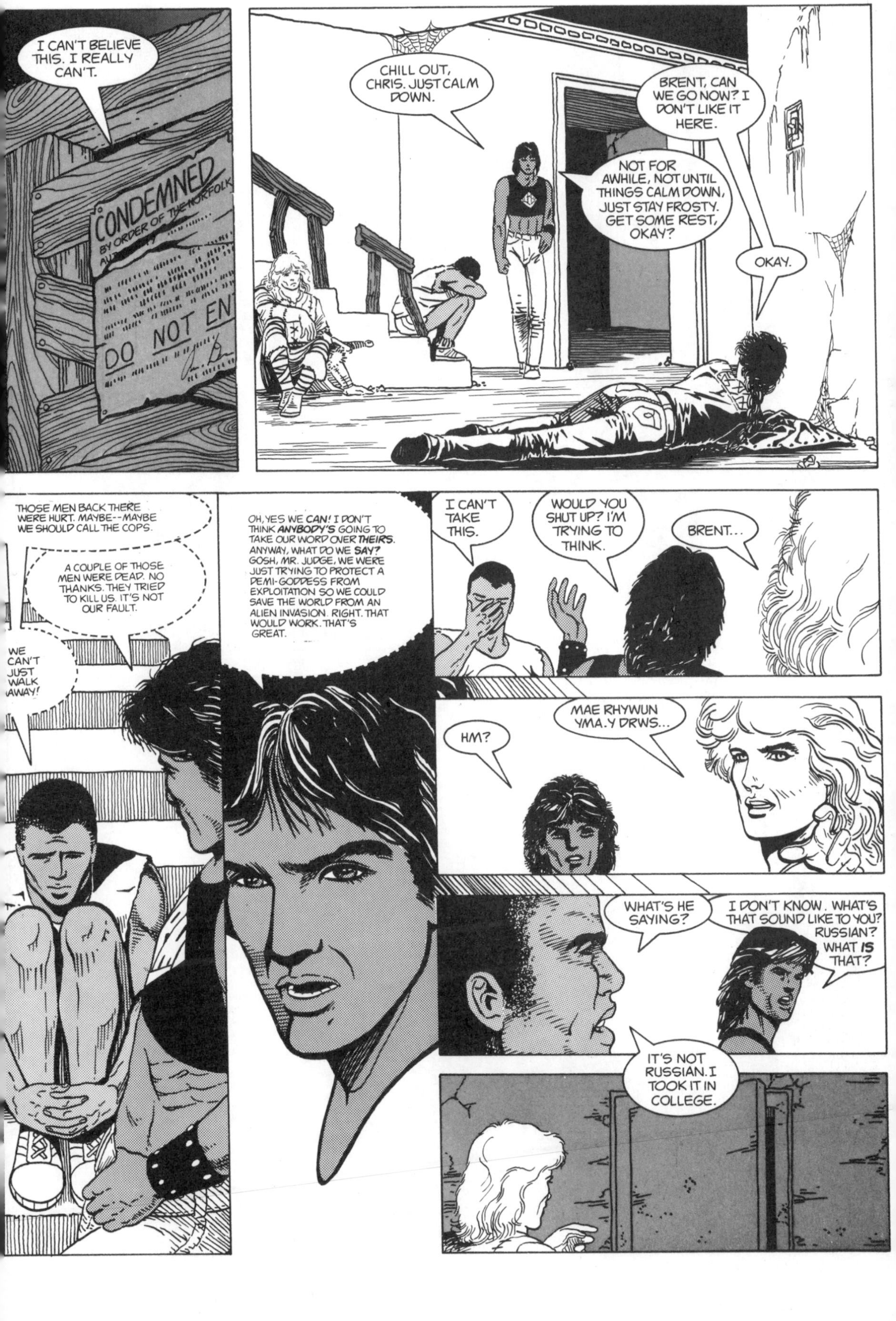
I CAN'T BELIEVE THIS. I REALLY CAN'T.
CONDEMNED
BY ORDER OF THE NORFOLK
DO NOT ENT
CHILL OUT, CHRIS. JUST CALM DOWN.
BRENT, CAN WE GO NOW? I DON'T LIKE IT HERE.
NOT FOR AWHILE, NOT UNTIL THINGS CALM DOWN, JUST STAY FROSTY. GET SOME REST, OKAY?
OKAY.
THOSE MEN BACK THERE WERE HURT. MAYBE--MAYBE WE SHOULD CALL THE COPS.
A COUPLE OF THOSE MEN WERE DEAD. NO THANKS. THEY TRIED TO KILL US. IT'S NOT OUR FAULT.
WE CAN'T JUST WALK AWAY!
OH, YES WE CAN! I DON'T THINK ANYBODY'S GOING TO TAKE OUR WORD OVER THEIRS. ANYWAY, WHAT DO WE SAY? GOSH, MR. JUDGE, WE WERE JUST TRYING TO PROTECT A DEMI-GODDESS FROM EXPLOITATION SO WE COULD SAVE THE WORLD FROM AN ALIEN INVASION. RIGHT. THAT WOULD WORK. THAT'S GREAT.
I CAN'T TAKE THIS.
WOULD YOU SHUT UP? I'M TRYING TO THINK.
BRENT...
HM?
MAE RHYWUN YMA.Y DRWS...
WHAT'S HE SAYING?
I DON'T KNOW. WHAT'S THAT SOUND LIKE TO YOU? RUSSIAN? WHAT IS THAT?
IT'S NOT RUSSIAN. I TOOK IT IN COLLEGE.

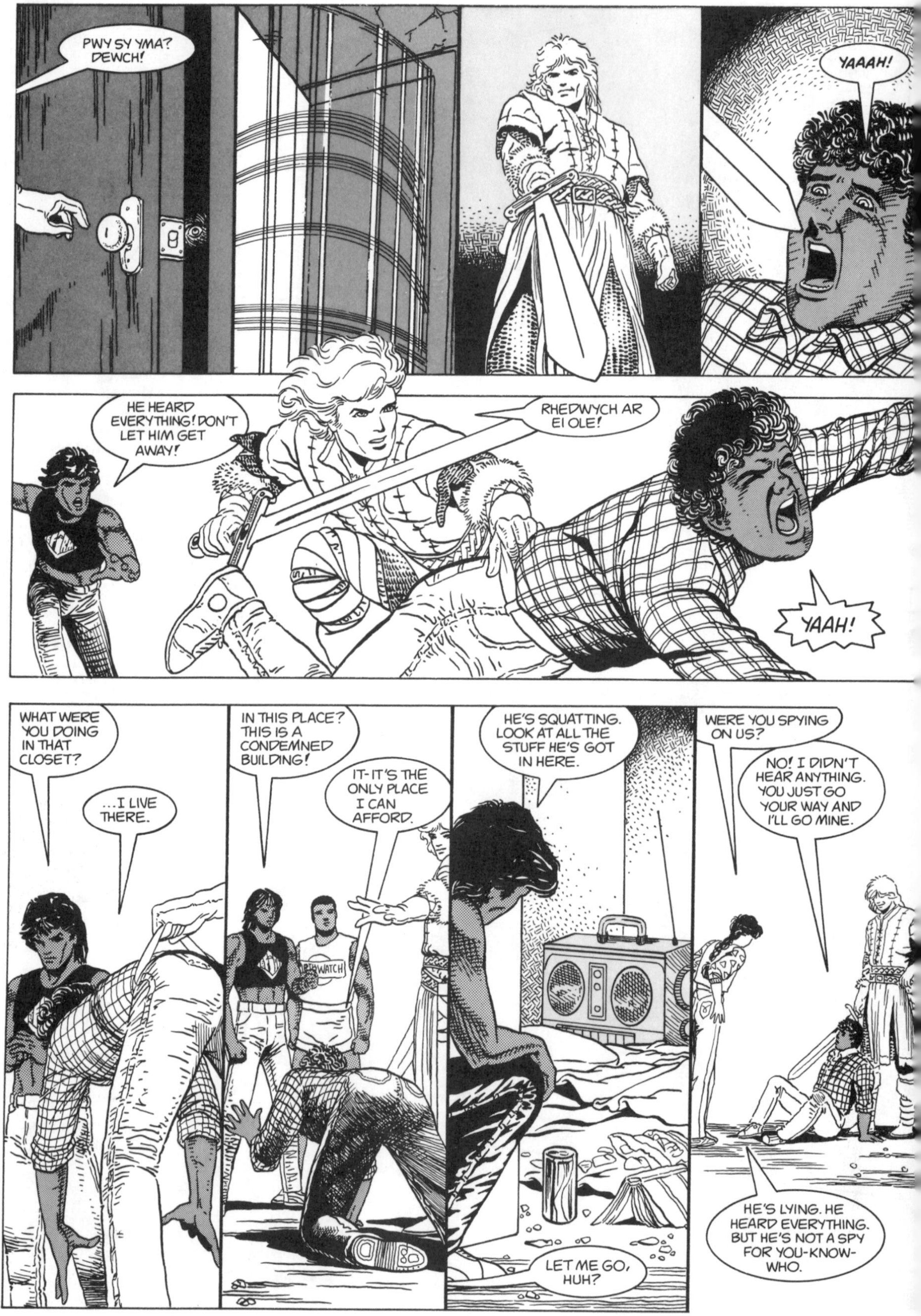
PWY SY YMA? DEWCH!
YAAAH!
HE HEARD EVERYTHING! DON'T LET HIM GET AWAY!
RHEDWYCH AR EI OLE!
YAAH!
WHAT WERE YOU DOING IN THAT CLOSET?
...I LIVE THERE.
IN THIS PLACE? THIS IS A CONDEMNED BUILDING!
IT-IT'S THE ONLY PLACE I CAN AFFORD.
HE'S SQUATTING. LOOK AT ALL THE STUFF HE'S GOT IN HERE.
LET ME GO, HUH?
WERE YOU SPYING ON US?
NO! I DIDN'T HEAR ANYTHING. YOU JUST GO YOUR WAY AND I'LL GO MINE.
HE'S LYING. HE HEARD EVERYTHING. BUT HE'S NOT A SPY FOR YOU-KNOW-WHO.

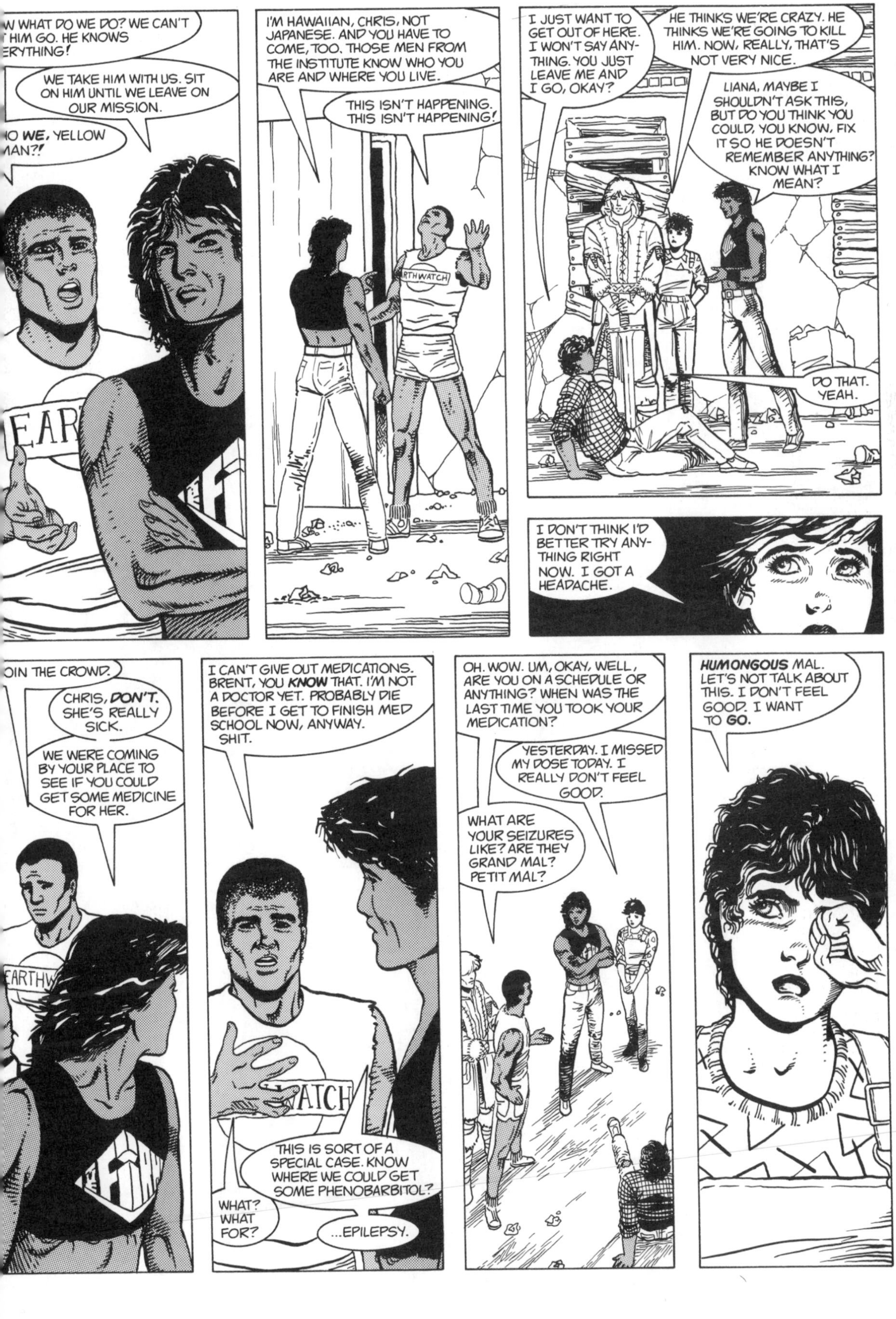
W WHAT DO WE DO? WE CAN'T
T HIM GO. HE KNOWS
ERYTHING!
WE TAKE HIM WITH US. SIT ON HIM UNTIL WE LEAVE ON OUR MISSION.
O WE, YELLOW
MAN?!
I'M HAWAIIAN, CHRIS, NOT JAPANESE. AND YOU HAVE TO COME, TOO. THOSE MEN FROM THE INSTITUTE KNOW WHO YOU ARE AND WHERE YOU LIVE.
THIS ISN'T HAPPENING. THIS ISN'T HAPPENING!
I JUST WANT TO GET OUT OF HERE. I WON'T SAY ANYTHING. YOU JUST LEAVE ME AND I GO, OKAY?
HE THINKS WE'RE CRAZY. HE THINKS WE'RE GOING TO KILL HIM. NOW, REALLY, THAT'S NOT VERY NICE.
LIANA, MAYBE I SHOULDN'T ASK THIS, BUT DO YOU THINK YOU COULD, YOU KNOW, FIX IT SO HE DOESN'T REMEMBER ANYTHING? KNOW WHAT I MEAN?
DO THAT. YEAH.
I DON'T THINK I'D BETTER TRY ANYTHING RIGHT NOW. I GOT A HEADACHE.
OIN THE CROWD.
CHRIS, DON'T. SHE'S REALLY SICK.
WE WERE COMING BY YOUR PLACE TO SEE IF YOU COULD GET SOME MEDICINE FOR HER.
I CAN'T GIVE OUT MEDICATIONS. BRENT, YOU KNOW THAT. I'M NOT A DOCTOR YET. PROBABLY DIE BEFORE I GET TO FINISH MED SCHOOL NOW, ANYWAY. SHIT.
THIS IS SORT OF A SPECIAL CASE. KNOW WHERE WE COULD GET SOME PHENOBARBITOL?
WHAT? WHAT FOR?
...EPILEPSY.
OH. WOW. UM, OKAY, WELL, ARE YOU ON A SCHEDULE OR ANYTHING? WHEN WAS THE LAST TIME YOU TOOK YOUR MEDICATION?
YESTERDAY. I MISSED MY DOSE TODAY. I REALLY DON'T FEEL GOOD.
WHAT ARE YOUR SEIZURES LIKE? ARE THEY GRAND MAL? PETIT MAL?
HUMONGOUS MAL. LET'S NOT TALK ABOUT THIS. I DON'T FEEL GOOD. I WANT TO GO.

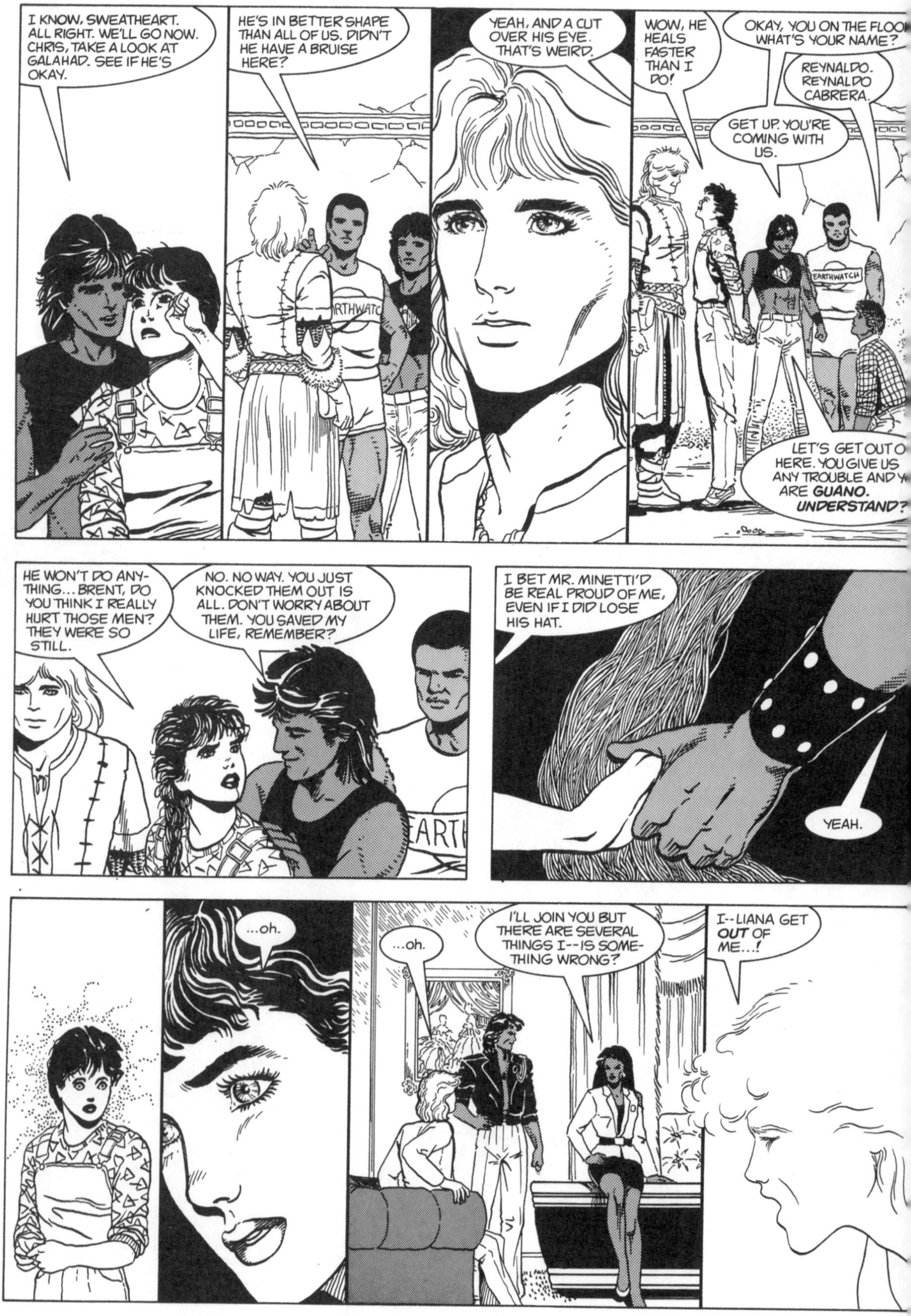
I KNOW, SWEATHEART. ALL RIGHT. WE'LL GO NOW. CHRIS, TAKE A LOOK AT GALAHAD. SEE IF HE'S OKAY.
HE'S IN BETTER SHAPE THAN ALL OF US. DIDN'T HE HAVE A BRUISE HERE?
YEAH, AND A CUT OVER HIS EYE. THAT'S WEIRD.
WOW, HE HEALS FASTER THAN I DO!
EARTHWATCH
OKAY, YOU ON THE FLOO WHAT'S YOUR NAME?
REYNALDO. REYNALDO CABRERA.
GET UP. YOU'RE COMING WITH US.
EARTHWATCH
LET'S GET OUT O HERE. YOU GIVE US ANY TROUBLE AND Y ARE **GUANO. UNDERSTAND?**
HE WON'T DO ANY-THING... BRENT, DO YOU THINK I REALLY HURT THOSE MEN? THEY WERE SO STILL.
NO. NO WAY. YOU JUST KNOCKED THEM OUT IS ALL. DON'T WORRY ABOUT THEM. YOU SAVED MY LIFE, REMEMBER?
EARTH
I BET MR. MINETTI'D BE REAL PROUD OF ME, EVEN IF I DID LOSE HIS HAT.
YEAH.
...oh.
...oh.
I'LL JOIN YOU BUT THERE ARE SEVERAL THINGS I--IS SOME-THING WRONG?
I--LIANA GET **OUT** OF ME...!

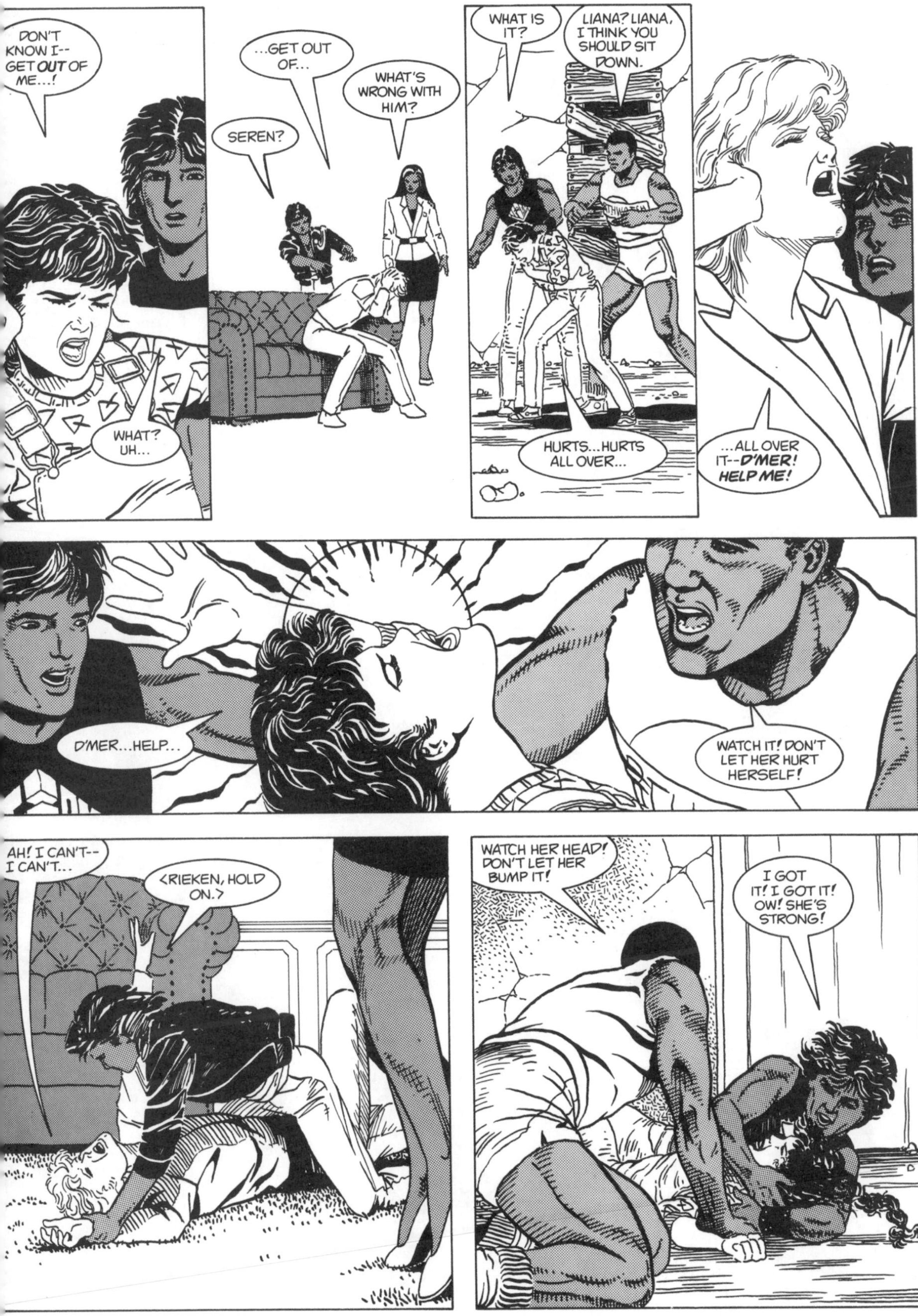
DON'T KNOW I-- GET OUT OF ME...!
WHAT? UH...
SEREN?
...GET OUT OF...
WHAT'S WRONG WITH HIM?
WHAT IS IT?
LIANA? LIANA, I THINK YOU SHOULD SIT DOWN.
HURTS...HURTS ALL OVER...
...ALL OVER IT--D'MER! HELP ME!
D'MER...HELP...
WATCH IT! DON'T LET HER HURT HERSELF!
AH! I CAN'T-- I CAN'T...
<RIEKEN, HOLD ON.>
WATCH HER HEAD! DON'T LET HER BUMP IT!
I GOT IT! I GOT IT! OW! SHE'S STRONG!

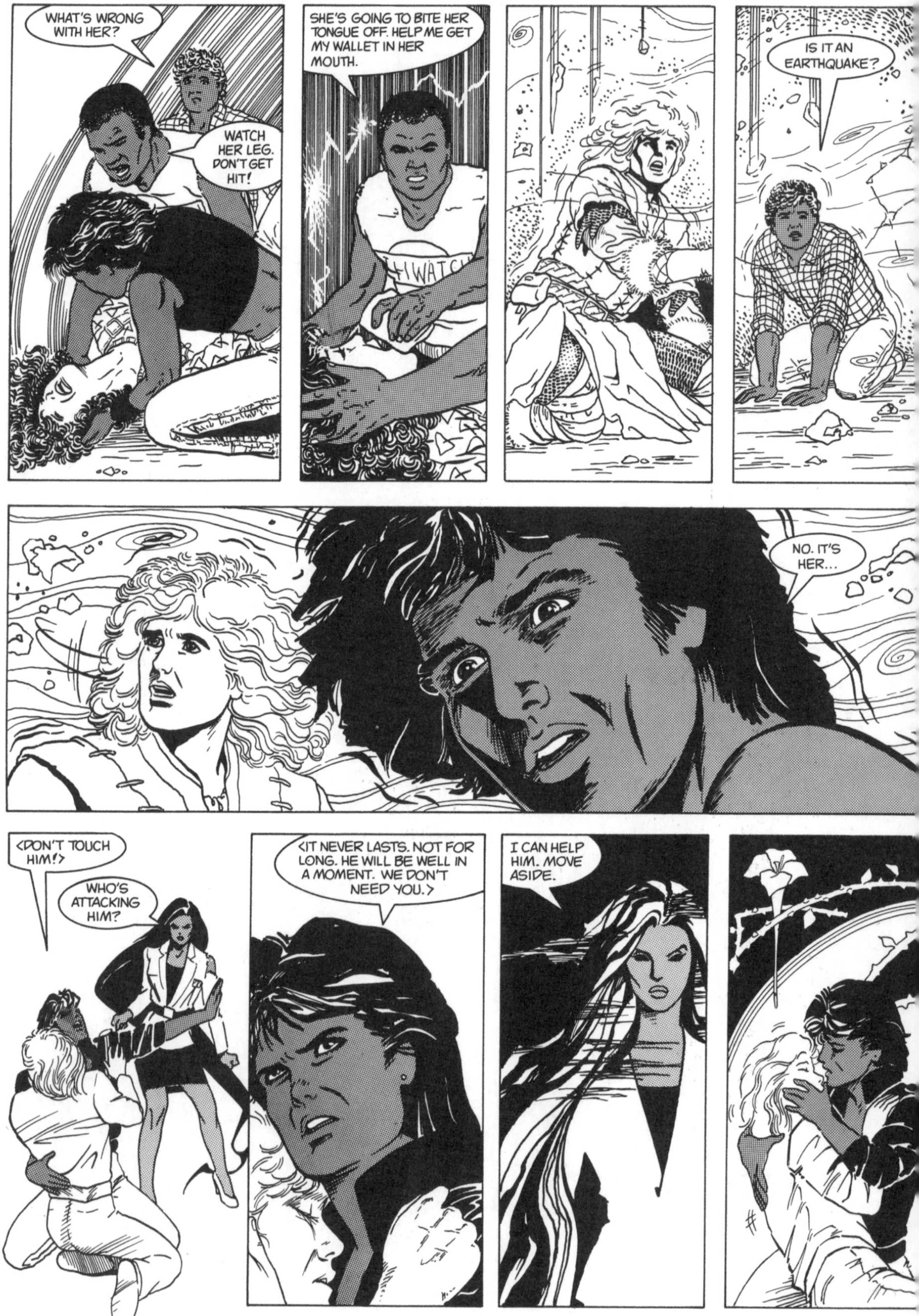
WHAT'S WRONG WITH HER?
WATCH HER LEG. DON'T GET HIT!
SHE'S GOING TO BITE HER TONGUE OFF. HELP ME GET MY WALLET IN HER MOUTH.
IS IT AN EARTHQUAKE?
NO. IT'S HER...
<DON'T TOUCH HIM!>
WHO'S ATTACKING HIM?
<IT NEVER LASTS. NOT FOR LONG. HE WILL BE WELL IN A MOMENT. WE DON'T NEED YOU.>
I CAN HELP HIM. MOVE ASIDE.

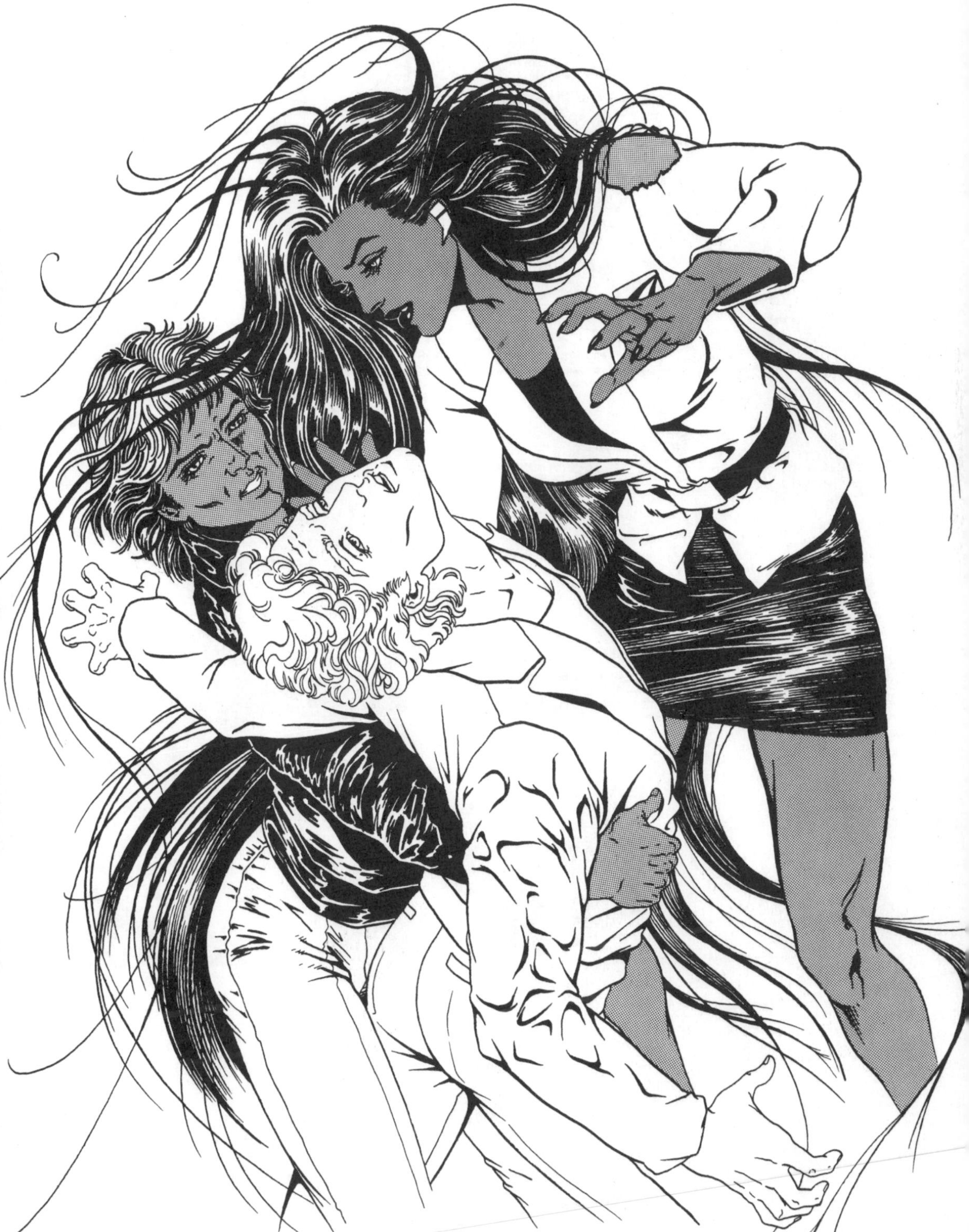

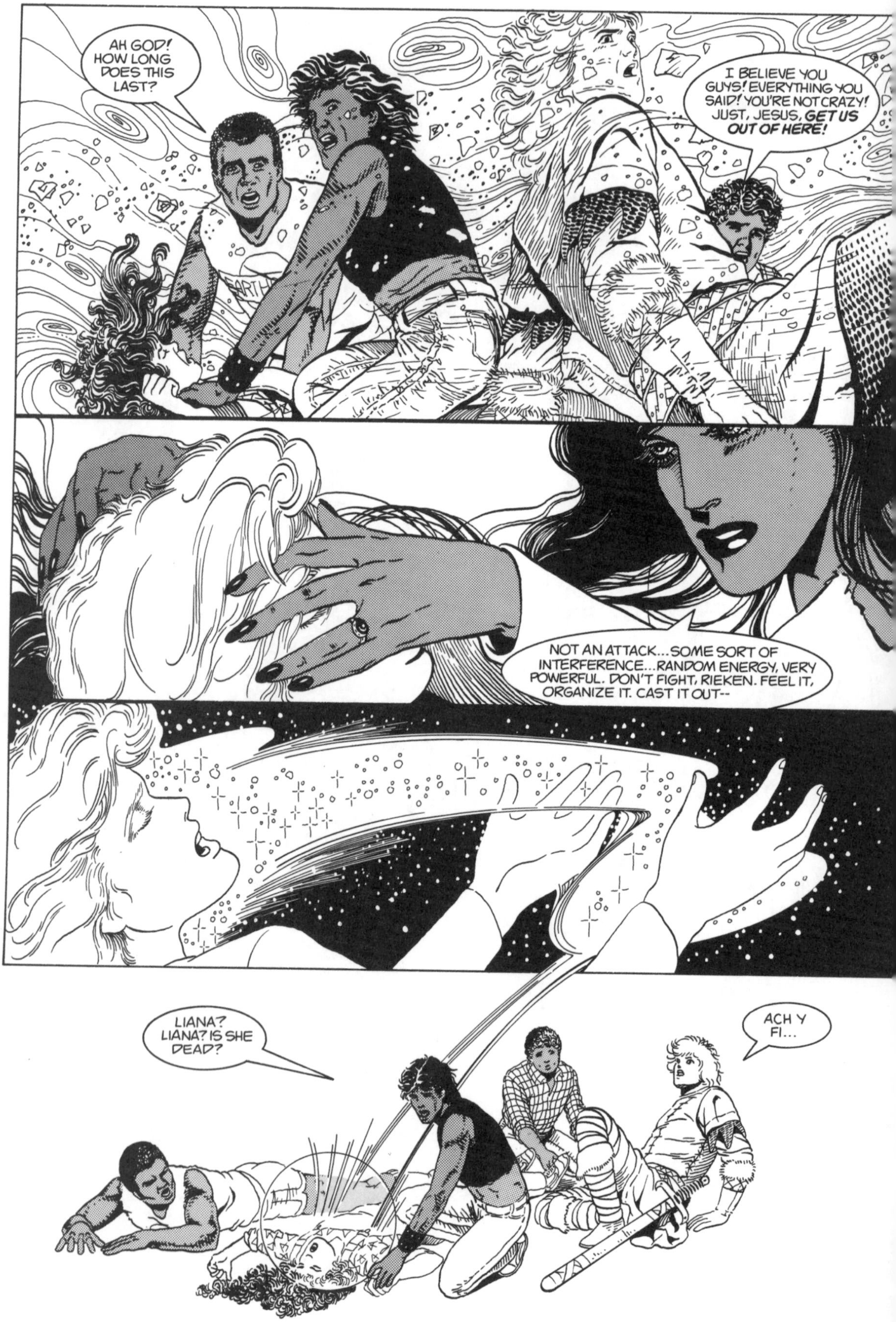
AH GOD! HOW LONG DOES THIS LAST?
I BELIEVE YOU GUYS! EVERYTHING YOU SAID! YOU'RE NOT CRAZY! JUST, JESUS, GET US OUT OF HERE!
NOT AN ATTACK...SOME SORT OF INTERFERENCE...RANDOM ENERGY, VERY POWERFUL. DON'T FIGHT, RIEKEN. FEEL IT, ORGANIZE IT. CAST IT OUT--
LIANA? LIANA? IS SHE DEAD?
ACH Y FI...

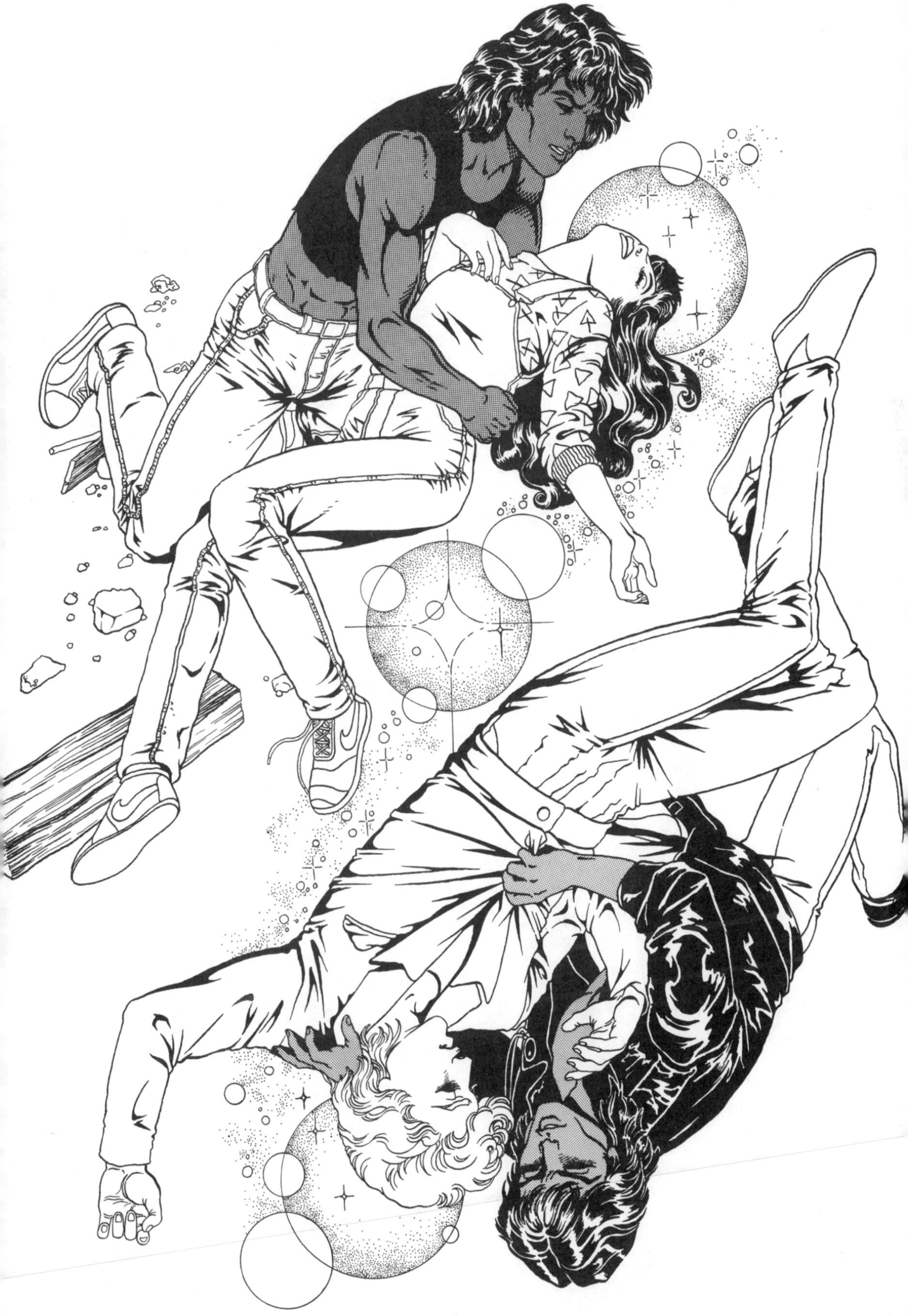

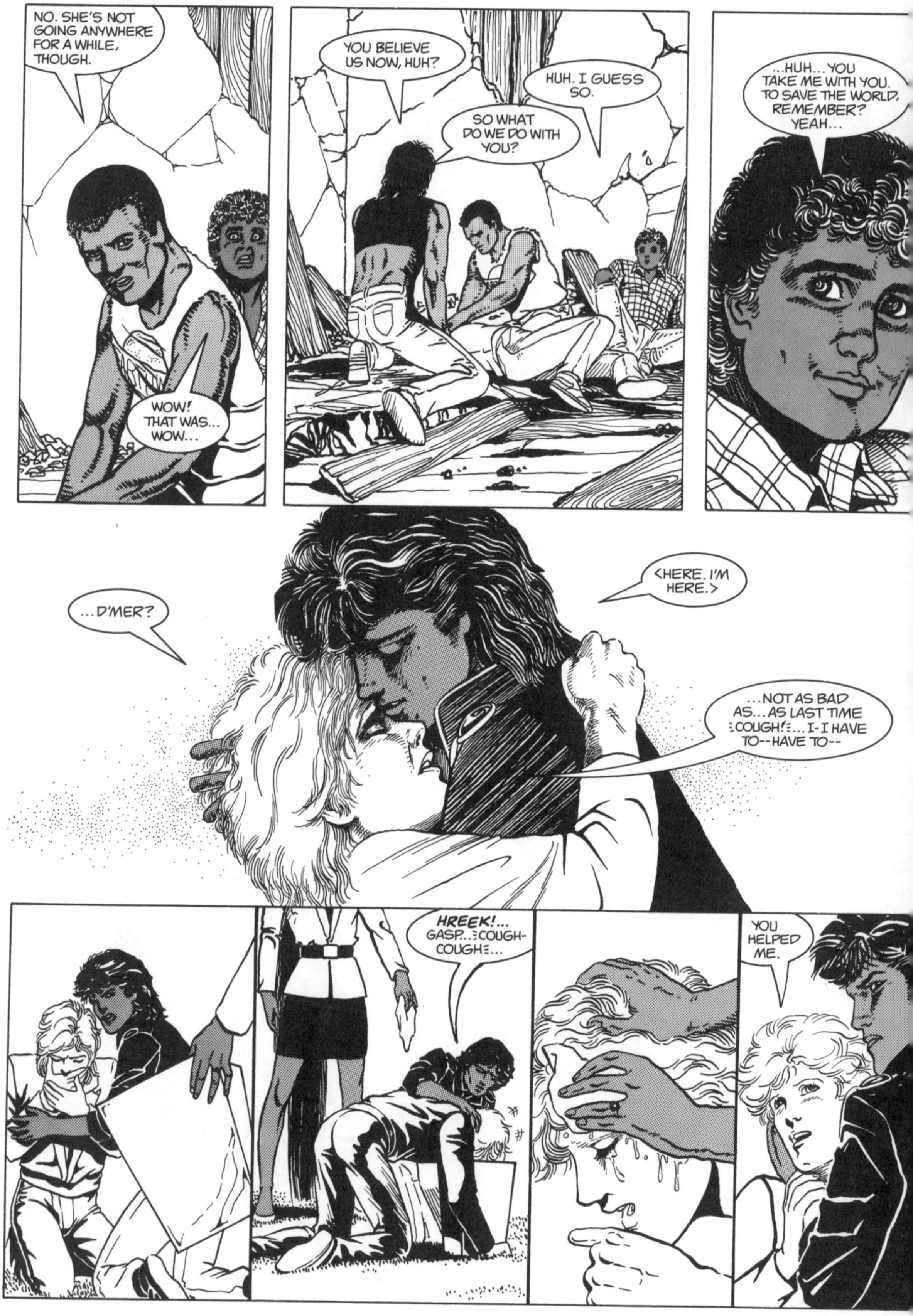
NO. SHE'S NOT GOING ANYWHERE FOR A WHILE, THOUGH.
WOW! THAT WAS... WOW...
YOU BELIEVE US NOW, HUH?
SO WHAT DO WE DO WITH YOU?
HUH. I GUESS SO.
...HUH... YOU TAKE ME WITH YOU. TO SAVE THE WORLD, REMEMBER? YEAH...
...D'MER?
<HERE. I'M HERE.>
...NOT AS BAD AS... AS LAST TIME =COUGH!=... I-I HAVE TO--HAVE TO--
HREEK!... GASP... =COUGH-COUGH=...
YOU HELPED ME.

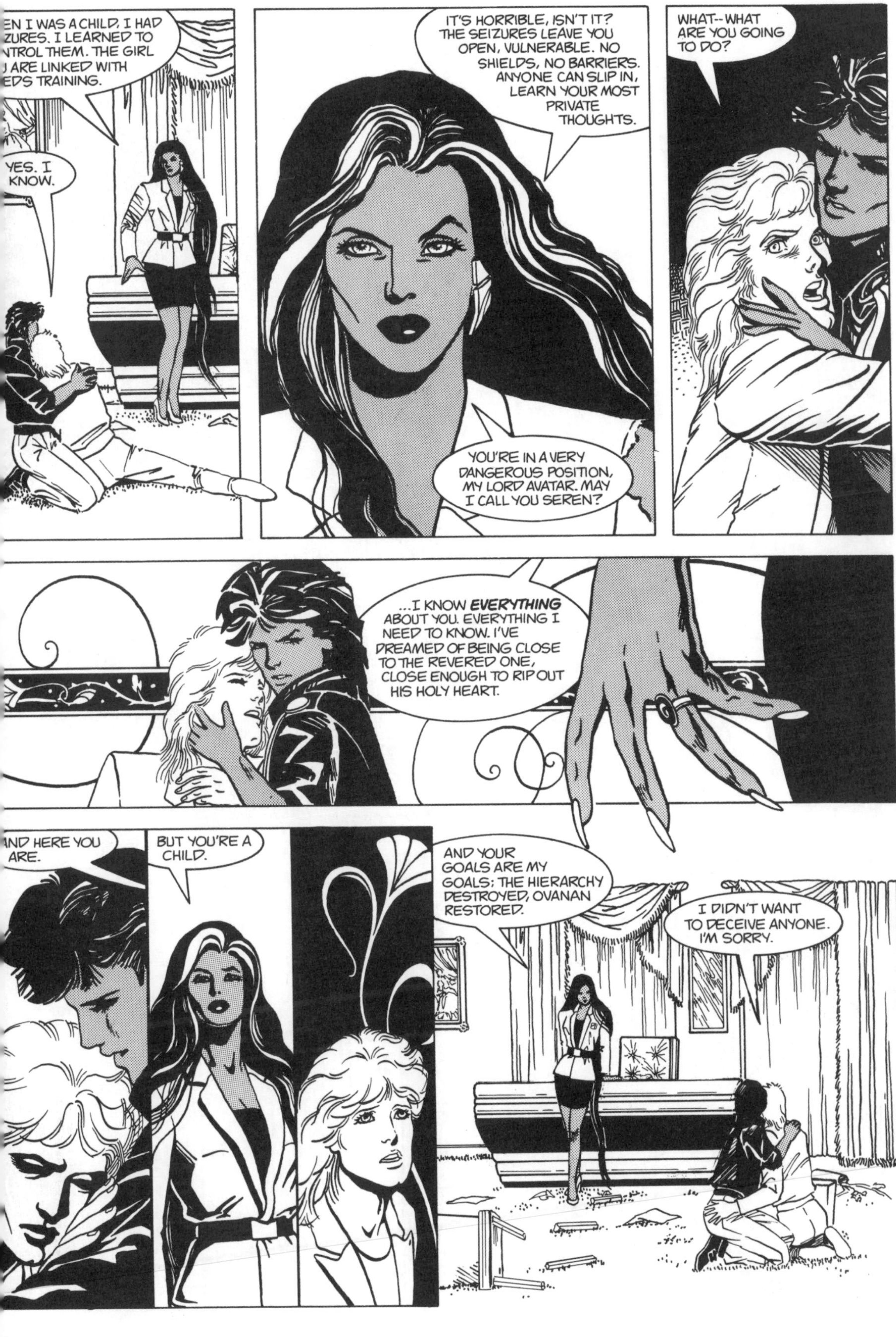

EN I WAS A CHILD, I HAD ZURES. I LEARNED TO NTROL THEM. THE GIRL J ARE LINKED WITH EDS TRAINING.
YES. I KNOW.
IT'S HORRIBLE, ISN'T IT? THE SEIZURES LEAVE YOU OPEN, VULNERABLE. NO SHIELDS, NO BARRIERS. ANYONE CAN SLIP IN, LEARN YOUR MOST PRIVATE THOUGHTS.
YOU'RE IN A VERY DANGEROUS POSITION, MY LORD AVATAR. MAY I CALL YOU SEREN?
WHAT--WHAT ARE YOU GOING TO DO?
...I KNOW **EVERYTHING** ABOUT YOU. EVERYTHING I NEED TO KNOW. I'VE DREAMED OF BEING CLOSE TO THE REVERED ONE, CLOSE ENOUGH TO RIP OUT HIS HOLY HEART.
ND HERE YOU ARE.
BUT YOU'RE A CHILD.
AND YOUR GOALS ARE MY GOALS; THE HIERARCHY DESTROYED, OVANAN RESTORED.
I DIDN'T WANT TO DECEIVE ANYONE. I'M SORRY.

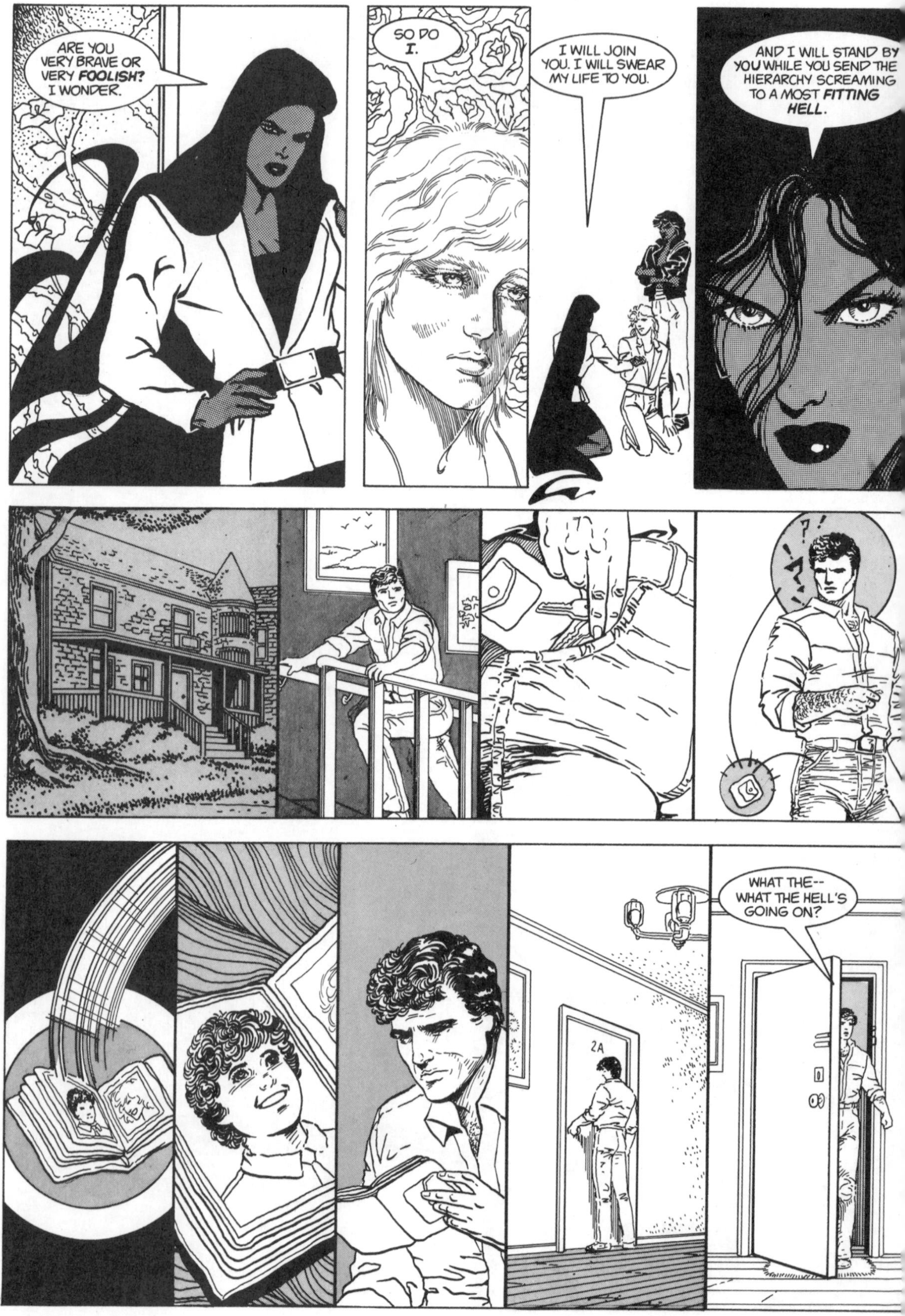

ARE YOU VERY BRAVE OR VERY FOOLISH? I WONDER.
SO DO I.
I WILL JOIN YOU. I WILL SWEAR MY LIFE TO YOU.
AND I WILL STAND BY YOU WHILE YOU SEND THE HIERARCHY SCREAMING TO A MOST FITTING HELL.
2A
WHAT THE-- WHAT THE HELL'S GOING ON?

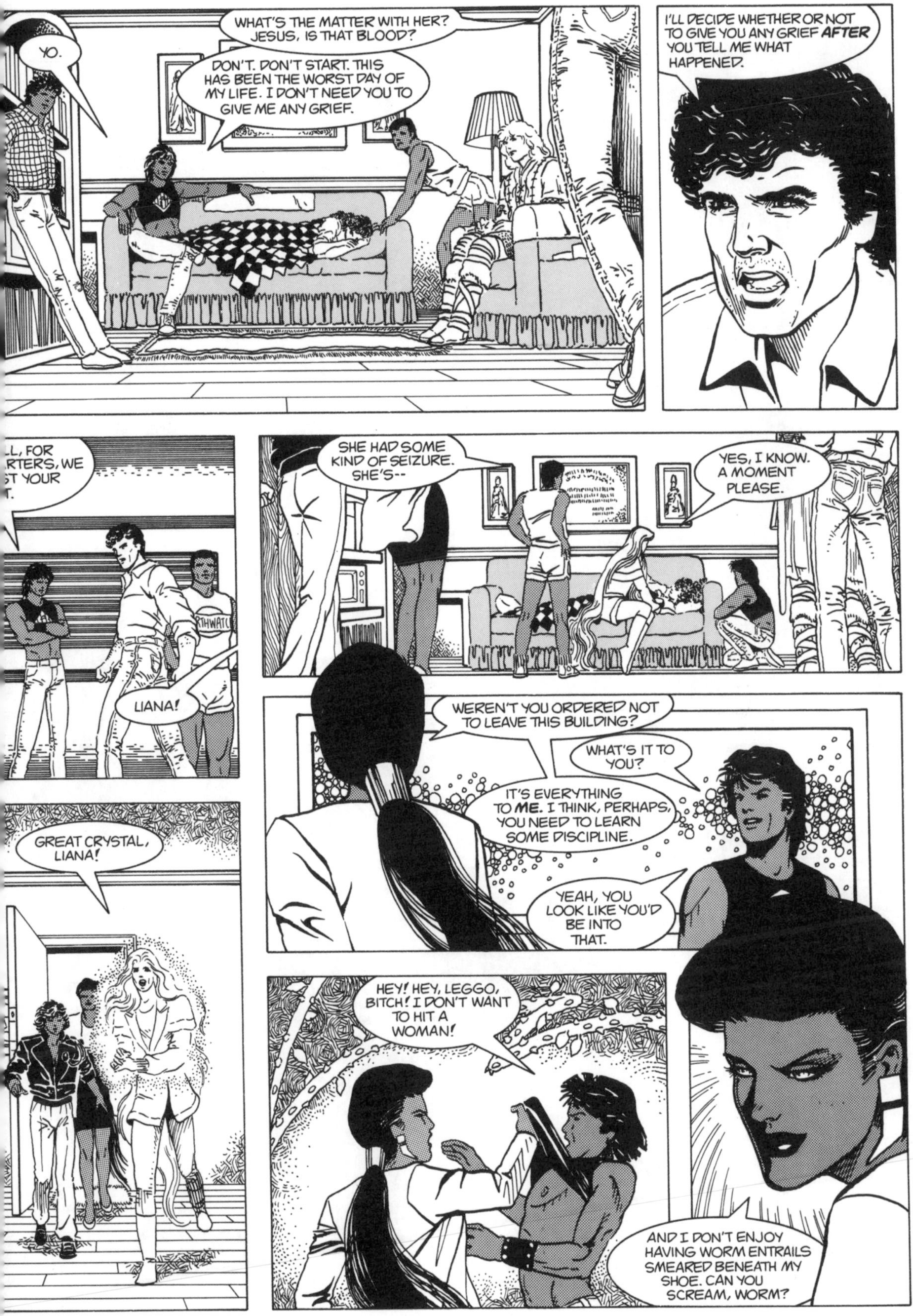
YO.
WHAT'S THE MATTER WITH HER? JESUS, IS THAT BLOOD?
DON'T. DON'T START. THIS HAS BEEN THE WORST DAY OF MY LIFE. I DON'T NEED YOU TO GIVE ME ANY GRIEF.
I'LL DECIDE WHETHER OR NOT TO GIVE YOU ANY GRIEF **AFTER** YOU TELL ME WHAT HAPPENED.
LL, FOR RTERS, WE ST YOUR T.
LIANA!
SHE HAD SOME KIND OF SEIZURE. SHE'S--
YES, I KNOW. A MOMENT PLEASE.
GREAT CRYSTAL, LIANA!
WEREN'T YOU ORDERED NOT TO LEAVE THIS BUILDING?
WHAT'S IT TO YOU?
IT'S EVERYTHING TO **ME.** I THINK, PERHAPS, YOU NEED TO LEARN SOME DISCIPLINE.
YEAH, YOU LOOK LIKE YOU'D BE INTO THAT.
HEY! HEY, LEGGO, BITCH! I DON'T WANT TO HIT A WOMAN!
AND I DON'T ENJOY HAVING WORM ENTRAILS SMEARED BENEATH MY SHOE. CAN YOU SCREAM, WORM?

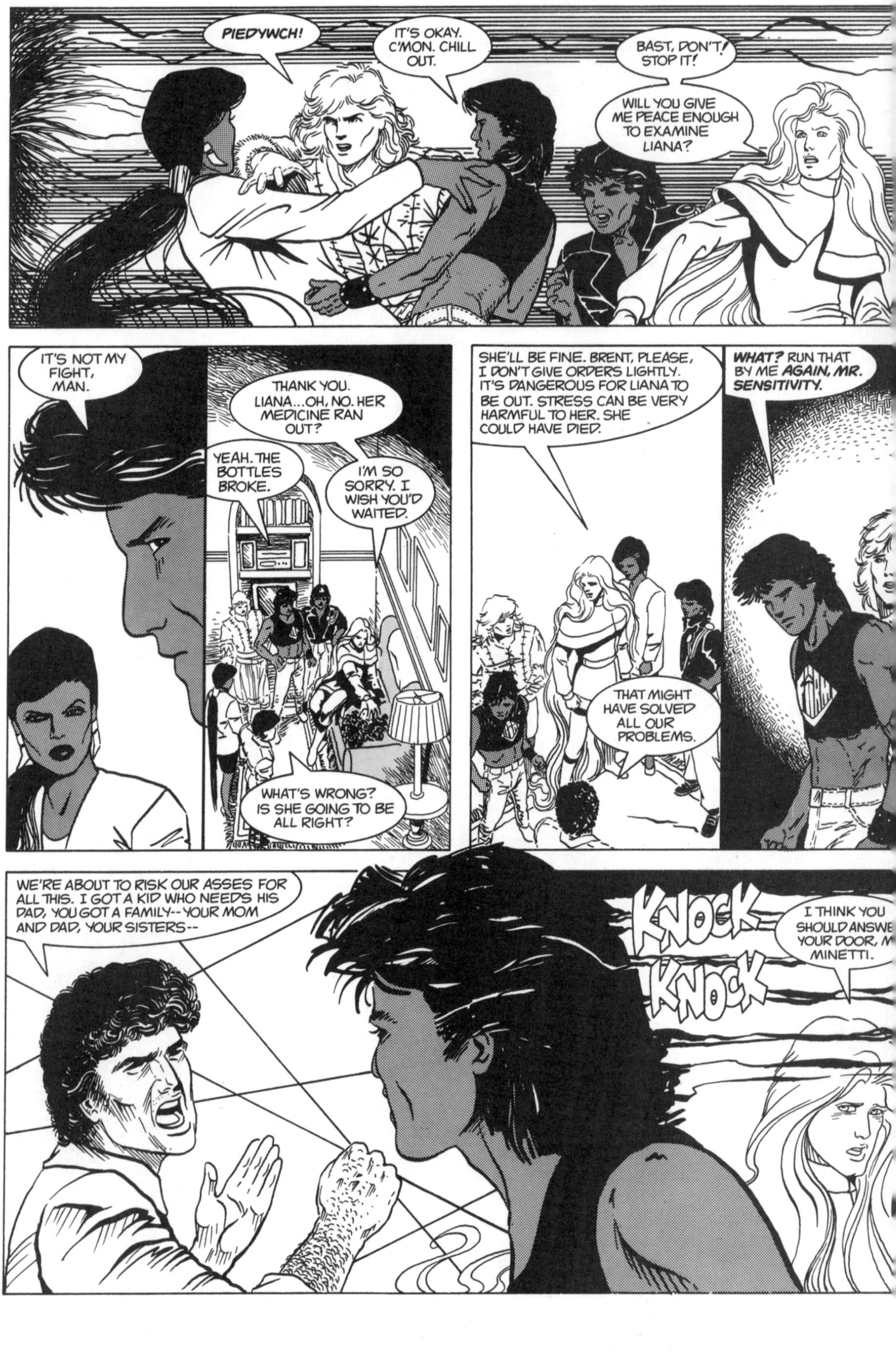
PIEDYWCH!
IT'S OKAY. C'MON. CHILL OUT.
BAST, DON'T! STOP IT!
WILL YOU GIVE ME PEACE ENOUGH TO EXAMINE LIANA?
IT'S NOT MY FIGHT, MAN.
THANK YOU. LIANA...OH, NO. HER MEDICINE RAN OUT?
YEAH. THE BOTTLES BROKE.
I'M SO SORRY. I WISH YOU'D WAITED.
WHAT'S WRONG? IS SHE GOING TO BE ALL RIGHT?
SHE'LL BE FINE. BRENT, PLEASE, I DON'T GIVE ORDERS LIGHTLY. IT'S DANGEROUS FOR LIANA TO BE OUT. STRESS CAN BE VERY HARMFUL TO HER. SHE COULD HAVE DIED.
THAT MIGHT HAVE SOLVED ALL OUR PROBLEMS.
WHAT? RUN THAT BY ME AGAIN, MR. SENSITIVITY.
WE'RE ABOUT TO RISK OUR ASSES FOR ALL THIS. I GOT A KID WHO NEEDS HIS DAD, YOU GOT A FAMILY-- YOUR MOM AND DAD, YOUR SISTERS--
KNOCK KNOCK
I THINK YOU SHOULD ANSWE YOUR DOOR, M MINETTI.

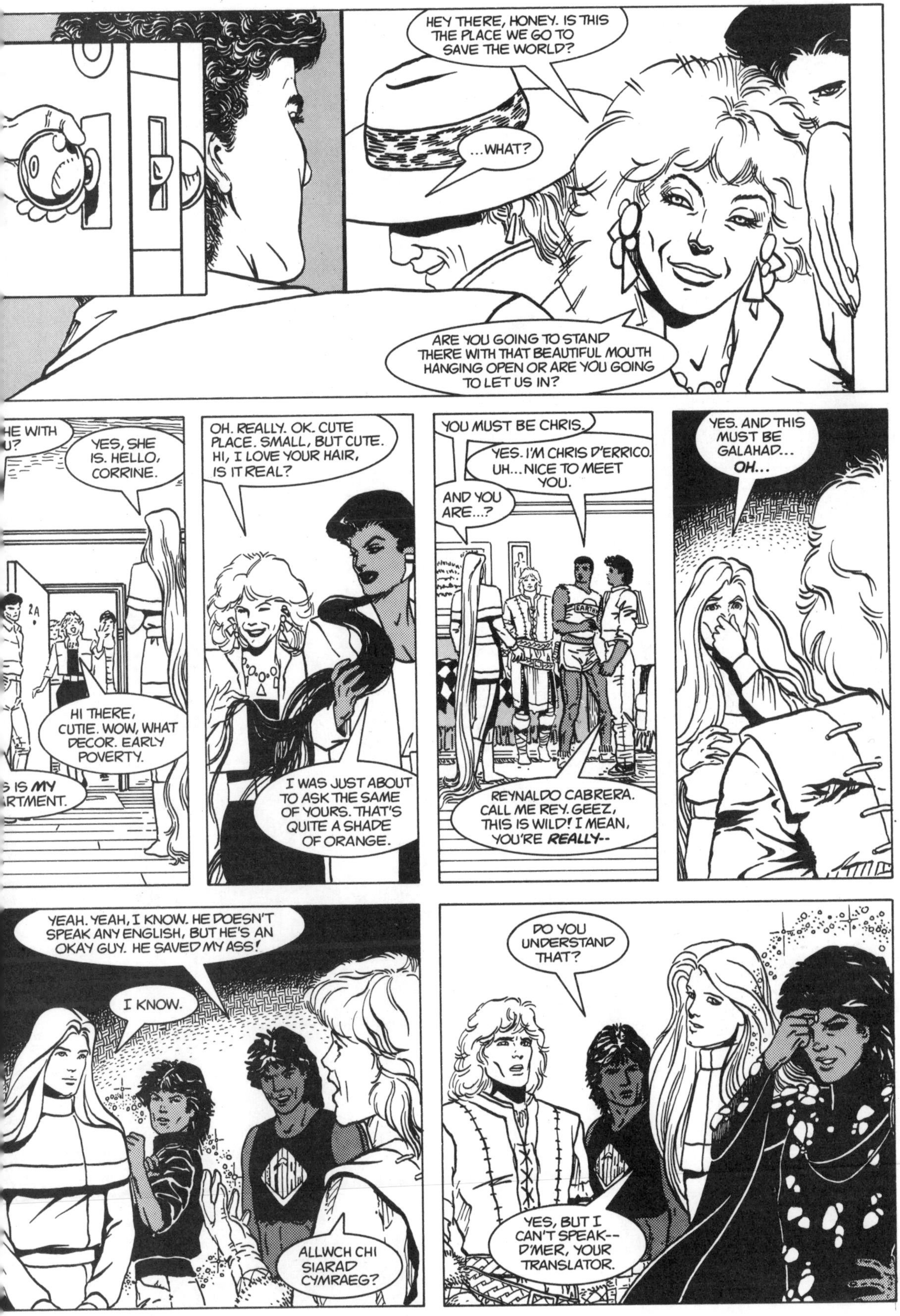
HEY THERE, HONEY. IS THIS THE PLACE WE GO TO SAVE THE WORLD?
...WHAT?
ARE YOU GOING TO STAND THERE WITH THAT BEAUTIFUL MOUTH HANGING OPEN OR ARE YOU GOING TO LET US IN?
HE WITH U?
YES, SHE IS. HELLO, CORRINE.
2A
HI THERE, CUTIE. WOW, WHAT DECOR. EARLY POVERTY.
S IS MY ARTMENT.
OH. REALLY. OK. CUTE PLACE. SMALL, BUT CUTE. HI, I LOVE YOUR HAIR, IS IT REAL?
I WAS JUST ABOUT TO ASK THE SAME OF YOURS. THAT'S QUITE A SHADE OF ORANGE.
YOU MUST BE CHRIS.
YES. I'M CHRIS D'ERRICO. UH...NICE TO MEET YOU.
AND YOU ARE...?
EARTH
REYNALDO CABRERA. CALL ME REY. GEEZ, THIS IS WILD! I MEAN, YOU'RE REALLY--
YES. AND THIS MUST BE GALAHAD... OH...
YEAH. YEAH, I KNOW. HE DOESN'T SPEAK ANY ENGLISH, BUT HE'S AN OKAY GUY. HE SAVED MY ASS!
I KNOW.
ALLWCH CHI SIARAD CYMRAEG?
DO YOU UNDERSTAND THAT?
YES, BUT I CAN'T SPEAK-- D'MER, YOUR TRANSLATOR.

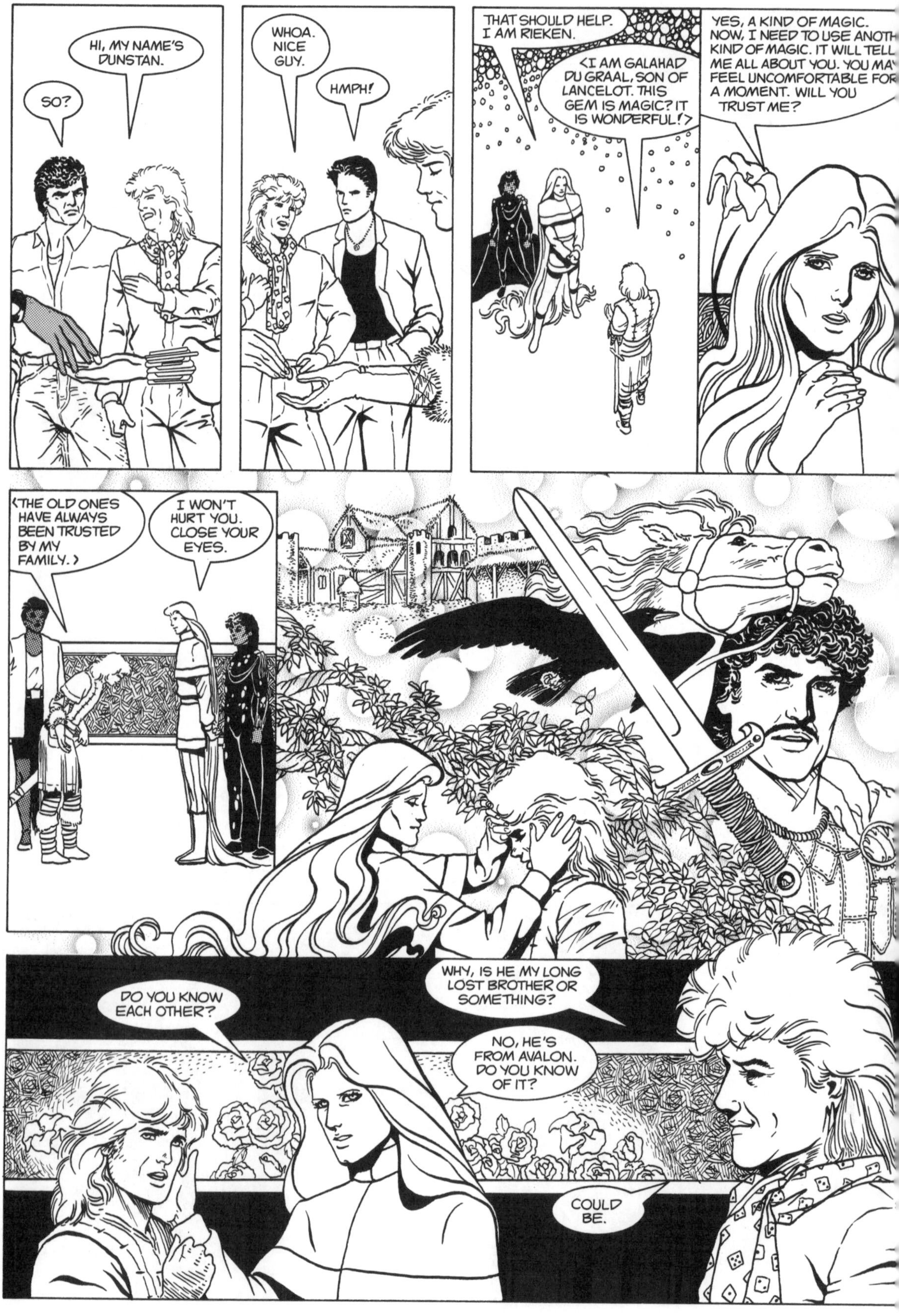

HI, MY NAME'S DUNSTAN.
SO?
WHOA. NICE GUY.
HMPH!
THAT SHOULD HELP. I AM RIEKEN.
<I AM GALAHAD DU GRAAL, SON OF LANCELOT. THIS GEM IS MAGIC? IT IS WONDERFUL!>
YES, A KIND OF MAGIC. NOW, I NEED TO USE ANOTH KIND OF MAGIC. IT WILL TELL ME ALL ABOUT YOU. YOU MA FEEL UNCOMFORTABLE FOR A MOMENT. WILL YOU TRUST ME?
<THE OLD ONES HAVE ALWAYS BEEN TRUSTED BY MY FAMILY.>
I WON'T HURT YOU. CLOSE YOUR EYES.
DO YOU KNOW EACH OTHER?
WHY, IS HE MY LONG LOST BROTHER OR SOMETHING?
NO, HE'S FROM AVALON. DO YOU KNOW OF IT?
COULD BE.

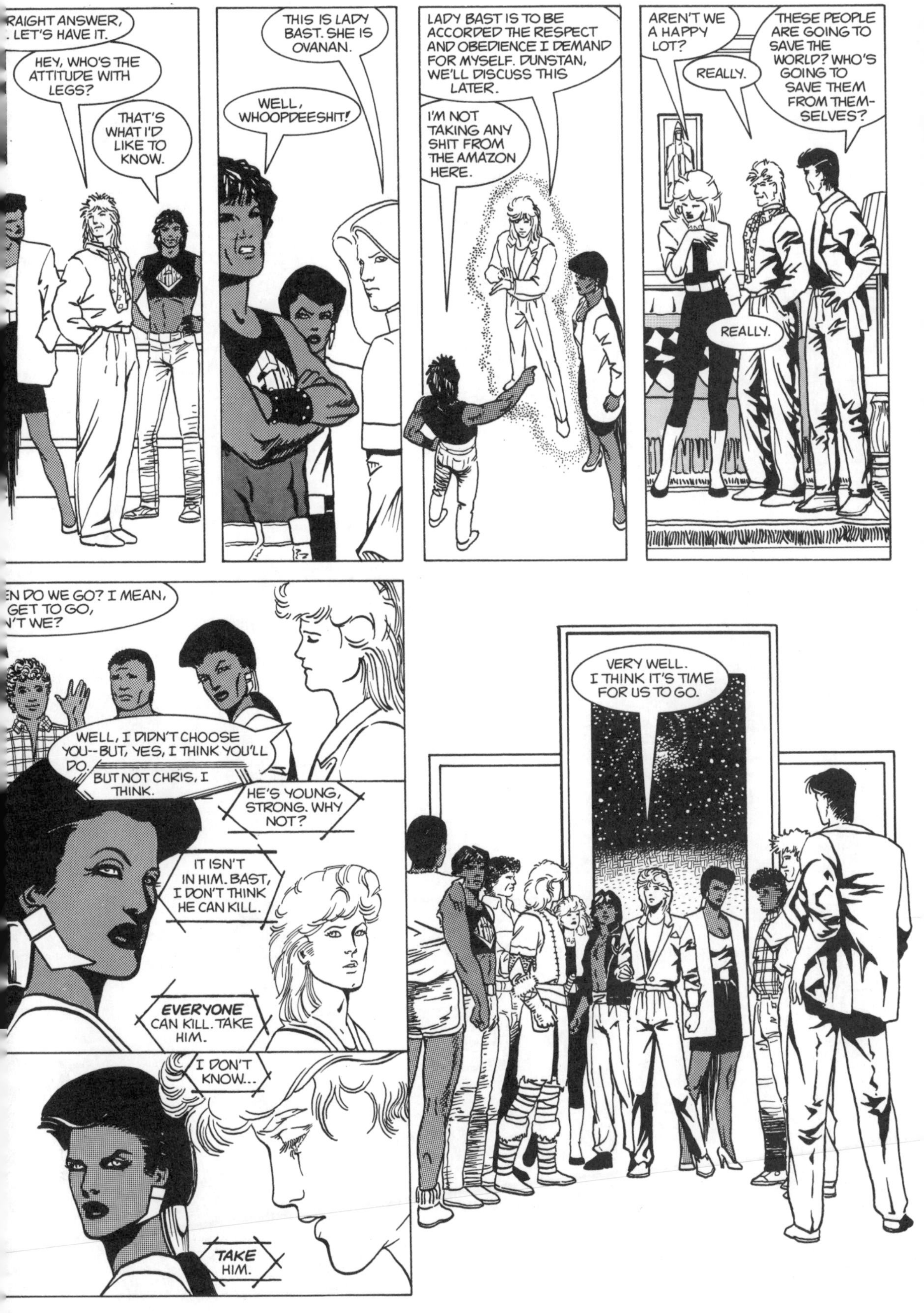
RAIGHT ANSWER,
. LET'S HAVE IT.
HEY, WHO'S THE ATTITUDE WITH LEGS?
THAT'S WHAT I'D LIKE TO KNOW.
THIS IS LADY BAST. SHE IS OVANAN.
WELL, WHOOPDEESHIT!
LADY BAST IS TO BE ACCORDED THE RESPECT AND OBEDIENCE I DEMAND FOR MYSELF. DUNSTAN, WE'LL DISCUSS THIS LATER.
I'M NOT TAKING ANY SHIT FROM THE AMAZON HERE.
AREN'T WE A HAPPY LOT?
REALLY.
THESE PEOPLE ARE GOING TO SAVE THE WORLD? WHO'S GOING TO SAVE THEM FROM THEM-SELVES?
REALLY.
EN DO WE GO? I MEAN, GET TO GO, N'T WE?
WELL, I DIDN'T CHOOSE YOU--BUT, YES, I THINK YOU'LL DO.
BUT NOT CHRIS, I THINK.
HE'S YOUNG, STRONG. WHY NOT?
IT ISN'T IN HIM. BAST, I DON'T THINK HE CAN KILL.
EVERYONE CAN KILL. TAKE HIM.
I DON'T KNOW...
TAKE HIM.
VERY WELL. I THINK IT'S TIME FOR US TO GO.

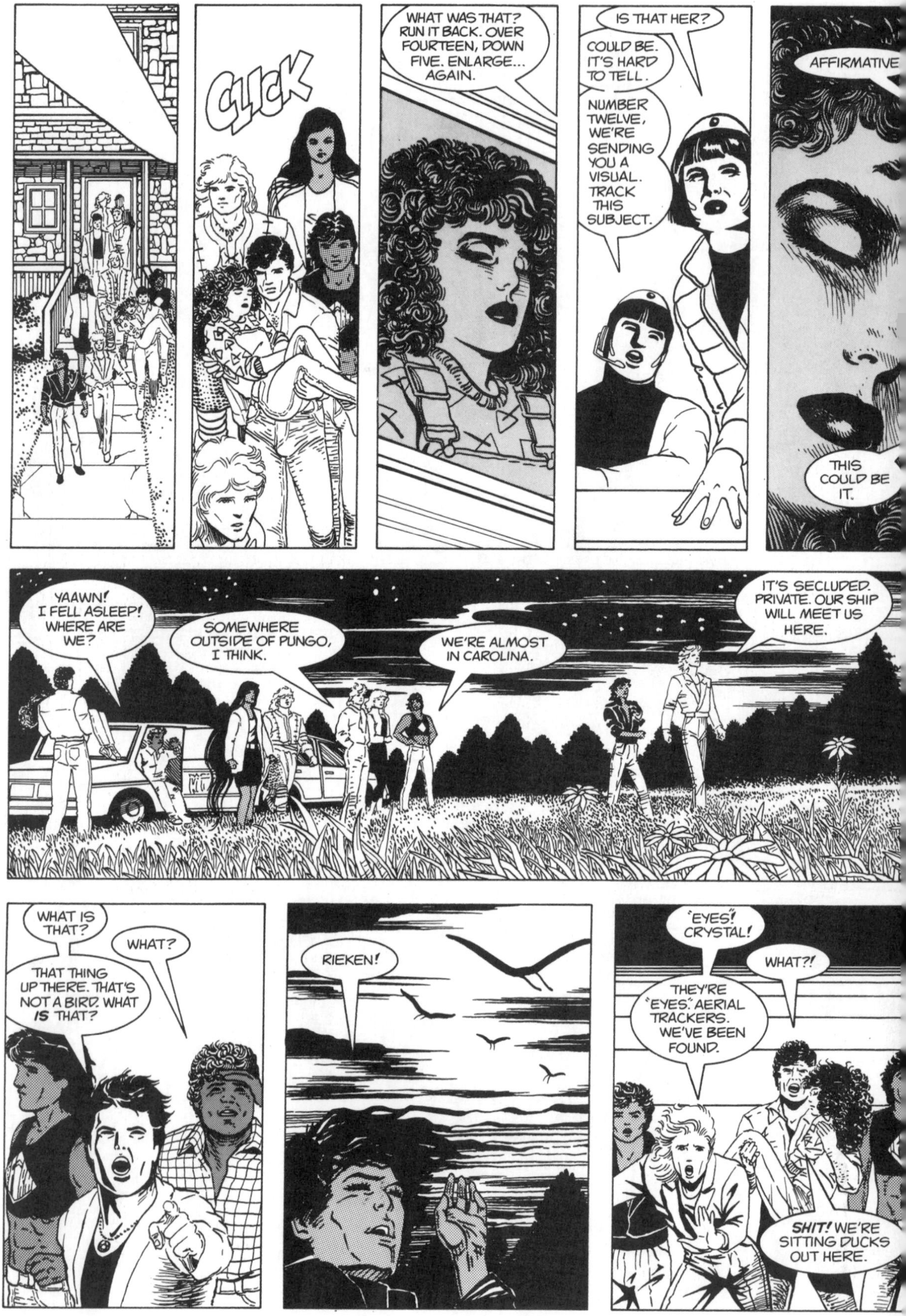
CLICK
WHAT WAS THAT? RUN IT BACK. OVER FOURTEEN, DOWN FIVE. ENLARGE... AGAIN.
IS THAT HER?
COULD BE. IT'S HARD TO TELL.
NUMBER TWELVE, WE'RE SENDING YOU A VISUAL. TRACK THIS SUBJECT.
AFFIRMATIVE
THIS COULD BE IT.
YAAWN! I FELL ASLEEP! WHERE ARE WE?
SOMEWHERE OUTSIDE OF PUNGO, I THINK.
WE'RE ALMOST IN CAROLINA.
IT'S SECLUDED. PRIVATE. OUR SHIP WILL MEET US HERE.
WHAT IS THAT?
WHAT?
THAT THING UP THERE. THAT'S NOT A BIRD. WHAT IS THAT?
RIEKEN!
"EYES!" CRYSTAL!
WHAT?!
THEY'RE "EYES." AERIAL TRACKERS. WE'VE BEEN FOUND.
SHIT! WE'RE SITTING DUCKS OUT HERE.

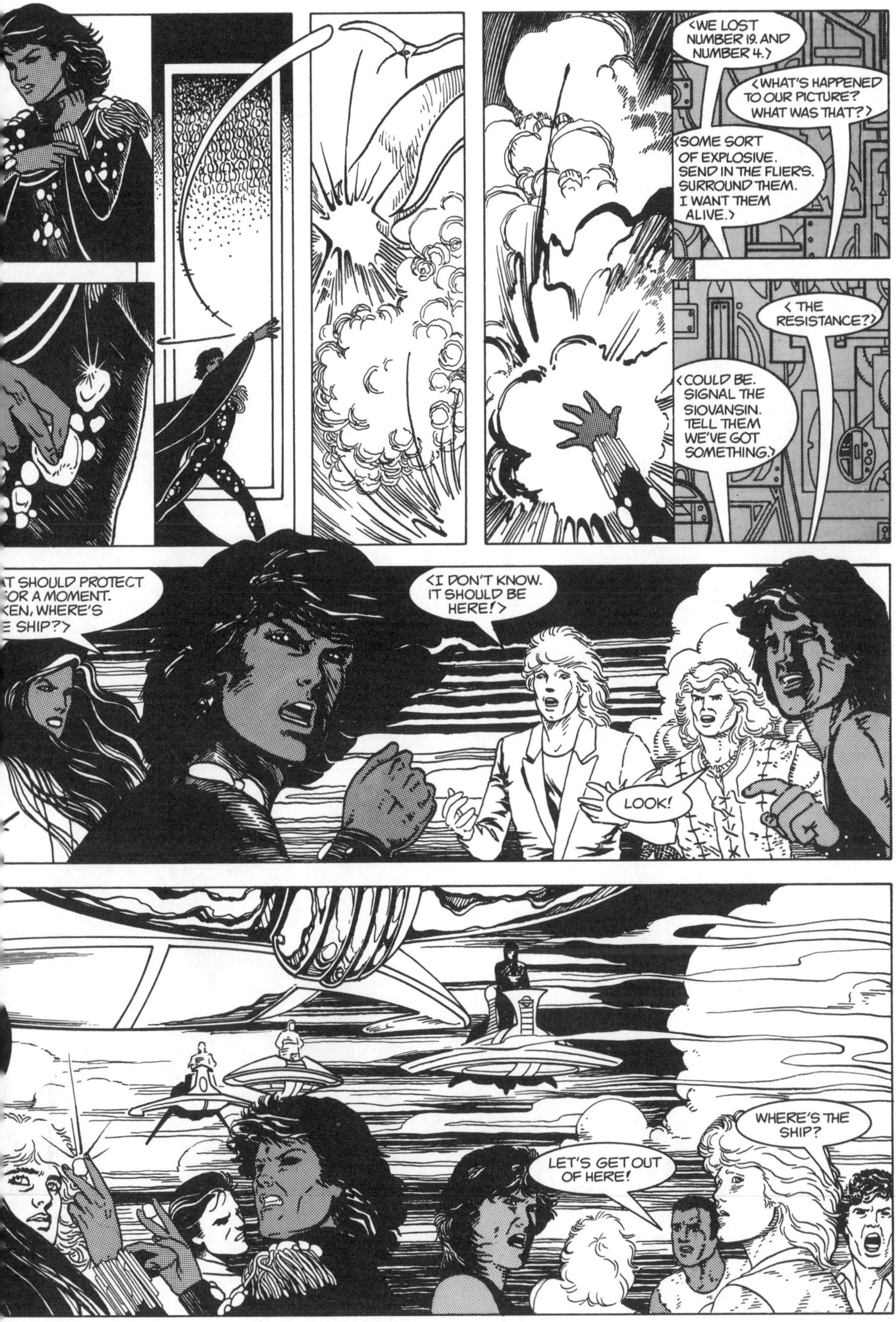

<WE LOST NUMBER 19. AND NUMBER 4.>
<WHAT'S HAPPENED TO OUR PICTURE? WHAT WAS THAT?>
<SOME SORT OF EXPLOSIVE. SEND IN THE FLIERS. SURROUND THEM. I WANT THEM ALIVE.>
< THE RESISTANCE?>
<COULD BE. SIGNAL THE SIOVANSIN. TELL THEM WE'VE GOT SOMETHING.>
AT SHOULD PROTECT OR A MOMENT. KEN, WHERE'S E SHIP?>
<I DON'T KNOW. IT SHOULD BE HERE!>
LOOK!
WHERE'S THE SHIP?
LET'S GET OUT OF HERE!

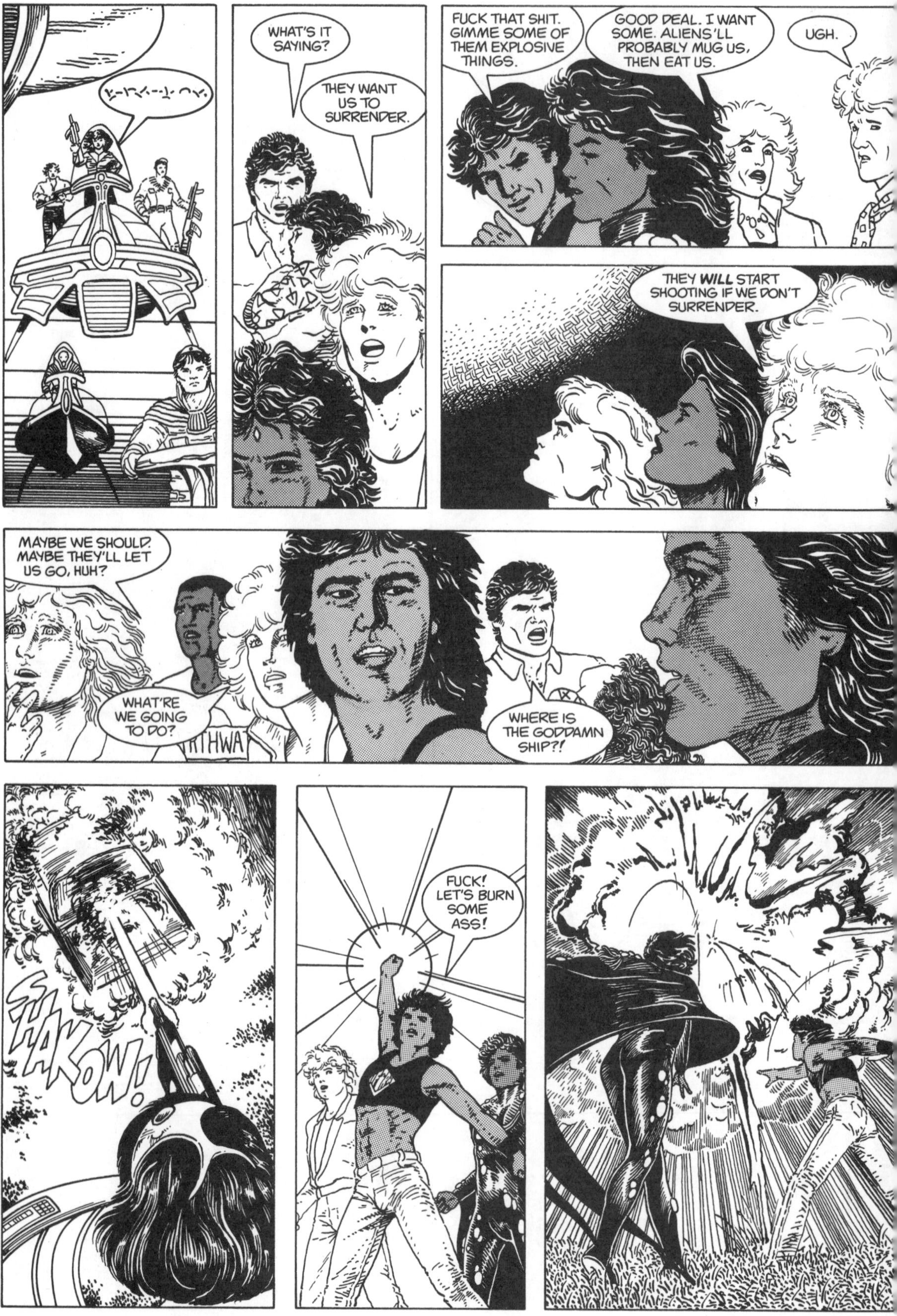

WHAT'S IT SAYING?
THEY WANT US TO SURRENDER.
FUCK THAT SHIT. GIMME SOME OF THEM EXPLOSIVE THINGS.
GOOD DEAL. I WANT SOME. ALIENS'LL PROBABLY MUG US, THEN EAT US.
UGH.
THEY WILL START SHOOTING IF WE DON'T SURRENDER.
MAYBE WE SHOULD. MAYBE THEY'LL LET US GO, HUH?
WHAT'RE WE GOING TO DO?
WHERE IS THE GODDAMN SHIP?!
SHAKOW!
FUCK! LET'S BURN SOME ASS!

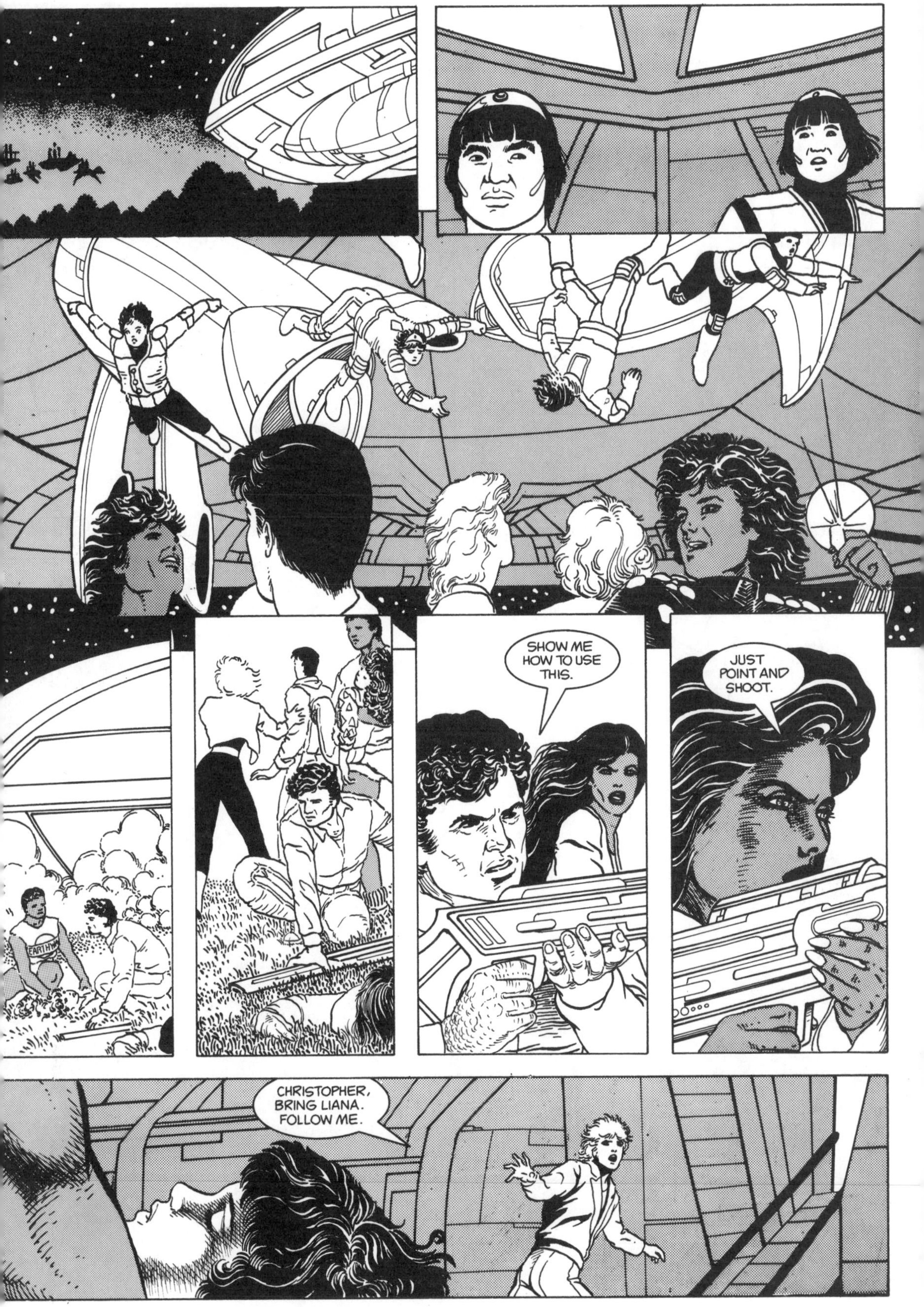

SHOW ME HOW TO USE THIS.
JUST POINT AND SHOOT.
CHRISTOPHER, BRING LIANA. FOLLOW ME.

IT'S BIG IN HERE. WHERE DO I--

PUT HER ANY-WHERE. I'LL BE BACK IN A MOMENT.

THEIR MOTHER SHIP MUST BE CLOSE.

I HAVE TO JAM THEIR TRANSMISSION BEFORE THEY RELAY ANY INFORMATION TO THE SIOVANSIN. THERE!

WHAT SHIP IS THAT? I DON'T SEE ANY IDENTIFICATION--

BZZZ

WE'VE LOST OUR TRANSMISSION.

WHAT ABOUT THE SIOVANSIN?

ALL WE GET STATIC.

LET'S SE WHAT'S GO ON OVER THERE. TA US IN.

WE HAVE TO GET OUT OF HERE! EVERY-ONE ON TO THE SHIP! OH!

ZOT!

ZOT!

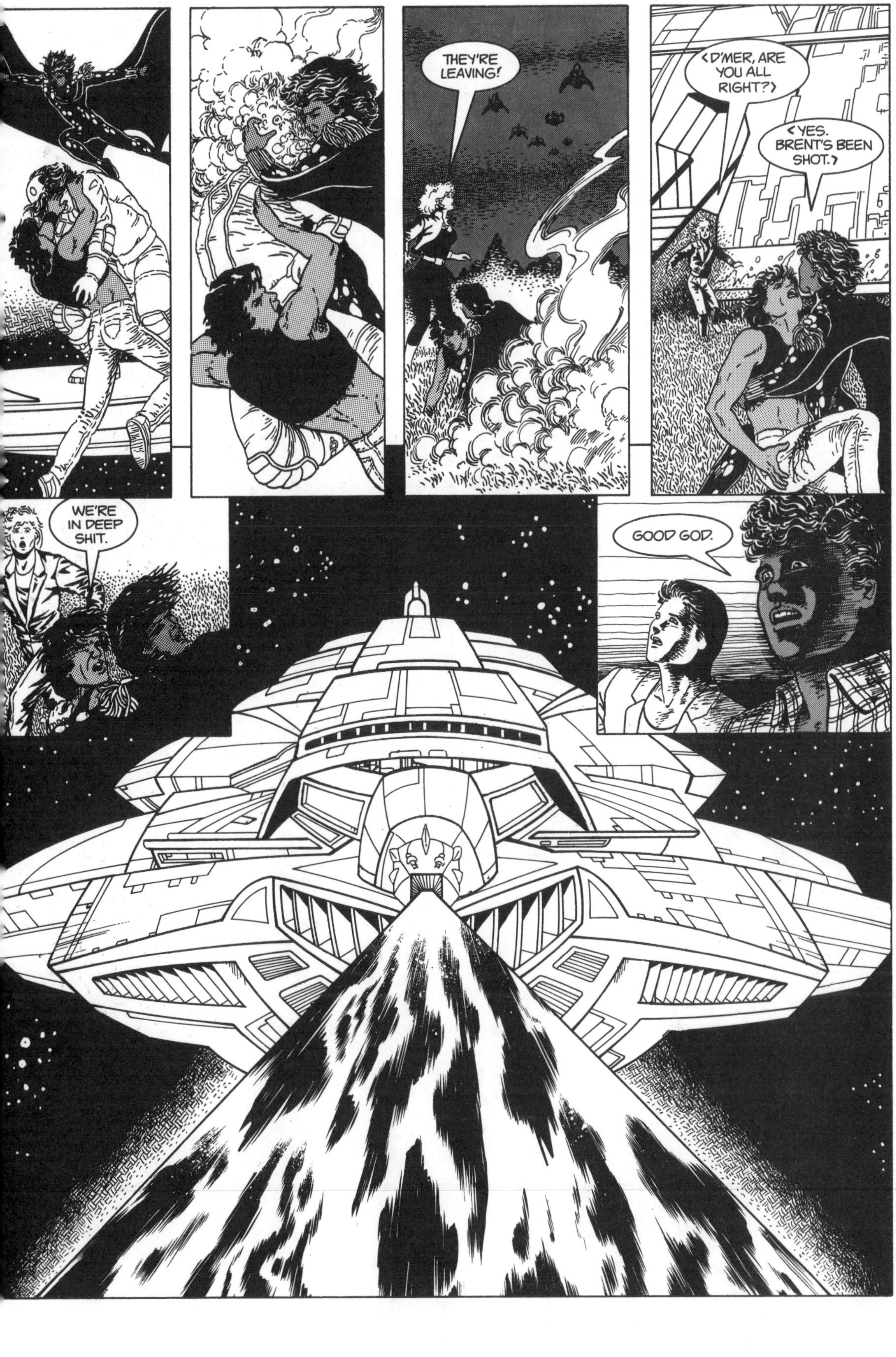
THEY'RE LEAVING!
<D'MER, ARE YOU ALL RIGHT?>
<YES. BRENT'S BEEN SHOT.>
WE'RE IN DEEP SHIT.
GOOD GOD.

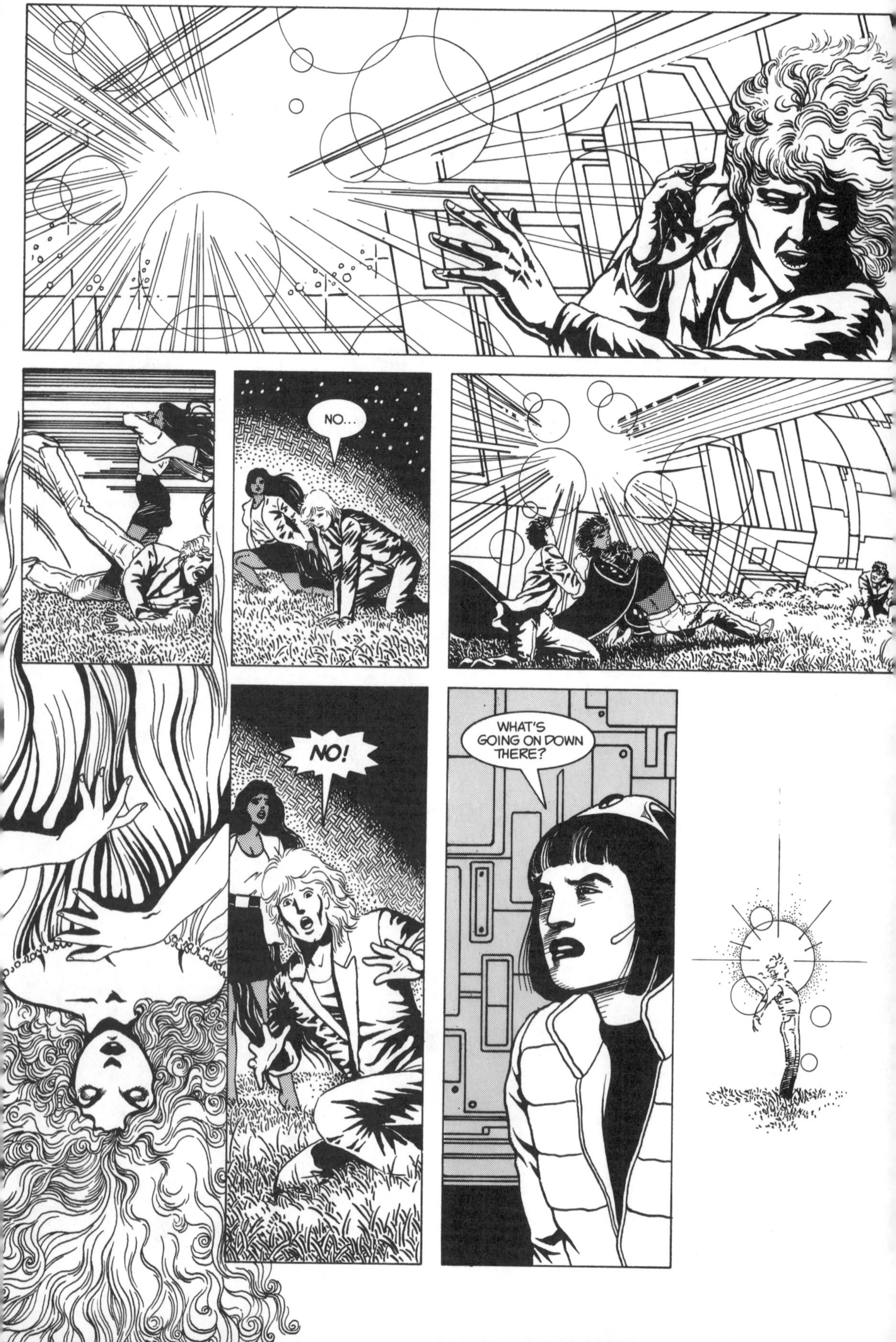
NO...
NO!
WHAT'S GOING ON DOWN THERE?

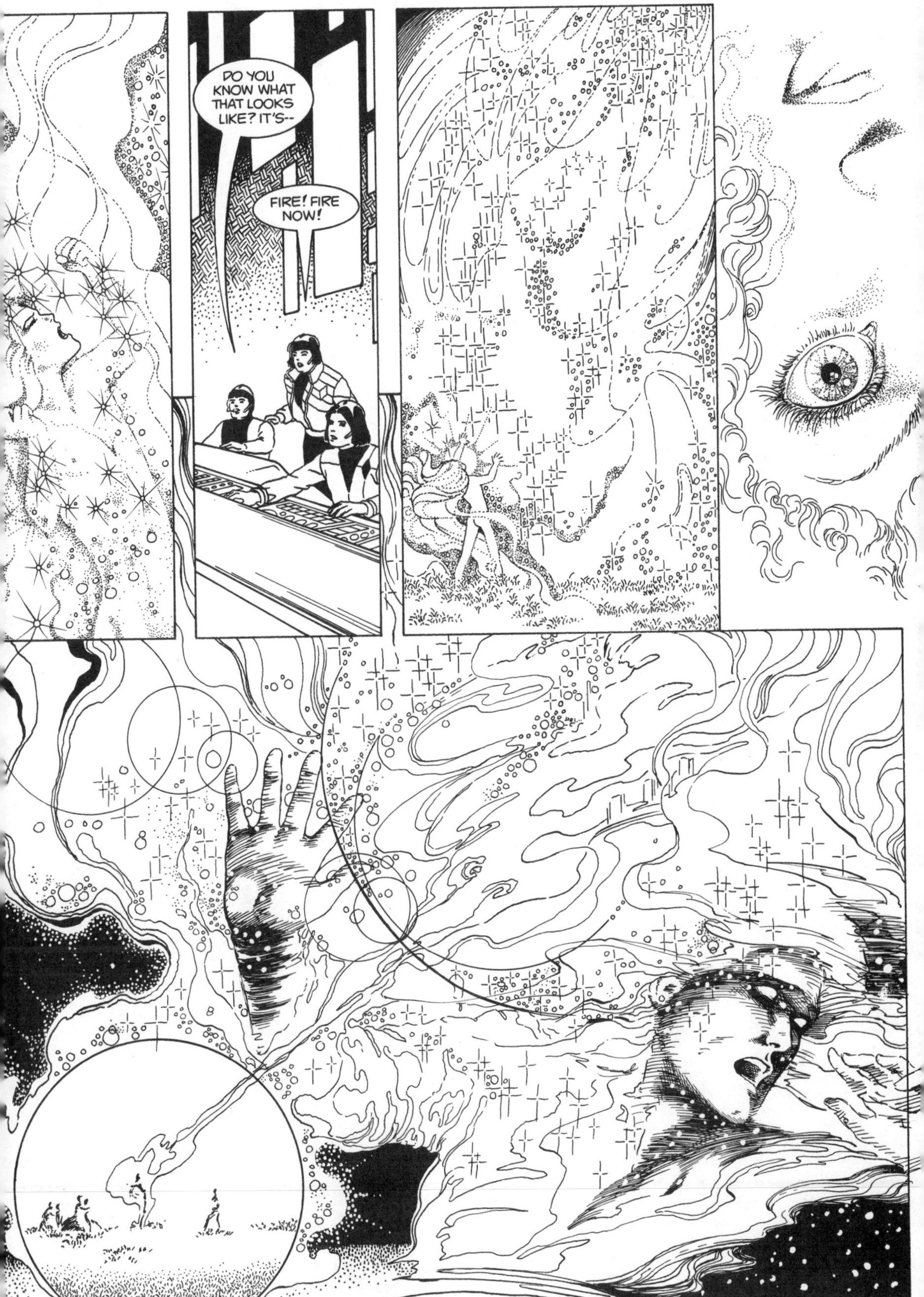
DO YOU KNOW WHAT THAT LOOKS LIKE? IT'S--
FIRE! FIRE NOW!

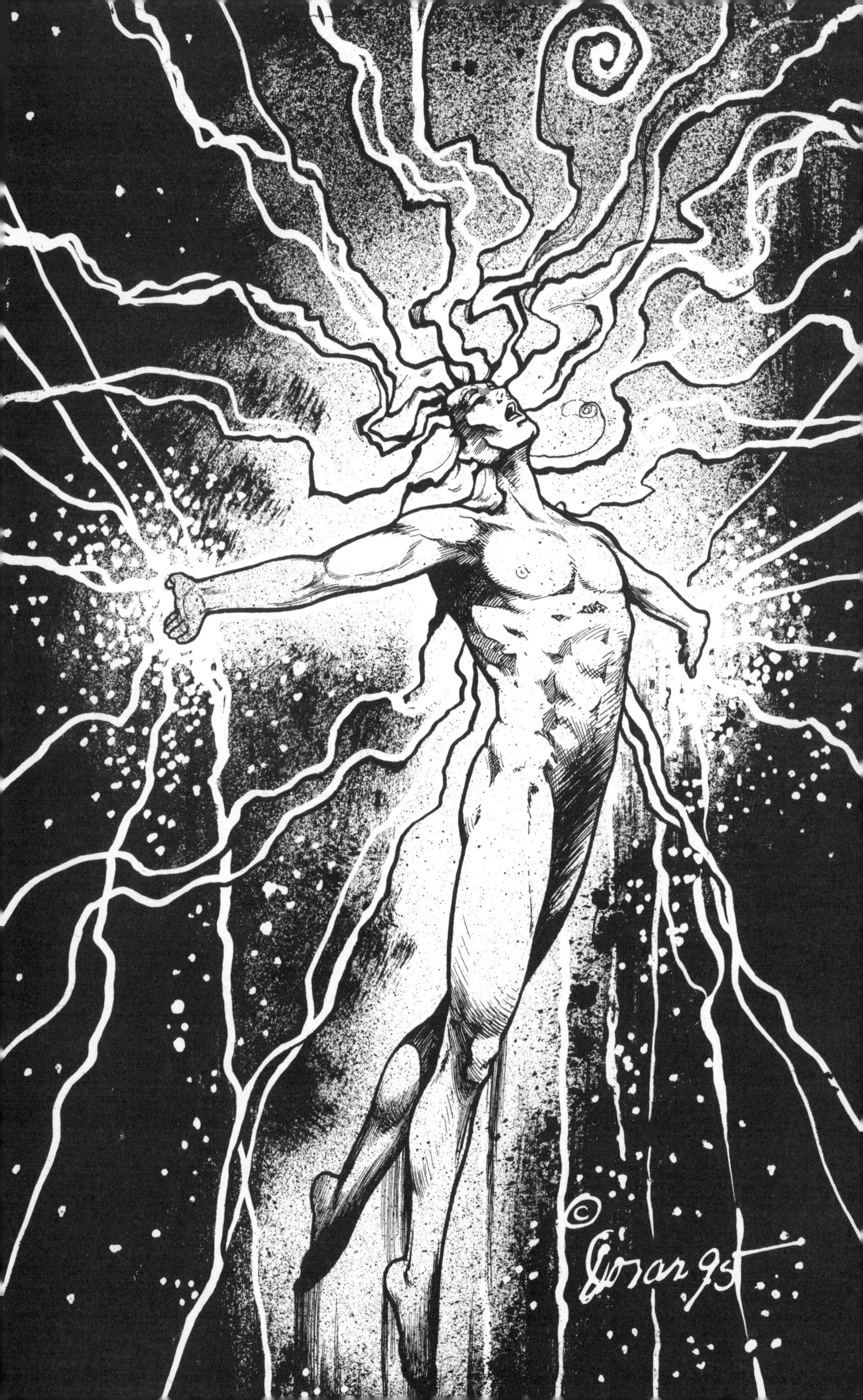

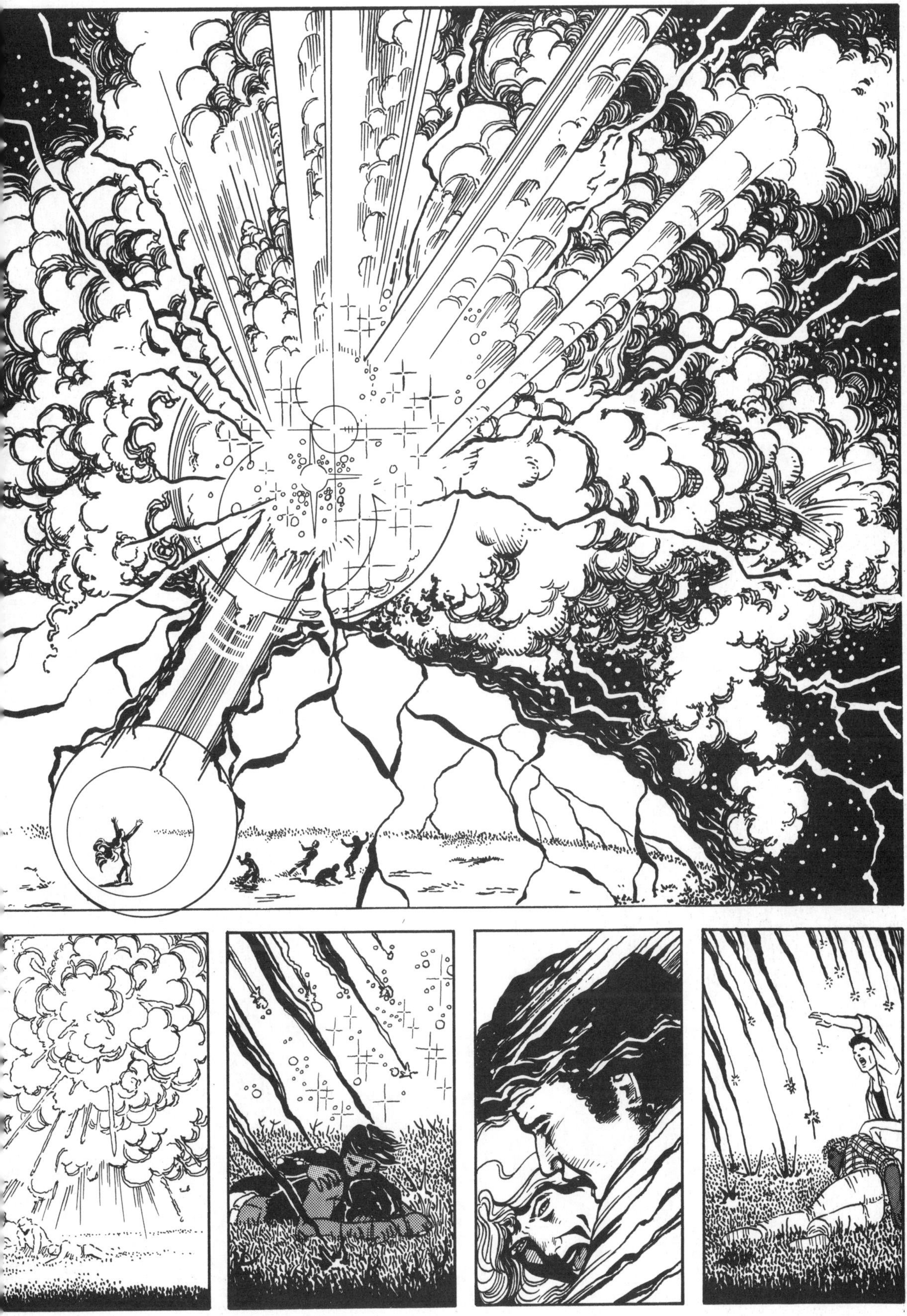

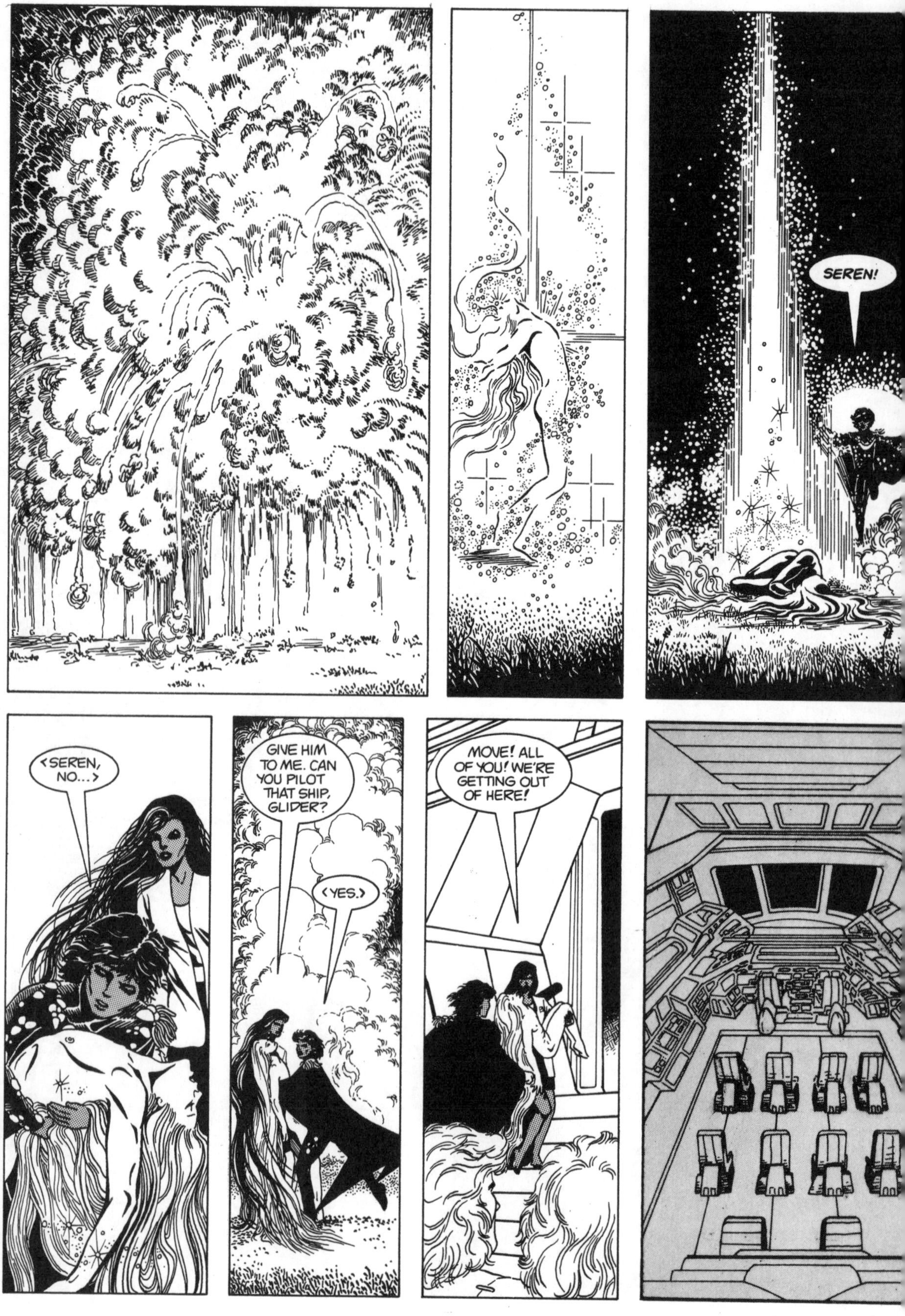
SEREN!
<SEREN, NO...>
GIVE HIM TO ME. CAN YOU PILOT THAT SHIP, GLIDER?
<YES.>
MOVE! ALL OF YOU! WE'RE GETTING OUT OF HERE!

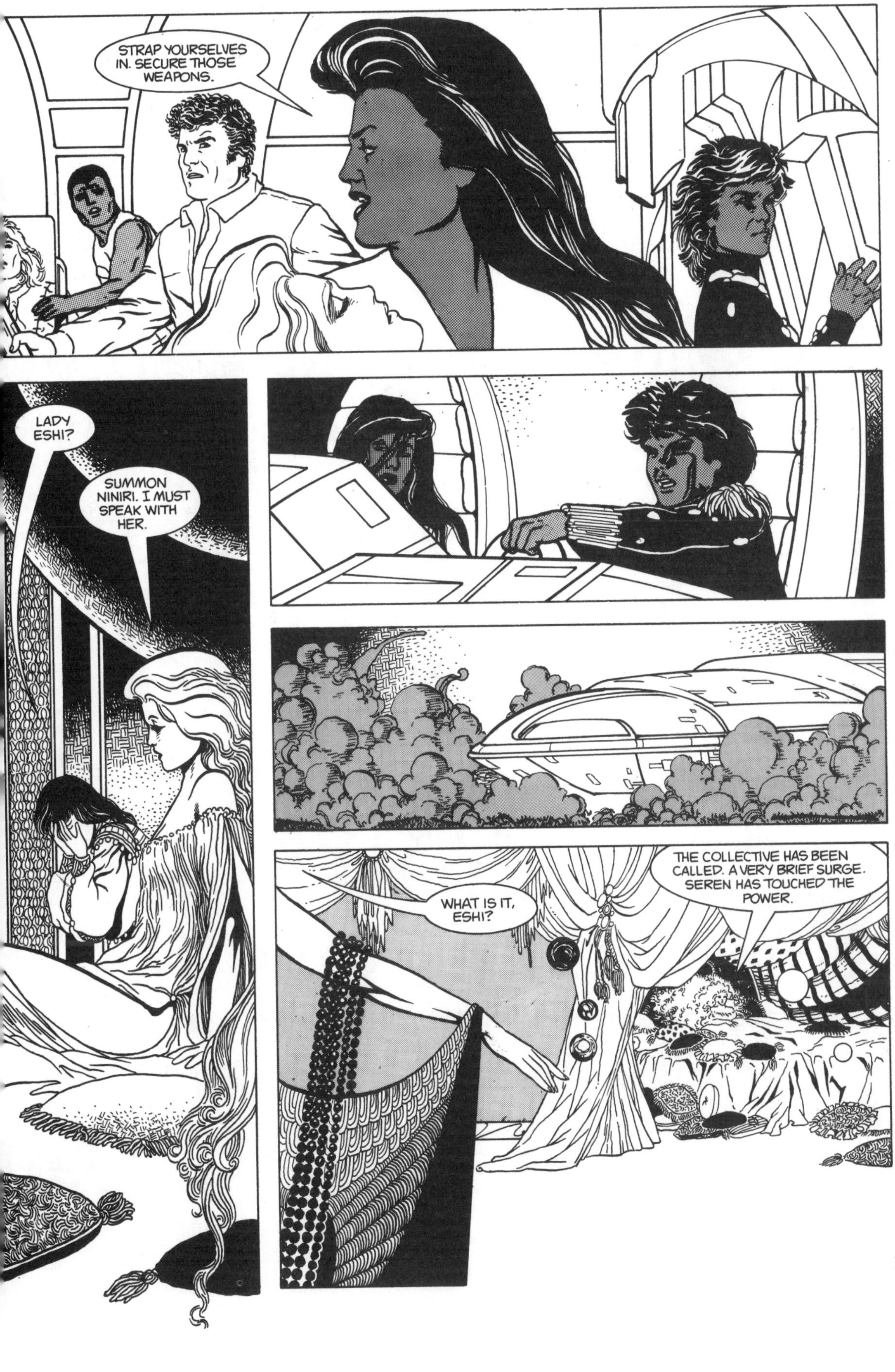
STRAP YOURSELVES IN. SECURE THOSE WEAPONS.
LADY ESHI?
SUMMON NINIRI. I MUST SPEAK WITH HER.
WHAT IS IT, ESHI?
THE COLLECTIVE HAS BEEN CALLED. A VERY BRIEF SURGE. SEREN HAS TOUCHED THE POWER.

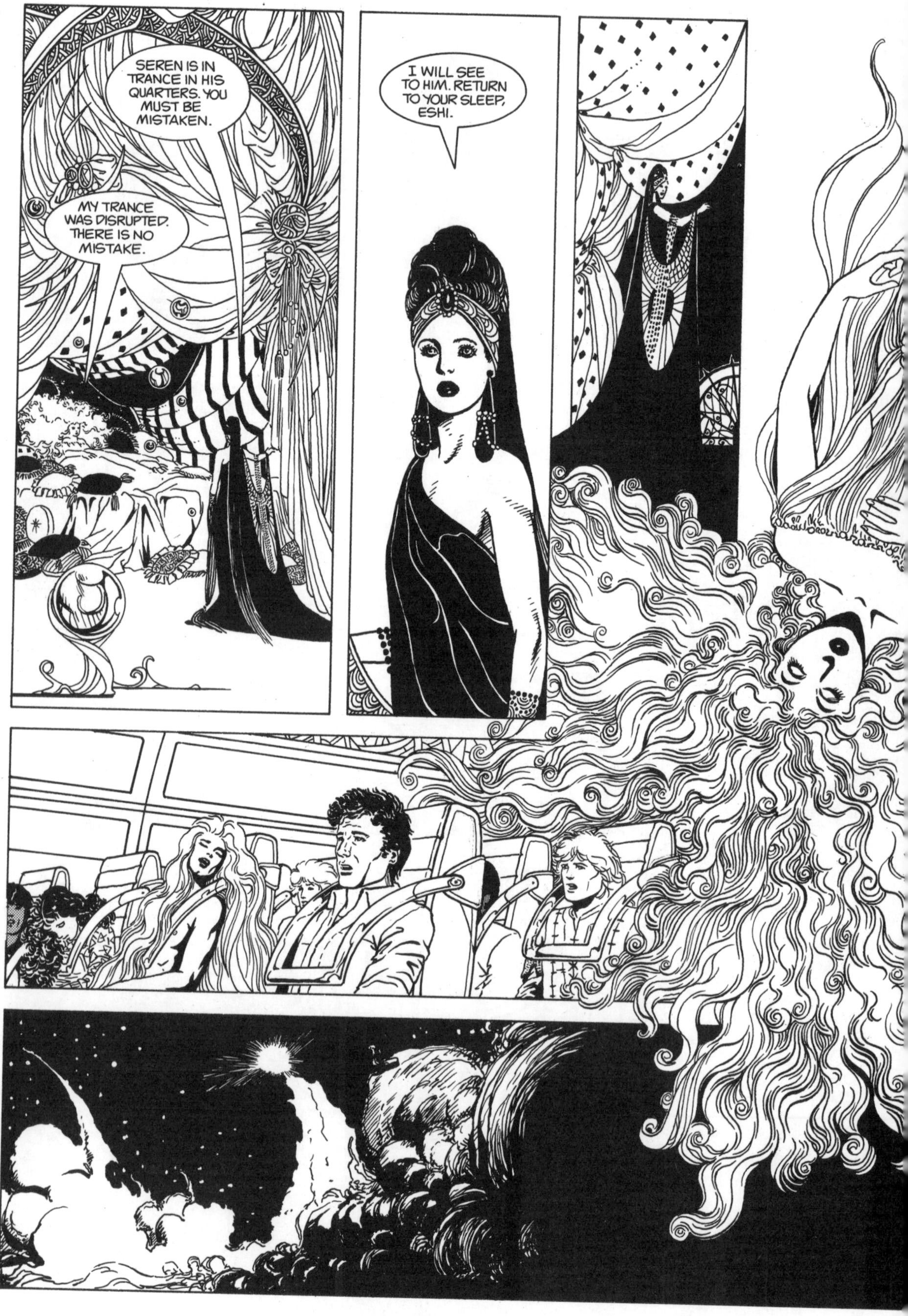
SEREN IS IN TRANCE IN HIS QUARTERS. YOU MUST BE MISTAKEN.
MY TRANCE WAS DISRUPTED. THERE IS NO MISTAKE.
I WILL SEE TO HIM. RETURN TO YOUR SLEEP, ESHI.

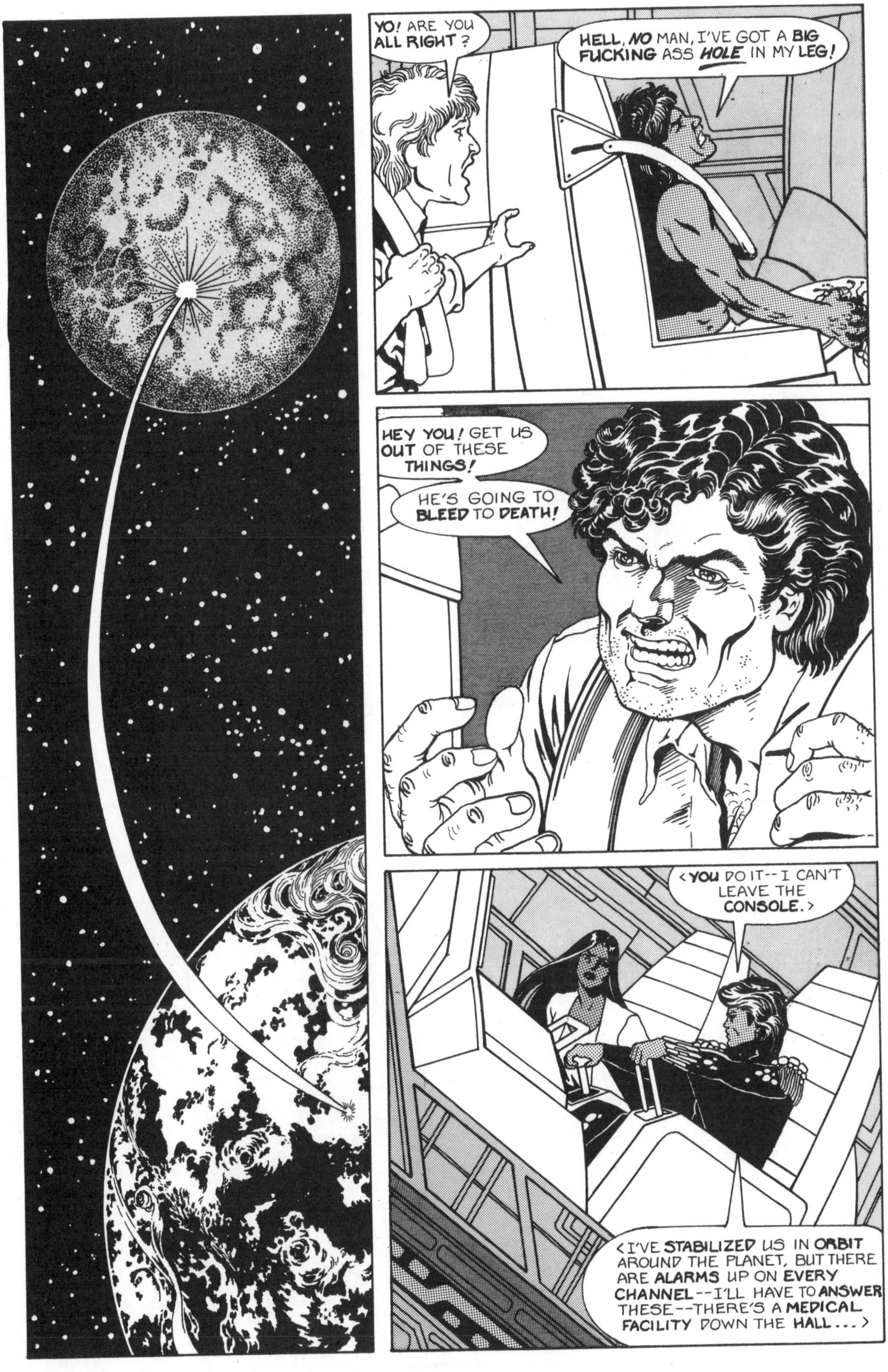
YO! ARE YOU ALL RIGHT?
HELL, NO MAN, I'VE GOT A BIG FUCKING ASS HOLE IN MY LEG!
HEY YOU! GET US OUT OF THESE THINGS!
HE'S GOING TO BLEED TO DEATH!
<YOU DO IT--I CAN'T LEAVE THE CONSOLE.>
<I'VE STABILIZED US IN ORBIT AROUND THE PLANET, BUT THERE ARE ALARMS UP ON EVERY CHANNEL--I'LL HAVE TO ANSWER THESE--THERE'S A MEDICAL FACILITY DOWN THE HALL...>

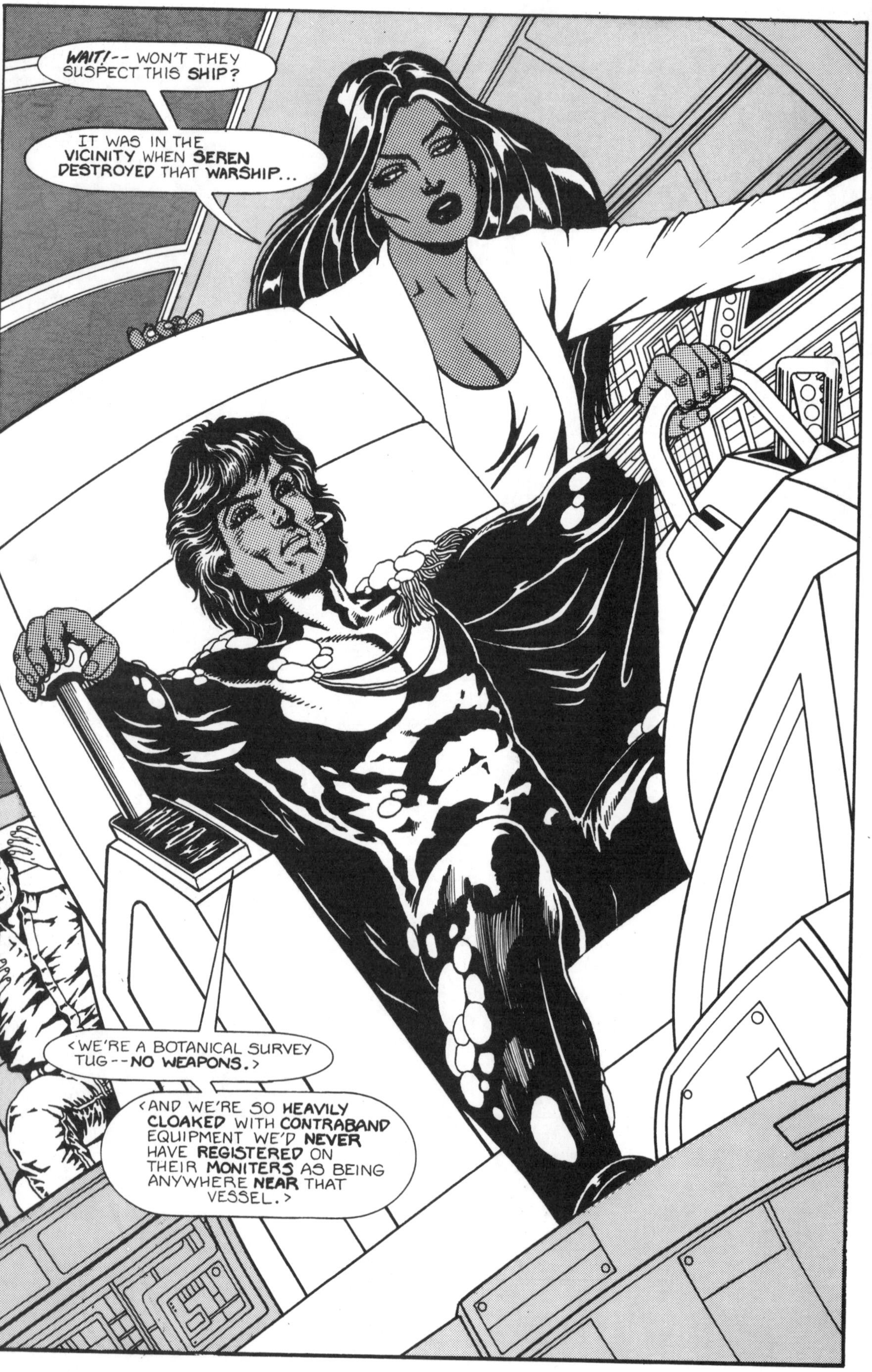
WAIT!-- WON'T THEY SUSPECT THIS SHIP?
IT WAS IN THE VICINITY WHEN SEREN DESTROYED THAT WARSHIP...
<WE'RE A BOTANICAL SURVEY TUG--NO WEAPONS.>
<AND WE'RE SO HEAVILY CLOAKED WITH CONTRABAND EQUIPMENT WE'D NEVER HAVE REGISTERED ON THEIR MONITERS AS BEING ANYWHERE NEAR THAT VESSEL.>

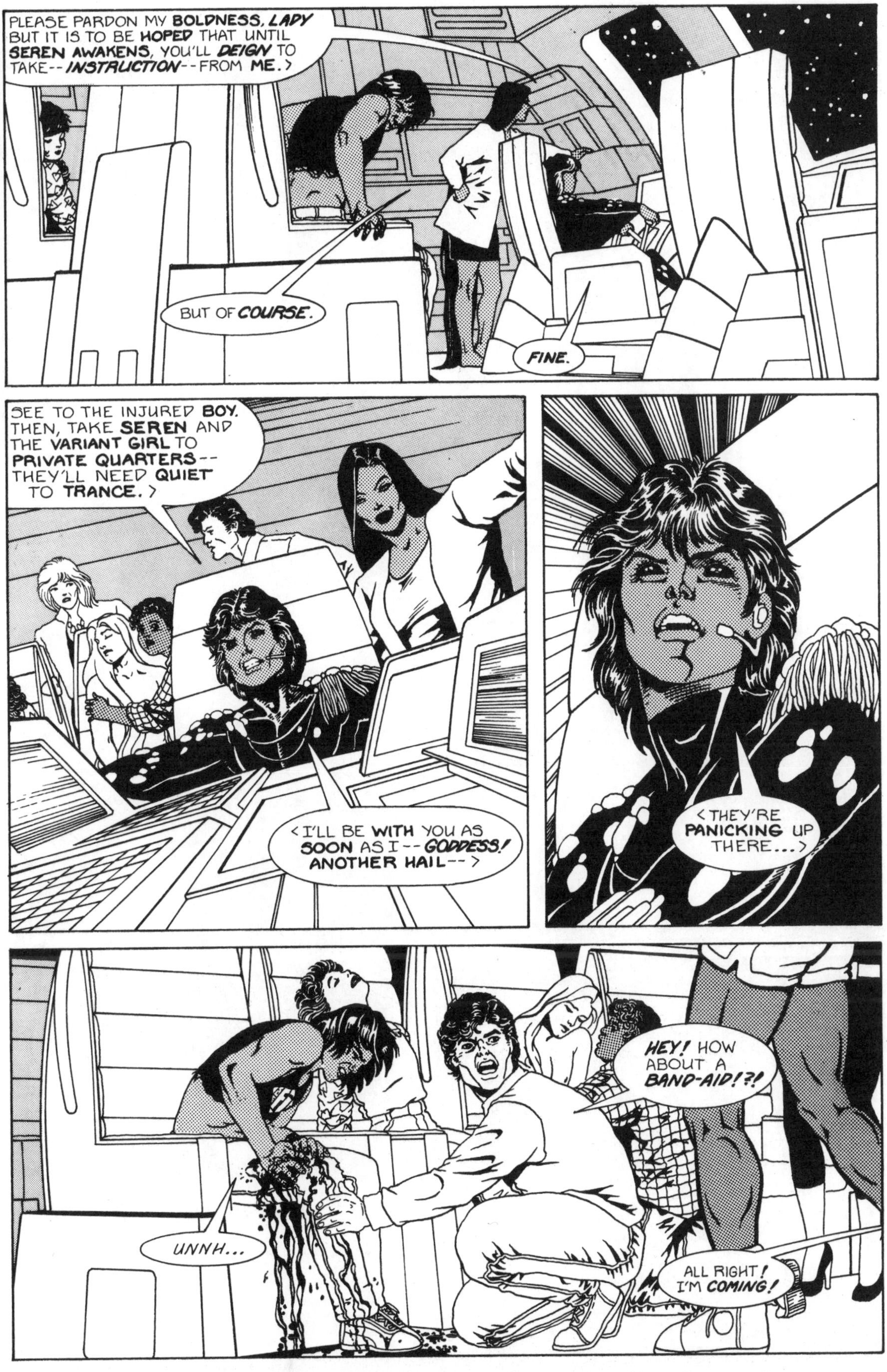
PLEASE PARDON MY BOLDNESS, LADY BUT IT IS TO BE HOPED THAT UNTIL SEREN AWAKENS, YOU'LL DEIGN TO TAKE--INSTRUCTION--FROM ME.>
BUT OF COURSE.
FINE.
SEE TO THE INJURED BOY. THEN, TAKE SEREN AND THE VARIANT GIRL TO PRIVATE QUARTERS--THEY'LL NEED QUIET TO TRANCE.>
<I'LL BE WITH YOU AS SOON AS I--GODDESS! ANOTHER HAIL-->
<THEY'RE PANICKING UP THERE...>
HEY! HOW ABOUT A BAND-AID!?!
UNNH...
ALL RIGHT! I'M COMING!

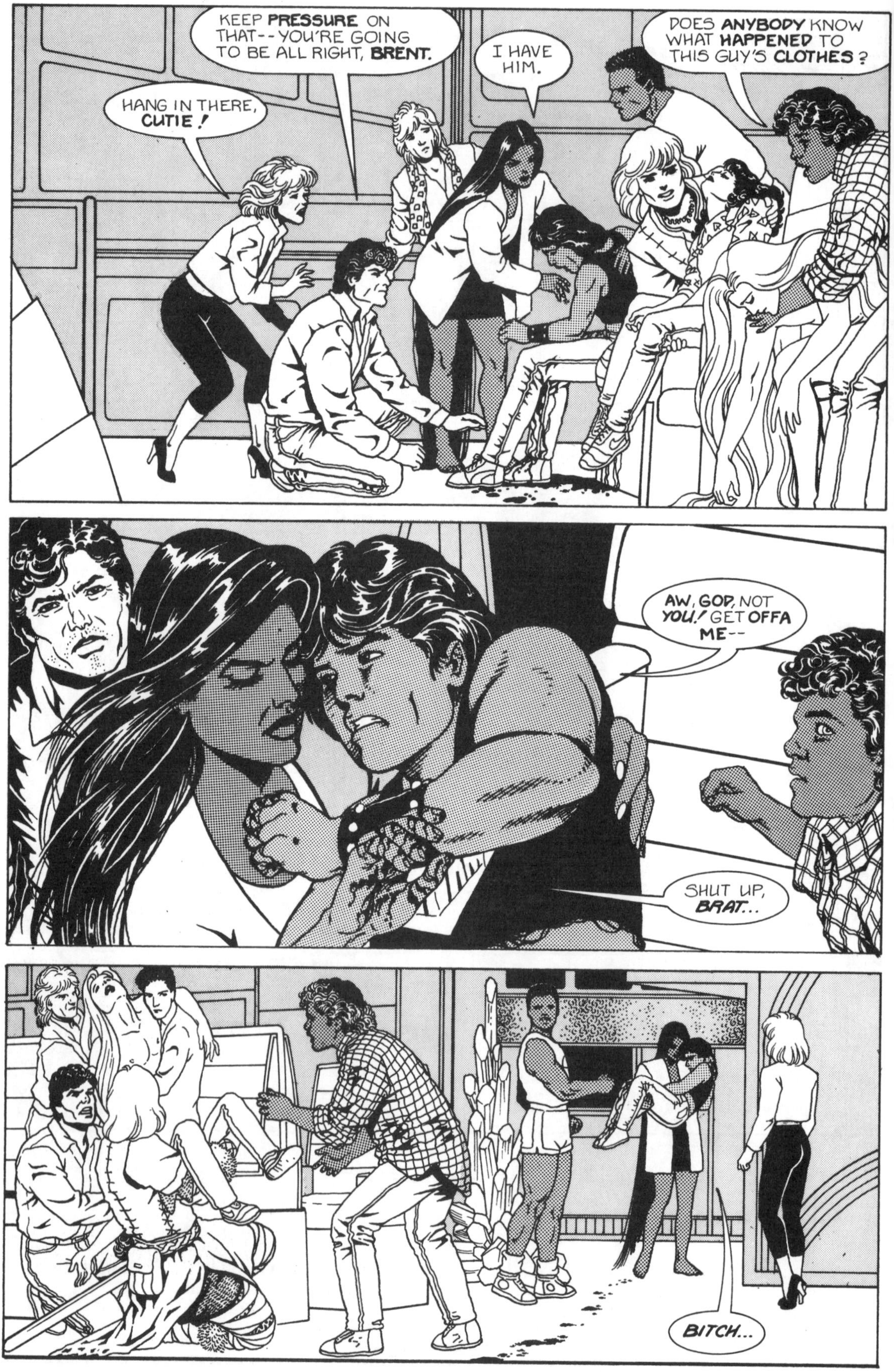
HANG IN THERE, CUTIE!
KEEP PRESSURE ON THAT--YOU'RE GOING TO BE ALL RIGHT, BRENT.
I HAVE HIM.
DOES ANYBODY KNOW WHAT HAPPENED TO THIS GUY'S CLOTHES?
AW, GOD, NOT YOU! GET OFFA ME--
SHUT UP, BRAT...
BITCH...

THE AVATAR'S CHAMBERS ABOARD THE **SIOVANSIN**...

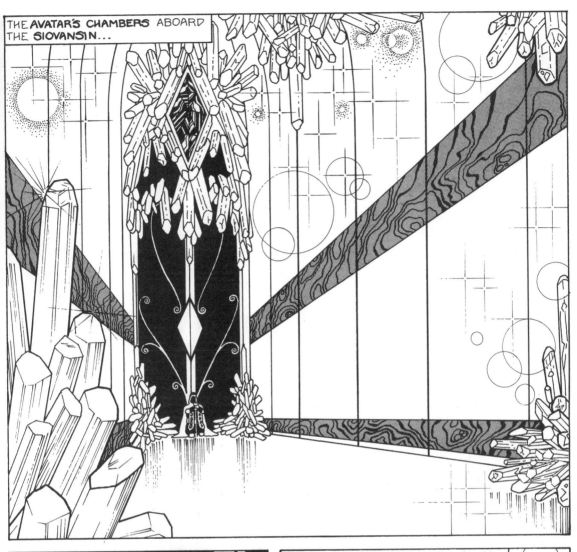

HOW DARE YOU DISTURB THE SANCTITY OF THE ADYTUM!

MAJOR KOVAR, I BEG YOUR INDULGENCE. HIERARCHY TROOPS ARE HERE.

THERE'S A **COURIER** WITH A **HIERARCHY SEAL**, DEMANDING AN **AUDIENCE** WITH **YOU**.

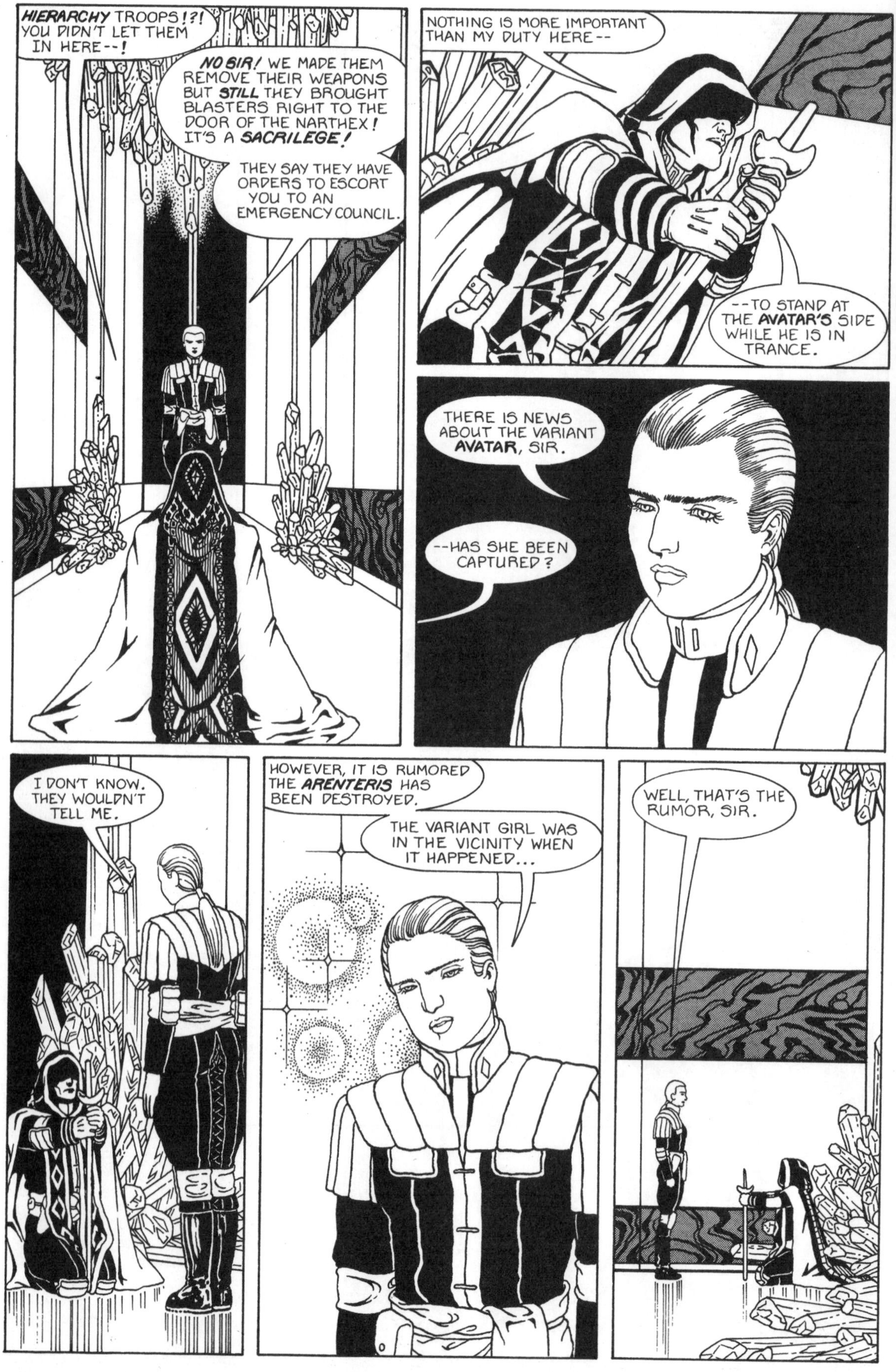
HIERARCHY TROOPS!?! YOU DIDN'T LET THEM IN HERE--!
NO SIR! WE MADE THEM REMOVE THEIR WEAPONS BUT STILL THEY BROUGHT BLASTERS RIGHT TO THE DOOR OF THE NARTHEX! IT'S A SACRILEGE!
THEY SAY THEY HAVE ORDERS TO ESCORT YOU TO AN EMERGENCY COUNCIL.
NOTHING IS MORE IMPORTANT THAN MY DUTY HERE--
--TO STAND AT THE AVATAR'S SIDE WHILE HE IS IN TRANCE.
THERE IS NEWS ABOUT THE VARIANT AVATAR, SIR.
--HAS SHE BEEN CAPTURED?
I DON'T KNOW. THEY WOULDN'T TELL ME.
HOWEVER, IT IS RUMORED THE ARENTERIS HAS BEEN DESTROYED.
THE VARIANT GIRL WAS IN THE VICINITY WHEN IT HAPPENED...
WELL, THAT'S THE RUMOR, SIR.

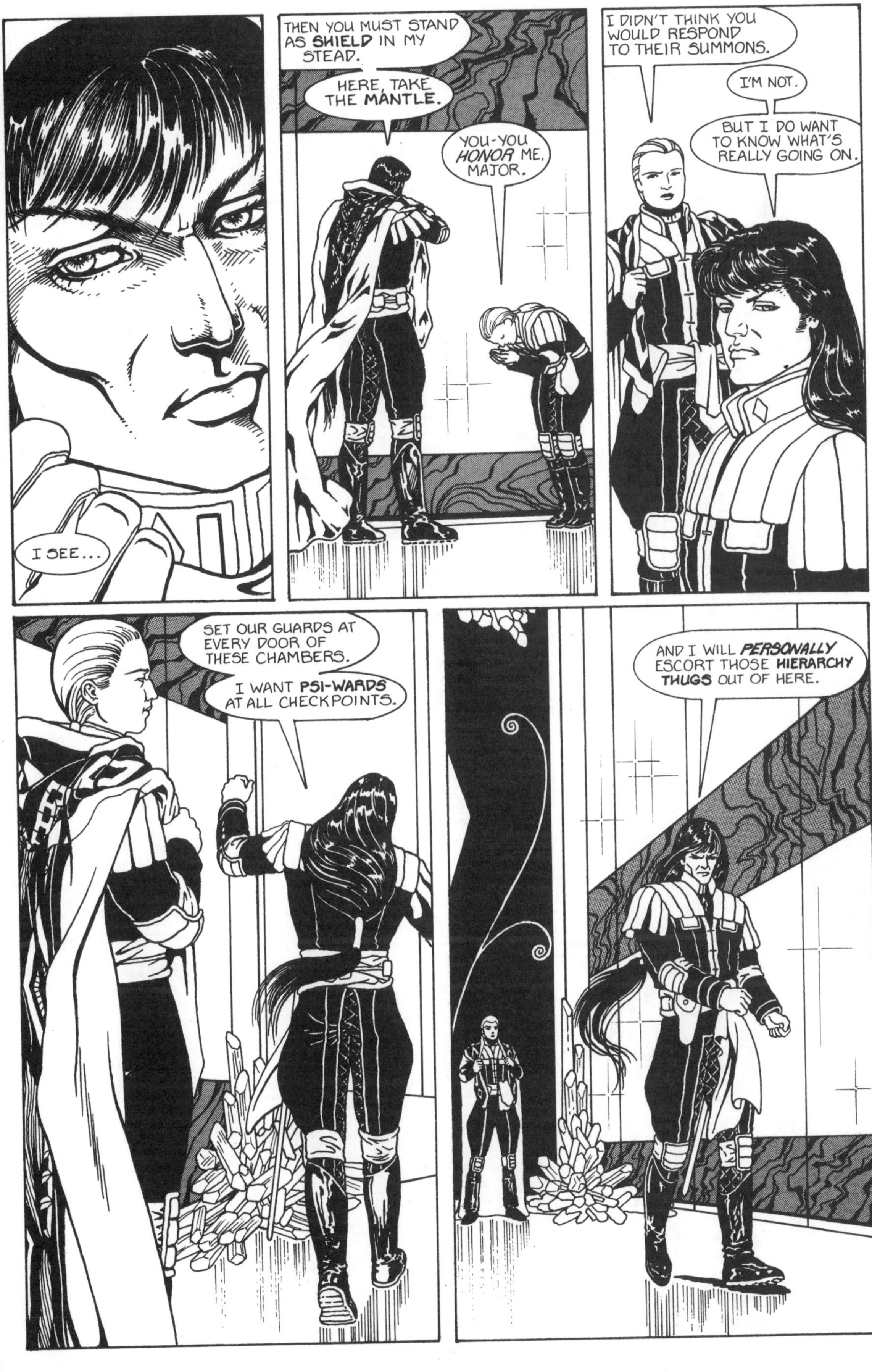
I SEE...
THEN YOU MUST STAND AS **SHIELD** IN MY STEAD.
HERE, TAKE THE **MANTLE.**
YOU-YOU *HONOR* ME, MAJOR.
I DIDN'T THINK YOU WOULD RESPOND TO THEIR SUMMONS.
I'M NOT.
BUT I DO WANT TO KNOW WHAT'S REALLY GOING ON.
SET OUR GUARDS AT EVERY DOOR OF THESE CHAMBERS.
I WANT **PSI-WARDS** AT ALL CHECKPOINTS.
AND I WILL ***PERSONALLY*** ESCORT THOSE **HIERARCHY THUGS** OUT OF HERE.

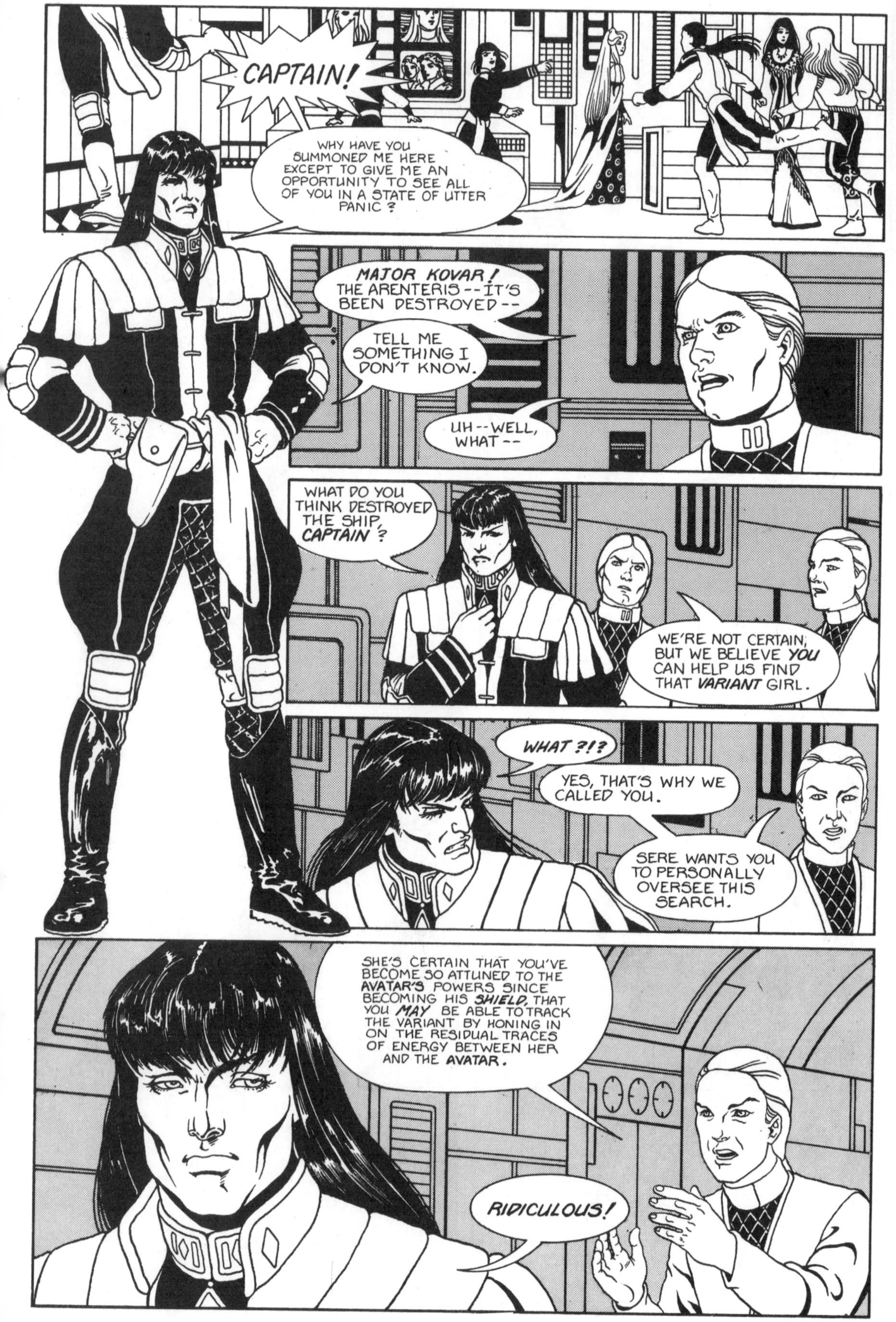
CAPTAIN!
WHY HAVE YOU SUMMONED ME HERE EXCEPT TO GIVE ME AN OPPORTUNITY TO SEE ALL OF YOU IN A STATE OF UTTER PANIC?
MAJOR KOVAR! THE ARENTERIS -- IT'S BEEN DESTROYED --
TELL ME SOMETHING I DON'T KNOW.
UH -- WELL, WHAT --
WHAT DO YOU THINK DESTROYED THE SHIP, CAPTAIN?
WE'RE NOT CERTAIN, BUT WE BELIEVE YOU CAN HELP US FIND THAT VARIANT GIRL.
WHAT?!?
YES, THAT'S WHY WE CALLED YOU.
SERE WANTS YOU TO PERSONALLY OVERSEE THIS SEARCH.
SHE'S CERTAIN THAT YOU'VE BECOME SO ATTUNED TO THE AVATAR'S POWERS SINCE BECOMING HIS SHIELD, THAT YOU MAY BE ABLE TO TRACK THE VARIANT BY HONING IN ON THE RESIDUAL TRACES OF ENERGY BETWEEN HER AND THE AVATAR.
RIDICULOUS!

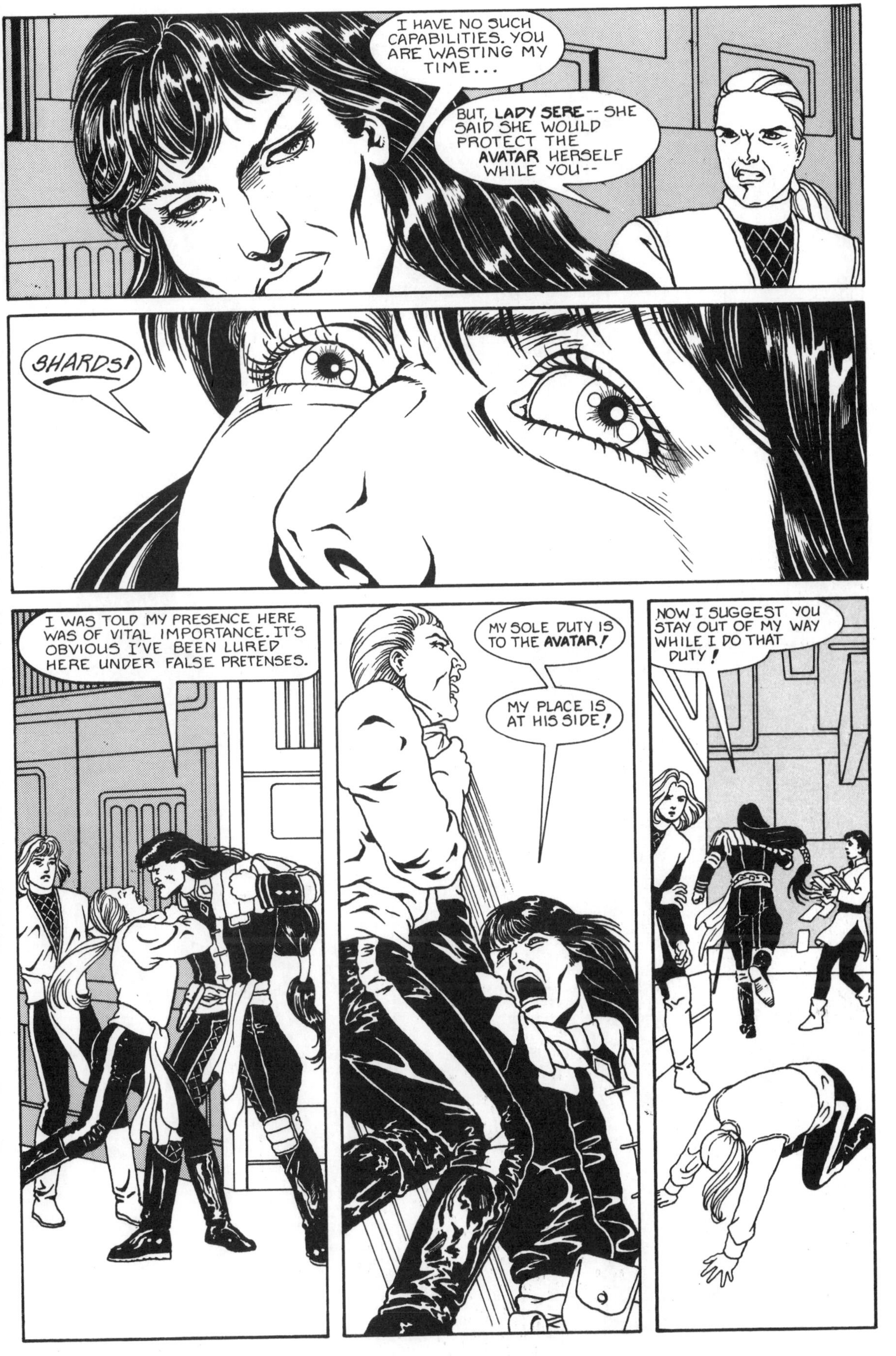
I HAVE NO SUCH CAPABILITIES. YOU ARE WASTING MY TIME...
BUT, **LADY SERE**-- SHE SAID SHE WOULD PROTECT THE **AVATAR** HERSELF WHILE YOU--
SHARDS!
I WAS TOLD MY PRESENCE HERE WAS OF VITAL IMPORTANCE. IT'S OBVIOUS I'VE BEEN LURED HERE UNDER FALSE PRETENSES.
MY SOLE DUTY IS TO THE **AVATAR**!
MY PLACE IS AT HIS SIDE!
NOW I SUGGEST YOU STAY OUT OF MY WAY WHILE I DO THAT DUTY!

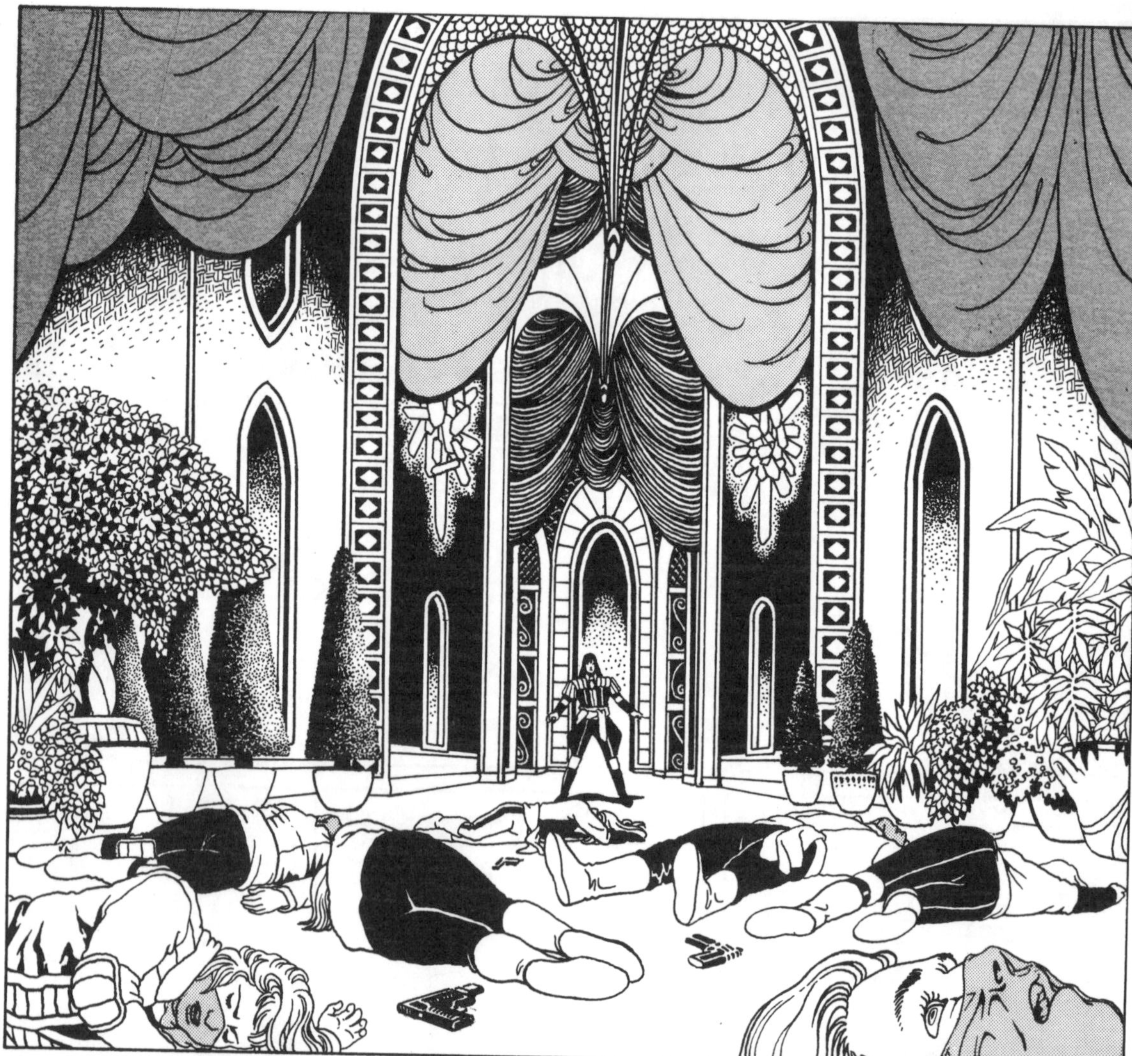

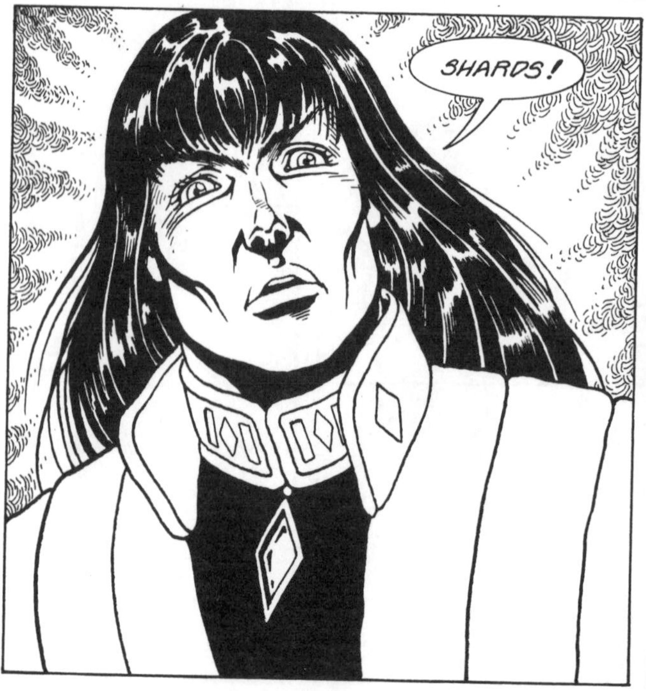
SHARDS!

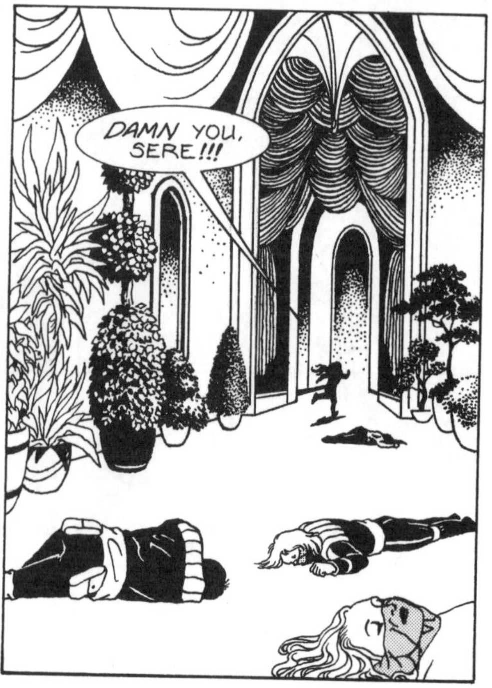
DAMN YOU, SERE!!!

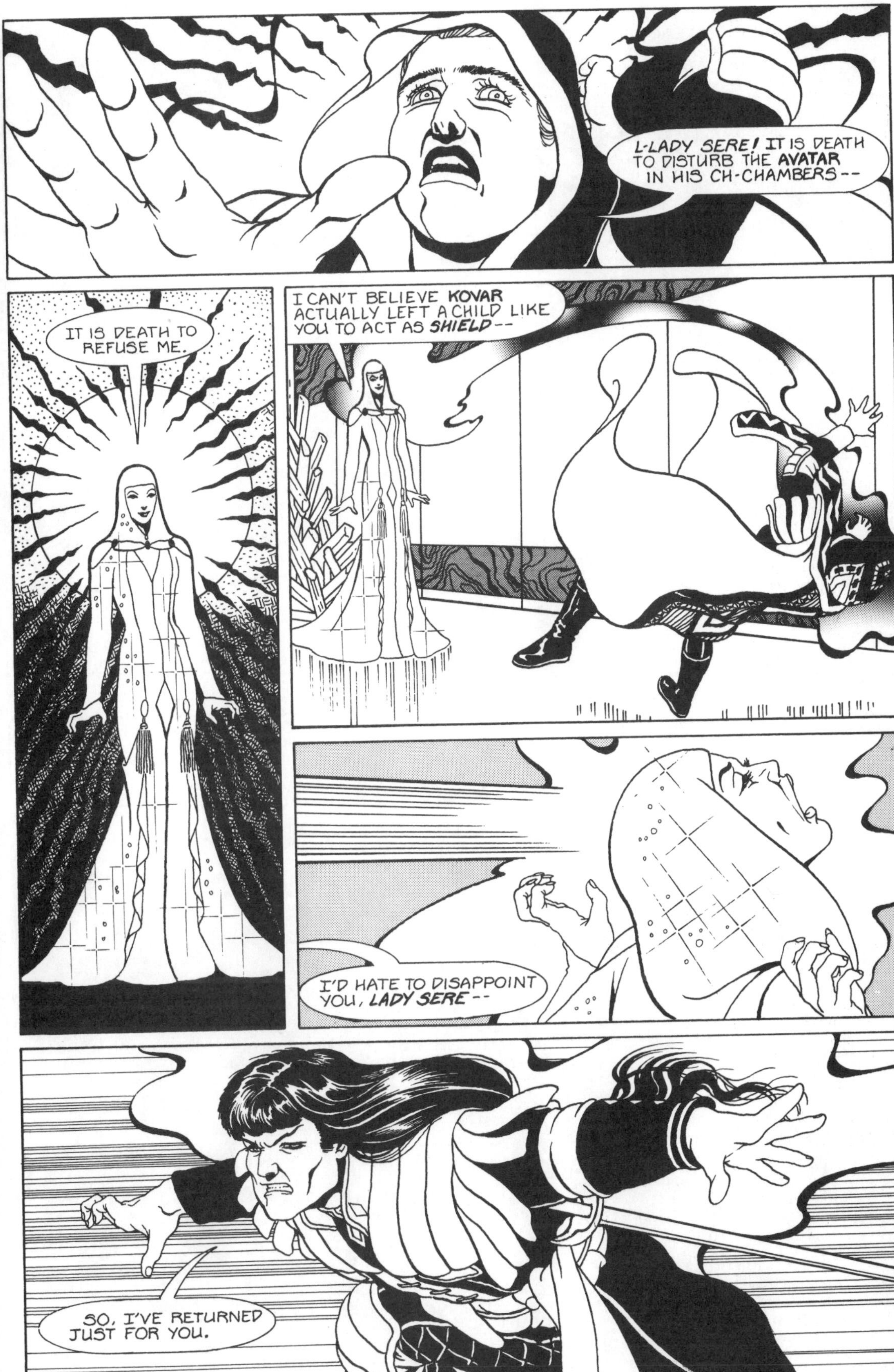
L-LADY SERE! IT IS DEATH TO DISTURB THE AVATAR IN HIS CH-CHAMBERS--
IT IS DEATH TO REFUSE ME.
I CAN'T BELIEVE KOVAR ACTUALLY LEFT A CHILD LIKE YOU TO ACT AS SHIELD--
I'D HATE TO DISAPPOINT YOU, LADY SERE--
SO, I'VE RETURNED JUST FOR YOU.

AH, I'M TRULY DELIGHTED, **MAJOR.** SO MANY OF YOUR COLLEAGUES HAVE **MARTYRED** THEMSELVES IN SERVICE TO THE **AVATAR** THIS DAY.

I'D BE PLEASED TO PERFORM THE SAME SERVICE FOR YOU.

YOU CAN TRY.

NAUGHTY MAN, WHAT ARE YOU **DOING** HERE? I BELIEVE I SPECIFICALLY ORDERED YOU TO--

LADY, MY LOYALTY IS TO THE **AVATAR'S** HOUSEHOLD. YOU HAVE NO POWER OVER ME.

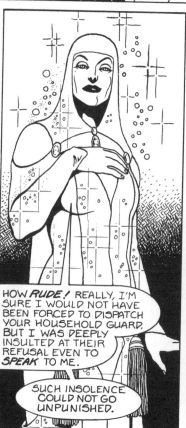

HOW **RUDE!** REALLY, I'M SURE I WOULD NOT HAVE BEEN FORCED TO DISPATCH YOUR HOUSEHOLD GUARD, BUT I WAS DEEPLY INSULTED AT THEIR REFUSAL EVEN TO **SPEAK** TO ME.

SUCH INSOLENCE COULD NOT GO UNPUNISHED.

SURELY, LADY, YOU CAN'T FAIL TO HAVE NOTICED THE **AVATAR'S** GUARD IS **VEILED,** INDICATING THEY'VE TAKEN A VOW OF SILENCE AND ARE **FORBIDDEN** TO SPEAK EXCEPT TO THE **AVATAR** HIMSELF...

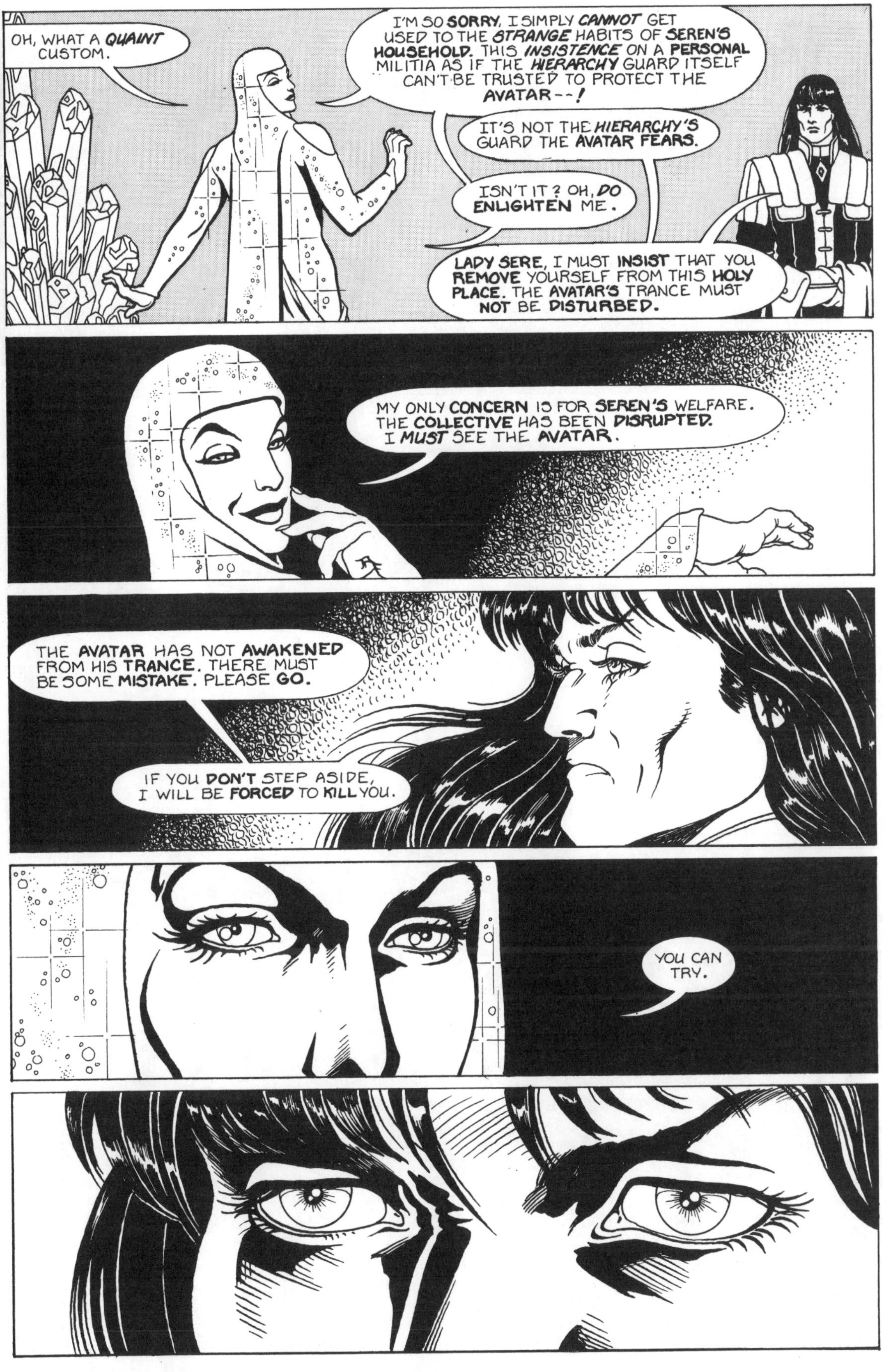
OH, WHAT A QUAINT CUSTOM.
I'M SO SORRY, I SIMPLY CANNOT GET USED TO THE STRANGE HABITS OF SEREN'S HOUSEHOLD. THIS INSISTENCE ON A PERSONAL MILITIA AS IF THE HIERARCHY GUARD ITSELF CAN'T BE TRUSTED TO PROTECT THE AVATAR--!
IT'S NOT THE HIERARCHY'S GUARD THE AVATAR FEARS.
ISN'T IT? OH, DO ENLIGHTEN ME.
LADY SERE, I MUST INSIST THAT YOU REMOVE YOURSELF FROM THIS HOLY PLACE. THE AVATAR'S TRANCE MUST NOT BE DISTURBED.
MY ONLY CONCERN IS FOR SEREN'S WELFARE. THE COLLECTIVE HAS BEEN DISRUPTED. I MUST SEE THE AVATAR.
THE AVATAR HAS NOT AWAKENED FROM HIS TRANCE. THERE MUST BE SOME MISTAKE. PLEASE GO.
IF YOU DON'T STEP ASIDE, I WILL BE FORCED TO KILL YOU.
YOU CAN TRY.

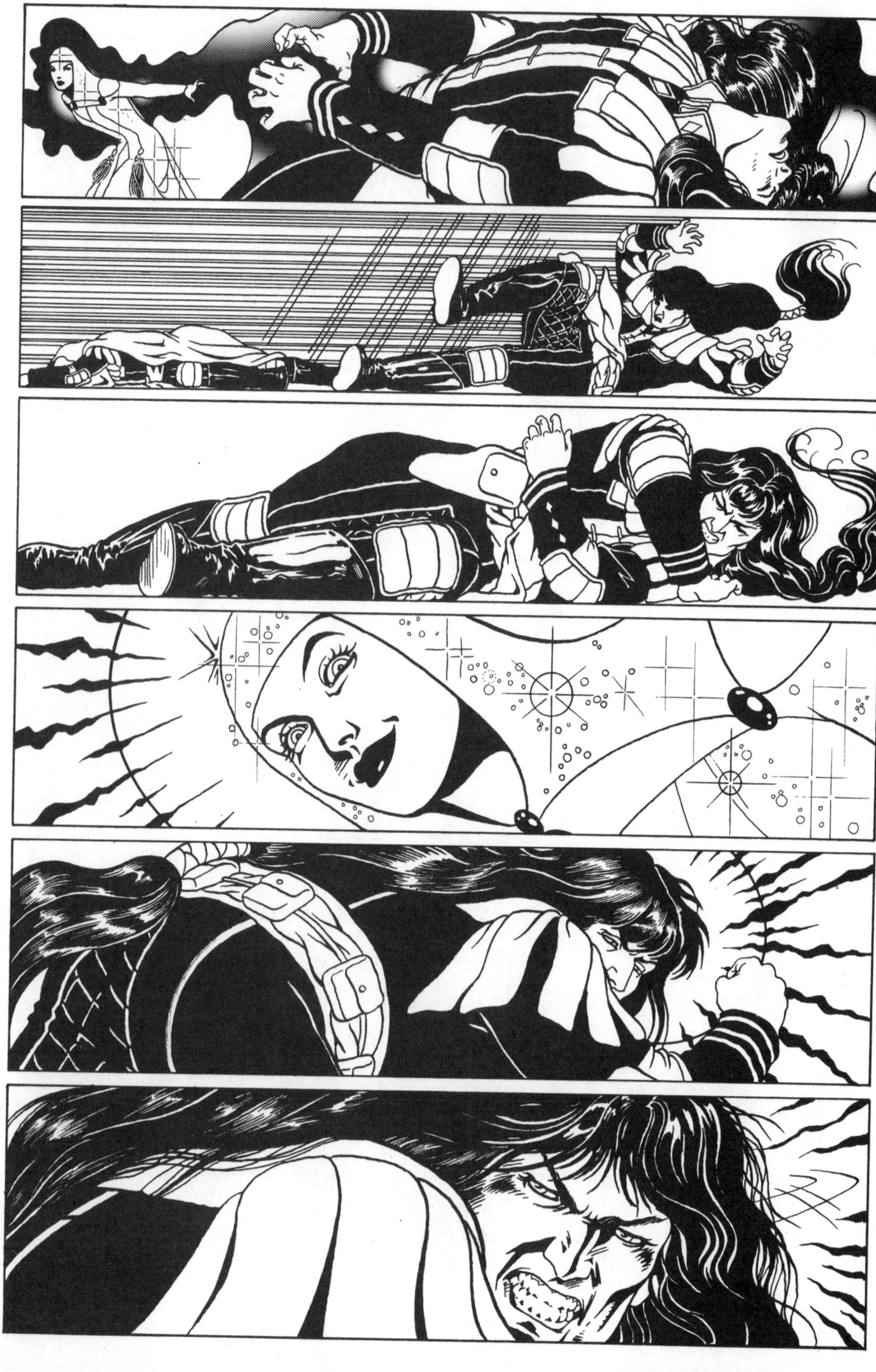

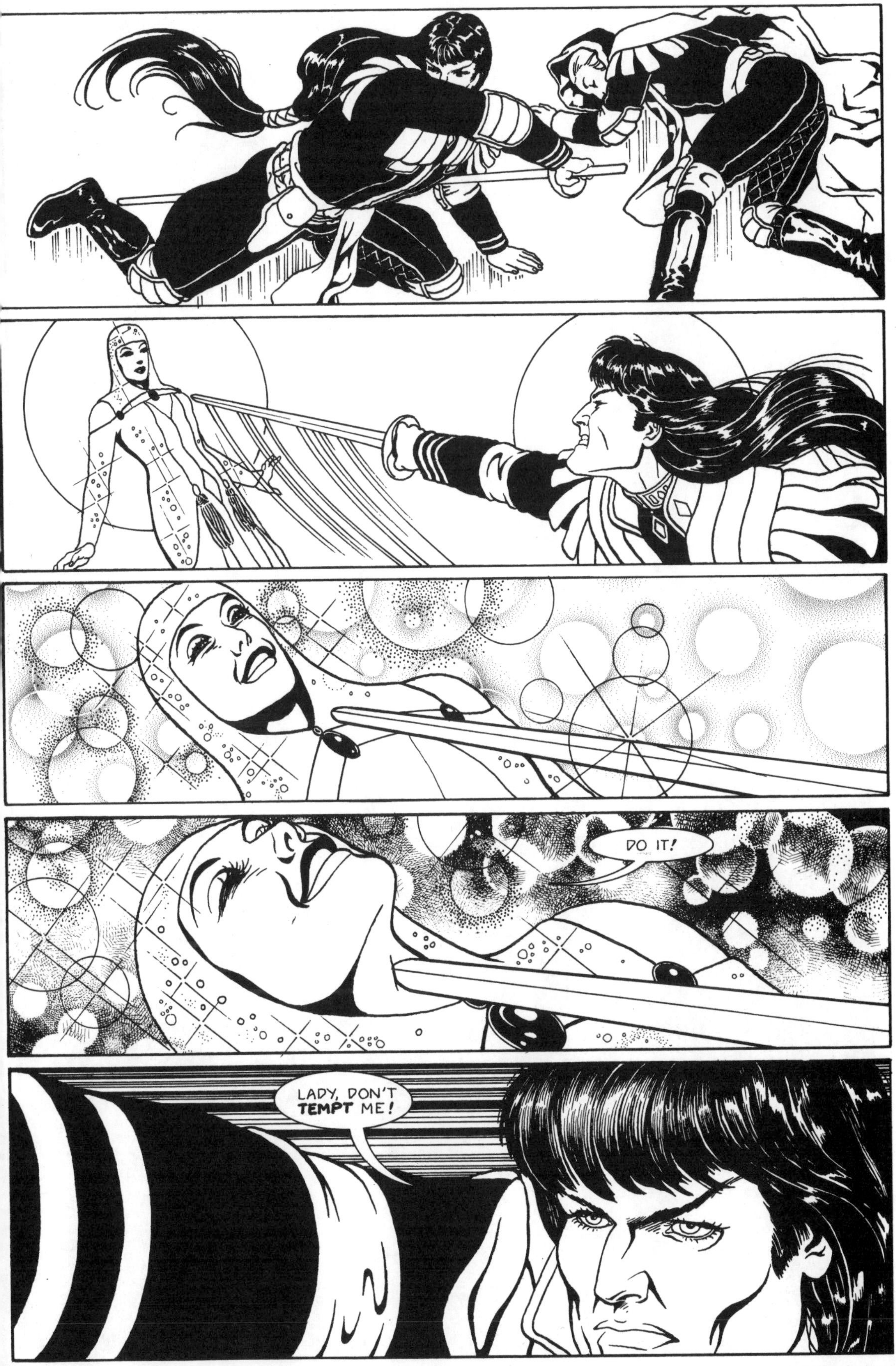
DO IT!
LADY, DON'T TEMPT ME!

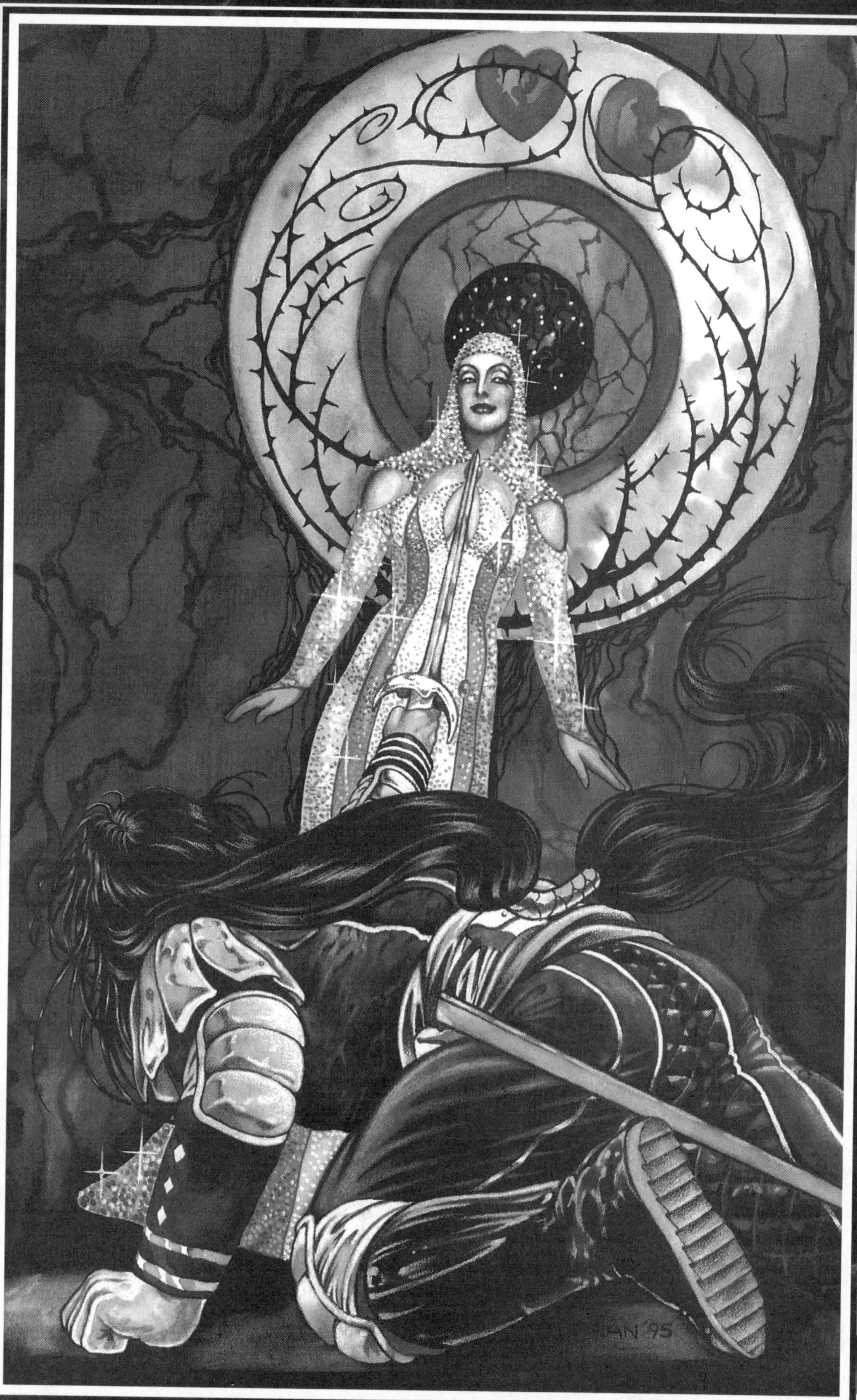

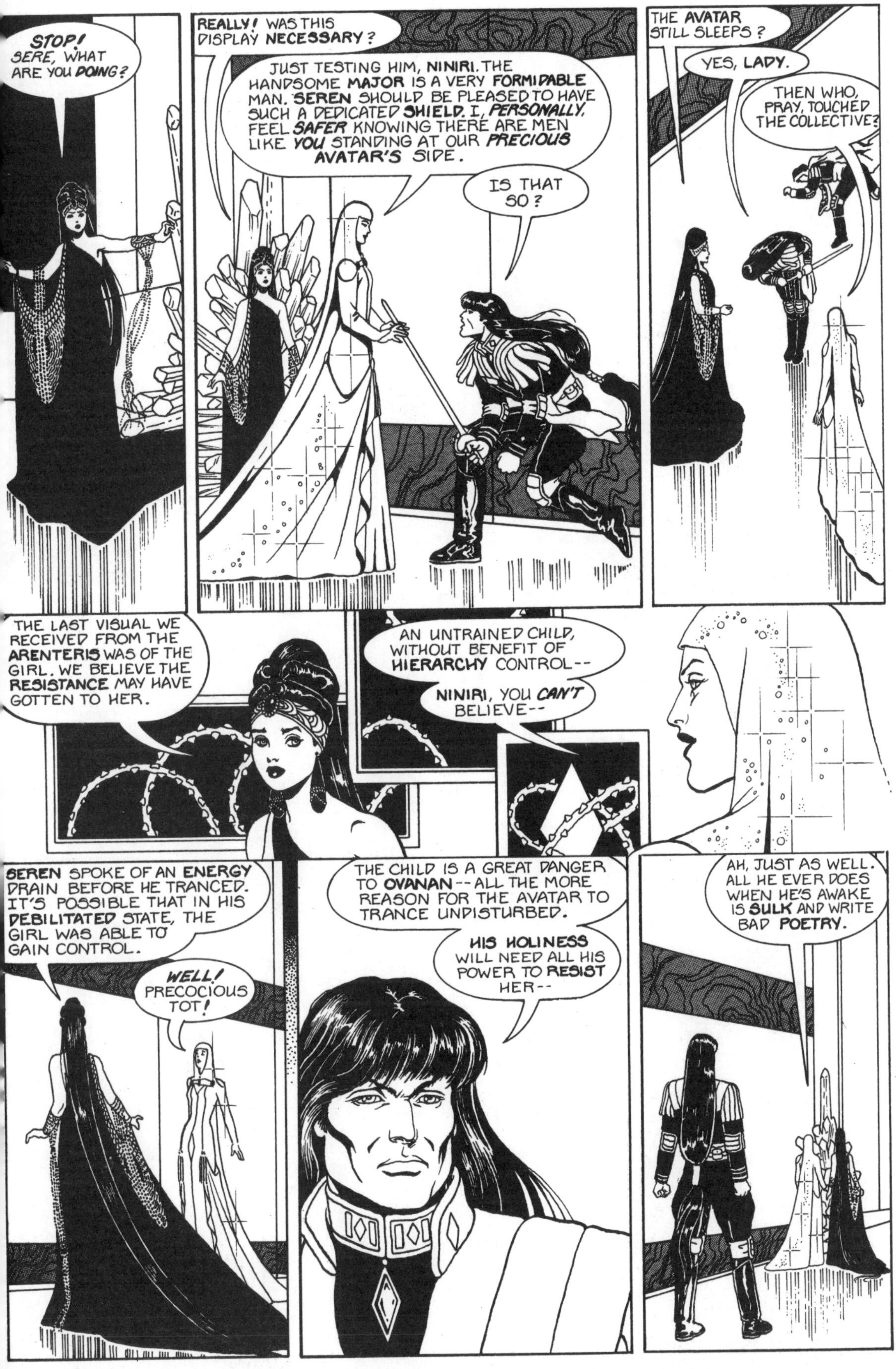
STOP! SERE, WHAT ARE YOU DOING?
REALLY! WAS THIS DISPLAY NECESSARY?
JUST TESTING HIM, NINIRI. THE HANDSOME MAJOR IS A VERY FORMIDABLE MAN. SEREN SHOULD BE PLEASED TO HAVE SUCH A DEDICATED SHIELD. I, PERSONALLY, FEEL SAFER KNOWING THERE ARE MEN LIKE YOU STANDING AT OUR PRECIOUS AVATAR'S SIDE.
IS THAT SO?
THE AVATAR STILL SLEEPS?
YES, LADY.
THEN WHO, PRAY, TOUCHED THE COLLECTIVE?
THE LAST VISUAL WE RECEIVED FROM THE ARENTERIS WAS OF THE GIRL. WE BELIEVE THE RESISTANCE MAY HAVE GOTTEN TO HER.
AN UNTRAINED CHILD, WITHOUT BENEFIT OF HIERARCHY CONTROL--
NINIRI, YOU CAN'T BELIEVE--
SEREN SPOKE OF AN ENERGY DRAIN BEFORE HE TRANCED. IT'S POSSIBLE THAT IN HIS DEBILITATED STATE, THE GIRL WAS ABLE TO GAIN CONTROL.
WELL! PRECOCIOUS TOT!
THE CHILD IS A GREAT DANGER TO OVANAN--ALL THE MORE REASON FOR THE AVATAR TO TRANCE UNDISTURBED.
HIS HOLINESS WILL NEED ALL HIS POWER TO RESIST HER--
AH, JUST AS WELL. ALL HE EVER DOES WHEN HE'S AWAKE IS SULK AND WRITE BAD POETRY.

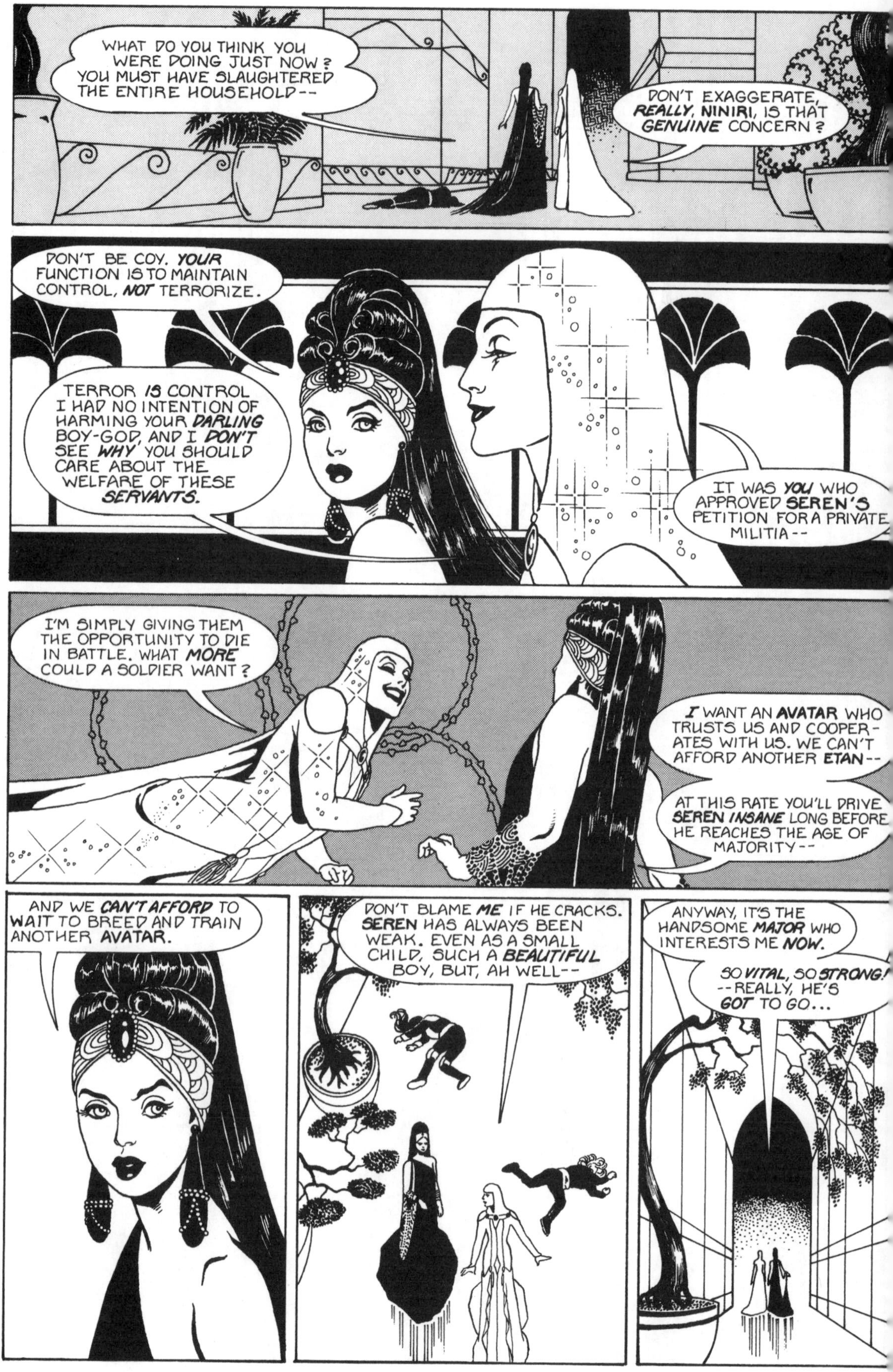
WHAT DO YOU THINK YOU WERE DOING JUST NOW? YOU MUST HAVE SLAUGHTERED THE ENTIRE HOUSEHOLD--
DON'T EXAGGERATE, REALLY, NINIRI, IS THAT GENUINE CONCERN?
DON'T BE COY. YOUR FUNCTION IS TO MAINTAIN CONTROL, NOT TERRORIZE.
TERROR IS CONTROL I HAD NO INTENTION OF HARMING YOUR DARLING BOY-GOD, AND I DON'T SEE WHY YOU SHOULD CARE ABOUT THE WELFARE OF THESE SERVANTS.
IT WAS YOU WHO APPROVED SEREN'S PETITION FOR A PRIVATE MILITIA--
I'M SIMPLY GIVING THEM THE OPPORTUNITY TO DIE IN BATTLE. WHAT MORE COULD A SOLDIER WANT?
I WANT AN AVATAR WHO TRUSTS US AND COOPERATES WITH US. WE CAN'T AFFORD ANOTHER ETAN--
AT THIS RATE YOU'LL DRIVE SEREN INSANE LONG BEFORE HE REACHES THE AGE OF MAJORITY--
AND WE CAN'T AFFORD TO WAIT TO BREED AND TRAIN ANOTHER AVATAR.
DON'T BLAME ME IF HE CRACKS. SEREN HAS ALWAYS BEEN WEAK. EVEN AS A SMALL CHILD, SUCH A BEAUTIFUL BOY, BUT, AH WELL--
ANYWAY, IT'S THE HANDSOME MAJOR WHO INTERESTS ME NOW.
SO VITAL, SO STRONG! --REALLY, HE'S GOT TO GO...

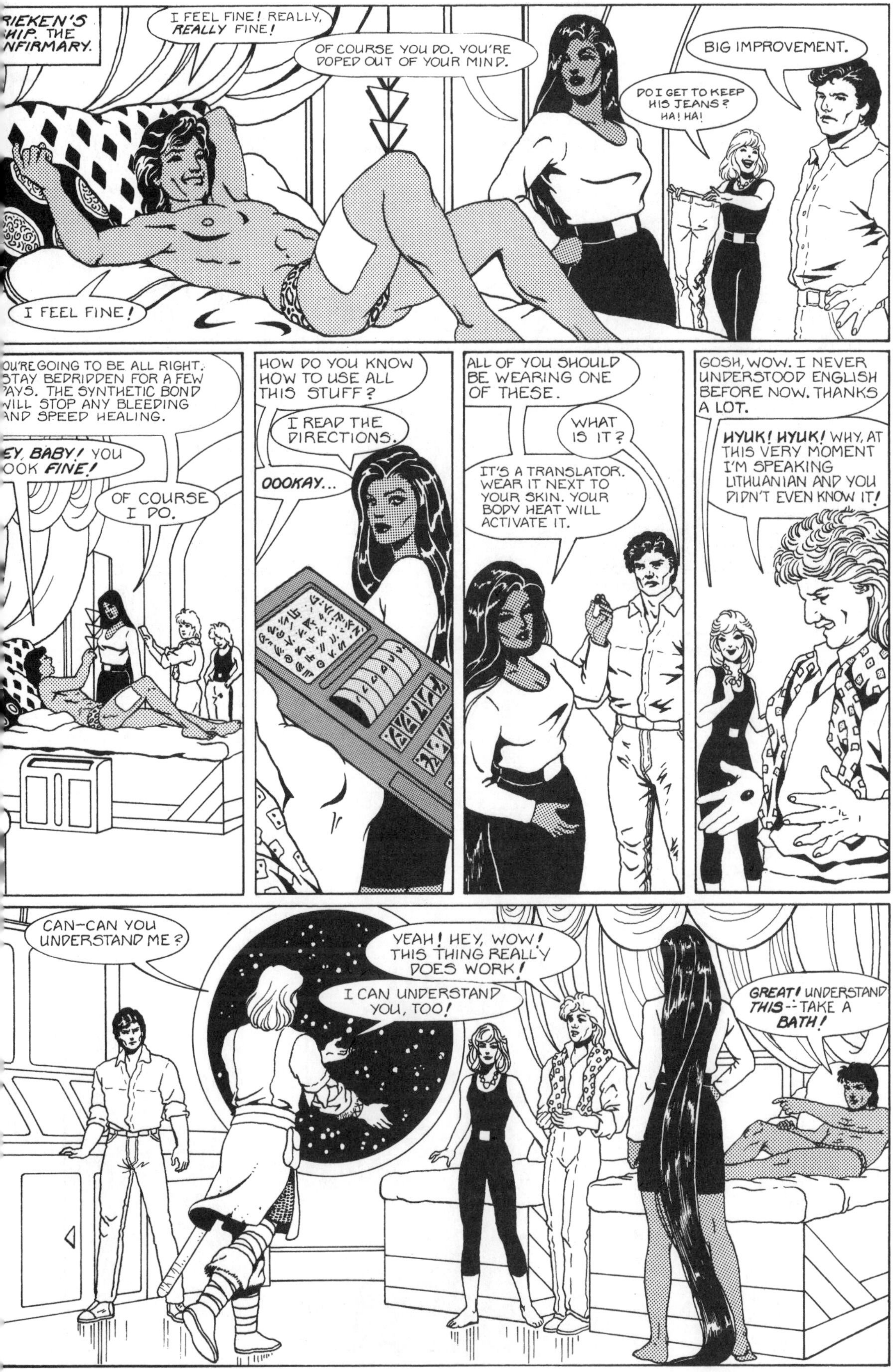
RIEKEN'S SHIP. THE INFIRMARY.
I FEEL FINE! REALLY, REALLY FINE!
OF COURSE YOU DO. YOU'RE DOPED OUT OF YOUR MIND.
I FEEL FINE!
DO I GET TO KEEP HIS JEANS? HA! HA!
BIG IMPROVEMENT.
OU'RE GOING TO BE ALL RIGHT. STAY BEDRIDDEN FOR A FEW DAYS. THE SYNTHETIC BOND WILL STOP ANY BLEEDING AND SPEED HEALING.
EY, BABY! YOU OOK FINE!
OF COURSE I DO.
HOW DO YOU KNOW HOW TO USE ALL THIS STUFF?
I READ THE DIRECTIONS.
OOOKAY...
ALL OF YOU SHOULD BE WEARING ONE OF THESE.
WHAT IS IT?
IT'S A TRANSLATOR. WEAR IT NEXT TO YOUR SKIN. YOUR BODY HEAT WILL ACTIVATE IT.
GOSH, WOW. I NEVER UNDERSTOOD ENGLISH BEFORE NOW. THANKS A LOT.
HYUK! HYUK! WHY, AT THIS VERY MOMENT I'M SPEAKING LITHUANIAN AND YOU DIDN'T EVEN KNOW IT!
CAN-CAN YOU UNDERSTAND ME?
YEAH! HEY, WOW! THIS THING REALLY DOES WORK!
I CAN UNDERSTAND YOU, TOO!
GREAT! UNDERSTAND THIS--TAKE A BATH!

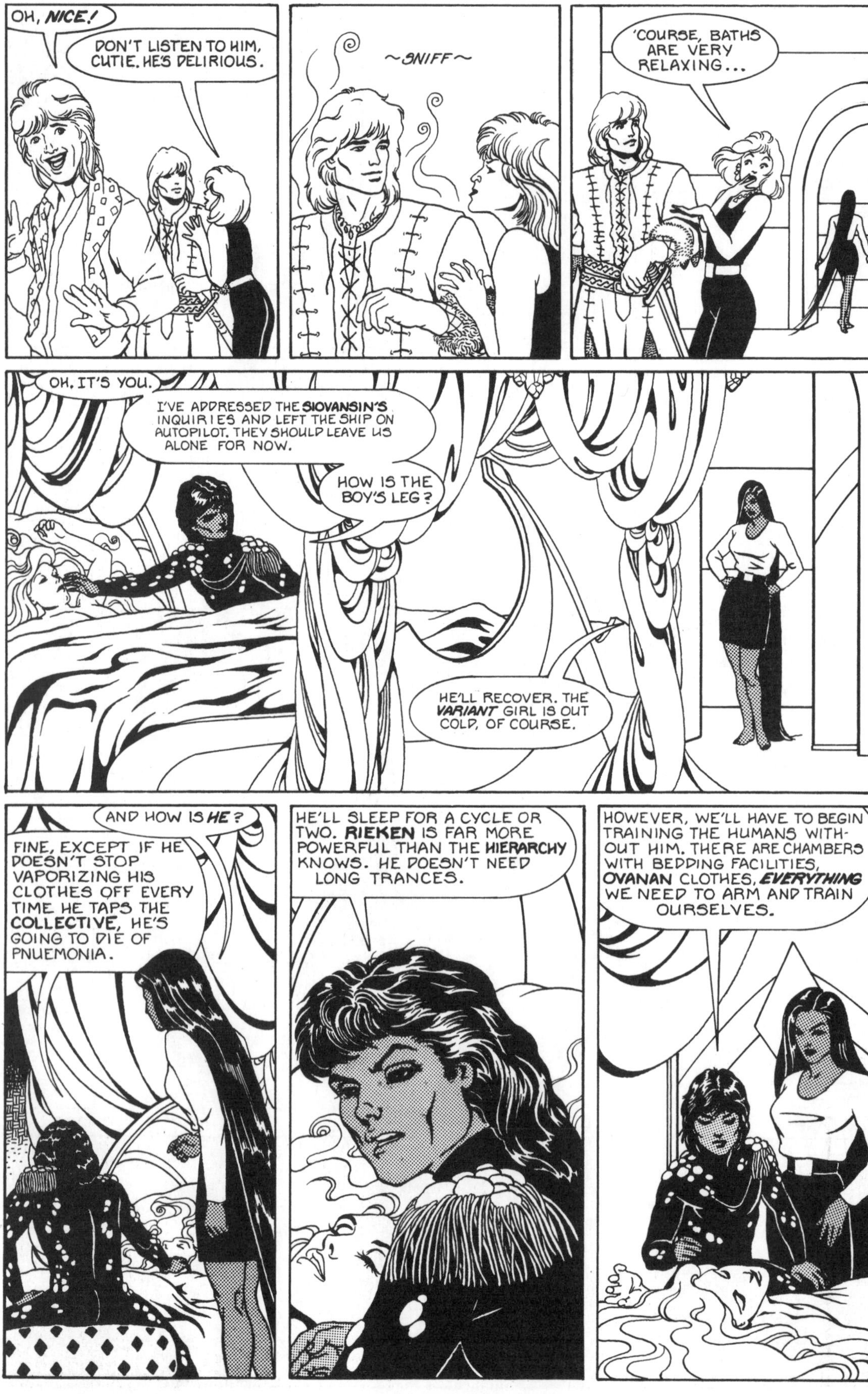
OH, NICE!
DON'T LISTEN TO HIM, CUTIE. HE'S DELIRIOUS.
~SNIFF~
'COURSE, BATHS ARE VERY RELAXING...
OH, IT'S YOU.
I'VE ADDRESSED THE SIOVANSIN'S INQUIRIES AND LEFT THE SHIP ON AUTOPILOT. THEY SHOULD LEAVE US ALONE FOR NOW.
HOW IS THE BOY'S LEG?
HE'LL RECOVER. THE VARIANT GIRL IS OUT COLD, OF COURSE.
AND HOW IS HE?
FINE, EXCEPT IF HE DOESN'T STOP VAPORIZING HIS CLOTHES OFF EVERY TIME HE TAPS THE COLLECTIVE, HE'S GOING TO DIE OF PNUEMONIA.
HE'LL SLEEP FOR A CYCLE OR TWO. RIEKEN IS FAR MORE POWERFUL THAN THE HIERARCHY KNOWS. HE DOESN'T NEED LONG TRANCES.
HOWEVER, WE'LL HAVE TO BEGIN TRAINING THE HUMANS WITHOUT HIM. THERE ARE CHAMBERS WITH BEDDING FACILITIES, OVANAN CLOTHES, EVERYTHING WE NEED TO ARM AND TRAIN OURSELVES.

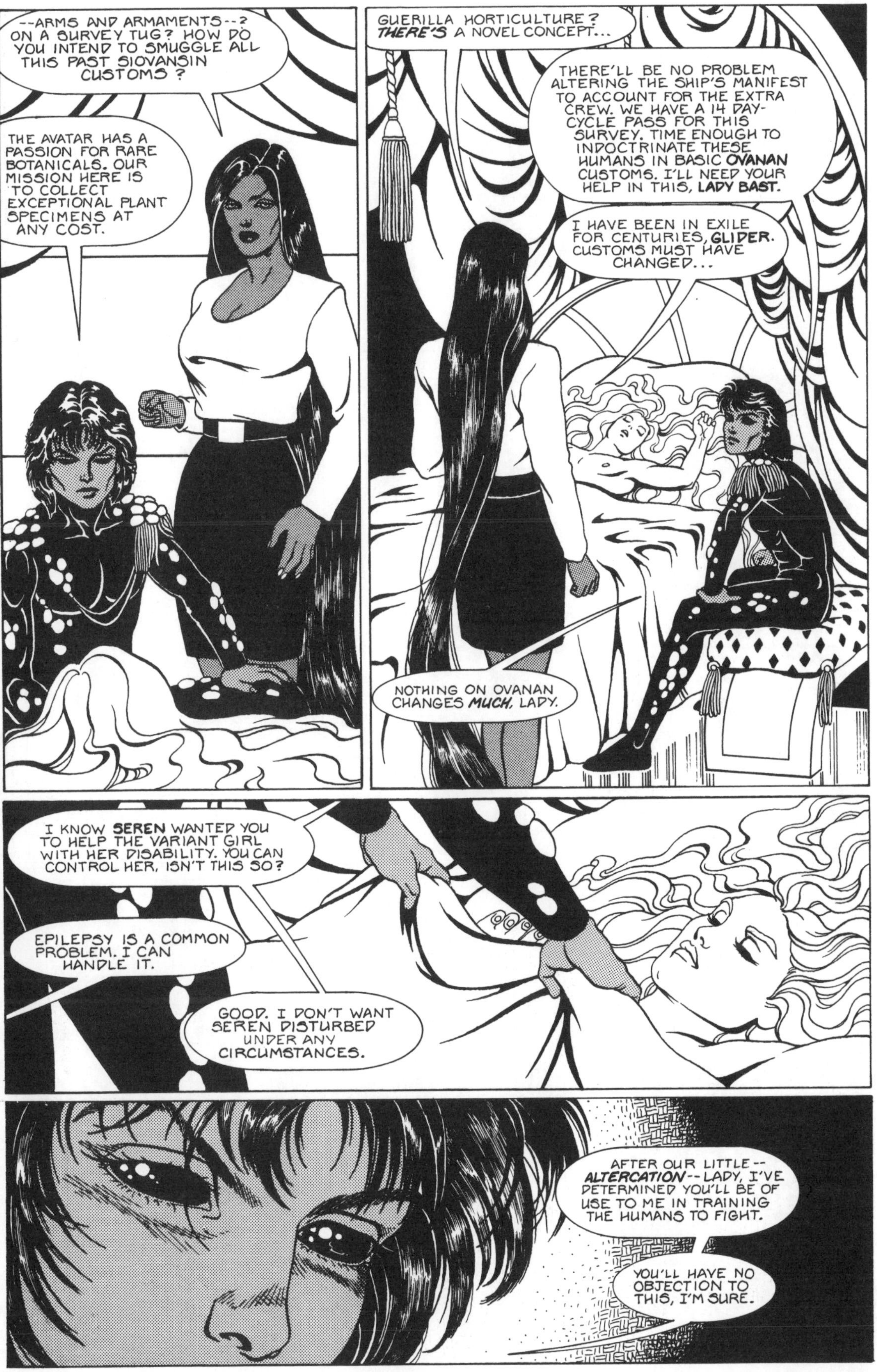
--ARMS AND ARMAMENTS--? ON A SURVEY TUG? HOW DO YOU INTEND TO SMUGGLE ALL THIS PAST SIOVANSIN CUSTOMS?
THE AVATAR HAS A PASSION FOR RARE BOTANICALS. OUR MISSION HERE IS TO COLLECT EXCEPTIONAL PLANT SPECIMENS AT ANY COST.
GUERILLA HORTICULTURE? THERE'S A NOVEL CONCEPT...
THERE'LL BE NO PROBLEM ALTERING THE SHIP'S MANIFEST TO ACCOUNT FOR THE EXTRA CREW. WE HAVE A 14 DAY-CYCLE PASS FOR THIS SURVEY. TIME ENOUGH TO INDOCTRINATE THESE HUMANS IN BASIC OVANAN CUSTOMS. I'LL NEED YOUR HELP IN THIS, LADY BAST.
I HAVE BEEN IN EXILE FOR CENTURIES, GLIDER. CUSTOMS MUST HAVE CHANGED...
NOTHING ON OVANAN CHANGES MUCH, LADY.
I KNOW SEREN WANTED YOU TO HELP THE VARIANT GIRL WITH HER DISABILITY. YOU CAN CONTROL HER, ISN'T THIS SO?
EPILEPSY IS A COMMON PROBLEM. I CAN HANDLE IT.
GOOD. I DON'T WANT SEREN DISTURBED UNDER ANY CIRCUMSTANCES.
AFTER OUR LITTLE--ALTERCATION--LADY, I'VE DETERMINED YOU'LL BE OF USE TO ME IN TRAINING THE HUMANS TO FIGHT.
YOU'LL HAVE NO OBJECTION TO THIS, I'M SURE.

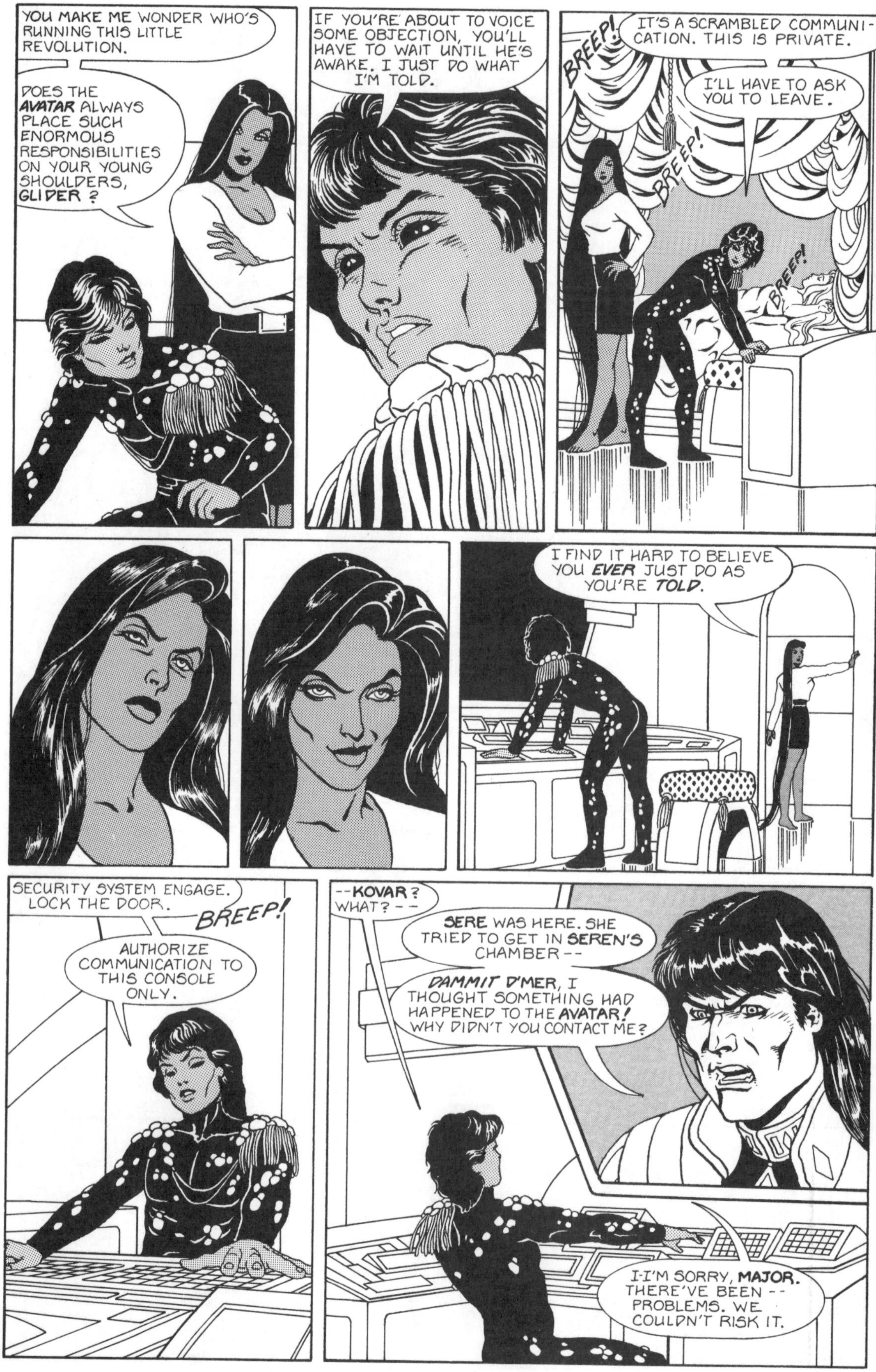
YOU MAKE ME WONDER WHO'S RUNNING THIS LITTLE REVOLUTION.
DOES THE AVATAR ALWAYS PLACE SUCH ENORMOUS RESPONSIBILITIES ON YOUR YOUNG SHOULDERS, GLIDER ?
IF YOU'RE ABOUT TO VOICE SOME OBJECTION, YOU'LL HAVE TO WAIT UNTIL HE'S AWAKE. I JUST DO WHAT I'M TOLD.
BREEP!
IT'S A SCRAMBLED COMMUNICATION. THIS IS PRIVATE.
BREEP!
I'LL HAVE TO ASK YOU TO LEAVE.
BREEP!
I FIND IT HARD TO BELIEVE YOU EVER JUST DO AS YOU'RE TOLD.
SECURITY SYSTEM ENGAGE. LOCK THE DOOR.
BREEP!
AUTHORIZE COMMUNICATION TO THIS CONSOLE ONLY.
--KOVAR? WHAT?--
SERE WAS HERE. SHE TRIED TO GET IN SEREN'S CHAMBER--
DAMMIT D'MER, I THOUGHT SOMETHING HAD HAPPENED TO THE AVATAR! WHY DIDN'T YOU CONTACT ME?
I-I'M SORRY, MAJOR. THERE'VE BEEN -- PROBLEMS. WE COULDN'T RISK IT.

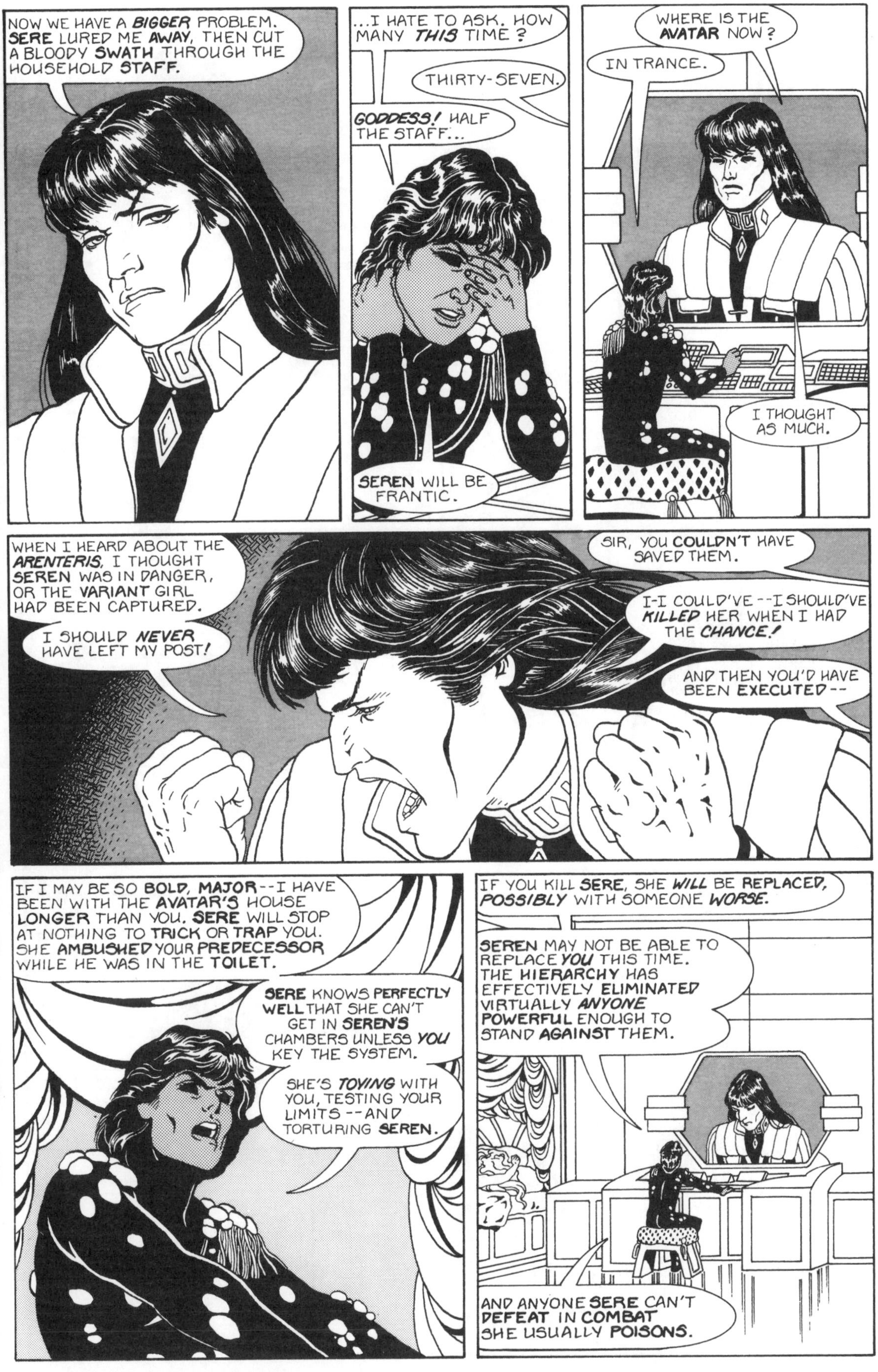
NOW WE HAVE A BIGGER PROBLEM. SERE LURED ME AWAY, THEN CUT A BLOODY SWATH THROUGH THE HOUSEHOLD STAFF.
...I HATE TO ASK. HOW MANY THIS TIME?
THIRTY-SEVEN.
GODDESS! HALF THE STAFF...
SEREN WILL BE FRANTIC.
WHERE IS THE AVATAR NOW?
IN TRANCE.
I THOUGHT AS MUCH.
WHEN I HEARD ABOUT THE ARENTERIS, I THOUGHT SEREN WAS IN DANGER, OR THE VARIANT GIRL HAD BEEN CAPTURED.
I SHOULD NEVER HAVE LEFT MY POST!
SIR, YOU COULDN'T HAVE SAVED THEM.
I-I COULD'VE--I SHOULD'VE KILLED HER WHEN I HAD THE CHANCE!
AND THEN YOU'D HAVE BEEN EXECUTED--
IF I MAY BE SO BOLD, MAJOR--I HAVE BEEN WITH THE AVATAR'S HOUSE LONGER THAN YOU. SERE WILL STOP AT NOTHING TO TRICK OR TRAP YOU. SHE AMBUSHED YOUR PREDECESSOR WHILE HE WAS IN THE TOILET.
SERE KNOWS PERFECTLY WELL THAT SHE CAN'T GET IN SEREN'S CHAMBERS UNLESS YOU KEY THE SYSTEM.
SHE'S TOYING WITH YOU, TESTING YOUR LIMITS--AND TORTURING SEREN.
IF YOU KILL SERE, SHE WILL BE REPLACED, POSSIBLY WITH SOMEONE WORSE.
SEREN MAY NOT BE ABLE TO REPLACE YOU THIS TIME. THE HIERARCHY HAS EFFECTIVELY ELIMINATED VIRTUALLY ANYONE POWERFUL ENOUGH TO STAND AGAINST THEM.
AND ANYONE SERE CAN'T DEFEAT IN COMBAT SHE USUALLY POISONS.

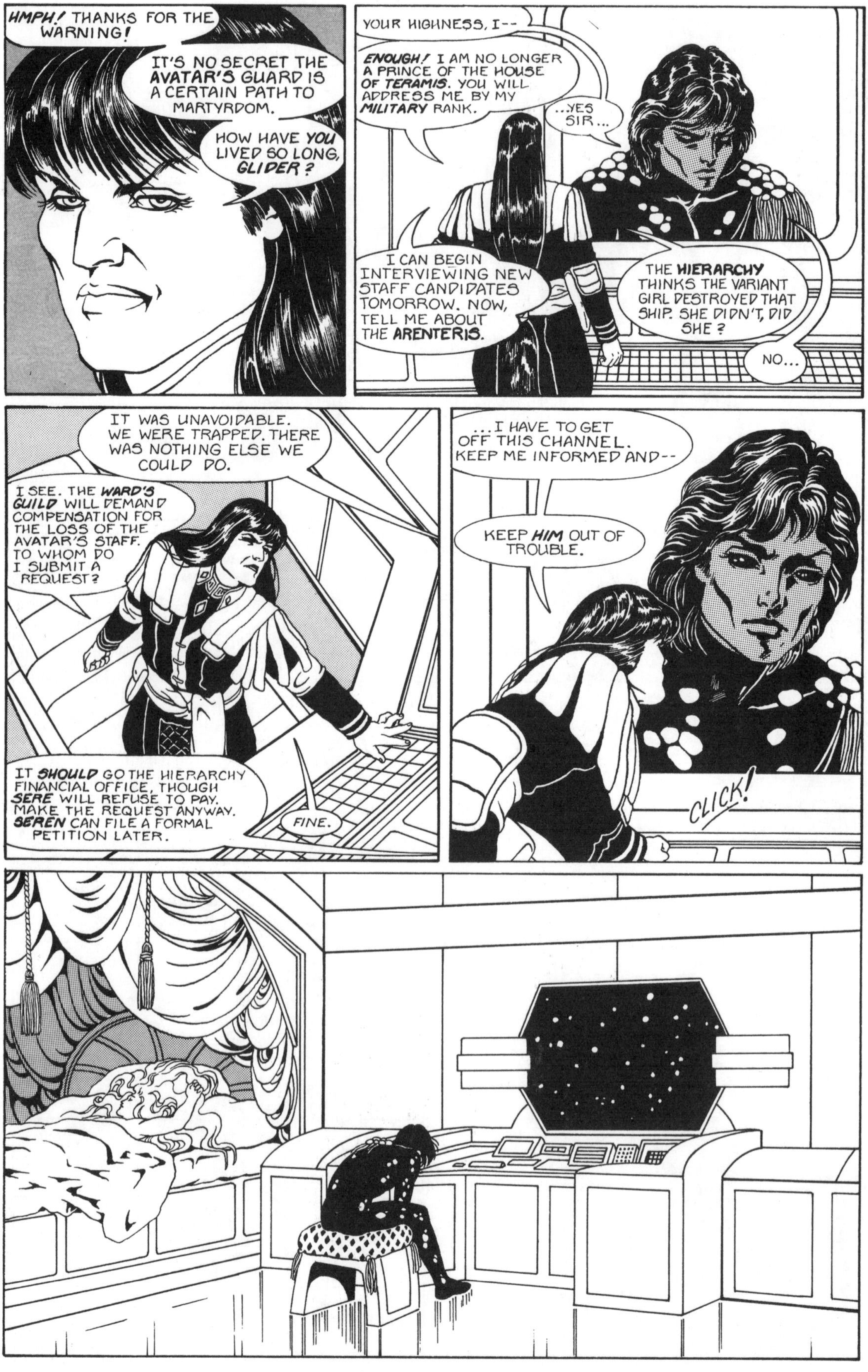
HMPH! THANKS FOR THE WARNING!
IT'S NO SECRET THE AVATAR'S GUARD IS A CERTAIN PATH TO MARTYRDOM.
HOW HAVE YOU LIVED SO LONG, GLIDER?
YOUR HIGHNESS, I--
ENOUGH! I AM NO LONGER A PRINCE OF THE HOUSE OF TERAMIS. YOU WILL ADDRESS ME BY MY MILITARY RANK.
...YES SIR...
I CAN BEGIN INTERVIEWING NEW STAFF CANDIDATES TOMORROW. NOW, TELL ME ABOUT THE ARENTERIS.
THE HIERARCHY THINKS THE VARIANT GIRL DESTROYED THAT SHIP. SHE DIDN'T, DID SHE?
NO...
IT WAS UNAVOIDABLE. WE WERE TRAPPED. THERE WAS NOTHING ELSE WE COULD DO.
I SEE. THE WARD'S GUILD WILL DEMAND COMPENSATION FOR THE LOSS OF THE AVATAR'S STAFF. TO WHOM DO I SUBMIT A REQUEST?
IT SHOULD GO THE HIERARCHY FINANCIAL OFFICE, THOUGH SERE WILL REFUSE TO PAY. MAKE THE REQUEST ANYWAY. SEREN CAN FILE A FORMAL PETITION LATER.
FINE.
...I HAVE TO GET OFF THIS CHANNEL. KEEP ME INFORMED AND--
KEEP HIM OUT OF TROUBLE.
CLICK!

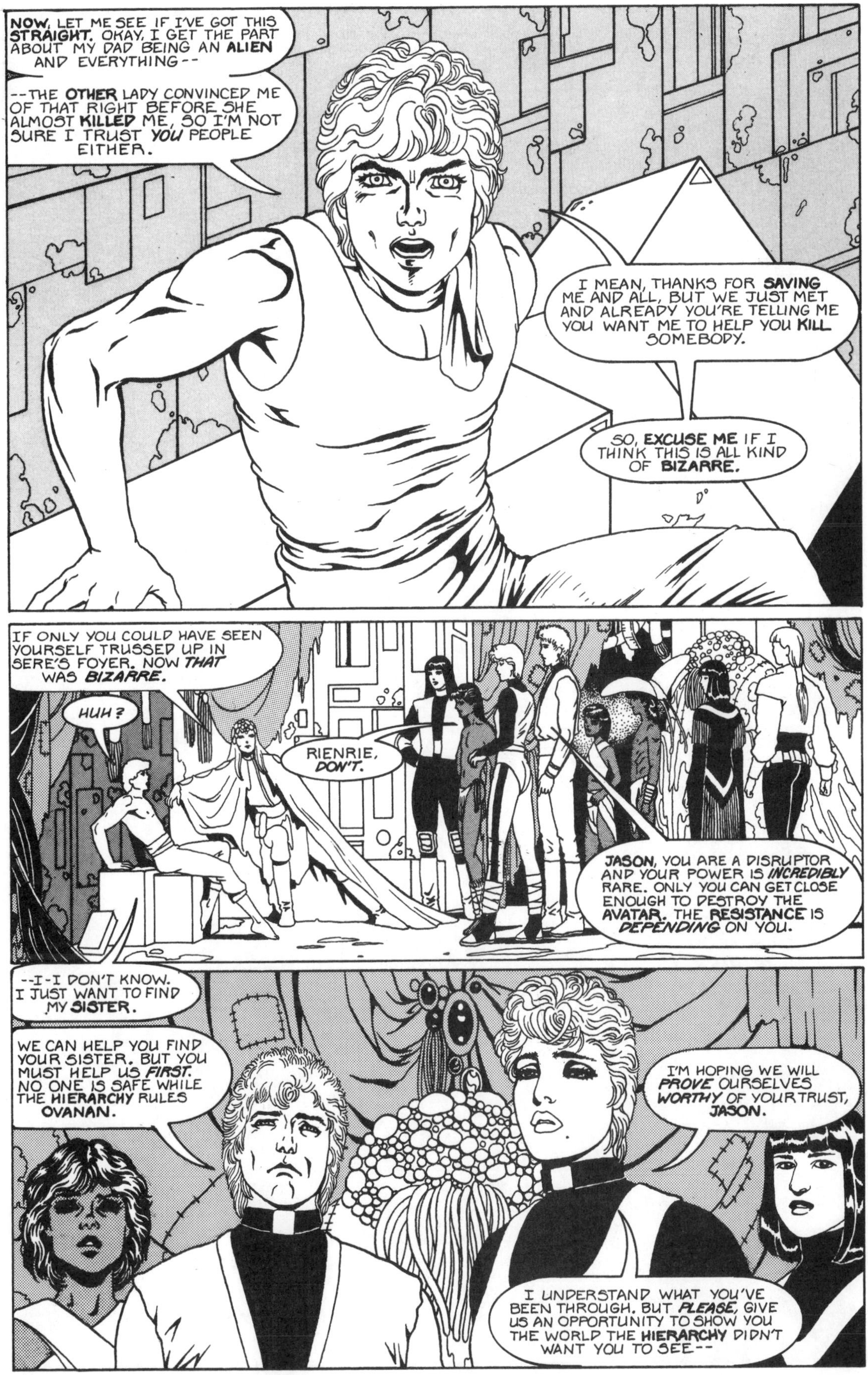
NOW, LET ME SEE IF I'VE GOT THIS STRAIGHT. OKAY, I GET THE PART ABOUT MY DAD BEING AN ALIEN AND EVERYTHING--
--THE OTHER LADY CONVINCED ME OF THAT RIGHT BEFORE SHE ALMOST KILLED ME, SO I'M NOT SURE I TRUST YOU PEOPLE EITHER.
I MEAN, THANKS FOR SAVING ME AND ALL, BUT WE JUST MET AND ALREADY YOU'RE TELLING ME YOU WANT ME TO HELP YOU KILL SOMEBODY.
SO, EXCUSE ME IF I THINK THIS IS ALL KIND OF BIZARRE.
IF ONLY YOU COULD HAVE SEEN YOURSELF TRUSSED UP IN SERE'S FOYER. NOW THAT WAS BIZARRE.
HUH?
RIENRIE, DON'T.
JASON, YOU ARE A DISRUPTOR AND YOUR POWER IS INCREDIBLY RARE. ONLY YOU CAN GET CLOSE ENOUGH TO DESTROY THE AVATAR. THE RESISTANCE IS DEPENDING ON YOU.
--I-I DON'T KNOW. I JUST WANT TO FIND MY SISTER.
WE CAN HELP YOU FIND YOUR SISTER. BUT YOU MUST HELP US FIRST. NO ONE IS SAFE WHILE THE HIERARCHY RULES OVANAN.
I'M HOPING WE WILL PROVE OURSELVES WORTHY OF YOUR TRUST, JASON.
I UNDERSTAND WHAT YOU'VE BEEN THROUGH. BUT PLEASE, GIVE US AN OPPORTUNITY TO SHOW YOU THE WORLD THE HIERARCHY DIDN'T WANT YOU TO SEE--

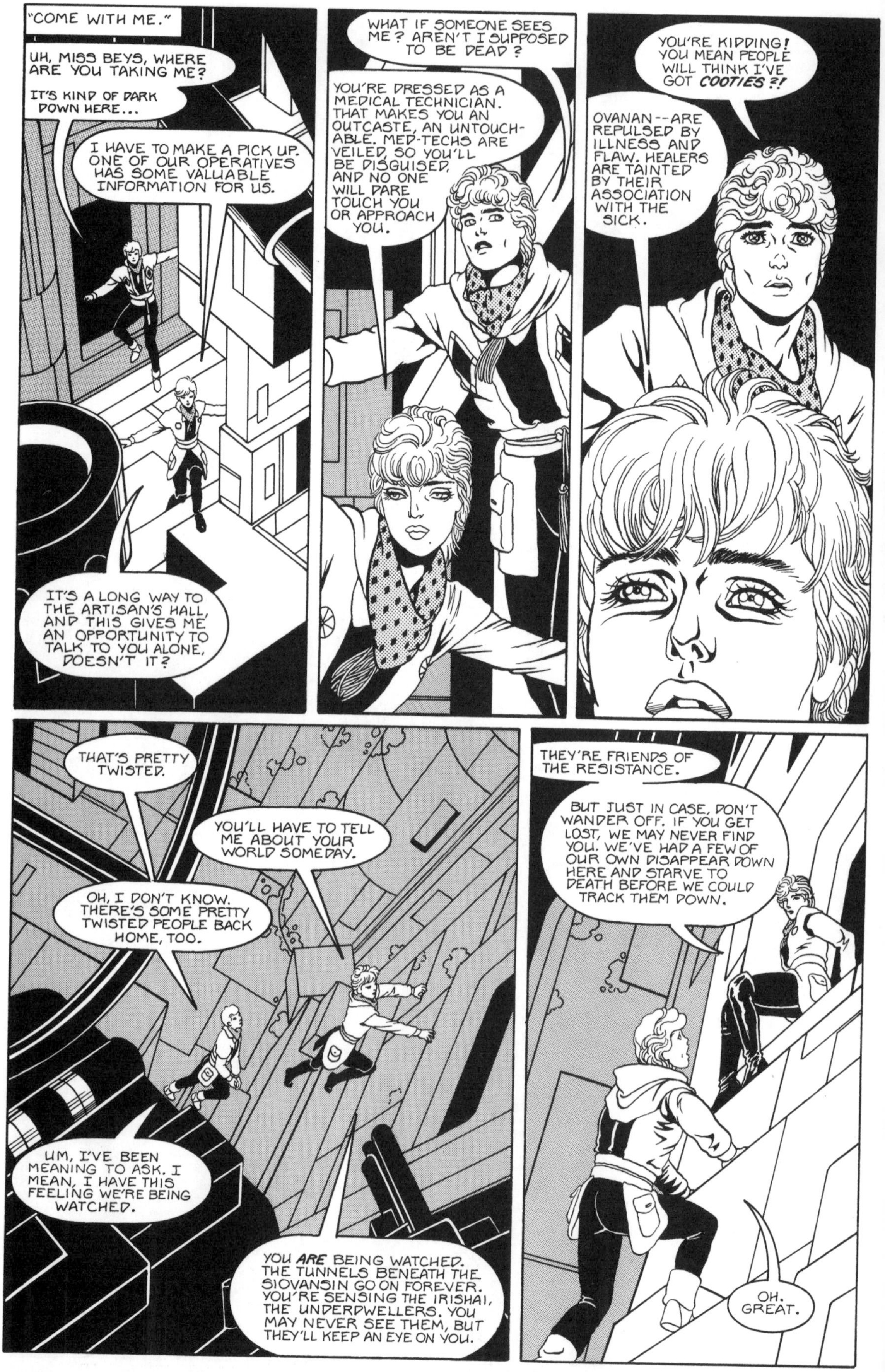
"COME WITH ME."
UH, MISS BEYS, WHERE ARE YOU TAKING ME?
IT'S KIND OF DARK DOWN HERE...
I HAVE TO MAKE A PICK UP. ONE OF OUR OPERATIVES HAS SOME VALUABLE INFORMATION FOR US.
IT'S A LONG WAY TO THE ARTISAN'S HALL, AND THIS GIVES ME AN OPPORTUNITY TO TALK TO YOU ALONE, DOESN'T IT?
WHAT IF SOMEONE SEES ME? AREN'T I SUPPOSED TO BE DEAD?
YOU'RE DRESSED AS A MEDICAL TECHNICIAN. THAT MAKES YOU AN OUTCASTE, AN UNTOUCHABLE. MED-TECHS ARE VEILED, SO YOU'LL BE DISGUISED, AND NO ONE WILL DARE TOUCH YOU OR APPROACH YOU.
YOU'RE KIDDING! YOU MEAN PEOPLE WILL THINK I'VE GOT *COOTIES*?!
OVANAN--ARE REPULSED BY ILLNESS AND FLAW. HEALERS ARE TAINTED BY THEIR ASSOCIATION WITH THE SICK.
THAT'S PRETTY TWISTED.
YOU'LL HAVE TO TELL ME ABOUT YOUR WORLD SOMEDAY.
OH, I DON'T KNOW. THERE'S SOME PRETTY TWISTED PEOPLE BACK HOME, TOO.
UM, I'VE BEEN MEANING TO ASK. I MEAN, I HAVE THIS FEELING WE'RE BEING WATCHED.
YOU *ARE* BEING WATCHED. THE TUNNELS BENEATH THE SIOVANSIN GO ON FOREVER. YOU'RE SENSING THE IRISHAI, THE UNDERDWELLERS. YOU MAY NEVER SEE THEM, BUT THEY'LL KEEP AN EYE ON YOU.
THEY'RE FRIENDS OF THE RESISTANCE.
BUT JUST IN CASE, DON'T WANDER OFF. IF YOU GET LOST, WE MAY NEVER FIND YOU. WE'VE HAD A FEW OF OUR OWN DISAPPEAR DOWN HERE AND STARVE TO DEATH BEFORE WE COULD TRACK THEM DOWN.
OH. GREAT.

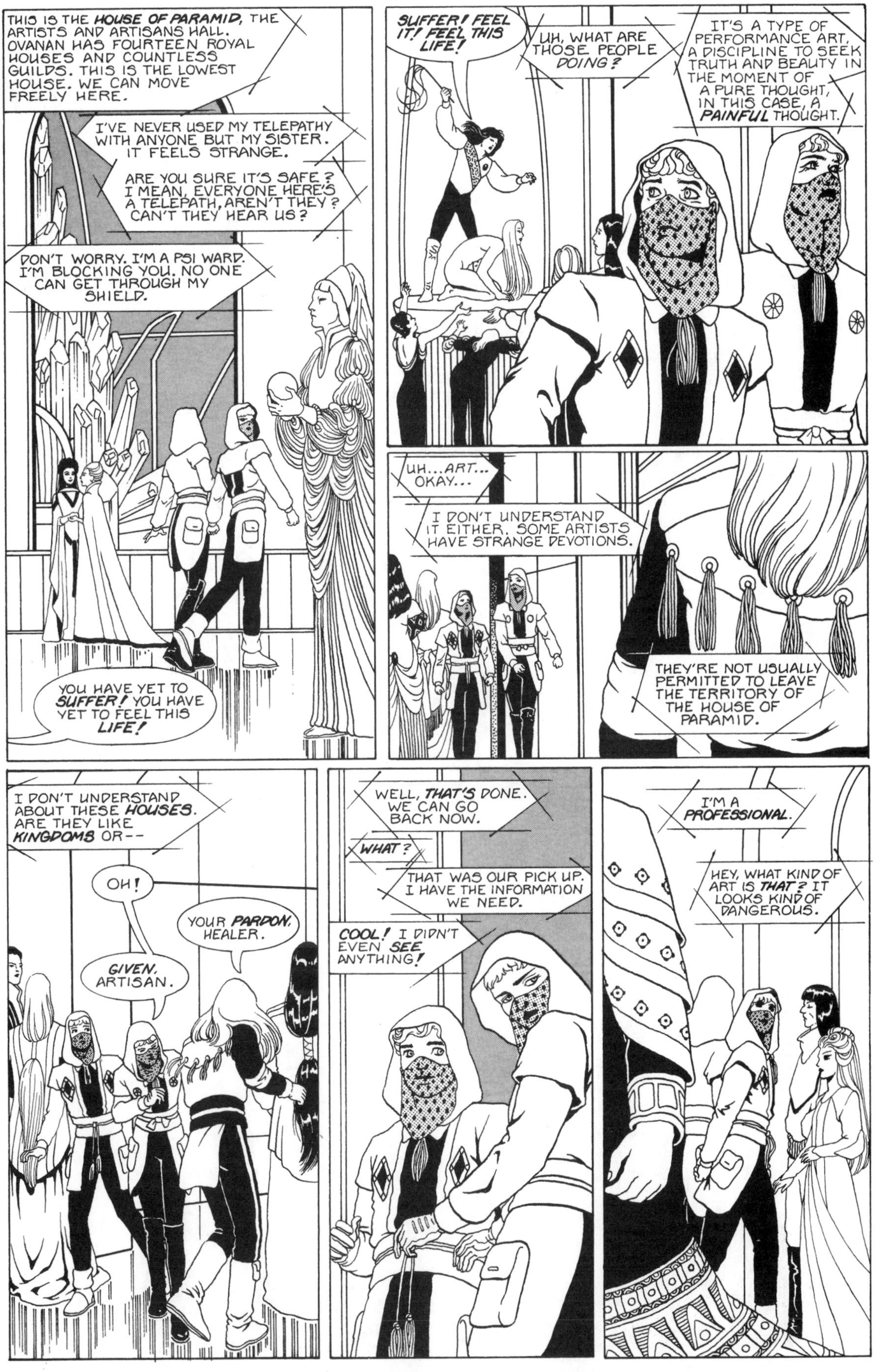

THIS IS THE HOUSE OF PARAMID, THE ARTISTS AND ARTISANS HALL. OVANAN HAS FOURTEEN ROYAL HOUSES AND COUNTLESS GUILDS. THIS IS THE LOWEST HOUSE. WE CAN MOVE FREELY HERE.
I'VE NEVER USED MY TELEPATHY WITH ANYONE BUT MY SISTER. IT FEELS STRANGE.
ARE YOU SURE IT'S SAFE? I MEAN, EVERYONE HERE'S A TELEPATH, AREN'T THEY? CAN'T THEY HEAR US?
DON'T WORRY. I'M A PSI WARD. I'M BLOCKING YOU. NO ONE CAN GET THROUGH MY SHIELD.
YOU HAVE YET TO SUFFER! YOU HAVE YET TO FEEL THIS LIFE!
SUFFER! FEEL IT! FEEL THIS LIFE!
UH, WHAT ARE THOSE PEOPLE DOING?
IT'S A TYPE OF PERFORMANCE ART, A DISCIPLINE TO SEEK TRUTH AND BEAUTY IN THE MOMENT OF A PURE THOUGHT, IN THIS CASE, A PAINFUL THOUGHT.
UH...ART... OKAY...
I DON'T UNDERSTAND IT EITHER. SOME ARTISTS HAVE STRANGE DEVOTIONS.
THEY'RE NOT USUALLY PERMITTED TO LEAVE THE TERRITORY OF THE HOUSE OF PARAMID.
I DON'T UNDERSTAND ABOUT THESE HOUSES. ARE THEY LIKE KINGDOMS OR--
OH!
YOUR PARDON, HEALER.
GIVEN, ARTISAN.
WELL, THAT'S DONE. WE CAN GO BACK NOW.
WHAT?
THAT WAS OUR PICK UP. I HAVE THE INFORMATION WE NEED.
COOL! I DIDN'T EVEN SEE ANYTHING!
I'M A PROFESSIONAL.
HEY, WHAT KIND OF ART IS THAT? IT LOOKS KIND OF DANGEROUS.

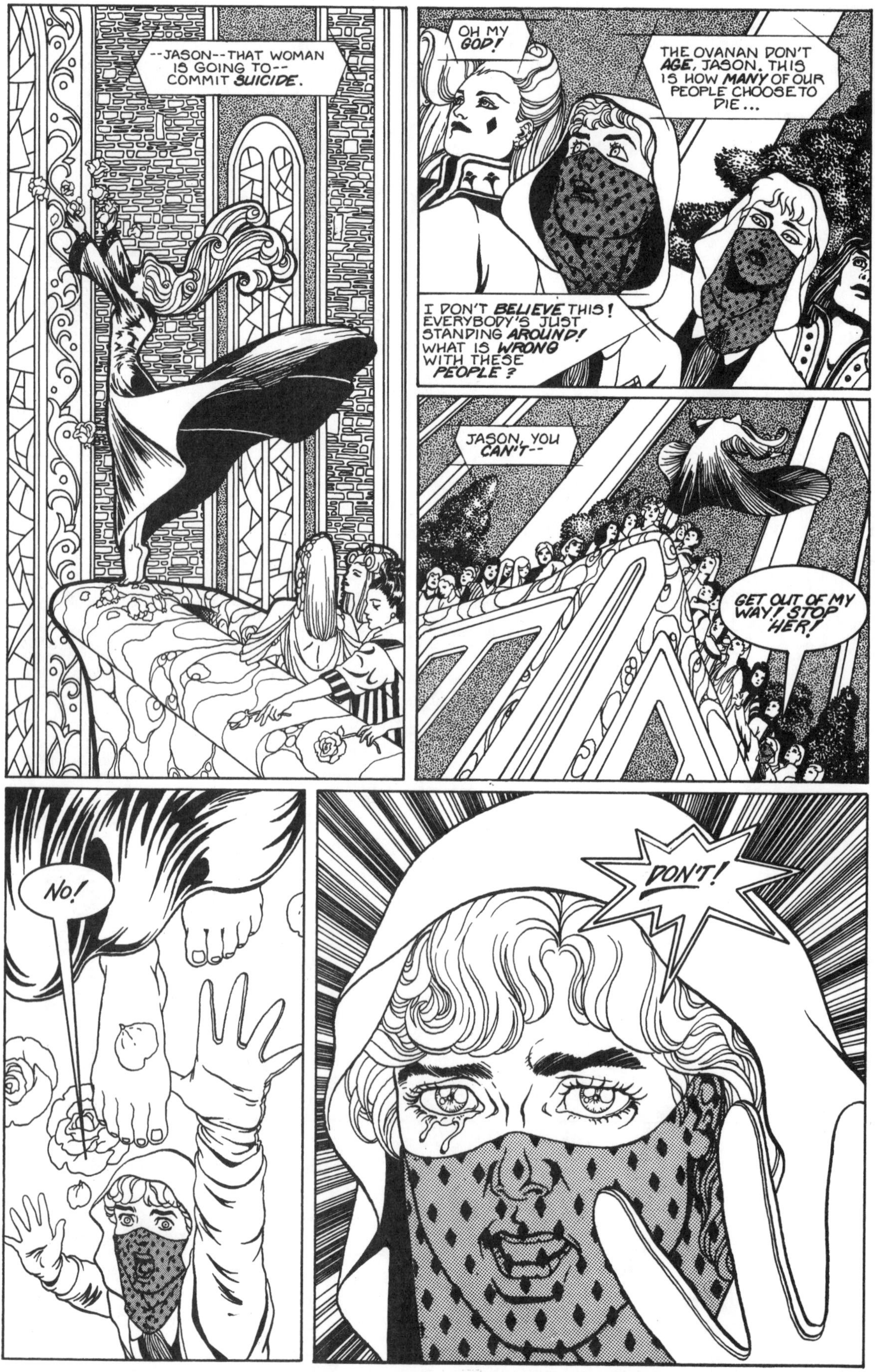
--JASON--THAT WOMAN IS GOING TO-- COMMIT SUICIDE.
OH MY GOD!
THE OVANAN DON'T AGE, JASON. THIS IS HOW MANY OF OUR PEOPLE CHOOSE TO DIE...
I DON'T BELIEVE THIS! EVERYBODY'S JUST STANDING AROUND! WHAT IS WRONG WITH THESE PEOPLE?
JASON, YOU CAN'T--
GET OUT OF MY WAY! STOP HER!
No!
DON'T!

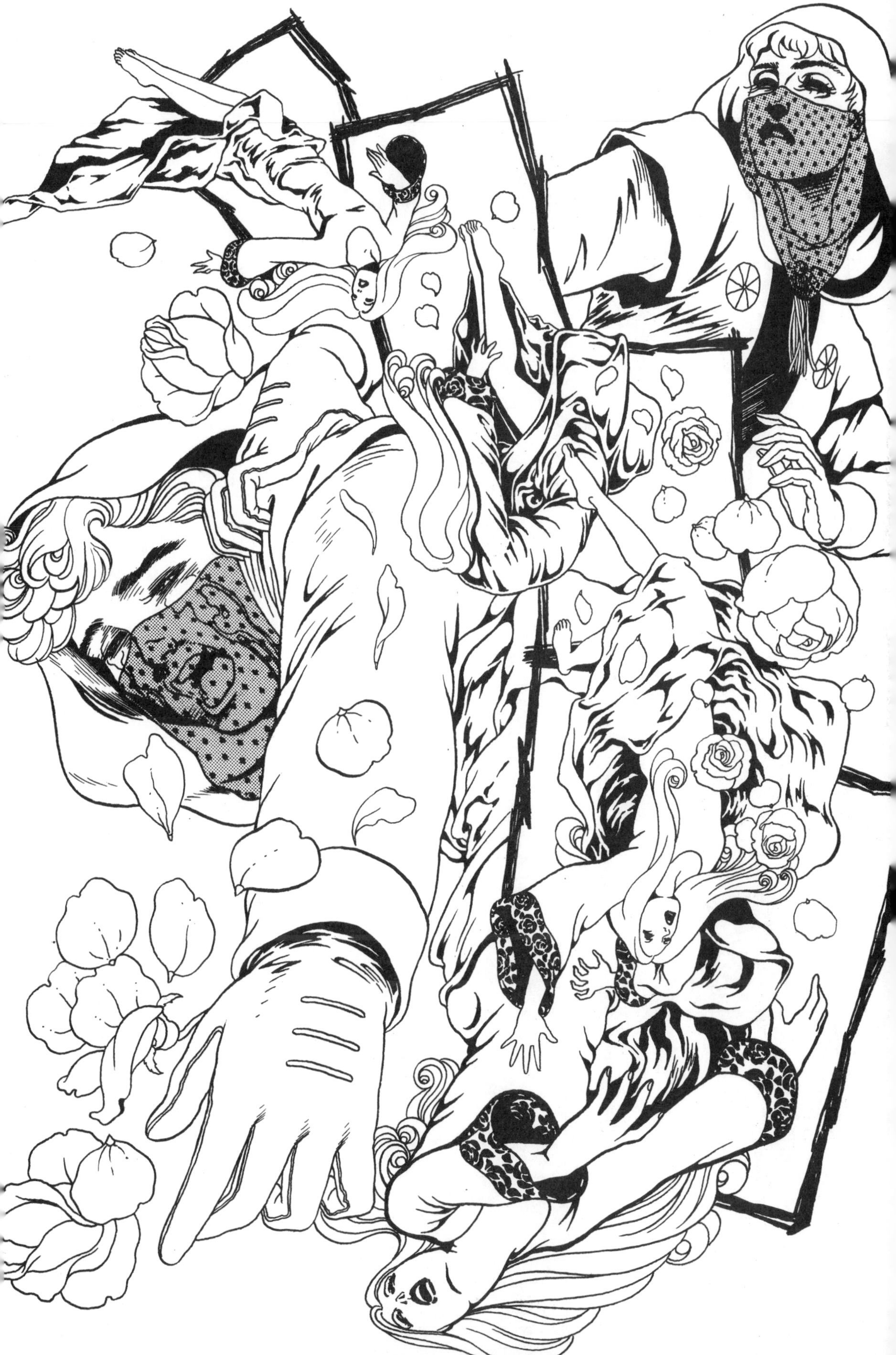

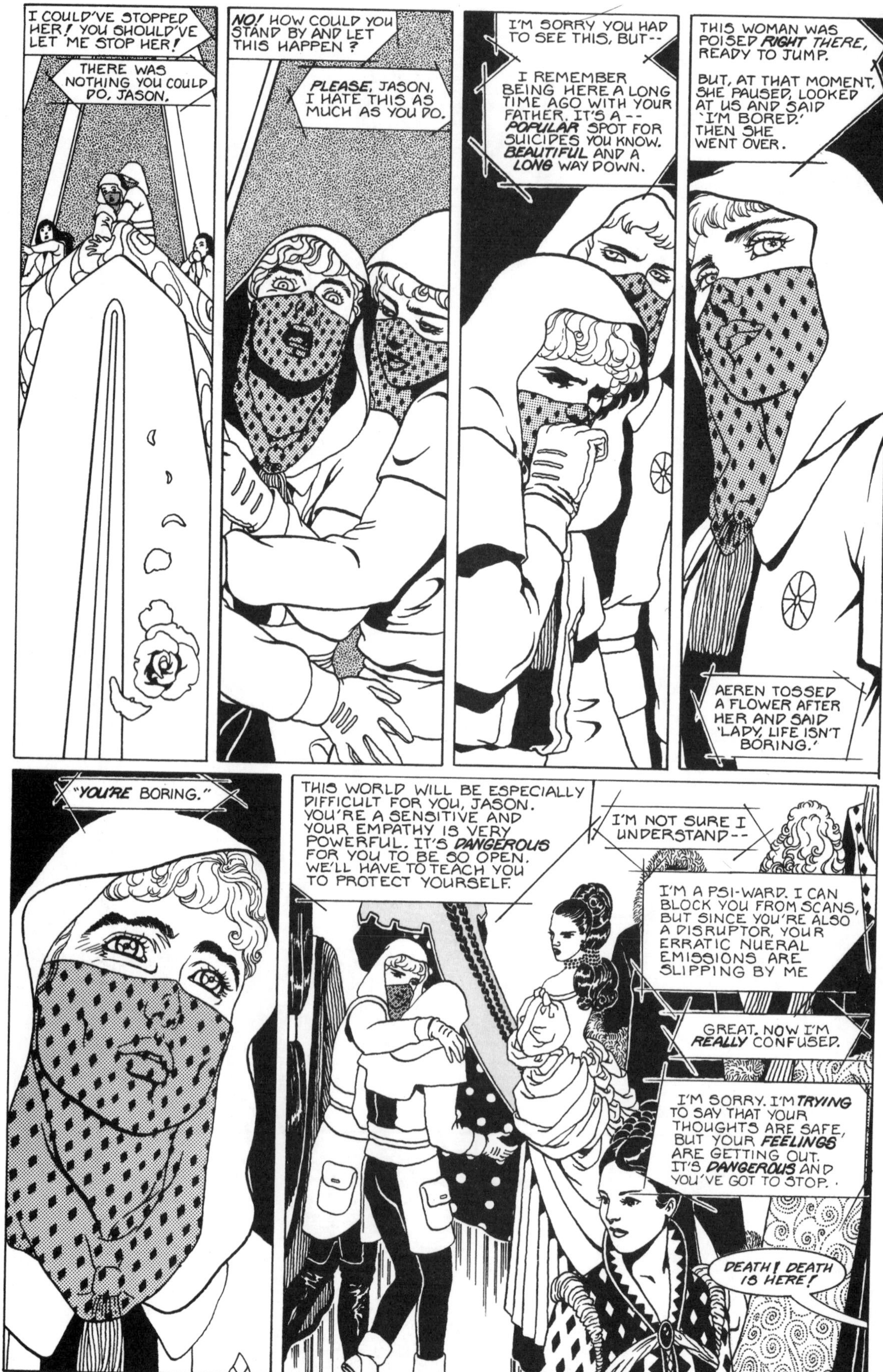
I COULD'VE STOPPED HER! YOU SHOULD'VE LET ME STOP HER!
THERE WAS NOTHING YOU COULD DO, JASON.
NO! HOW COULD YOU STAND BY AND LET THIS HAPPEN?
PLEASE, JASON, I HATE THIS AS MUCH AS YOU DO.
I'M SORRY YOU HAD TO SEE THIS, BUT--
I REMEMBER BEING HERE A LONG TIME AGO WITH YOUR FATHER. IT'S A-- POPULAR SPOT FOR SUICIDES YOU KNOW. BEAUTIFUL AND A LONG WAY DOWN.
THIS WOMAN WAS POISED RIGHT THERE, READY TO JUMP.
BUT, AT THAT MOMENT, SHE PAUSED, LOOKED AT US AND SAID 'I'M BORED.' THEN SHE WENT OVER.
AEREN TOSSED A FLOWER AFTER HER AND SAID 'LADY, LIFE ISN'T BORING.'
"YOU'RE BORING."
THIS WORLD WILL BE ESPECIALLY DIFFICULT FOR YOU, JASON. YOU'RE A SENSITIVE AND YOUR EMPATHY IS VERY POWERFUL. IT'S DANGEROUS FOR YOU TO BE SO OPEN. WE'LL HAVE TO TEACH YOU TO PROTECT YOURSELF.
I'M NOT SURE I UNDERSTAND--
I'M A PSI-WARD. I CAN BLOCK YOU FROM SCANS, BUT SINCE YOU'RE ALSO A DISRUPTOR, YOUR ERRATIC NUERAL EMISSIONS ARE SLIPPING BY ME
GREAT. NOW I'M REALLY CONFUSED.
I'M SORRY. I'M TRYING TO SAY THAT YOUR THOUGHTS ARE SAFE, BUT YOUR FEELINGS ARE GETTING OUT. IT'S DANGEROUS AND YOU'VE GOT TO STOP.
DEATH! DEATH IS HERE!

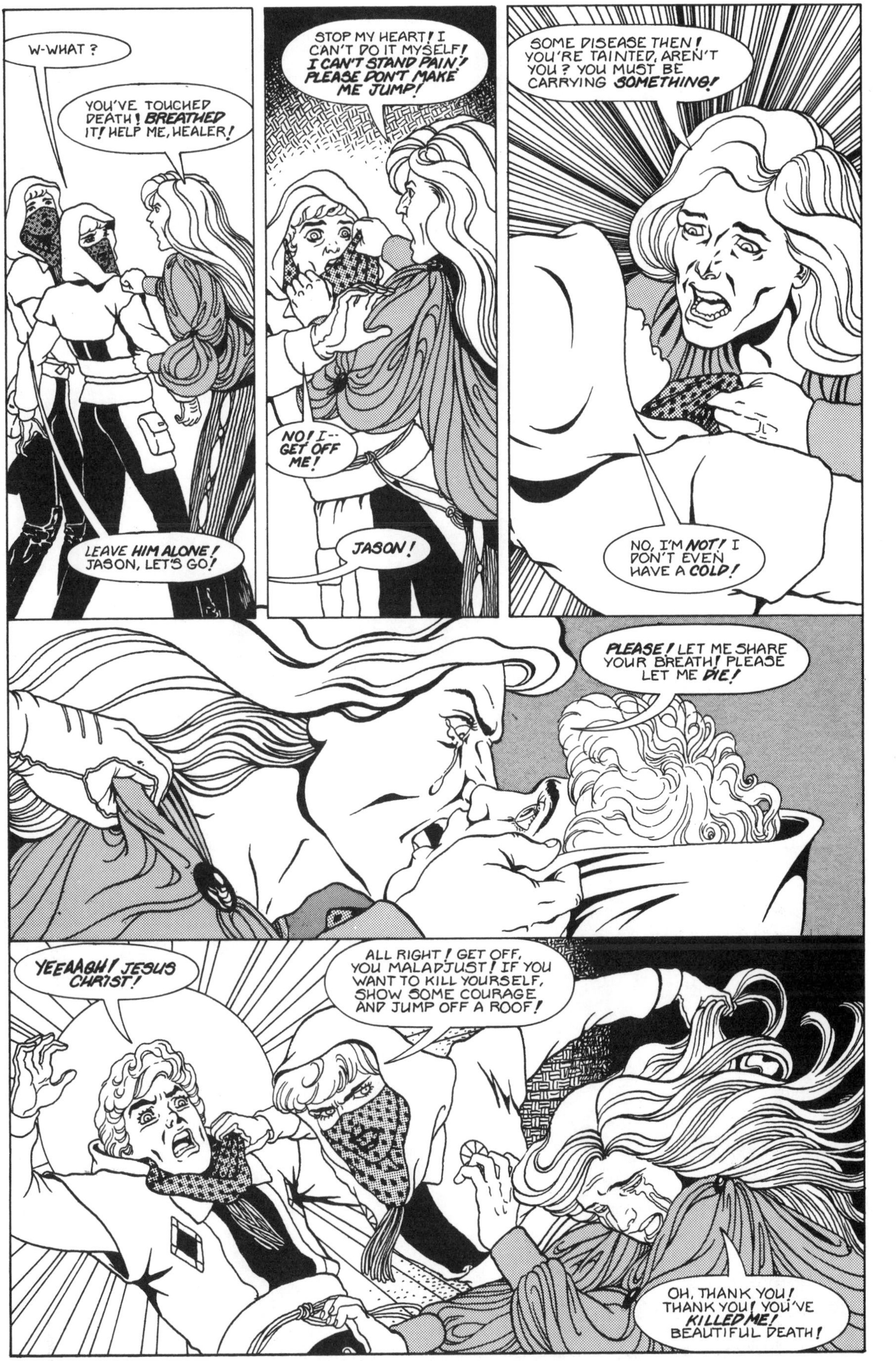
W-WHAT ?
YOU'VE TOUCHED DEATH! BREATHED IT! HELP ME, HEALER!
LEAVE HIM ALONE! JASON, LET'S GO!
STOP MY HEART! I CAN'T DO IT MYSELF! I CAN'T STAND PAIN! PLEASE DON'T MAKE ME JUMP!
NO! I-- GET OFF ME!
JASON!
SOME DISEASE THEN! YOU'RE TAINTED, AREN'T YOU ? YOU MUST BE CARRYING SOMETHING!
NO, I'M NOT! I DON'T EVEN HAVE A COLD!
PLEASE! LET ME SHARE YOUR BREATH! PLEASE LET ME DIE!
YEEAAGH! JESUS CHRIST!
ALL RIGHT! GET OFF, YOU MALADJUST! IF YOU WANT TO KILL YOURSELF, SHOW SOME COURAGE AND JUMP OFF A ROOF!
OH, THANK YOU! THANK YOU! YOU'VE KILLED ME! BEAUTIFUL DEATH!

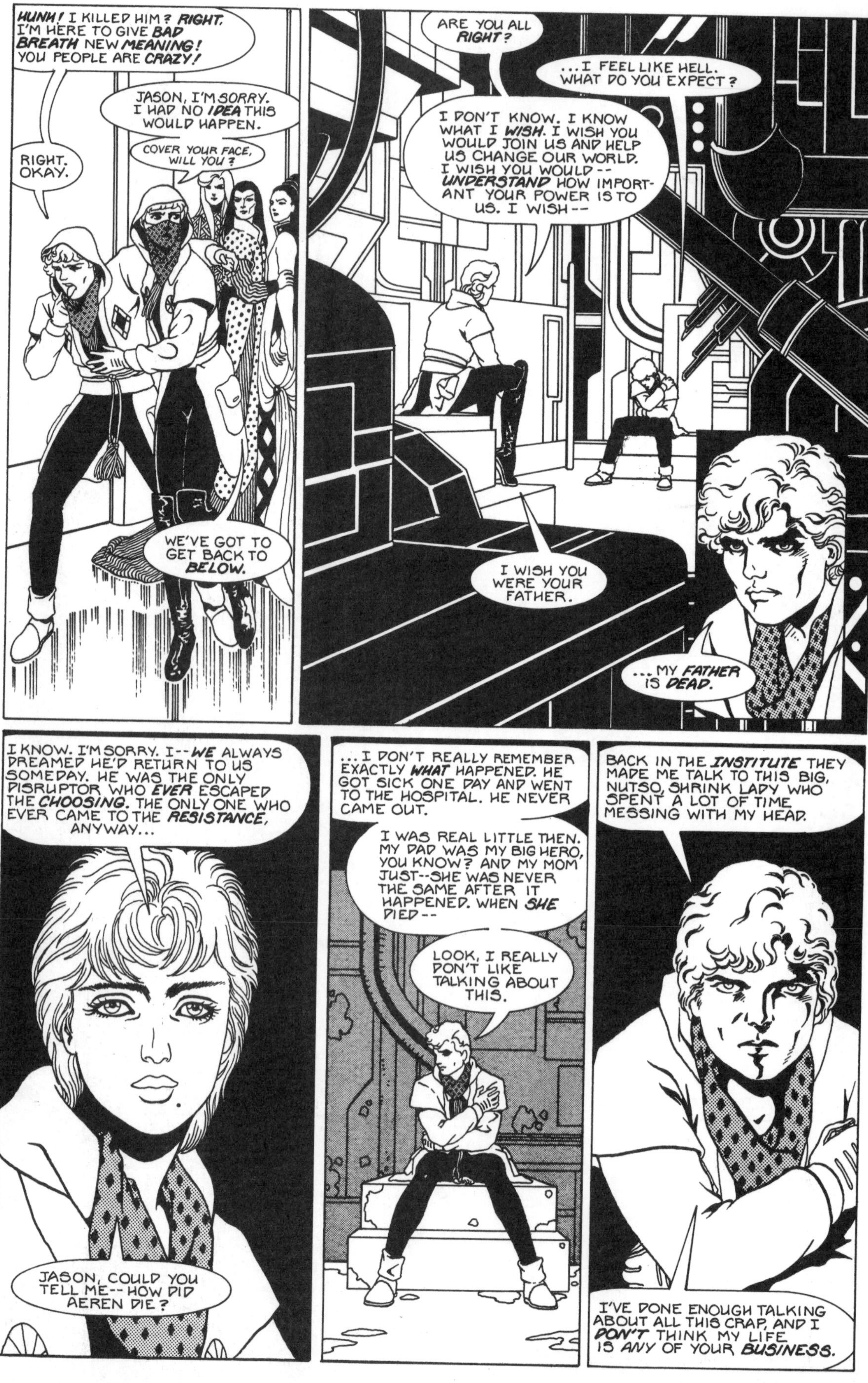
HUNH! I KILLED HIM? RIGHT. I'M HERE TO GIVE BAD BREATH NEW MEANING! YOU PEOPLE ARE CRAZY!
JASON, I'M SORRY. I HAD NO IDEA THIS WOULD HAPPEN.
RIGHT. OKAY.
COVER YOUR FACE, WILL YOU?
WE'VE GOT TO GET BACK TO BELOW.
ARE YOU ALL RIGHT?
...I FEEL LIKE HELL. WHAT DO YOU EXPECT?
I DON'T KNOW. I KNOW WHAT I WISH. I WISH YOU WOULD JOIN US AND HELP US CHANGE OUR WORLD. I WISH YOU WOULD -- UNDERSTAND HOW IMPORTANT YOUR POWER IS TO US. I WISH --
I WISH YOU WERE YOUR FATHER.
...MY FATHER IS DEAD.
I KNOW. I'M SORRY. I-- WE ALWAYS DREAMED HE'D RETURN TO US SOMEDAY. HE WAS THE ONLY DISRUPTOR WHO EVER ESCAPED THE CHOOSING. THE ONLY ONE WHO EVER CAME TO THE RESISTANCE, ANYWAY...
JASON, COULD YOU TELL ME-- HOW DID AEREN DIE?
...I DON'T REALLY REMEMBER EXACTLY WHAT HAPPENED. HE GOT SICK ONE DAY AND WENT TO THE HOSPITAL. HE NEVER CAME OUT.
I WAS REAL LITTLE THEN. MY DAD WAS MY BIG HERO, YOU KNOW? AND MY MOM JUST--SHE WAS NEVER THE SAME AFTER IT HAPPENED. WHEN SHE DIED --
LOOK, I REALLY DON'T LIKE TALKING ABOUT THIS.
BACK IN THE INSTITUTE THEY MADE ME TALK TO THIS BIG, NUTSO, SHRINK LADY WHO SPENT A LOT OF TIME MESSING WITH MY HEAD.
I'VE DONE ENOUGH TALKING ABOUT ALL THIS CRAP, AND I DON'T THINK MY LIFE IS ANY OF YOUR BUSINESS.

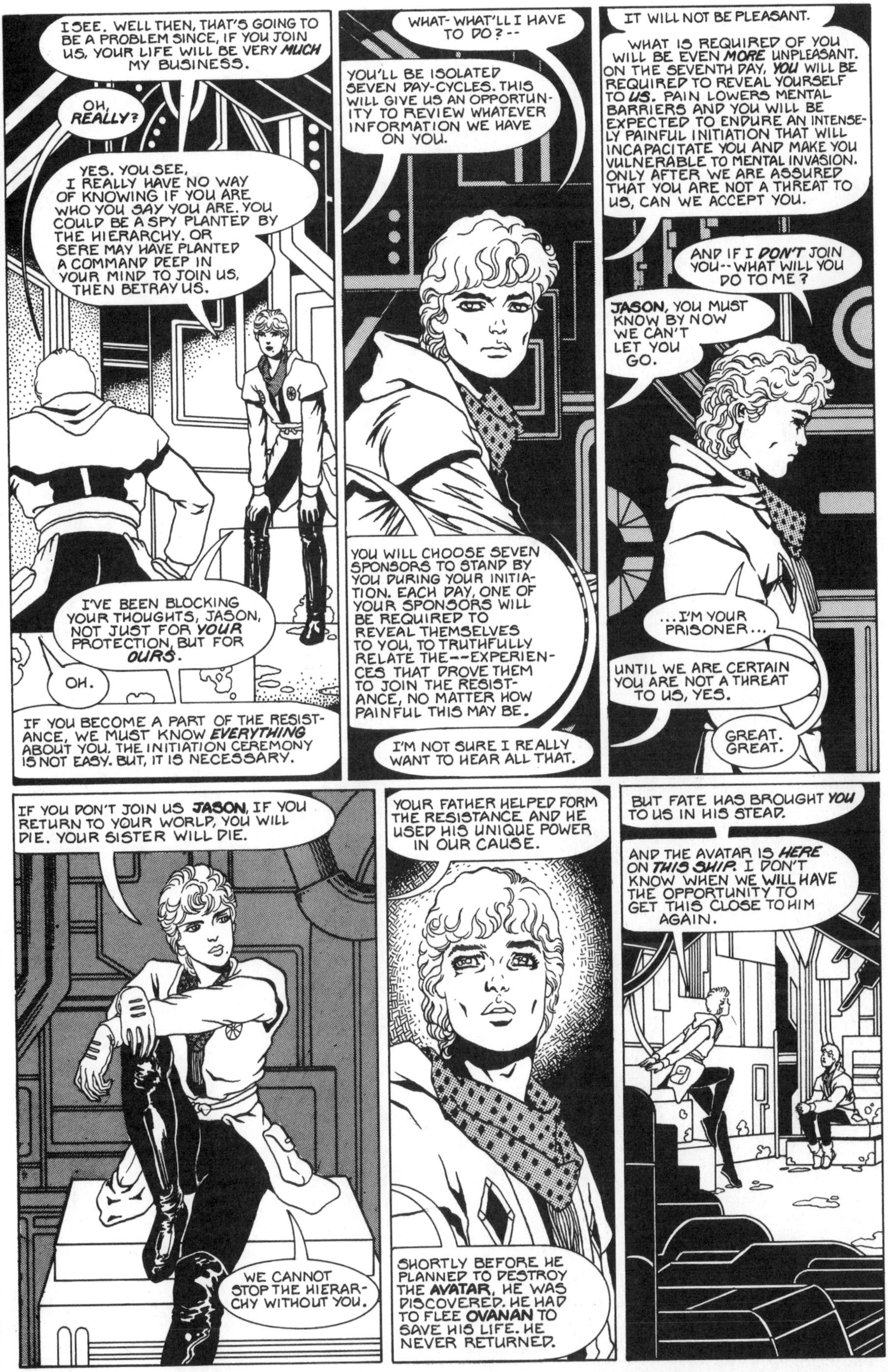
I SEE. WELL THEN, THAT'S GOING TO BE A PROBLEM SINCE, IF YOU JOIN US, YOUR LIFE WILL BE VERY MUCH MY BUSINESS.
OH, REALLY?
YES. YOU SEE, I REALLY HAVE NO WAY OF KNOWING IF YOU ARE WHO YOU SAY YOU ARE. YOU COULD BE A SPY PLANTED BY THE HIERARCHY. OR SERE MAY HAVE PLANTED A COMMAND DEEP IN YOUR MIND TO JOIN US, THEN BETRAY US.
I'VE BEEN BLOCKING YOUR THOUGHTS, JASON, NOT JUST FOR YOUR PROTECTION, BUT FOR OURS.
OH.
IF YOU BECOME A PART OF THE RESISTANCE, WE MUST KNOW EVERYTHING ABOUT YOU. THE INITIATION CEREMONY IS NOT EASY. BUT, IT IS NECESSARY.
WHAT- WHAT'LL I HAVE TO DO?--
YOU'LL BE ISOLATED SEVEN DAY-CYCLES. THIS WILL GIVE US AN OPPORTUNITY TO REVIEW WHATEVER INFORMATION WE HAVE ON YOU.
YOU WILL CHOOSE SEVEN SPONSORS TO STAND BY YOU DURING YOUR INITIATION. EACH DAY, ONE OF YOUR SPONSORS WILL BE REQUIRED TO REVEAL THEMSELVES TO YOU, TO TRUTHFULLY RELATE THE--EXPERIENCES THAT DROVE THEM TO JOIN THE RESISTANCE, NO MATTER HOW PAINFUL THIS MAY BE.
I'M NOT SURE I REALLY WANT TO HEAR ALL THAT.
IT WILL NOT BE PLEASANT.
WHAT IS REQUIRED OF YOU WILL BE EVEN MORE UNPLEASANT. ON THE SEVENTH DAY, YOU WILL BE REQUIRED TO REVEAL YOURSELF TO US. PAIN LOWERS MENTAL BARRIERS AND YOU WILL BE EXPECTED TO ENDURE AN INTENSELY PAINFUL INITIATION THAT WILL INCAPACITATE YOU AND MAKE YOU VULNERABLE TO MENTAL INVASION. ONLY AFTER WE ARE ASSURED THAT YOU ARE NOT A THREAT TO US, CAN WE ACCEPT YOU.
AND IF I DON'T JOIN YOU--WHAT WILL YOU DO TO ME?
JASON, YOU MUST KNOW BY NOW WE CAN'T LET YOU GO.
...I'M YOUR PRISONER...
UNTIL WE ARE CERTAIN YOU ARE NOT A THREAT TO US, YES.
GREAT. GREAT.
IF YOU DON'T JOIN US JASON, IF YOU RETURN TO YOUR WORLD, YOU WILL DIE. YOUR SISTER WILL DIE.
WE CANNOT STOP THE HIERARCHY WITHOUT YOU.
YOUR FATHER HELPED FORM THE RESISTANCE AND HE USED HIS UNIQUE POWER IN OUR CAUSE.
SHORTLY BEFORE HE PLANNED TO DESTROY THE AVATAR, HE WAS DISCOVERED. HE HAD TO FLEE OVANAN TO SAVE HIS LIFE. HE NEVER RETURNED.
BUT FATE HAS BROUGHT YOU TO US IN HIS STEAD.
AND THE AVATAR IS HERE ON THIS SHIP. I DON'T KNOW WHEN WE WILL HAVE THE OPPORTUNITY TO GET THIS CLOSE TO HIM AGAIN.

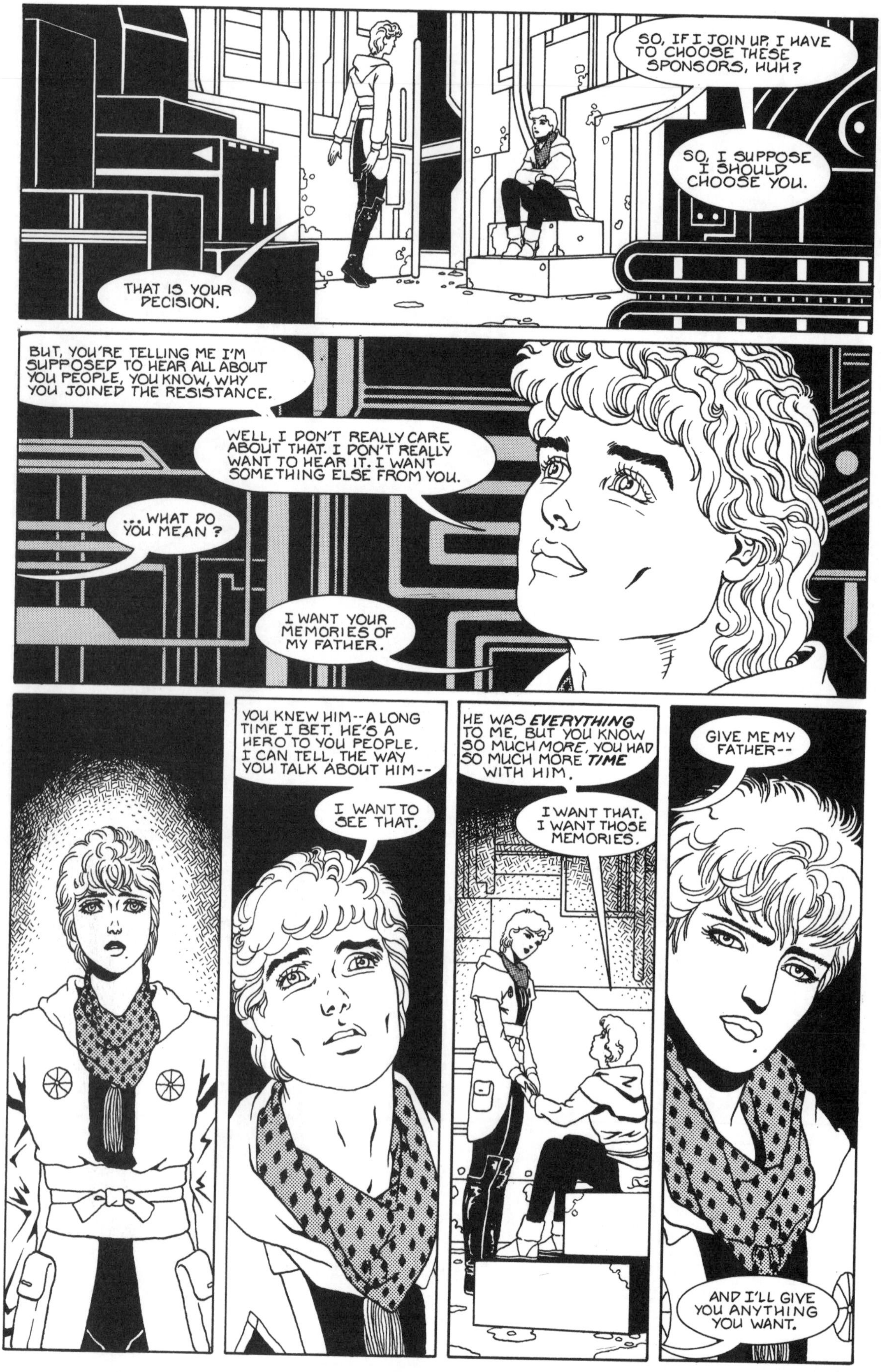
SO, IF I JOIN UP, I HAVE TO CHOOSE THESE SPONSORS, HUH?
SO, I SUPPOSE I SHOULD CHOOSE YOU.
THAT IS YOUR DECISION.
BUT, YOU'RE TELLING ME I'M SUPPOSED TO HEAR ALL ABOUT YOU PEOPLE, YOU KNOW, WHY YOU JOINED THE RESISTANCE.
WELL, I DON'T REALLY CARE ABOUT THAT. I DON'T REALLY WANT TO HEAR IT. I WANT SOMETHING ELSE FROM YOU.
...WHAT DO YOU MEAN?
I WANT YOUR MEMORIES OF MY FATHER.
YOU KNEW HIM--A LONG TIME I BET. HE'S A HERO TO YOU PEOPLE. I CAN TELL, THE WAY YOU TALK ABOUT HIM--
I WANT TO SEE THAT.
HE WAS EVERYTHING TO ME, BUT YOU KNOW SO MUCH MORE, YOU HAD SO MUCH MORE TIME WITH HIM.
I WANT THAT. I WANT THOSE MEMORIES.
GIVE ME MY FATHER--
AND I'LL GIVE YOU ANYTHING YOU WANT.

A Distant Soil

The story continues in

A DISTANT SOIL:
The Ascendant

&

A DISTANT SOIL:
The Aria,

available now from
Image Comics.

www.adistantsoil.com

—AFTERWORD—

When I was five, I won an art contest sponsored by Disney and got free tickets for me and my family to Disney on Ice. Ever since then I dreamed of growing up to be a cartoonist. Only ten years later, I was granted my first professional assignment and got my first check, a whopping $50.00!

There is something vaguely bizarre about starting a professional career in publishing while still in high school. Sometimes I wonder if my books didn't sell, would I even be capable of doing anything else for a living?

Fortunately, I've never had to face that problem! I've spent my entire adult life, and the last of my childhood bent over a drawing board and a typewriter, telling stories. I even eventually realized my dream of working for Disney studios, so I've been very fortunate!

Because I was so young when I began my work, I got taken advantage of by some rather unscrupulous types, but I am grateful for every experience since I had the opportunity to learn and grow and I write fabulous villains now.

I have been surrounded by some wonderful people who supported me and gave me the wonderful gift of their love and friendship.

First and foremost, my love to my family: my mother Anita who so often works at my side, handling the mail and the bookkeeping and the incredibly dull task of cutting and pasting those tone sheets, running interference, and bestowing big sloppy hugs. She is beautiful and looks rather like Greta Garbo and is a classy dame; also, my love and thanks to my Dad, Chief Ron Doran who worries for me, and slipped me money when I was poor and has visions of starving artists dancing at the back of his consciousness but supports me absolutely. He also shares fab stories about life as a cop which have found new life in the form of a certain Sergeant Minetti; my brother Richard, also a cop, who actually helped out on some of the goblins and armor, and who isn't a creepy big brother at all.

Eternal thanks to Erik Larsen, who knows that the best way to get me to do anything is to leave me the heck alone, and to all the staff at Image, and also to Jim Valentino for over a decade of friendship and support.

Thanks and apologies to the now defunct Lee Moyer studio. Lee's staff actually helped me ink some of the backgrounds in A DISTANT SOIL for a brief period about ten years ago, but cranky, picky girl that I am, I ended up redrawing virtually every line later, so this contribution has been largely obliterated.

To my pookie Neil Gaiman, for nearly a decade of the treasure of friendship, a lovely introduction and a room full of faces. Neil didn't even take revenge for the dreadful roast I gave him in a story I wrote and drew about him some years back, which proves he has a sense of humor on top of all his other fine qualities.

Bob Pinaha no longer letters A DISTANT SOIL since I eventually learned the craft and took up the job myself, but be assured that the good lettering in this volume is his work, and the less than fine lettering in this book is mine.

George Beahm was the only good thing that came from a very bad publisher. He is wise and kind and dear.

My never ending thanks to my beloved Frank Kelly Freas, friend and teacher.

To Dave Sim. He knows why.

Thanks, Mary Gray. I can't proofread for anything.

To Dawn Bromley, Margaret Cubberly, Spencer Beck, Caesar, Ivan and Susan Clark, Trina Robbins, Jeff Smith, all those jolly HaRoSFAns, and to all the very faithful A DISTANT SOIL readers for many years of support.

There are many others to thank for all they have given me over the years, but I'd need another book to write them all down.

Colleen Doran
July 1997

A Distant Soil™ Items

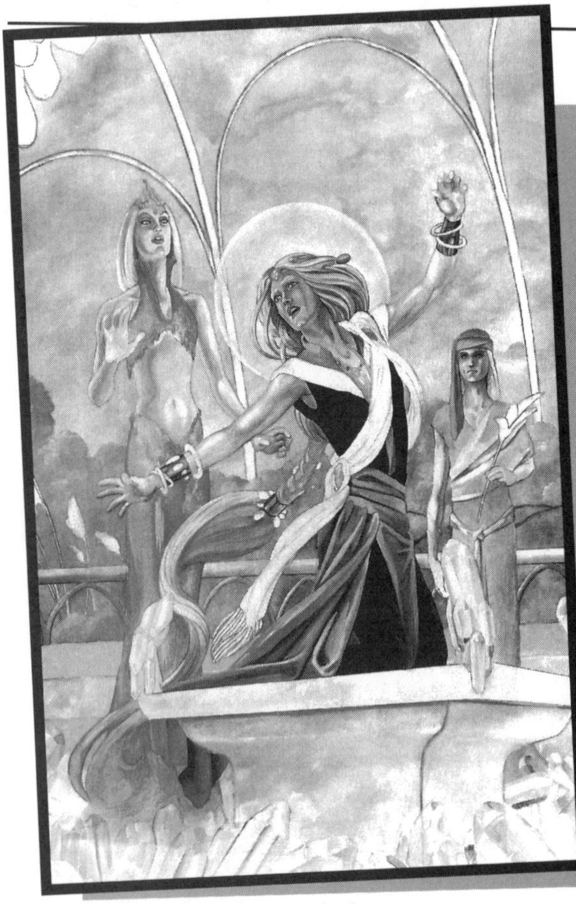

A DISTANT SOIL: THE GATHERING

Volume 1 of the acclaimed graphic novel series collects the first 13 issues of the lead story of the comic book in a big, 240 page, beautifully illustrated trade paperback! With a lovely, gold foil enhanced cover, A DISTANT SOIL: THE GATHERING is available for only $19.95!

A DISTANT SOIL II: THE ASCENDANT

240 page softcover edition for only $18.95!
Also available in a limited edition hardcover, A DISTANT SOIL: THE ASCENDANT, signed and numbered, is only $29.95 and includes a limited edition print and beautiful foil stamped cover.

The hardcover remarqued edition is all that *and* an original full page character drawing for $74.95.

A DISTANT SOIL: The Aria

Volume III in the A DISTANT SOIL saga! The story continues in this all new, beautiful collection! 164 pages of passion and intrigue, politics and betrayal! Available in a signed, numbered hardcover limited edition for $29.95 of only 150 copies. Also available in a remarqued edition of 100 copies, each featuring a hand drawn character portrait of your choice! Only $74.95 (available after July 2001.) Or get the trade paperback edition with handsome, foil enhanced cover for $16.95.

IMAGES OF A DISTANT SOIL

A gallery of original work inspired by A DISTANT SOIL, this 32 page book from Image showcases stellar talents: Charles Vess, Frank Kelly Freas, Dave Sim and Gerhard, Jim Valentino, David Mack, Dave Lapham, Nick Cardy, Curt Swan, Joe Szekeres and others. With full color covers, character biographies and an eight page short story from A DISTANT SOIL! Only $2.95!

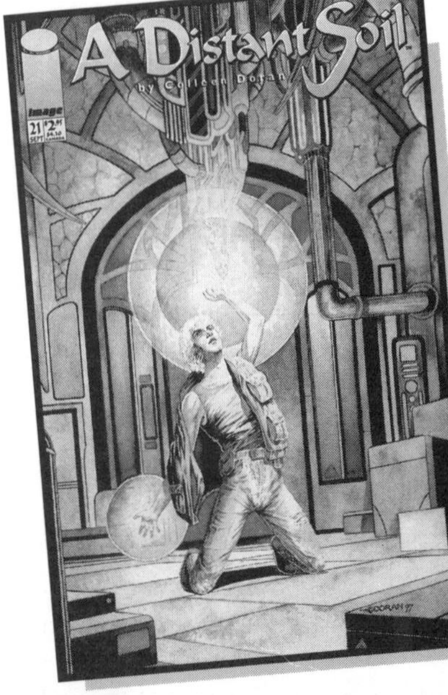
A Distant Soil
by Colleen Doran
image

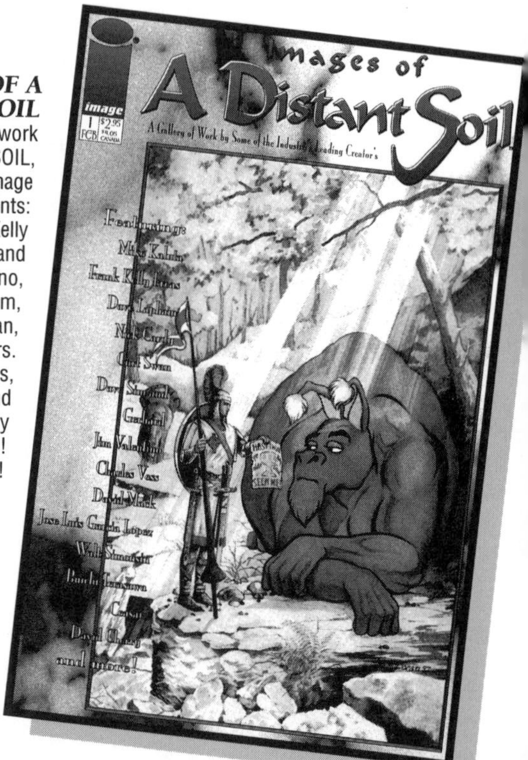
Images of
A Distant Soil
image

For more information about
A DISTANT SOIL, including never before
published art, online
interviews with
creator Colleen Doran and
other great features, visit our website!

www.adistantsoil.com

To find *A DISTANT SOIL*
comics and graphic novels,
as well as other work
by Colleen Doran and
your favorite Image artists,
call: 1-888-COMIC-BOOK

Send to:
Colleen Doran, Colleen Doran Studios
435-2 Oriana Road PMB 610
Newport News • VA 23608 • USA

If you are paying by credit card, please fill this out:

Type of credit card: _____

Card Number: _____

Expiration Date: _____

Your name as imprinted on the card: _____

Your signature: _____

Your Name: _____

Street address: _____

City • State • Zip: _____

ITEM ORDERED	QUANTITY	PRICE EACH	TOTAL

subtotal	
shipping charge	
Total enclosed:	

• *Important ordering information:*
All orders must be in U.S. funds

• *Shipping charges:*
U.S. orders under $20.00, add $3.00. Over $20.00, add $4.00
Canada, Mexico, overseas: Add $5.00 for order under $20.00.
Add $10.00 for orders over $20.00

• *Virginia residents:* add 4.5% sales tax

Biography

Colleen Doran began publishing **A Distant Soil** while still a teenager and the series has gone on to sell some 500,000 copies. She manages her production company Colleen Doran Studios and continues to publish her **A Distant Soil** comic book series through Image Comics.

Her work has also appeared in Neil Gaiman's *Sandman*, Anne Rice's *The Master of Rampling Gate*, Clive Barker's *Nightbreed* and Clive Barker's *Hellraiser*, *Amazing Spiderman*, *Walt Disney's Beauty and the Beast*, *The Star Wars Galaxy*, *Excalibur*, *Captain America*, *The Legion of Superheroes*, *Wonder Woman: The Once and Future Story* , *X-Factor*, *Excalibur* and various stories for Paradox Press's *Big Books* series.

With some 400 credits, Doran has been a professional illustrator since the age of fifteen. She's also illustrated a SWAT team training manual, designed toys and games, and created corporate designs and illustrations.

Her work has been profiled in *The Anne Rice Companion*, *Comic Book Rebels*, *Censorship: War of Words* and *Women and the Comics*.

She has received a number of awards and nominations for her work. In 1989 she received a grant from the Delphi Institute to attend a multicultural, cross-country tour of the U.S. to study American pop culture with participants from diverse nations such as Zimbabwe, Nigeria, Hungary, Czechoslovakia, The Philippines and Egypt. She has also received the Amy Shultz Memorial Award for using her work to heighten awareness of Child Sexual Abuse. In 1997, she was chosen by Tezuka Productions to attend a week long comics/manga seminar in Japan with Oscar/Pulitzer Prize winning cartoonist Jules Ffeiffer, acclaimed *Bone* creator Jeff Smith, syndicated *Sylvia* cartoonist Nicole Hollander, and Dreamworks animator Denys Cowan. Colleen is just full of herself and you can tell, since she wrote this bio.

She enjoys gardening, hiking, reading and being able to afford a housekeeper. This is a picture of what Colleen Doran looks like now: